P9-BYE-686

"*Opening Doors* meets all my expectations for **a remarkable developmental reading text. The explanations** are **precise** and **easily understood.** The design is **aesthetically pleasing.** It is **inviting** to students and the **layout is easy to follow. I especially like the chapter objectives** that are invaluable in helping students identify the most important aspects of each chapter. I **found the comprehension and vocabulary quizzes to be an excellent means of evaluating student performance.** They are **thorough** and provide **a reliable means of checking student comprehension** of the material as well as **provide a systematic means for building vocabulary skills** . . . a **well-written, user-friendly** textbook."

—*Barbara Doyle, Arkansas State University*

"*Opening Doors* provides an **effective balance of theory, rigorous application, and formative assessment** to meet the challenges of preparing students for college-level reading. The inclusion of three reading selections in each chapter provides **much flexibility for instruction, application, and testing.**"

—*TC Stuwe, Salt Lake Community College*

"*Opening Doors* is **an ideal textbook** for students starting their college education."

—*Maureen Connolly, Elmhurst College*

"The **reading selections are current and interesting,** often introducing new fields to my students . . . . The **topics** are **varied and representative.** *Opening Doors* **covers the skills needed** for college-level reading and includes **excellent selections and supplements** to use in applying these skills."

—*Sherry Prather, Austin Community College*

"**This is *the* textbook to use** if you want to prepare your students for intelligent critical reading and thinking in all content areas."

—*Barbara Belroy, Cerritos College*

"It is refreshing to read a text **written by instructors 'in the trenches' who understand the complexities of today's student** and the demand of college reading."

—*Marlys Cordoba, College of the Siskiyous*

"I **have recommended this text to many others** . . . I like the **use of color** within chapter sections because it **gets students' attention. Pictures** are **strategically placed** but not overdone. The **textbook aids** are **consistent from chapter to chapter,** which is important for developmental students. I currently use *Opening Doors* for my online class. I think it is one of the easiest texts to choose for an online class. It covers the typical reading skills, but more importantly, it **employs the concept of metacognition.** This concept is critical in any class, but when an instructor is not available on a face-to-face basis, it is essential that the text emphasize this skill."

—*John Lyon, Aviation Institute of Maintenance*

"The text covers **all of the important skills developmental students need** to learn in order to become successful college students."

—*Richard J. Richards, St. Petersburg College*

About the Authors

Joe Cortina

Janet Elder

Joe Cortina and Janet Elder began their writing collaboration as colleagues in the Human and Academic Development Division at Richland College, a member of the Dallas County Community College District. Professor Elder now writes full time; professor Cortina currently teaches reading at Richland and serves as the developmental reading program coordinator. Both are trained reading specialists and are highly experienced in teaching basic and advanced reading improvement and study skills courses. Their combined teaching experience spans elementary, secondary, and undergraduate levels, as well as clinical remediation.

Dr. Cortina and Dr. Elder began collaborating in 1985. Their first textbook was *Comprehending College Textbooks: Steps to Understanding and Remembering What You Read.* Their beginning-level textbook, *New Worlds: An Introduction to College Reading,* is now in its third edition. Dr. Elder is also the author of a new introductory-level text, *Entryways into College Reading and Learning,* and an intermediate- to upper-level college reading improvement textbook, *Exercise Your College Reading Skills: Developing More Powerful Comprehension.* Both authors are long-standing members of the College Reading and Learning Association (CRLA) and the National Association for Developmental Education (NADE). Dr. Cortina is also a member of the Texas counterparts of these national organizations, Texas-CRLA and TADE, and Dr. Elder has given numerous presentations at their conferences over the years.

Joe Cortina earned his B.A. degree in English from San Diego State University and his master's degree and doctoral degree in curriculum and instruction in reading from the University of North Texas. He has taught undergraduate teacher education courses in reading at the University of North Texas and Texas Woman's University. In 1981 he was selected to represent the Dallas County Community College District as a nominee for the Piper Award for Teaching Excellence. In addition, Dr. Cortina was selected as his division's nominee for Richland's Excellence in Teaching Award in 1987, 1988, and 1993. In 1992 he was selected as an honored alumnus by the Department of Elementary, Early Childhood and Reading Education of the University of North Texas and in 1994 he was a recipient of an Excellence Award given by the National Institute for Staff and Organizational Development. In addition to teaching reading courses at Richland College, Dr. Cortina has served on interdisciplinary teaching teams for honors English courses and has served as a faculty leader of Richland's writing-across-the-curriculum program. Dr. Cortina conducts in-service training and serves as a mentor to both new full-time and adjunct faculty at Richland College.

Janet Elder was graduated summa cum laude from the University of Texas in Austin with a B.A. in English and Latin, and is a member of Phi Beta Kappa. She was the recipient of a government fellowship for Southern Methodist University's Reading Research Program, which resulted in a master's degree. Her Ph.D. in curriculum and instruction in reading is from Texas Woman's University where the College of Education presented her the Outstanding Dissertation Award. After teaching reading and study skills courses at Richland for several years, she implemented the college's Honors Program and directed it for six years before returning to teaching full time. She was a three-time nominee for excellence in teaching awards. Disability Services students also selected her three times as the recipient of a special award for "exceptional innovation, imagination, and consideration in working with students with disabilities." She is a recipient of the National Institute for Staff and Organizational Development's Excellence Award. In fall, 2004, she left teaching in order to write full time, but she continues her affiliation with Richland as a professor emerita. A frequent presenter at professional conferences and in-service workshops, she has a deep interest and expertise in "brain-friendly" instruction.

Opening Doors

Understanding College Reading

FIFTH EDITION

Joe Cortina   Janet Elder

Richland College
Dallas County Community College District

Boston   Burr Ridge, IL   Dubuque, IA   Madison, WI   New York   San Francisco   St. Louis
Bangkok   Bogotá   Caracas   Kuala Lumpur   Lisbon   London   Madrid   Mexico City
Milan   Montreal   New Delhi   Santiago   Seoul   Singapore   Sydney   Taipei   Toronto

Higher Education

Published by McGraw-Hill, a business unit of The McGraw-Hill Companies, Inc., 1221 Avenue of the Americas, New York, NY, 10020. Copyright © 2008 by The McGraw-Hill Companies, Inc. All rights reserved. No part of this publication may be reproduced or distributed in any form or by any means, or stored in a database or retrieval system, without the prior written consent of The McGraw-Hill Companies, Inc., including, but not limited to, in any network or other electronic storage or transmission, or broadcast for distance learning. Some ancillaries, including electronic and print components, may not be available to cutomers outside the United States.

This book is printed on acid-free paper.

3 4 5 6 7 8 9 0 DOC/DOC 0 9

ISBN: 978-0-07-340713-5
MHID: 0-07-340713-5
AIE ISBN: 978-0-07-329545-9
AIE MHID: 0-07-329545-0

Vice President and Editor-in-Chief: *Emily Barrosse*
Publisher: *Lyn Uhl*
Sponsoring Editor: *John Kindler*
Director of Development: *Carla Samodulski*
Editorial Assistant: *Jesse Hassenger*
Marketing Manager: *Tamara Wederbrand*
Text Permissions Editor: *Marty Moga*
Production Editor: *Leslie LaDow*
Art Editor: *Emma Ghiselli*

Designer: *Gino Cieslik*
Photo Research Coordinator: *Alexandra Ambrose*
Photo Researcher: *Jennifer Blankenship*
Media Project Manager: *Brian Jones*
Media Producer: *Alexander Rohrs*
Production Supervisor: *Randy Hurst*
Composition: *10.5/12 Times Roman by Thompson Type*
Printing: *45 # Pub Matte Plus, R. R. Donnelley & Sons*

Credits: The credits section for this book begins on page C-1 and is considered an extension of the copyright page.
Cover photo: Copyright © Richard Cummins/SuperStock

Library of Congress Cataloging-in-Publication Data

Cortina, Joe.
  Opening doors : understanding college reading / Joe Cortina, Janet Elder.—5th ed.
    p. cm.
  ISBN-13: 978-0-07-340713-5 (pbk. : alk. paper)
  ISBN-10: 0-07-340713-5 (pbk. : alk. paper)
   1. College readers. 2. Reading (Higher education). I. Elder, Janet. II. Title.
  PE1122.C637 2008
428.6—dc22

2006051485

The Internet addresses listed in the text were accurate at the time of publication. The inclusion of a website does not indicate an endorsement by the authors or McGraw-Hill, and McGraw-Hill does not guarantee the accuracy of the information presented at these sites.

www.mhhe.com

Brief Contents

v

Contents

PART TWO

Comprehension:
Understanding College Textbooks by Reading for Ideas   205

CHAPTER 4

CHAPTER 5

To the Instructor

Opening Doors is designed to help college students move from a precollege reading level to a college reading level. It also presents a systematic way of approaching college textbook material that can make students more efficient in the study skills integral to their college success.

While the scope of this book is broad, the focus is ultimately on comprehension. Comprehension skills are introduced early in the text and are integrated throughout subsequent chapters so that students learn how to apply them. Though the emphasis is on main ideas and essential supporting details (Part Two, Comprehension), the book gives thorough attention to skills that range from predicting and questioning actively as you read (Part One, Orientation), to selecting, organizing, and rehearsing texbook material to be learned for a test (Part Three, Systems for Studying Textbooks). In Part Three, students learn how to use textbook features to full advantage, how to underline and annotate textbook material, and how to organize material in writing so that it can be mastered for a test.

Although *Opening Doors* is designed for developmental readers, we have chosen to use only college textbook excerpts and other materials students would be likely to encounter in college. The selections are the result of field-testing with hundreds of our students over several semesters to identify material that is interesting, informative, and appropriate. We believe that this extensive field-testing provides a much more useful indicator of appropriateness than a readability formula. Field-testing revealed that, with coaching and guidance from the instructor, students can comprehend these selections. Equally important is that students like dealing with "the real thing"—actual college textbook material—since that is what they will encounter in subsequent college courses. This type of practice enables them to transfer skills to other courses and to avoid the frustration and disappointment of discovering that their reading improvement course did not prepare them for "real" college reading. Finally, these passages help students acquire and expand their background knowledge in a variety of subjects.

Extensive and varied exercises accompany the reading selections in *Opening Doors.* (These are described in "To the Student.") The exercises prepare students to read the selection and give them an opportunity to apply comprehension and study skills during and after reading. Each selection in Chapters 1–9 is accompanied by a three-part Reading Selection Quiz. The comprehension questions are the same type that content-area teachers ask on tests. All vocabulary words in each vocabulary exercise are from the reading selections and are presented in context. Reading skills application exercises include the types of questions that might appear on standardized reading tests. There are also Respond in Writing activities that include short-answer and essay-type questions with options for students to work collaboratively. The final exercise following each reading selection includes websites and keywords so that students can read more about each topic on their own.

Opening Doors is also accompanied by a Student Online Learning Center that contains a wealth of exercises and activities, such as video and audio clips of key terms and comprehension-monitoring questions, sets of "flashcards" for each chapter, and interactive chapter tests and reading selection quizzes with feedback. Also included on the Student Online Learning Center are journal writing prompts for reading selections and crossword puzzles containing vocabulary from the reading selections.

PROVEN FEATURES

- An extensive "comprehension core" as the heart of the text (Part Two, Chapters 4–9).
- Clear explanations and understandable examples of each essential comprehension skill.
- Numerous textbook excerpts and longer passages for application of reading and study skills.
- Three full-length reading selections in each of the first nine chapters. Chapters 10 and 11 each presents a chapter-length reading selection.
- Exercises that integrate writing and reading and call for both objective and essay responses.
- Cumulative review and continued application of skills taught in the comprehension core.
- Presentation of vocabulary and study skills as they relate to learning from college textbooks and other college-level materials.
- Flexibility, allowing instructors to adapt assignments to the specific needs of their particular students.
- Skills typically included on state-mandated reading competency tests are addressed, as well as tips for scoring well on standardized reading tests.
- Consistency in philosophy and approach with *Entryways, New Worlds,* and *Exercise Your College Reading Skills,* other reading comprehension textbooks in the Cortina/Elder series.
- An extensive **Online Learning Center** that contains a **Test Bank** of 14 supplemental reading selections, chapter review tests, comprehension review tests, and additional comprehension practice exercises. Also included are annotated answer keys, teaching strategies, and pages that can be printed out to make transparency masters.

ENHANCEMENTS AND NEW MATERIAL IN THE FIFTH EDITION

- New reading selections with accompanying exercises, quizzes, and activities:

  2-1 "Making It Happen: Creating Positive Change to Become a Peak Performer" (Student Success)

  2-2 "Fighting Terrorism in a Global Age" (History)

  5-2 "Violence in Television and Video Games: Does the Media's Message Matter? (Psychology)

  6-2 "America's Most Popular Drug: Caffeine" (Health)

  7-1 "E-Commerce? It's E-Normous!" (Business)

9-1 "Poverty in America and Improving Social Welfare through Public Education" (Government)

- New material and enhanced material by chapter:

Chapter One: Revised *Weekly Study Schedule*

Chapter Two: New *Standardized Test Tips for Answering Vocabulary in Context and Figurative Language Questions*

Chapter Three: Improved *Three-Step Process for Reading & Studying* table

Chapter Five: Enhanced chart of *Formulas for Implied Main Ideas*

Chapter Seven: Expanded definitions and explanations of *Author's Writing Patterns:*

List pattern (division/classification)
Sequence/time order pattern (process)
Definition pattern (definition-example)
Comparison-contrast pattern (ideas in opposition)
Cause-effect pattern

New section on *Spatial Order Pattern (Place Order)*
New section on *Relationships within and between Sentences:*

Clarification; Example; Addition; Sequence; Comparison; Contrast; Cause-effect; Problem-solution; Spatial order; Summary

New "study card" samples that illustrate comparison-contrast and cause-effect

Chapter Nine: New *Annotation Practice Exercises* for *Identifying Controversial Topics*

Chapter Ten: New excerpts in *Textbook Features* section; new charts and graphs in *Interpreting Graphic Material* section

New and revised appendixes:

Appendix 1   Glossary of Key Reading and Study Skills Terms

Appendix 2   A List of Word Parts: Prefixes, Roots and Suffixes

Appendix 3   United States Map, World Map and List of World Capitals

Appendix 4   New *Master Vocabulary List* from the *Vocabulary in Context* exercises for each *Reading Selection*

- New material and enhanced material in each chapter:

Updated *Read More about This Topic on the World Wide Web* sections with each reading selection with current websites and suggested keywords to encourage students to discover more about each topic on their own

Redesigned *Chapter Review Cards* with page prompts for Chapters 1–6 and without page prompts for Chapters 7–11

- New material and enhancements to the Instructor's Online Learning Center:

Fourteen Supplemental Reading Selections that may be assigned as extra practice exercises or given as tests:

"Music Revolution: Napster" (Mass Communications)
"The Yellow Ribbon" (Short Story)
"The Changing Roles of Men and Women" (Sociology)
"Ben & Jerry's Homemade" (Business)
"Career Choice: Choosing Your Own Future" (Personal Finance)
"Why Vote?" (Government)
"Walter Anderson: Hero on Parade" (Nonfiction)
"What Is on the Web? (Information Technology)
"How to Find Time to Read" (Essay)
"Laugh Your Stress Away" (Magazine Article)
"Benjamin Franklin: Man for All Reasons" (Newspaper Article)
"The Time Message" (Study Skills)
"Intercultural Communication" (Speech Communications)
"Communication" (Psychology)

Eleven *Chapter Review Tests* addressing the essential elements of each chapter; each test contains 10 multiple choice items

Six *Comprehension Review Tests* addressing the comprehension skills presented in Chapters 4–9 (the "comprehension core")

We wish you success in using *Opening Doors* to prepare your students to read textbooks effectively and to be more successful in college. We hope the endeavor will be enjoyable and rewarding for both you and your students.

SUPPLEMENTS TO *OPENING DOORS*

Print Resources

- *Annotated Instructor's Edition* (AIE) (0-07-329545-0)
  The *AIE* contains the full text of the student edition of the book with answers as well as marginal notes that provide a rich variety of teaching tips, related resources, and relevant quotations.

Digital Resources

- *Opening Doors* Student Online Learning Center
  This resource provides students with a rich multimedia extension of the text's content. Each module of the OLC is tied to a chapter of the text, featuring interactive quizzes with feedback for both right and wrong answers, video and audio clips, crossword puzzles, Web links, journal activities, and an Internet primer. (www.mhhe.com/opening doors).
- Instructor's Online Learning Center
  This resource provides specific suggestions for teaching each topic in the text, suggested course sequences, and a test bank of chapter quizzes. This resource also contains downloads that can be printed out to make transparencies, as well as 14 additional reading selections (with accompanying quizzes) from previous editions of *Opening Doors*. These reading selections and quizzes can be used in a variety of ways.
- PageOut: The Course Website Development Center
  Let us help you build your own course website. PageOut lets you offer students instant access to your syllabus and lecture notes, original material, recommended website addresses, and related material from the *P.O.W.E.R. Learning* website. Students can even check their grades online. PageOut also provides a discussion board where you and your students can exchange questions and post announcements, as well as an area for students to build personal Web pages.
  To find out more about PageOut: The Course Website Development Center, ask your McGraw-Hill representative for details, or fill out the form at www.mhhe.com/pageout.

Additional Value-Added Packaging Options

- *Random House Webster's College Dictionary* (0-07-366069-8) and *Student Notebook* (0-07-243099-0)
  Updated for the twenty-first century, the dictionary is available for a nominal cost when packaged with the text.

ACKNOWLEDGMENTS

We are grateful to John Kindler, Senior Sponsoring Editor, for helping make this beautiful, full-color edition fifth edition of *Opening Doors* a reality. Development Editor Carla Samodulski was a pleasure to work with, and we benefited greatly from her meticulous attention to detail. We were fortunate once again to have Senior Designer Gino Cieslik apply his magic to this new edition. Manuscript Editor Susan Nodine brought a superb eye to the manuscript. We are also indebted to Editorial Coordinator Jesse Hassenger for helping us in myriad ways throughout the project. In addition, we are grateful to Marketing Manager Tamara Wederbrand, Production Supervisor Randy Hurst, Text Permissions Editor Marty Moga, and Photo Researcher Jennifer Blankenship. We thank Paul Banks, Senior Media Development Editor, and Media Producer Alexander Rohrs for lending their technology- and media-related expertise. As in the past, Online Learning Center Content Specialist Heather Severson has enhanced our OLC content. In particular, our heartfelt thanks go to Senior Project Manager Rebecca Komro, and we dedicate this book to her. We have enjoyed the great good fortune to have worked with Becky on several editions of various books. Her organizational skills, ability to juggle dozens of things simultaneously and gracefully, and creative problem-solving ability are unsurpassed. We were doubly fortunate because Leslie LaDow, who inherited the role of Production Editor, was able to see the project to completion so skillfully and gracefully.

As always, we are indebted both to Richland College's talented and dedicated adjunct reading faculty and to students in developmental reading classes. All provided ongoing feedback and encouragement. Our admiration and appreciation for Mary Darin, Executive Dean of the Human and Academic Development Division, remains well deserved and ever constant.

The thoughtful, constructive comments and suggestions provided by the following reviewers contributed greatly to this new edition, and we thank them.

Maureen Connolly, Elmhurst College
Barbara Doyle, Arkansas State University
Mary Dubbe, Thomas Nelson Community College
Suzanne Hughes, Florida Community College at Jacksonville
John Lyon, Aviation Institute of Maintenance
Shirley Melcher, Austin Community College–Pinnacle
Sherry Prather, Austin Community College
Carrie Pyhrr, Austin Community College
TC Stuwe, Salt Lake Community College

We hope that using *Opening Doors* will be a rewarding experience for both you and your students.

Joe Cortina   **Janet Elder**

To the Student

> *Didn't I realize that reading would open up whole new worlds?*
> *A book could open doors for me. It could introduce me to people*
> *and show me places I never imagined existed.*
>
> Richard Rodriguez, *Hunger of Memory*

Welcome to *Opening Doors*. We hope that this reading improvement textbook will, in fact, "open doors" for you, doors to success in college.

Opening Doors is designed to help you acquire and practice the reading and study skills that will make you a success in college. Described below are the special features that will help you learn efficiently from this book.

SPECIAL FEATURES OF *OPENING DOORS*

Opening Doors is organized into three parts. Each part focuses on skills that are essential to your college success.

Part I: Orientation—Preparing and Organizing Yourself for Success in College
(Chapters 1–3)

This section includes chapters on goal-setting, motivation, time management, learning styles, making sense of college reading, and approaching textbook assignments effectively. Each chapter in this section includes three reading selections from a variety of subjects.

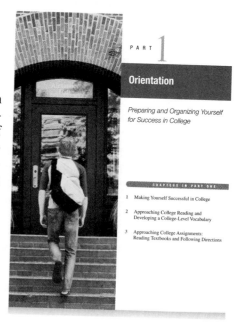

PART 1

Orientation

Preparing and Organizing Yourself for Success in College

CHAPTERS IN PART ONE

1 Making Yourself Successful in College

2 Approaching College Reading and Developing a College-Level Vocabulary

3 Approaching College Assignments: Reading Textbooks and Following Directions

Part II: Comprehension—Understanding Your College Textbooks by Reading for Ideas
(Chapters 4–9)

Comprehending what you read is vital to your success as a college student. This section is the "heart" of the book—the "comprehension core." This section will help you:

- Identify the topic and stated main idea
- Formulate implied main idea sentences

- Identify supporting details
- Understand the organization of the details (the authors' writing patterns)
- Read critically
- Think critically

Each chapter in this section includes three reading selections from a variety of subjects.

Part III: Study Systems—Developing a Textbook Study System That Works for You
(Chapters 10–11)

This part teaches you how to select and organize essential textbook information in order to prepare for a test. Both chapters in this section include a chapter-length textbook reading selection. We think you will enjoy applying the study skills to actual textbook chapters.

BUILT-IN LEARNING AIDS

Chapter Opening Page

Each chapter has major headings and subheadings that make the chapter's organization clear. Pertinent quotations begin each chapter.

Key Term Boxes

Important terms appear in Key Term Boxes in the margins so that the terms and their definitions are easy to locate.

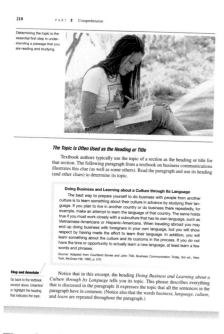

Stop and Annotate Exercises

These exercises give you the opportunity to "stop and annotate" actual college textbook excerpts. You will learn actively by underlining or highlighting stated main idea sentences, writing formulated main ideas in the margin, or numbering the important supporting details in a passage, for example.

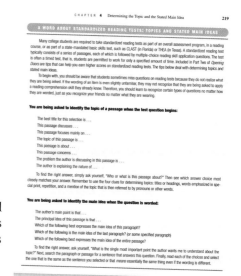

Tips for Standardized Reading Tests

Chapter 2 and each chapter in Part Two includes special tips for scoring well on standardized reading tests. These tips illustrate various reading skills as well as specific strategies for handling different types of questions.

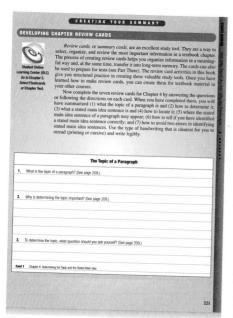

Chapter Review Cards

These simulated index cards allow you to create your own summary of the important points in the chapter. Each card includes questions, and Chapters 1–6 include prompts with page numbers to direct you to the significant information.

CHAPTER READING SELECTIONS FOR CHAPTERS 1 THROUGH 9

All the reading selections in Chapters 1 through 9 (three selections per chapter) are excerpts taken from widely used introductory-level college textbooks, news magazines, and literary selections of the type you are likely to encounter in college. These selections provide important practice, and they will increase your background knowledge in a variety of interesting subjects. They were chosen to give you the practice, skill, and confidence you need to handle subsequent college courses successfully.

Each reading selection is accompanied by preliminary and follow-up exercises. In order, the exercises are:

Prepare Yourself to Read

This exercise allows you to use techniques (such as previewing and making predictions) that will help you read the selection more actively and effectively.

Introduction to the Selection and Annotation Practice Exercises

Each selection begins with an introduction that provides background information about the selection's topic. The Annotation Practice Exercises give you the opportunity to apply to the selection the reading skills you are learning.

SELECTION 5-1　**Identity Theft: You Are at Risk**
Personal Finance

Prepare Yourself to Read

Directions: Do these exercise *before* you read Selection 5-1.

1. First, read and think about the title. What do you already know about identity theft?

2. Next, complete your preview by reading the following:
   Introduction (in *italics*)
   Headings
   The first two paragraphs (paragraphs 1 and 2)
   First sentence of each of the other paragraphs

   Now that you have previewed the selection, tell what identity theft is, and write one or two ways you could reduce your risk of becoming an identity theft victim.

Apply Comprehension Skills

Directions: Do the Annotation Practice Exercises *as you read* Selection 5-1. Apply the skills from this chapter.

Formulate implied main ideas. Follow these general steps: First determine the topic; then ask what the author's most important point about the topic is; then create a sentence that expresses the author's most important point. Use the appropriate formula to "formulate" an implied main idea sentence based on information in the paragraph.

Check your formulated main idea sentences. Be sure each of your main idea sentences meets the requirements on page 276.

Complete the Annotation Practice Exercises. In these exercises, you will work only with paragraphs that have implied main ideas.

283

284　PART **2**　Comprehension

IDENTITY THEFT: YOU ARE AT RISK

Identity theft is rapidly increasing. Chances are that even if you yourself are not a victim of identity theft, you know someone who has been and you know the devastating effects this crime can have. College students, in particular, can be easy targets for identity thieves. The following selection explains the crime, the techniques these thieves use, and some ways to reduce your risk of becoming an identity theft victim.

The Crime of Identity Theft

1 Don't think it can't happen to you. Your credit card bill arrives with charges for items you never purchased. You pay your bills on time and always have. Suddenly, though, creditors start hounding you for payment of past-due bills, but you never ordered any of the goods or services they're demanding payment for. The grocery store and drugstore where you've always shopped are now refusing to accept your checks because of your bad credit history. Perhaps you even receive a summons to show up in court for a traffic ticket you never paid—and, in fact, which you never received. Guess what: You're now among the hundreds of thousands of people each year who become victims of identity theft.

2 In this fast-growing crime, perpetrators steal or gather data on individuals. The data that these criminals steal include Social Security numbers, driver's license numbers, dates of birth, bank account numbers, and credit card numbers, as well as credit cards and ATM cards. They use several methods of acquiring these. Once they have enough information, the thieves impersonate the victim. They spend as much money as possible as quickly as possible, charging the purchases to the victim. Then they do the same thing all over again, using someone else's identity and credit.

Forms of Identity Theft

3 There are two forms of this theft. The first type is "account takeover" theft, in which the thief uses existing credit information to make purchases. The criminal may use an actual credit card or may simply charge purchases by phone or online using the credit card number and expiration date. The victim discovers the "theft" when the monthly account statement arrives. The second type of identity theft

Annotation Practice Exercises

Directions: For each exercise below,
· Write the topic of the paragraph on the lines provided.
· Formulate the implied main idea of the paragraph and write it on the lines provided.

This will help you remember the topic and the main idea.

Practice Exercise
· Topic of paragraph 2:

· Formulate the implied main idea of paragraph 2:

CHAPTER **5**　Formulating Implied Main Ideas　　285

is "application fraud" (or "true name fraud"). Using the victim's information, the thief opens new accounts in the victim's name. The thief has the monthly statements sent to a different address, so considerable time may elapse before the victim realizes what has happened.

4 If there is any good news, it is this: in general, credit and banking fraud victims are liable for no more than the first $50 of loss. Many times, the victim will not have to pay for any of the loss.

5 The bad news is that victims are left with a time-consuming, frustrating mess to clear up. Because their credit has been wrecked, they may be denied credit and loans. They may have difficulty leasing an apartment, or even getting a job. Unfortunately, victims get little help from authorities as they try to untangle the problem.

Thieves' Information Sources

6 How do thieves obtain the information that enables them to "steal" someone else's identity? The easiest way is by stealing the person's wallet. For thieves, it's like one-stop shopping, since wallets usually contain credit cards, a driver's license and other pieces of information, such as the person's Social Security number.

7 There are many other techniques thieves use. These include:
· Stealing documents from unlocked mailboxes and breaking into locked ones. Thieves look especially for boxes of checks, new credit cards, bank statements, tax documents, insurance statements, and credit card statements.
· Searching through trash receptacles ("dumpster diving") for unshredded documents with identifying Social Security numbers, unused pre-approved credit card applications, loan applications, and so forth.
· Using personnel files or customer files in the workplace to improperly access names, Social Security numbers, and other data.
· Obtaining people's credit reports fraudulently by impersonating an employer, a landlord, or a loan officer at a financial institution.
· "Shoulder surfing" at phone booths and ATMs to obtain people's PIN numbers (personal identification numbers).
· Going to Internet sites that provide identifying information and public records.

Practice Exercise
· Topic of paragraph 3:

· Formulate the implied main idea of paragraph 3:

Practice Exercise
· Topic of paragraph 6:

· Formulate the implied main idea of paragraph 6:

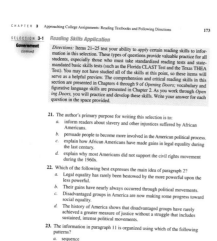

Reading Selection Quizzes

The Reading Selection Quizzes include three types of exercises: comprehension, vocabulary in context, and reading skills application.

Comprehension

These exercises test your comprehension (understanding) of the material in the selection. These questions are the type a content area instructor (such as a business professor) would ask on a test over this material.

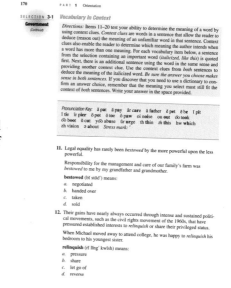

Vocabulary in Context

These exercises test your skill in determining the meaning of words by using context clues.

Reading Skills Application

In these exercises, you will apply certain reading skills to the material in the selection. These are the types of questions that might appear on standardized reading tests and state-mandated basic skills tests.

Respond in Writing

These short-answer and essay-type exercises ask you to write about the selection. They will extend your understanding and help you relate the material to your own experiences. They will also give you practice in determining the overall main idea of the selection.

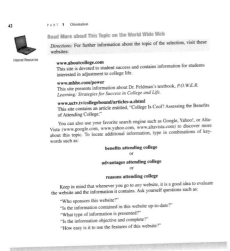

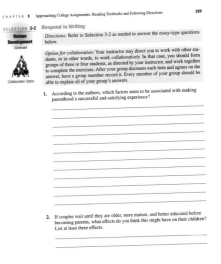

Read More about This Topic on the World Wide Web

This consists of a list of websites related to the topic or author of the selection. It also contains suggested keywords so you can use your favorite search engine such as Google, Yahoo!, or AltaVista to discover more about this topic on your own. This gives you an opportunity to explore the topic further.

SPECIAL STUDY SKILLS FEATURES IN CHAPTERS 10 AND 11

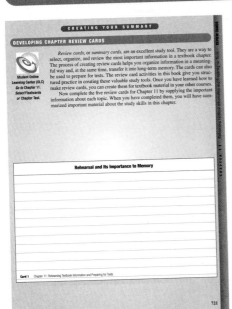

Chapter Review Cards

Chapters 10 and 11 give you specific strategies that enable you to understand and remember important information in your college textbooks. In order to give you a "real-life" simulation of studying textbook material, the Chapter Review Cards for Chapters 10 and 11 do not contain any prompts.

Full-Length Reading Selections

Chapters 10 and 11 each contain a chapter-length selection rather than three shorter reading selections. Instead of taking a Reading Selection Quiz, you are asked to highlight and annotate the selection as you read. You are then asked to prepare an outline, study map, test review cards, etc., for specific subsections of the reading selection.

In addition to the built-in learning aids that occur in each chapter, *Opening Doors* offers you photos, summary charts, diagrams, cartoons, study maps, outlines, and other learning aids. As you work through this book, we hope that you will take advantage of all of its features and that you will discover that you are becoming a better reader and a more effective, efficient student.

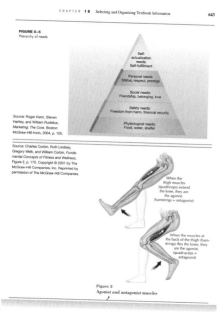

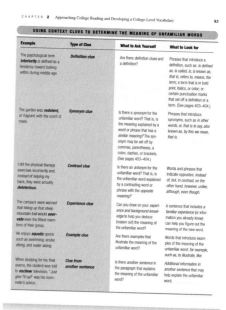

We welcome you to *Opening Doors*. We hope your journey through this textbook is an enjoyable and rewarding experience.

Joe Cortina   **Janet Elder**

PART 1

Orientation

*Preparing and Organizing Yourself
for Success in College*

CHAPTERS IN PART ONE

1   Making Yourself Successful in College

2   Approaching College Reading and
    Developing a College-Level Vocabulary

3   Approaching College Assignments:
    Reading Textbooks and Following Directions

1

Making Yourself Successful in College

In this chapter you will learn the answers to these questions:

- What do successful college students do?

- How can I motivate myself to do well in college?

- How can I set goals for myself?

- What are learning styles?

- How can I manage my time more effectively?

SKILLS

Doing What Successful Students Do

Motivating Yourself

Setting Your Goals

Identifying Your Learning Style

Managing Your Time

- Setting Up a Weekly Study Schedule
- Making the Most of Your Study Time
- Planning Further Ahead: Creating a Monthly Assignment Calendar and Using a Daily To Do List

CREATING YOUR SUMMARY

Developing Chapter Review Cards

READINGS

Selection 1-1 *(Study Skills)*
"Why Go to College?" from *P.O.W.E.R. Learning: Strategies for Success in College and Life*
by Robert S. Feldman

Selection 1-2 *(Business)*
"Getting Ready for Prime Time: Learning the Skills Needed to Succeed Today and Tomorrow" from *Understanding Business*
by William Nickels, James McHugh, and Susan McHugh

Selection 1-3 *(Literature)*
"Saved" from *The Autobiography of Malcolm X,*
as told to Alex Haley

Education is our passport to the future, for tomorrow belongs to the people who prepare for it today.

Malcolm X

Industry and patience are the surest means to plenty.

Benjamin Franklin

DOING WHAT SUCCESSFUL STUDENTS DO

Some students are more successful than others. Why? One answer is that successful students know how to motivate themselves, set goals for themselves, and manage their time. They also have identified their learning style, the way they learn best. In this chapter, you will learn how to do all of these things. If you start now and consistently apply the techniques and strategies in this chapter, you will become a more successful college student. Getting off to a good start is important because, as the proverb says, "Well begun is half done." This is just a way of saying that a good beginning goes a long way toward your ultimate success.

Moreover, the Greek philosopher Aristotle observed, "We are what we repeatedly do. Excellence then is not an act, but a habit." This is valuable advice. If you make good study techniques and time management a habit, each semester you can become a better, more effective student.

It is helpful to look more closely at exactly what successful students do. One especially interesting research study involved college students who were highly effective *despite the fact that they did not have high entrance scores*. In other words, anyone looking at these students' test scores would not have predicted that they would do well in college. The researchers asked the students themselves what it was that enabled them to be so successful. They learned from these effective students that they all shared five important characteristics:

1. **Effective students are highly motivated.** Successful students have an inner drive to do well. They are goal-oriented; they have specific careers in mind. They believe that they are responsible for their own success or failure; they attribute nothing to "good luck" or "bad luck."

2. **Effective students plan ahead.** Successful students are organized. They develop good study habits. They establish a study schedule and stick to it. They study at the same time each day, and in the same place.

3. **Effective students focus on understanding.** Successful students use instructors' oral and written feedback to monitor their progress and make changes if necessary. They assess their own strengths and weaknesses on the basis of instructors' comments in class, evaluations of homework assignments, and grades on tests. If they start to do poorly or fall behind in a subject, they adjust their schedule to spend more time on it, and they immediately seek help from an instructor, a tutor, or a friend. Moreover, successful students are familiar with

5

their learning style—the way they learn best—and they take steps to use this learning style when they study.

4. **Effective students are highly selective.**   Successful students concentrate on main ideas and important supporting details when they read assignments. To identify important information, they pay attention to how paragraphs are organized and to signals and clue words in their textbooks and class notes. They do not try to memorize everything when they study. They use instructors' suggestions, course outlines, textbook features, and class notes to guide their efforts.

5. **Effective students are involved and attentive.**   Successful students focus on their academic work in class and outside of class. In class, they pay attention, take notes, and participate in discussions. They make a point of arriving early, and they help themselves concentrate by sitting near the front. Outside of class, they study in quiet places to avoid distractions. They put academic work ahead of social life, and they limit time spent watching television, playing video and computer games, and surfing the Internet. They find a "study buddy" or join a study group so that they can study with others who are serious about school. They take advantage of their college's tutoring center and other resources. If supplemental instruction is available, they participate in it. They concentrate on the present rather than worrying about the past or daydreaming too much about the future.

Source: Adapted from John Q. Easton, Don Barshis, and Rick Ginsberg, "Chicago Colleges Identify Effective Teachers, Students," *Community and Junior College Journal,* December–January 1983–1984, pp. 27–31.

Perhaps the most interesting aspect of these characteristics of successful college students is that there is nothing that is especially complicated or difficult about achieving them. With planning and determination, any student can make these behaviors part of his or her own life in college.

Another, more recent study also looked at students who had low high school grades and low college entrance scores. Although these students were not expected to do well in college, half of them achieved a relatively high college grade point average (GPA). The rest were on scholastic probation after several semesters. Researchers wanted to know, What was the difference between those who succeeded and those who did not?

Careful interviews with all the students revealed these characteristics of the successful students:

1. They attend and participate in class.

2. They are prepared for class.

3. They perceive instructors as experts.

4. They adhere to an organized study routine.

5. They develop a repertoire of study skills and strategies.

6. They take responsibility for their own learning.

Sounds familiar, doesn't it? The findings were strikingly similar to those of the earlier study conducted by different researchers at a different college. The unsuccessful students in this study "readily admitted that they did not engage in these behaviors and explained that their social lives held higher priority." Clearly, practicing these obvious "success behaviors" and making your college education a priority can make you more successful too.

Source: JoAnn Yaworski, Rose-Marie Weber, and Nabil Ibrahim, "What Makes Students Succeed or Fail? The Voices of Developmental College Students," *Journal of College Reading and Learning,* vol. 30, no. 2 (Spring 2000), pp. 195–221.

MOTIVATING YOURSELF

In college, you are responsible for motivating yourself. Developing an interest in and a commitment to your courses is not your instructors' responsibility; it is your responsibility. Developing the discipline and commitment to make yourself successful is not your parents' responsibility; it is your responsibility. If you assume the responsibility, then you can feel justifiably proud when you succeed, because the credit goes to you. The truly valuable and worthwhile things in life are seldom easy, but that is one of the things that gives them their value.

Fortunately, motivating yourself is easier than you may think. For one thing, college is a stimulating place to be! As you progress through college, you will find how pleasurable and satisfying learning can be. Also, there are specific, effective self-motivation techniques you can use. Here are a dozen strategies that you can use to get motivated and to stay motivated throughout the semester.

1. **Write down your educational goals for the semester.** The act of writing down semester goals can be motivating in and of itself. Clear goals can also motivate you to use your time well. Specific goals (for class attendance and participation, homework, and grades) help you select activities that will move you toward your goals. In addition, achieving any worthwhile goal is a deeply satisfying experience that will motivate you to achieve more goals. (Goal-setting is discussed on pages 10–12.)

2. **Visualize your success.** Visualize successful outcomes that you want to make happen in the near future, such as earning a high grade on an assignment or completing the semester successfully. Then visualize the future further ahead: Imagine yourself in a cap and gown being handed your college diploma; imagine an employer offering you the job you've dreamed of. Make your mental images as sharp and vivid as possible. Imagine the feelings as well, such as the happiness and pride you will feel in your accomplishment.

3. **Think of classes as your easiest learning sessions.** If you spend three hours a week in class for a course, view those hours as your *easiest* three hours of learning and studying for the course. Remind yourself of this when you feel frustrated by a course or when you are tempted to skip class. Your instructor, who is an expert, is there to explain and to answer questions. Adopting this perspective can make a big difference.

Simply doing the things that successful students do can enable you to succeed in college.

4. **View your courses as opportunities.**   Especially if a course is difficult, consider it a challenge rather than a problem or an obstacle. The brain grows only when it is challenged. Accept the fact that you are required to take a variety of courses to broaden your educational background. Later in life, you will most likely come to appreciate these courses more than you can now. Taking the "long view" can be motivating.

5. **Develop emotional strategies for dealing with difficult courses.**   For example, to keep from feeling overwhelmed, a good strategy is to focus on the material you are studying at the time rather than worrying about what is coming next or whether it will be difficult. Another strategy is to consider the feeling of accomplishment and pride that will come from succeeding at a challenging subject. Realize, too, that you can enjoy a subject even if you never make a top grade or become an expert in it.

6. **Seek advice and study tips from good students in your courses.**   Ask them what they are doing to be successful. If they like a course that seems difficult or boring to you, ask them why they enjoy the subject. Ask them how they approach assignments and prepare for tests.

7. **Choose the right friends.**   By "right" friends, we mean friends who support and encourage your class participation and studying. Find a "study buddy" or form a small study group with others who are serious about college. It is also helpful to find a mentor (a wise and trusted counselor or instructor) who can give you advice, support, and encouragement.

8. **Divide big projects into smaller parts.** To motivate yourself, break large projects into smaller, more manageable tasks. (For instance, a 20-page reading assignment can be divided into four shorter readings of 5 pages each, and you may even want to read these during short study sessions on two different days.) Sometimes you will find it necessary to set priorities or to sequence the smaller tasks. (For example, to write a paper, you might have to get information from library books or the Internet, take notes, write an outline of your paper, and so forth.)

9. **Give yourself rewards.** Reward yourself for successfully completing an activity such as a homework assignment or studying for a test. For example, have a snack or take a short walk.

10. **Make positive "self-talk" a habit.** Say encouraging things to yourself, such as, "I think I can do this assignment, even though it might take a while" and "If other students in my class can do this, I can too." Over time, this actually changes your beliefs. Also, use a technique called *thought stopping* to shut off negative self-talk, such as, "I'll never learn this!" or "This test is impossible." When you find that you are giving yourself negative feedback, just say "Stop!" and substitute some *positive* self-talk. Don't let frustration overcome you and destroy your productivity. Recognizing that frustration is a normal part of learning (and of life) will help you develop tolerance for it.

11. **Think in terms of being satisfied if you do your best.** Reassure yourself that if you truly do your best, you can feel satisfied with your effort, regardless of the outcome. You will never have to wonder whether you could have done better if only you had tried harder. Best of all, you will have no regrets.

12. **Remind yourself that motivation and success reinforce each other.** Motivation leads to success; success increases motivation; increased motivation leads to more success; and so on! In other words, motivation and success go hand in hand. Celebrate each small success and use it as a springboard to even greater success.

From this list, pick at least two strategies that are new to you and that you think would work for you. Add them to your short-term goals list, and then use them throughout the semester to increase your motivation.

Some students who are having a difficult time in a subject mistakenly believe that the subject is easy for those who are doing well in it. They do not realize that those students are successful *because* they are working very hard. Some students who are having difficulty in a course tell themselves that they just don't have the ability to do well, and therefore, there is no reason to try. Of course, the very way you become better at a subject is by working at it. Thinking that a subject is easy for everyone else or that you just don't have the ability is really just an excuse for not trying very hard or for not trying at all. Don't fall into this trap.

SETTING YOUR GOALS

Most successful students (in fact, most successful people) have this in common: They establish goals, and they put their goals *in writing*. They write down *what they want to accomplish* and the *length of time* in which they plan to accomplish it. Putting your goals in writing is a very simple technique that can help you turn wishes into reality.

Why should you bother to write out your goals? There are several reasons. First, goals that are not written down are not much better than wishes. ("I wish I had a college degree." "I wish I had a career I enjoyed.") Unwritten goals will probably remain just wishes. Second, writing your goals helps you make a commitment to them. If a goal is not even important enough to write down, how likely do you think you are to accomplish it? Third, writing out your goals gives you a yardstick, a written record, that you can use to measure your progress. Finally, no one wants to look back and feel regret about things he or she might have done or accomplished but hasn't. When your life is over, what do you want to be remembered for? Surely that is important enough to write down. Another way to think about setting goals is to ask yourself what you *don't* want to be doing a year from now, several years from now, or several decades from now.

You may find it helpful to put your goals into categories, such as educational, financial, spiritual, personal (including family matters), physical (health and fitness), and career. An example of an educational goal might be, "To complete all my courses this semester and earn at least a grade of B in each." An example of a financial goal might be, "To save enough money during the next year to make a down payment on a new car."

Sometimes it becomes necessary to choose between two or more competing goals. For example, suppose that you wanted to attend college full time and work full time. You would have to give up the second goal in order to have enough time for studying. Or you would have to modify both goals, deciding to attend college part time and work part time. Competing goals do not always make it necessary to give up a goal, but they do make it necessary to be realistic, to set priorities, and to adjust your time and efforts.

A famous expert in time management, Alan Lakein, gives these recommendations for setting goals:

- **Be specific.**   An example of a specific goal is, "I will exercise for 30 minutes five days a week for the next three months." A vague goal such as "I will get more exercise" is not very helpful.

- **Be realistic.**   "I will exercise for 30 minutes five days a week" is also an example of a realistic goal. An unrealistic goal would be "I will exercise two hours a day for the rest of the year." Unrealistic goals are not helpful, and they can be frustrating and discouraging as well.

- **Revise your goals at regular intervals.**   People change, and so do their situations and priorities. Therefore, it is important to review your goals regularly and revise them whenever necessary.

Source: Alan Lakein, *How to Get Control of Your Time and Your Life* (New York: Signet, 1973), pp. 30–37, pp. 64–65.

KEY TERMS

long-term goal

Goal you want to
accomplish during
your lifetime.

intermediate goal

Goal you want to
accomplish within the
next 3 to 5 years

short-term goal

Goal you want to
accomplish within
3 to 6 months.

Lakein also recommends setting three types of goals based on how important the goals are and the amount of time required to accomplish or achieve them. The three types of goals are long-term, intermediate, and short-term. **Long-term goals** are ones you want to accomplish during your lifetime; **intermediate goals** are ones you want to achieve within the next three to five years; **short-term goals** are ones you want to accomplish within three to six months. (As a student, you may find it helpful to think of short-term goals as ones you would like to accomplish during the semester.) Your short-term goals should help you achieve your intermediate goals, which in turn should help you achieve your long-term, lifetime goals. For instance, improving your reading skills is a short-term goal that will contribute to the intermediate goal of earning a college degree, and ultimately to the long-term goal of an interesting, satisfying career. Of course, some goals will fall between half a year and three years. Regardless of the precise length of time, it's still helpful to think in terms of long-term, intermediate, and short-term goals.

The box below will give you an opportunity to formulate and record your long-term, intermediate, and short-term goals. When you have put your goals in writing, identify one or two from each category that are especially important to you now. Whenever you must decide how to use your time, choose activities that will help you reach those goals.

Keep a list of your goals where you can see and read them often. You might keep them at the front of a notebook, for instance, or on your desk. Some of your

---

PUTTING YOUR GOALS IN WRITING

Take a few minutes to write down your goals. Write at least three goals for each category. (These are personal and private, and they do not have to be shared with anyone.)

What are my long-term goals?

On the lines below, write three things you want to accomplish and achieve during your lifetime.

1. plan my work very well
2. try to make positive
3. And make changes

What are my intermediate goals?

On the lines below, write three things you want to accomplish during the next 3 to 5 years.

1. get good jobs
2. planing financial goal
3.

What are my short-term goals?

On the lines below, write three things you want to accomplish this semester.

1.
2.
3.

goals will be achieved quickly and removed from your list, but you may find that others will remain on your list for a long time, perhaps even a lifetime.

IDENTIFYING YOUR LEARNING STYLE

In addition to managing your study time, you need to identify your learning style, or how you learn best. To gain insight into your learning style, complete the learning styles inventory below. When you have completed the survey and totaled your responses, read the rest of this section.

IDENTIFYING YOUR LEARNING STYLE

To gain insight into your learning style, answer the following questions. For each item, circle all the answers that describe you.

1. When I go someplace I have not been before, I usually
   A.   trust my intuition about the right direction or route to take.
   B.   ask someone for directions.
   C.   look at a map.

2. I like to go to places where
   A.   there is lots of space to move around.
   B.   people are talking or there is music that matches my mood.
   C.   there is good "people watching" or there is something interesting to see.

3. If I have lots of things to do, I generally
   A.   feel nervous or fidgety until I get most of them done.
   B.   repeat things to myself so I won't forget to do them.
   C.   jot them down on a list or write them on a calendar or organizer.

4. When I have free time, I like to
   A.   work on a handicraft or hobby, or do an activity such as play a sport or exercise.
   B.   listen to a tape, a CD, or the radio, or talk on the phone.
   C.   watch television, play a computer or video game, or see a movie.

5. When I am talking with other people, I typically
   A.   pay attention to their gestures or move close to them so I can get a feel for what they are telling me.
   B.   listen carefully so I can hear what they are saying.
   C.   watch them closely so that I can see what they are saying.

6. When I meet someone new, I usually pay most attention to
   A.   the way the person walks or moves, or the gestures the person makes.
   B.   the way the person speaks, what the person says, and how his or her voice sounds.
   C.   the way the person looks and is dressed.

(Continued on next page)

(Continued from previous page)

7. When I select books, magazines, or articles to read, I generally choose ones that
  A. deal with sports or fitness, hobbies and crafts, or other activities.
  B. tell me about something that happened or tell a story.
  C. include lots of photos, pictures, or illustrations.

8. Learning something is easier for me when I can
  A. use a hands-on approach.
  B. have someone explain it to me.
  C. watch someone show me how to do it.

Total up your As, then total up your Bs, and your Cs.

_____ As   _____ Bs   _____ Cs

If your highest total is As, you are a tactile *or* kinesthetic *learner.*
If your highest total is Bs you are an auditory *learner.*
If your highest total is Cs, you are a visual *learner.*

KEY TERMS

learning style

The modality through which an individual learns best.

visual learner

One who prefers to see or read information to be learned.

auditory learner

One who prefers to hear information to be learned.

tactile or kinesthetic learner

One who prefers to touch and manipulate materials physically or to incorporate movement when learning.

Learning style refers to the modality through which an individual learns best. Everyone has a *modality,* or sensory channel, through which he or she prefers to learn because learning is easier and more efficient that way. Your learning style, of course, is the way you learn best.

The three primary modalities for learning are seeing (visual modality), hearing (auditory modality), and touch (tactile modality) or movement (kinesthetic modality). People who are **visual learners** prefer to see or read the material to be learned and will benefit from books, class notes, concept maps, review cards, test review sheets, and the like. Others are **auditory learners,** preferring to hear the material in the form of lectures and discussions. Auditory learners often benefit from reciting material or reading aloud to themselves, making or using audiotapes, and participating in study groups. Still others are **tactile learners,** who benefit from touching and manipulating materials, or **kinesthetic learners,** who benefit from physical movement. Tactile learners prefer laboratory work and other hands-on projects. Kinesthetic learners like to "go through the motions" of doing something; they also benefit from writing things down or typing out material to be learned. (The three basic learning styles are summarized in the box on page 14.)

Of course, people learn in more than one way, and most people use some combination of modalities simultaneously. And even though most people prefer to use one modality more heavily than the others, a person's learning style can change as he or she acquires more practice and skill in using the other modalities.

Did your results on the learning style survey surprise you, or did they simply confirm what you already knew about how you prefer to learn? If you know your learning style, you can put yourself in situations in which you learn best; you can utilize study techniques and strategies that take advantage of your strengths. Moreover, when material is presented in a way that does not match your learning style, you can take steps to compensate and "work around" the problem by studying the material the way *you* learn best.

There is one other aspect of learning that you might also want to think about: whether you prefer to work by yourself or with others. If you prefer working alone, make it a priority to find a quiet place where you will not be disturbed. You may also find that self-paced courses, computer-assisted instruction, telecourses, or other on-line or distance-learning options work well for you. On the other hand, if you are a person who finds it advantageous to study with others, you will benefit from being part of a study group or having a study partner. When selecting study partners, remember to select other students who are serious and motivated. Also, keep in mind that participating in a study group does not guarantee success. You must prepare yourself to work with a group: You must read and study on your own first.

THREE LEARNING STYLES

If This Is Your Learning Style . . .	Then These Activities Are the Most Helpful to Your Learning
Visual learner (prefers to read or see information)	Reading textbooks and seeing information in print Reviewing class notes and concept maps Reading your chapter review cards Studying test review sheets
Auditory learner (prefers to hear information)	Listening to class lectures and discussions Reciting material (saying it out loud) Reading aloud to yourself Listening to audiotapes Participating in study groups
Tactile or kinesthetic learner (prefers to manipulate materials physically or incorporate movement)	Taking notes from lectures and from textbooks Making concept maps Rewriting lecture notes after class Preparing study cards Doing laboratory work (computer labs, science labs, etc.) Actually going through steps or procedures in a process Taking hands-on classes (science, computer science, engineering, and other technical or vocational subjects)

MANAGING YOUR TIME

Time, like money, is valuable, and, like money, it should be spent wisely. Managing your time means making decisions about how you choose to spend time. When you look at the numbers in the box below, you will realize how much decision making is necessary in order to gain control of your time.

Fortunately, there are several strategies that you can use to control your time. In this section, you'll learn how to set up a weekly study schedule and make the most of your study sessions; you'll also look at two other important planning tools: a monthly calendar and a daily To Do list.

HOW DO YOU CHOOSE TO SPEND YOUR TIME?

There are 168 hours in a week.

If you sleep 8 hours a night, you spend 56 hours a week sleeping.

If you spend 1 hour at each meal, you spend 21 hours a week eating.

If you have a full college schedule, you spend about 12 to 20 hours a week attending classes and labs.

This leaves you about 70 hours a week, or 10 hours a day, for everything else: studying, work, recreation, personal chores, and so on.

For at least 10 out of every 24 hours, you make decisions about how you will spend your time.

KEY TERM

study schedule

Weekly schedule with specific times set aside for studying.

Setting Up a Weekly Study Schedule

If you tell yourself that you will study "whenever you find time," you may never "find time," or at least not *enough* time. To be a truly effective student, you must set aside time specifically for studying. In other words, it is essential to have a study schedule. A weekly **study schedule** is just what it sounds like: a weekly schedule with specific times set aside for studying. A realistic, well thought-out weekly schedule will assure you of ample study time.

Most college students say that they have too much to do in too little time. In fact, they cite this as their number one source of stress. Scheduling your time can lower this stress and reduce tension, worry, and inefficiency. A realistic schedule does not turn you into a robot; rather, it frees you from constant decision making (and indecision!) and lets you make the best use of your time.

It's important to balance study time and leisure time, but here's the rule successful students go by: Study first; then relax or have fun. If you stick to this rule, you will have more free time. Also, you will genuinely enjoy that free time because you won't feel guilty about unfinished work. These become your rewards for completing your studying first.

To develop your weekly study schedule, use the planning form on page 18, and follow these steps:

• **Step 1.** Identify times that are already committed to other activities (such as classes, meals, work, organizations, commuting, sleeping, etc.) since those times are definitely not available for study. Write those fixed activities in the appropriate places on your weekly study schedule, or type them in if you keep your schedule on your computer or PDA.

- **Step 2.**   Identify other times when you probably would not be able to study (for example, times devoted to household and personal chores, family, rest, and leisure activities). Post these on your weekly study schedule. These are somewhat more flexible parts of your schedule because you have more control over when you do many of them.

- **Step 3.**   Identify the best general times for you to study. On the list below, circle the time periods when you are most alert and energetic:

Early morning (6–9 A.M.)

Midmorning (9 A.M. to noon)

Early afternoon (12–3 P.M.)

Late afternoon (3–6 P.M.)

Early evening (6–9 P.M.)

Late evening (9 P.M. to midnight)

Late night (after midnight)

Studying during daylight hours and when you are alert and rested allows you to accomplish more in less time. Try to schedule as much studying as possible, however, during the hours you identified as *your* best times.

- **Step 4.**   Determine how much study time you need. Allow a *minimum* of one hour of study time for each hour you spend in class. (For a typical three-credit course, that means a minimum of three hours of study time per week; difficult courses may require more time. You will need to schedule more study time if you are a slow reader or if you have not yet developed efficient study skills.) Set aside an appropriate number of study hours for each course; it is better to overestimate than to underestimate. College students are expected to be much more independent in their learning than high school students, and many new college students are surprised at how much time studying takes. To meet the challenge of college courses, plan as much study time as you think you will possibly need.

- **Step 5.**   From the times that are still available, select the specific times you will study and mark them on your schedule. Also, be specific about what you intend to study at each time (such as "Study psychology," "Computer science homework," or "Study history" rather than "study"). A sample weekly study schedule on page 17 has been filled in to show you how a typical study schedule might look. You may want to highlight the times you plan to study.

Once you have set up your study schedule, keep it where you can see it—*then follow it.* You will probably need about three weeks to become accustomed to a new schedule. This is because it takes approximately three weeks to establish a new habit or to break an old one. Don't get discouraged if using a schedule feels awkward at first. That's normal.

If your work schedule changes each week or if your school or personal activity times vary, you will have to create an updated schedule each week. Successful students often gain great satisfaction from organizing their time in this manner. As you gain experience making weekly schedules, you will discover that it becomes easier to "find" enough time for studying.

SAMPLE WEEKLY STUDY SCHEDULE

Here is a sample of a weekly study schedule that has been completed according to the directions on pages 15–16. Notice that *specific study times have been identified for each course*. Use the blank form on page 18 to create your own weekly study schedule.

Time	Sunday	Monday	Tuesday	Wednesday	Thursday	Friday	Saturday
6:00 A.M.				Get ready for school			
7:00				Travel to school			
8:00		Computer Science	Read English	Computer Science	Review English	Computer Science	Workout
9:00		History	English	History	English	History	Tennis
10:00	Family time	Sociology	Biology	Sociology	Biology	Sociology	
11:00		Lunch		Lunch		Lunch	
12:00 noon		Computer Science homework		Computer Science homework		Computer Science homework	Work
1:00 P.M.		English assignment	Lunch	English assignment	Lunch	English assignment	
2:00	Workout		Biology lab		Biology study group		
3:00	Tennis	Study biology		Study biology		Snack	
4:00		Dinner		Dinner	Workout		
5:00		Work	Read history text	Work	Read history text	Work	
6:00	Read biology assignment						Spend time with friends
7:00			Dinner		Dinner		
8:00	English assignment		Read sociology text		Read sociology text		
9:00	English assignment						
10:00	Sleep	Relax/watch news	Relax/watch news	Relax/watch news	Relax/watch news	Go out	
11:00		Sleep	Sleep	Sleep	Sleep	Sleep	Sleep
12:00 midnight							
1:00 A.M.							

WEEKLY STUDY SCHEDULE

Time	Sunday	Monday	Tuesday	Wednesday	Thursday	Friday	Saturday
6:00 A.M.							
7:00							
8:00							
9:00							
10:00							
11:00							
12:00 noon							
1:00 P.M.							
2:00							
3:00							
4:00							
5:00							
6:00							
7:00							
8:00							
9:00							
10:00							
11:00							
12:00 midnight							
1:00 A.M.							

Remember: Adjust your weekly schedule if you need to, but then make every effort to stick to it. Each time you deviate from your schedule, returning to it becomes harder. Sticking with it will get you past one big obstacle to studying: simply getting started. Having a regular study routine makes it easier to become a more effective, successful student.

Making the Most of Your Study Time

Once you have set up a weekly study schedule, it is important to make your study time as productive as possible. There are various strategies you can use to get the most out of your study sessions. Try these proven techniques:

1. **Find or create a suitable place to study.**   Your study place can be at home or elsewhere. A library or any other quiet place on campus can serve as well. Buy whatever materials and supplies you will need, and have them at hand in a drawer or book bag. *Use your study place* only *for studying.* This reinforces the message that when you are in your study place, you are there to study!

2. **Study in the same place at the same time every day.**   This helps you "get into" studying immediately because it makes studying automatic, a habit. Knowing when, where, and what you are going to study keeps you from indecision and procrastination.

3. **Make your study time more productive, not longer.**   Strive for, say, one or two productive study hours rather than three or four unproductive hours. To keep your study time productive, you must stay focused. Remember that just sitting at a desk is not studying, and just looking at a book is not reading. If you find yourself daydreaming, stop and refocus your thinking. If you begin to tire, and your ability to concentrate decreases, take a five-minute break or switch to another subject to maintain your efficiency. Be sure, however, to take your break at a logical stopping point—not in the middle of a task that is going well. It is also helpful to stand up or stretch at least every half hour while you are studying.

4. **Study as soon as possible after lecture classes.**   One hour spent studying immediately or soon after a lecture class will do as much to develop your understanding and recall of the material as several hours of studying would a few days later. Review and improve your lecture notes while they are still fresh in your mind. Start assignments while your understanding of the directions and the material is still accurate. If there are points you do not understand, take steps immediately to clear them up: look up an unknown word, make a note to ask the instructor about something that confused you, etc.

5. **Take advantage of short periods of free time for studying.**   Brief periods of time (for instance, periods of 15 to 45 minutes before, between, and after classes) are often wasted. Use these brief periods for study or review. Before a lecture class, for example, it's wise to spend a few minutes reviewing your notes from the previous lecture or going over the reading assignment. When you look for short periods of free time to use, keep in mind that (in general) daytime study is more efficient than nighttime study: What you can accomplish in one hour

during the day might take two hours at night. Also, look for time on Saturdays and Sundays.

6. **Don't try to study your most difficult subject last.**   You may have favorite subjects that you enjoy studying. It is tempting to focus on these subjects first and leave the harder subjects until last. But if you do this, you will often find that you have run out of time for a difficult subject or are too tired to work on it effectively. Study your most difficult subjects when you still have the time and energy to do a good job on them.

7. **If you can't study at your scheduled time, take some time from another, nonstudy activity.**   When unexpected events arise that take up time you had scheduled for studying, decide immediately where in your schedule you can make up the study session you missed, and make a temporary adjustment in your schedule. Don't overlook weekends, including Saturday and Sunday evening. Successful students often take advantage of weekends by using part of them for productive, unhurried study times.

8. **Experiment to develop study strategies and techniques that work for you.**   Try out techniques that allow you to capitalize on your learning style or make learning easier. Be creative. If you get sleepy when you read your textbook assignments, try standing up and walking back and forth in your room as you read. Try reading out loud or taking notes. Try reviewing your week's class notes and textbook markings to help you learn and remember the material. Study hard for 45 minutes, then take a 15-minute break. The key is to discover the particular strategies that work for you.

9. **Don't let friends, your phone, or television interfere with your study time.**   Students say over and over again that, along with working too many hours, these are the main reasons they do not get all of their studying done. Every time you interrupt your study session to visit with friends, talk on the phone, play a video game, or watch a TV program, you make your study session longer and less effective. Honor your commitment to your study time.

10. **Improve your concentration.**   You can do this by dealing immediately with any external and internal distractions. To deal with external distractors in your environment, you may need to find a place that is quieter or has better light, adjust the room temperature, etc. To deal with internal (emotional) distractors, you will need to develop strategies to reduce worrying and daydreaming. The last section of the box on page 78 in Chapter 2 describes some techniques that work. Your instructor or a counselor can give you additional suggestions.

Planning Further Ahead: Creating a Monthly Assignment Calendar and Using a Daily To Do List

Two useful tools for planning ahead are a monthly assignment calendar and a daily To Do list. In this section you'll learn about each of these.

Students sometimes discover too late that they have three tests, a paper, and a project all due in the same week. In contrast, effective students alert themselves to upcoming weeks that will be especially busy: They give themselves an overview of

KEY TERM
monthly assignment calendar

Calendar showing test dates and due dates in all courses for each month of a semester.

the semester by creating a **monthly assignment calendar.** A monthly assignment calendar is a calendar that shows the test dates and due dates in *all* your courses for each month of the semester. A monthly assignment calendar helps you plan ahead so that you can meet each deadline and produce better work. As a result, you feel more in control, experience less stress, and enjoy the semester more.

Setting up a monthly calendar is simple. As soon as you receive the syllabi for your courses, transfer all the test dates and due dates (for projects, papers, oral reports, etc.) to *one* calendar. It could be a regular paper calendar or one you keep on your computer. Whenever a test or due date is announced, add it to your calendar. When you see that several due dates coincide in one week, plan to finish some of the projects ahead of time. (To complete a project comfortably in advance of its deadline, remember the motivational strategy of breaking big projects into smaller parts.) Or, if several tests coincide, begin reviewing for each of them well ahead of time.

Pages 22–23 show monthly assignment calendars. The sample has been filled in to give you an idea of how a typical student's calendar might look. You can make several photocopies of the blank calendar on page 23 and create your own monthly calendar for each month of the semester.

Another effective tool for time management is a daily **To Do list,** a prioritized list of things to be done in a single day. To Do lists are a proven way to get more accomplished. Make your list every morning or, if you prefer, make it each evening for the coming day. Regardless of when you make it, be sure to make a list for each day. An index card, which is both small and sturdy, works well for a To Do list. Keep your list with you so that you can refer to it throughout the day and check off items as you complete them. The steps for creating a To Do list are described below.

KEY TERM
To Do list

Prioritized list of items to be accomplished in a single day.

The most valuable feature of a To Do list is that you identify which items you consider high priorities and which ones you consider less important. This is what makes the To Do list so useful: It helps you resist the temptation to do easy, unimportant tasks first rather than the important, often more challenging ones. And, of course, a To Do list also helps you avoid *procrastination*—putting off doing something or postponing a task, especially out of habit. If you use a To Do list daily, you will be more productive and have more free time.

Here are the steps for making a daily To Do list:

- **Step 1. Write down everything you would like to accomplish today** (or tomorrow, if you are making the list the night before). Some activities will be school-related (such as "buy graph paper at bookstore"). Others will not be related to school (such as "make appointment for haircut"). You can include activities related to long-term goals ("practice the piano" or "exercise for 45 minutes") as well as ones related to short-term goals. Do not include routine activities ("eat lunch" or "go to work").

- **Step 2. On the basis of how important it is to accomplish each item that day, rate each as being an A, B, or C.** Mark an item A if accomplishing it that day is *very* important. Mark an item B if it is moderately important. Mark it C if it is *less* important. In other words, set priorities. This step is crucial: If you do not set priorities, you are likely to spend your time on easy but unimportant items while the important items are left undone.

SAMPLE MONTHLY ASSIGNMENT CALENDAR

Month of September

Sunday	Monday	Tuesday	Wednesday	Thursday	Friday	Saturday
			1	2	3	4
5	6 History group report	7	8	9	10	11
12	13	14	15 Computer Science project due	16	17 English paper due	18
19	20	21	22	23	24	25
26	27					

Month of October

Sunday	Monday	Tuesday	Wednesday	Thursday	Friday	Saturday
					1 Psychology midterm	2
3	4 History test	5 Math test	6	7	8	9
10	11	12	13 English paper due	14	15	16
17	18	19	20	21	22	23
24 / 31	25					

Month of November

Sunday	Monday	Tuesday	Wednesday	Thursday	Friday	Saturday
		1	2	3 English oral report due	4	5	6
7	8	9	10	11	12 Psychology project due	13
14	15	16 Math test	17	18	19	20
21	22	23	24	25	26	27
28	29					

Month of December

Sunday	Monday	Tuesday	Wednesday	Thursday	Friday	Saturday
			1	2	3	4
5	6 History test	7	8	9	10 English paper due	11
12 Finals begin	13 History exam	14	15 Psy & English exams	16 Math exam	17 Computer Science exam	18
19	20	21	22	23	24	25
26	27	28	29	30	31	

MONTHLY ASSIGNMENT CALENDAR

Sunday	Monday	Tuesday	Wednesday	Thursday	Friday	Saturday

• **Step 3. Now you must set final priorities by ranking all your As, then all your Bs, and then your Cs.**   Consider the As and label them A-1, A-2, A-3, etc., according to the importance of each. Do the same for the Bs and Cs. This gives you the *overall* order in which you should do the items on the list. (You may want to rewrite the list at this point or transfer it to your computer, putting the items in their final order.) Try to do all of your A items first, starting with item A-1. When you complete it, tackle item A-2. When you have completed all your A items, start on the B items, beginning with B-1, and so forth. Even if you are unable to complete everything on your list, you will have accomplished the most important ones.

The box below shows a sample of a finished To Do list.

When you make the To Do list for the following day, look at the items on the previous day's list that you did not complete. If some of them still need to be done, carry them over to the new list. Priorities may change from day to day, of course. An item that was priority C on Tuesday ("pick up suit at cleaners") may become an A item on Friday (if you plan to wear the suit that night).

SAMPLE TO DO LIST

A-1	Study for history test
A-2	Write draft of English paper
A-3	Schedule dental appointment
A-4	Pay bills
B-1	Return library books
B-2	Cleaners
B-3	Birthday present for Pat
C-1	Buy stamps
C-2	Call Lynn
C-3	Wash car

SELECTION **1-1**

Study Skills

Why Go to College?

From *P.O.W.E.R. Learning: Strategies for Success in College and Life*
By Robert S. Feldman

Prepare Yourself to Read

Directions: Do these exercises *before* you read Selection 1-1.

1. Read and think about the title of this selection. Why are *you* going to college? Write 1, 2, and 3 next to the *three most important* reasons that you have for attending college:

   _____ I want to get a good job when I graduate.

   _____ My parents want me to go.

   _____ I couldn't find a job.

   _____ I want to get away from home.

   _____ I want to get a better job as soon as possible.

   _____ I want to gain a general education and appreciation of ideas.

   _____ I want to improve my reading and study skills.

   _____ I want to become a more cultured person.

   _____ I want to make more money.

   _____ I want to learn more about things that interest me.

   _____ A mentor or role model encouraged me to go.

   _____ I want to prove to others that I can succeed.

   How do you think your reasons compare with those of other first-year students?

   _____

   _____

   _____

   _____

2. Next, complete your preview by reading the following:

   Introduction (in *italics*)

   Chart

   First sentence of each paragraph

   On the basis of your preview, what does the selection seem to be about?

   _____

   _____

   _____

   _____

29

Apply Comprehension Skills

Directions: Do these exercises *before* you read Selection 1-1. Apply two skills from this chapter:

Set your goal for reading. What do you expect to discover about the reasons for pursuing a college education?

_____

_____

Plan your time. Estimate how long it will take you to read Selection 1-1.

_____

_____

WHY GO TO COLLEGE?

In 2006 there were more than 17 million students in the United States enrolled in college. Why are so many people willing to devote the effort, time, and money a college education requires? What would your answer be if you were asked the question, "Why are you going to college?"

This selection comes from the study skills textbook P.O.W.E.R. Learning: Strategies for Success in College and Life *by Robert S. Feldman, professor of psychology at the University of Massachusetts at Amherst. At the beginning of this selection Professor Feldman presents the reasons that first-year college students cited most frequently when they were asked, "Why are you going to college?" Then, to support his belief that "the value of college extends far beyond dollars and cents," Professor Feldman presents five other important reasons for going to college that first-year students may be unaware of.*

1   Congratulations. You're in college.

2   Why?

3   Although it seems as if it should be easy to say why you're continuing your education, for most students it's not that simple. The reasons that people go to college vary. Some people want to go to college for practical reasons ("I want to get a good job"). Some reasons for going to college are lofty ("I want to learn about people and the world"). And some reasons are unreflective ("Why not?—I don't have anything better to do"). Think about your own reasons for attending college.

4   Surveys of first-year college students show that almost three-quarters say they want to get a better job and make money (see Figure 1). But most students also have additional goals in mind: They want to learn about things that interest them (74 percent) and gain a general education and appreciation of ideas (61 percent).

5   And, in fact, it's not wrong to expect that a college education helps people find better jobs. The average person with a college degree earns about 50 percent more each year than the average person with only a high school education. Furthermore, as jobs become increasingly complex and technologically sophisticated, college will become more and more a necessity.

6   But the value of college extends far beyond dollars and cents. Consider these added reasons for pursuing a college education:

7   **You'll learn to think and communicate better.** Here's what one student said about his college experience after he graduated: "It's not about what you major in or which classes you take. . . . It's really about learning to *think* and to *communicate.* Wherever you end up, you'll need to be able to analyze and solve problems—to figure out what needs to be done and do it."

8   Education improves your ability to understand the world—understand it as it now is, and prepare to understand

College can be the starting point for a more successful and satisfying journey through life.

Figure 1
Choosing College
These are the most
frequently cited
reasons that first-
year college students
gave for why they
enrolled in college
when asked in a
national survey.

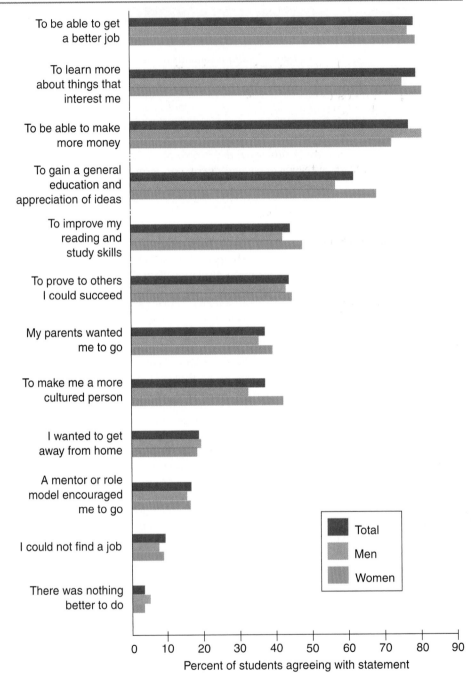

it as it will be. By showing you how to develop your capacity for critical and creative thinking, education will increase your abilities to think clearly and to communicate more effectively with others.

9   **You'll be able to better deal with advances in knowledge and technology that are changing the world.** Genetic engineering . . . drugs to reduce forgetfulness . . . computers that respond to our voices. Innovations such as these—and the ones that haven't even been thought of yet—illustrate how rapidly the world is changing.

10   No one knows what the future will hold, but education can provide you with the intellectual tools that you can apply regardless of the specific situation in which you find yourself. You can't anticipate what the future holds, but you can prepare for it through a college education.

11   **You'll be better prepared to live in a world of diversity.** The United States is changing rapidly. In fact, by the middle of the twenty-first century, non-Hispanic whites will become a minority group. You'll be working and living with people whose backgrounds, lifestyles, and ways of thinking may be entirely different from your own.

12   The greater diversity of the United States, along with the fact that we live in a global society, necessitates a deeper understanding of other cultures. Culture provides a lens through which people view the world. You won't be prepared for the future unless you understand others and their cultural backgrounds—as well as how your own cultural background affects you.

13   **You'll make learning a lifelong habit.** Higher education isn't the end of your education. If you make the most of college, you will develop a thirst for more knowledge, a lifelong quest that can never be fully satisfied. Education will build upon your natural curiosity about the world, and it will make you aware that learning is a rewarding and never-ending journey.

14   **You'll understand the meaning of your own contributions to the world.** No matter who you are, you are poised to make your own contributions to society and the world. Higher education provides you with a window to the past, present, and future, and it allows you to understand the significance of your own contributions. Your college education provides you with a compass to discover who you are, where you've been, and where you're going.

Source: Adapted from Robert S. Feldman, *P.O.W.E.R. Learning: Strategies for Success and Life*, pp. 3–5. Copyright © 2000 by The McGraw-Hill Companies, Inc. Reprinted by permission of The McGraw-Hill Companies.

Study Skills
(continued)

Reading Selection Quiz

This quiz has three parts. Your instructor may assign some or all of them.

Comprehension

Directions: Items 1–10 test your comprehension (understanding) of the material of this selection. These questions are the type a content area instructor (such as a psychology professor) would ask on a test over this material. You should be able to answer these questions after studying this selection. For each comprehension question below, use information from the selection to determine the correct answer. Refer to the selection as you answer each question. Write your answer in the space provided.

As an example, the answer to the first item and an explanation for it are given below.

True or False

_____F_____   **1.** Professor Feldman believes that the value of a college education should be measured mainly in terms of dollars and cents.

Explanation

In paragraph 6 Professor Feldman states, "But the value of college extends far beyond dollars and cents." He then goes on to present five other important reasons for pursuing a college education. Consequently, this statement is false because Professor Feldman does *not* believe that "the value of a college education should be measured mainly in terms of dollars and cents."

_____   **2.** The average person with only a high school education earns about 50 percent less each year than the average person with a college degree.

_____   **3.** According to the national survey results presented in Figure 1, first-year college students most frequently cited being able to make more money as their reason for enrolling in college.

_____   **4.** Surveys show that 61 percent of first-year college students cite gaining a general education and appreciation of ideas as their reason for enrolling in college.

_____   **5.** Professor Feldman believes that college can help you develop your capacity for creative and critical thinking.

Multiple-Choice

_____ **6.** Of the following, which is cited more often by women than men as a reason for enrolling in college?

    a. the ability to make money

    b. there was nothing better to do

    c. to improve my reading and study skills

    d. to get away from home

_____ **7.** Of the following, which is cited more often by men than women as a reason for attending college?

    a. to make me a more cultured person

    b. to prove to others I could succeed

    c. my parents wanted me to go

    d. to be able to make more money

_____ **8.** The author states that college will become more and more of a necessity because

    a. higher incomes will be required in the future.

    b. jobs are becoming increasingly complex and technologically sophisticated.

    c. the economy of the United States is becoming global.

    d. there will be fewer jobs in the future.

_____ **9.** Which of the following is *not* listed as a beneficial reason for pursuing a college education?

    a. to understand the meaning of your own contributions to the world

    b. to make learning a lifelong habit

    c. to be better prepared to live in a world of diversity

    d. to anticipate what will be required in the future

_____ **10.** The author states that college can provide students with

    a. skills that will help them find a better job.

    b. a deeper understanding of other cultures.

    c. intellectual tools.

    d. all of the above

Vocabulary in Context

Directions: Items 11–20 test your ability to determine the meaning of a word by using context clues. *Context clues* are words in a sentence that allow the reader to deduce (reason out) the meaning of an unfamiliar word in that sentence. Context clues also enable the reader to determine which meaning the author intends, when a word has more than one meaning. For each vocabulary item below, a sentence from the selection containing an important word (*italicized, like this*) is quoted first. Next, there is an additional sentence using the word in the same sense and providing another context clue. Use the context clues from *both* sentences to deduce the meaning of the italicized word. *Be sure the answer you choose makes sense in both sentences.* If you discover that you need to use a dictionary to confirm an answer choice, remember that the meaning you select must still fit the context of *both* sentences. Write your answer in the space provided. *Note:* Chapter 2, "Approaching College Reading and Developing a College-Level Vocabulary," presents the skill of using context clues.

Pronunciation Key: ă pat ā pay âr **care** ä father ĕ pet ē be ĭ pit
ī tie îr **pier** ŏ pot ō toe ô **paw** oi **noise** ou **out** ŏŏ **took**
ōō **boot** ŭ **cut** yōō abuse ûr **urge** th **thin** *th* **this** hw **which**
zh vision ə about *Stress mark:* ′

Because the skill of using context clues is not introduced until the next chapter, the answer to the first vocabulary item and an explanation are given below.

___*d*___ **11.** The reasons that people go to college *vary*.

Prices of new homes *vary* depending on their size and location.

vary (vâr′ ē) means:

a. disappear

b. decrease

c. remain the same

d. differ

Explanation

- Answer choice **a,** *disappear* (meaning *to vanish* or *to cease to exist*), does not make sense in either sentence.
- Answer choice **b,** *decrease* (meaning *to grow smaller*), also does not make sense in either sentence.
- Answer choice **c,** *remain the same* (meaning *does not change*), does not make sense in the second sentence.

- Answer choice **d,** *differ* (meaning *to be different*), is the only choice that makes sense in *both* sentences: "The reasons that people go to college *differ*" and "Prices of new homes *differ* depending on their size and location."

_____ **12.** Some people want to go to college for *practical* reasons ("I want to get a good job").

Patricia's *practical* knowledge of Spanish helped her have a successful business trip to Mexico City.

practical (prăk′ tĭ kəl) means:

a. private
b. useful
c. enjoyable
d. limited

_____ **13.** Consider these added reasons for *pursuing* a college education.

In *pursuing* his goal to become a commercial airline pilot, Ted spent many years training.

pursuing (pər soo′ ĭng) means:

a. chasing or running after
b. attending
c. studying
d. striving to gain or accomplish

_____ **14.** By showing you how to develop your *capacity* for critical and creative thinking, education will increase your abilities to think clearly and to communicate more effectively with others.

Ms. Nichols has an amazing *capacity* for remembering the first and last names of everyone she meets.

capacity (kə păs′ ĭ tē) means:

a. ability to do something
b. creativity
c. maximum amount
d. ability to communicate

_____ **15.** But education can provide you with the *intellectual* tools that you can apply regardless of the specific situation in which you find yourself.

Cassandra preferred *intellectual* activities such as playing chess and bridge, reading, working crossword puzzles, and writing poetry.

intellectual (ĭn tə lĕk′ choo əl) means:

a. helpful
b. interesting
c. pertaining to the ability to learn
d. challenging; difficult to grasp

_____ **16.** You can't *anticipate* what the future holds, but you can prepare for it through a college education.

Studying for an exam is easier if you can *anticipate* some of the questions that you may be asked.

anticipate (ăn tĭs′ ə pāt) means:
- *a.* prevent; avoid
- *b.* foresee; predict
- *c.* change; alter
- *d.* study; remember

_____ **17.** You'll be better prepared to live in a world of *diversity*.

New York City is famous for the *diversity* of its ethnic restaurants—Italian, Chinese, French, Indian, Russian, Vietnamese, you name it!

diversity (dĭ vûr′ sĭ tē) means:
- *a.* opportunity
- *b.* variety
- *c.* difficulty
- *d.* quantity

_____ **18.** The greater diversity of the United States, along with the fact that we live in a global society, *necessitates* a deeper understanding of other cultures.

Being successful as a full-time student often *necessitates* reducing the number of hours that you work and spending less time socializing.

necessitates (nə sĕs′ ĭ tāts) means:
- *a.* creates
- *b.* provides
- *c.* requires
- *d.* reduces

_____ **19.** If you make the most of college, you will develop a thirst for more knowledge, a lifelong *quest* that can never be fully satisfied.

Michael's *quest* for an exciting and challenging sport ended when he discovered the thrill of motorcycle racing.

quest (kwĕst) means:
- *a.* search
- *b.* problem
- *c.* question
- *d.* habit

_____ **20.** No matter who you are, you are *poised* to make your own contributions to society and the world.

After graduating from college, Kim was *poised* for the challenges and responsibilities of her first full-time job.

poised (poizd) means:

a. afraid

b. positioned

c. required

d. allowed

SELECTION **1-1**

Study Skills
(continued)

Reading Skills Application

Directions: Items 21–25 test your ability to *apply* certain reading skills to information in this selection. These types of questions provide valuable practice for all students, especially those who must take standardized reading tests and state-mandated basic skills tests (such as the Florida CLAST Test and the Texas THEA Test). You may not have studied all of the skills at this point, so these items will serve as a helpful preview. The comprehension and critical reading skills in this section are presented in Chapters 4 through 9 of *Opening Doors;* vocabulary and figurative language skills are presented in Chapter 2. As you work through *Opening Doors,* you will practice and develop these skills. Write your answer for each question in the space provided.

_____ **21.** In paragraph 12 the author uses the word *lens* to mean:

a. an unexpected way.

b. a distorted way.

c. a particular way.

d. a constantly changing way.

_____ **22.** According to the selection, by the middle of the 21st century, non-Hispanic whites will become:

a. the greatest source of first-year college students.

b. a window to the past, the present, and the future.

c. the largest number of college graduates.

d. a minority group.

_____ **23.** Which of the following statements from the selection represents an opinion rather than a fact:

a. The average person with a college degree earns about 50 percent more each year than the average person with only a high school education.

b. If you make the most of college, you will develop a thirst for more knowledge, a lifelong quest that can never be fully satisfied.

c. Surveys of first-year college students show that almost three-quarters say they want to get a better job and make more money.

d. The reasons that most people go to college vary.

_____ **24.** The author's primary purpose in writing this selection is to:

    a. persuade all students to attend college.

    b. broaden students' understanding of the value of college.

    c. encourage more research on the value of college.

    d. convince first-year college students to complete their college education.

_____ **25.** In paragraph 12, the author uses which of the following patterns to organize the information?

    a. cause and effect

    b. comparison and contrast

    c. sequence

    d. list

S E L E C T I O N **1-1**

Study Skills
(continued)

Respond in Writing

Directions: As Oliver Wendell Holmes observed, "Writing is good for us because it brings our thoughts out into the open." These essay-type exercises will help you bring your thoughts into the open. Refer to Selection 1-1 as needed to answer them.

Collaboration Option

Option for collaboration: It has been said that "None of us is as smart as all of us." Adults, in particular, learn well from each other. For this reason, your instructor may direct you to work with other students on one or more of these items, or in other words, to work *collaboratively.* In that case, you should form groups of three or four students, as directed by your instructor, and work together to complete the exercises. After your group discusses an item and agrees on the answer, have a group member record it. Each member of your group should be able to explain all of your group's answers.

1. In paragraph 6 Professor Feldman states, "But the value of college extends far beyond dollars and cents." He then goes on to present five other important reasons for pursuing a college education. In the space below, list these five reasons.

_____

_____

_____

_____

_____

_____

_____

2. Why does Professor Feldman believe that it is valuable to make learning a lifelong habit? List the three reasons he cites.

_____

_____

_____

_____

_____

3. In some cases, men's and women's reasons for attending college are quite different. What are these differences?

Men more often say that they enrolled in college:

_____

_____

_____

_____

Women more often say that they enrolled in college:

_____

_____

_____

_____

4. **Overall main idea.** What is the overall main idea the author wants you to understand about reasons for pursuing a college education? Answer this question in one sentence. Notice that the phrase *pursuing a college education* appears in the overall main idea sentence.

   Because this is the first time you are asked to write an overall main idea, the answer and an explanation are given below. (Chapters 4 and 5 present the skills of identifying and expressing main ideas. These chapters include examples and practice exercises.)

   There are several valuable reasons for pursuing a college education beyond getting

   a better job, making more money, and learning interesting things.

   _____

Explanation

   Notice that this sentence expresses the one most important point the author wants readers to understand after reading the *entire* selection.

Internet Resources

Read More about This Topic on the World Wide Web

Directions: For further information about the topic of the selection, visit these websites:

www.aboutcollege.com
This site is devoted to student success and contains information for students interested in adjustment to college life.

www.mhhe.com/power
This site presents information about Dr. Feldman's textbook, *P.O.W.E.R. Learning: Strategies for Success in College and Life.*

www.uctv.tv/collegebound/articles-a.shtml
This site contains an article entitled, "College Is Cool? Assessing the Benefits of Attending College."

You can also use your favorite search engine such as Google, Yahoo!, or Alta-Vista (www.google.com, www.yahoo.com, www.altavista.com) to discover more about this topic. To locate additional information, type in combinations of key-words such as:

benefits attending college

or

advantages attending college

or

reasons attending college

Keep in mind that whenever you go to *any* website, it is a good idea to evaluate the website and the information it contains. Ask yourself questions such as:

"Who sponsors this website?"

"Is the information contained in this website up-to-date?"

"What type of information is presented?"

"Is the information objective and complete?"

"How easy is it to use the features of this website?"

SELECTION 1-2
Business

Getting Ready for Prime Time: Learning the Skills Needed to Succeed Today and Tomorrow

From *Understanding Business*
By William Nickels, James McHugh, and Susan McHugh

Prepare Yourself to Read

Directions: Do these exercises *before* you read Selection 1-2.

1. First, read and think about the title. What do you already know about the skills that are needed for success?

_____

_____

_____

2. Next, complete your preview by reading the following:

Introduction (in *italics*)
Headings
All of the first paragraph (paragragh 1)
First sentence of each of the other paragraphs

On the basis of your preview, what two kinds of success are the authors addressing?

_____

_____

_____

_____

Apply Comprehension Skills

Directions: Do these exercises *before* you read Selection 1-2. Apply two skills from this chapter:

Set your goal for reading. What do you expect to discover about the skills needed for success?

_____

_____

Plan your time. Estimate how long it will take you to read Selection 1-2.

_____

_____

43

GETTING READY FOR PRIME TIME: LEARNING THE SKILLS NEEDED TO SUCCEED TODAY AND TOMORROW

You've probably done it lots of times: arranged your evening in order to watch prime time TV. But have you ever thought about getting ready for the "prime time" of your life? In other words, are you preparing yourself for the most important or significant time in your life—your future? This selection from the introduction to a business textbook addresses this challenge. In it, the authors present a variety of techniques and behaviors students can adopt in order to be successful both in college and also in their chosen careers. As you will discover when you read this selection, taking an introduction to business course can be beneficial even if you are majoring in a different subject. The suggestions included throughout this selection can help any student, and not just students who are majoring in business.

1   Your life is full. You're starting a new semester, perhaps even beginning your college career, and you're feeling pulled in many directions. Why take time to read this introductory section? Because your success is no joking matter. The purpose of this introduction is to help you learn principles, strategies, and skills for success that will help you not only in this course but also in your career and entire life. Whether or not you learn these skills is up to you. Learning them won't guarantee success, but not learning them—well, you get the picture.

Succeeding in This Course and in Life

2   Since you've signed up for this course, we're guessing you already know the value of a college education. But just to give you some numerical backup, you should know that the gap between the earnings of high school graduates and college graduates, which is growing every year, now ranges from 60 to 70 percent. According to the U.S. Census Bureau, the holders of bachelor's degrees will make an average of $40,478 per year as opposed to just $22,895 for high school graduates. That's a whopping additional $17,583 a year. Thus, what you invest in a college education is likely to pay you back many times. See Figure 1 to get an idea of how much salary difference a college degree makes by the end of a 30-year career. That doesn't mean that there aren't good careers available to non–college graduates. It just means that those with an education are more likely to have higher earnings over their lifetime.

3   The value of a college education is more than just a larger paycheck. Other benefits include increasing your ability to think critically and communicate your ideas to others, improving your ability to use technology, and preparing yourself to live in a diverse world. Knowing you've met your goals and earned a college degree also gives you the self-confidence to continue to strive to meet your future goals.

Figure 1
Salary Comparison of High School versus College Graduates
Source: Adapted from William G. Nickels, James M. McHugh, and Susan M. McHugh, *Understanding Business,* 7th ed. Copyright © 2005 by The McGraw-Hill Companies, Inc. Reprinted by permission of The McGraw-Hill Companies.

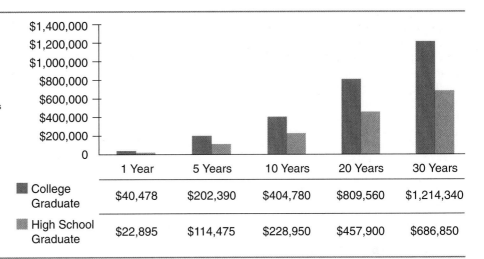

	1 Year	5 Years	10 Years	20 Years	30 Years
■ College Graduate	$40,478	$202,390	$404,780	$809,560	$1,214,340
■ High School Graduate	$22,895	$114,475	$228,950	$457,900	$686,850

Many people return to college to improve their skills in areas such as computers and writing. Others return because they realize, once they enter the marketplace, how important a college education is. Can you see the advantage of going back to school periodically during your career to keep your skills current?

4   Experts say it is likely that today's college graduates will hold seven or eight different jobs (often in several different careers) in their lifetime. There are many returning students in college today who are changing their careers and their plans for life. In fact, 41 percent of the people enrolled in college today are 25 or older. More than 1.6 million students are over 40. Talk to them and learn from their successes and mistakes. You too may want to change careers someday. Often, that is the path to long-term happiness and success. That means you will have to be flexible and adjust your strengths and talents to new opportunities. Many of the best jobs of the future don't even exist today. Learning has become a lifelong

job. You will have to constantly update your skills if you want to achieve and remain competitive.

5   If you're typical of many college students, you may not have any idea what career you'd like to pursue. That isn't necessarily a big disadvantage in today's fast-changing job market. There are no perfect or certain ways to prepare for the most interesting and challenging jobs of tomorrow. Rather, you should continue your college education, develop strong computer skills, improve your verbal and written communication skills, and remain flexible while you explore the job market.

Using This Course to Prepare for Your Career

6   One of the objectives of this course is to help you choose an area in which you might enjoy working and in which you might succeed. This textbook and this course together may be one of your most important learning experiences ever. They're meant to help you understand business so that you can use business principles throughout your life. You'll learn about production, marketing, finance, accounting, management, economics, and more. At the end of the course, you should have a much better idea about what careers would be best for you and what careers you would *not* enjoy.

7   But you don't have to be in business to use business principles. You can use marketing principles to get a job and to sell your ideas to others. You can use your knowledge of financial planning to invest wisely in the stock market. Similarly, you'll be able to use management skills and general business knowledge wherever you go and whatever career you pursue— including government agencies, charities, and social causes.

Learning to Behave Like a Professional

8   Good manners are back, and for a good reason. As the world becomes increasingly competitive, the gold goes to the individuals and the teams that have an extra bit of polish. The person who makes a good impression will be the one who gets the job, wins the promotion, or clinches the deal. Manners and professionalism must become second nature to anyone who wants to achieve and maintain a competitive edge.

9   Often, students focus on becoming experts in their particular field and neglect other concerns, including proper attire and etiquette. Their résumés look great and they may get through the interview process, but then they get in the workplace and may not succeed. Their behavior, including their verbal behavior, is so unacceptable that they are rejected by their peers.

10   The lesson is this: You can have good credentials, but a good presentation is everything. You can't neglect etiquette, or somewhere in your career you will be at a competitive disadvantage because of your inability to use good manners or to

maintain your composure in tense situations. You must constantly practice the basics until they become second nature to you. Such basics include saying "Please" and "Thank you" when you ask for something. They also include opening doors for others, standing when an older person enters the room, and using a polite tone of voice. You may want to take a course in etiquette to learn the proper way to act at a formal party, and so on. Of course, it is also critical that you are honest, reliable, dependable, and ethical at all times.

11   You can probably think of sports stars who have earned a bad reputation by not acting professionally (for example, swearing or criticizing teammates in front of others). People in professional sports are fined if they are late to meetings or refuse to follow the rules established by the team and coach. Business professionals also must follow set rules. Many of these rules are not formally written anywhere, but every successful businessperson learns them through experience.

12   You can develop the habits *now* while you are in college so that you will have the skills needed for success when you start your career. These good habits include the following:

13   *Making a good first impression.* An old saying goes, "You never get a second chance to make a good first impression." You have just a few seconds to make an impression. Therefore, how you dress and look are important. Take a clue as to what is appropriate in a college classroom or at any specific company by studying the people there who are most successful. What do they wear? How do they act?

14   *Focusing on good grooming.* Be aware of your appearance and its impact on those around you. Consistency is essential—you can't project a good image by dressing up a few times a week and then show up looking like you're getting ready to mow a lawn. Wear appropriate, clean clothing and accessories. For example, revealing shirts, nose rings, and such may not be appropriate in a work setting. It is not appropriate for men to wear hats inside buildings. It is also not appropriate, usually, to wear wrinkled clothing or to have shirttails hanging out of your pants. Many businesses are adopting "business casual" policies, but others still require traditional attire, so it may be helpful to ask what the organization's policies are and choose your wardrobe accordingly. What is business casual to some may not be acceptable to others, but there are a few guidelines most organizations accept. First of all, casual doesn't mean sloppy or shabby. For women, casual attire includes simple skirts and slacks (no jeans), cotton shirts, sweaters (not too tight), blazers, low-heeled shoes or boots (always with socks or stockings). For men, acceptable casual attire includes khaki trousers,

sport shirts with collars, sweaters or sport jackets, casual loafers or lace-up shoes (no athletic shoes).

15   *Being on time.* When you don't come to class or to work on time, you're sending a message to your professor or boss. You are saying, "My time is more important than your time. I have more important things to do than be here." In addition to the lack of respect tardiness shows to your professor or boss, it rudely disrupts the work of your colleagues. Promptness may not be a priority in some circles, but in the workplace promptness is essential. But being punctual doesn't always mean just being on time. You have to pay attention to the corporate culture. Sometimes you have to come earlier than others and leave later to get that promotion you desire. To develop good work habits and get good grades, it is important to get to class on time and not leave early.

16   *Practicing considerate behavior.* Considerate behavior includes listening when others are talking—for example, not reading the newspaper or eating in class. Don't interrupt others when they are speaking. Wait for your turn to present your views in classroom or workplace discussions. Of course, eliminate all words of profanity from your vocabulary. Use appropriate body language by sitting up attentively and not slouching. Sitting up has the added bonus of helping you stay awake! Professors and managers get a favorable impression from those who look and act alert. That may help your grades in college and your advancement in work.

17   *Practicing good "netiquette."* Computer technology, particularly e-mail, can be a great productivity tool. The basic courtesy rules of face-to-face communication also apply to e-mail exchanges. As in writing a letter, you should introduce yourself at the beginning of your first e-mail message. Next, you should let your recipients know how you got their names and e-mail addresses. Then you can proceed with your clear but succinct message, and finally, close the e-mail with your signature.

18   *Practicing good cell phone manners.* Cellular phones are a vital part of today's world, but it is important to be polite when using a phone. Turn off the phone when you are in class or a business meeting unless you are expecting a critical call. If you are expecting a critical call, turn off the audible phone ring and use the vibrating ring if your phone has that feature. If you do have to have your cellular phone turned on, sit by the aisle and near the door to leave if the phone rings. Leave the room before answering the call. Apologize to the professor after class and explain the nature of the emergency. Most professors are more sympathetic when you explain why you left the room abruptly.

19   *Being prepared.* A business person would never show up for a meeting without reading materials assigned for the meeting and being prepared to discuss the topics of the day. *To become a professional, you must practice acting like a professional.* For students, that means reading assigned materials before class, asking questions and responding to questions in class, and discussing the material with fellow students.

20   From the minute you enter your first job interview until the day you retire, people will notice whether you follow the proper business etiquette. Just as traffic laws enable people to drive more safely, business etiquette allows people to conduct business with the appropriate amount of dignity. How you talk, how you eat, and how you dress all create an impression on others.

Doing Your Best in College

21   The skills you need to succeed in college are the same skills you need to succeed in life after college. Career, family, and hobbies all involve the same organizational and time management skills. Applying these skills during your college years will ensure that you will have the life skills you need for a successful career. We will try to help you hone your skills by offering hints for improving your study habits, taking tests, and managing your time.

22   Success in any venture comes from understanding basic principles and having the skills to *apply* those principles effectively. What you learn now could help you be a success—for the rest of your life. If you use the suggestions we've presented here, you will not simply "take a course in business." Instead, you will be "getting ready for prime time" by participating in a learning experience that will help you greatly in your chosen career.

Source: Adapted from William G. Nickels, James M. McHugh, and Susan M. McHugh, *Understanding Business,* 7th ed., pp. P-3, P-4, P-6–P-9. Copyright © 2005 by The McGraw-Hill Companies, Inc. Reprinted by permission of The McGraw-Hill Companies.

Reading Selection Quiz

This quiz has three parts. Your instructor may assign some or all of them.

Comprehension

Directions: Items 1–10 test your comprehension (understanding) of the material of this selection. These questions are the type a content area instructor (such as a business professor) would ask on a test over this material. You should be able to answer these questions after studying this selection. For each comprehension question below, use information from the selection to determine the correct answer. Refer to the selection as you answer the questions. Write your answer in the space provided.

_____ **1.** A college education will:
  a. guarantee that you will be able to find a high-paying job.
  b. give you the self-confidence to continue to strive to meet your future goals.
  c. enable you to keep the same job for your entire career.
  d. provide you with a salary that is 41 percent higher than that of a high school graduate.

_____ **2.** According to the salary comparison in Figure 1, by the end of a 30-year career a college graduate is likely to earn:
  a. $22,895.
  b. $40,478.
  c. $686,850.
  d. $1,214,340.

_____ **3.** Students who graduate from college will:
  a. prepare themselves to live in a diverse world.
  b. increase their ability to think critically and communicate their ideas to others.
  c. improve their ability to use technology.
  d. all of the above

_____ **4.** College graduates should remain flexible throughout their careers and adjust their strengths and talents to new opportunities because:
  a. this is the path to the highest salaries.
  b. they may want or need to change careers someday.
  c. this is the only way to keep a good job.
  d. there will be fewer jobs in the future.

_____ **5.** What percent of college students today are 25 or older?

   a. 4%

   b. 10%

   c. 25%

   d. 41%

_____ **6.** In addition to being reliable, dependable, and ethical, behaving like a professional requires you to:

   a. have a great-looking résumé and to present yourself well during an interview.

   b. use good manners and maintain your composure in tense situations.

   c. dress in a sophisticated and fashionable manner.

   d. have outstanding credentials.

_____ **7.** Professional behavior involves:

   a. being prepared and being on time.

   b. following the basic rules of courtesy during face-to-face and e-mail exchanges.

   c. practicing considerate behavior and focusing on good grooming.

   d. all of the above

_____ **8.** If you are sending e-mails to persons whom you do not know, "netiquette" dictates that you should:

   a. let them know how you got their names and e-mail addresses.

   b. present your message in a friendly, casual manner.

   c. begin your message with a clear but succinct statement.

   d. understand that e-mail is a great productivity tool.

_____ **9.** The best way for a student to develop the skills needed for a successful career is to:

   a. take an introduction to business course.

   b. complete a college education before the age of 25.

   c. practice acting like a professional while in college.

   d. take a course in etiquette.

_____ **10.** To be successful in any venture, you must understand basic principles, but you must also:

   a. have the skills to apply those principles effectively.

   b. make a good first impression.

   c. participate in a learning experience.

   d. enjoy what you are doing.

Directions: Items 11–20 test your ability to determine the meaning of the word by using context clues. *Context clues* are words in a sentence that allow the reader to deduce (reason out) the meaning of an unfamiliar word in that sentence. Context clues also enable the reader to determine which meaning the author intends when a word has more than one meaning. For each vocabulary item below, a sentence from the selection containing an important word (*italicized, like this*) is quoted first. Next, there is an additional sentence using the word in the same sense and providing another context clue. Use the context clues from *both* sentences to deduce the meaning of the italicized word. *Be sure the answer you choose makes sense in both sentences.* If you discover that you need to use a dictionary to confirm an answer choice, remember that the meaning you select must still fit the context for *both* sentences. Write your answer in the space provided.

Pronunciation Key: ă pat   ā **pay**   âr **care**   ä father   ĕ pet   ē be   ĭ pit
ī tie   îr **pier**   ŏ pot   ō toe   ô **paw**   oi **noise**   ou **out**   ŏŏ **took**
ōō **boot**   ŭ **cut**   yōō abuse   ûr **urge**   th **thin**   *th* **this**   hw **which**
zh vision   ə **about**   *Stress mark:* '

---

11. But have you ever thought about getting ready for the *prime* time of your life?

Our retired neighbor, Fred Thomas, said that the time he served as mayor of our city was the *prime* experience of his career.

prime (prīm) means:

a. earliest

b. easiest time in a person's career

c. most important period or part

d. most exciting

12. Other benefits include increasing your ability to think critically and communicate your ideas to others, improving your ability to use technology, and preparing yourself to live in a *diverse* world.

Most first-time visitors are amazed by the *diverse* collection of artwork displayed at the Museum of Modern Art in New York City—sculpture, paintings, drawings, collages—something for every taste!

diverse (dĭ vûrs') means:

a. complicated

b. modern

c. having variety in form

d. involving many styles and preferences

_____ **13.** Knowing you've met your goals and earned a college degree also gives you the self-confidence to continue to *strive* to meet your future goals.

Pamela vowed to *strive* to pay off her student loan in less than three years, even if it meant postponing buying a new car and riding the bus to work.

strive (strīv) means:

a. to accomplish

b. to budget

c. to prepare for the future; to plan

d. to exert much effort; to struggle

_____ **14.** Rather, you should continue your college education, develop strong computer skills, improve your *verbal* and written communication skills, and remain flexible while you explore the job market.

A telemarketing salesperson must have good *verbal* skills in order to catch and keep your interest and discourage you from hanging up the phone.

verbal (vûr′ bəl) means:

a. grammar skills

b. spoken rather than written; oral

c. computer and communication skills

d. keeps your attention; interesting

_____ **15.** Similarly, you'll be able to use management skills and general business knowledge wherever you go and whatever career you *pursue*, including government agencies, charities, and social causes.

My two-month internship at a community hospital during high school encouraged me to *pursue* a degree in nursing.

pursue (pər sōo′) means:

a. to chase; overtake

b. to study; examine

c. to strive to accomplish; attain

d. to volunteer; participate

_____ **16.** You can't neglect etiquette, or somewhere in your career you will be at a competitive disadvantage because of your inability to use good manners or to maintain your *composure* in tense situations.

When a flight is delayed, airline ticket counter personnel must try to preserve their *composure* and assist annoyed and impatient customers.

composure (kəm pō′ zhər) means:

a. advantage

b. behavior

c. interest

d. calmness

_____ **17.** You may want to take a course in *etiquette* to learn the proper way to act at a formal party, and so on.

Because Charles' mother and father insisted that he learn rules of *etiquette,* he felt comfortable at business functions, banquets, and other social events.

etiquette (ĕt′ ĭ kĕt) means:

a. speech communication

b. behavior

c. rules for business

d. good manners

_____ **18.** Of course, it is also critical that you are honest, reliable, dependable, and *ethical* at all times.

Although Cecilia was tempted for a moment to keep the wallet full of cash that she found, she knew that the *ethical* thing to do would be to contact the owner and return it.

ethical (ĕth′ ĭ kəl) means:

a. dependable

b. likely to be successful

c. honorable

d. safe

_____ **19.** Be aware of your appearance and its *impact* on those around you.

My brother's good study habits and excellent grades throughout his time in college had a powerful *impact* on my desire to become a successful student.

impact (ĭm′ păkt) means:

a. awareness

b. influence

c. desire

d. habit

_____ **20.** Then you can proceed with your clear but *succinct* message.

Because our professor's explanation of the procedure for logging on to our new computer network was so *succinct* and easy to understand, we began working immediately and had plenty of time to finish our work.

succinct (sək sĭngkt′) means:

a. clear

b. successful

c. challenging

d. brief

SELECTION 1-2

Business
(Continued)

Reading Skills Application

Directions: Items 21–25 test your ability to *apply* certain reading skills to the information in this selection. These types of questions provide valuable practice for all students, especially those who must take standardized reading tests and state-mandated basic skills tests (such as the Florida CLAST Test and the Texas THEA Test). You may not have studied all of the skills at this point, so these items will serve as a helpful preview. The comprehension and critical reading skills in this section are presented in Chapters 4 through 9 of *Opening Doors;* vocabulary and figurative language skills are presented in Chapter 2. As you work through *Opening Doors,* you will practice and develop these skills. Write your answer for each question in the space provided.

_____ **21.** What is the meaning of the word *clinches* as it is used in paragraph 8?

    a. misses; loses

    b. closes; finalizes

    c. creates; invents

    d. proposes; presents

_____ **22.** What is the main point of paragraph 7?

    a. You can use your knowledge of financial planning to invest wisely in the stock market.

    b. You can use marketing principles to get a job and to sell your ideas to others.

    c. You'll be able to use management skills and general business knowledge wherever you go.

    d. You don't have to be in business to use business principles.

_____ **23.** The information in paragraph 17 is organized using which of the following patterns?

    a. cause-effect

    b. comparison-contrast

    c. sequence

    d. problem-solution

_____ **24.** Which of the following statements represents an opinion rather than a fact?

    a. Holders of bachelor's degrees will make an average of $40,478 per year.

    b. The gap between the earnings of high school graduates and college graduates is growing every year.

    c. High school graduates will make an average of $22,895 per year.

    d. What you invest in a college education is likely to pay you back many times.

_____ **25.** The authors' purpose in writing this selection is to:

    a. convince students that they must find a suitable career when they graduate.

    b. persuade students to select a job that they can keep for a lifetime.

  c. present principles, strategies, and
   skills for success that will help
   students not only in their college
   courses but throughout their careers
   and entire lives as well.

  d. prove to students that a college
   degree is required in order to obtain
   a job with a good salary.

SELECTION **1-2**

Business
(Continued)

Collaboration Option

Respond in Writing

Directions: These essay-type exercises will help you bring your thoughts into the open. Refer to Selection 1-1 as needed to answer them.

Option for collaboration: It has been said that "None of us is as smart as all of us." Adults, in particular, learn well from each other. For this reason, your instructor may direct you to work with other students on one or more of these items, or in other words, to work *collaboratively.* In that case, you should form groups of three or four students, as directed by your instructor, and work together to complete the exercises. After your group discusses an item and agrees on the answer, have a group member record it. Each member of your group should be able to explain all of your group's answers.

1. Do you agree with the authors' point of view that success requires you to "behave like a professional"? Explain why or why not.

  _____

  _____

  _____

  _____

  _____

2. Create a "Top 10" list of behaviors or techniques that you believe can help people succeed in college as well as in their careers. You may use some or all of the suggestions included in the selection or you may include your own suggestions. (Item #1 on your list should be what you view as the *most* important success behavior.)

  #1 _____

  #2 _____

  #3 _____

  #4 _____

#5 _____

#6 _____

#7 _____

#8 _____

#9 _____

#10 _____

3. **Overall main idea.** What is the overall main idea the authors want the reader to understand about the skills that are needed for success? Answer this question in one sentence. Be sure to include the words *success* (or *succeed*) and *professional* in your overall main idea sentence.

_____

_____

_____

_____

_____

_____

_____

_____

_____

_____

Internet Resources

Read More about This Topic on the World Wide Web

Directions: For further information about the topic of the selection, visit these websites:

http://suemorem.com
This website contains general information about becoming a success in the business world. Click on the "Tips" button and select from categories such as "Etiquette," "Job Search Secrets," and "Interviewing Tips" to read advice from Sue Morem, a business consultant. This website also offers videos for sale on various topics.

http://wlb.monster.com/articles/etiquette/
This link contains an article titled "Business Etiquette You Should Know," by Susan Bryant, a contributing writer to Monster.com, the popular job search website.

You can also use your favorite search engine such as Google, Yahoo!, or Alta-Vista (www.google.com, www.yahoo.com, www.altavista.com) to discover more about this topic. To locate additional information, type in combinations of key-words such as:

career success

or

professional etiquette

or

workplace success

or

success skills

or

characteristics of professional behavior

Keep in mind that whenever you go to *any* website, it is a good idea to evaluate the website and the information it contains. Ask yourself questions such as:

"Who sponsors this website?"

"Is the information contained in this website up-to-date?"

"What type of information is presented?"

"Is the information objective and complete?"

"How easy is it to use the features of this website?"

SELECTION **1-3**

Literature

Saved

From *The Autobiography of Malcolm X*
As Told to Alex Haley

Prepare Yourself to Read

Directions: Do these exercises *before* you read Selection 1-3.

1. First, read and think about the title. What do you already know about Malcolm X?

   _____

   _____

   _____

   _____

2. Next, complete your preview by reading the following:
   Introduction (in *italics*)
   First paragraph (paragraph 1)
   All of the last paragraph (paragraph 19)

   On the basis of your preview, what aspect of Malcolm X's life do you think will be discussed?

   _____

   _____

   _____

Apply Comprehension Skills

Directions: Do these exercises *before* you read Selection 1-3. Apply two skills from this chapter:

Set your goal for reading. What do you hope to learn about Malcolm X?

_____

_____

Plan your time. Estimate how long it will take you to read Selection 1-3.

_____

_____

SAVED

Born Malcolm Little in 1925, Malcolm X was a member of the American Black Muslims (1952–1963), an organization that advocated separatism and black pride. Before Malcolm X became a prominent Black Muslim and political leader, he served time in prison.

In this selection, Malcolm X describes a life-changing experience he had while he was in prison. His desire to write letters to Elijah Muhammad during this time motivated Malcolm X to make this profound change in his life. (Elijah Muhammad, a black American, was an activist and leader of the Nation of Islam from 1934 to 1975. He favored political and social equality, as well as economic independence for black Americans.)

Malcolm X, however, eventually separated from the Black Muslims and converted to orthodox Islam, a religion that believes in the unity of the human race. He founded the Organization of Afro-American Unity in 1964. In 1965, Malcolm X was assassinated in Harlem as he was about to give a speech.

In 1992 Warner Studios produced the film Malcolm X, *directed by Spike Lee and starring Denzel Washington. And in 1995 A&E Network produced a documentary on Malcolm X for its* Biography *series. In 1999 the United States Postal Service issued a stamp in honor of Malcolm X (El-Hajj Malik El-Shabazz).*

1   It was because of my letters that I happened to stumble upon starting to acquire some kind of a homemade education.

2   I became increasingly frustrated at not being able to express what I wanted to convey in letters that I wrote, especially those to Mr. Elijah Muhammad. In the street, I had been the most articulate hustler out there—I had commanded attention when I said something. But now, trying to write simple English, I not only wasn't articulate, I wasn't even functional. How would I sound writing in slang, the way I would say it, something such as, "Look, daddy, let me pull your coat about a cat, Elijah Muhammad—"

3   Many who today hear me somewhere in person, or on television, or those who read something I've said, will think I went to school far beyond the eighth grade. This impression is due entirely to my prison studies.

4   It had really begun back in the Charlestown Prison, when Bimbi first made me feel envy of his stock of knowledge. Bimbi had always taken charge of any conversation he was in, and I had tried to emulate him. But every book I picked up had few sentences which didn't contain anywhere from one to nearly all of the words that might as well have been in Chinese. When I just skipped those words, of course, I really ended up with little idea of what the book said. So I had come to the Norfolk Prison Colony still going through only book-reading motions. Pretty soon, I would have quit even these motions, unless I had received the motivation that I did.

5   I saw that the best thing I could do was get hold of a dictionary—to study, to learn some words. I was lucky enough to reason also that I should try to improve my penmanship. It was sad. I couldn't even write in a straight line. It was both

ideas together that moved me to request a dictionary along with some tablets and pencils from the Norfolk Prison Colony school.

6   I spent two days just rifling uncertainly through the dictionary's pages. I'd never realized so many words existed! I didn't know which words I needed to learn. Finally, just to start some kind of action, I began copying.

7   In my slow, painstaking, ragged handwriting, I copied into my tablet everything printed on that first page, down to the punctuation marks.

8   I believe it took me a day. Then, aloud, I read back, to myself, everything I'd written on the tablet. Over and over, aloud, to myself, I read my own handwriting.

9   I woke up the next morning, thinking about those words—immensely proud to realize that not only had I written so much at one time, but I'd written words that I never knew were in the world. Moreover, with a little effort, I also could remember what many of these words meant. I reviewed the words whose meanings I didn't remember. Funny thing, from the dictionary first page right now, that "aardvark" springs to my mind. The dictionary had a picture of it, a long-tailed, long-eared, burrowing African mammal, which lives off termites caught by sticking out its tongue as an anteater does for ants.

Malcolm X (1925–1965)

10   I was so fascinated that I went on—I copied the dictionary's next page. And the same experience came when I studied that. With every succeeding page, I also learned of people and places and events from history. Actually the dictionary is like a miniature encyclopedia. Finally the dictionary's A section had filled a whole tablet—and I went on into the B's. That was the way I started copying what eventually became the entire dictionary. It went a lot faster after so much practice helped me to pick up handwriting speed. Between what I wrote in my tablet, and writing letters, during the rest of my time in prison I would guess I wrote a million words.

11   I suppose it was inevitable that as my word-base broadened, I could for the first time pick up a book and read and now begin to understand what the book was saying. Anyone who has read a great deal can imagine the new world that opened. Let me tell you something: from then until I left that prison, in every free moment I had, if I was not reading in the library, I was reading on my bunk. You couldn't have gotten me out of books with a wedge. Between Mr. Muhammad's teachings, my correspondence, my visitors—usually Ella and Reginald—and my reading of books, months passed without my even thinking about being imprisoned. In fact, up to then, I never had been so truly free in my life.

12   The Norfolk Prison Colony's library was in the school building. A variety of classes was taught there by instructors who came from such places as Harvard and Boston universities. The weekly debates between inmate teams were also

held in the school building. You would be astonished to know how worked up convict debaters and audiences would get over subjects like "Should Babies Be Fed Milk?"

13   Available on the prison library's shelves were books on just about every general subject. Much of the big private collection that Parkhurst had willed to the prison was still in crates and boxes in the back of the library—thousands of old books. Some of them looked ancient: covers faded, old-time parchment-looking binding. Parkhurst, I've mentioned, seemed to have been principally interested in history and religion. He had the money and the special interest to have a lot of books that you wouldn't have in general circulation. Any college library would have been lucky to get that collection.

14   As you can imagine, especially in a prison where there was heavy emphasis on rehabilitation, an inmate was smiled upon if he demonstrated an unusually intense interest in books. There was a sizable number of well-read inmates, especially the popular debaters. Some were said by many to be practically walking encyclopedias. They were almost celebrities. No university would ask any student to devour literature as I did when this new world opened to me, of being able to read and *understand.*

15   I read more in my room than in the library itself. An inmate who was known to read a lot could check out more than the permitted maximum number of books. I preferred reading in the total isolation of my own room.

16   When I had progressed to really serious reading, every night at about ten P.M. I would be outraged with the "lights out." It always seemed to catch me right in the middle of something engrossing.

17   Fortunately, right outside my door was a corridor light that cast a glow into my room. The glow was enough to read by, once my eyes adjusted to it. So when "lights out" came, I would sit on the floor where I could continue reading in that glow.

18   At one-hour intervals the night guards paced past every room. Each time I heard the approaching footsteps, I jumped into bed and feigned sleep. And as soon as the guard passed, I got back out of bed onto the floor area of that light-glow, where I would read for another fifty-eight minutes—until the guard approached again. That went on until three or four every morning. Three or four hours of sleep a night was enough for me. Often in the years in the streets I had slept less than that. . . .

19   I have often reflected upon the new vistas that reading opened to me. I knew right there in prison that reading had changed forever the course of my life. As I see it today, the ability to read awoke inside me some long dormant craving to be mentally alive. I certainly wasn't seeking any degree, the way a college confers a status symbol upon its students. My homemade education gave me, with every additional book

    a. involving great speed and dexterity
    b. involving significant physical pain
    c. involving considerable boredom
    d. involving great effort or care

_____ **15.** With every *succeeding* page, I also learned of people and places and events from history.

In the years *succeeding* his presidency, Bill Clinton wrote his memoirs and devoted his time to several humanitarian causes.

succeeding (sək sēd′ ĭng) means:
    a. coming next or after
    b. coming before
    c. inserted or inserted in
    d. preceding

_____ **16.** I suppose it was *inevitable* that as my word-base broadened, I could for the first time pick up a book and read and now begin to understand what the book was saying.

It is *inevitable* that summer follows spring.

inevitable (ĭn ĕv′ ĭ tə bəl) means:
    a. likely to happen
    b. uncertain
    c. incapable of being prevented or avoided
    d. unreasonable

_____ **17.** Much of the big private collection that Parkhurst had *willed* to the prison was still in crates and boxes in the back of the library—thousands of old books.

Since my grandmother is no longer alive, I treasure the piano she *willed* to me, and I play it often.

willed (wĭld) means:
    a. kept in storage
    b. taken back
    c. received as a gift
    d. granted in a legal will; bequeathed

_____ **18.** As you can imagine, especially in a prison where there was heavy emphasis on *rehabilitation,* an inmate was smiled upon if he demonstrated an unusually intense interest in books.

It took three months of *rehabilitation* for the actor to recover fully from his drug and alcohol addiction.

rehabilitation (rē hĭ bĭl ĭ tā′ shən) means:

    a. regaining useful life through education or therapy

    b. hard physical labor

    c. rest and relaxation

    d. cooperation

_____ **19.** Fortunately, right outside my door was the *corridor* light that cast a glow in the room.

When the fire alarm sounded, students quickly left their classrooms and walked down the *corridor* to the exit.

corridor (kôr′ ĭ dər) means:

    a. door that leads to an exit

    b. large room

    c. passageway with rooms opening into it

    d. an open area outside a building

_____ **20.** Each time I heard the approaching footsteps, I jumped into bed and *feigned* sleep.

Have you ever *feigned* illness so that you wouldn't have to go to work?

feigned (fānd) means:

    a. endured

    b. experienced

    c. pretended; gave a false appearance of

    d. suffered or felt pain

SELECTION **1-3**

Literature
(Continued)

Reading Skills Application

Directions: Items 21–25 test your ability to *apply* certain reading skills to the information in this selection. These types of questions provide valuable practice for all students, especially those who must take standardized reading tests and state-mandated basic skills tests (such as the Florida CLAST Test and the Texas THEA Test). You may not have studied all of the skills at this point, so these items will serve as a helpful preview. The comprehension and critical reading skills in this section are presented in Chapters 4 through 9 of *Opening Doors;* vocabulary and figurative language skills are presented in Chapter 2. As you work through *Opening Doors,* you will practice and develop these skills. Write your answer for each question in the space provided.

_____ **21.** What is the meaning of *devour* in paragraph 14?

    a. eat greedily

    b. read large quantities of

    c. destroy

    d. copy by hand

_____ **22.** According to this selection, Malcolm X's formal
education ended:

    a.   after 6th grade.

    b.   with the 8th grade.

    c.   after high school.

    d.   after his first year of college.

_____ **23.** Which of the following conclusions can be logically
based on the selection?

    a.   Malcolm X would probably have returned to the
same type of life he led before prison if he had not
spent the time in prison reading and educating himself.

    b.   Malcolm X could have qualified for a college scholarship if he had not
gone to prison.

    c.   Malcolm X was envied and disliked by the other prison inmates because
he became so knowledgeable.

    d.   Malcolm X willed his books to the Charlestown Prison library when he died.

_____ **24.** The writer's primary purpose for telling about his experience is to:

    a.   instruct others about how to improve their reading skills.

    b.   persuade young men to stay out of prison.

    c.   describe what life in prison is like.

    d.   persuade readers of the value of reading and
education.

_____ **25.** Which of the following best expresses the writer's point
of view in this selection?

    a.   Education can change lives.

    b.   Prisons should offer inmates educational courses.

    c.   Prisoners should be allowed to read as late at
night as they like.

    d.   No one should ever be sent to prison.

SELECTION **1-3**

Literature
(Continued)

Collaboration Option

Respond in Writing

Directions: Refer to Selection 1-3 as needed to answer the essay-type questions
below.

Option for collaboration: Your instructor may direct you to work with other students on one or more of these items, or in other words, to work *collaboratively.*
In that case, you should form groups of three or four students, as directed by
your instructor, and work together to complete the exercises. After your group
discusses an item and agrees on the answer, have a group member record it. Each
member of your group should be able to explain all of your group's answers.

1. List at least three surprising or interesting facts you learned about Malcolm X.

   _____

   _____

   _____

   _____

   _____

   _____

   _____

   _____

   _____

   _____

2. Although Malcolm X may not have realized it, he used many of the same study and learning techniques that effective college students use. What were some of them?

   _____

   _____

   _____

   _____

   _____

   _____

   _____

   _____

   _____

3. By the end of 2001, about 1 in every 37 U.S. adults was either imprisoned or had been at one time. That's 5.6 million people with "prison experience." Malcolm X used his time in prison to change his life. What, in your opinion, can be done to help those in prison benefit from the time they spend there?

   _____

   _____

   _____

   _____

_____

_____

_____

4. What are at least two ways in which Malcolm X's prison experience may have "saved" him while he was in prison and after he was released?

_____

_____

_____

_____

_____

_____

_____

_____

5. **Overall main idea.** What is the overall main idea the author wants the reader to understand about Malcolm X's experience in prison? Answer this question in one sentence. Be sure to include the words _Malcolm X_ and _saved_ in your overall main idea sentence.

_____

_____

_____

_____

Internet Resources

Read More about This Topic on the World Wide Web

Directions: For further information about the topic of the selection, visit these websites:

www.wabash.edu/mxi/history.htm
The site is sponsored by the Malcolm X Institute of Black Studies at Wabash College.

www.brothermalcolm.net/
This site contains general information about Malcolm X and is sponsored by the Africana Studies Program of the University of Toledo.

www.refdesk.com
Click on "Reference Desk: Site Map," then choose "World Religions" to read more about _Islam._

You can also use your favorite search engine such as Google, Yahoo!, or Alta-Vista (www.google.com, www.yahoo.com, www.altavista.com) to discover more about this topic. To locate additional information, type in combinations of key-words such as:

Malcolm X

or

Malcolm X and reading

or

autodidact

Keep in mind that whenever you go to *any* website, it is a good idea to evaluate the website and the information it contains. Ask yourself questions such as:

"Who sponsors this website?"

"Is the information contained in this website up-to-date?"

"What type of information is presented?"

"Is the information objective and complete?"

"How easy is it to use the features of this website?"

CHAPTER 2

Approaching College Reading and Developing a College-Level Vocabulary

In this chapter you will learn the answers to these questions:

- What do I need to know about the reading process?

- How can I improve my reading?

- Why should I make predictions as I read?

- How can I monitor my comprehension while I read?

- What do I need to know about adjusting my reading rate?

- How can I develop a college-level vocabulary?

- What are denotations and connotations?

- What is figurative language?

SKILLS

Understanding the Reading Process

Improving Your Reading

- Predicting as You Read
- Monitoring Your Comprehension
- Adjusting Your Reading Rate

Developing a College-Level Vocabulary

- Using Context Clues
- Using Word-Structure Clues
- Using a Dictionary Pronunciation Key
- Understanding Denotations and Connotations of Words
- Understanding Figurative Language

CREATING YOUR SUMMARY

Developing Chapter Review Cards

READINGS

Selection 2-1 *(Student Success)*
"Making It Happen: Creating Positive Change to Become a Peak Performer"
from *Peak Performance: Success in College and Beyond*
by Sharon K. Ferrett

Selection 2-2 *(History)*
"Fighting Terrorism in a Global Age" from *Nation of Nations:*
A Narrative History of the American Republic
by James Davidson et al.

Selection 2-3 *(Biology)*
"A Whale of a Survival Problem" from *The Nature of Life*
by John Postlethwait and Janet Hopson

To read without reflecting is like eating without digesting.

Edmund Burke

The difference between the almost-right *word and the* right *word is really a large matter—it's the difference between the lightning bug and the lightning.*

Mark Twain

UNDERSTANDING THE READING PROCESS

Understanding the reading process can make you a better reader and help you study more effectively. You should be aware of these important points about reading:

1. **Reading is a form of thinking.** It is your brain that does the reading, not your eyes. The role of your eyes is to transmit images to the brain. (To understand this, consider a blind person reading Braille: In this case, the fingertips transmit input to the brain.) Therefore, improving your reading means improving your *thinking*. Remember that meaning resides in the reader's mind, not in symbols printed on a page. It is the readers who construct meaning by associating their knowledge and experience with what is on the printed page.

2. **Reading requires no unique mental or physical abilities.** The processes you typically use when you read are the same processes of vision, reasoning, and memory that you use in other areas of your daily life.

3. **The reading process includes three stages.** The three stages of reading are *preparing yourself to read, processing information,* and *reacting to what you read.* These stages overlap, but all three are needed for the reading process to be complete. In Chapter 3, this process will be explained as it applies to college reading.

4. **Effective reading is active and interactive.** Effective reading requires that you interact with the material you are reading. One way to interact with an author's ideas is to mentally ask yourself questions as you read and then seek answers to these questions. Another way to interact with material you are reading is by relating the author's ideas to your own experience and knowledge. Reading actively also means being aware of how the material is organized. Finally, active reading means that you *monitor your comprehension* as you read and that you take steps to correct the situation when you are not comprehending. (Monitoring your comprehension will be discussed later in this chapter.)

5. **Comprehension problems often result from a reader's lack of background knowledge.** Many comprehension problems are not strictly reading comprehension problems but instead are more general comprehension problems that occur when the reader lacks sufficient background knowledge. To put it another way, comprehension problems occur when a reader does not possess enough information about a subject to understand what an author is saying about it. This means that if you are having difficulty understanding new or unfamiliar material, you may need to increase your background knowledge. (For example, you

Developing strong reading and vocabulary skills will make you more successful in college.

could read a simplified explanation in an encyclopedia first.) Finding out more about an unfamiliar topic can often clear up this kind of problem. It stands to reason that the greater the amount of background knowledge you have, the more things you can understand. Every bit of information you acquire can help you learn new information more efficiently and easily.

6. **Comprehension, background knowledge, and reading rate are interrelated.**   The more you know about a topic and the better you understand the material, the faster you can read it. Conversely, if you know very little about a topic, you must reduce your reading rate. For this reason, it is meaningless to try to improve your reading rate by artificial means, such as moving your eyes or hand down the page in a certain manner. Reading rate is a by-product of comprehension. To be precise, the goal is to *comprehend* more rapidly (efficiently). This is the work of the brain and does not depend on special eye or hand movements.

7. **Your reading strategies should fit your purpose for reading.**   You read for many different purposes, and your reason for reading any particular material affects the way you approach it. (For example, your approach to reading a newspaper article or a letter from a friend will be different from your approach to reading and studying a college textbook.) You should choose reading strategies that fit your purpose.

With these things in mind, let's look at general ways you can improve your reading and your reading rate.

IMPROVING YOUR READING

Predicting as You Read

Predicting means anticipating or making educated guesses about what is coming next as you read. Predicting is a natural part of reading, but you may not always do it when you are reading college textbooks. As you read an assignment, you should make a conscious effort to anticipate not only what is coming next, but also the author's writing pattern. (Chapter 7 discusses authors' writing patterns.)

Of course, when you preview a chapter or reading selection, you are predicting in a general way what it will be about and how the material is organized. (The title or heading usually tells you or gives you a clue.) However, when you actually read and study it carefully, you should continue to make predictions as you read. For example, if an author presents one side of an issue, you might predict that he or she is going to discuss the other side as well. If a paragraph in a psychology textbook begins with the question "Why do people have nightmares?" you would expect the author to explain the reason or reasons.

Predicting helps you concentrate and comprehend; it focuses your attention because it makes you want to keep reading to see if your prediction is correct. In other words, predicting helps you stay involved with the material you are reading.

Instead of passively waiting to see what comes up next when you are reading, try to anticipate what the author will say or present. You will discover that making predictions helps you become a more active and effective reader.

Monitoring Your Comprehension

Monitoring your comprehension means periodically evaluating your understanding as you read and correcting the problem whenever you realize that you are not comprehending. You should monitor your comprehension whenever you read and study college textbooks. If you are reading a difficult textbook or section, you may need to monitor your comprehension paragraph by paragraph. At other times, you may need to stop and monitor at the end of each section.

To monitor your comprehension, follow this procedure:

- First, ask yourself, "*Am I understanding what I am reading?*"
- If you do not understand what you are reading, ask yourself, "*Why* don't I understand?"
- Once you determine why you are not comprehending, do whatever is necessary to correct the situation.

Specific types of comprehension problems and strategies for correcting them are listed in the box on page 78. Strive to make monitoring your comprehension a habit. After all, unless you comprehend what you are reading, you are not really reading.

COMPREHENSION MONITORING:
STRATEGIES FOR CORRECTING COMMON COMPREHENSION PROBLEMS

Problems	Solutions
I am not understanding because the subject is completely new to me, and I do not have enough background knowledge. College reading frequently introduces you to subjects you have not learned about before. Textbooks frequently contain a great deal of new information.	• Keep reading to see if the material becomes clearer. • Ask for a brief explanation from someone who is knowledgeable about the topic. • Read supplemental material or simpler material on the same topic (perhaps an encyclopedia, another textbook, or a book from the library) in order to build background knowledge.
I am not understanding because there are too many words I do not know. College material contains unfamiliar words and specialized or technical vocabulary that you must learn. Also, college textbooks in general are written at a higher level than other materials.	• Try to use the context (the rest of the sentence or paragraph) to figure out the meaning of an unfamiliar word. • Look up unfamiliar words in a dictionary or in the glossary at the back of the textbook. (Online dictionaries make this simple to do.) • Ask someone the meaning of unfamiliar words.
I am not understanding because I am not concentrating as I read. I am allowing distractors to interfere with my concentration. Your mind may sometimes wander while you are reading long or difficult passages.	• Identify what is bothering you. Is it a *physical distraction* (such as a noisy room or being tired), or is it a *psychological distraction* (such as being worried or daydreaming)? • Take some action that will help you deal with environmental distractions. For example, close the door or move to a quiet room. Turn off the television. Turn off the music. Move out of sight of the computer screen. Don't answer your phone. • If you are worrying about finding time for other important tasks or errands, jot the items down on a To Do list. Then, after studying, tackle your To Do list. If you are worrying about a personal problem, tell yourself, "I'll address this after I finish studying." The point is to take some action to prevent distractors from interfering with your concentration while you are studying. • Make a conscious decision to concentrate on what you are reading. Concentration does not happen automatically.

Adjusting Your Reading Rate

Have you ever been asked, "What's your reading rate?" The fact is that each reader has, or should have, *several* reading rates. Reading everything at the same rate is a sign of poor reading. "Reading" at any rate without comprehending, even if the rate is a fast one, isn't really reading.

Having a range of reading rates is an important skill. You will find it helpful to develop flexibility in your reading rates. The information below provides a brief introduction to adjusting your reading rate. A range of reading rates and when to use each are presented in the box below.

Factors Influencing Reading Rate: Purpose and Difficulty

To be a flexible, efficient reader you must adjust your reading rate according to two factors: your *purpose* for reading and *how difficult* the material is for you.

Obviously, you read for many different purposes. For instance, your purpose in reading a textbook chapter may be to understand and learn the material thoroughly and study for a test. Or there may be some specific bit of information you are searching for, such as the definition of a term in a textbook, a name in an index, or the starting time of a movie in a newspaper listing. Sometimes, of course, you read a magazine or a book just for pleasure.

FLEXIBLE READING: INFORMATION-GATHERING RATES AND READING RATES

	Approximate rate (wpm)	Uses
Information-gathering rates:		
Scanning	1,500 words per minute (wpm) or more	To find a particular piece of information (such as a name, date, or phone number)
Skimming	800–1,000 wpm	To get an overview of the highlights of the material
Reading rates:		
Rapid reading	300–500 wpm	For relatively easy material; when you want only important facts or ideas; for leisure reading
Reading rates:		
Average reading	200–300 wpm	For textbooks, complex magazines and journals, and literature
Study reading	50–200 wpm	For new vocabulary, complex concepts, technical material, and retaining details (such as legal documents, material to be memorized and material of great interest or importance)

What determines how difficult material will be for you to read? Actually, there are several factors, such as vocabulary level, writing style, and "idea density." The most important factor, however, is your background knowledge, or *how much you already know about the subject.* If you are reading about computers, for instance, and you already know a great deal about them, then you will easily understand the terms and concepts you encounter. The information will make much more sense to you than it would to someone who knows nothing about computers.

When you are assigned to read a textbook chapter, you should preview it first. (The techniques that comprise previewing are presented in Chapter 3.) Ask yourself why you are reading it and how much you already know about the subject. If the material is new to you, then you will need to read more slowly. If you are very familiar with the subject, you can probably read at a much faster rate. The point is to read flexibly, adjusting your rate as needed.

Often, you must adjust your rate *as* you are reading. How can you tell when you should slow down and when you should speed up? The following lists describe situations in which you should do each.

When to Slow Down

Here are some situations in which you should slow down your reading:

- You know little or nothing about the topic.
- It is complicated or technical material that you need to learn.
- There are details you need to remember.
- There is new or difficult vocabulary in the selection.
- There are directions that you must follow.
- The material includes charts or graphs to which you must shift your attention as you read.
- The material requires you to visualize something in your mind (for example, visualizing a heart value as you read a section in your biology text).
- Beautiful, artistic, descriptive, or poetic writing that invites you to linger and enjoy each word. (You may want to read such material aloud to yourself.)
- The material contains ideas you want to consider carefully (such as two sides of an argument) or "words to live by" (such as philosophical, religious, or inspirational writing).

When to Speed Up

Here are some situations in which you can speed up your reading:

- The whole passage is easy; there are no complicated sentences, no complex ideas, and no difficult terms.
- There is an easy passage within a longer, more difficult section.
- A passage gives an example of something you already understand, or merely explains it in different words.
- You are already knowledgeable about the topic.

- You want only main ideas and are not concerned about details.

- The material is not related to your purpose for reading (for example, a section of a magazine article that does not pertain to the topic you are researching).

Here is a technique for increasing your reading rate on leisure reading material:

1. Practice regularly with easy, interesting material, such as a newspaper, a magazine (like *Reader's Digest*), or a short, easy novel.

2. Read for 15 minutes each day, pushing yourself to read at a rate that is slightly too fast for you—in other words, a rate that is slightly uncomfortable. Once it becomes comfortable, push yourself a little more.

3. Strive for good concentration. If you are momentarily distracted, return immediately to your reading.

4. Keep track of the number of pages or articles you read each day.

As you continue to practice, you will find that you are able to read more in the same amount of time. You will also find that you can usually understand many of the important points in a passage even though you are reading it at a faster rate. There is another bonus: as you read each day, you will be adding to your background knowledge. This will enable you to read related material more effectively in the future.

DEVELOPING A COLLEGE-LEVEL VOCABULARY

Developing a powerful vocabulary is a process that takes time, but every time you read, you have an opportunity to expand your vocabulary. The more you read, the better your vocabulary can become—*if* you develop a real interest in words and their meanings. Remember that writers take special care to select words that convey precisely what they want to say.

Improving your vocabulary will make your college work easier, and your speech and your writing will become more interesting and more precise. If all those benefits are not enough, your increased vocabulary may even lead to an increased salary. Research tells us that the size of a person's vocabulary correlates with his or her income. Thinking of each word you learn as "money in the bank" may be an incentive for you to pay attention to new words and add them to your vocabulary! And, needless to say, a broad vocabulary helps create a favorable impression in a job interview.

Here are three techniques that you can use to develop and expand your vocabulary as you read:

1. **Use context clues.**   This means that you reason out the meaning of an unfamiliar word from clues provided by the surrounding words and sentences.

2. **Use word-structure clues.**   That is, determine a word's meaning on the basis of its parts (prefix, root, and suffix).

3. Use a dictionary.   Use a dictionary to determine a word's meaning (and perhaps pronunciation) as it is used in the passage you are reading.

The vocabulary exercises that follow each of the reading selections in *Opening Doors* will give you ongoing opportunities to use context clues and practice pronouncing words correctly.

Using Context Clues

Writers want you to understand what they have written. When they use words that they think might be unfamiliar to their readers, they often help the reader by offering various clues in the rest of the sentence so that the reader can deduce (reason out) the meaning of the word. Such clues are called **context clues.** (The word *context* refers to the sentence and the paragraph in which the word appears.) Since context clues can help you figure out the meaning of an unfamiliar word, think of them as gifts the writer is giving you to make your job easier.

How can you take advantage of these "gifts"? You can do so by reading the sentence carefully and by paying attention to the words and other sentences surrounding the unfamiliar word. The most common types of context clues are summarized in the box on page 83.

Using Word-Structure Clues

Although context clues will be your greatest aid in determining the meaning of unknown words, **word-structure clues** or *word-part clues* can help you determine meanings. They can also help you confirm the educated guess you made based on context clues. A list of important and useful word parts appears in Appendix 3.

To use word-structure clues, examine an unfamiliar word to see if it has any of the following word parts:

- **Root:** Base word that has a meaning of its own.
- **Prefix:** Word part attached to the beginning of a root that adds its meaning to the meaning of the root.
- **Suffix:** Word part attached to the end of a root word.

Prefixes and suffixes are also called *affixes,* since they are "fixed" (attached or joined) to a root or base word. Words may consist of a:

Root only (such as the word *graph*)

Prefix and root (such as the word *telegraph*)

Root and suffix (such as the word *graphic*)

Prefix, root, and suffix (such as the word *telegraphic*)

Learning about prefixes and suffixes not only increases your vocabulary but can help you improve your spelling as well. For instance, if you know the meaning of the prefix *mis* ("bad" or "wrong"), then you will understand why the word *misspell* has two *s*'s: One is in the prefix (*mis*) and one is in the root word (*spell*).

USING CONTEXT CLUES TO DETERMINE THE MEANING OF UNFAMILIAR WORDS

Example	Type of Clue	What to Ask Yourself	What to Look for
The psychological term **interiority** *is defined* as a tendency toward looking within during middle age.	*Definition clue*	Are there *definition clues* and a definition?	Phrases that introduce a definition, such as: *is defined as, is called, is, is known as, that is, refers to, means, the term;* a term that is in bold print, italics, or color; or certain punctuation marks that set off a definition or a term. (See pages 403–404.)
The garden was **redolent,** *or fragrant,* with the scent of roses.	*Synonym clue*	Is there a *synonym* for the unfamiliar word? That is, is the meaning explained by a word or phrase that has a *similar meaning?* The synonym may be set off by commas, parentheses, a colon, dashes, or brackets. (See pages 403–404.)	Phrases that introduce synonyms, such as *in other words, or, that is to say, also known as, by this we mean, that is.*
I did the physical therapy exercises incorrectly and, *instead of helping* my back, they were actually **deleterious.**	*Contrast clue*	Is there an *antonym* for the unfamiliar word? That is, is the unfamiliar word explained by a contrasting word or phrase with the *opposite meaning?*	Words and phrases that indicate opposites: *instead of, but, in contrast, on the other hand, however, unlike, although, even though.*
The campers *were warned that hiking up that steep mountain trail* would **enervate** even the fittest members of their group.	*Experience clue*	Can you draw on your *experience and background knowledge* to help you deduce (reason out) the meaning of the unfamiliar word?	A sentence that includes *a familiar experience* (or information you already know) can help you figure out the meaning of the new word.
He enjoys **aquatic** sports *such as swimming, scuba diving,* and *water skiing.*	*Example clue*	Are there *examples* that illustrate the meaning of the unfamiliar word?	Words that introduce examples of the meaning of the unfamiliar word: *for example, such as, to illustrate, like.*
When studying for his final exams, the student was told to **eschew** television. "*Just give TV up!*" was his roommate's advice.	*Clue from another sentence*	Is there *another sentence* in the paragraph that explains the meaning of the unfamiliar word?	*Additional information in another sentence* that may help explain the unfamiliar word.

KEY TERM
root

Base word that has a
meaning of its own.

Roots are powerful vocabulary-building tools because whole "families" of words in English come from the same root. For example, if you know that the root *aud* means "to hear," then you will understand the connection between *audience* (people who come to *hear* something or someone), *auditorium* (a place where people come to *hear* something), *audit* (enrolling in a course just to *hear* about a subject, rather than taking it for credit), *auditory* (pertaining to *hearing*, as in auditory learner), and *audiologist* (a person trained to evaluate *hearing*). Knowing the meaning of a word's root also makes it easier to remember the meaning of the word.

KEY TERM
prefix

Word part attached to
the beginning of a root
word that adds its
meaning to that of the
base word.

Prefixes change the meaning of a root by adding their meaning to the meaning of the root. For example, adding the prefix *tele* ("distant" or "far") to the root word *scope* ("to see") creates the word *telescope,* a device that lets you *see* things that are *far* away. Try adding the prefixes *pre* ("before") and *re* ("back") to the root *cede* ("to go" or "to move"). *Precede* means "to go before" something or someone else; *recede* means "to move back."

Think of roots and prefixes as parts of a puzzle that can often help you figure out the meaning of an unfamiliar word. Remember, however, that although a word may begin with the same letters as a prefix, it does not necessarily contain that prefix. The words *malt, mall, male,* and *mallard* (a type of duck), for example, have no connection with the prefix *mal* ("wrong" or "bad") as in words such as *malnourished* or *maladjusted.*

KEY TERM
suffix

Word part attached to
the end of a root word.

Suffixes are word parts that are attached to the end of a root word. Some add their meaning to a root. Other suffixes change a word's part of speech or inflection. For example, consider these forms of the word *predict:* predic*tion,* predict*ability,* predict*or* (nouns); predict*able* (adjective); predict*ably* (adverb). Examples of suffixes that serve as inflectional endings include adding *s* to make a word plural or *ed* to make a verb past tense.

Comprehension
Monitoring Question
for Word-Structure
Clues

Are there roots, prefixes,
or suffixes that give me
clues to the meaning of
an unfamiliar word?

Suffixes are not as helpful as roots or prefixes in determining the meaning of unfamiliar words because many suffixes have similar or even the same meanings. Also, some root words change their spelling before a suffix is added. For instance, when suffixes are added to *happy* the *y* becomes an *i: happier, happiness, happily.*

The most common and helpful roots, prefixes, and suffixes in English come from Latin and ancient Greek. These Latin and Greek word parts not only help you figure out the meaning of a word, but also serve as built-in memory aids that make it easy to recall the meaning.

Spanish, French, Italian, Portuguese, and Romanian are called *romance languages* because they draw so heavily on Latin. (Latin was the "Roman" language because it was spoken in ancient Rome.) Although English is not one of the romance languages (it is a Germanic language), English still has many words derived from Latin and ancient Greek. In particular, a considerable number of terms in science, medicine, and technology are derived from Latin and Greek, so learning word parts from these two older languages can be useful to you if you are considering a career in one of those fields.

KEY TERM
etymology

The origin and history
of a word.

A word's **etymology** (origin and history) indicates whether it contains Latin or Greek word parts. Because a word's etymology can help you understand and remember a word's meaning, dictionaries typically give the etymology of a word in brackets [ ] before or after the definition. When you look up a word in the dictionary, take an extra minute to check its etymology for word parts that you might recognize. This technique of checking a word's etymology will also help you learn and remember the meaning of many roots and affixes.

Take time to familiarize yourself with the common roots, prefixes, and suffixes in Appendix 2. Then watch for them in new words you encounter. Use word-structure clues whenever possible to help you determine the meaning of an unfamiliar word or confirm an "educated guess" you based on context clues.

Using a Dictionary Pronunciation Key

Most college students already know how to locate a word in the dictionary efficiently and accurately, and how to determine which definition is appropriate for their needs. But, like many students, you may still not be proficient at or feel confident using a dictionary pronunciation key. Being able to use a pronunciation key is important, because when you need to remember words, one of the most helpful things you can do is say them aloud. Checking and then practicing a word's pronunciation takes only a moment or two.

A complete pronunciation key appears at the beginning of a dictionary. Most of them look similar to the example shown in the box on page 86.

DICTIONARY PRONUNCIATION KEY

A list of pronunciation symbols used in this dictionary is given below in the column headed **AHD** [*American Heritage Dictionary*]. The column headed **Examples** contains words chosen to illustrate how the **AHD** symbols are pronounced. The letters that correspond in sound to the **AHD** symbols are shown in boldface. The third column, headed **IPA** (International Phonetic Alphabet), gives the equivalent transcription symbols most often used by scholars. Although similar, the **AHD** and **IPA** symbols are not precisely the same because they were conceived for different purposes.

Examples	AHD	IPA
p**a**t	ă	æ
p**ay**	ā	e
c**are**	âr	∈r, er
f**a**ther	ä	ɑ:, ɑ
bi**b**	b	b
chur**ch**	ch	tʃ
dee**d**, mill**ed**	d	d
p**e**t	ĕ	∈
b**ee**	ē	i
fi**fe**, **ph**ase, rou**gh**	f	f
ga**g**	g	g
hat	h	h
which	hw	hw (also ʍ)
p**i**t	ĭ	ɪ
p**ie**, b**y**	ī	aɪ
p**ier**	îr	ɪr, ir
ju**dge**	j	dʒ
ki**ck**, **c**at, pi**que**	k	k
lid, need**le***	l (nēd′l)	l, ļ [′nidļ]
mu**m**	m	m
no, sudd**en***	n (sŭd′n)	n, ņ [′sʌdņ]
thi**ng**	ng	ŋ
p**o**t	ŏ	ɑ
t**oe**	ō	o
c**augh**t, p**aw**,	ô	ɔ
n**oi**se	oi	ɔɪ
t**oo**k	o͝o	ʊ
b**oo**t	o͞o	u
out	ou	aʊ

Examples	AHD	IPA
po**p**	p	p
roar	r	ɹ
sau**ce**	s	s
ship, di**sh**	sh	ʃ
tigh**t**, stopp**ed**	t	t
thin	th	θ
this	*th*	ð
cut	ŭ	ʌ
urge, t**er**m, f**ir**m word, h**ear**d	ûr	ɜ, ɜr
val**ve**	v	v
with	w	w
yes	y	j
zebra, **x**ylem	z	z
vi**s**ion, plea**s**ure, gara**ge**	zh	ʒ
about, it**e**m, ed**i**ble, gall**o**p, circ**u**s	ə	ə
butt**er**	ər	ɚ

Foreign	AHD	IPA
French f**eu**		ø
German sch**ö**n	œ	
French **oeu**f		œ
German zw**ö**lf		
French t**u**	ü	y
German **ü**ber		
German i**ch**		ç
German a**ch**	кн	
Scottish lo**ch**		x
French bo**n****	ɴ (bôɴ)	~ [bõ]

*In English the consonants *l* and *n* often constitute complete syllables by themselves.
**The IPA symbols show nasality with a diacritic mark over the vowel, whereas the dictionary uses ɴ to reflect that the preceding vowel is nasalized. In French four nasalized vowels occur, as in the phrase *un bon vin blanc:* AHD (œn *bôn* văn blän), IPA | œ bõ væ blä].

In most dictionaries an *abridged* (shortened) *pronunciation key,* showing only vowel sounds and the more unusual consonant sounds, appears at or near the bottom of each page. It looks something like this:

Pronunciation Key: ă **pat**   ā **pay**   âr **care**   ä **father**   ĕ **pet**   ē **be**   ĭ **pit**
ī **tie**   îr **pier**   ŏ **pot**   ō **toe**   ô **paw**   oi **noise**   ou **out**   ŏo **took**
ōō **boot**   ŭ **cut**   yōō **abuse**   ûr **urge**   th **thin**   *th* **this**   hw **which**
zh **vision**   ə **about**   *Stress mark:* '

Your instructor can give you guidance in using a dictionary pronunciation key. In *Opening Doors,* you will have numerous opportunities to practice this skill because the pronunciation is given for each term in the vocabulary quizzes that accompany the reading selections. To help you interpret the symbols, an abridged pronunciation key is repeated in each vocabulary section.

Understanding Denotations and Connotations of Words

The literal, explicit meaning of a word—its dictionary definition—is called its **denotation.** But many words also have connotations. A **connotation** is an additional, nonliteral meaning associated with a word. For example, the two words *weird* and *distinctive* have similar denotations (both of them describe something that is different or out of the ordinary). It is their connotations that cause us to choose one of these words instead of the other when describing someone or something. You might describe the traits of someone you admire as *distinctive* but those of someone you dislike as *weird,* because *distinctive* has a positive connotation and *weird* has a negative one. Most people, for example, would rather be thought of as having *distinctive* clothes than *weird* clothes. *Distinctive* and *weird* have opposite connotations. *Distinctive* is associated with positive qualities; *weird* is associated with negative ones.

As explained above, many words have positive or negative connotative meanings that are very different from their more neutral denotative meanings. The first column in the chart on page 88 presents a sentence containing an italicized word whose denotation is neutral. In the other two columns, the italicized word has been replaced by other words that have a similar denotation, but have a positive or negative connotation.

EXAMPLES OF DENOTATIONS AND CONNOTATIONS

Denotation (Neutral)	Similar Word with Positive Connotation	Similar Word with Negative Connotation
Sofia has *different* tastes.	Sofia has *distinctive* tastes.	Sofia has *weird* tastes.
When I was younger, I was *thin*.	When I was younger, I was *slender*.	When I was younger, I was *skinny*.
I purchased a *used* car.	I purchased a *preowned* car.	I purchased a *secondhand* car.
She's a computer *expert*.	She's a computer *whiz*.	She's a computer *nerd*.
His behavior was *abnormal*.	His behavior was *unusual*.	His behavior was *peculiar*.
She *wants* power.	She *desires* power.	She *craves* power.
Lou spent time in *jail*.	Lou spent time in a *correctional facility*.	Lou spent time in a *penitentiary*.
Hector has joined a *club*.	Hector has joined an *association*.	Hector has joined a *gang*.
The patient *died*.	The patient *passed on*.	The patient *croaked*.

Comprehension Monitoring Question for Connotative Meaning

Is there a positive or negative association in addition to the literal meaning of a word?

Careful readers ask themselves, "Does this word have a connotation as well as a denotation?" That is, "Is there a positive or negative association in addition to the word's literal meaning?"

Understanding Figurative Language

Figurative language is language that uses imagery—unusual comparisons or vivid words that create certain effects—to paint a picture in the reader's or listener's mind. Figurative expressions are also called *figures of speech*. You use figurative language every day, although you may not know it by that name. Whenever you say something such as "That chemistry test was a monster" or "My mother is a saint," you are using figurative language.

KEY TERM
figurative language

Words that create unusual comparisons or vivid pictures in the reader's mind.

Figurative expressions are also known as *figures of speech*.

Because figures of speech do not literally mean what the words say, the reader or listener must *interpret* their meaning. If you say, "My landlord is a prince," you do not actually or literally mean that he is a member of a royal family. You expect your listener to interpret your words to mean that you appreciate your landlord, perhaps because he is cooperative and pleasant. If you say, "My landlord is a rat," you do not literally mean that he is a rodent. You expect your listener to interpret your words to mean that you dislike your landlord, perhaps because he has proved to be untrustworthy or unfair.

Four common figures of speech are *metaphor, simile, hyperbole,* and *personification.* Let's look at each of these.

Metaphors and similes both make comparisons. A **metaphor** is an implied comparison between two things that seem very different from each other on the sur-

KEY TERM

metaphor

Figure of speech suggesting a comparison between two essentially dissimilar things, usually by saying that one of them *is* the other.

KEY TERM

simile

Figure of speech presenting a comparison between two essentially dissimilar things by saying that one of them is *like* the other.

KEY TERMS

hyperbole

Figure of speech using obvious exaggeration for emphasis and effect.

personification

Figure of speech in which nonhuman or nonliving things are given human traits or attributes.

Comprehension Monitoring Question for Figurative Language

Should these words or this expression be interpreted figuratively?

face yet are alike in some significant way. A metaphor usually states that one thing is something else. The author assumes that readers will not take his or her words literally, but instead will understand that it is figurative language. (That is, the sentence is to be taken figuratively, not literally.) For example, in the sentence "Mae's *garden is a rainbow,*" the writer is making a comparison between a garden and a rainbow to help the reader envision the colorful array of flowers in the garden. To interpret this metaphor correctly, the reader must compare a garden and a rainbow and determine what they might have in common: a multitude of colors. (The author does not mean that the garden was literally a rainbow.) Another example of a metaphor would be "Joe's *desk was a mountain of paper.*" It creates a vivid image of how high ("a mountain") the paper was stacked on the desk. As noted, a metaphor usually states that one thing is something else (in these cases, that a garden *is* a rainbow or that a stack of papers *was* a mountain).

A **simile** is also a comparison between two essentially dissimilar things, but instead of saying that one thing *is* something else, the author says that one thing is *like* something else. In fact, a simile is usually introduced by the words *like* or *as.* "Nancy felt *like a lottery winner* when she received the scholarship" and "The marine stood at attention *as rigid as an oak tree*" are examples of similes. In the first sentence, receiving a scholarship is compared with winning a lottery. The author wants us to understand that receiving the scholarship made Nancy feel as excited as if she had won a great deal of money in the lottery. In the second example, a marine, because of his stiff posture, is compared with an oak tree. To repeat: A simile says that one thing is *like* another. To understand a simile, you must determine which things are being compared and the important way in which the author considers them to be similar.

Another type of figurative language is **hyperbole** (pronounced hī *pĕr'* bə lē), in which obvious exaggeration is used for emphasis. "My parents will explode if I get one more speeding ticket!" is an example of hyperbole. The parents would not literally "explode," but the exaggeration conveys how angry they would be.

In **personification,** nonliving or nonhuman things are given human characteristics or qualities. "My car groaned, coughed, and wheezed, then crawled to a stop" gives human attributes to an automobile to suggest that the car made strange noises and then quit running. Cars, of course, cannot groan, cough, wheeze, and crawl in the same sense that a person would do these things. That's what makes it personification.

Careful readers ask themselves, "Is the author using figurative language?" "What things are being compared, and how are they alike?" "What exaggeration is being made, and why? What human traits are being given to a nonliving thing?"

The chart on page 90 summarizes metaphor, simile, hyperbole, and personification and presents examples of each.

FOUR TYPES OF FIGURATIVE LANGUAGE

Figures of Speech	Examples
Metaphor	
Implied comparison between two essentially dissimilar things, usually using the word *is* or *was.*	My grandfather's face is a raisin. TV was my babysitter, my teacher, and my friend. Shyness was my prison. One person's trash is another person's treasure. The midnight sky was diamonds on black velvet. He believes losing his old job turned out to be a great gift.
Simile	
Stated comparison between two essentially dissimilar things, usually introduced by the word *like* or *as.*	Roberto's garden is like a supermarket. After the party, Ted's apartment looked as if it had been hit by a tornado. Monica's closet is like a shoe store. The ice hockey player looked as if he'd gone 10 rounds in a boxing ring—and lost. My allergies made my head feel like a block of wood. The sleet hit our faces like tiny knives.
Hyperbole	
Obvious exaggeration for emphasis and effect.	I'm so hungry I could eat a horse! Smoke came out of the coach's ears when the penalty was called. My grandmother's biscuits are so light they float off the plate. I'm buried in homework this weekend. My backpack weighs a ton.
Personification	
Attribution of human characteristics or qualities to nonhuman or nonliving things.	The ATM machine ate my debit card! The old house looked tired and unhappy until it received a face-lift. The mystery hooked me on the opening page and then reeled me in. When the theater lights dimmed, the cell phones couldn't wait to begin screaming. Even though it seemed far off and unlikely, a college degree beckoned me.

A WORD ABOUT STANDARDIZED READING TESTS: CONTEXT CLUES AND FIGURATIVE LANGUAGE

Many college students are required to take standardized reading tests as part of an overall assessment program, in a reading course, or as part of a state-mandated basic skills test. Examples of these tests include the Nelson-Denny Reading Test, COMPASS, ASSET, ACCUPLACER, CLAST (in Florida), and THEA (in Texas). A standardized reading test typically consists of a series of passages, each of which is followed by multiple-choice reading skill application questions. The test is often a timed test. That is, students are permitted to work for only a specified amount of time.

The tips below, along with the ones in each chapter in Part Two, can help you earn higher scores on standardized reading tests. The tips for this chapter deal with context clues and figurative language. Many tests, such as the CLAST and THEA test, include context clue questions, and the THEA test has figurative language items as well.

On tests, vocabulary-in-context questions will be worded:

As used in line [#] . . .

As used in paragraph [#] . . .

The [vocabulary word] in the first paragraph means . . .

In the fifth paragraph, the meaning of [word] is . . .

As used in the last paragraph, [the term] means . . .

To determine the correct answer, ask yourself, "What would this word have to mean in order to make sense in this sentence?" Most words have more than one meaning, so be sure to refer to the sentence in which the word appears. Reread the sentence and, if necessary, the sentences that come immediately before and after it. Look for definition clues, synonym clues (including punctuation clues), contrast clues (antonyms), experience clues, example clues, and clues from other sentences. You may be able to use word parts (prefixes and roots) to help confirm your answer choice. Keep in mind that you may occasionally be asked the meaning of a phrase in context. For example, in context, the phrase *to take a swing at it* might mean *to attempt* or *to try*. The process for determining the correct meaning will still be to ask yourself what the phrase would have to mean in order to make sense in the sentence. Be sure to read all the answer choices before choosing one.

Figurative language questions might be worded:

The author uses the metaphor of a ship to represent . . .

In paragraph 2 the author compares old age to . . .

In the selection, *winter* is personified as being . . .

In using the simile "Peace negotiations are a high-stakes chess game," the author is suggesting . . .

The author uses the hyperbole "On 9/11, *the world stood still* in order to indicate that . . .

In the metaphor in paragraph 4, a bridge is compared with . . .

The comparison between the brain and a computer is an example of which figure of speech?

To find the right answer, think about the type of figure of speech. If it is a *simile* or *metaphor*, decide which two things are being compared and how they are alike. If it is a *hyperbole*, decide what effect the author is trying to achieve—humor, shock, persuasion, etc. If it is *personification*, decide what inanimate object is being compared with a person and the important way it might be like a person. Be sure to read all the answer choices before choosing one.

Monitoring Your Understanding of Vocabulary

1. What question should you ask yourself in order to take advantage of context clues? (See page 82.)

2. What question should you ask yourself in order to take advantage of word-structure clues? (See page 84.)

3. What question should you ask yourself in order to understand the connotation of a word? (See page 88.)

4. What question should you ask yourself in order to understand figurative language? (See page 89.)

Card 8   Chapter 2: Approaching College Reading and Developing a College-Level Vocabulary

SELECTION **2-1**

Student Success

Making It Happen: Creating Positive Change to Become a Peak Performer

From *Peak Performance: Success in College and Beyond,* 5th ed.

By Sharon K. Ferrett

Prepare Yourself to Read

Directions: Do these exercises *before* you read Selection 2-1.

1. First, read and think about the title. What do you know about making positive changes and becoming a peak performer?

   _____

   _____

   _____

   _____

   _____

2. Next, complete your preview by reading the following:

   First paragraph

   Headings

   Bold print

   Last paragraph (paragraph 20)

   Now that you have previewed the selection, what points do you think the author is making about creating positive changes?

   _____

   _____

   _____

   _____

   _____

   _____

   _____

Apply Comprehension Skills

Directions: Do these exercises *as* you read Selection 2-1. Apply three skills from this chapter:

Adjust your reading rate. On the basis of your preview and your prior knowledge of how to change a habit, do you think you should read Selection 2-1 slowly or more rapidly?

_____

_____

Develop a college-level vocabulary. Did you notice any unfamiliar words while you were previewing Selection 2-1? If so, list them here.

_____

_____

_____

_____

Predict as you read. As you read Selection 2-1, make predictions about what the author will discuss next. Write your predictions in the blanks provided throughout the selection.

MAKING IT HAPPEN: CREATING POSITIVE CHANGE TO BECOME A PEAK PERFORMER

The first paragraph of this selection serves as an introduction.

1   You can use many strategies for doing well in your school, career, and personal life. Many techniques are also available on how to manage your time, how to succeed at taking tests, and how to develop healthy relationships. Reading about and discussing them is one thing, but actually making these techniques and strategies part of your everyday life is another. You will find that embracing them will prove rewarding and helpful as you begin developing and working on your goals. Knowing that you have the motivational skills to succeed in school and in your career can give you the confidence to risk, grow, contribute, and overcome life's setbacks. You have what it takes to keep going even when you feel frustrated and unproductive. This selection will show you how to take strategies and turn them into lasting habits. It will also look at the importance of effort and commitment, without which there is no great achievement. Look at great athletes. The difference in their levels of physical skill is often not dramatic, but their sense of commitment is what separates the good from the truly great. Peak performers also achieve results by being committed.

Prediction Exercises

Directions: At each of the points indicated below, answer the question, "What do you predict will be discussed next?"

Make a Commitment to Change Your Habits

2   Most people resist change. Even when you are aware of a bad habit, it is difficult to change it. Consequently, you may find it hard to integrate into your life some of the skills and strategies that you know would benefit you.

3   Old habits become comfortable, familiar parts of your life. Giving them up leaves you feeling insecure. For example, you want to get better grades, and you know it's a good idea to study only in a quiet study area rather than while watching television or listening to the radio. However, you have always read your assignments while watching television. You might even try studying at your desk for a few days, but then you lapse into your old habit. Many people give up at this point rather than acknowledge their resistance. Some find it useful to take stock of what common resistors, or barriers, keep them from meeting their goals. However, as a potential peak performer, you will begin to adopt positive techniques to help change your old habits.

Prediction Exercise

What do you predict will be discussed in this section?

_____

_____

Use Strategies for Creating Positive Change

4   If you have trouble making changes, realize that habits are learned and can be unlearned. Adopting new habits

Prediction Exercise

What do you predict will be discussed in this section?

_____

_____

requires a desire to change, consistent effort, time, and a commitment. Try the following ten strategies for eliminating old habits and acquiring new ones.

5 1. **You must want to change.** To change, you must have a real desire and see the value of the change. It helps to identify important goals: "I really want to get better grades. I have a real desire to graduate from business college and start my own small retail business. I see the benefit and value in continuing my education." Your motivation has to be channeled into constructive action.

6 2. **Develop specific goals.** Setting specific goals is a beginning for change. Statements such as "I wish I could get better grades" or "I hope I can study more" are too general and only help to continue your bad habits. Stating goals such as "I will study for 40 minutes, two times a day, in my study area" are specific and can be assessed and measured for achievement.

7 3. **Change only one habit at a time.** You will become discouraged if you try to change too many things about yourself at the same time. If you have decided to study for 40 minutes, two times a day, in your study area, then do this for a month, then two months, then three, and so on, it will become a habit. After you have made one change move on to the next. Perhaps you want to exercise more, or give better speeches, or get up earlier.

8 4. **Be patient.** It takes at least 30 days to change a habit. Lasting change requires a pattern of consistent behavior. With time and patience, the change will eventually begin to feel comfortable and normal. Don't become discouraged and give up if you haven't seen a complete change in your behavior in a few weeks. Give yourself at least a month of progressing toward your goal. If you fall short one day, get back on track the next. Don't expect to get all A's the first few weeks of studying longer hours. Don't become discouraged if you don't feel comfortable instantly studying at your desk instead of lying on the couch.

9 5. **Imagine success.** Imagine yourself progressing through all the steps toward your desired goal. For example, see yourself sitting at your desk in your quiet study area. You are calm and find it easy to concentrate. You enjoy studying and feel good about completing projects. Think back to a time in your life when you had these same positive feelings. Think of a time when you felt warm, confident, safe, and relaxed. Imagine enjoying these feelings and create that same state of mind. Remember, the mind and body produce your state of mind, and this state determines your behaviors.

10 6. **Observe and model others.** How do successful people think, act, and relate to others? Do students who get good grades have certain habits that contribute to their success? Basic success principles produce successful results. Research indicates that successful students study regularly in a quiet study area. They regularly attend classes, are punctual, and sit in or near the front row. Observe successful students. Are they interested, involved, and well prepared in class? Do they seem confident and focused? Now model this behavior until it feels comfortable and natural. Form study groups with people who are good students, are motivated, and have effective study habits.

11 7. **Self-awareness.** Sometimes paying attention to your own behavior can help you change habits. For example, you may notice that the schoolwork you complete late at night is not as thorough as the work you complete earlier in the day. Becoming aware of this characteristic may prompt you to change your time frame for studying and completing schoolwork.

12 8. **Reward yourself.** One of the best ways to change a habit is to reward yourself when you've made a positive change. Increase your motivation with specific payoffs. Suppose you want to reward yourself for studying for a certain length of time in your study

area or for completing a project. For example, you might say to yourself, "After I outline this chapter, I'll watch television for 20 minutes," or "When I finish reading these two chapters, I'll call a friend and talk for 10 minutes." The reward should always come after the results are achieved and be limited in duration.

13   **9. Use affirmations.** Talking to yourself means that you are reprogramming your thoughts, a successful technique for making change. When you have negative thoughts, tell yourself, "Stop!" Counter negative thoughts with positive statements. Replace the negative thought with something like "I am centered and focused. I have control over my thoughts. When they wander, I gently bring them back. I can concentrate for the next 40 minutes, and then I'll take a short break."

14   **10. Write a contract for change.** Write a contract with yourself for overcoming your barriers. State the payoffs for meeting your goals: "I agree to take an honest look at where I am now and at my resistors, my shortcomings, my negative thoughts, the ways I sabotage myself, and the barriers I experience. I agree to learn new skills, choose positive thoughts and attitudes, and try new behaviors. I will reward myself for meeting my goals." You may want to discuss this with a study partner.

Make a Commitment to Contribute

15   As a peak performer, you can make a contribution to the world. By improving yourself, giving to your family, and volunteering your time in the community, you will make the world a better place. You will be leaving a legacy that is positive and inspiring to others. Try to focus on more than just financial success, possessions, prestige, and career advancement. Your family and friends will think of you as being a giving and service-minded person. Consider the contribution you make, the kind of person you want to be, and ways in which you can make a positive impact in your community and personal life.

Prediction Exercise

What do you predict will be discussed in this section?

_____

_____

Make a Commitment to Develop a Positive Attitude

16   Achieving excellence is a combination of a positive attitude and specific skills. When you commit yourself to being successful, you learn to go with your own natural energy and strengths. You learn to be your own best friend by working for yourself. You begin by telling the truth about who you are: your current skills, abilities, goals, barriers, and both good and bad habits. You learn to be aware of the common barriers and setbacks that cause others to fail. Then you set goals to focus your energy on a certain path. Next, you create the specific thoughts and behaviors that will produce the results you want.

17   Everyone loses course at times; thus, it is important to build in observation and feedback so that you can correct

Prediction Exercise

What do you predict will be discussed in this section?

_____

_____

and modify. You will learn to alter your actions to get back on track. Even when you are equipped with the best skills, self-understanding, and a motivated attitude, you will still face occasional setbacks and periods of frustration. At times you may question your decisions, become discouraged, and feel your confidence and self-esteem dip. Focus on the positive and learn to be resilient.

Make a Commitment to Be Resilient

18   The key to being a peak performer is to make adversity work for you. Successful people see their failures as temporary setbacks and learning experiences; unsuccessful people see their failures as barriers and dead ends. Use the power of reframing to see your setbacks as stepping-stones to your final goal. Children have a natural resiliency and can bounce back after a disappointment. You can reclaim resiliency by using your creativity to see what options are still available.

Make a Commitment to Be a Person of Character and Integrity

19   The word integrity comes from the Latin word *integer,* meaning "a sense of wholeness." It is important to use the *whole* of your intelligence for school and job success. When you have a sense of wholeness, you are confident about thinking, speaking, living, and taking the right path. You know that you can trust yourself to do the right thing, keep your commitments, and play by the rules. You are a complete human being when you use your skills, competencies, and essential personal qualities, such as integrity. You have effective communication skills, strive to be sociable and personable, but you put character first. It is not difficult to work out a code of ethics or a moral code that most of us can agree on. Most people believe in core values of honesty, truthfulness, fairness, kindness, compassion, and respect for others. Doing the right thing is a decision and a habit. The key is to assess your integrity as you would any skill and use critical thinking to reflect on your actions.

20   As an adult, you teach values by example. To choose to teach deliberately and consistently is the challenge. Becoming a responsible, motivated, emotionally mature person makes you smarter than you think. You may have a high IQ, talent, skills, and experience, but if you lack responsibility, effort, commitment, a positive attitude, interpersonal skills, and especially character and integrity, you will have difficulty in college, in the workplace, and in your relationships.

Prediction Exercise

What do you predict will be discussed in this section?

_____

_____

Prediction Exercise

What do you predict will be discussed in this section?

_____

_____

_____

Source: Adapted from Sharon Ferrett, *Peak Performance: Success in College and Beyond,* 5th ed., pp. 13-2–13-4, 13-7–13-9, 13-12.
Copyright © 2006 by The McGraw-Hill Companies, Inc. Reprinted with permission of The McGraw-Hill Companies.

SELECTION **2-1**   **Reading Selection Quiz**

Student Success
(Continued)

This quiz has three parts. Your instructor may assign some or all of them.

Comprehension Quiz

Directions: Items 1–10 test your comprehension (understanding) of the material of this selection. These questions are the type a content area instructor would ask on a test over this material. You should be able to answer these questions after studying this selection. For each comprehension question below, use information from the selection to determine the correct answer. Refer to the selection as you answer the questions. Write your answer in the space provided.

True or False

_____ **1.** The difference between good athletes and great ones is often their commitment and not their levels of physical skill.

_____ **2.** Changing several habits at once is more effective and efficient than changing them one at a time.

_____ **3.** It takes approximately a month to change a habit.

_____ **4.** A goal of "I will work out for an hour three times a week" is more likely to lead to positive change than a goal of "I will get in better shape physically."

_____ **5.** Peak performers, like other successful people, view failures as temporary setbacks and as opportunities to learn.

_____ **6.** As an adult, you teach values by telling others how to think and behave.

Multiple-Choice

_____ **7.** Using affirmations refers to:
  a. being around others who are positive models.
  b. being patient with yourself while you make changes.
  c. saying positive things to yourself to reprogram your thoughts.
  d. visualizing yourself being successful.

_____ **8.** To be a peak performer, it is important to commit to contribute and to commit to:
  a. develop a positive attitude.
  b. be resilient.
  c. be a person of character and integrity.
  d. all of the above

_____ **9.** When writing a contract for change, it is important to:
  a. state the payoffs for meeting your goals.
  b. include affirmations.

     c.   observe and model others.

     d.   be patient.

_____ **10.** When you use the strategy of imagining success, you should:

     a.   be with other people who are motivated.

     b.   alter your actions to get back on track rather than become discouraged.

     c.   reward yourself for having a positive attitude.

     d.   visualize yourself progressing through the steps to your goal.

SELECTION **2-1**

Student Success
(Continued)

Vocabulary in Context

Directions: Items 11–20 test your ability to determine the meaning of a word by using context clues. *Context clues* are words in a sentence that allow the reader to deduce (reason out) the meaning of an unfamiliar word in that sentence. Context clues also enable the reader to determine which meaning the author intends, when a word has more than one meaning. For each vocabulary item below, a sentence from the selection containing an important word (*italicized, like this*) is quoted first. Next, there is an additional sentence using the word in the same sense and providing another context clue. Use the context clues from *both* sentences to deduce the meaning of the italicized word. *Be sure the answer you choose makes sense in both sentences.* If you discover that you need to use a dictionary to confirm an answer choice, remember that the meaning you select must still fit the context of *both* sentences. Write your answer in the space provided.

Pronunciation Key: ă pat ā pay âr **care** ä father ě pet ē be ĭ pit
ī tie îr **pier** ŏ pot ō toe ô **paw** oi **noise** ou **out** ŏŏ **took**
ōō **boot** ŭ **cut** yōō abuse ûr **urge** th **thin** *th* **this** hw **which**
zh vision ə about   *Stress mark:* ′

_____ **11.** *Peak* performers also achieve results by being committed.

Florists report *peak* sales on Valentine's Day and Mother's Day.

peak (pēk) means:

     a.   well-known; well-documented

     b.   less than expected

     c.   busy

     d.   approaching the highest or maximum

_____ **12.** You might even try studying at your desk for a few days, but then you *lapse* into your old habit.

Dieters should remove inappropriate food in the house so that they do not *lapse* into unhealthy eating habits.

lapse (lăps) means:

    a. to fall to a previous or lower level

    b. to improve upon

    c. to refuse to cooperate or go along with

    d. to struggle against

_____ **13.** Your motivation has to be channeled into *constructive* action.

Because of the new coach's *constructive* criticism, the team's morale was the best ever, and they won the college championship.

constructive (kən strŭk′ tĭv) means:

    a. creating negative feelings

    b. nonstop; continuous

    c. helpful; intended to result in improvement

    d. hurtful; insulting

_____ **14.** The reward should always come after the results are achieved and be limited in *duration*.

The audience lost interest quickly, but politely suffered through the *duration* of the guest speaker's long presentation.

duration (dŏo rā′ shən) means:

    a. period of time something lasts

    b. final few minutes

    c. excitement

    d. a brief period of time

_____ **15.** *Counter* negative thoughts with positive statements.

During a trial, the defense attorney's job is to *counter* the charges and evidence presented by the prosecuting attorney.

counter (koun′ tər) means:

    a. to ignore; to dismiss as unimportant

    b. to oppose; to offer in response

    c. to reveal

    d. to accept; to welcome

_____ **16.** I agree to take an honest look at where I am now and at my resistors, my shortcomings, my negative thoughts, the ways I *sabotage* myself, and the barriers I experience.

The soldiers were shocked when a member of their unit attempted to *sabotage* their mission.

sabotage (săb′ ə täzh) means:

    a. to defeat by betraying faith or trust

    b. to cause to happen

    c. to complete alone without aid

    d. to celebrate

_____ **17.** You will be leaving a *legacy* that is positive and inspiring to others.

Because my grandfather often took us camping and hiking, part of his *legacy* to us was a deep love for nature.

legacy (lĕg′ ə sē) means:
  a. written document that explains or describes
  b. something passed from one generation to another
  c. time spent oneself
  d. outdoor activities

_____ **18.** Try to focus on more than just financial success, possessions, *prestige,* and career advancement.

Because of her *prestige* in the community, she is often asked to lend her name to charitable causes and to chair important civic projects.

prestige (prĕ stēzh′) means:
  a. lack of respect
  b. living in the same place for a long time
  c. a person's high standing among others
  d. questionable reputation

_____ **19.** The key to being a peak performer is to make *adversity* work for you.

For children who live in poverty, hunger, and danger, *adversity* is a never-changing way of life.

adversity (ăd vûr′ sĭ tē) means:
  a. sadness; unhappiness
  b. lack of money
  c. depression
  d. misfortune; hardship

_____ **20.** Children have a natural *resiliency* and can bounce back after a disappointment.

Writer William Faulkner expressed *resiliency* of the human spirit in his Nobel Prize acceptance speech when he said, "I believe that man will not merely endure: He will prevail."

resiliency (rĭ zĭl′ yən sē) means:
  a. tendency to give up easily
  b. ability to stretch
  c. ability to recover quickly from misfortune
  d. tendency to deceive oneself

SELECTION **2-1** *Reading Skills Application*

Student Success
(Continued)

Directions: Items 21–25 test your ability to *apply* certain reading skills to information in this selection. These types of questions provide valuable practice for all students, especially those who must take standardized reading tests and state-mandated basic skills tests (such as the Florida CLAST Test and the Texas THEA Test). You may not have studied all of the skills at this point, so these items will serve as a helpful preview. The comprehension and critical reading skills in this section are presented in Chapters 4 through 9 of *Opening Doors;* vocabulary and figurative language skills are presented in Chapter 2. As you work through *Opening Doors,* you will practice and develop these skills. Write your answer for each question in the space provided.

_____ **21.** Based on the information in the selection, it can be inferred that the author believes:

  a. only people with high IQs can become peak performers.

  b. talent, skills, and experience are the most important factors in becoming a peak performer.

  c. it takes several years to become a peak performer.

  d. anyone can make positive changes and become a peak performer.

_____ **22.** In paragraph 3, the writer says, "Some find it useful to take stock of what common resistors, or barriers, keep them from meeting their goals." *To take stock of* means:

  a. change

  b. eliminate; do away with

  c. assess; take an inventory of

  d. ignore; pay no attention to

_____ **23.** Which pattern is used to organize the information in the passage?

  a. definition

  b. comparison

  c. sequence

  d. cause-effect

_____ **24.** The information in the selection is based on which of the following assumptions held by the author?

  a. It is very difficult to persuade other people to change their habits.

  b. Only a few people can successfully change their own habits and attitudes.

  c. Making positive changes is more trouble than it is worth.

  d. People have a desire to make positive changes and perform at higher levels.

_____ **25.** As an example of how observing and modeling others can be helpful, the author mentions:

    a. imagining yourself enjoying studying and
feeling good about completing projects.

    b. giving to your family and volunteering
time in the community.

    c. forming study groups with motivated stu-
dents who have effective study habits.

    d. striving to be sociable and personable.

SELECTION **2-1**

Student Success
(Continued)

Collaboration Option

Respond in Writing

Directions: Refer to Selection 2-1 as needed to answer the essay-type questions
below.

Option for collaboration: Your instructor may direct you to work with other students on one or more of these items, or in other words, to work *collaboratively*. In
that case, you should form groups of three or four students, as directed by your
instructor, and work together to complete the exercises. After your group discusses an item and agrees on the answer, have a group member record it. Each
member of your group should be able to explain all of your group's answers.

1. In your opinion, how realistic is the author's approach for making changes?
What do you base your opinion on?

_____

_____

_____

2. Write one habit you would like to change, and then describe how you could
use at least three of the strategies in the selection to accomplish that change.

_____

_____

_____

_____

3. Which of the four commitments—to contribute, to develop a positive attitude,
to be resilient, to be a person of character and integrity—do you think is most
important for success? Why do you think that?

_____

_____

_____

_____

4. In addition to the 10 strategies described in the selection, what are at least two other strategies that could help a person create positive changes?

_____

_____

_____

_____

5. Overall main idea. What is the overall main idea the author wants you to understand about "changing habits and making positive changes"? Answer this question in one sentence. Be sure that your overall main idea sentence includes the topic (_changing habits and positive change_) and tells the overall most important point about it. Do _not_ begin your sentence with "The overall main idea is . . ." or "The author wants us to understand . . ." Just _state_ the overall main idea.

_____

_____

_____

_____

_____

Internet Resources

Read More about This Topic on the World Wide Web

Directions: For further information about the topic of this selection, visit these websites:

http://www.feinet.com/pubs/200101/eapost/articles/nuhabit.htm
This website outlines a helpful procedure for breaking old habits.

http://www.cob.fsu.edu/jmi/articles/habits.asp
This Florida State University College of Business website presents a short essay about changing habits.

You can also use your favorite search engine such as Google, Yahoo!, or Alta-Vista (www.google.com, www.yahoo.com, www.altavista.com) to discover more about this topic. To locate additional information, type in combinations of key-words such as:

changing habits

or

breaking habits

Keep in mind that whenever you go to *any* website, it is a good idea to evaluate the website and the information it contains. Ask yourself questions such as:

"Who sponsors this website?"

"Is the information contained in this website up-to-date?"

"What type of information is presented?"

"Is the information objective and complete?"

"How easy is it to use the features of this website?"

Fighting Terrorism in a Global Age

From *Nation of Nations: A Narrative History of the American Republic*
By James Davidson et al.

Prepare Yourself to Read

Directions: Do these exercises *before* you read Selection 2-2.

1. First, read and think about the title. What comes to mind when you think about the word *terrorism?*

_____

_____

_____

_____

2. Next, complete your preview by reading the following:

    Introduction (in *italics*)

    Headings

    Captions accompanying the photographs

Now that you have completed your preview, what aspects of fighting terrorism does this selection seem to be about?

_____

_____

_____

_____

3. Most adults say that they can remember where they were or what they were doing on the morning of September 11, 2001. How did you learn of the news that planes had struck the World Trade Center and the Pentagon?

_____

_____

_____

_____

_____

Apply Comprehension Skills

Directions: Do these exercises *as* you read Selection 2-2. Apply three skills from this chapter.

Adjust your reading rate. On the basis of your preview and your prior knowledge of terrorism, do you think you should read Selection 2-2 slowly or more rapidly?

_____

_____

Develop a college-level vocabulary. Did you notice any unfamiliar words while you were previewing Selection 2-2? If so, list them here.

_____

_____

_____

_____

Predict as you read. As you read Selection 2-2, make predictions about what the author will discuss next. Write your predictions in the blanks provided throughout the selection.

FIGHTING TERRORISM IN A GLOBAL AGE

This selection from a U.S. history textbook explains how a world already connected in so many ways found those connections challenged and shattered by a terrorist movement that was itself global. The attack on the World Trade Center and the Pentagon on September 11, 2001, reoriented American priorities, causing President George W. Bush's administration to wage a war on terror both at home and abroad. While an invasion of Afghanistan in October, 2001, received widespread support, the decision to invade Iraq on March 19, 2003, without the support of the United Nations, signaled a more controversial foreign policy. The fight against terrorism became a challenging yet urgent national priority.

1   Along the northeast coast of the United States, September 11, 2001, dawned bright and clear. One New Yorker on the way to work remembered that it was the day of the Democratic mayoral primary. He decided to vote before going to his job at the World Trade Center. There, at about the same time, Francis Ledesma was sitting in his office on the sixty-fourth floor of the South Tower when a friend suggested they go for coffee. Francis seldom took breaks that early, but he decided to make an exception. Almost everyone makes similar small choices every day. But this was no ordinary day, and the choices proved to be life-saving.

2   In the cafeteria Francis heard and felt a muffled explosion. He thought a boiler had burst, but then saw bricks and glass falling by the window. Although he intended to head back to his office for a nine o'clock meeting, his friend insisted they leave immediately. Out on the street Francis noticed the smoke and gaping hole where American Airlines Flight 11 had hit the North Tower. At that moment a huge fireball erupted as United Airlines Flight 175 hit their own South Tower. "We kept looking back," Francis recalled as they escaped the area, "and then all of a sudden our building, Tower 2, collapsed. I didn't believe what I had seen; I really thought that it was a mirage.

3   Both planes had left Boston's Logan Airport that morning carrying passengers—and a full load of jet fuel—for their flights to Los Angeles. Once the planes were aloft, terrorists commandeered their controls and turned them into lethal missiles. And that was only the beginning of the horror to follow. American Airlines Flight 77 to San Francisco left half an hour later from Dulles Airport in Washington, D.C. Shortly after takeoff it veered from its path and crashed into the Pentagon, the headquarters of the United States Defense Department. News of the terrorist attacks began to spread. Several passengers on United Airlines Flight 93 from Newark to San Francisco heard the news over their cell phones. But hijackers seized that plane as well. Rather than allow another disaster, several passengers stormed the cockpit. Moments later the plane crashed into a wooded area of western Pennsylvania.

Prediction Exercises

Directions: At each of the points indicated below, answer the question "What do you predict will be discussed next?"

Prediction Exercise

What do you predict will be discussed in this section?

_____

_____

_____

_____

_____

_____

The Cold War of the 1950s had imagined a Manhattan like this: debris everywhere, buildings in ruin, the city shrouded in smoke and fumes. On September 11, 2001, however, disaster on such a large scale came not from confrontation with another superpower but through the actions of international terrorists. The attack made clear that in a post–Cold War world, global threats could come from small groups as well as powerful nations.

The 38 passengers, 5 flight attendants, and 2 pilots, as well as the hijackers, all died instantly.

4   President Bush was in Sarasota, Florida, that morning to promote educational reform. He learned about the attacks while reading to schoolchildren. Aides rushed him to Air Force One, which then flew to a secure area at Barksdale Air Force Base in Louisiana. There the president addressed a shaken nation. He called the crashes a "national tragedy" and condemned those responsible. "Freedom itself was attacked this morning by a faceless coward, and freedom will be defended," he assured the American people.

5   The attack on the World Trade Center left New York City in chaos. The airports shut down, tunnels and bridges closed, and masses of people struggled to leave lower Manhattan. Fearing a potentially staggering loss of life, 10,000 rescue workers swarmed to the scene, where as many as 50,000 people had worked. Firefighters and police, arriving just after the explosions, did what they were trained to do with little regard for their personal safety. They rushed into the burning towers hoping to save as many people as they could. Some victims trapped on the top floors jumped to their deaths to escape the deadly flames. Then, with little warning, the two towers collapsed, one after the other, trapping inside thousands of office workers. With them died nearly 100 Port Authority and city police officers and some 343 fire fighting personnel.

6   At the Pentagon in Washington rescue workers struggled with similar heroism to evacuate victims and extinguish the intense flames. Eighty-four people died there along with the 64 people aboard Flight 77.

In 2002 Paraguay issued a stamp memorializing the events that occurred on September 11, 2001, with the slogan "No to Terrorism."

Global Dimensions of the World Trade Center Attack

7   In an age of instant global communications, the entire world watched as the tragedy unfolded. Three minutes after the first plane hit the World Trade Center's North Tower, Diane Sawyer of *ABC News* announced that an explosion had rocked the towers. British television was already covering the fire when the second plane reached its target at 9:03. Japanese networks were on the air with coverage of the Pentagon crash about an hour later, around midnight their time. *TV Azteca* in Mexico carried President Bush's statement from Barksdale Air Force Base, and China Central Television was not far behind. For this was, indeed, an international tragedy. The aptly named World Trade Center was a hub for global trade and finance. Citizens of more than 50 nations had died in the attack, hailing from states as diverse as Argentina and Belarus to Yemen and Zimbabwe. Expressions of sorrow flowed in from around the world. Paraguay, for example, issued a stamp memorializing the event, with the slogan "No to Terrorism."

8   The events of September 11, 2001, changed the United States profoundly. Not since the surprise attack by the Japanese on Pearl Harbor in 1941 had the nation experienced such a devastating attack on its homeland. Most directly, the attack on the World Trade Center claimed approximately 3,000 lives. Some 2,000 children lost a parent in the attack. More than 20,000 residents living nearby had to evacuate their homes. Officials estimated the cost to the New York City economy at over $83 billion.

Prediction Exercise

What do you predict will be discussed in this section?

_____

_____

_____

_____

_____

_____

Economic Downturn and Threats to National Security

9   Before September 11 the booming economy of the 1990s had already shown serious signs of strain. Shares in many once high-flying dot-com Internet companies had plummeted, sending the stock market into a sharp decline. Telecommunications companies were among the biggest losers. Having spent vast sums on broadband connections for the Internet, they found themselves awash in debt they could not repay. The disruptions of September 11 and its aftermath shocked and, in many ways, weakened an economy already sliding into recession.

10   Added to those economic worries were new fears for American security. The attacks seemed to be the work not of enemy nations but of an Islamic terrorist group known as al Qaeda, led by a shadowy figure, Saudi Arabian national Osama bin Laden. Members of al Qaeda had moved freely around the United States for years, attended flight training schools, and found jobs. How many more undetected terrorist cells were preparing to commit acts of sabotage? Malls, high-rise buildings, and sports stadiums all loomed as possible targets.

11   What had also changed was the nature of the threat. Following World War II, the possibility of atomic war reduced American confidence that the United States could remain safely isolated from the great-power conflicts of the Old World. The attack on the World Trade Center proved that nations were no longer the only threat to our national security. Smaller groups—subnational or international—possessed the capability of using weapons of mass destruction to make war against the most powerful nation on Earth.

Wars on Terrorism

12   But September 11 changed perspectives both at home and around the world. "This is not only an attack on the United States but an attack on the civilized world," insisted German chancellor Gerhard Schroeder, while French Prime Minister Lionel Jospin expressed his feelings of "sadness and horror." Even normally hostile nations like Cuba and Libya conveyed their shock and regrets. At home President Bush seemed energized by the crisis. In a speech to the nation he vowed that "the United States will hunt down and punish those responsible for these cowardly acts." At the same time he was careful to note that Americans would wage war on terrorism, not the religion of Islam. He distinguished between the majority of "peace loving" Muslims and "evil-doers" like Osama bin Laden. This war would produce no smashing victories nor a quick end, he warned, but the adversary's identity was clear: "Our enemy is a radical network of terrorists and

Prediction Exercise

What do you predict will be discussed in this section?

_____

_____

_____

_____

_____

Prediction Exercise

What do you predict will be discussed in this section?

_____

_____

_____

_____

_____

every government that supports them." Other countries now had a simple choice: "Either you are with us or you are with the terrorists." The war would end only when terrorism no longer threatened the world.

13 But a war with so many shadowy opponents was not always easy to reduce to an *either/or* proposition, because it was not always easy to agree on which radical groups or even which nations threatened American security directly. The "radical network of terrorists" worked underground, communicated secretly, and was spread across dozens of nations. Even the states most hospitable to al Qaeda proved hard to single out. Afghanistan was an obvious target, as it had long been a haven to bin Laden and the seat of the Taliban Islamic fundamentalists who ruled the country. Yet 15 of the 19 hijackers in the World Trade Center attacks hailed from Saudi Arabia, long an ally of the United States. During 2003 and 2004, as the administration widened its campaign to root out terrorism, there seemed to be not one war on terror but several—waged both abroad and at home.

14 Over forty years earlier President John F. Kennedy had warned against a global mission that overreached the nation's powers. With only 6 percent of the world's population, our nation could not readily impose its will on the other 94 percent, he observed. Nor could the United States "right every wrong or reverse every adversity." In the end, "there cannot be an American solution to every world problem," he concluded. Only time would tell whether our nation could act successfully to police an uncertain world.

Source: Adapted from James Davidson et al., *Nation of Nations: A Narrative History of the American Republic,* 5th ed., pp. 1136–1138, 1141–1142, 1150. Copyright © 2005 by The McGraw-Hill Companies, Inc. Reprinted by permission of The McGraw-Hill Companies.

Reading Selection Quiz

This quiz has three parts. Your instructor may assign some or all of them.

Comprehension

Directions: Items 1–10 test your comprehension (understanding) of the material of this selection. These questions are the type a content area instructor (such as a history professor) would ask on a test over this material. You should be able to answer these questions after studying this selection. For each comprehension question below, use information from the selection to determine the correct answer. Refer to the selection as you answer the questions. Write your answer in the space provided.

True or False

_____ **1.** Two planes that left Boston's Logan Airport on September 11, 2001, crashed into the Pentagon half an hour later.

_____ **2.** Both planes that had departed from Boston's Logan Airport were scheduled to land in Los Angeles.

_____ **3.** Fifteen of the 19 hijackers involved in the World Trade Center attacks hailed from Afghanistan.

_____ **4.** The disruptions of September 11, 2001, and its aftermath weakened the U.S. economy.

_____ **5.** The attack on the World Trade Center proved that smaller, subnational groups possessed the capability of using weapons of mass destruction to wage war against the United States.

Multiple-Choice

_____ **6.** On September 11, 2001, United Airlines Flight 93 from Newark to San Francisco crashed into:
   a. the World Trade Center, South Tower.
   b. the World Trade Center, North Tower.
   c. the Pentagon.
   d. a wooded area in western Pennsylvania.

_____ **7.** The al Qaeda leader Osama bin Laden was born in:
   a. Saudi Arabia.
   b. Afghanistan.
   c. Iraq.
   d. Libya.

_____ **8.** Fighting international terrorism is especially difficult because terrorists:

    a. work underground and communicate secretly.

    b. have networks that are spread across dozens of nations.

    c. sometimes hail from countries who are allies of the United States.

    d. all of the above

_____ **9.** The World Trade Center attack and its aftermath shocked the U.S. economy, which was:

    a. already sliding into recession by the end of the 1990s.

    b. remarkably strong as a result of the dot-com Internet industry.

    c. experiencing a telecommunications boom.

    d. all of the above

_____ **10.** One reason Afghanistan was an obvious target in the war against terrorism was because:

    a. it was the birthplace of Osama bin Laden.

    b. most of the hijackers were citizens of Afghanistan.

    c. it was the seat of the Taliban Islamic fundamentalists.

    d. all of the above

SELECTION **2-2**   *Vocabulary in Context*

History
(Continued)

Directions: Items 11–20 test your ability to determine the meaning of the word by using context clues. *Context clues* are words in a sentence that allow the reader to deduce (reason out) the meaning of an unfamiliar word in that sentence. Context clues also enable the reader to determine which meaning the author intends, when a word has more than one meaning. For each vocabulary item below, a sentence from the selection containing an important word (*italicized, like this*) is quoted first. Next, there is an additional sentence using the word in the same sense and providing another context clue. Use the context clues from *both* sentences to deduce the meaning of the italicized word. *Be sure the answer you choose makes sense in both sentences.* If you discover that you need to use a dictionary to confirm an answer choice, remember that the meaning you select must still fit the context of *both* sentences. Write your answer in the space provided.

Pronunciation Key: ă pat   ā pay   âr **care**   ä father   ĕ pet   ē be   ĭ pit
ī tie   îr **pier**   ŏ pot   ō toe   ô paw   oi **noise**   ou **out**   ŏŏ took
ōō **boot**   ŭ cut   yōō abuse   ûr **urge**   th **thin**   *th* **this**   hw **which**
zh vision   ə **about**   *Stress mark:* '

_____ **11.** Once the planes were aloft, terrorists commandeered their controls and turned them into *lethal* missiles.

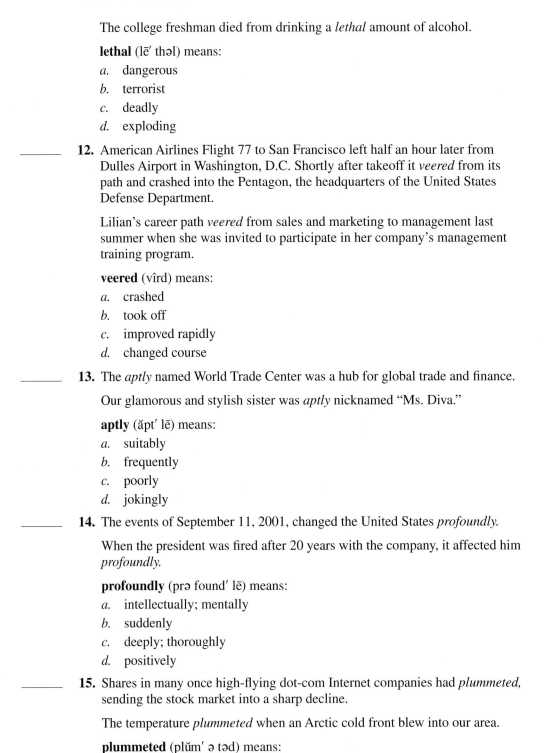

The college freshman died from drinking a *lethal* amount of alcohol.

lethal (lē′ thəl) means:

a. dangerous

b. terrorist

c. deadly

d. exploding

_____ **12.** American Airlines Flight 77 to San Francisco left half an hour later from Dulles Airport in Washington, D.C. Shortly after takeoff it *veered* from its path and crashed into the Pentagon, the headquarters of the United States Defense Department.

Lilian's career path *veered* from sales and marketing to management last summer when she was invited to participate in her company's management training program.

veered (vîrd) means:

a. crashed

b. took off

c. improved rapidly

d. changed course

_____ **13.** The *aptly* named World Trade Center was a hub for global trade and finance.

Our glamorous and stylish sister was *aptly* nicknamed "Ms. Diva."

aptly (ăpt′ lē) means:

a. suitably

b. frequently

c. poorly

d. jokingly

_____ **14.** The events of September 11, 2001, changed the United States *profoundly.*

When the president was fired after 20 years with the company, it affected him *profoundly.*

profoundly (prə found′ lē) means:

a. intellectually; mentally

b. suddenly

c. deeply; thoroughly

d. positively

_____ **15.** Shares in many once high-flying dot-com Internet companies had *plummeted,* sending the stock market into a sharp decline.

The temperature *plummeted* when an Arctic cold front blew into our area.

plummeted (plŭm′ ə təd) means:

   a. dropped down sharply

   b. lost value

   c. froze

   d. rose suddenly; skyrocketed

_____ **16.** How many more *undetected* terrorist cells were preparing to commit acts of sabotage?

   Jennifer's diabetes had remained *undetected* for years but was discovered when she finally went to her doctor for a physical exam.

   undetected (ŭn də tĕkt′ dĭd) means:

   a. controlled

   b. undiscovered

   c. dangerous

   d. secret

_____ **17.** He *distinguished* between the majority of "peace loving" Muslims and "evil-doers" like Osama bin Laden.

   Professor Martin *distinguished* between his students who were attentive and eager to learn and those who were indifferent.

   distinguished (dĭ stĭng′ gwĭshd) means:

   a. realized a difference

   b. judged to be outstanding

   c. disliked

   d. compared

_____ **18.** This war would produce no smashing victories nor a quick end, he warned, but the *adversary's* identity was clear: "Our enemy is a radical network of terrorists and every government that supports them."

   Procrastination is often a college student's greatest *adversary*.

   adversary (ăd′ vĕr sĕr ē) means:

   a. problem

   b. challenge

   c. identity

   d. enemy

_____ **19.** Afghanistan was an obvious target, as it had long been a *haven* to bin Laden and the seat of the Taliban Islamic fundamentalists who ruled the country.

   When Joey was in his early teens the Boys' Club was a *haven* from his dangerous neighborhood and his overcrowded school.

   haven (hā′ vən) means:

   a. obvious target

   b. place of safety; refuge

    c. secret hiding place

    d. dangerous environment

20. Nor could the United States "right every wrong or reverse every *adversity.*"

Learning how to overcome *adversity* is an important part of maintaining happiness and success in life.

adversity (ăd vûr′ sĭ tē) means:

    a. misfortune; hardship

    b. evil; wrong

    c. reversal; change of attitude

    d. decision; commitment

S E L E C T I O N **2-2**   *Reading Skills Application*

History
(Continued)

Directions: Items 21–25 test your ability to *apply* certain reading skills to information in this selection. These types of questions provide valuable practice for all students, especially those who must take standardized reading tests and state-mandated basic skills tests (such as the Florida CLAST Test and the Texas THEA Test). You may not have studied all of the skills at this point, so these items will serve as a helpful preview. The comprehension and critical reading skills in this section are presented in Chapters 4 through 9 of *Opening Doors;* vocabulary and figurative language skills are presented in Chapter 2. As you work through *Opening Doors,* you will practice and develop these skills. Write your answer for each question in the space provided.

21. In paragraph 14 the authors use the word *police* to mean:

    a. to hire security officers

    b. to eliminate threats of terrorism

    c. to regulate and keep in order

    d. to find a solution to a problem

22. Which of the following best expresses the main idea of paragraph 8?

    a. More than 3,000 people lost their lives and 2,000 children lost a parent in the attack on the World Trade Center.

    b. Officials estimated the cost to the New York City economy at more than $83 billion.

    c. More than 20,000 residents living near the World Trade Center had to evacuate their homes.

    d. The events of September 11, 2001, changed the United States profoundly because the nation had not experienced such a devastating attack on its homeland since the attack on Pearl Harbor in 1941.

_____ **23.** The authors mention Diane Sawyer of *ABC News,* British television, and *TV Azteca* in Mexico to show that:

    a. we are living in an age of instant global communications.

    b. the war against terrorism is a war against "faceless cowards."

    c. television networks were slow to report information about the World Trade Center attacks.

    d. it was difficult to agree on which terrorist groups were responsible for the attacks.

_____ **24.** Which writing pattern did the authors use to organize the main idea and supporting details in paragraph 3?

    a. chronological order

    b. comparison-contrast

    c. definition

    d. listing

_____ **25.** Which of the following expresses an opinion rather than a fact?

    a. One hundred Port Authority and city police officers and 343 fire fighting personnel died when the World Trade Center towers collapsed.

    b. Firefighters and police rushed into the burning towers to save as many people as they could.

    c. The tragic attack on the World Trade Center caused widespread chaos and panic throughout New York City.

    d. Following the attack on the World Trade Center, New York airports shut down, and tunnels and bridges were closed.

SELECTION 2-2

History
(Continued)

Collaboration Option

Respond in Writing

Directions: Refer to Selection 2-2 as needed to answer the essay-type questions below.

Option for collaboration: Your instructor may direct you to work with other students on one or more of these items, or, in other words, to work *collaboratively.* In that case, you should form groups of three or four students as directed by your instructor and work together to complete the exercises. After your group discusses each item and agrees on the answer, have a group member record it. Every member of your group should be able to explain all of your group's answers.

1. On the morning of September 11, 2001, we now know that 19 hijackers commandeered four planes—almost simultaneously. In the spaces below, list the facts given for each aircraft that was involved in the attack.

American Airlines Flight 11:

_____

_____

United Airlines Flight 175:

_____

_____

American Airlines Flight 77:

_____

_____

United Airlines Flight 93:

_____

_____

_____

2. On September 11, President Bush said, "Freedom itself was attacked this morning by a faceless coward." List several reasons terrorist attacks against the United States are so difficult, perhaps impossible, to prevent.

_____

_____

_____

_____

_____

3. In the early 1960s President John Kennedy warned that "There cannot be an American solution to every world problem." What message did he hope to convey to both Americans and other nations with this remark?

_____

_____

_____

_____

4. **Overall main idea.** What is the overall main idea the author wants the reader to understand about the relationship between terrorism and the September 11 attacks? Answer this question in one sentence. Be sure to begin your sentence with the phrase "The attack on the World Trade Center and the Pentagon on September 11, 2001. . . ." and include the word *terrorism* in your overall main idea.

_____

_____

_____

_____

Internet Resources

Read More about This Topic on the World Wide Web

Directions: For further information about the topic of the selection, visit these websites:

http://www.whitehouse.gov/infocus/homeland/index.html
This is the site for the U.S. government's Department of Homeland Security, a federal agency whose primary mission is to help prevent, protect against, and respond to acts of terrorism on United States soil.

http://www.buildthememorial.org/site/PageServer?pagename=homepage2
This website is sponsored by the World Trade Center Memorial Foundation, the not-for-profit builder and caretaker of the Memorial and the Memorial Museum. This foundation hopes to bring together the global community of people who care about 9/11 and provide regular updates on the building progress. Construction of the Memorial and the Memorial Museum began in the spring of 2006.

You can also use your favorite search engine such as Google, Yahoo!, or Alta-Vista (www.google.com, www.yahoo.com, www.altavista.com) to discover more about this topic. To locate additional information, type in combinations of keywords such as:

terrorism United States
or
World Trade Center Memorial

Keep in mind that whenever you go to *any* website, it is a good idea to evaluate the website and the information it contains. Ask yourself questions such as:

"Who sponsors this website?"
"Is the information contained in this website up-to-date?"
"What type of information is presented?"
"Is the information objective and complete?"
"How easy is it to use the features of this website?"

A Whale of a Survival Problem

From *The Nature of Life*

By John Postlethwait and Janet Hopson

Prepare Yourself to Read

Directions: Do these exercises *before* you read Selection 2-3.

1. First, read and think about the title. What kinds of things do you think threaten the survival of blue whales?

    _____

    _____

2. Next, complete your preview by reading the following:

    Introduction (in *italics*)

    First paragraph (paragraph 1)

    First sentence of each paragraph

    Words in *italics*

    Diagram

    All of the last paragraph (paragraph 4)

    On the basis of your preview, what specific problem of blue whale survival do you think will be discussed?

    _____

    _____

    _____

Apply Comprehension Skills

Directions: Do these exercises *as* you read Selection 2-3. Apply three skills from this chapter.

Adjust your reading rate. On the basis of your preview and your prior knowledge of how blue whales survive, do you think you should read Selection 2-3 slowly or more rapidly?

_____

Develop a college-level vocabulary. Did you notice any unfamiliar words while you were previewing Selection 2-3? If so, list them here.

_____

Predict as you read. As you read Selection 2-3, make predictions about what the authors will discuss next. Write your predictions in the blanks provided throughout the selection.

A WHALE OF A SURVIVAL PROBLEM

Blue whales are the largest animals on earth. Unfortunately, they have been hunted almost to extinction and are now on the endangered species list. Human predators have not been their only problem, however. Their size alone presents unique challenges for survival. This textbook selection explores the biological adaptations this immense creature has had to make in order to survive.

1   An intrepid visitor to the perpetually frozen Antarctic could stand at the coastline, raise binoculars, and witness a dramatic sight just a few hundred meters offshore: a spout as tall and straight as a telephone pole fountaining upward from the blowhole of a blue whale (*Balaenoptera musculus*), then condensing into a massive cloud of water vapor in the frigid air. The gigantic animal beneath the water jet would be expelling stale air from its 1-ton lungs after a dive in search of food. Then, resting at the surface only long enough to take four deep breaths of fresh air, the streamlined animal would raise its broad tail, thrust mightily, and plunge into the ocean again. The observer on shore might see such a sequence only twice per hour, since the blue whale can hold its breath for 30 minutes as it glides along like a submarine, swallowing trillions of tiny shrimplike animals called krill.

2   It is difficult to comprehend the immense proportions of the blue whale, the largest animal ever to inhabit our planet. At 25 to 30 m (80 to 100 ft) in length, this marine mammal is longer than three railroad boxcars and bigger than any dinosaur that ever lumbered on land. It weighs more than 25 elephants or 1600 fans at a basketball game. Its heart is the size of a beetle—a Volkswagen beetle. And that organ pumps 7200 kg (8 tons) of blood through nearly 2 million kilometers (1.25 million miles) of blood vessels, the largest of which could accommodate an adult person crawling on hands and knees. The animal has a tongue the size of a grown elephant. It has 45,500 kg (50 tons) of muscles to move its 54,500 kg (60 tons) of skin, bones, and organs. And this living mountain can still swim at speeds up to 48 km (30 mi) per hour!

Prediction Exercises

Directions: At each of the points indicated below, answer the question, "What do you predict will be discussed next?"

The blue whale is the largest creature on earth.

3   Leviathan proportions aside, it is difficult to grasp the enormous problems that so large an organism must overcome simply to stay alive. For starters, a blue whale is a warm-blooded animal with a relatively high metabolic rate; to stay warm and active in an icy ocean environment, it must consume and burn 1 million kilocalories a day. This it does by straining 3600 kg (8000 lb) of krill from the ocean water each day on special food-gathering sieve plates. In addition, each of the trillions of cells in the whale's organs must exchange oxygen and carbon dioxide, take in nutrients, and rid itself of organic wastes, just as a single-celled protozoan living freely in seawater must do. Yet a given whale cell—a liver cell, let's say—can lie deep in the body, separated from the environment by nearly 2 m (6 ft) of blubber, muscle, bone, and other

Prediction Exercise

What do you predict will be discussed in paragraph 3?

_____

_____

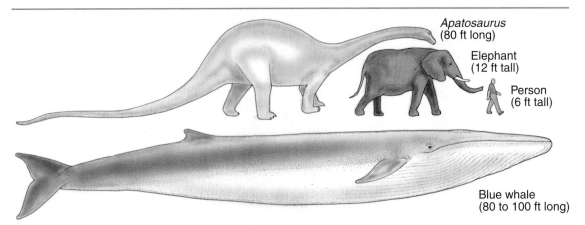

Apatosaurus
(80 ft long)

Elephant
(12 ft tall)

Person
(6 ft tall)

Blue whale
(80 to 100 ft long)

A whale to scale. A blue whale is longer and far heavier than an elephant or even an *Apatosaurus* (formerly *Brontosaurus*), the longest land animal that ever lived.

tissues. For this reason, the whale needs elaborate transport systems to deliver oxygen and nutrients and to carry away carbon dioxide and other wastes. Finally, the galaxy of living cells inside a whale must be coordinated and controlled by a brain, a nervous system, and chemical regulators (hormones) so that the organism can function as a single unit.

4   Although blue whales are the largest animals that have ever lived, they share with all other animals the same fundamental physical problems of day-to-day survival: how to extract energy from the environment; how to exchange nutrients, wastes, and gases; how to distribute materials to all the cells in the body; how to maintain a constant internal environment despite fluctuations in the external environment; how to support the body; and how to protect it from attackers or from damaging environmental conditions. Blue whales have evolved with unique adaptations of form and function that meet such challenges and leave the animals suited to their way of life.

Prediction Exercise

What do you predict will be discussed in paragraph 4?

_____

_____

1. Describe any three comparisons the author uses to illustrate the enormous size of the blue whale.

First comparison:

_____

_____

Second comparison:

_____

_____

Third comparison:

_____

_____

2. Because of its size, what are three special problems that blue whales must overcome to survive?

One problem:

_____

_____

Another problem:

_____

_____

A third problem:

_____

_____

3. Explain why the title of this selection is clever.

_____

_____

_____

4. **Overall main idea.** What is the overall main idea the authors want the reader to understand about the survival of the blue whale? Answer this question in one sentence. Be sure to include *blue whale* and *survive* (or *survival*) in your overall main idea sentence.

_____

_____

_____

Internet Resources

Read More about This Topic on the World Wide Web

Directions: For further information about the topic of the selection, visit these websites:

www.physics.helsinki.fi/whale/
This website is part of the World Wide Web Virtual Library. It contains many interesting links related to whale watching. Click on links for research, pictures, slide shows, videos, and even interspecies communication.

www.unisci.com/aboutunisci.shtml
Unisci was the first science daily news site on the Web and remains the only one that selects stories on the basis of their scientific importance. For more information on whale survival, type "whale" into the archive search box.

www.pacificwhale.org/
This is the website of the nonprofit Pacific Whale Foundation in Maui, Hawaii. It is dedicated to saving the oceans and the life they contain, especially the species of whales that are threatened with extinction. (The organization does not focus on blue whales alone.) The foundation stresses marine research, education, and conservation.

You can also use your favorite search engine such as Google, Yahoo!, or Alta-Vista (www.google.com, www.yahoo.com, www.altavista.com) to discover more about this topic. To locate additional information, type in combinations of keywords such as:

blue whales

or

blue whale survival

Keep in mind that whenever you go to *any* website, it is a good idea to evaluate the website and the information it contains. Ask yourself questions such as:

"Who sponsors this website?"

"Is the information contained in this website up-to-date?"

"What type of information is presented?"

"Is the information objective and complete?"

"How easy is it to use the features of this website?"

CHAPTER 3

Approaching College Assignments: Reading Textbooks and Following Directions

In this chapter you will learn the answers to these questions:

- What is an effective way to read and study a college textbook?

- How can I prepare to read an assignment?

- How can I guide my reading by asking questions?

- How can I review material by rehearsing?

- What are the keys to following directions on college assignments and tests?

SKILLS

College Textbooks: A Process for Reading and Studying Effectively

- Step 1: Prepare to Read
- Step 2: Ask and Answer Questions to Enhance Your Reading
- Step 3: Review by Rehearsing the Answers to Your Questions

Following Directions in Textbooks and on Tests

- Guidelines for Following Directions
- Example: Directions from a Textbook
- Example: Directions for a Test

CREATING YOUR SUMMARY

Developing Chapter Review Cards

READINGS

Selection 3-1 *(Government)*
"African Americans: The Struggle for Equality" from *The American Democracy*
by Thomas E. Patterson

Selection 3-2 *(Human Development)*
"Parenthood: Now, Later, . . . Never?" from *Human Development*
by Diane E. Papalia, Sally Wendkos Olds, and Ruth Feldman

Selection 3-3 *(Art Appreciation)*
"Art in the Service of Religion" from *Living with Art*
by Rita Gilbert

If you need a helping hand, look at the end of your sleeve.

Proverb

The book that can be read without any trouble
was probably written without any trouble also.

Oscar Wilde

COLLEGE TEXTBOOKS: A PROCESS FOR READING AND STUDYING EFFECTIVELY

Students often ask, "When should I start studying for final exams?" The answer is, "At the beginning of the semester." From the first day of classes, you should read and study your textbook assignments as if you were preparing for the final exam. If you read and study your assignments effectively the first time, you won't have to start over again and reread them when it is time for a unit test, a major exam, or even a final exam.

Reading your textbooks requires more than casually looking at the pages. Reading and studying take time and effort. Moreover, you must make reading and studying textbook material an active process, not a passive one.

How can you understand and remember what you read in your textbooks? This chapter presents an effective approach for reading a college textbook assignment that will ultimately save you time. This approach is based on doing it right the first time, so that when you prepare for a test, you will not have to spend additional hours rereading textbook chapters. This approach helps you learn more the first time you read your textbook assignments.

The three basic steps of this study-reading process are:

- Step 1: Prepare to read.
- Step 2: Ask and answer questions to enhance your reading.
- Step 3: Review by rehearsing the answers to your questions.

It is important to have a process for reading and studying college textbooks effectively.

SUMMARY OF THE THREE-STEP PROCESS FOR READING AND STUDYING COLLEGE TEXTBOOKS

Step 1: Prepare to Read

Preview the selection to see what it contains and how it is organized.

- Read the title.
- Read the introduction.
- Read headings and subheadings in each section.
- Read words in italics or bold print.
- Look over illustrations, charts, and diagrams.
- Read any questions that are included in the chapter or a study guide.
- Read the summary.

Consider the topics being presented. Ask yourself, "What topics does the author seem to be emphasizing?" and "How are the topics organized?"

Assess your prior knowledge. Ask yourself, "What do I already know about the topic?" and "How familiar am I with this topic?"

Plan your reading and study time. Ask yourself, "How long will it take me to read this assignment?" and "Do I need to divide the assignment into smaller units?"

Step 2: Ask and Answer Questions to Enhance Your Reading

Guide your reading by asking and answering questions.

- Turn chapter headings into questions.
- Create questions based on what the paragraphs or sections appear to be about.
- If the author has included questions, use them.
- Use questions in a study guide, if there is one.
- Use questions given by the instructor.

Read actively.

- Look for answers to your questions.

Record the answers to your questions.

- Write the answers on notebook paper or in the margins of the textbook.
- Create notes for the material.
- Emphasize the answers by highlighting or underlining them.

Step 3: Review by Rehearsing the Answers to Your Questions

Review the material and transfer it into long-term memory by rehearsing.

- Recite (say aloud) the answers to your questions, and then review any you missed.
- Rewrite the important points from memory, and then fill in any missing information.

KEY TERMS

preparing to read

Previewing the material, assessing your prior knowledge, and planning your reading and studying time.

previewing

Examining material to determine its topic and organization before actually reading it.

Comprehension Monitoring Questions for Previewing

What topics does the author seem to be emphasizing? How are the topics organized?

KEY TERM

assessing your prior knowledge

Determining what you already know about a topic.

Step 1: Prepare to Read

Before you begin to read a textbook assignment, you should spend a few minutes preparing to read. **Preparing to read** involves previewing the chapter, assessing your prior knowledge, and planning your reading and study time.

Preview the Selection

Previewing means examining material to determine its topic and organization before actually reading it. This gives you a general idea of what an entire assignment will be about and allows you to see how the material is organized. This not only helps you comprehend what you read but also helps improve your concentration, your motivation, and your interest in what you are about to read. (That is why each reading selection in *Opening Doors* is preceded by the activity called "Prepare Yourself to Read.")

To preview a chapter assignment:

- **First, read the chapter title.** This should tell you the overall topic of the chapter.

- **Next, read the chapter introduction.** A chapter introduction (if there is one) usually presents some of the important points in the chapter, or it may give background information that you will need.

- **Read the heading and subheadings of each section.** Turn through the chapter to read the headings and subheadings. These tell you the topics the author has included and they provide an outline of the information in the chapter.

- **Read words in *italics,* bold print, or color.** Notice any words that appear in special print (italics or bold print) or in color; these are important terms you will be expected to understand and remember.

- **Look over illustrations, charts, and diagrams.** Look at pictures, charts, diagrams, and graphs you find in the chapter. These give you visual representations of the material.

- **Read questions that accompany a chapter or appear in a study guide.** They alert you to important information you should watch for as you read.

- **Finally, read the chapter summary.** A chapter summary contains in brief form many of the important ideas of the chapter. A chapter summary (like a chapter introduction) is especially useful. Take advantage of it.

As you preview, ask yourself questions about the chapter you are about to read. Ask yourself, "What topics does the author seem to be emphasizing?" and "How are the topics organized?"

Assess Your Prior Knowledge

As you learned in Chapter 2, when you lack background knowledge in a subject—and this is often the case when you are reading college textbooks—you may have to take additional steps to comprehend the material. **Assessing your prior knowledge,** that is, determining what you already know about the topic, will enable you to decide whether you need help with the assignment and whether you need to allow additional time. To assess your prior knowledge, simply ask yourself, "What do I already know about this topic?" and "How familiar am I with this topic?" Previewing the chapter can help you determine this. By introducing you to the chapter topics, previewing allows you to predict whether or not you will be dealing with familiar material.

If the material is new to you, you may need to take extra steps to deal with an assignment successfully. While you are previewing, while you are reading, or after you finish reading, you may discover that you do not understand the material adequately, and you may decide that you need more background knowledge. If so, it is your responsibility to take some or all of these steps to fill in missing background information:

Comprehension Monitoring Questions for Assessing Your Prior Knowledge

What do I already know about this topic? How familiar am I with this topic?

- Reading other, perhaps easier, textbooks on the same subject (these might be other college textbooks or more general study aids, such as an outline of American history or a book with a title such as *Accounting Made Easy*).
- Consulting an encyclopedia, a good dictionary, or some other reference book, or going online to get information from the Internet.
- Talking with someone who is knowledgeable about the subject.

These steps require effort, and obviously there are no shortcuts. But going the extra mile to get necessary background information is part of being a responsible, mature learner and student. As a bonus, you may discover that it is exciting and satisfying to understand new or difficult material through your own efforts. You may also find that when you take responsibility for your own learning, you will feel good about yourself as a student. (Remember that a *student* is someone who *studies.*)

Plan Your Reading and Study Time

Comprehension Monitoring Questions for Planning Your Study Time

How long will it take me to read and study this assignment? Do I need to divide the assignment into smaller units?

By previewing an assignment, you will be able to decide whether you can read the entire assignment in just one study session or whether you need to divide it into smaller parts.

If you decide that you need more than one study session, you should divide the assignment into several shorter segments and read them at times when you know you can concentrate best. For example, a 24-page chapter may be too much for you to read and study effectively all at once. You could divide the assignment in half and read it over two days. Or you could divide this long assignment into three 8-page segments and read them during three 1-hour study sessions on the same day, perhaps at 1, 5, and 8 P.M. In any case, plan your study-reading session and follow your plan. (Then reward yourself after you complete your studying!)

Step 2: Ask and Answer Questions to Enhance Your Reading

The second step in reading and studying a college textbook assignment is enhancing your reading by asking and answering questions. To read and study effectively, you need to read and understand each paragraph or section. This means that you must determine what is important to learn and remember in each section.

To put it another way, you need to read for a specific purpose. Reading for a specific purpose will increase your interest and concentration, and it will enable you to monitor (evaluate) your comprehension while you are reading. One of the best ways to learn the material in a reading assignment is to ask and answer questions about the material as you read.

Ask Questions as You Read

Creating one or more questions for each section of a reading assignment will guide you to the pertinent, important information and help you remember that information. When you read to seek answers to questions, you will be reading with a specific purpose; in other words, you will be reading selectively and purposefully.

Turning chapter headings and subheadings into questions is the easiest way to accomplish this. For example, if a section in a history textbook has a heading "The War in Iraq," you might want to ask, "Why did the war begin?" You may also want to ask, "When did it begin?" (In Chapters 10 and 11 you will be working with actual college textbook chapters that have headings that can be turned into useful questions.)

Comprehension Monitoring Question for Asking and Answering Questions as You Read

Am I understanding the important information the author and my instructor expect me to know?

When a section or paragraph has no heading, it is a good idea to create a question based on what that section or paragraph appears to be about. If you see a term or phrase in bold print, italics, or color you might create a question about that term or phrase. You can also create questions about names of people, places, events, and so on. Of course, you will be able to refine your questions later, when you read the material more carefully.

In addition to creating your own questions as you read each section of a textbook, you may find that the author has included questions for you. These may appear at the end of a chapter, at the beginning of a chapter, throughout a chapter (perhaps in the margins), or in an accompanying study guide. If a textbook chapter contains such questions, read them before you read the chapter. Then keep them in mind as you read. When you have finished reading the chapter, you should be able to answer these questions. In fact, you will probably be asked some of these same questions on a test.

Finally, your instructor may give you questions to guide you as you read a chapter. Of course, you should be able to answer these questions by the time you finish reading and studying the chapter. Chapter questions, regardless of the source, enable you to monitor your comprehension: Are you understanding the important information the author and your instructor expect you to know? Identifying important information lets you begin preparing for tests from the day you first read the assignment.

Answer Questions When You Come to the End of Each Section

As you read each paragraph or section, look for answers to your questions. Then, after you have finished reading that section, record the answers by writing them down. A word of warning: Do not try to record answers *while* you are reading a section. Constantly switching between reading and writing disrupts your comprehension and will greatly slow you down. The time to write your answers is immediately after you *finish* reading a section, not while you are reading it for the first time.

There are several effective ways to record your answers. One of the most effective is to write answers on notebook paper or in the margins of your textbook. Another effective way of recording answers is to make review cards for the material. With either of these techniques, be sure your answer makes it clear which question you are answering. In addition to writing out your answers, you may want to mark information in the textbook that answers your questions.

What if you cannot locate or formulate an answer to one of your questions? In that case, there are several things you can do:

- Read ahead to see if the answer becomes apparent.
- If the question involves an important term you need to know, look the term up in the glossary or in a dictionary.
- Go back and reread a paragraph or a section.
- Do some extra reading, ask a classmate, or ask your instructor about it.
- If you still cannot answer all of your questions after you have read an assignment, note which questions remain unanswered. Put a question mark in the margin, or make a list of the unanswered questions. One way or another, be sure to find the answers.

As you can see, actively seeking answers to questions encourages you to concentrate and focus on *understanding* as you read. Reading for a purpose—to answer specific questions—can help you remember more and ultimately score higher on tests. Often, you will discover that questions on tests are identical to the questions you asked yourself as you studied. When this happens, you will be glad that you took the time to use this technique while you were studying.

Step 3: Review by Rehearsing the Answers to Your Questions

Experienced college students know that if they want to remember what they read in their textbooks and the answers they wrote to questions, they need to take certain steps to make it happen. They also know that it is essential to take these steps immediately after they finish reading a section or a chapter, while the material is still in short-term memory—that is, while the material is still fresh in their minds. Good readers know that forgetting occurs rapidly and that they need to rehearse material immediately in order to remember it; or in other words, to transfer it into long-term (permanent) memory. (Rehearsal and memory are discussed in Chapter 11.) The shocking fact is that unless you take some special action immediately after you finish studying your textbook, you will forget at least half of what you learned.

Finally, you should rehearse important points in a chapter by reading your questions and *reciting* answers from the material. Simply rereading your answers is not good enough; you should say them *aloud.* Remember, "If you can't say it, you don't know it."

If you still need more practice with the material, or when you need to prepare for a test, you should continue to rehearse important points by *reciting or rewriting the material from memory.* When you give yourself a "practice test" in either of these ways, you transfer the material into long-term memory. When you check your answers, make corrections and add any information needed to make your answers complete. (Writing the information allows you to learn the correct spelling of important terms, names, and so forth. This is especially helpful if you will have an essay test.)

Taking the time to review and rehearse immediately after you finish reading a chapter will not only help you remember what you learned. It will also give you a feeling of accomplishment, which in turn will encourage you to continue learning. One success will build on another.

Comprehension Monitoring Question for Reviewing by Rehearsing Your Answers

Can I recite answers to questions about the material and write the answers from memory?

To recapitulate, here is the three-step process: (1) Prepare to read by previewing, assessing your prior knowledge, and planning your study time. (2) Ask and answer questions to enhance your reading. (3) Review by rehearsing the answers to your questions. This process will enable you to learn more as you complete your textbook reading assignments, and it will also be a foundation for effective test preparation.

Remember that preparing for a test *begins* with reading each textbook assignment effectively. Specific techniques for preparing for tests are discussed in Chapters 10 and 11. They include annotating textbooks by writing marginal study notes, outlining, "mapping," writing summaries, creating review cards, and developing test review sheets. Part of doing well on any test, of course, is following the directions. The next section focuses on this important skill.

FOLLOWING DIRECTIONS IN TEXTBOOKS AND ON TESTS

An important part of success in college is following written directions. In particular, it is important for you to understand directions in order to do your assignments correctly, carry out procedures in classes and labs (such as computer labs and science labs), and earn high grades on tests. Most people are not as good at following directions as they think they are.

You have probably learned from experience that problems arise from misunderstanding or failing to follow directions. Perhaps you have answered an entire set of test questions instead of some specific number stated in the directions ("Answer any *two* of the following five essay questions"). Or you may have had points deducted from your grade on a research paper because you did not follow the correct format ("Double-space your paper and number the pages"). When you do not follow directions, you can waste time and lower your grade.

Guidelines for Following Directions

There are a few simple things to remember about following written directions:

- **Read the entire set of directions carefully before doing any of the steps.** This is a time when you must slow down and pay attention to every word. Even though most students *know* they should do this, they make the mistake of jumping in without doing it. Resist this temptation and read *all* of the directions!
- **Make sure you understand all the words in the directions.** Although directions may use words you hear or see often, you may still not know precisely

what each word means. For example, on an essay test you might be asked to compare two poems or contrast two pieces of music. Do you know the difference between *compare* and *contrast?* Unless you do, you cannot answer the question correctly. Other typical words in test questions include *enumerate, justify, explain,* and *illustrate.* Each has a specific meaning. General direction words include *above, below, consecutive, preceding, succeeding, former,* and *latter.* In addition, directions in college textbooks and assignments often include many specialized terms that you must understand. For example, in a set of directions for a biology lab experiment, you might be instructed to "stain a tissue sample on a slide." The words *stain, tissue,* and *slide* have specific meanings in biology.

- **Circle signals that announce steps in directions and underline key words.** Not every step in a set of directions will have a signal word, of course, but steps in sets of directions frequently are introduced by bullets (• • •), letters and numbers (*a, b, c,* or 1, 2, 3, etc.), and words such as *first, second, third, next, then, finally,* and *last* to indicate the sequence or order of the steps.

You should mark directions *before* you begin following them, since you must understand what you are to do *before* you try to do it. This means finding and numbering steps if they are not already numbered. Be aware that a single sentence sometimes contains more than one step. (For example, "Type your name, enter your I.D. number, and press the Enter key.") When you are busy working on a test or an assignment, it is easy to become distracted and do the steps in the wrong order or leave a step out. Another reason it is important to number steps in a set of directions is that even though the steps may not include signal words, you are still responsible for finding each step. Especially on tests, then, you should number each step and mark key words in directions.

Example: Directions from a Textbook

Look at the following box, which shows a set of directions that explain how to "log on" (establish a connection) with a network so that you can use e-mail and visit Internet websites.

LOGGING ON

To log on to the host site, complete the following steps:

1. Turn on system.
2. Type Host Name: LOCAL
3. Username: (Enter your assigned username.)
4. Password: (Enter the last four digits of Soc. Sec. #.)
5. The first time you use your password, you must verify it. Enter your four-digit password again. Remember your password, or you will not be able to log in again.
6. A prompt will appear. You are now logged on to the network.
7. When you are finished, exit the system by typing "logout" or "lo."

Notice that the steps in the directions are numbered. If you were actually following these directions, you would want to read the entire set first, then mark key words.

Notice also that before you can carry out these directions, you must understand certain terms (such as *system, host name, username,* and *prompt*) and know certain information (such as your assigned username and the last four digits of your Social Security number). Notice also that step 5 consists of several sentences. This makes it easy to overlook the fact that there are two important parts in this step: After typing your password the first time, you must verify it by typing it again.

Example: Directions for a Test

The first box on page 154 shows a set of directions for a unit test in a psychology course. Read these directions carefully.

Notice that this unit has two distinct parts: Part I—Content Questions, and Part II—Discussion Questions. Part I of the test consists of multiple-choice questions, whereas Part II requires the student to write essay answers.

Notice that each multiple-choice question in Part I is worth 2 points (for a total of 50 points) and that the student must use a machine-scorable answer sheet and a number two pencil. Also, notice that Part I is to be completed before beginning Part II.

In Part II, notice that each question is worth a possible 25 points (for a total of 50 points). Next, notice a key point in the directions: Only two of the four discussion questions are to be answered. Notice that notebook paper is required for these two essay answers, but either pen or pencil may be used. Finally, notice that the answer to each discussion question must be at least three paragraphs long, but not longer than five paragraphs.

Marking the test directions as shown in the second box on page 154 would help you follow them accurately.

SAMPLE OF DIRECTIONS FOR UNIT TEST: PSYCHOLOGICAL DISORDERS

Directions:

    Part I—Content Questions   (2 points each) Answer the 25 multiple-choice questions using the machine-scorable answer sheet provided. (You must use a number two pencil on this answer sheet.) Complete this part of the test before you begin Part II.

    Part II—Discussion Questions   (25 points each) Answer two of the four discussion questions, using notebook paper. (You may use pen or pencil for this portion of the test.) The answer to each discussion question should be 3–5 paragraphs in length.

SAMPLE OF MARKED DIRECTIONS FOR UNIT TEST: PSYCHOLOGICAL DISORDERS

Directions:

(50 points)   (1)

Part I—Content Questions   (2 points each) Answer the 25 multiple-choice questions using the machine-scorable answer sheet provided. (You must use a number two pencil on this answer sheet.) Complete this part of the test before you begin Part II.

(50 points)   (2)

Part II—Discussion Questions   (25 points each) Answer two of the four discussion questions, using notebook paper. (You may use pen or pencil for this portion of the test.) The answer to each discussion question should be 3–5 paragraphs in length.

DEVELOPING CHAPTER REVIEW CARDS

**Student Online
Learning Center (OLC)**
Go to Chapter 3.
Select Flashcards
or Chapter Test.

Review cards, or *summary cards,* are an excellent study tool. They are a way to select, organize, and review the most important information in a textbook chapter. The process of creating review cards helps you organize information in a meaningful way and, at the same time, transfer it into long-term memory. The cards can also be used to prepare for tests (see Part Three). The review card activities in this book give you structured practice in creating these valuable study tools. Once you have learned how to make review cards, you can create them for textbook material in your other courses.

Now complete the eight review cards for Chapter 3 by answering the questions or following the directions on each card. When you have completed them, you will have summarized important information about (1) preparing to read, (2) previewing a textbook chapter, (3) assessing your prior knowledge, (4) guiding your reading, (5) answering questions as you read, (6) reviewing by rehearsing, (7) following directions in textbooks and on tests, and (8) monitoring your comprehension as you read. Use the type of handwriting that is clearest for you to reread (printing or cursive) and write legibly. You will find it easier to complete the review cards if you remove these pages before filling them in.

The Three-Step Process for Reading and Studying: Step 1

What is the first step of the three-step study-reading process? (See page 147.)

Step 1:

Step 1 involves these three parts: (See pages 147–48.)

1.

2.

3.

Card 1 Chapter 3: Approaching College Assignments

Previewing a Textbook Chapter

One part of step 1 in the study-reading process is previewing a chapter. List seven things to do when previewing.

(See page 147.)

1.

2.

3.

4.

5.

6.

7.

Card 2   Chapter 3: Approaching College Assignments

Assessing Your Prior Knowledge

Assessing your prior knowledge is part of step 1 in the study-reading process. Define *prior knowledge.* (See page 147.)

List three things you can do if you need to increase your prior knowledge about a topic. (See page 148.)

1.

2.

3.

Card 3   Chapter 3: Approaching College Assignments

The Three-Step Process for Reading and Studying: Step 2

What is the second step of the three-step study-reading process? (See page 148.)

Step 2:

List at least four chapter features or other sources on which you can base your own questions to ask as you read. (See page 149.)

1.

2.

3.

4.

Card 4   Chapter 3: Approaching College Assignments

Answering Questions as You Read

When should you record the answers to your questions about a passage? (See page 149.)

List three ways to record your answers. (See page 150.)

1.

2.

3.

Describe four things you can do if any of your questions remain unanswered when you have finished a passage. (See page 150.)

1.

2.

3.

4.

Card 5   Chapter 3: Approaching College Assignments

The Three-Step Process for Reading and Studying: Step 3

What is the third step of the three-step study-reading process? (See page 150.)

Step 3:

When should you rehearse the answers to your questions about material in a reading assignment? (See page 150.)

List two effective ways to rehearse. (See pages 150–51.)

1.

2.

Card 6   Chapter 3: Approaching College Assignments

Following Directions

List three things to remember about following written directions. (See pages 151–52.)

1.

2.

3.

Card 7   Chapter 3: Approaching College Assignments

Monitoring Your Comprehension as You Read and Study College Textbooks
1. What questions should you ask yourself while you are previewing a chapter? (See page 147.)
2. What questions should you ask yourself to assess your prior knowledge? (See page 148.)
3. What questions should you ask yourself while you are planning your study time? (See page 148.)
4. What question should you ask yourself as you are asking and answering questions as you read? (See page 149.)
5. What question should you ask yourself as you review a chapter by rehearsing your answers? (See page 151.)
Card 8   Chapter 3: Approaching College Assignments

SELECTION **3-1**

Government

African Americans: The Struggle for Equality

From *The American Democracy*

By Thomas E. Patterson

Prepare Yourself to Read

Directions: Do these exercises *before* you read Selection 3-1.

1. First, read and think about the title. What do you already know about African Americans' struggle for equality?

   _____

   _____

   _____

   _____

   _____

2. Next, complete your preview by reading the following:

   Introduction (in *italics*)

   Headings

   All of the first paragraph (paragraph 1)

   First sentence of each of the other paragraphs

   On the basis of your preview, what aspects of African Americans' struggle for equality does the selection seem to be about?

   _____

   _____

   _____

   _____

   _____

   _____

   _____

Apply Comprehension Skills

Directions: Do these exercises *as* you read Selection 3-1. Apply three skills from this chapter:

Ask and answer questions as you read. Complete the practice exercises by creating questions based on what each paragraph seems to be about.

Read actively to find answers to your questions. Record the answers to your questions. Write the answer in the margin or highlight the answer in the text.

Review by rehearsing the answers to your questions. Recite your answers or write them down from memory.

AFRICAN AMERICANS: THE STRUGGLE FOR EQUALITY

Most historians and political scientists would agree that African Americans have made great progress toward social and judicial equality since the Civil War, but this progress has not come without a struggle. This selection from a government textbook explains how Supreme Court decisions and the civil rights movement altered the concept of equality for African Americans.

1   *Equality* has always been the least fully developed of America's founding concepts. Not even Thomas Jefferson, who had a deep admiration for the "common man," believed that broad meaning could be given to the claim of the Declaration of Independence that "all men are created equal." To Jefferson, "equality" had a restricted, though significant, meaning: people are of equal moral worth and, as such, deserve equal treatment under the law. Even then, Jefferson made a distinction between free men and slaves, who were not entitled to legal equality.

2   The history of America shows that disadvantaged groups have rarely achieved a greater measure of justice without a struggle. Legal equality has rarely been bestowed by the more powerful upon the less powerful. Their gains have nearly always occurred through intense and sustained political movements, such as the civil rights movement of the 1960s, that have pressured established interests to relinquish or share their privileged status.

3   Of all America's problems, none has been as persistent as the white race's unwillingness to yield a fair share of society's benefits to members of the black race. The ancestors of most African Americans came to this country as slaves, after having been captured in Africa, shipped in chains across the Atlantic, and sold in open markets in Charleston and other seaports.

Creating Questions Exercises

Directions: For each paragraph:

- Create a question based on what the paragraph seems to be about. Ask *who, what, when, where, why,* or *how.*
- Write your question in the spaces provided.
- Write the answer to your question in the margin or highlight it in the text.

Doing this will help you understand and remember the material.

Creating Questions Exercise

Question about paragraph 1:

_____

_____

_____

Creating Questions Exercise

Question about paragraph 2:

_____

_____

_____

Creating Questions Exercise

Question about paragraph 3:

_____

_____

_____

4   It took a civil war to bring slavery to an end, but the battle did not end institutionalized racism. When Reconstruction ended in 1877 with the withdrawal of federal troops from the South, whites in the region regained power and gradually reestablished racial segregation by enacting laws that prohibited black citizens from using the same public facilities as whites. In *Plessy v. Ferguson* (1896), the Supreme Court endorsed these laws, ruling the "separate" facilities for the two races did not violate the Constitution as long as the facilities were "equal." "If one race be inferior to the other socially," the Court argued, "the Constitution of the United States cannot put them on the same plane." The *Plessy* decision became a justification for the separate and *unequal* treatment of African Americans. Black children, for example, were forced into separate schools that rarely had libraries and had few teachers; they were given worn-out books that had been used previously in white schools.

5   Black leaders challenged these discriminatory state and local policies through legal action, but not until the late 1930s did the Supreme Court begin to respond favorably to their demands. The Court began modestly by ruling that where no public facilities existed for African Americans, they must be allowed to use those reserved for whites.

The *Brown* Decision

6   Substantial judicial relief for African Americans was finally achieved in 1954 with *Brown v. Board of Education of Topeka,* arguably the most significant ruling in Supreme Court history. The case began when Linda Carol Brown, a black child in Topeka, Kansas, was denied admission to an all-white elementary school that she passed every day on her way to her all-black school, which was twelve blocks farther away. In its decision, the Court fully reversed its *Plessy* doctrine by declaring that racial segregation of public schools "generates [among black children] a feeling of inferiority as to their status in the community that may affect their hearts and minds in a way unlikely ever to be undone. . . . Separate educational facilities are inherently unequal."

7   As a 1954 Gallup poll indicated, a sizable majority of southern whites opposed the *Brown* decision, and billboards were erected along southern roadways that called for the impeachment of Chief Justice Earl Warren. In the so-called Southern Manifesto, southern congressmen urged their state governments to "resist forced integration by any lawful means." In 1957, rioting broke out when Governor Orval Faubus called out the Arkansas National Guard to block the entry of black children to the Little Rock public schools. To restore order and carry out the desegregation of the Little Rock schools, President Dwight D. Eisenhower used his

Creating Questions Exercise

Question about paragraph 4:

_____

_____

_____

Creating Questions Exercise

Question about paragraph 5:

_____

_____

_____

Creating Questions Exercise

Question about paragraph 6:

_____

_____

_____

Creating Questions Exercise

Question about paragraph 7:

_____

_____

_____

power as the nation's commander-in-chief to place the Arkansas National Guard under federal control. For their part, northern whites were neither strongly for nor strongly against school desegregation. A Gallup poll revealed that only a slim majority of whites outside the South agreed with the *Brown* decision.

The Black Civil Rights Movement

8   After *Brown,* the struggle of African Americans for their rights became a political movement. Perhaps no single event turned national public opinion so dramatically against segregation as a 1963 march led by Dr. Martin Luther King Jr. in Birmingham, Alabama. An advocate of nonviolent protest, King had been leading peaceful demonstrations and marches for nearly eight years before that fateful day in Birmingham. As the nation watched in disbelief on television, police officers led by Birmingham's sheriff, Eugene "Bull" Connor, attacked King and his followers with dogs, cattle prods, and fire hoses.

9   The modern civil rights movement peaked with the triumphant March on Washington for Jobs and Freedom of August 2, 1963. Organized by Dr. King, and other civil rights leaders, it attracted 250,000 marchers, one of the largest

Creating Questions Exercise

Question about paragraph 8:

_____

_____

_____

Creating Questions Exercise

Question about paragraph 9:

_____

_____

_____

Two police dogs attack a black civil rights activist during the 1963 Birmingham demonstrations. Such images of hatred and violence shook many white Americans out of their complacency regarding race relations.

gatherings in the history of the nation's capital. "I have a dream," the Reverend King told the gathering, "that my four little children will one day live in a nation where they will not be judged by the color of their skin but by the content of their character."

10   A year later, after a months-long fight in Congress that was marked by every parliamentary obstacle that racial conservatives could muster, the Civil Rights Act of 1964 was enacted. The legislation provided African Americans and other minorities with equal access to public facilities and prohibited job discrimination. Even then, southern states resorted to legal maneuvering and other delaying tactics to blunt the new law's impact. The state of Virginia, for example, established a commission to pay the legal expenses of white citizens who were brought to court for violation of the federal act. Nevertheless, momentum was on the side of racial equality. The murder of two civil rights workers during a voter registration drive in Selma, Alabama, helped sustain the momentum. President Lyndon Johnson, who had been a decisive force in the battle to pass the Civil Rights Act, called for new legislation that would end racial barriers to voting. Congress's answer was the 1965 Voting Rights Act.

The Aftermath of the Civil Rights Movement

11   Although the most significant progress in history toward the legal equality of all Americans occurred during the 1960s, Dr. King's dream of a color-blind society has remained elusive. Even the legal rights of African Americans do not, in practice, match the promise of the civil rights movement. Studies have found, for example, that African Americans accused of crime are more likely to be convicted and to receive stiffer sentences than are white Americans on trial for comparable offenses. Federal statistics from the National Office of Drug Control Policy and the U.S. Sentencing Commission revealed that in 1997 black Americans accounted for more than 75 percent of crack cocaine convictions but only about 35 percent of crack cocaine users. It is hardly surprising that many African Americans believe that the nation has two standards of justice, an inferior one for blacks and a higher one for whites.

Martin Luther King Jr. (1929–1968) is the only American of the 20th century to be honored with a national holiday. The civil rights leader was the pivotal figure in the movement to gain legal and political rights for black Americans. The son of the Baptist minister, King used rhetorical skills and nonviolent protest to sweep aside a century of governmental discrimination and to inspire other groups, including women and Hispanics, to assert their rights. Recipient of the Nobel Peace Prize in 1964 (the youngest person ever to receive that honor), King was assassinated in Memphis in 1968.

Creating Questions Exercise

Question about paragraph 10:

_____

_____

_____

Creating Questions Exercise

Question about paragraph 11:

_____

_____

_____

12   One area in which African Americans have made substantial progress since the 1960s is the winning of election to public office. Although the percentage of black elected officials is still far below the proportion of African Americans in the population, it has risen sharply over recent decades. As of 2000, there were more than 20 black members of Congress and 400 black mayors—including the mayors of some of this country's largest cities.

Creating Questions Exercise

Question about paragraph 12:

_____ ____

_____

_____

Source: Adapted from Thomas E. Patterson, *The American Democracy,* Alternate Edition, 6th ed., pp. 132–35. Copyright © 2003 by The McGraw-Hill Companies, Inc. Reprinted by permission of The McGraw-Hill Companies.

SELECTION **3-1**   **Reading Selection Quiz**

Government
(Continued)

This quiz has three parts. Your instructor may assign some or all of them.

Comprehension

Directions: Items 1–10 test your comprehension (understanding) of the material of this selection. These questions are the type a content area instructor (such as a government instructor) would ask on a test over this material. You should be able to answer these questions after studying this selection. For each comprehension question below, use information from the selection to determine the correct answer. Refer to the selection as you answer the questions. Write your answer in the space provided.

_____   **1.**   To Thomas Jefferson, equality meant that:
 a.   all men and women are created equal.
 b.   people are of equal moral worth and as such deserve equal treatment under the law.
 c.   there should be no distinction between free men and slaves.
 d.   there should be two standards of justice.

_____   **2.**   When Civil War Reconstruction ended in 1877:
 a.   whites in the South gradually reestablished racial segregation.
 b.   slaves were sold in open markets in Charleston and other seaports.
 c.   legal equality for African Americans was achieved.
 d.   the Arkansas National Guard was placed under federal control.

_____   **3.**   Significant judicial relief for African Americans was achieved with the:
 a.   1896 Supreme Court ruling *Plessy v. Ferguson.*
 b.   1954 Supreme Court ruling *Brown v. Board of Education of Topeka.*
 c.   1957 desegregation of Little Rock public schools.
 d.   1963 March on Washington led by Dr. Martin Luther King, Jr.

_____   **4.**   The *Brown* decision ruled that:
 a.   separate educational facilities for blacks and whites did not violate the Constitution.
 b.   separate educational facilities for blacks and whites were inherently unequal.
 c.   black children could be denied admission to all-white schools.
 d.   racial segregation of public schools was acceptable as long as the facilities were "equal."

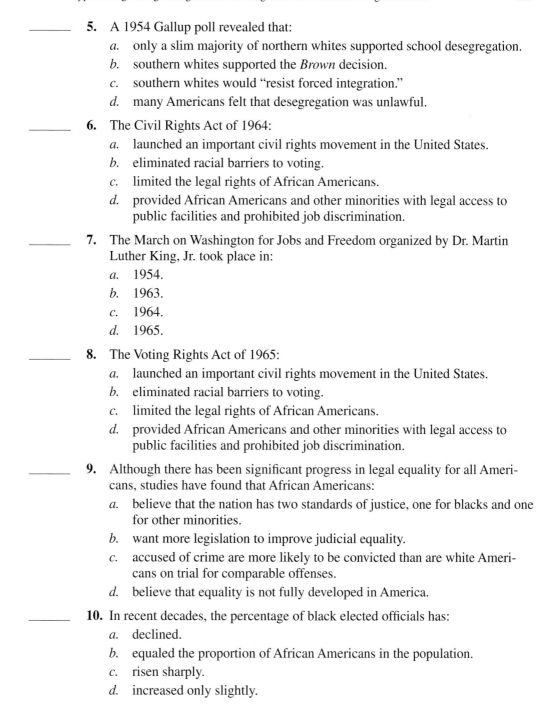

_____ **5.** A 1954 Gallup poll revealed that:
  a. only a slim majority of northern whites supported school desegregation.
  b. southern whites supported the *Brown* decision.
  c. southern whites would "resist forced integration."
  d. many Americans felt that desegregation was unlawful.

_____ **6.** The Civil Rights Act of 1964:
  a. launched an important civil rights movement in the United States.
  b. eliminated racial barriers to voting.
  c. limited the legal rights of African Americans.
  d. provided African Americans and other minorities with legal access to public facilities and prohibited job discrimination.

_____ **7.** The March on Washington for Jobs and Freedom organized by Dr. Martin Luther King, Jr. took place in:
  a. 1954.
  b. 1963.
  c. 1964.
  d. 1965.

_____ **8.** The Voting Rights Act of 1965:
  a. launched an important civil rights movement in the United States.
  b. eliminated racial barriers to voting.
  c. limited the legal rights of African Americans.
  d. provided African Americans and other minorities with legal access to public facilities and prohibited job discrimination.

_____ **9.** Although there has been significant progress in legal equality for all Americans, studies have found that African Americans:
  a. believe that the nation has two standards of justice, one for blacks and one for other minorities.
  b. want more legislation to improve judicial equality.
  c. accused of crime are more likely to be convicted than are white Americans on trial for comparable offenses.
  d. believe that equality is not fully developed in America.

_____ **10.** In recent decades, the percentage of black elected officials has:
  a. declined.
  b. equaled the proportion of African Americans in the population.
  c. risen sharply.
  d. increased only slightly.

Vocabulary in Context

Directions: Items 11–20 test your ability to determine the meaning of a word by using context clues. *Context clues* are words in a sentence that allow the reader to deduce (reason out) the meaning of an unfamiliar word in that sentence. Context clues also enable the reader to determine which meaning the author intends when a word has more than one meaning. For each vocabulary item below, a sentence from the selection containing an important word (*italicized, like this*) is quoted first. Next, there is an additional sentence using the word in the same sense and providing another context clue. Use the context clues from *both* sentences to deduce the meaning of the italicized word. *Be sure the answer you choose makes sense in both sentences.* If you discover that you need to use a dictionary to confirm an answer choice, remember that the meaning you select must still fit the context of *both* sentences. Write your answer in the space provided.

Pronunciation Key: ă pat ā pay âr care ä father ĕ pet ē be ĭ pit
ī tie îr pier ŏ pot ō toe ô paw oi noise ou out ŏŏ took
ōō boot ŭ cut yōō abuse ûr urge th thin th this hw which
zh vision ə about *Stress mark:* ʹ

---

11. Legal equality has rarely been *bestowed* by the more powerful upon the less powerful.

Responsibility for the management and care of our family's farm was *bestowed* to me by my grandfather and grandmother.

bestowed (bĭ stōdʹ) means:
a. negotiated
b. handed over
c. taken
d. sold

12. Their gains have nearly always occurred through intense and sustained political movements, such as the civil rights movement of the 1960s, that have pressured established interests to *relinquish* or share their privileged status.

When Michael moved away to attend college, he was happy to *relinquish* his bedroom to his youngest sister.

relinquish (rĭ lĭngʹ kwĭsh) means:
a. pressure
b. share
c. let go of
d. reverse

_____ **13.** Of all America's problems, none has been as *persistent* as the white race's unwillingness to yield a fair share of society's benefits to members of the black race.

Yolanda's *persistent* headaches finally forced her to see a specialist.

persistent (pər sĭs′ tənt) means:

a. painful

b. mysterious; confusing

c. terrible

d. continuing; lasting

_____ **14.** "If one race be inferior to the other socially," the Court argued, "the Constitution of the United States cannot put them on the same *plane*."

In a perfect world, every child would begin elementary school on the same *plane*.

plane (plān) means:

a. level surface

b. level of development or existence

c. grade

d. place or destination

_____ **15.** The Supreme Court declared that "separate educational facilities are *inherently* unequal."

Many people claim that men and women are *inherently* opposite from each other.

inherently (ĭn hîr′ ənt lē) means:

a. unfairly; unjustly

b. slightly; partly

c. intellectually; mentally

d. essentially; intrinsically

_____ **16.** The modern civil rights movement *peaked* with the triumphant March on Washington for Jobs and Freedom of August 2, 1963.

As usual, the holiday shopping season *peaked* on Christmas Eve, December 24th, when last-minute-gift buyers flooded the shopping malls.

peaked (pēkt) means:

a. reached a maximum of development

b. improved

c. flooded; clogged

d. came to an end; dissolved

_____ **17.** A year later, after a months-long fight in Congress that was marked by every parliamentary obstacle that racial conservatives could muster, the Civil Rights Act of 1964 was *enacted.*

Before the Miranda ruling was *enacted,* a person could be arrested without being informed of his or her legal rights.

enacted (ĕn ăk′ təd) means:

a. acted out, as on a stage

b. abandoned; given up

c. made into law

d. overturned

_____ **18.** Although the most significant progress in history toward the legal equality of all Americans occurred during the 1960s, Dr. King's dream of a color-blind society has remained *elusive.*

Despite intensive research during the last decade, a cure for breast cancer has remained *elusive.*

elusive (ĭ lōō′ sĭv) means:

a. difficult to grasp or attain

b. likely to be unsuccessful

c. impossible

d. unlikely to be controlled

_____ **19.** One area in which African Americans have made *substantial* progress since the 1960s is the winning of election to public office.

In 2000, 2001, and 2002, many investors lost *substantial* sums of money in the stock market.

substantial (səb stăn′ shəl) means:

a. solidly built; strong

b. considerable; large

c. possessing wealth; well-to-do

d. substandard; unimportant

_____ **20.** Although the percentage of black elected officials is still far below the proportion of African Americans in the population, it has risen sharply over recent *decades.*

Many people say the 1960s and 1970s were the most socially permissive *decades* in our country's history.

decades (dĕk′ ādz) means:

a. attitudes

b. developments

c. periods of ten years

d. times

SELECTION **3-1**   *Reading Skills Application*

Government
(Continued)

Directions: Items 21–25 test your ability to *apply* certain reading skills to information in this selection. These types of questions provide valuable practice for all students, especially those who must take standardized reading tests and state-mandated basic skills tests (such as the Florida CLAST Test and the Texas THEA Test). You may not have studied all of the skills at this point, so these items will serve as a helpful preview. The comprehension and critical reading skills in this section are presented in Chapters 4 through 9 of *Opening Doors;* vocabulary and figurative language skills are presented in Chapter 2. As you work through *Opening Doors,* you will practice and develop these skills. Write your answer for each question in the space provided.

_____ **21.** The author's primary purpose for writing this selection is to:

   a. inform readers about slavery and other injustices suffered by African Americans.

   b. persuade people to become more involved in the American political process.

   c. explain how African Americans have made gains in legal equality during the last century.

   d. explain why most Americans did not support the civil rights movement during the 1960s.

_____ **22.** Which of the following best expresses the main idea of paragraph 2?

   a. Legal equality has rarely been bestowed by the more powerful upon the less powerful.

   b. Their gains have nearly always occurred through political movements.

   c. Disadvantaged groups in America are now making some progress toward social equality.

   d. The history of America shows that disadvantaged groups have rarely achieved a greater measure of justice without a struggle that includes sustained, intense political movements.

_____ **23.** The information in paragraph 11 is organized using which of the following patterns?

   a. sequence

   b. comparison-contrast

   c. definition

   d. list

_____ **24.** Which of the following statements represents an opinion rather than a fact?

   a. Substantial judicial relief for African Americans was finally achieved in 1954 with *Brown v. Board of Education of Topeka,* arguably the most significant ruling in Supreme Court history.

   b. In 1957, rioting broke out when Governor Orval Faubus called out the Arkansas National Guard to block the entry of black children to the Little Rock public schools.

     c.   Organized by Dr. King and other civil rights leaders, the March on Washington attracted 250,000 marchers, one of the largest gatherings in the history of the nation's capital.

     d.   A year after the March on Washington, the Civil Rights Act of 1964 was enacted.

_____ **25.** Which of these is a logical conclusion that can be inferred from the information in the selection?

     a.   African Americans no longer need to struggle for equality.

     b.   Equality has always been the least fully developed of America's founding concepts.

     c.   It is likely that the percentage of African Americans elected to public office will increase.

     d.   Many African Americans believe there is now one standard of justice for both whites and blacks.

Respond in Writing

Directions: Refer to Selection 3-1 as needed to answer the essay-type questions below.

Collaboration Option

Option for collaboration: Your instructor may direct you to work with other students on one or more of these items, or in other words, to work *collaboratively.* In that case, you should form groups of three or four students, as directed by your instructor, and work together to complete the exercises. After your group discusses an item and agrees on the answer, have a group member record it. Each member of your group should be able to explain all of your group's answers.

1. Dr. Martin Luther King, Jr. is certainly one of America's best-known advocates for judicial equality and civil rights. What other persons (past or present) can you name who have contributed to the civil rights or equal rights movement for any groups in America?

_____

_____

_____

_____

2. Complete the chronological list of the Supreme Court Decisions, civil rights demonstrations, and congressional acts that were mentioned in this selection.

1896: _____

1954: _____

1963: _____

1964: _____

1965: _____

3. **Overall main idea.** What is the overall main idea the authors want the reader to understand about African Americans and their struggle for equality? Answer this question in one sentence. Be sure to include the words *African Americans* and *equality* in your overall main idea sentence.

_____

_____

_____

_____

_____

_____

_____

Internet Resources

Read More about This Topic on the World Wide Web

Directions: For further information about the topic of the selection, visit these websites:

http://www.naacp.org
The website of the National Association for the Advancement of Colored People (NAACP); includes historical and current information on the struggle of African Americans for equal rights.

http://www.nclr.org
The website for the National Council of La Raza (NCLR), an organization dedicated to improving the lives of Hispanics; contains information on public policy, immigration, citizenship, and other subjects.

http://www.rci.rutgers.edu/_cawp
The website of the Center for the American Woman and Politics (CAWP) at Rutgers University's Eagleton Institute of Politics.

http://www.airpi.org/
The website for the American Indian Policy Center, which was established by Native Americans in 1992; includes a political and legal history of Native Americans and examines current issues affecting them.

You can also use your favorite search engine such as Google, Yahoo!, or AltaVista (www.google.com, www.yahoo.com, www.altavista.com) to discover more about this topic. To locate additional information, type in combinations of keywords such as:

civil rights movement

or

equality African Americans

Keep in mind that whenever you go to *any* website, it is a good idea to evaluate the website and the information it contains. Ask yourself questions such as:

"Who sponsors this website?"

"Is the information contained in this website up-to-date?"

"What type of information is presented?"

"Is the information objective and complete?"

"How easy is it to use the features of this website?"

SELECTION **3-2**

**Human
Development**

Parenthood: Now, Later, . . . Never?

From *Human Development*

By Diane E. Papalia, Sally Wendkos Olds, and Ruth Feldman

Prepare Yourself to Read

Directions: Do these exercises *before* you read Selection 3-2.

1. It has been said that "parenthood is the hardest job in the world if you do it right." Do you agree? Why or why not?

_____

_____

_____

_____

2. Next, complete your preview by reading the following:

> Introduction (in *italics*)
> First paragraph (paragraph 1)
> Headings for each section
> The first sentence of paragraphs 2–17
> Line graph and explanation beside it

On the basis of your preview, what aspects of parenthood do you think will be discussed?

_____

_____

_____

_____

Apply Comprehension Skills

Directions: Do these exercises *as* you read Selection 3-2.

Ask and answer questions as you read. Complete the practice exercises by creating questions based on what each paragraph seems to be about.

Read actively to find answers to your questions. Record the answers to your questions. Write the answer in the margin or highlight the answer in the text.

Review by rehearsing the answers to your questions. Recite your answers or write them down from memory.

PARENTHOOD: NOW, LATER, . . . NEVER?

"Just wait until you have children of your own!" At one time or another in our lives, we have all heard those words from our parents. Becoming a parent and being a parent affect every area of a person's life. In this selection, the authors present some new, interesting, and sometimes surprising research findings about parenthood in the 21st century.

1   Although the institution of the family is universal, the "traditional" family—a husband, a wife, and their biological children—is not. In many African, Asian, and Latin American cultures the extended-family household is the traditional form. In western industrialized countries, family size, composition, structure, and division of labor have changed dramatically. Most mothers now work for pay, in or outside the home, and a small but growing number of fathers are primary caregivers. More single women and cohabiting couples are having or adopting children and raising them. Millions of children live with gay or lesbian parents or with stepparents.

2   On the other hand, an increasing number of couples remain childless by choice. Some of these couples want to concentrate on careers or social causes. Some feel more comfortable with adults or think they would not make good parents. Some want to retain the intimacy of the honeymoon. Some enjoy an adult lifestyle, with freedom to travel or to make spur-of-the-moment decisions. Some women worry that pregnancy will make them less attractive and that parenthood will change their relationship with their spouse.

3   Some people may be discouraged by the financial burdens of parenthood and the difficulty of combining parenthood with employment. In 2000 the estimated expenditures to raise a child to age 18 in a middle-income two-parent, two-child family were $165,630. Better childcare and other support services might help couples make truly voluntary decisions.

Creating Questions Exercises

Directions: For each paragraph:

- Create a question based on what the paragraph seems to be about. Ask *who, what, when, where, why,* or *how.*
- Write your question in the spaces provided.
- Write the answer to your question in the margin or highlight it in the text.

Doing this will help you understand and remember the material.

Creating Questions Exercise

Question about paragraph 1:

_____

_____

_____

Creating Questions Exercise

Question about paragraph 2:

_____

_____

_____

Creating Questions Exercise

Question about paragraph 3:

_____

_____

_____

Becoming Parents

4   At one time, a blessing offered to newlyweds in the Asian country of Nepal was, "May you have enough sons to cover the hillsides!" Today, Nepali couples are wished, "May you have a very bright son." While sons still are preferred over daughters, even boys are not wished for in such numbers as in the past.

5   In preindustrial farming societies, large families were a necessity: children helped with the family's work and would eventually care for aging parents. The death rate in childhood was high, and having many children made it more likely that some would reach maturity. Today, infant and child mortality rates have improved greatly, and, in industrial societies, large families are no longer an economic asset. In developing countries, too, where overpopulation and hunger are major problems, there is recognition of the need to limit family size and to space children further apart.

6   Not only do people typically have fewer children today, but they also start having them later in life, often because they spend their early adult years getting an education and establishing a career. Today the median age of first-time mothers in the United States is 24.6, having risen consistently for three decades. Since the mid-1970s the percentage of women who give birth in their thirties and even after 40 has increased steadily, often thanks to fertility treatments. Meanwhile, birthrates for women in their late twenties, which had declined after 1990, are again on the rise. For the first time in almost thirty years, the total fertility rate in 2000 (a projected total of 2.1 births per woman) exceeded "replacement level," the number of births needed to offset deaths. The U.S. fertility rate is higher than in several other developed countries.

7   Economically, delaying childbirth may pay off for women who intend to work later on. Among women born between 1944 and 1954, the first cohort to combine child raising and employment on a large scale, those who gave birth between ages 20 and 27 tend to earn less than women who gave birth at later ages. Further research may show whether this holds true in later cohorts.

8   Babies of older mothers may benefit from their mothers' greater ease with parenthood. When 105 new mothers ages 16 to 38 were interviewed and observed with their infants, the older mothers reported more satisfaction with parenting and spent more time at it. They were more affectionate and sensitive to their babies and more effective in encouraging desired behavior. And, among a large, nationally representative sample, men who became fathers after their thirty-fifth birthdays spent more leisure time with their children, had higher expectations for the children's behavior, and were more nurturing than a comparison group who became fathers before age 35. On the other hand, looking far down the road, older parents

Creating Questions Exercise

Question about paragraph 4:

_____

_____

_____

Creating Questions Exercise

Question about paragraph 5:

_____

_____

_____

Creating Questions Exercise

Question about paragraph 6:

_____

_____

_____

Creating Questions Exercise

Question about paragraph 7:

_____

_____

_____

Creating Questions Exercise

Question about paragraph 8:

_____

_____

_____

Figure 1

Birthrates by age of mother, 1960 to 2000.
(Martin, J., Park, M., and Sutton, P. (2002). Births: Preliminary data for 2001. *National Vital Statistics Reports* 50(10). Hyattsville, MD. National Center for Health Statistics.)

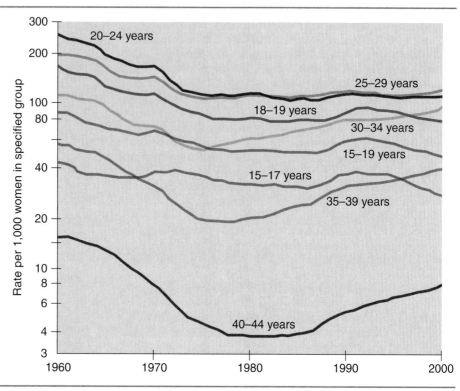

Couples today tend to have fewer children than in past generations, and to have them later in life. Infants may benefit from mature parents' ease with parenthood and willingness to invest more time in it.

are more likely to become a burden when their children reach middle age.

Parenthood as a Developmental Experience

9   A first baby marks a major transition in parents' lives. This totally dependent new person changes individuals and changes relationships. As children develop, parents do, too.

Men's and Women's Involvement in Parenthood

10   Both women and men often have mixed feelings about becoming parents. Along with excitement, they may feel anxiety about the responsibility of caring for a child and the commitment of time and energy it entails.

11   Fathers today are more involved in their children's lives, and even in childcare and housework, than ever before. Still, most are not nearly as involved as mothers are. In a study of parents of 4-year-olds in 10 European, Asian, and African countries and the United States, fathers averaged less than 1 hour a day in sole charge of their children during the work week, while U.S. mothers spent an average of nearly 11 hours each weekday caring for preschoolers—more than mothers in any of the other 10 countries.

12   Even working mothers are the primary caregivers in most families. This is especially true on weekdays, according to time diaries kept by a nationally representative sample of 2,400 intact U.S. families in 1997. However, the time fathers spend with children becomes more nearly equal to mothers' on weekends, and increases as children get older. Fathers spend considerably *more* time with children than mothers in television or video viewing, outdoor play, and coaching or teaching sports.

13   Some fathers do much more, sharing parenting equally with mothers. Such a choice challenges still-prominent social expectations that fathers are primarily breadwinners and mothers are primarily responsible for child raising. Equally sharing parents do not reverse roles; instead, both parents make job adjustments and career choices compatible with their parenting responsibilities.

14   Today, fathers are the primary caregivers for 11.4 percent of preschoolers with employed mothers. Studies show that fathers who are primary caregivers can be nearly as nurturing as mothers.

Creating Questions Exercise

Question about paragraph 9:

_____

_____

_____

Creating Questions Exercise

Question about paragraph 10:

_____

_____

_____

Creating Questions Exercise

Question about paragraph 11:

_____

_____

_____

Creating Questions Exercise

Question about paragraph 12:

_____

_____

Creating Questions Exercise

Question about paragraph 13:

_____

_____

Creating Questions Exercise

Question about paragraph 14:

_____

_____

15   Besides time spent in direct childcare, fatherhood may change men in other ways. Among 5,226 men ages 19 to 65, fathers living with their dependent children were less involved in outside social activities than those who had no children, but more likely to be engaged in school-related activities, church groups, and community service organizations. They tended to work more hours and were less likely to be unemployed. The most involved fathers were more satisfied with their lives and more involved in work, family, community, and socializing.

Creating Questions Exercise

Question about paragraph 15:

_____

_____

_____

How Parenthood Affects Marital Satisfaction

16   Marital satisfaction typically declines during the child-raising years. In a ten-year longitudinal study of predominantly white couples who married in their late twenties, both husbands and wives reported a sharp decline in satisfaction during the first four years, followed by a plateau and then another decline. Spouses who had children, especially those who became parents early in their marriage and those who had many children, showed a steeper decline. Although there was a high attrition rate—429 out of the original 522 couples divorced or separated during the course of the study or did not complete it—the presumably greater dissatisfaction of the couples who ultimately left the study did not seriously skew the findings while they were in it. The pattern of decline held true, though less strongly, even when this factor was controlled.

Creating Questions Exercise

Question about paragraph 16:

_____

_____

_____

17   Of course, this statistical pattern is an average; it is not necessarily true of all couples. One research team followed 128 middle- and working-class couples in their late twenties from the first pregnancy until the child's third birthday. Some marriages got stronger, while others deteriorated, especially in the eyes of the wives. In these marriages, the partners tended to be younger and less well educated, to earn less money, to have been married a shorter time, and to have lower self-esteem. The mothers who had the hardest time were those whose babies had difficult temperaments. Surprisingly, women who had planned their pregnancies were unhappier, possibly because they had expected life with a baby to be better than it turned out to be.

Creating Questions Exercise

Question about paragraph 17:

_____

_____

_____

18   Among young Israeli first-time parents, fathers who saw themselves as caring, nurturing, and protecting experienced less decline in marital satisfaction than other fathers and felt better about parenthood. Men who were less involved with their babies, and whose wives were more involved, tended to be more dissatisfied. The mothers who became most dissatisfied with their marriages were those who saw themselves as disorganized and unable to cope with the demands of motherhood.

Creating Questions Exercise

Question about paragraph 18:

_____

_____

_____

SELECTION **3-2**   **Reading Selection Quiz**

Human Development
(Continued)

This quiz has three parts. Your instructor may assign some or all of them.

Comprehension

Directions: Items 1–10 test your comprehension (understanding) of the material of this selection. These questions are the type a content area instructor (such as a human development professor) would ask on a test over this material. You should be able to answer these questions after studying this selection. For each comprehension question below, use information from the selection to determine the correct answer. Refer to the selection as you answer each question. Write your answer in the space provided.

True or False

_____   **1.** Over the years there have been few changes in family size, composition, structure, or division of labor in western industrialized countries.

_____   **2.** People today typically have fewer children and have them later in life.

_____   **3.** Older mothers tend to be more satisfied with their parenting and to spend more time on it.

_____   **4.** Having a baby changes the individual parents and their relationship.

_____   **5.** Both men and women often have mixed feelings about becoming parents.

Multiple-Choice

_____   **6.** During child-raising years, parents' marital satisfaction typically:
   a.   declines.
   b.   stays the same.
   c.   increases.
   d.   cannot be assessed.

_____   **7.** In most families the primary caregivers are:
   a.   the mothers.
   b.   the fathers.
   c.   both parents.
   d.   relatives other than the parents.

_____   **8.** In marriages that deteriorated between pregnancy and the child's third birthday, the partners tended to:
   a.   be younger and less well educated.
   b.   earn less money.
   c.   have been married a shorter time.
   d.   all of the above

_____ **9.** Parents who share equally in child raising:

      a. typically reverse their roles.

      b. make adjustments in their job and career choices.

      c. make no adjustments.

      d. tend to have higher divorce rates.

_____ **10.** During the last three decades the median age for first-time mothers in the United States has:

      a. consistently decreased.

      b. stayed the same.

      c. fluctuated up and down.

      d. consistently risen.

S E L E C T I O N **3-2**   *Vocabulary in Context*

Human Development
(Continued)

Directions: Items 11–20 test your ability to determine the meaning of a word by using context clues. *Context clues* are words in a sentence that allow the reader to deduce (reason out) the meaning of an unfamiliar word in that sentence. Context clues also enable the reader to determine which meaning the author intends when a word has more than one meaning. For each vocabulary item below, a sentence from the selection containing an important word (*italicized, like this*) is quoted first. Next, there is an additional sentence using the word in the same sense and providing another context clue. Use the context clues from *both* sentences to deduce the meaning of the italicized word. *Be sure the answer you choose makes sense in both sentences.* If you discover that you need to use a dictionary to confirm an answer choice, remember that the meaning you select must still fit the context of *both* sentences. Write your answer in the space provided.

Pronunciation Key: ă pat   ā pay   âr care   ä father   ĕ pet   ē be   ĭ pit
ī tie   îr pier   ŏ pot   ō toe   ô paw   oi noise   ou out   ŏŏ took
ōō boot   ŭ cut   yōō abuse   ûr urge   th thin   *th* this   hw which
zh vision   ə about   *Stress mark:* ′

_____ **11.** Although the institution of the family is *universal,* the "traditional" family—a husband, a wife, and their biological children—is not.

Love is a *universal* emotion.

universal (yōō nə vûr′ səl) means:

      a. knowledgeable about many subjects

      b. existing all over the world

      c. pertaining to the universe

      d. cosmic

_____ **12.** More single women and *cohabiting* couples are having or adopting children and raising them.

Many religious groups disapprove of *cohabiting* couples.

cohabiting (kō hăb′ ĭt ĭng) means:

a. legally married

b. marrying late in life

c. living together in a sexual relationship, especially when not legally married

d. legally married and living in the same house

_____ **13.** In *preindustrial* farming societies, large families were a necessity; children helped with the family's work and would eventually care for aging parents.

In *preindustrial* times, many items that are now mass-produced by machines were produced singly, by hand.

preindustrial (prē ĭn dŭs′ trē əl) means:

a. relating to a society whose industries do not yet produce manufactured goods on a large scale

b. relating to a society in which all individuals are engaged in industry

c. relating to a society in which all industry exists for profit

d. relating to a society whose economic well-being rests only on the production of manufactured goods

_____ **14.** In a study of parents of 4-year-olds in 10 European, Asian, and African countries and the United States, fathers averaged less than 1 hour a day in *sole* charge of their children during the work week, while U.S. mothers spent an average of nearly 11 hours each weekday caring for preschoolers—more than mothers in any of the other 10 countries.

The child, the *sole* survivor of the plane crash, was adopted by her aunt and uncle.

sole (sōl) means:

a. total, complete

b. fortunate, lucky

c. being religious in nature

d. being the only one

_____ **15.** Even working mothers are the *primary* caregivers in most families.

College students report that for them the *primary* cause of stress is having too much to do and not enough time in which to do it.

primary (prī′ mĕr ē) means:

a. highest paid

b. main, principal

   c. dissatisfied

   d. temporary

_____ **16.** Such a choice challenges still-prominent social expectations that fathers are primarily *breadwinners* and mothers are primarily responsible for child raising.

In some families wives are the *breadwinners* and husbands enjoy staying home caring for the children.

breadwinners (brĕd′ wĭn′ ərz) means:

   a. those whose earnings are the main source of support for dependents

   b. those who are the main source of meals for dependents

   c. those who are lucky in gambling

   d. those who have training as bakers

_____ **17.** In a ten-year longitudinal study of *predominantly* white couples who married in their late twenties, both husbands and wives reported a sharp decline in satisfaction during the first four years, followed by a plateau and then another decline.

His undergraduate grades are *predominantly* A's; he has only four B's on his entire transcript.

predominantly (prĭ dŏm′ ə nənt lē) means:

   a. occasionally

   b. a few

   c. completely, totally

   d. mainly, mostly

_____ **18.** In a ten-year longitudinal study of predominantly white couples who married in their late twenties, both husbands and wives reported a sharp decline in satisfaction during the first four years, followed by a *plateau* and then another decline.

Mortgage rates increased, reached a *plateau* during the summer, and then declined.

plateau (plă tō′) means:

   a. an uneven level

   b. a relatively stable level or period

   c. a period of constant change

   d. an unexplained change

_____ **19.** Although there was a high *attrition* rate—429 out of the original 522 couples divorced or separated during the course of the study or did not complete it— the presumably greater dissatisfaction of the couples who ultimately left the study did not seriously skew the findings while they were in it.

An unusually high number of retirements and resignations caused our employee *attrition* rate to be higher last year.

attrition (ə trĭsh′ ən) means:

a. frustration

b. dissatisfaction

c. reduction

d. achievement

_____ **20.** Although there was a high attrition rate—429 out of the original 522 couples divorced or separated during the course of the study or did not complete it— the presumably greater dissatisfaction of the couples who ultimately left the study did not seriously *skew* the findings while they were in it.

If there are patients in the study who do not take their medications consistently, it will *skew* the results and make the research meaningless.

skew (skyo͞o) means:

a. distsort, influence unfairly

b. confirm, verify

c. improve

d. publish

SELECTION **3-2** *Reading Skills Application*

Human Development
(Continued)

Directions: Items 21–25 test your ability to *apply* certain reading skills to information in this selection. These types of questions provide valuable practice for all students, especially those who must take standardized reading tests and state-mandated basic skills tests (such as the Florida CLAST Test and the Texas THEA Test). You may not have studied all of the skills at this point, so these items will serve as a helpful preview. The comprehension and critical reading skills in this section are presented in Chapters 4 through 9 of *Opening Doors;* vocabulary and figurative language skills are presented in Chapter 2. As you work through *Opening Doors,* you will practice and develop these skills. Write your answer for each question in the space provided.

_____ **21.** In paragraph 2, the authors use the term *spur-of-the-moment* to describe decisions made:

a. by adults only.

b. under extreme pressure.

c. hastily on impulse.

d. after careful consideration.

_____ **22.** In paragraph 5 a comparison is made between family size in:

a. preindustrial societies and industrial societies today.

b. preindustrial farming societies and developing countries today.

c. industrial societies and developing countries today.

d. preindustrial farming societies and in industrial societies and developing countries today.

_____ **23.** Based on the information in the selection, it can be logically concluded that:

    a. couples who enter into parenthood with a realistic understanding of its demands, challenges, and rewards are likely to find the experience more satisfying.

    b. the greater number of children, the more unhappy parents are likely to become.

    c. children born to younger, immature couples are likely to have no more problems than children born to older, more mature couples.

    d. couples who are unprepared for parenthood usually adjust fairly quickly once the baby is born.

_____ **24.** The author would be most likely to agree with which of the following statements?

    a. Parenthood is a rewarding experience that ideally every couple should experience.

    b. Because parenthood causes changes in so many aspects of a couple's life, they should consider carefully whether they want to have children and, if so, when.

    c. There is nothing that can be done to prepare couples for the transition to parenthood.

    d. People who do not have children are self-centered.

_____ **25.** Which of the following represents an opinion rather than a fact?

    a. Babies of older mothers may benefit from their mothers' greater ease with parenthood.

    b. When 105 new mothers ages 16 to 38 were interviewed and observed with their infants, the older mothers reported more satisfaction with parenting and spent more time at it.

    c. They were more affectionate and sensitive to their babies and more effective in encouraging desired behavior.

    d. And, among a large, nationally representative sample, men who became fathers after their 35th birthdays spent more leisure time with their children, had higher expectations for the children's behavior, and were more nurturing than a comparison group who became fathers before age 35.

SELECTION **3-2**   **Respond in Writing**

**Human
Development**
(Continued)

Collaboration Option

Directions: Refer to Selection 3-2 as needed to answer the essay-type questions below.

Option for collaboration: Your instructor may direct you to work with other students, or in other words, to work *collaboratively*. In that case, you should form groups of three or four students, as directed by your instructor, and work together to complete the exercises. After your group discusses each item and agrees on the answer, have a group member record it. Every member of your group should be able to explain all of your group's answers.

1. According to the authors, which factors seem to be associated with making parenthood a successful and satisfying experience?

   _____

   _____

   _____

   _____

   _____

   _____

   _____

   _____

   _____

   _____

   _____

2. If couples wait until they are older, more mature, and better educated before becoming parents, what effects do you think this might have on their children? List at least three effects.

   _____

   _____

   _____

   _____

   _____

3. If most couples were older, more mature, and better educated when they become parents, what possible effects do you think this might have on society? List at least three effects.

_____

_____

_____

_____

_____

_____

_____

_____

4. **Overall main idea.** What is the overall main idea the authors want the reader to understand about parenthood? Answer this question in one sentence. Be sure to include the word *parenthood* in your overall main idea sentence.

_____

_____

_____

_____

_____

_____

_____

_____

Internet Resources

Read More about This Topic on the World Wide Web

Directions: For further information about the topic of the selection, visit these websites:

www.family.com
This website has hundreds of links for family activities, health, parenting, crafts for kids, family vacations, etc.

www.familyeducation.com
This is the Family Education Network Home Page. The mission of FEN is to help children succeed in school and in life. FEN is an interactive community that links parents, teachers, students, and schools to timely resources, to educational activities, and to each other.

www.aak.com
All About Kids website.

www.disney.com
The Disney.com website is great fun. Check it out with young family members or relatives.

You can also use your favorite search engine such as Google, Yahoo!, or Alta-Vista (www.google.com, www.yahoo.com, www.altavista.com) to discover more about this topic. To locate additional information, type in combinations of key-words such as:

successful parenting

or

transition to parenthood

Keep in mind that whenever you go to any website, it is a good idea to evaluate the website and the information it contains. Ask yourself questions such as:

"Who sponsors this website?"

"Is the information contained in this website up-to-date?"

"What type of information is presented?"

"Is the information objective and complete?"

"How easy is it to use the features of this website?"

Art in the Service of Religion

From *Living with Art*
By Rita Gilbert

Prepare Yourself to Read

Directions: Do these exercises *before* you read Selection 3-3.

1. First, read and think about the title. What factors do you think architects must consider when they design churches, temples, or other places of religious worship?

    _____

    _____

    _____

2. Next, complete your preview by reading the following:

    Introduction (in *italics*)

    First paragraph (paragraph 1)

    First sentence of each paragraph

    Words in italics

    Picture and caption

    All of the last paragraph (paragraph 12)

    On the basis of your preview, how do you think architecture is used to serve religion?

    _____

    _____

    _____

    _____

    _____

    _____

Apply Comprehension Skills

Directions: Do these exercises *as* you read Selection 3-3.

Ask and answer questions as you read. Complete the practice exercises by creating questions based on what each paragraph seems to be about.

Read actively to find answers to your questions. Record the answers to your questions. Write the answers in the margin or highlight the answers in the text.

Review by rehearsing the answers to your questions. Recite your answers or write them down from memory.

ART IN THE SERVICE OF RELIGION

Think about various churches, synagogues, mosques, temples, shrines, and other religious structures you have seen, attended, or visited. Have you ever considered how the architecture of a place of worship is related to the activities that occur there? In this selection from an art appreciation textbook, the author explains the relationship between three different religions and the architecture of some of their well-known places of worship.

1   Since earliest times art has served religion in two important ways. First, artists have erected the sacred temples where believers join to profess their faith and follow the observances faith requires. Second, art attempts to make specific and visible something that is, by its very nature, spiritual, providing images of the religious figures and events that make up the fabric of faith. In other words, art attempts to make concrete that which is abstract. In this section we shall explore how the theme of religious art has been adapted for different purposes, for different faiths, in different parts of the world.

2   A very large portion of the magnificent architecture we have was built in the service of religion. Naturally the architectural style of any religious structure reflects the culture in which it was built, but it is also dependent on the particular needs of a given religion. Three examples will show this.

3   On a high hill, the Acropolis, overlooking the city of Athens stands the shell of what many consider the most splendid building ever conceived: the Parthenon. The Parthenon was erected in the 5th century B.C. as a temple to the goddess Athena, patroness of the city, and at one time its core held a colossal statue of the goddess. However, the religion associated with the Parthenon was not confined to worship of a deity. In ancient Greece, veneration of the gods was closely allied to the political and social ideals of a city-state that celebrated its own greatness.

4   Rising proudly on its hill, visible from almost every corner of the city, and for miles around, the Parthenon functioned as a symbol of the citizens' aspirations. Its structure as a religious shrine seems unusual for us in that it turns outward, toward the city, rather than in upon itself. Worshipers were not meant to gather inside the building; actually, only priests could enter the inner chamber, or *cella,* where the statue of Athena stood. Religious ceremonies on festal occasions focused on processions, which began down in the city, wound their way up the steep path on the west side of the Acropolis, and circled the Parthenon and other sacred buildings at the top.

Creating Questions Exercises

Directions: For each paragraph:

• Create a question based on what the paragraph seems to be about. Ask *who, what, when, where, why,* or *how.*

• Write your question in the spaces provided.

• Write the answer to your question in the margin or highlight it in the text.

Doing this will help you understand and remember the material.

Creating Questions Exercise

Question about paragraph 1:

_____

_____

Creating Questions Exercise

Question about paragraph 2:

_____

_____

Creating Questions Exercise

Question about paragraph 3:

_____

_____

Creating Questions Exercise

Question about paragraph 4:

_____

_____

5   Most of the Parthenon's architectural embellishment was intended for the appreciation of the worshipers outside. All four walls of the exterior were decorated with sculptures high up under the roof, and originally portions of the marble façade were painted a vivid blue and red. We shall concentrate on the theme of religion and on the Parthenon's purpose, which is both religious *and* political exaltation.

6   At about the same time the Parthenon was being constructed in Athens, but half a continent away, one of the world's great religions was developing and beginning to form its own architecture. Buddhism derives its principles from the teachings of Gautama Siddhartha, later known as the Buddha, who was born in India about 563 B.C. Although of noble birth, the Buddha renounced his princely status and life of ease. When he was about twenty-nine, he began a long period of wandering and meditation, seeking enlightenment. He began with the supposition that humans are predisposed to live out lives of suffering, to die, then to be reborn and repeat the pattern. Ultimately, he worked out a doctrine of moral behavior that he believed could break the painful cycle of life and death, and he attracted many followers.

7   Buddhism is predominantly a personal religion, and its observances depend less on communal worship than on individual contemplation. It places great emphasis on symbolism, much of it referring to episodes in the Buddha's life. Both of these aspects—the personal and the symbolic—are evident in one of Buddhism's finest early shrines, the Great Stupa at Sanchi, in India. Like the Parthenon, the Great Stupa turns more outward than inward, but its moundlike form is more sculptural, intended as a representation of the cosmos. At the very top is a three-part "umbrella," symbolizing the three major aspects of Buddhism—the Buddha, the Buddha's law, and the Monastic Order.

8   Buddhist shrines—the word *stupa* means "shrine"— often housed relics of the Buddha, and worship rituals called for circumambulation ("walking around") of the stupa. Thus, on the outside of the Great Stupa of Sanchi we see a railed pathway, where pilgrims could take the ritual clockwise walk following the Path of Life around the World Mountain. Elsewhere the stupa is embellished richly with carvings and sculpture evoking scenes from the Buddha's life. Every part of the stupa is geared to the pursuit of personal enlightenment and transcendence.

The Parthenon on the Acropolis. Athens, Greece. 447–432 B.C.

Creating Questions Exercise

Question about paragraph 5:

_____

_____

Creating Questions Exercise

Question about paragraph 6:

_____

_____

Creating Questions Exercise

Question about paragraph 7:

_____

_____

Creating Questions Exercise

Question about paragraph 8:

_____

_____

9   If the Buddhist temple is dedicated to private worship, then its extreme opposite can be found in the total encompassment of a community religious experience: the medieval Christian cathedral. And the supreme example of that ideal is the Cathedral of Notre Dame de Chartres, in France. Chartres Cathedral was built, rebuilt, and modified over a period of several hundred years, but the basic structure, which is in the Gothic style, was established in the 13th century. A cathedral—as opposed to a church—is the bishop's domain and therefore is always in a town or a city. This one fact is crucial to understanding the nature of Chartres and the role it played in the people's lives.

10   The cathedral towers magnificently over the surrounding city, much as the Parthenon does over Athens, but here the resemblance ends. Whereas the Parthenon is above and apart from the city, accessible only by a steep path, Chartres Cathedral is very much a living presence *within* the city. In the Middle Ages houses and shops clustered right up to its walls, and one side of the cathedral formed an edge of the busy marketplace. The cathedral functioned as a hub of all activities, both sacred and secular, within the town.

11   Medieval France had one dominant religion, and that was the Christianity of Rome. One could assume that almost every resident of the town of Chartres professed exactly the same faith, and so the church was an integral part of everyday life. Its bells tolled the hours of waking, starting work, praying, and retiring for the evening rest. Its feast days were the official holidays. Chartres Cathedral and its counterparts served the populace not only as a setting for religious worship but as meeting hall, museum, concert stage, and social gathering place. Within its walls business deals were arranged, goods were sold, friends met, young couples courted. Where else but inside the cathedral could the townsfolk hear splendid music? Where else would they see magnificent art?

The Great Stupa, Sanchi, India. Third century B.C. to first century A.D.

Creating Questions Exercise

Question about paragraph 9:

_____

_____

Creating Questions Exercise

Question about paragraph 10:

_____

_____

Creating Questions Exercise

Question about paragraph 11:

_____

_____

Chartres Cathedral,
France,
c. 1194–1260.

12   Three religious structures: the Parthenon, the Great Stupa, and Chartres Cathedral. Each was built in the service of religion but for each we can find another slightly different purpose. For the Parthenon the purpose is also *political;* for the Great Stupa there is the purely *private* observance of religion; and for Chartres the *social* role is as important as the religious.

SELECTION **3-3**

Art Appreciation
(Continued)

Student Online
Learning Center (OLC)
Go to Chapter 3.
Choose Reading
Selection Quiz.

Reading Selection Quiz

This quiz has three parts. Your instructor may assign some or all of them.

Comprehension

Directions: Items 1–10 test your comprehension (understanding) of the material of this selection. These questions are the type a content area instructor (such as an art appreciation professor) would ask on a test over this material. You should be able to answer these questions after studying this selection. For each comprehension question below, use information from the selection to determine the correct answer. Refer to the selection as you answer each question. Write your answer in the space provided.

True or False

_____ 1. Throughout history, art has served religion in three important ways. *false*

_____ 2. The Parthenon was built as a temple to the Greek goddess Diana. *false*

_____ 3. Greek citizens gathered inside the Parthenon to worship their gods. *false*

_____ 4. Many consider the Parthenon the most splendid building ever constructed. *true*

_____ 5. Buddhism was beginning to form its own architecture in India at approximately the same time as the Parthenon was being constructed in Greece. *true*

_____ 6. "Circumambulation" is a Buddhist religious ritual that involves walking clockwise around a stupa, a Buddhist shrine. *true*

Multiple-Choice

_____ 7. Which of the following does not describe early Buddhism?
   a. It was a personal religion.
   b. It required individual contemplation and a search for enlightenment.
   c. It required communal worship.
   d. It involved a ritual of walking around the shrine.

_____ 8. One of the finest Buddhist shrines, the Great Stupa of Sanchi in India, is characterized by all of the following except which?
   a. It contained a railed pathway.
   b. It resembled the cosmos with its moundlike form.
   c. It did not contain any carving or sculptures.
   d. It housed relics of the Buddha.

_____ **9.** In medieval France, the cathedral served as a:

  a. place of worship.

  b. concert stage and meeting hall.

  c. museum housing fine religious paintings and sculpture.

  d. all of the above

_____ **10.** Chartres Cathedral in France was built, rebuilt, and modified over a period of:

  a. 25 years.

  b. 50 years.

  c. 100 years.

  d. several hundred years.

SELECTION **3-3**   *Vocabulary in Context*

Art Appreciation
(Continued)

Directions: Items 11–20 test your ability to determine the meaning of a word by using context clues. *Context clues* are words in a sentence that allow the reader to deduce (reason out) the meaning of an unfamiliar word in that sentence. Context clues also enable the reader to determine which meaning the author intends, when a word has more than one meaning. For each vocabulary item below, a sentence from the selection containing an important word (*italicized, like this*) is quoted first. Next, there is an additional sentence using the word in the same sense and providing another context clue. Use the context clues from *both* sentences to deduce the meaning of the italicized word. *Be sure the answer you choose makes sense in both sentences.* If you discover that you need to use a dictionary to confirm an answer choice, remember that the meaning you select must still fit the context of *both* sentences. Write your answer in the space provided.

Pronunciation Key: ă pat   ā pay   âr care   ä father   ĕ pet   ē be   ĭ pit
ī tie   îr pier   ŏ pot   ō toe   ô paw   oi noise   ou out   ŏŏ took
ōō boot   ŭ cut   yōō abuse   ûr urge   th thin   th this   hw which
zh vision   ə about   *Stress mark:* ʹ

_____ **11.** First, artists have erected the sacred temples where believers join to *profess* their faith and follow the observances faith requires.

Although the visiting scientists tried to *profess* loyalty to the host country, they were nevertheless deported as spies.

profess (prə fĕsʹ) means:

  a. discuss

  b. lie about

  c. deny

  d. declare

_____ **12.** In ancient Greece, *veneration* of the gods was closely allied to the political and social ideals of a city-state that celebrated its own greatness.

In Asian cultures older people, such as grandparents, are treated with great respect and *veneration.*

veneration (věn ə rā′ shən) means:
- *a.* reverence
- *b.* courtesy
- *c.* fondness
- *d.* patience

_____ **13.** All four walls of the exterior were decorated with sculptures high up under the roof, and originally, portions of the marble *façade* were painted a vivid blue and red.

The architect updated the *façade* of the old hotel by adding a beautiful new brick exterior and elegant bronze doors.

façade (fə säd′) means:
- *a.* front of a building
- *b.* decorative trim
- *c.* columns; pillars
- *d.* steps or stairs

_____ **14.** Although of noble birth, the Buddha *renounced* his princely status and life of ease.

When my brother became a Catholic priest, he *renounced* all of his worldly possessions and took a vow of poverty.

renounced (rǐ nounst′) means:
- *a.* ignored
- *b.* gave up, especially by formal announcement
- *c.* described in someone else's words
- *d.* collected; gathered together

_____ **15.** He began with the *supposition* that humans are predisposed to live out lives of suffering, to die, then to be reborn and repeat the pattern.

Under the American judicial system, we begin with the *supposition* that a person is considered innocent until proven guilty.

supposition (sŭp ə zǐsh′ ən) means:
- *a.* scientific conclusion
- *b.* religious belief
- *c.* assumption
- *d.* hope

16. Like the Parthenon, the Great Stupa turns more outward than inward, but its moundlike form is more sculptural, intended as a representation of the *cosmos*.

Because human beings have always wondered how life began, every culture has its own explanation of the creation of the *cosmos*.

cosmos (kŏz′ mōs) means:

   a.   city

   b.   mountains and other significant geological features

   c.   the universe regarded as an orderly, harmonious whole

   d.   life after death

17. Buddhist shrines—the word "stupa" means "shrine"—often housed *relics* of the Buddha, and worship rituals called for circumambulation ("walking around") of the stupa.

The museum presented a splendid exhibit of Russian icons, altar pieces, and other religious *relics*.

relics (rĕl′ ĭks) means:

   a.   objects of religious reverence

   b.   pieces of art

   c.   personal belongings

   d.   paintings

18. Elsewhere the stupa is *embellished* richly with carvings and sculpture evoking scenes from the Buddha's life.

The Sistine Chapel in Rome is *embellished* with magnificent frescoes by Michelangelo.

embellished (ĕm bĕl′ ĭsht) means:

   a.   made colorful and bright

   b.   painted

   c.   made in a shape of a bell

   d.   adorned; made beautiful

19. Every part of the stupa is geared to the pursuit of personal enlightenment and *transcendence*.

The monk spent his days in solitude, meditation, and prayer as a way of seeking *transcendence*.

transcendence (trăn sĕn′ dĕns) means:

   a.   suffering; punishment

   b.   existence beyond or independent of the material universe

   c.   a change from one physical place to another

   d.   public recognition

1. The Great Stupa of Sanchi was designed strictly for the private observance of religion by individuals. However, the Parthenon and Chartres Cathedral served other purposes besides private observance. In addition to religious worship, what *other purposes* did each of them serve?

   Parthenon:

   _____

   _____

   Chartres Cathedral:

   _____

   _____

2. **Overall main idea.** What is the overall main idea the author wants the reader to understand about religious structures such as the Parthenon, the Great Stupa of Sanchi, and Chartres Cathedral? Answer this question in one sentence. Be sure to use the words *art* and *religion* in your overall main idea sentence.

   _____

   _____

   _____

   _____

   _____

   _____

   _____

   _____

Internet Resources

Read More about This Topic on the World Wide Web

Directions: For further information about the topic of the selection, visit these websites:

www.greatbuildings.com
This is one of the leading architecture sites on the Web. *Great Buildings Online* is a gateway to architecture around the world and across history. It documents 1,000 buildings and hundreds of leading architects; it includes photographic images, architectural drawings, three-dimensional models, commentaries, bibliographies, Web links, and more. Type in *Parthenon, Chartres Cathedral,* and *Great Stupa of Sanchi.*

www.refdesk.com
Click on "Reference Desk: Site map," then choose "World Religions" to read more about Buddhism.

You can also use your favorite search engine such as Google, Yahoo!, or Alta-Vista (www.google.com, www.yahoo.com, www.altavista.com) to discover more about this topic. To locate additional information, type in combinations of key-words such as:

Parthenon

or

Great Stupa of Sanchi

or

Chartres Cathedral

or

Acropolis

or

circumambulation

Keep in mind that whenever you go to *any* website, it is a good idea to evaluate the website and the information it contains. Ask yourself questions such as:

"Who sponsors this website?"

"Is the information contained in this website up-to-date?"

"What type of information is presented?"

"Is the information objective and complete?"

"How easy is it to use the features of this website?"

PART 2

Comprehension

Understanding College Textbooks by Reading for Ideas

CHAPTER 4

Determining the Topic and the Stated Main Idea

In this chapter you will learn the answers to these questions:

- Why is it important to determine the topic of a paragraph?

- How can I determine the topic of a paragraph?

- Why is the stated main idea of a paragraph important?

- How can I locate the stated main idea sentence of a paragraph?

SKILLS

The Topic of a Paragraph

- What Is the Topic of a Paragraph, and Why Is It Important?
- Determining and Expressing the Topic

The Stated Main Idea of a Paragraph

- What Is a Stated Main Idea, and Why Is It Important?
- Locating the Stated Main Idea Sentence
- How to Tell If You Have Identified the Stated Main Idea Sentence
- How to Avoid Two Common Errors in Locating a Stated Main Idea
- Stated Overall Main Ideas in Longer Passages

A Word about Standardized Reading Tests: Topics and Stated Main Ideas

CREATING YOUR SUMMARY

Developing Chapter Review Cards

READINGS

Selection 4-1 *(Magazine Article)*
"The New Workforce: People with Disabilities" from *BusinessWeek*
by Michelle Conlin

Selection 4-2 *(Sociology)*
"Latinos: An Emerging Influence in the United States"
from *Sociology: An Introduction*
by Richard J. Gelles and Ann Levine

Selection 4-3 *(History)*
"Muhammad" from *The 100: A Ranking of the Most
Influential Persons in History*
by Michael K. Hart

Reading is to the mind like exercise is to the body.

Sir Richard Steele

A person who does not read good books
has no advantage over a person who cannot read.

Mark Twain

THE TOPIC OF A PARAGRAPH

KEY TERM

topic

Word, name, or phrase that tells who or what the author is writing about.

The topic is also known as the *subject,* or the *subject matter.*

Student Online Learning Center (OLC)
Go to Chapter 4.
Select Video.

Comprehension Monitoring Question for Determining the Topic

Who or what is this paragraph about?

What Is the Topic of a Paragraph, and Why Is It Important?

Every paragraph has a topic, because every paragraph is written about something. That "something" is the topic. A **topic** is a word, name, or phrase that tells what the author is writing about in a paragraph. (There are other names for the topic of a paragraph. In a writing course or an English course, you may hear the topic referred to as the *subject* or *subject matter.* These are simply different terms for the topic.)

The topic is always expressed as a single word (for example, *procrastination*) or a name (for instance, *Bill Gates* or *the Mississippi River*) or as a phrase consisting of two or more words (for instance, *the increasing use of computers in education*). Each sentence in a paragraph should relate in some way to the topic (explain it, tell more about it, give examples of it, etc.). For this reason, the topic may be mentioned several times within a paragraph.

Determining the topic focuses your attention and helps you understand complex paragraphs precisely. It is the essential first step in understanding a passage that you are reading and studying. As you will learn later in this chapter, it is also a key to locating the stated main idea of a paragraph.

Determining and Expressing the Topic

You know from Chapter 2 that effective readers are active and interactive readers who ask questions as they read. When you read a paragraph, you can determine its topic by asking yourself, "Who or what is this paragraph about?" and then answering this question. Paragraphs, especially paragraphs in textbooks, contain various clues that will help you answer this question.

One or more of the following clues often make the topic of a textbook paragraph obvious. The topic is a word, name, or phrase that:

- appears as a *heading* or *title*
- appears in *special type* such as **bold print,** *italics,* or color
- is *repeated* throughout the paragraph
- appears at the beginning of the paragraph and is then referred to throughout the paragraph by *pronouns* (or other words)

A paragraph does not usually contain all of these clues, but every paragraph has at least one of them. Let's look at each clue in more detail.

Determining the topic is the essential first step in understanding a passage that you are reading and studying.

The Topic Is Often Used as the Heading or Title

Textbook authors typically use the topic of a section as the heading or title for that section. The following paragraph from a textbook on business communications illustrates this clue (as well as some others). Read the paragraph and use its heading (and other clues) to determine its topic.

> **Doing Business and Learning about a Culture through Its Language**
>
> The best way to prepare yourself to do business with people from another culture is to learn something about their culture in advance by studying their language. If you plan to live in another country or do business there repeatedly, for example, make an attempt to learn the language of that country. The same holds true if you must work closely with a subculture that has its own language, such as Vietnamese-Americans or Hispanic-Americans. When traveling abroad you may end up doing business with foreigners in your own language, but you will show respect by having made the effort to learn their language. In addition, you will learn something about the culture and its customs in the process. If you do not have the time or opportunity to actually learn a new language, at least learn a few words and phrases.
>
> *Source:* Adapted from Courtland Bovée and John Thill, *Business Communication Today,* 3rd ed., New York: McGraw-Hill, 1992, p. 570.

Stop and Annotate

Go back to the textbook excerpt above. Underline or highlight the heading that indicates the topic.

Notice that in this excerpt, the heading *Doing Business and Learning about a Culture through Its Language* tells you its topic. This phrase describes everything that is discussed in the paragraph: It expresses the topic that all the sentences in the paragraph have in common. (Notice also that the words *business, language, culture,* and *learn* are repeated throughout the paragraph.)

It is important to understand that although the heading of a paragraph is often a clue to the topic, it may not always express the topic completely or accurately. To determine the topic, do not rely *only* on headings; you must also read the paragraph and ask yourself, "Who or what is this paragraph about?"

The Topic Often Appears in Special Print

A second clue to the topic of a paragraph is the use of special print (such as **bold** print, *italics,* or color) to emphasize a word, name, or phrase. The paragraph below is from a textbook on criminal justice. As you read this paragraph, watch for special print that indicates its topic.

> Depending on the nature and severity of the punishment, crimes are considered to be felonies, misdemeanors, or violations. **Felonies** are serious crimes that are subject to punishments of a year or more in prison to capital punishment. **Misdemeanors** are less serious than felonies and are subject to a maximum sentence of one year in jail or a fine. **Violations** are infractions of the law for which normally only a fine can be imposed. Fines can also be imposed for felonies and misdemeanors.
>
> *Source:* Adapted from Freda Adler, Gerhard O. W. Mueller, and William S. Laufer, *Criminal Justice: An Introduction,* 3rd ed., p. 91. Copyright © 2003 by The McGraw-Hill Companies, Inc. Reprinted with permission of The McGraw-Hill Companies.

Stop and Annotate

Go back to the textbook excerpt above. Underline or highlight the words in bold print that indicate the topic.

Notice the three words in bold print: **felonies, misdemeanors,** and **violations.** These words, together, indicate the topic. The paragraph discusses *felonies, misdemeanors* and *violations,* and the differences among these three types of crimes. Keep in mind that the topic can also appear in italics, and that in many college textbooks such key words are printed in color. Special print, then, can often help you identify the topic.

The Topic Is Often Repeated throughout the Paragraph

A third clue to the topic is repetition of a word, name, or phrase throughout a paragraph. Read the paragraph below from a psychology textbook and use this clue to determine its topic.

> Claustrophobia. Acrophobia. Xenophobia. Although these sound like characters in a Greek tragedy, they are actually members of a class of psychological disorders known as phobias. Phobias are intense, irrational fears of specific objects or situations. For example, claustrophobia is a fear of enclosed places, acrophobia a fear of high places, and xenophobia a fear of strangers. Although the objective danger posed by an anxiety-producing stimulus is typically small or nonexistent, to the individual suffering from the phobia it represents great danger, and a full-blown panic attack may follow exposure to the stimulus.
>
> *Source:* Robert S. Feldman, *Understanding Psychology,* 6th ed., p. 479. Copyright © 2002 by The McGraw-Hill Companies, Inc. Reprinted by permission of The McGraw-Hill Companies.

Stop and Annotate

Go back to the textbook excerpt above. Underline or highlight the repeated words that indicate the topic.

Notice that the word *phobias* or *phobia* appears three times in this paragraph, indicating that this is the topic. In addition, three specific types of phobias are given as examples.

The Topic Sometimes Appears Only Once, but Is Then Referred to by Pronouns or Other Words

A fourth clue to the topic of a paragraph is a word, name, or phrase that often appears near the beginning of the paragraph and is then referred to throughout the paragraph by a pronoun (such as *he, she, it, they, his, her, its,* etc.) or other words. Here is a paragraph from a physics textbook. Use this clue to determine the topic of the paragraph.

> Before the age of 30, Isaac Newton had invented the mathematical methods of calculus, demonstrated that white light contained all the colors of the rainbow, and discovered the law of gravitation. Interestingly, this mathematical genius led a lonely and solitary life. His father died before he was born, and after his mother remarried, he was raised by an aged grandmother. In 1661, he was admitted to Cambridge University, where he worked for the next eight years, except for one year at home to escape the plague. During those years, he made his major discoveries, although none were published at that time. His genius was nonetheless recognized, and in 1669 he was appointed Lucasion Professor of Mathematics at Cambridge University, a position he retained until 1695. His major scientific work was completed prior to 1692, when he suffered a nervous breakdown. After his recovery, he determined to lead a more public life, and soon became the Master of the Mint in London. He was elected president of the Royal Society in 1703, and held that position until his death.
>
> *Source:* Adapted from Frederick Bueche, *Principles of Physics,* 5th ed., p. 70. Copyright © 1988 by The McGraw-Hill Companies, Inc. Reprinted by permission of The McGraw-Hill Companies.

Stop and Annotate

Go back to the textbook excerpt above. Underline or highlight the topic, the pronouns, and other words that refer to the topic.

Notice that Newton's name appears only in the first sentence, but it is obvious from the words *this mathematical genius* and the pronouns *he* and *his* that the rest of the paragraph continues to discuss him. Therefore, *Isaac Newton* is the topic of this paragraph.

Be sure you understand that authors sometimes present the topic (a word, name, or phrase) at or near the beginning of a paragraph, but then refer to the topic by one or more *other* words, rather than just by pronouns. For instance, a paragraph might begin "Pneumonia is . . ." and then might say something such as "This disease is characterized by . . ." and "The condition worsens when . . ." and "The disorder is typically treated by . . ." In this case, the words *disease, condition,* and *disorder* refer to *pneumonia* and indicate that pneumonia is the topic of the paragraph. (In the preceding example, you saw *Isaac Newton* referred to as *this mathematical genius* as well as by pronouns.)

It is important to be precise when you express the topic of a paragraph. If you choose a word or a phrase that is too general or too specific, it will not describe the topic accurately. A topic described in terms that are *too general,* or too broad, will go beyond what is discussed in the paragraph. A topic described in terms that are *too specific,* or too narrow, will fail to cover everything discussed in the paragraph. Suppose, for instance, that the topic of a paragraph is the phrase *causes of gang violence.* The word *gangs,* the word *violence,* or the phrase *gang violence,* would be too general to express this topic precisely. The paragraph could be about many different things that pertain to gangs or violence. On the other hand, the phrase *lack of parental supervision as a cause of gang violence* would be too specific, even though "lack of parental supervision" might be mentioned in the paragraph as one of the causes.

Keep in mind that it is often possible to express a topic correctly in more than one way. For example, the topic of a paragraph could be correctly expressed as *Winston Churchill's childhood, the childhood of Winston Churchill, Churchill's life as a child, Churchill's boyhood,* or *Churchill's youth,* since all these phrases mean the same thing. Keep in mind, too, that (as the examples show) the topic is *never* expressed as a complete sentence. You must always express the topic as a single word or as a phrase (a group of words).

Determining a topic precisely is the starting point in comprehending as you read. It is also a key to locating the main idea sentence in a paragraph, as you will see in the next section of this chapter.

THE STATED MAIN IDEA OF A PARAGRAPH

What Is a Stated Main Idea, and Why Is It Important?

KEY TERM

stated main idea

The sentence in a paragraph that contains both the topic and the author's single most important point about this topic.

A stated main idea sentence is also known as the *topic sentence.*

Student Online Learning Center (OLC)
Go to **Chapter 4.**
Select **Video.**

Every paragraph has a main idea. A **stated main idea** is a sentence within a paragraph that contains both the topic and the author's single most important point about this topic. (There are various terms for a stated main idea. In a writing course or an English course, the main idea sentence of a paragraph may be called the *topic sentence.*) Unlike the topic, which is always a single word, name, or phrase, the main idea is always expressed as a complete sentence.

Do not select a question from a paragraph as the stated main idea, because the stated main idea is always written as a statement. The stated main idea is *never* written in the form of a question, but the stated main idea sentence will often be the *answer* to a question the author presents at the beginning of a paragraph.

As you learned at the beginning of this chapter, the topic of a paragraph tells who or what the paragraph is about. The topic is always expressed as a word, name, or phrase, never as a sentence. A stated main idea, however, is always a *sentence.* It goes further than the topic because this sentence expresses the author's *one most important point* about the topic. For example, the main idea sentence in a paragraph whose topic is *procrastination* might be, "Procrastination is the major cause of stress for college students." This sentence includes the topic, *procrastination,* and tells the important point the author is making about *procrastination.* Because the word *main* means "most important," there can be only *one* main, or most important, idea in any paragraph. This is only logical: Two or three different sentences can't all be the one most important sentence.

A main idea is called a *stated main idea* when the author presents it (in other words, the author *states* it) as one of the sentences in the paragraph. An author can place his or her stated main idea sentence anywhere in the paragraph: at the beginning, end, or even in the middle. In this chapter, you will practice only with paragraphs that contain stated main ideas. Sometimes, however, an author does not state the main idea of a paragraph directly. In that case, the main idea is called an *implied main idea,* and the reader must create a sentence that states the author's main point. (Implied main ideas are discussed in Chapter 5.)

There are several reasons it is important to determine main ideas when you are studying:

* To increase your comprehension
* To enable you to mark textbooks effectively and take notes as you study
* To enable you to write summaries and outlines
* To help you identify and remember important material for tests

For these reasons, effective readers focus on main ideas.

Locating the Stated Main Idea Sentence

Steps to Follow

Comprehension Monitoring Question for Stated Main Idea

What is the single most important point the author wants me to understand about the topic of this paragraph?

Student Online Learning Center (OLC)
Go to Chapter 4.
Select Video.

Because a stated main idea is one of the sentences in the paragraph, your task is simply to determine *which* sentence is the main idea. Often, the stated main idea will be obvious. To identify the stated main idea sentence, find the sentence that contains both the topic and the most important point about it.

To locate the stated main idea, follow these two steps:

* **Step 1.**   After you have read the paragraph, determine the topic by asking yourself, "Who or what is the passage about?" and then answering this question. (Use the clues you learned earlier in this chapter for determining the topic.)

* **Step 2.**   Locate the main idea sentence by asking yourself, "What is the single most important point the author wants me to understand about the topic of this paragraph?" Then search the paragraph for the sentence that answers this question. That sentence is the stated main idea.

Here is a simple formula that gives the essential parts of any stated main idea sentence:

| The *topic* | + | Author's *most important point* about the topic | = | Main idea sentence |

Authors can put a stated main idea sentence anywhere in a paragraph. However, they usually put it at the beginning of a paragraph. The next most common place is at the end of a paragraph. Of course, a stated main idea can also be placed elsewhere within the paragraph. Let's look at examples of each.

Where a Stated Main Idea Sentence May Appear in a Paragraph

Authors often put their stated main idea sentence at the beginning of the paragraph. Although authors could put the main idea sentence anywhere in the paragraph, they often put it first because it makes it easier for the reader to comprehend the single most important point in the paragraph. Especially in textbooks, authors are likely to start a paragraph with the main idea.

The following excerpt from a textbook on career planning is an example in which the main idea has been stated at the beginning of the paragraph. The topic of this paragraph is *beginning a new job.* Read the paragraph and ask yourself, "What is the most important point the authors want me to understand about beginning a new job?" The sentence that answers this question, the first sentence, is the main idea.

> Beginning a new job is always exciting and sometimes intimidating. There is an invigorating feeling of a fresh start and a clean slate. You face new challenges and draw on a renewed sense of energy as you approach them. But you may also feel apprehensive about this new adventure. Will it actually turn out as well as you hope? You are entering a strange environment, and you must learn to work with new associates. If you were laid off or fired from your last job, you may feel particularly sensitive. "What if it happens again?" you ask yourself.
>
> *Source:* William Morin and James Cabrera, *Parting Company: How to Survive the Loss of a Job and Find Another,* San Diego, CA: Harcourt, Brace, 1982, p. 238.

Stop and Annotate

Go back to the textbook excerpt above. Underline or highlight the stated main idea sentence.

The first sentence in the excerpt is a general one that mentions two different types of feelings people often have as they start a new job. Since the most important point the authors want you to understand is that people may have *both* types of feelings, this sentence is the main idea of the paragraph: *Beginning a new job is always exciting and sometimes intimidating.* The rest of the paragraph presents specific details that support this sentence as the main idea: The first half of the paragraph explains why starting a new job is *exciting,* and the last half of the paragraph explains why it can be *intimidating.* In this paragraph, then, the first sentence states the main idea, and the rest of the sentences are details that tell more about it.

The author may place a stated main idea sentence at the end of a paragraph. Frequently, the last sentence of a paragraph is the stated main idea. Authors sometimes prefer to lead up to their main point, and so they place it at the end of the paragraph. They know it can be helpful to the reader if they first give an explanation, provide background information or present examples, and then state their main idea.

Read the excerpt below from a sociology textbook. The topic of this paragraph is *ethnocentrism.* As you read the paragraph, ask yourself, "What is the most important point the author wants me to understand about the term *ethnocentrism?*" The sentence that answers this question, the last sentence, is the stated main idea.

> It is tempting to evaluate the practices of other cultures on the basis of our own perspectives. For example, Westerners who think cattle are to be used for food might look down on India's Hindu religion and culture, which views the cow as sacred. Or people in one culture may dismiss as unthinkable the mate-selection or child-rearing practices of another culture. Sociologist William Graham Sumner (1906) coined the term **ethnocentrism** to refer to the tendency to assume that one's culture and way of life represent the norm or are superior to all others.
>
> *Source:* Adapted from Richard Schaefer, *Sociology,* 9th ed., p. 73. Copyright © 2005 by The McGraw-Hill Companies, Inc. Reprinted with permission of The McGraw-Hill Companies.

Stop and Annotate

Go back to the textbook excerpt above. Underline or highlight the stated main idea sentence.

In this paragraph, the first sentence is an introductory one. The second and third sentences give examples of how people in one culture might look down on or reject aspects of other cultures. The last sentence is the main idea because it states the author's most important point: that *ethnocentrism* is the term used to describe the tendency to assume that one's culture and way of life represent the norm or are superior to all others. Notice that this stated main idea sentence contains the topic and that the topic is in bold.

Authors sometimes put the stated main idea sentence within the paragraph. Sometimes the stated main idea sentence is neither the first nor the last sentence of a paragraph, but rather one of the other sentences in the paragraph. That is, the stated main idea appears within the paragraph. Sometimes authors begin a paragraph with an introductory comment or question designed to get the reader's attention, or with some background information. Then they present their main idea. The rest of the information in the paragraph then explains or tells more about the main idea, or gives examples. (Helpful hint: Whenever a paragraph begins with a question, expect the author to then answer that important question. Moreover, the answer is often the main idea of the paragraph.)

Here is a paragraph from a government textbook in which the second sentence is the main idea sentence. The topic is *television commercials and presidential campaigns.* As you read this paragraph, ask yourself, "What is the most important point the author wants me to understand about television commercials and presidential campaigns?"

> In addition to television interviews and debates, presidential campaigns include political advertising in the form of televised commercials. Television commercials are by far the most expensive part of presidential campaigns. Since 1976, political commercials on television have accounted for about half of the candidates' expenditures in the general election campaign. In 1992 Bush and Clinton each spent more than $30 million on advertising in the general election, and Perot spent even more. Perot relied heavily on "infomercials"—30-minute and hour-long commercials that emphasized substance over slogans.
>
> *Source:* Thomas E. Patterson, *The American Democracy,* 3rd ed., p. 398. Copyright © 1996 by The McGraw-Hill Companies, Inc. Reprinted by permission of The McGraw-Hill Companies.

The author's second sentence presents his most important point: *Television commercials are by far the most expensive part of presidential campaigns.* The first sentence introduces the use of televised commercials in presidential campaigns. Each of the other sentences presents facts or examples that demonstrate how expensive television campaign commercials have become.

How to Tell If You Have Identified the Stated Main Idea Sentence

Stated Main Idea Checklist

How can you tell if you have *correctly* identified an author's stated main idea sentence in a paragraph? You have found the stated main idea sentence if the sentence has these five characteristics:

- The sentence contains the topic.
- The sentence states the *single* most important point about the topic.
- The sentence is general enough to cover all the information in the paragraph.
- The sentence makes complete sense by itself (in other words, a reader could understand it without having to read the rest of the paragraph).
- The other sentences introduce, explain, or tell more about the main idea sentence.

Here is an example of the last item on the list. The following sentence could be a main idea sentence since it makes sense by itself: *Most historians consistently rank Abraham Lincoln among the five greatest presidents of the United States.* On the other hand, this sentence would not be meaningful by itself since the reader would not know who "him" refers to: *Most historians consistently rank him among the five greatest presidents of the United States.* This sentence could not be a correct main idea sentence because it says "him" rather than "Abraham Lincoln."

When you locate a stated main idea sentence in your textbooks, you should highlight or underline it. Be sure to mark the entire sentence. (Marking textbooks is discussed in Chapter 11.)

How to Avoid Two Common Errors in Locating a Stated Main Idea

You have learned that a stated main idea sentence is most often the first or last sentence of a paragraph, and so you may be tempted to try to take a shortcut by reading only the first and last sentences. This is a common error you should avoid. You must read the entire paragraph to identify the main idea accurately. You will not be able to compare the sentences to evaluate which is the most important unless you read the entire paragraph. And you may miss a stated main idea sentence that occurs within the paragraph.

A second common error can occur when a paragraph is difficult. In this case, you may be tempted to select a sentence as the main idea simply because it contains familiar or interesting information, or because it seems to "sound important." These are not valid reasons for choosing a sentence as the stated main idea. To avoid this mistake, remind yourself that the stated main idea sentence must always answer the question, "What is the *single most important point* the author wants me to understand about the topic of this paragraph?"

Stated Overall Main Ideas in Longer Passages

Locating stated main ideas is a skill that can also be applied to passages longer than a single paragraph, such as sections of a textbook chapter, short reading selections, and essays. You will sometimes discover a sentence in a longer passage (usually an introductory or concluding sentence) that expresses the most important point or the overall message of the *entire passage.* This sentence is called the *overall main idea.* (There are various terms for an overall main idea. In a writing course or an English course, the overall main idea of an essay or an article may be called the *thesis statement* or *thesis.*) The chapter reading selections in *Opening Doors* include an exercise called Respond in Writing. As you may have noticed, the final item gives you practice in determining the overall main idea of the entire selection.

A WORD ABOUT STANDARDIZED READING TESTS: TOPICS AND STATED MAIN IDEAS

Many college students are required to take standardized reading tests as part of an overall assessment program, in a reading course, or as part of a state-mandated basic skills test, such as CLAST (in Florida) or THEA (in Texas). A standardized reading test typically consists of a series of passages, each of which is followed by multiple-choice reading skill application questions. The test is often a timed test, that is, students are permitted to work for only a specified amount of time. Included in Part Two of *Opening Doors* are tips that can help you earn higher scores on standardized reading tests. The tips below deal with determining topics and stated main ideas.

To begin with, you should be aware that students sometimes miss questions on reading tests because they do not realize what they are being asked. If the wording of an item is even slightly unfamiliar, they may not recognize that they are being asked to apply a reading comprehension skill they already know. Therefore, you should learn to recognize certain types of questions no matter how they are worded, just as you recognize your friends no matter what they are wearing.

You are being asked to identify the topic of a passage when the test question begins:

The best title for this selection is . . .

This passage discusses . . .

This passage focuses mainly on . . .

The topic of this passage is . . .

This passage is about . . .

This passage concerns . . .

The problem the author is discussing in this passage is . . .

The author is explaining the nature of . . .

To find the right answer, simply ask yourself, "Who or what is this passage about?" Then see which answer choice most closely matches your answer. Remember to use the four clues for determining topics: titles or headings, words emphasized in special print, repetition, and a mention of the topic that is then referred to by pronouns or other words.

You are being asked to identify the main idea when the question is worded:

The author's main point is that . . .

The principal idea of this passage is that . . .

Which of the following best expresses the main idea of this paragraph?

Which of the following is the main idea of the last paragraph? (or some specified paragraph)

Which of the following best expresses the main idea of the entire passage?

To find the right answer, ask yourself, "What is the single most important point the author wants me to understand about the topic?" Next, search the paragraph or passage for a sentence that answers this question. Finally, read each of the choices and select the one that is the same as the sentence you selected or that *means* essentially the same thing even if the wording is different.

SELECTION **4-1**

Magazine Article

The New Workforce: People with Disabilities

From *BusinessWeek*
By Michelle Conlin

Prepare Yourself to Read

Directions: Do these exercises *before* you read Selection 4-1.

1. Magazine articles are typically written in a straightforward, journalistic style. Preview this selection by reading the following:

    Introduction

    Title

    First paragraph (paragraph 1)

    First sentence of each paragraph

    Last paragraph (paragraph 20)

2. After you have previewed the selection, answer these questions:

    Who do you think the "new workforce" might be?

    _____

    _____

    _____

    Why do you think these people are now entering the workforce in large numbers?

    _____

    _____

    _____

    _____

Apply Comprehension Skills

Directions: Do the Annotation Practice Exercises *as* you read Selection 4-1. Apply the two skills from this chapter:

Determine the topic. When you read a paragraph, ask yourself, "Who or what is this about?"

Identify the stated main idea. As you read, ask yourself, "What is the most important point the author wants me to understand about the topic?" Then search for the sentence that answers this question.

Complete the Annotation Practice Exercises. In these exercises, you will work only with paragraphs that have stated main ideas.

THE NEW WORKFORCE: PEOPLE WITH DISABILITIES

Did you know that one out of every five people in the United States has a disability? This means that there are more than 54 million American men, women, and children who are disabled. Ready for an even more shocking figure? According to researchers' estimates, as the population ages, one in every three persons in our country will become disabled in some way. Some will experience a temporary disability; for others, the disability will be permanent. The disability may be present at birth, may come on gradually (as with a progressive illness), or may occur suddenly (from an accident, for example). This means that virtually all of us will know disability either firsthand or through the experience of family members, friends, or coworkers. Fortunately, attitudes toward the disabled, especially in the workforce, are changing for a variety of reasons. The article below, from BusinessWeek magazine, explores why this change is occurring and examines some barriers that still remain between the disabled and a good job.

1   The Gap's emporium of affordable chic in midtown Manhattan throbs with New Economy action. Salesclerks sporting headsets race across the store to wait on tourists and time-starved New Yorkers. Stockboys heave huge boxes overflowing with clothes. At the center of this retail hubbub is Gap's "wild man in a wheelchair," supersalesman Wilfredo "Freddy" Laboy, a fast-talking, goateed 36-year-old who lost his legs when he fell off a freight train at age 9. Freddy dances across the store, popping wheelies and spinning himself around to the bouncy pop music. Little kids stare as he hops off his chair and onto the floor to grab a tangerine-colored T-shirt and then pulls himself up on his stump to reach for another pair of khakis. Instead of using the elevator, he prefers to horrify colleagues by scooting himself down the stairs. "It's faster," he says.

2   Freddy loves the Gap, and the Gap loves Freddy. But just six months ago, the story was altogether different. An amateur wheelchair basketball star who pulled himself through the New York City Marathon, Freddy was used to letting nothing stand in his way. But even with New York City's unemployment level at record lows, he couldn't find a job. Once prospective employers caught sight of his legless torso, they lost interest.

3   Still, on a whim, Freddy wheeled himself into the Gap last October. To his astonishment, they hired him. "I finally got accepted somewhere because they didn't just see the wheelchair," says the married father of three. "They saw me."

4   Freddy may well be at the cusp of a huge change rocking the world of the workplace, marking the first time in history that people with disabilities have been poised to enter Corporate America en masse—many of them with the help of wheelchairs and seeing-eye dogs.

Annotation Practice Exercises

Directions: For each exercise below,

- Write the topic of the paragraph on the lines beside the paragraph.
- Underline or highlight the stated main idea sentence of the paragraph.

This will help you remember the topic and the stated main idea.

5   Facing the worst labor shortage in modern history, recruiters are tapping the kinds of workers they would have easily blown off just 10 years ago: prepubescent wireheads, grandmothers—even convicted murderers. Next up are the disabled, who may prove to be the last great hope—if only because they're the only labor pool that hasn't been completely drained. At the same time, groundbreaking technology is creating ways for people with disabilities to better perform jobs, helping to erase the deep divisions that once existed between them and everybody else.

6   Sure, a few companies have a long record of hiring workers with disabilities. In the 1980s—still the Dark Ages of the movement—Marriott International Inc. was doing the unheard-of: paying adults with Down's Syndrome $7 an hour to work 40 hours a week cleaning rooms and sweeping floors. But that was the exception. Despite the Americans with Disabilities Act (ADA), passed in July 1990, only 25 percent of the country's 15 million disabled who are also of working age are employed. Of the 75 percent who aren't working, Harris Polls indicate that two-thirds of them wish they could be. Says Paul H. Wehman, director of the rehabilitation research center at Virginia Commonwealth University: "The dirty little secret of the welfare-to-work movement is that people with disabilities got left out."

7   That may be about to change. Never before has it been so easy and made so much economic sense for companies to invest in workers with disabilities by making accommodations for them. "We can use new technologies to contribute to society in ways that weren't really possible when I started 25 years ago," says Michael Coleman, IBM's vice-president for global operations. Coleman, who lost both his hands in Vietnam when he was trying to defuse a bomb, is IBM's top-ranking disabled worker. He is also chairing the company's task force to find ways to employ more workers with disabilities.

8   Crestar Bank has already found ways to make that happen. Newfangled voice-activated technology means that callers to the bank never know that customer service representative Chris Harmon is a quadriplegic. He is so disabled that the recruiter who hired him had to stick a pen in his mouth so he could sign the employment application. At the company's Richmond (Va.) call center, he simply tells his computer what to do and the information appears on the screen in a flash.

9   Crestar is one of a growing list of businesses that is mining the ranks of the disabled to solve labor crises they say would otherwise have been catastrophic. Turns out that what began as a last-ditch maneuver to stem this worker drought has yielded an unexpected boon that veteran employers of people with disabilities have long known about: The disabled

Salesman extraordinaire Freddy Laboy couldn't find a job until he wheeled himself into a Gap in Midtown Manhattan.

Practice Exercise

• Topic of paragraph 7:

_____

_____

• Underline or highlight the stated main idea of paragraph 7.

are often more proficient, productive, and efficient than "normies," according to researchers.

10   A 30-year study by DuPont revealed that job performance by workers with disabilities was equal to or better than that of fully functioning peers. The disabled had a 90% above-average job performance, with safety and attendance records that were far above the norm, too. Perhaps most enticing to human-resource heads pulling their hair out over the dot-com-induced worker exodus is the fact that people with disabilities can often be far more loyal to the employers who gave them a break and are therefore less likely to be lured away by a boss dangling a bigger paycheck.

11   But until recently, the disabled were actually penalized for finding a job because even a minimum-wage gig flipping burgers or mopping floors meant the automatic loss of Medicaid benefits. That huge barrier to employment fell in December 1999, when President Clinton signed the Workers Incentives Improvement Act, clearing the path for states to change Medicaid laws to let the disabled hang on to much-needed benefits while entering the workforce.

12   The move came none too soon. Already, temporary agency Manpower Inc. is raiding the ranks of the disabled to fill its employee rolls. The National Disability Council reports a 50% jump in requests for workers with disabilities from companies as diverse as Merrill Lynch & Co. and Microsoft Corp.

13   In fact, Microsoft is so eager to hire such workers that the software company is spearheading the Able to Work program, a consortium of 22 businesses scrambling to find the best ways to place disabled people in jobs. Says Microsoft's director of diversity, Santiago Rodriguez: "Until now, the whole country has been at a loss as to how to do this."

14   To many advocates for the disabled, this confusion is a disappointment. The ADA was passed with great hopes of creating jobs and access for America's disabled population of 54 million. It prohibited employers from refusing to hire qualified applicants who also had disabilities. It also mandated that the disabled have access to telecommunications equipment and public transportation.

15   But barriers standing between most people with disabilities and a good, solid job haven't exactly been wiped out by employee sensitivity training courses and curb-cut accessible sidewalks. Those and other strides have helped, but problems still abound. Cities such as Chicago and New Orleans face lawsuits for failing to bring their public transportation systems into compliance.

16   There are also, disability advocates say, still too many lawsuits like the one brought on behalf of a mentally retarded janitor, Don Perkl, who loved scrubbing toilets for Chuck E. Cheese in Madison, Wis. A district manager, a lawsuit alleges, fired him after saying "We don't hire people like that." The

Practice Exercise

- Topic of paragraph 10:

_____

_____

_____

- Underline or highlight the stated main idea of paragraph 10.

Practice Exercise

- Topic of paragraph 15:

_____

_____

_____

- Underline or highlight the stated main idea of paragraph 15.

pizza parlor's local manager and two other employees quit in protest because they claimed the perennially upbeat Perkl was doing such a stellar job. Last year, a jury in federal court in the Western District of Wisconsin agreed with them, slapping the company with $13 million in punitive damages—the largest ADA award ever for a single plaintiff. A judge is still reviewing the jury's verdict. Chuck E. Cheese claims that Perkl "wasn't dismissed due to his disability but because he couldn't perform the job," says company spokesman Jon Rice.

17   Plenty of other lawsuits brought under the ADA have caused critics to question its scope. Some worry that the act is not broad enough, pointing to a recent Supreme Court ruling that established that people with treatable disabilities don't qualify for protection. Others say the ADA is straying into the realm of the absurd, noting such cases as the employee with bad body odor who argued she should be protected from getting fired because her glandular problem qualified her as disabled.

18   But most of the country's workers with disabilities face challenges that are far more clear-cut: They are deaf, blind, paralyzed, or emotionally impaired. Some have been burdened with disabilities since they were born. Others, like Booz, Allen & Hamilton Inc. principal Jeffrey Schaffer, are new to the minority—a group that one in three people will be a part of during their lives. Three years ago, Schaffer's car was in a head-on collision with another vehicle that swerved into his lane on a windy back road in West Virginia. It took paramedics an hour to cut him from the wreckage.

19   After learning he would be confined to a wheelchair, Schaffer says, the thought of returning to work was the thing that kept him going. "Getting back to work was critical to my sense of well-being," says Schaffer from the bed of a hospital where he has just undergone his sixth operation since the accident. "Work ends up being a defining characteristic for self-worth."

20   For worker-starved companies, spreading that kind of self-worth around is looking more and more like the only answer to today's labor-shortage woes. Still, the real test will be when the economy cools and companies can afford to get picky about choosing between applicants with disabilities and everyone else. By then, though, it may be a lot harder to tell the difference.

Practice Exercise

• Topic of paragraph 17:

_____

_____

_____

• Underline or highlight the stated main idea of paragraph 17.

Source: Michelle Conlin, "The New Workforce," *BusinessWeek,* March 20, 2000, pp. 64–68. Reprinted with permission.

SELECTION **4-1**

Magazine Article
(Continued)

Reading Selection Quiz

This quiz has three parts. Your instructor may assign some or all of them.

Comprehension

Directions: Items 1–10 test your comprehension (understanding) of the material of this selection. These questions are the type a content area instructor (such as a business professor) would ask on a test over this material. You should be able to answer these questions after studying this selection. For each comprehension question below, use information from the selection to determine the correct answer. Refer to the selection as you answer each questions. Write your answer in the space provided.

True or False

_____ 1. The Americans with Disabilities Act has been highly effective in helping disabled Americans enter the workforce.

_____ 2. People with disabilities tend to be more loyal than other workers to employers who give them a chance.

_____ 3. Seventy-five percent of disabled Americans who are not working wish they could be.

_____ 4. One study revealed that 90 percent of disabled workers had an above-average job performance, but their safety and attendance records were far below the norm.

Multiple-Choice

_____ 5. More disabled people are now entering the workforce because of the:
   a. new economy.
   b. worst labor shortage in modern history.
   c. new technologies that make it easier for companies to accommodate workers with disabilities.
   d. all of the above

_____ 6. Until recently the disabled were actually penalized for finding a job because:
   a. they were paid less than other workers.
   b. they lost their Medicaid benefits if they entered the workforce.
   c. their disabilities made the workplace less safe for them.
   d. they had to work harder than "normies."

_____ **7.** The number of disabled Americans is:

    a. 54 million.

    b. 36 million.

    c. 22 million.

    d. 15 million.

_____ **8.** How many people will become disabled during their lives?

    a. three in four

    b. one in two

    c. one in three

    d. four in five

_____ **9.** Which of the following would be a violation of the Americans with Disabilities Act?

    a. refusing to hire qualified applicants who have disabilities

    b. lack of accessible telecommunications equipment

    c. unavailability of public transportation

    d. all of the above

_____ **10.** Companies' attitudes toward hiring the disabled:

    a. have not changed in decades.

    b. have worsened.

    c. have improved dramatically.

    d. should begin to change during the next decade.

SELECTION **4-1**

Magazine Article

(Continued)

Vocabulary in Context

Directions: Items 11–20 test your ability to determine the meaning of a word by using context clues. *Context clues* are words in a sentence that allow the reader to deduce (reason out) the meaning of an unfamiliar word in that sentence. Context clues also enable the reader to determine which meaning the author intends when a word has more than one meaning. For each vocabulary item below, a sentence from the selection containing an important word (*italicized, like this*) is quoted first. Next, there is an additional sentence using the word in the same sense and providing another context clue. Use the context clues from *both* sentences to deduce the meaning of the italicized word. *Be sure the answer you choose makes sense in both sentences.* If you discover that you need to use a dictionary to confirm an answer choice, remember that the meaning you select must still fit the context of *both* sentences. Write your answer in the space provided.

Pronunciation Key: ă **pat** ā **pay** âr **care** ä **father** ě **pet** ē **be** ĭ **pit**
ī **tie** îr **pier** ŏ **pot** ō **toe** ô **paw** oi **noise** ou **out** o͝o **took**
o͞o **boot** ŭ **cut** yo͞o **abuse** ûr **urge** th **thin** *th* **this** hw **which**
zh **vision** ə **about** *Stress mark:* ′

11. Once *prospective* employers caught sight of his legless torso, they lost interest.

Prospective students are often invited to visit and take a tour of a college they are considering attending.

prospective (prə spĕk′ tĭv) means:

a. highly intelligent

b. likely to be or become

c. inclined to be competitive

d. tending to be selfish

12. Newfangled voice-activated technology means that callers to the bank never know that customer service representative Chris Harmon is a *quadriplegic.*

After the mountain climber broke his neck in a fall and became a *quadriplegic,* all he could move was his head.

quadriplegic (kwŏd rə plē′ jĭk) means:

a. person who is completely paralyzed from the neck down

b. person whose lower body is paralyzed

c. person whose arms are paralyzed

d. person whose vocal cords are paralyzed

13. Crestar is one of a growing list of businesses that is mining the ranks of the disabled to solve labor crises that they say would otherwise be *catastrophic.*

The entire town was destroyed by the *catastrophic* tornado.

catastrophic (kă tə strŏ′ fĭk) means:

a. having an unknown outcome

b. having a disastrous outcome

c. having an undetermined outcome

d. having a unexpectedly pleasant outcome

14. Turns out that what began as a last-ditch maneuver to stem the worker drought has yielded an unexpected *boon* that veteran employers have long known about: The disabled are often more proficient, productive, and efficient than "normies," according to researchers.

Receiving the scholarship was a real *boon* to Luis because it enabled him to quit work and go to school full time.

boon (boon) means:

a. side effect

b. problem

c. benefit

d. hindrance

_____ **15.** Perhaps most *enticing* to human-resource heads pulling their hair out over the dot-com-induced worker exodus is the fact that people with disabilities are often far more loyal to the employers who gave them a break and are therefore less likely to be lured away by a boss dangling a bigger paycheck.

The aroma of the fresh-baked cookies was so *enticing* that we went into the bakery and bought a dozen.

enticing (ĕn tī′ sĭng) means:

a.   upsetting

b.   causing puzzlement or confusion

c.   attracting by arousing desire

d.   misunderstood

_____ **16.** Perhaps the most enticing to human-resource heads pulling their hair out over the dot-com-induced worker *exodus* is the fact that people with disabilities are often far more loyal to the employers who gave them a break and are therefore less likely to be lured away by a boss dangling a bigger paycheck.

When rumors began to spread of a possible terrorist attack, there was an *exodus* from the city.

exodus (ĕk′ sə dəs) means:

a.   general, widespread panic

b.   a closing off or enclosing

c.   redistribution of people

d.   departure of a large number of people

_____ **17.** It also *mandated* that the disabled have access to telecommunications equipment and public transportation.

Desegregation of public schools was *mandated* in 1954 by the Supreme Court decision in a case known as *Brown v. Board of Education of Topeka.*

mandated (măn′ dā təd) means:

a.   required

b.   overturned

c.   questionable

d.   changed

_____ **18.** But the barriers standing between most people with disabilities and a good, solid job haven't exactly been wiped out by employee sensitivity training courses and curb-cut *accessible* sidewalks.

Wheelchair ramps, electric door openers, and elevators were added to make the public library *accessible* to the elderly and the disabled.

accessible (ăk sĕs′ ə bəl) means:

a.   off-limits

b.   more pleasing

       c.   more attractive

       d.   easily approached or entered

_____ **19.** Cities such as Chicago and New Orleans face lawsuits for failing to bring their public transportation systems into *compliance.*

The company reviewed its accounting procedures to be sure they were in *compliance* with the new laws.

compliance (kəm plī′ əns) means:

    a.   disagreement

    b.   agreement with a demand

    c.   popularity

    d.   good repair

_____ **20.** There are also, disability *advocates* say, still too many lawsuits like the one brought on behalf of a mentally retarded janitor, Don Perkl, who loved scrubbing toilets for Chuck E. Cheese in Madison, Wis.

Advocates for animal rights staged a demonstration in front of the department store to protest the sale of fur coats.

advocates (ăd′ və kəts) means:

    a.   protesters

    b.   advisers

    c.   teachers

    d.   supporters

SELECTION **4-1**   *Reading Skills Application*

Magazine Article
(Continued)

Directions: Items 21–25 test your ability to *apply* certain reading skills to information in this selection. These types of questions provide valuable practice for all students, especially those who must take standardized reading tests and state-mandated basic skills tests (such as the Florida CLAST Test and the Texas THEA Test). You may not have studied all of the skills at this point, so these items will serve as a helpful preview. The comprehension and critical reading skills in this section are presented in Chapters 4 through 9 of *Opening Doors;* vocabulary and figurative language skills are presented in Chapter 2. As you work through *Opening Doors,* you will practice and develop these skills. Write your answer for each question in the space provided.

_____ **21.** Which of the following is the meaning of *normies* as it is used in paragraph 9?

    a.   employers

    b.   workers

    c.   people without disabilities

    d.   people with disabilities

_____ **22.** The author mentions the Able to Work Program to show that:

    a. corporations are now interested in the best ways to place disabled workers in jobs.

    b. people with disabilities are able to work.

    c. technology can help disabled workers.

    d. some employers still refuse to hire disabled persons.

_____ **23.** The primary reason the author wrote this selection was to:

    a. explain how and why the disabled are now entering the workforce in significant numbers.

    b. convince employers to hire disabled workers.

    c. change people's attitudes towards the disabled.

    d. increase public awareness of the Americans with Disabilities Act.

_____ **24.** The author would be most likely to agree with which of the following?

    a. Discrimination in employment against the disabled has finally ended.

    b. More disabled people should seek jobs.

    c. Most corporations treat their disabled workers unfairly.

    d. Being able to work elevates a person's sense of self-esteem.

_____ **25.** The information in paragraph 11 is organized using which of these patterns?

    a. comparison

    b. problem-solution

    c. sequence

    d. contrast

SELECTION **4-1**

Magazine Article
(Continued)

Collaboration Option

Respond in Writing

Directions: Refer to Selection 4-1 as needed to answer the essay-type questions below.

Option for collaboration: Your instructor may direct you to work with other students on one or more of these items, or in other words, to work *collaboratively.* In that case, you should form groups of three or four students, as directed by your instructor, and work together to complete the exercises. After your group discusses an item and agrees on the answer, have a group member record it. Each member of your group should be able to explain all of your group's answers.

1. How would you react to seeing an obviously disabled person such as Freddy Laboy working in a Gap store? How would the presence of such an employee influence your opinion of the store?

  _____

  _____

  _____

2. Some able-bodied people treat the disabled as if they were invisible. Why do you think this happens?

_____

_____

_____

3. What are some ways that technology could be used to adapt the workplace for disabled workers? Give at least three examples.

_____

_____

_____

4. According to the selection, one-third of all Americans will become disabled to some extent during their lives. List at least five ways in which a person could become disabled.

_____

_____

_____

_____

_____

5. **Overall main idea.** What is the overall main idea the author wants you to understand about the "new workforce?" Answer this question in one sentence. Be sure that your overall main idea sentence includes the topic (*disabled people* or the new workforce) and tells the overall most important point about it. Do not begin your sentence with "The overall main idea is . . ." or "The author wants us to understand . . ." Just *state* the overall main idea.

_____

_____

_____

_____

Internet Resources

Read More about This Topic on the World Wide Web

Directions: For further information about the topic of the selection, visit these websites:

www.nod.org
This is the website for the National Organization on Disability (NOD), which promotes full and equal participation in all aspects of life by America's 54 million men, women, and children with disabilities. NOD is the only national disability network organization concerned with all disabilities, all age groups, and all issues related to disability.

www.ablelink.org
Ability OnLine is a friendly and safe computer friendship network (electronic bulletin board) where young people with disabilities or chronic illnesses connect to each other as well as to their friends, family members, caregivers, and supporters. Free and easy to use.

janweb.icdi.wvu.edu
The Job Accommodation Network (JAN) is not a job placement service, but an international toll-free consulting service that provides information about job accommodations and the employability of people with disabilities. JAN also provides information regarding the Americans with Disabilities Act (ADA). More than 250 links.

You can also use your favorite search engine such as Google, Yahoo!, or AltaVista (www.google.com, www.yahoo.com, www.altavista.com) to discover more about this topic. To locate additional information, type in combinations of keywords such as:

disabled workers

or

services for disabled workers

or

jobs for disabled workers

Keep in mind that whenever you go to *any* website, it is a good idea to evaluate the website and the information it contains. Ask yourself questions such as:

"Who sponsors this website?"

"Is the information contained in this website up-to-date?"

"What type of information is presented?"

"Is the information objective and complete?"

"How easy is it to use the features of this website?"

SELECTION **4-2**

Sociology

Latinos: An Emerging Influence in the United States

From *Sociology: An Introduction*

By Richard J. Gelles and Ann Levine

Prepare Yourself to Read

Directions: Do these exercises *before* you read Selection 4-2.

1. First, read and think about the title. What are the countries of origin of the Latinos who live in your city or closest to the area in which you live?

   _____

   _____

   _____

2. Latinos have made many contributions to our country's culture—in the arts, literature, politics, science, medicine, the military, sports, and music and other entertainment fields. Who are some distinguished or famous Latinos you are already aware of?

   _____

   _____

   _____

   _____

   _____

3. Next, complete your preview by reading the following:
   Introduction (in *italics*)
   All of the first paragraph (paragraph 1)
   First sentence of each paragraph
   Charts
   Map
   All of the last paragraph (paragraph 7)

   On the basis of your preview, what does the selection now seem to be about?

   _____

   _____

   _____

   _____

   _____

Apply Comprehension Skills

Directions: Do the Annotation Practice Exercises *as* you read Selection 4-2. Apply the two skills from this chapter:

Determine the topic. When you read a paragraph, ask yourself, "Who or what is this about?"

Identify the stated main idea. As you read, ask yourself, "What is the most important point the authors want me to understand about the topic?" Then search for the sentence that answers this question.

Complete the Annotation Practice Exercises. In these exercises, you will work only with paragraphs that have stated main ideas.

LATINOS: AN EMERGING INFLUENCE IN THE UNITED STATES

According to political scientist Thomas E. Patterson of Harvard, demographers were surprised when the 2000 census revealed that there were 33 million Hispanics compared with 31 million African Americans. In 2003 the Bureau of the Census estimated that there were 38.8 million Hispanics living in the United States, making them the nation's largest minority group. Only 14.6 million Hispanics lived in the United States in 1980. It is estimated that by 2010 one out of every five Americans will be Latino. Latinos have immigrated to the United States from Mexico, Central America, South America, Cuba, and Puerto Rico. They live in virtually every state in the United States, but they are concentrated in nine states that together control 75% of the electoral votes a candidate would need to win the presidency.

Although recent arrivals have helped make Latinos the nation's largest minority group. Hispanics are one of the country's oldest ethnic groups. Some Hispanics are descendants of people who helped colonize the areas of California, Texas, Florida, New Mexico, and Arizona before those areas became part of the United States. The earliest Hispanics were here before the landing of the Mayflower.

Although Latinos are one of the oldest ethnic groups in the United States and now are the most rapidly growing segment of our population, many people are still unaware of their achievements and contributions to our culture. Latinos have made contributions in science and medicine, literature and the arts, politics and government, education, the military, sports, and entertainment. Nevertheless, Latinos as a whole are among the less educated and less well-to-do in our society. Their impact on American life and culture will only increase. Consequently, young Latinos must begin to educate themselves for professional careers and prepare themselves for the leadership roles that many of them will be called upon to assume.

The selection below, from a sociology textbook, gives an overview of this increasingly important segment of our population.

1   By the year 2000, Latinos had become the largest minority in the United States. They now outnumber African Americans, in part because of immigration, and in part because many Latinos are in their childbearing years and tend to have larger families than non-Hispanics. People of Spanish heritage have lived in what is now the United States since the sixteenth century, but nearly two-thirds of those who identify themselves as Latino or Hispanic today are immigrants or the children of immigrants. A diverse population, they come from varied national backgrounds and social classes and have followed different immigration and settlement patterns. Latinos may have European, Amerindian, or African ancestors or—perhaps most often—some combination thereof. Latinos have been described as the "in-between" minority, whose ethnic status lies between European Americans and African Americans.

Annotation Practice Exercises

Directions: For each exercise below,

- Write the topic of the paragraph on the lines beside the paragraph.
- Underline or highlight the stated main idea sentence of the paragraph.

This will help you remember the topic and the stated main idea.

2   In socioeconomic terms, Latinos are among the most dis-advantaged groups in our society. Many Latino families are solidly middle-class: one in five has a household income of $50,000 or more, about the same percentage as for African Americans. But more than one-quarter (28 percent) have in-comes below the poverty level. Latinos have the lowest rates of high school and college graduation of any major population group. On average, Mexican Americans have the lowest edu-cation levels and incomes, and Cuban Americans the highest (though below levels for non-Hispanic whites). Why do Lati-nos have such low incomes and high poverty levels? Many are recent immigrants who have few marketable skills, speak little English, and work for entry-level salaries at low-level jobs. Many face discrimination in the workplace, particularly if they are dark-skinned and have strong accents. In school, Latino young people face numerous barriers, including limited proficiency in English, low expectations on the part of teach-ers, and overcrowded and poorly funded schools. Although Latinos make up 11 percent of the population, in 1997 only 1 percent of all elected officials and 17 members of Congress were Latino.

3   The Latino population includes three main ethnic groups (as well as many smaller ones, including many recent immi-grants from Central and South America). The largest group, Mexican Americans, are concentrated in the southwest. Some trace their ancestry to colonial days, while others are recent immigrants. Up through the 1960s, a majority worked as agricultural laborers. The Anglo majority viewed Mexican Americans as "peasants" and "foreigners," and little effort was made to assimilate them. In the 1970s and 1980s, Mexi-can Americans began moving into cities, where eight out of ten reside today. But the pattern of low levels of education and low-wage employment, especially among recent immi-grants, has continued.

4   The second-largest group is Puerto Ricans, most of whom live in New York City. Puerto Ricans were declared American citizens in 1917, but the first large wave of immi-grants did not arrive until the 1950s, when airlines introduced relatively inexpensive flights between the island and the mainland. By 1970 there were half as many Puerto Ricans on the mainland as in Puerto Rico, but migration back and forth is common. Owing to low levels of education, poor English, recent entry into the labor force, and discrimination, espe-cially against those who are dark-skinned, Puerto Ricans are among the poorest Latinos.

5   Another prominent group of Latinos in the United States is Cuban Americans, who began arriving in 1959, the year Fidel Castro seized control of the Cuban government. The first large group of refugees to move to the United States

Latinos are the largest minority in the United States.

Practice Exercise

• Topic of paragraph 2:

_____

_____

• Underline or highlight the stated main idea of paragraph 2.

Latino Americans.
Although a majority of Latino immigrants are from Mexico, immigration from countries in Central and South America is increasing.
Source: Adapted from Richard J. Gelles and Ann Levine, *Sociology: An Introduction,* 6th ed. Boston: McGraw-Hill, 1999, p. 348. Reprinted by permission from Richard J. Gelles and Ann Levine.

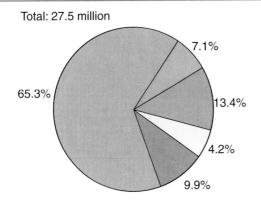

Total: 27.5 million

7.1%

13.4%

65.3%

4.2%

9.9%

Mexican

Puerto Rican

Cuban

Central and South American*

Other

*Includes El Salvadorians, Guatemalans, Nicaraguans, Hondurans, Panamanians, Colombians, Ecuadorians, Peruvians, and Argentinians, among others.

Countries of origin of Hispanic immigrants, 1980s and 1990s.
Source: J. del Pinal and A. Singer, "Generations of Diversity: Latinos in the United States," *Population Bulletin* 52(3), October 1997, p. 10, fig. 8.

United States

Mexico

Cuba

Dominican Republic

Puerto Rico

Guatemala

Honduras

El Salvador

Nicaragua

Panama

Venezuela

Colombia

Ecuador

Peru

Brazil

Argentina

N

en masse, Cuban Americans have also been one of the most successful non-English-speaking immigrant groups.

6   Cuban Americans differ from Mexican Americans and Puerto Ricans in a number of ways. Many of the early Cuban refugees were educated urban business owners and professionals. They arrived not as poor individuals but as a relatively well-off group with established social networks. As political refugees, they had access to government programs not available to other immigrants. A majority settled in Miami, where they established an economic enclave with businesses run by and catering to Cubans. As a result they did not have to learn a new language and new ways of doing business or to accept entry-level jobs in the mainstream economy. Subsequent waves of Cuban (and other Latino) immigrants supplied both the labor and the consumers to maintain and expand this enclave.

7   Second- and third-generation Latinos tend to be "bicultural" as well as bilingual. Although Americanized in some ways, they have maintained their language, religion (Roman Catholicism), family traditions, and contacts with their homelands over the generations.

Practice Exercise

- Topic of paragraph 6:

  _____

  _____

  _____

- Underline or highlight the stated main idea of paragraph 6.

Practice Exercise

- Topic of paragraph 7:

  _____

  _____

  _____

- Underline or highlight the stated main idea of paragraph 7.

Source: Adapted from Richard J. Gelles and Ann Levine, *Sociology: An Introduction,* 6th ed. Boston: McGraw-Hill, 1999, pp. 347–49. Reprinted by permission from Richard J. Gelles and Ann Levine.

enclave (ŏn′ klāv) means:

a.   suburb of a large city

b.   an area enclosed within a larger area

c.   industrial area

d.   restricted area

_____   **19.** *Subsequent* waves of Cuban (and other Latino) immigrants supplied both the labor and the consumers to maintain and expand this enclave.

I made a low score on my first history test, but I have scored well on all *subsequent* tests this semester.

subsequent (sŭb′ sĭ kwĕnt) means:

a.   advanced

b.   unexpected

c.   following

d.   harder

_____   **20.** Second- and third-generation Latinos tend to be "*bicultural*" as well as bilingual. Although Americanized in some ways, they have maintained their language, religion (Roman Catholicism), family traditions, and contacts with their homelands over the generations.

Montreal is considered a *bicultural* city because it has strong influences from both the French and the English.

bicultural (bī kŭl′ chûr əl) means:

a.   pertaining to the arts

b.   pertaining to two distinct cultures

c.   pertaining to manners

d.   able to speak two languages

SELECTION **4-2**

Sociology

(Continued)

Reading Skills Application

Directions: Items 21–25 test your ability to *apply* certain reading skills to information in this selection. These types of questions provide valuable practice for all students, especially those who must take standardized reading tests and state-mandated basic skills tests (such as the Florida CLAST Test and the Texas THEA Test). You may not have studied all of the skills at this point, so these items will serve as a helpful preview. The comprehension and critical reading skills in this section are presented in Chapters 4 through 9 of *Opening Doors;* vocabulary and figurative language skills are presented in Chapter 2. As you work through *Opening Doors,* you will practice and develop these skills. Write your answer for each question in the space provided.

_____ **21.** The word *catering* as it is used in paragraph 6 means:

    a. preparing food for.

    b. providing entertainment for.

    c. attending to the wants and needs of.

    d. anticipating the desires of.

_____ **22.** According to information presented in paragraph 4, the next to the largest group of Latinos in this country is:

    a. Mexican Americans.

    b. Guatemalans.

    c. Puerto Ricans.

    d. Cubans.

_____ **23.** Which of the following contrasts is presented in paragraph 6 of the selection?

    a. Cuban Americans are contrasted with Mexican Americans and Puerto Ricans.

    b. Cuban Americans are contrasted with Mexican Americans.

    c. Mexican Americans are contrasted with Puerto Ricans.

    d. Puerto Ricans are contrasted with Cubans.

_____ **24.** The authors' tone in this selection can best be described as:

    a. factual.

    b. nostalgic.

    c. hostile.

    d. sarcastic.

_____ **25.** Which of the following gives the best evidence of the authors' credibility?

    a. individual case studies of Latinos

    b. the authors' extensive experience with Latinos

    c. the authors' ongoing observation of Latinos

    d. research findings and statistics

SELECTION **4-2**

Sociology
(Continued)

Collaboration Option

Respond in Writing

Directions: Refer to Selection 4-2 as needed to answer the essay-type questions below.

Option for collaboration: Your instructor may direct you to work with other students on one or more of these items, or in other words, to work *collaboratively*. In that case, you should form groups of three or four students, as directed by your instructor, and work together to complete the exercises. After your group discusses an item and agrees on the answer, have a group member record it. Each member of your group should be able to explain all of your group's answers.

1. Name any Latino groups represented in your school, city, or region of the country.

    _____

    _____

2. What are some of the advantages and disadvantages of being an "in-between" or "bicultural" group such as the Latinos? Does every group that is new to a country experience being an "in-between" or "bicultural" group? (Be sure to answer both questions.)

    _____

    _____

    _____

3. What can any group of immigrants do to assimilate itself into the culture of the country to which it has immigrated?

    _____

    _____

4. In what ways do immigrants who settle in a country enrich that country's culture? List at least four ways.

    _____

    _____

    _____

5. Give the names and describe the achievements of at least four famous Americans of Latino descent. These individuals may have lived in the past or may be living presently. (If necessary, you may do research to answer this question.)

    _____

    _____

6. **Overall main idea.** What is the overall main idea the author wants the reader to understand about Latinos? Answer this question in one sentence. Be sure that your overall main idea sentence includes the topic (*Latinos*) and tells the overall most important point about it.

_____

_____

_____

Internet Resources

Read More about This Topic on the World Wide Web

Directions: For further information about the topic of the selection, visit these websites:

www.hisp.com
This site provides links to Latino news and politics. There is also information about Latino arts, entertainment, lifestyles, and interests; resources for business, careers, and education; and other resources.

www.zonalatina.com
"Zona Latina" is a site that contains links to media and marketing. There are virtually thousands of media Web links: newspapers, magazines, radio, and television. Also included are resources on individual Latin American countries, music, children's resources, book reviews, and more. Most sites are in English, but there are also many in español.

www.mundolatino.org/
Esta sitio contiene enlaces a los siguientes sectores: educación, cultura, noticias, empleo, correo electrónico, y mucho más. Disponible solamente en español.

You can also use your favorite search engine such as Google, Yahoo!, or AltaVista (www.google.com, www.yahoo.com, www.altavista.com) to discover more about this topic. To locate additional information, type in combinations of keywords such as:

United States Latinos

or

Mexican Americans

or

Puerto Ricans

or

United States ethnic groups

Keep in mind that whenever you go to *any* website, it is a good idea to evaluate the website and the information it contains. Ask yourself questions such as:

"Who sponsors this website?"

"Is the information contained in this website up-to-date?"

"What type of information is presented?"

"Is the information objective and complete?"

"How easy is it to use the features of this website?"

SELECTION **4-3**

History

Muhammad

From *The 100: A Ranking of the Most Influential Persons in History*

By Michael K. Hart

Prepare Yourself to Read

Directions: Do these exercises *before* you read Selection 4-3.

1. First, read and think about the title. What do you already know about Muhammad?

   _____

   _____

   _____

2. Next, complete your preview by reading the following:

   Introduction (in *italics*)

   First paragraph (paragraph 1)

   First sentence of each paragraph

   Words in *italics*

   Last paragraph (paragraph 9)

   On the basis of your preview, what information about Muhammad does this selection seem to present?

   _____

   _____

   _____

   _____

Apply Comprehension Skills

Directions: Do the Annotation Practice Exercises *as* you read Selection 4-3. Apply the two skills from this chapter:

Determine the topic. When you read a paragraph, ask yourself, "Who or what is this about?"

Identify the stated main idea. As you read, ask yourself, "What is the most important point the author wants me to understand about the topic?" Then search for the sentence that answers this question.

Complete the Annotation Practice Exercises. In these exercises, you will work only with paragraphs that have stated main ideas.

MUHAMMAD

Of the billions of human beings who have populated the earth, which ones do you think have most influenced the world and the course of history? The historian Michael Hart attempts to answer this fascinating question in his book, The 100: A Ranking of the Most Influential Persons in History. *He emphasizes that he was seeking to identify the "most influential" persons in history, not necessarily the "greatest." On his list of the top 100, the first 10 are: (1) Muhammad, (2) Isaac Newton, (3) Jesus Christ, (4) Buddha, (5) Confucius, (6) St. Paul, (7) Ts'ai Lun, (8) Johannes Gutenberg, (9) Christopher Columbus, and (10) Albert Einstein. Perhaps you were surprised to see Muhammad listed first. In the selection below, Hart explains why he considers Muhammad to be the "most influential person in history."*

This selection will be especially useful to you if you do not already know who Muhammad is. Every well-educated person should be familiar with the names and accomplishments of individuals who have significantly influenced the history and culture of the world.

Keep in mind that it does not matter whether or not you agree with Michael Hart that Muhammad is the most influential person in history. Michael Hart does not expect everyone to agree with him. As you read, your goal should be to understand and consider the reasons Michael Hart gives for his selection of Muhammad as the most influential person who has ever lived.

1   My choice of Muhammad to lead the list of the world's most influential persons may surprise some readers and may be questioned by others, but he was the only man in history who was supremely successful on both the religious and the secular level.

2   Of humble origins, Muhammad founded and promulgated one of the world's great religions, and became an immensely effective political leader. Today, thirteen centuries after his death, his influence is still powerful and pervasive.

3   The majority of the persons in this book had the advantage of being born and raised in centers of civilization, highly cultured and politically pivotal nations. Muhammad, however, was born in the year 570, in the city of Mecca, in southern Arabia, at that time a backward area of the world, far from the centers of trade, art, and learning. Orphaned at age six, he was reared in modest surroundings. Islamic tradition tells us that he was illiterate. His economic position improved when, at the age of twenty-five, he married a wealthy widow. Nevertheless, as he approached forty, there was little outward indication that he was a remarkable person.

4   Most Arabs at that time were pagans, who believed in many gods. There were, however, in Mecca, a small number of Jews and Christians; it was from them no doubt that Muhammad first learned of a single, omnipotent God who ruled the entire universe. When he was forty years old, Muhammad became convinced that this one true God (Allah) was speaking to him, and had chosen him to spread the true faith.

Annotation Practice Exercises

Directions: For each exercise below,

- Write the topic of the paragraph on the lines beside the paragraph.

- Underline or highlight the stated main idea sentence of the paragraph.

This will help you remember the topic and the stated main idea.

Practice Exercise

- Topic of paragraph 4:

  _____

  _____

  _____

- Underline or highlight the stated main idea of paragraph 4.

5   For three years, Muhammad preached only to close friends and associates. Then, about 613, he began preaching in public. As he slowly gained converts, the Meccan authorities came to consider him a dangerous nuisance. In 622, fearing for his safety, Muhammad fled to Medina (a city some 200 miles north of Mecca), where he had been offered a position of considerable political power.

6   The flight, called the Hegira (hĕj′ ər ə, hĭ jī′ rə), was the turning point of the Prophet's life. In Mecca, he had had a few followers. In Medina, he had many more, and he soon acquired an influence that made him a virtual dictator. During the next few years, while Muhammad's following grew rapidly, a series of battles were fought between Medina and Mecca. This war ended in 630 with Muhammad's triumphant return to Mecca as conqueror. The remaining two and one-half years of his life witnessed the rapid conversion of the Arab tribes to the new religion. When Muhammad died, in 632, he was the effective ruler of all of southern Arabia.

7   How, then, is one to assess the overall impact of Muhammad on human history? Like all religions, Islam exerts an enormous influence upon the lives of its followers. It is for this reason that the founders of the world's great religions all figure prominently in this book. Since there are roughly twice as many Christians as Moslems in the world, it may initially seem strange that Muhammad has been ranked higher than Jesus. There are two principal reasons for that decision. First, Muhammad played a far more important role in the development of Islam than Jesus did in the development of Christianity. Although Jesus was responsible for the main ethical and moral precepts of Christianity (insofar as these differed from Judaism), St. Paul was the main developer of Christian theology, its principal proselytizer, and the author of a large portion of the New Testament.

8   Muhammad, however, was responsible for both the theology of Islam and its main ethical and moral principles. In addition, he played the key role in proselytizing the new faith, and in establishing the religious practices of Islam. Moreover, he is the author of the Muslim holy scriptures, the *Koran* [Qu'ran], a collection of certain of Muhammad's insights that he believed had been directly revealed to him by Allah. Most of these utterances were copied more or less faithfully during Muhammad's lifetime and were collected together in authoritative form not long after his death. The Koran, therefore, closely represents Muhammad's ideas and teachings and to a considerable extent his exact words. No such detailed compilation of the teachings of Christ has survived. Since the Koran is at least as important to Muslims as the Bible is to Christians, the influence of Muhammad through the medium of the Koran has been enormous. It is probable that the relative influence of

Muhammad, A.D. 570–632

Practice Exercise

• Topic of paragraph 6:

_____

_____

_____

• Underline or highlight the stated main idea of paragraph 6.

Muhammad on Islam has been larger than the combined influence of Jesus Christ and St. Paul on Christianity. On the purely religious level, then, it seems likely that Muhammad has been as influential in human history as Jesus.

9   Furthermore, Muhammad (unlike Jesus) was a secular as well as a religious leader. In fact, as the driving force behind the Arab conquests, he may well rank as the most influential political leader of all time.

Source: From Michael K. Hart, *The 100: A Ranking of the Most Influential Persons in History.* Copyright © 1978, 1992 Michael H. Hart, Inc. All rights reserved. Reprinted by arrangement with Kensington Publishing Corp. www.kensingtonbooks.com.

Practice Exercise

• Topic of paragraph 9:

_____

_____

_____

• Underline or highlight the stated main idea of paragraph 9.

SELECTION **4-3**

History
(continued)

**Student Online
Learning Center (OLC)**
Go to **Chapter 4.**
Choose **Reading
Selection Quiz.**

Reading Selection Quiz

This quiz has three parts. Your instructor may assign some or all of them.

Comprehension

Directions: Items 1–10 test your comprehension (understanding) of the material of this selection. These questions are the type a content area instructor (such as a history professor) would ask on a test over this material. You should be able to answer these questions after studying this selection. For each comprehension question below, use information from the selection to determine the correct answer. Refer to the selection as you answer each question. Write your answer in the space provided.

True or False

_____ **1.** The author believes that everyone will agree with his choice of Muhammad as the most influential person in history.

_____ **2.** The author chose Muhammad solely because of Muhammad's success as a religious leader.

_____ **3.** Muhammad was born and raised in what was then called Arabia, a highly cultured and pivotal nation.

_____ **4.** According to the author, Muhammad learned about a single, all-powerful God from the small number of Christians and Jews living in Mecca.

Multiple-Choice

_____ **5.** Muhammad began preaching that Allah was the one true God when Muhammad was:
  a. still in his teens.
  b. 26 years old.
  c. 30 years old.
  d. 40 years old.

_____ **6.** The *Hegira* was Muhammad's flight:
  a. from Arabia.
  b. from Medina to Mecca.
  c. from Mecca to Medina.
  d. to southern Arabia.

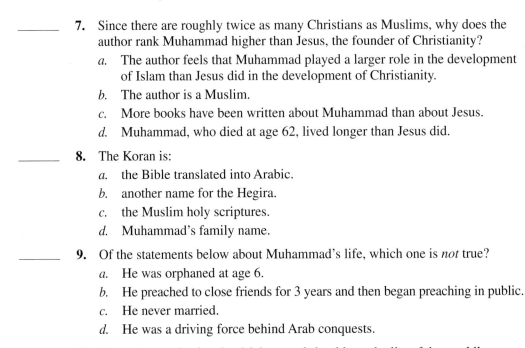

_____ **7.** Since there are roughly twice as many Christians as Muslims, why does the author rank Muhammad higher than Jesus, the founder of Christianity?

    a. The author feels that Muhammad played a larger role in the development of Islam than Jesus did in the development of Christianity.

    b. The author is a Muslim.

    c. More books have been written about Muhammad than about Jesus.

    d. Muhammad, who died at age 62, lived longer than Jesus did.

_____ **8.** The Koran is:

    a. the Bible translated into Arabic.

    b. another name for the Hegira.

    c. the Muslim holy scriptures.

    d. Muhammad's family name.

_____ **9.** Of the statements below about Muhammad's life, which one is *not* true?

    a. He was orphaned at age 6.

    b. He preached to close friends for 3 years and then began preaching in public.

    c. He never married.

    d. He was a driving force behind Arab conquests.

_____ **10.** The author maintains that Muhammad should top the list of the world's most influential persons because:

    a. Muhammad was responsible for the theology of Islam and its main principles.

    b. In Mecca, he became a virtual dictator.

    c. Muhammad was a great military leader.

    d. Muhammad was an influential religious leader and secular leader.

SELECTION **4-3**

History
(continued)

Vocabulary in Context

Directions: Items 11–20 test your ability to determine the meaning of the word by using context clues. *Context clues* are words in a sentence that allow the reader to deduce (reason out) the meaning of an unfamiliar word in that sentence. Context clues also enable the reader to determine which meaning the author intends when a word has more than one meaning. For each vocabulary item below, a sentence from the selection containing an important word (*italicized, like this*) is quoted first. Next, there is an additional sentence using the word in the same sense and providing another context clue. Use the context clues from *both* sentences to deduce the meaning of the italicized word. *Be sure the answer you choose makes sense in both sentences.* If you discover that you need to use a dictionary to confirm an answer choice, remember that the meaning you select must still fit the context of *both* sentences. Write your answer in the space provided.

Pronunciation Key: ă pat ā pay âr care ä father ĕ pet ē be ĭ pit ī tie îr pier ŏ pot ō toe ô paw oi noise ou out ŏŏ took ōō boot ŭ cut yōō abuse ûr urge th thin *th* this hw which zh vision ə about *Stress mark: ′*

_____ **11.** Of humble origins, Muhammad founded and *promulgated* one of the world's great religions, and became an immensely effective political leader.

In the State of the Union speech, the president *promulgated* the new administration's policy on gun control.

promulgated (prŏm′ əl gāt əd) means:

a. reversed or changed

b. made known or put into effect by public declaration

c. refused to reveal

d. denounced as untrue

_____ **12.** Today, 13 centuries after his death, his influence is still powerful and *pervasive.*

The drug problem in the United States is difficult to deal with because the problem is so *pervasive.*

pervasive (pər vā′ sĭv) means:

a. important

b. widespread

c. decreasing or diminishing

d. popular

_____ **13.** The majority of the persons in this book had the advantage of being born and raised in centers of civilization, highly cultured or politically *pivotal* nations.

Supreme Court Justice O'Connor's opinion was the *pivotal* one that reversed the lower court's decision.

pivotal (pĭv′ ə təl) means:

a. causing rotation or spinning

b. pertaining to religion or theology

c. determining a direction or effect; crucial

d. going in two different directions

_____ **14.** Orphaned at age six, he was reared in *modest* surroundings.

Even after the Smiths won the lottery, they continued to live in a *modest* apartment and to take the subway to work.

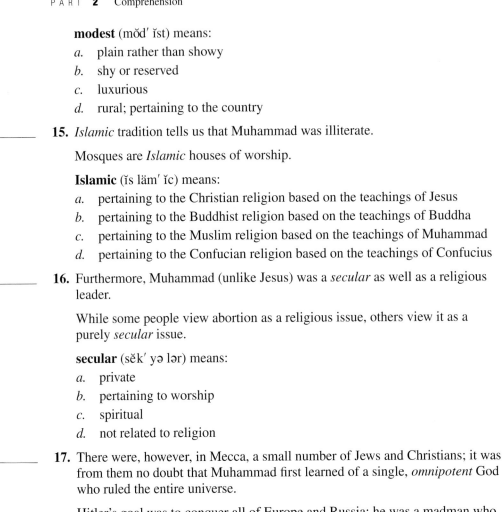

modest (mŏd′ ĭst) means:

a. plain rather than showy

b. shy or reserved

c. luxurious

d. rural; pertaining to the country

_____ **15.** *Islamic* tradition tells us that Muhammad was illiterate.

Mosques are *Islamic* houses of worship.

Islamic (ĭs läm′ ĭc) means:

a. pertaining to the Christian religion based on the teachings of Jesus

b. pertaining to the Buddhist religion based on the teachings of Buddha

c. pertaining to the Muslim religion based on the teachings of Muhammad

d. pertaining to the Confucian religion based on the teachings of Confucius

_____ **16.** Furthermore, Muhammad (unlike Jesus) was a *secular* as well as a religious leader.

While some people view abortion as a religious issue, others view it as a purely *secular* issue.

secular (sĕk′ yə lər) means:

a. private

b. pertaining to worship

c. spiritual

d. not related to religion

_____ **17.** There were, however, in Mecca, a small number of Jews and Christians; it was from them no doubt that Muhammad first learned of a single, *omnipotent* God who ruled the entire universe.

Hitler's goal was to conquer all of Europe and Russia; he was a madman who thought he could be *omnipotent*.

omnipotent (ŏm nĭp′ ə tənt) means:

a. having unlimited power or authority

b. having limited power or authority

c. having authority given by the citizens of a country

d. having no power or authority

_____ **18.** As he slowly gained *converts,* the Meccan authorities came to consider him a dangerous nuisance.

The new political party in India rapidly gained *converts*.

converts (kŏn′ vûrts) means:

a. people who revert to previously held beliefs

b. people who adopt a new religion or new beliefs

c. people who cling to long-held beliefs

d. people who have no religious beliefs

_____ **19.** Although Jesus was responsible for the main ethical precepts of Christianity, St. Paul was the main developer of Christian *theology,* its principal proselytizer, and the author of a large portion of the New Testament.

Although my uncle decided not to become a minister and left the seminary, he continued to read ancient and modern Christian *theology* throughout his life.

theology (thē ŏl′ ə jē) means:

a. system or school of opinions about God and religious questions

b. study of beliefs throughout the world

c. study of ancient religious rituals

d. study of the lives of saints

_____ **20.** In addition, Muhammad played the key role in *proselytizing* the new faith, and in establishing the religious practices of Islam.

The evangelists went door to door *proselytizing,* telling anyone who was willing to listen about their religious beliefs.

proselytizing (prŏs′ ə lə tīz ĭng) means:

a. speaking loudly or shouting

b. deceiving with trickery

c. declaring false or untrue

d. attempting to convert people from one belief or faith to another

SELECTION **4-3**

History

(continued)

Reading Skills Application

Directions: Items 21–25 test your ability to *apply* certain reading skills to information in this selection. These types of questions provide valuable practice for all students, especially those who must take standardized reading tests and state-mandated basic skills tests (such as the Florida CLAST Test and the Texas THEA Test). You may not have studied all of the skills at this point, so these items will serve as a helpful preview. The comprehension and critical reading skills in this section are presented in Chapters 4 through 9 of *Opening Doors;* vocabulary and figurative language skills are presented in Chapter 2. As you work through *Opening Doors,* you will practice and develop these skills. Write your answer for each question in the space provided.

_____ **21.** Which of the following best expresses the author's argument in this selection?

    a. My choice of Muhammad to lead the list of the world's most influential persons may surprise some readers and be questioned by others.

    b. As the driving force behind the Arab conquests, Muhammad may well rank as the most influential political leader of all time.

    c. When he was 40 years old, Muhammad became convinced that Allah had chosen him to spread the true faith.

    d. Because he was supremely successful as a religious and a secular leader, Muhammad can be viewed as the most influential person in history.

_____ **22.** The meaning of *humble* in paragraph 2 is:

    a. distinguished.

    b. famous.

    c. lowly.

    d. comfortable.

_____ **23.** In this selection the primary comparison and contrast the author presents is between:

    a. Jesus and Muhammad.

    b. Muhammad and his followers.

    c. pagans and Christians.

    d. secular and religious leaders.

_____ **24.** The author's tone in this selection can best be described as:

    a. persuasive.

    b. sympathetic.

    c. disapproving.

    d. sentimental.

_____ **25.** Which of the following represents an opinion rather than a fact?

    a. Islamic tradition tells us that Muhammad was illiterate.

    b. This war ended in 630 with Muhammad's triumphant return to Mecca as conqueror.

    c. Most Arabs at that time were pagans who believed in many gods.

    d. On a purely religious level, then, it seems likely that Muhammad has been as influential in human history as Jesus.

SELECTION **4-3**

History
(Continued)

Collaboration Option

Respond in Writing

Directions: Refer to Selection 4-3 as needed to answer these essay-type questions.

Option for collaboration: Your instructor may direct you to work with other students on one or more of these items, or in other words, to work *collaboratively.* In that case, you should form groups of three or four students, as directed by your instructor, and work together to complete the exercises. After your group discusses an item and agrees on the answer, have a group member record it. Each member of your group should be able to explain all of your group's answers.

1. List the three reasons the author chose Muhammad as the most influential person in history.

    Reason 1: _____

    _____

    _____

    Reason 2: _____

    _____

    _____

    Reason 3: _____

    _____

    _____

2. Michael Hart, the author of *The 100: A Ranking of the Most Influential Persons in History,* selected 99 other important people for his book. List five names *you* would include in a list of the world's most influential people, and state your reasons for including them. Remember, these must be people who have influenced the *world,* not just you. They must be actual *people* who have lived or are currently living. They should be people who have had the *most* influence, regardless of whether their influence on the world was positive or negative. Choose people who are *not* in Hart's top 10.

    Person 1: _____
    Reason: _____

    _____

    Person 2: _____
    Reason: _____

    _____

Person 3: _____

Reason: _____

_____

Person 4: _____

Reason: _____

_____

Person 5: _____

Reason: _____

_____

3. **Overall main idea.** What is the overall main idea the author wants the reader
to understand about Muhammad? Answer this question in one sentence. Be
sure that your overall main idea sentence includes the topic (*Muhammad*) and
tells the overall most important point about him.

_____

_____

Internet Resources

Read More about This Topic on the World Wide Web

Directions: For further information about the topic of the selection, visit these
websites:

www.usc.edu/dept/MSA/fundamentals/prophet
This website contains links to biographical information about Muhammad,
examples of his teachings and sayings, his last sermon, and quotations from
others about him. Try clicking on *What He Was Like.*

www.biography.com
Type *Mohammed* in the search box. (*Note that the spelling is slightly different.*)
Then click on "*Mohammed or Mahomet,*" and read a short biography of the
prophet of Islam.

You can also use your favorite search engine such as Google, Yahoo!, or Alta-
Vista (www.google.com, www.yahoo.com, www.altavista.com) to discover more
about this topic. To locate additional information, type in combinations of key-
words such as:

Muhammad

or

influence of prophet Muhammad

or

Michael Hart's ranking of influential persons

Keep in mind that whenever you go to *any* website, it is a good idea to evaluate the website and the information it contains. Ask yourself questions such as:

"Who sponsors this website?"

"Is the information contained in this website up-to-date?"

"What type of information is presented?"

"Is the information objective and complete?"

"How easy is it to use the features of this website?"

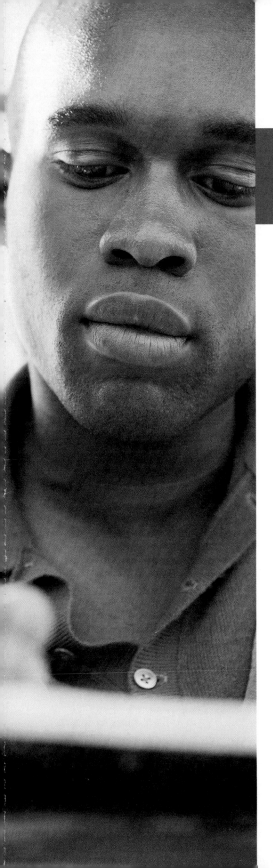

CHAPTER 5

Formulating Implied Main Ideas

In this chapter you will learn the answers to these questions:

- What is an implied main idea of a paragraph?

- Why is formulating implied main ideas important?

- How can I formulate implied main idea sentences?

- How can I know when a formulated main idea sentence is correct?

SKILLS

Implied Main Ideas in Paragraphs

- What Is an Implied Main Idea?
- Why Is Formulating Implied Main Ideas Important?

Formulating an Implied Main Idea

- Steps to Follow
- Three Formulas for Using Information in a Paragraph to Formulate the Main Idea
- Requirements for Correctly Formulated Main Idea Sentences
- Implied Overall Main Ideas in Longer Passages

A Word about Standardized Reading Tests: Implied Main Ideas

CREATING YOUR SUMMARY

Developing Chapter Review Cards

READINGS

Selection 5-1   *(Personal Finance)*
"Identity Theft: You Are at Risk"

Selection 5-2   *(Psychology)*
"Violence in Television and Video Games: Does the Media's Message Matter?"
from *Essentials of Understanding Psychology*
by Robert S. Feldman

Selection 5-3   *(Sociology)*
"Demography, the Study of Population"
from *Sociology: An Introduction*
by Richard J. Gelles and Ann Levine

If you want to climb mountains, do not practice on molehills.

IMPLIED MAIN IDEAS IN PARAGRAPHS

What Is an Implied Main Idea?

Student Online Learning Center (OLC)
Go to Chapter 5.
Select Video.

Every paragraph has a main idea, of course, but not every paragraph includes a *stated* main idea sentence. When an author gives you the information needed to understand the main point without stating it directly as a single sentence, the main idea is *implied*. When an author implies the main idea, you, the reader, must use information in the paragraph to *infer* (reason out) the main idea and *formulate* (create) a sentence that expresses it. In other words, the **implied main idea** is a sentence formulated by the reader that expresses the author's main point about the topic.

Sometimes you must infer that essential information needs to be added to an existing sentence to formulate the complete main idea. At other times, you must infer that information from two or more sentences in the paragraph has to be *combined* to formulate one complete main idea sentence. At still other times, you will have to formulate a *general* sentence that sums up the most important (but unstated) point the author is trying to illustrate or prove. That is, if a paragraph presents facts, descriptions, explanations, or examples that only *suggest* the main point the author wants you to understand, it is up to you to infer and formulate the main idea. When you grasp the main idea in these ways, you are *inferring* it.

Why Is Formulating Implied Main Ideas Important?

Your comprehension will be limited unless you understand main ideas, regardless of whether they are stated or implied. Just as you must be able to identify the main idea when it is stated, you must be able to formulate it when the author implies it. Of course, this will increase your comprehension, but you will also remember material better if you take the time and make the effort to formulate main ideas when they are implied. College instructors assume that students read carefully enough to understand paragraphs with implied main ideas. Instructors base test items on implied main ideas, just as they base items on more obvious stated main ideas.

To be an effective reader, then, you must be able to identify stated main ideas *and* be able to formulate main idea sentences for any paragraphs in which the main idea is implied.

269

FORMULATING AN IMPLIED MAIN IDEA

Steps to Follow

Of course, you will not know until you read a paragraph whether its main idea is stated or implied. Look first for a stated main idea sentence. If there is not a stated main idea sentence, formulate the implied main idea by following these steps:

* **Step 1.**   First, after you have read the paragraph, *determine the topic* by asking yourself, "Who or what is this passage about?"

* **Step 2.**   Next, *determine the main idea* by asking yourself, "What is the single most important point the author wants me to *infer* about the topic of this paragraph?"

* **Step 3.**   Then, use the information in the paragraph to *formulate a main idea sentence* that answers your question in step 2. The sentence you formulate will be the main idea of the paragraph.

Three Formulas for Using Information in a Paragraph to Formulate the Main Idea

Even when authors do not directly state a main idea as one sentence, they still provide you with all the information you need to infer and formulate a main idea sentence yourself. Authors may provide such information in three ways, and these three ways are the basis for three "formulas" for creating main idea sentences. Each of the three formulas and examples of its application is explained below.

As always, you must begin by reading the paragraph and determining its topic. Next, ask yourself the comprehension monitoring question, "What is the single most important point the author wants me to infer about the topic of this paragraph?" Then use one of the three formulas explained below to help you create the formulated main idea sentence. How can you determine which formula to use? The particular formula you will need to use will depend on the type of information presented in the paragraph.

Formula 1: Add an Essential Word or Phrase to a Sentence That Almost States the Main Idea

Sometimes, an author may express most of the main idea in one sentence of the paragraph, yet that sentence lacks some essential piece of information—a piece of information that you must insert to make the sentence a *complete* main idea sentence. To put it another way, a paragraph may contain a sentence that *almost* states the author's main idea, but you must add certain missing information to that sentence to make it express the main idea completely. For instance, a sentence may need to have the topic of the paragraph inserted to make it express the complete main idea.

When a sentence in the paragraph almost states the main idea but lacks an essential word or phrase, use **formula 1** to create a main idea sentence:

| Sentence that *almost* states the main idea | + | Essential word or phrase that needs to be added (usually the topic) | = | Formulated main idea sentence |

Here is an example of how an implied main idea sentence can be formulated using formula 1. The paragraph is from a sociology textbook. Its topic is *ethnocentrism.* The last sentence almost states the authors' most important point—the definition of ethnocentrism—but it lacks the topic, the word *ethnocentrism.* A complete main idea sentence can be formulated by adding *ethnocentrism* (the topic) to the last sentence of the paragraph. This formulated main idea sentence expresses the most important point the authors want you to understand about ethnocentrism, its definition.

Each person is born into a particular society that has its own particular culture. At an early age, children begin to learn many aspects of this culture, such as language, standards of behavior, and beliefs. They also begin to learn many of the group's values concerning judgments of good and bad, proper and improper, and right and wrong. This learning continues into and throughout adulthood as people internalize, accept, and identify with their group's way of living. This feeling is called **ethnocentrism.** It is the basic inclination to judge other cultures in terms of the values and norms of one's own culture.

Formulated Main Idea Sentence

_____

_____

_____

_____

_____

Source: Daniel Hebding and Leonard Glick, *Introduction to Sociology,* 4th ed. New York: McGraw-Hill, 1992, p. 62. Copyright © 1992 by The McGraw-Hill Companies, Inc.

Stop and Annotate

Go back to the textbook excerpt above. Write the formulated main idea sentence in the space provided by adding essential information to the sentence that almost states the main idea.

The last sentence becomes a complete main idea sentence when the essential word *ethnocentrism* is added: *Ethnocentrism is the basic inclination to judge other cultures in terms of the values and norms of one's own culture.*

Formula 2: Combine Two Sentences from the Paragraph into a Single Sentence

Sometimes two different sentences each give part of the main idea. The author assumes that the reader will understand that each contain part of the main idea and that the sentences, *together,* convey the main point. Whenever an author does this, *you* must combine the two sentences to formulate one sentence that expresses the complete main idea. (You already know that the main idea must be expressed as a single sentence.) Because both sentences contain important information, neither sentence by itself expresses the complete main idea. The two sentences may follow one another, or they may be separated. For example, the first sentence of the paragraph may present part of the main idea, and the last sentence may give the rest of the main idea.

When you realize that two sentences in a paragraph each give part of the main idea, use **formula 2** to combine them into a single sentence that is the complete main idea:

Sentence that expresses *part* of the main idea	+	Sentence that expresses *rest* of the main idea	=	Formulated main idea sentence

Here is an example of formula 2. The paragraph below is from a sociology textbook. Its topic is *tastes.* A main idea sentence for this paragraph can be formulated by combining its last two sentences into a single sentence. This formulated main idea sentence expresses the most important point the authors want you to understand about tastes.

Tastes—we all have them. You prefer certain styles of art, certain kinds of food and clothing, certain types of music, certain ways of decorating your room. The list could go on and on. *De gustibus non est disputandum,* the old Latin saying goes—there is no accounting for taste. Tastes just seem to spring from somewhere inside us, rather mysteriously. We can't really say why we prefer rock to Mozart, burgers to pâté, jeans to neatly pressed slacks. Tastes simply seem to be part of us, our individual selves. But tastes are also part of culture, which is a broader social phenomenon.

Formulated Main Idea Sentence

_____

_____

_____

_____

_____

_____

_____

Source: Craig Calhoun, Donald Light, and Suzanne Keller, *Sociology,* 6th ed. New York: McGraw-Hill, 1994, p. 68. Copyright © 1994 by The McGraw-Hill Companies, Inc.

The last two sentences in the paragraph are the important ones: "Tastes simply seem to be part of us, our individual selves" and "But tastes are also part of culture, which is a broader social phenomenon." Neither sentence by itself expresses the complete main idea. The first sentence addresses tastes on a personal level; the other sentence addresses tastes as part of culture. You must combine these two sentences in order to formulate the complete main idea the authors intended: *Tastes simply seem to be part of us, our individual selves, but tastes are also part of culture, which is a broader social phenomenon.* (Of course, it would be equally correct to express this same main idea in other ways, such as, *Although tastes simply seem to be part of our individual selves, tastes are also part of culture.*)

Stop and Annotate

Go back to the textbook excerpt above. Write the formulated main idea sentence in the space provided by combining the two sentences in the paragraph that together express the complete main idea.

Formula 3: Summarize Important Ideas into One Sentence or Write One Sentence That Gives a General Inference Based on the Details

For some paragraphs that have implied main ideas, you will either have to formulate a main idea sentence that *summarizes* the important information in the paragraph *or* formulate a sentence that gives a *general inference* based on the details. Which of these you do will depend upon the type of information you are given in the paragraph.

Sometimes a paragraph contains several parts of the main idea in different sentences throughout the paragraph. They must be combined in order to express the complete main idea. When this occurs, you must formulate a main idea sentence by *summarizing* this important information into one sentence. You will often have to use some of your own words when you create this kind of formulated main idea sentence.

Sometimes a paragraph consists only of details. When this is the case, you must formulate a main idea sentence by inferring the *general* point the author is illustrating or proving with the details, and then express this idea as a single sentence. This is not a matter of rewriting the details as one long sentence, but rather of writing a sentence that *sums up* the details the author presents. In other words, you have to create a general sentence that *summarizes* the details. When you write this formulated main idea sentence, you may also have to use some of your own words.

When a paragraph has important ideas included in several sentences or the paragraph consists only of details, **formula 3** should be used to formulate a main idea sentence.

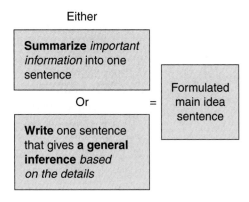

Here is an example of formulating an implied main idea using formula 3. The following excerpt is from a special section in an algebra textbook that introduces interesting information to be used in solving verbal problems. The topic of this paragraph is *pesticides*. The paragraph has an implied main idea that can be formulated by making a general inference based on the details presented throughout the paragraph. As you read the paragraph, try to reason out (infer) the most important general point the authors are making about pesticides.

Unfortunately, pesticides often kill plants and animals other than the pests they are intended for. Pesticides also pollute water systems. Over time, some pests develop immunity to frequently used pesticides and, therefore, more and more pesticides must be used. Some pesticides, such as DDT and its relatives, can remain in the environment for many years beyond the time necessary to do their intended job. Some pesticides have been linked to cancer and other health problems in humans.

Formulated Main Idea Sentence

_____

_____

_____

_____

_____

_____

Source: Adapted from James Streeter, Donald Hutchison, and Louis Hoelzle, *Beginning Algebra,* 3rd ed. New York: McGraw-Hill, 1993, p. 370. Copyright © 1993 by The McGraw-Hill Companies, Inc.

To formulate a main idea sentence for this paragraph, you must write a general inference that is based on the important information in *several* sentences. You need to examine the information, think about it, and ask yourself, "What is the most important general point the authors want me to understand about pesticides?" To answer that question, you will need to use some of your own words.

Although the phrase *dangerous effects* does not appear in this paragraph, it is obviously describing dangerous effects of pesticides. It is up to the reader to infer the main idea and reason out a general phrase such as *dangerous effects.* An example of a correctly formulated main idea sentence for the paragraph would be: *Pesticides can have dangerous, unintended effects on the environment, plants, animals, and human beings.* This formulated main idea sentence expresses the general point the authors want you to understand about pesticides.

The example given above for the formulated main idea sentence is not the only possible correct formulation. Another correct formulated main idea sentence would be: *Pesticides have several unintended, dangerous effects.* Still another possibility is: *Certain unintended side effects of pesticides are dangerous.* There are other possibilities as well. What is important is not the exact wording but that the sentence express the authors' main point.

Remember, when formulating implied main ideas, you must look at the type of information the author gives in the paragraph. The following chart summarizes what you must do to formulate the implied main idea once you determine what the author has given you to work with in the paragraph.

Stop and Annotate

Go back to the textbook excerpt above. Formulate a main idea sentence by making a general inference based on information from several sentences and write it in the space provided.

THREE WAYS TO FORMULATE IMPLIED MAIN IDEA SENTENCES

What the Author Gives You to Start with in the Paragraph	What You Must Do with the Information in Order to Formulate the Implied Main Idea
A sentence that *almost* states the main idea, but lacks some essential piece of information (usually the topic)	*Use Formula 1.* *Add* the essential piece of information that is missing to that sentence. *How to apply the formula:* Use the sentence from the paragraph and simply add the essential piece of information to that sentence.
Two sentences in the paragraph that each present *part* of the main idea	*Use Formula 2.* *Combine* them into one sentence. *How to apply the formula:* You will probably have to add a word or two in order to connect the two sentences (usually words such as *and, but, although,* etc.). *or* You can write the main idea in your own words, as long as the meaning is the same.
Details only *or* parts of the main idea occurring within several sentences throughout the paragraph	*Use Formula 3.* Write a *general sentence* that "sums up" the details or gives a general inference about the point the author is making. *How to apply the formula:* The sentence you write will contain several of your own words.

When the author does not state the main idea, the reader must *formulate* the author's main idea by "piecing together" important information.

Requirements for Correctly Formulated Main Idea Sentences

When you formulate an implied main idea sentence (in other words, when you use one of the three formulas above), there is a way to check to be sure that your formulated main idea sentence is correct. A correctly formulated implied main idea sentence is one that meets the requirements for *any* main idea (stated *or* implied).

- *A formulated main idea must be a complete sentence that includes the topic of the paragraph.*
- *A formulated main idea must express the author's most important general point about the topic.* In other words, if the formulated main idea sentence is placed at the beginning of the paragraph, the details explain, prove, or tell more about it.
- *A formulated main idea must make complete sense by itself (without the reader having to read the rest of the paragraph).* As you learned in Chapter 4, a stated main idea sentence must also be meaningful by itself (that is, even if the reader could not see the rest of the paragraph).

Remember that an implied main idea sentence can be expressed in various ways, as long as the sentence meets these three requirements. Keep in mind, however, that the formulated main idea sentence you write should express the author's most important point concisely. This means that there are many extraneous, or extra, words that you should *not* include in your formulated main idea sentence. For example, if the author's main idea is *Pesticides have several unintended dangerous effects,* you should write only that. You should *not* write a formulated main idea sentence with extraneous words such as the italicized ones shown here:

The author's main idea is that pesticides have several unintended dangerous effects.

The author says that pesticides have several unintended dangerous effects.

What the author wants us to understand is pesticides have several unintended dangerous effects.

The author is trying to say that pesticides have several unintended dangerous effects.

What the author means is that pesticides have several unintended dangerous effects.

When you formulate a main idea, it is enough merely to write the most important point the author wants readers to understand. In the examples above, for instance, you would use only the part of each sentence not in italics.

Implied Overall Main Ideas in Longer Passages

Of course, the ability to formulate implied main ideas is a skill that can be applied not only to paragraphs but also to longer passages, such as a section of a textbook chapter, a short reading selection, or an essay. In fact, you will often want to formulate the main idea of an entire passage in order to express its most important point, its overall message. These sentences are called overall main ideas. (As you learned in Chapter 4, there are various terms for an overall main idea. In a writing or English course, the overall main idea of an essay or an article may be called the *thesis statement* or *thesis.*) Throughout this book, the chapter reading selections include a Respond in Writing item that will give you practice in determining, and often formulating, the overall main idea sentence of the entire selection.

A WORD ABOUT STANDARDIZED READING TESTS: IMPLIED MAIN IDEAS

Many college students are required to take standardized reading tests as part of an overall assessment program, in a reading course, or as part of a state-mandated basic skills test. A standardized reading test typically consists of a series of passages followed by multiple-choice reading skill application questions, to be completed within a specified time limit. Here are some tips about formulating implied main ideas that should help you score as high as possible on standardized tests.

Remember that test items about implied main ideas may be worded in several different ways. Possible wordings of the test question stems include:

The author's main point is that . . .

The principal idea of this passage is that . . .

Which of the following best expresses the main idea of the entire passage?

Which of the following best expresses the main idea of this paragraph? (or a specifically identified paragraph)

To answer test items such as these, first determine the topic of the passage. Then ask yourself, "What is the most important idea the author wants me to understand about the topic?" If you cannot find a single sentence in the passage that answers this question, formulate a main idea sentence on scratch paper or in the margin next to the passage. Next, examine the answer choices, comparing each choice with your own formulation. Look for a choice that is similar *in meaning* to your own answer, but remember that the wording may be different. If none of the choices is at least partially similar to your formulation, you will need to reread the passage and make another attempt at formulating the main idea.

DEVELOPING CHAPTER REVIEW CARDS

Student Online Learning Center (OLC)
Go to Chapter 5.
Select Flashcards
or Chapter Test.

Review cards, or *summary cards,* are an excellent study tool. They are a way to select, organize, and review the most important information in a textbook chapter. The process of creating review cards helps you organize information in a meaningful way and, at the same time, transfer it into long-term memory. The cards can also be used to prepare for tests (see Part Three). The review card activities in this book give you structured practice in creating these valuable study tools. Once you have learned how to make review cards, you can create them for textbook material in your other courses.

Now complete the five review cards for Chapter 5 by answering the questions or following the directions on each card. When you have completed them, you will have summarized important information about implied main ideas: (1) what they are and why they are important, (2) what steps and (3) what formulas to follow in formulating them, (4) how to check to see if your formulations are correct, and (5) how to formulate main ideas in longer passages. Use the type of handwriting that is clearest for you to reread (printing or cursive) and write legibly.

Implied Main Ideas

1. What is an implied main idea? (See page 269.)

2. Why is formulating implied main ideas important? (See page 269.)

3. What question should you ask yourself in order to formulate the implied main idea of a paragraph? (See page 270.)

Card 1   Chapter 5: Formulating Implied Main Ideas

Steps to Follow in Formulating an Implied Main Idea Sentence

What are the three general steps to follow in formulating an implied main idea sentence? (See page 270.)

Step 1:

Step 2:

Step 3:

Card 2   Chapter 5: Formulating Implied Main Ideas

Formulas for Creating Implied Main Idea Sentences

Write out the three formulas for creating implied main idea sentences and draw the formula boxes. (See pages 270–73.)

Formula 1:

Formula 2:

Formula 3:

Card 3   Chapter 5: Formulating Implied Main Ideas

Requirements for Correctly Formulated Main Idea Sentences

What are three requirements for a correctly formulated main idea sentence? (See page 276.)

Requirement 1:

Requirement 2:

Requirement 3:

Card 4   Chapter 5: Formulating Implied Main Ideas

Implied Overall Main Ideas in Longer Passages

1.   Give examples of types of longer reading passages that might have implied main ideas. (See page 277.)

2.   Why would a reader need to formulate the main idea of an entire passage? (See page 277.)

Card 5   Chapter 5: Formulating Implied Main Ideas

Identity Theft: You Are at Risk

Prepare Yourself to Read

Directions: Do these exercise *before* you read Selection 5-1.

1. First, read and think about the title. What do you already know about identity theft?

   _____

   _____

   _____

2. Next, complete your preview by reading the following:

      Introduction (in *italics*)
      Headings
      The first two paragraphs (paragraphs 1 and 2)
      First sentence of each of the other paragraphs

   Now that you have previewed the selection, tell what identity theft is, and write one or two ways you could reduce your risk of becoming an identity theft victim.

   _____

   _____

   _____

   _____

   _____

Apply Comprehension Skills

Directions: Do the Annotation Practice Exercises *as* you read Selection 5-1. Apply the skills from this chapter:

Formulate implied main ideas. Follow these general steps: First determine the topic; then ask what the author's most important point about the topic is; then create a sentence that expresses the author's most important point. Use the appropriate formula to "formulate" an implied main idea sentence based on information in the paragraph.

Check your formulated main idea sentences. Be sure each of your main idea sentences meets the requirements on page 276.

Complete the Annotation Practice Exercises. In these exercises, you will work only with paragraphs that have implied main ideas.

IDENTITY THEFT: YOU ARE AT RISK

Identify theft is rapidly increasing. Chances are that even if you yourself are not a victim of identity theft, you know someone who has been and you know the devastating effects this crime can have. College students, in particular, can be easy targets for identity thieves. The following selection explains the crime, the techniques these thieves use, and some ways to reduce your risk of becoming an identity theft victim.

The Crime of Identity Theft

1   Don't think it can't happen to you. Your credit card bill arrives with charges for items you never purchased. You pay your bills on time and always have. Suddenly, though, creditors start hounding you for payment of past-due bills, but you never ordered any of the goods or services they're demanding payment for. The grocery store and drugstore where you've always shopped are now refusing to accept your checks because of your bad credit history. Perhaps you even receive a summons to show up in court for a traffic ticket you never paid—and, in fact, which you never received. Guess what: You're now among the hundreds of thousands of people each year who become victims of identity theft.

2   In this fast-growing crime, perpetrators steal or gather data on individuals. The data that these criminals steal include Social Security numbers, driver's license numbers, dates of birth, bank account numbers, and credit card numbers, as well as credit cards and ATM cards. They use several methods of acquiring these. Once they have enough information, the thieves impersonate the victim. They spend as much money as possible as quickly as possible, charging the purchases to the victim. Then they do the same thing all over again, using someone else's identity and credit.

Forms of Identity Theft

3   There are two forms of this theft. The first type is "account takeover" theft, in which the thief uses existing credit information to make purchases. The criminal may use an actual credit card or may simply charge purchases by phone or online using the credit card number and expiration date. The victim discovers the "theft" when the monthly account statement arrives. The second type of identity theft

Annotation Practice Exercises

Directions: For each exercise below,

•   Write the topic of the paragraph on the lines provided.

•   Formulate the implied main idea of the paragraph and write it on the lines provided.

This will help you remember the topic and the main idea.

Practice Exercise

•   Topic of paragraph 2:

_____

_____

•   Formulate the implied main idea of paragraph 2:

_____

_____

_____

_____

_____

_____

_____

is "application fraud" (or "true name fraud"). Using the victim's information, the thief opens new accounts in the victim's name. The thief has the monthly statements sent to a different address, so considerable time may elapse before the victim realizes what has happened.

4   If there is any good news, it is this: in general, credit and banking fraud victims are liable for no more than the first $50 of loss. Many times, the victim will not have to pay for any of the loss.

5   The bad news is that victims are left with a time-consuming, frustrating mess to clear up. Because their credit has been wrecked, they may be denied credit and loans. They may have difficulty leasing an apartment, or even getting a job. Unfortunately, victims get little help from authorities as they try to untangle the problem.

Thieves' Information Sources

6   How do thieves obtain the information that enables them to "steal" someone else's identity? The easiest way is by stealing the person's wallet. For thieves, it's like one-stop shopping, since wallets usually contain credit cards, a driver's license and other pieces of information, such as the person's Social Security number.

7   There are many other techniques thieves use. These include:

- Stealing documents from unlocked mailboxes and breaking into locked ones. Thieves look especially for boxes of checks, new credit cards, bank statements, tax documents, insurance statements, and credit card statements.

- Searching through trash receptacles ("dumpster diving") for unshredded documents with identifying Social Security numbers, unused pre-approved credit card applications, loan applications, and so forth.

- Using personnel files or customer files in the workplace to improperly access names, Social Security numbers, and other data.

- Obtaining people's credit reports fraudulently by impersonating an employer, a landlord, or a loan officer at a financial institution.

- "Shoulder surfing" at phone booths and ATMs to obtain people's PIN numbers (personal identification numbers).

- Going to Internet sites that provide identifying information and public records.

Practice Exercise

- Topic of paragraph 3:

_____

_____

- Formulate the implied main idea of paragraph 3:

_____

_____

_____

_____

_____

_____

Practice Exercise

- Topic of paragraph 6:

_____

_____

_____

_____

_____

- Formulate the implied main idea of paragraph 6:

_____

_____

_____

_____

How to Reduce the Risk of Identity Theft

Check your credit report.

8 The single best protection is to check your credit report at least once a year. If a thief has stolen your identity, you will become aware of it much sooner. You should order credit reports from the three credit reporting agencies: Equifax (800) 525-6285 or www.equifax.com, Experian (888) 397-3742 or www.experian.com, and TransUnion (800) 680-7289 or www.transunion.com. There is a charge for each report.

- Topic of paragraph 8:

_____

- Formulate the implied main idea of paragraph 8:

_____

_____

_____

_____

_____

_____

Minimize access to your personal information.

9 No one would carelessly leave money lying around in plain sight. It would be an open invitation to anyone who wanted to steal it. Unfortunately, most people are not as careful about their personal information, although they should be. You should protect your personal information with as much diligence as you protect your money.

10 In your wallet, carry only what you need. Carry only one or two credit cards and leave the rest at home. You should also cancel credit cards that you rarely use. Memorize your Social Security number. Leave the card at home unless you must have it with you for a specific reason. Do not carry any card in your wallet that has your SSN on it.

11 Know where your wallet or purse is at all times. Keep it in a safe place at work or, if you are a student, at school. In restaurants, airports, and other public places, such as school campuses, be careful about not leaving a wallet in an unattended book bag or purse. When you are eating, visiting, or waiting for someone, don't hang your book bag or purse on the back of the chair or stow it beneath your chair.

12 If mail is delivered to your home, install a lockable mailbox. Better yet, rent a box at a post office or commercial mailbox service and have your mail sent there. Use the post office box number rather than your home address printed on your checks. If you do not have a lockable home mailbox or rent a box, have checks you order mailed to your bank, and then pick them up there.

13 For maximum safety when you mail envelopes with checks in them, use the drop boxes inside the post office. Do not leave them in your mailbox for the mail carrier to pick up. Nor should you leave them in open "outgoing mail" baskets at work.

14 Remove your name from marketing lists. To minimize nationwide marketers having your name and address, sign up for the Direct Marketing Association's Mail Preference Service (P.O. Box 643, Carmel, NY 10512 or www.dmaconsumers .org/offmailinglist.html) and Telephone Preference Service (P.O. Box 155, Carmel, NY 10512). If your state has a "do not call" list, sign up for it as well. Use an unlisted phone number.

Protect credit cards, passwords,
15 ### *PINs, and receipts.*

You should know how to contact companies in the event your wallet and credit cards are stolen. Record the account numbers, expiration dates, and telephone contact information or photocopy the front and backsides of your credit cards. Store this information in a safe place. You need to be

16 prepared to act quickly if your credit cards are ever stolen.

Unless you initiated contact, do not give out personal information over the phone, by mail or over the Internet. Do not submit personal information to websites. Do not do business with companies online unless they provide transaction security protection. Beware, too, of phone scams in which the caller announces you have won a free trip or some other prize, and that all they need in order to verify that you are the winner is for you to give your Social Security number and a

17 credit card number and its expiration date.

When you are given a credit card receipt, be sure to take it with you. If you are in a store, put the receipt in your wallet and not in the sack. Don't throw credit card receipts in the

18 trash without first tearing them up or shredding them.

Shred pay stubs or file them in a safe place. They can

19 reveal a great deal of personal data.

Identity thieves know that many people use their birthdate, mother's maiden name, or the last four digits of their Social Security number as PIN numbers. Thieves can easily obtain this information, so don't use any of it. You should also avoid using your middle name, consecutive numbers, or other easy-to-remember sequences since these are also obvious choices. Instead, choose a combination of numbers and letters, and preferably at least six in total. For computer passwords, use a combination of 6–8 numbers and upper-

20 case and lowercase letters.

It goes without saying that carrying your passwords and PIN numbers in your wallet is asking for trouble. Memorize

21 them. Don't reveal them to others.

"Shoulder surfers" may stand nearby ATMs and pay telephones. They may even use binoculars or a video camera. For this reason, you should shield your hand when you punch in PIN numbers at ATMs or calling card numbers at payphones.

22 ## Handle Information Responsibly

Social Security numbers are the key to credit and bank accounts. Consequently, they are prime targets of identity thieves. Guard yours carefully, and release it only when

23 absolutely necessary.

Look through monthly statements that you receive for credit card transactions, phone usage, and bank transactions. File them, along with canceled checks (if your bank returns them), in a safe place.

24   Cut up old or unused credit cards and dispose of unwanted pre-approved credit card applications. College students in particular often receive numerous credit card offers, including pre-approved ones. Unwanted ones should be destroyed by tearing them into pieces or shredding them. (Office supply stores sell shredders at an affordable price. Cross-cut shredders are the best choice.) Many college students activate several or all of the pre-approved applications. Because they have so many cards, they not only get in over their heads in debt, they often do not realize it when a card is missing. With an actual card, an identity thief can do considerable damage in a short amount of time.

25   Although these measures require time and effort, they are much simpler than the time and effort required to try to undo the damage caused by identity theft. It takes years to build good credit. It can take even longer to restore it after it has been wrecked by an identity thief.

Further Information

26   If you would like more information about identity theft or privacy protection, there are several websites you can consult. The Privacy Rights Clearinghouse is a nonprofit consumer advocacy organization. At its website, www.privacyrights.org, you can take an "Identity Theft IQ Test" to see how at risk you are of becoming a victim of identity theft. The www.calpirg.org website, another nonprofit consumer advocacy website, also provides a wealth of information and links. In addition, the Identity Theft Resource Center, www.idtheftcenter.org, offers many resource guides for victims. The Federal Trade Commission (FTC) sponsors a tollfree Identity Theft Hotline (1-877-IDTHEFT; 438-4338, or you can visit the ID Theft website at www.consumer.gov/idtheft.

Source: Based on information from CALPIRG [California Public Interest Research Group] (Los Angeles, CA) and the Privacy Rights Clearinghouse (San Diego, CA).

Reading Selection Quiz

This quiz has three parts. Your instructor may assign some or all of them.

Comprehension

Directions: Items 1–10 test your comprehension (understanding) of the material of this selection. These questions are the type a content area instructor (such as a finance professor) would ask on a test over this material. You should be able to answer these questions after studying this selection. For each comprehension question below, use information from the selection to determine the correct answer. Refer to the selection as you answer the questions. Write your answer in the space provided.

_____ 1. One sign that you may have become the victim of identity theft is:
    a. your monthly credit card statement arrives a few days later than usual.
    b. a grocery store asks for your identification when you write a check.
    c. you receive a traffic ticket.
    d. creditors begin demanding payment for purchases you have not made.

_____ 2. It takes longer to detect application fraud theft because the thief:
    a. opens a new account in the victim's name but has the bills sent to a different address.
    b. keeps changing the name on the victim's credit card account.
    c. makes purchases only by phone or online.
    d. uses existing credit information to make purchases.

_____ 3. Until identity theft victims are able to resolve the problem, they may:
    a. find it difficult to lease an apartment.
    b. not be able to obtain credit or get a loan.
    c. have difficulty getting a job.
    d. all of the above

_____ 4. Stealing a wallet is the easiest way for identity thieves to obtain the information they need in order to steal someone else's identity because:
    a. so many people are careless with their wallets.
    b. it is easy to pickpocket a wallet.
    c. people usually carry so much personal information in their wallets.
    d. wallets are small, easy to conceal, and easy for thieves to dispose of.

_____ 5. Which of the following is the least safe place to have mail sent?
    a. a regular home mailbox
    b. a lockable home mailbox
    c. a post office box
    d. a box at a commercial mailbox service

_____ **6.** An example of a safer choice for a password or a PIN would be:

   a. numbers that represent a person's birthdate.

   b. a set of six sequential numbers.

   c. a six-digit number and lowercase and uppercase letter combination.

   d. the year a person was born.

_____ **7.** Credit card receipts should be:

   a. left on the counter.

   b. carried in your wallet rather than in the sack.

   c. thrown in the trash.

   d. given to the salesclerk to throw away.

_____ **8.** The one most effective way to protect yourself against identity theft is to:

   a. shred monthly account statements and canceled checks.

   b. check your three credit reports at least once a year.

   c. remove your name from marketing lists.

   d. photocopy the fronts and backs of all of your credit cards and keep the copy in a safe place.

_____ **9.** Identity thieves are especially interested in obtaining other people's Social Security numbers because SSNs are:

   a. the key to credit and bank accounts.

   b. prime targets.

   c. easy to steal.

   d. difficult to trace.

_____ **10.** One phone scam identity thieves use is to:

   a. pretend they are bank officers calling to verify account information.

   b. call the victim's house to see if anyone is home, and if not, to rob the house.

   c. pose as a representative of a credit card company and tell people they must select new PIN numbers.

   d. tell people they have won a prize, but must reveal personal data to confirm that they are the winner.

S E L E C T I O N **5-1**   *Vocabulary in Context*

Personal Finance
(Continued)

Directions: Items 11–20 test your ability to determine the meaning of a word by using context clues. *Context clues* are words in a sentence that allow the reader to deduce (reason out) the meaning of a unfamiliar word in that sentence. Context clues also enable the reader to determine which meaning the author intends when a word has more than one meaning. For each vocabulary item below, a sentence from the selection containing an important word (*italicized, like this*) is quoted first. Next, there is an additional sentence using the word in the same sense and providing another context clue. Use the context clues from *both* sentences to deduce the meaning of the italicized word. *Be sure the answer you choose makes sense in both sentences.* If you discover that you need to use a dictionary to confirm an answer choice, remember that the meaning you select must still fit the context of *both* sentences. Write your answer in the space provided.

Pronunciation Key: ă pat   ā pay   âr care   ä father   ĕ pet   ē be   ĭ pit
ī tie   îr **pier**   ŏ pot   ō toe   ô paw   oi **noise**   ou **out**   ŏŏ **took**
ōō **boot**   ŭ **cut**   yōō abuse   ûr **urge**   th **thin**   *th* **this**   hw **which**
zh vision   ə **about**   *Stress mark:* '

_____ **11.** Suddenly, though, creditors start *hounding* you for payment of past-due bills, but you never ordered any of the goods or services they're demanding payment for.

Mrs. Ditherwater finally stopped taking her six-year-old twins when she went to the grocery store because they were always *hounding* her to buy them cookies, candy, and toys.

hounding (haund' ĭng) means:
a. begging desperately
b. asking politely
c. harassing persistently
d. pouting childishly

_____ **12.** Perhaps you even receive a *summons* to show up in court for a traffic ticket you never paid—and, in fact, which you never received.

If a person ignores a *summons,* he or she can be arrested for failure to appear in court.

summons (sŭm' ənz) means:
a. citation to appear in court
b. jury verdict of guilty
c. unresolved legal dispute
d. judge's final ruling

_____ **13.** The second type of identity theft is "application *fraud*" (or "true name *fraud*").

The company was convicted of *fraud* for reporting that its previous year's earnings were several millions of dollars higher than they actually were.

fraud (frôd) means:

a.   lying in order to get out of an uncomfortable, embarrassing situation

b.   misrepresenting the truth in order to trick someone into giving up something of value

c.   pretending to be superior when that is not actually the case

d.   refusing to cooperate with authorities

_____ **14.** The thief has the monthly statements sent to a different address, so considerable time may *elapse* before the victim realizes what has happened.

The more time that is allowed to *elapse* before a child is reported missing, the less likely it is that they child can be found and safely returned home.

elapse (ĭ lăps′) means:

a.   hurry by

b.   pass or go by

c.   stay the same

d.   evaporate instantly

_____ **15.** If there is any good news, it is this: in general, credit and banking fraud victims are *liable* for no more than the first $50 of loss.

Since the movers dented my refrigerator when they were loading it into their truck, their company was *liable* for the damages and paid to have it repaired.

liable (lī′ ə bəl) means:

a.   punished

b.   excused or exempted from

c.   fined

d.   obligated by law

_____ **16.** One technique identity thieves use is obtaining people's credit reports fraudulently by *impersonating* an employer, a landlord, or a loan officer at a financial institution.

The imposter, who was dressed in an official uniform and directing traffic at a busy intersection, was arrested for *impersonating* a police officer.

impersonating (ĭm pûr′ sə nāt ĭng) means:

a.   pretending to be a relative of someone

b.   using a false name

c.   pretending to be someone you are not

d.   acting as if you know a person when you do not know them

_____ **17.** When you are eating, visiting, or waiting for someone, don't hang your book bag or purse on the back of your chair or *stow* it beneath your chair.

For safety, airline passengers are required to *stow* carry-on luggage beneath the seat in front of theirs or in the overhead storage compartments.

stow (stō) means:

a. to place carelessly

b. to lock up for safekeeping

c. to put someplace until future use

d. to dispose of in an orderly fashion

_____ **18.** Better yet, rent a box at a post office or *commercial* mailbox service and have your mail sent there

Professional truck drivers, bus drivers, and limousine drivers are required to have *commercial* driver's licenses for their work.

commercial (kə mər′ shəl) means:

a. pertaining to advertisements

b. pertaining to transportation

c. pertaining to mail delivery

d. pertaining to business

_____ **19.** Remove your name from *marketing* lists.

The dealership held a training session to familiarize its sales force with *marketing* material for their new models of cars.

marketing (mär′ kĭt ĭng) means:

a. related to the purchasing of new and used items

b. related to promoting, selling, and distributing a product or service

c. related to telephone sales

d. related to employee training and development

_____ **20.** Beware, too, of phone *scams* in which the caller announces you have won a free trip or some other prize, and that all they need in order to verify that you are the winner is for you to give your Social Security number and a credit card number and its expiration date.

Elderly people are often the victim of insurance *scams* and other deceptions designed to trick them out of their money.

scams (skămz) means:

a. fraudulent operations intended to cheat others

b. cruel practical jokes

c. false, nonexistent charities created to seek donations

d. a hoax designed to fool older people

Reading Skills Application

Directions: Items 21–25 test your ability to *apply* certain reading skills to information in this selection. These types of questions provide valuable practice for all students, especially those who must take standardized reading tests and state-mandated basic skills tests (such as the Florida CLAST Test and the Texas THEA Test). You may not have studied all of the skills at this point, so these items will serve as a helpful preview. The comprehension and critical reading skills in this section are presented in Chapters 4 through 9 of *Opening Doors;* vocabulary and figurative language skills are presented in Chapter 2. As you work through *Opening Doors,* you will practice and develop these skills. Write your answer for each question in the space provided.

_____ **21.** The author's purpose for including the section "How to Reduce the Risk of Identity Theft" is to:

    a. persuade readers not to become victims of identity theft.

    b. inform readers about identity theft scams.

    c. instruct readers how to lessen their likelihood of becoming identity theft victims.

    d. convince identity thieves to stop ruining other people's lives.

_____ **22.** Based on the information in the selection, it can be logically concluded that:

    a. avoiding identity theft requires ongoing diligence and effort.

    b. it is simple to avoid identity theft.

    c. the main problem identity theft victims face is paying off unfair credit charges.

    d. some identity theft victims can clear up the problem very quickly.

_____ **23.** The author uses the term "dumpster diving" to refer to:

    a. thieves' technique of searching through trash receptacles for documents that might enable them to steal someone else's identity.

    b. the process of placing documents with personal information at the bottom of dumpsters so that they are less likely to be found by thieves.

    c. shredding all personal information documents and putting them in dumpsters.

    d. companies' getting rid of outdated customer files by placing them in dumpsters.

_____ **24.** Which of the following statements represents an opinion rather than a fact?

    a. Many times, the victim will not have to pay for any of the loss.

    b. The bad news is that victims are left with a time-consuming, frustrating mess to clear up.

    c. Because their credit has been wrecked, they may be denied credit and loans.

    d. They may have difficulty leasing an apartment, or even getting a job.

_____ **25.** The author would most likely agree with which of the
following statements?

a. Authorities should do more to help identity theft
victims resolve the complicated problems they face.

b. The Social Security system should be done away
with since SSNs give identity thieves access to too
much information.

c. The crime of identity theft is likely to decrease in coming years.

d. There is really nothing anyone can do to avoid identity theft.

SELECTION **5-1**

Personal Finance
(Continued)

Collaboration Option

Respond in Writing

Directions: Refer to Selection 5-1 as needed to answer these essay-type questions.

Option for collaboration: Your instructor may direct you to work with other students on one or more of these items, or in other words, to work *collaboratively.* In that case, you should form groups of three or four students, as directed by your instructor, and work together to complete the exercises. After your group discusses an item and agrees on the answer, have a group member record it. Each member of your group should be able to explain all of your group's answers.

1. List at least four things you could do or change right away that would lessen your risk of becoming an identity theft victim.

_____

_____

_____

_____

_____

_____

2. If you were to become the victim of identity theft, describe *in order* the first three things you would do to begin to resolve the problem.

_____

_____

_____

_____

_____

_____

3. Do you think account takeover or application fraud identity theft would be harder to deal with as a victim? Tell which type and explain your reasoning.

_____

_____

_____

_____

_____

4. **Overall main idea.** What is the overall main idea the authors want the reader to understand about identity theft? Answer this question in one sentence. Be sure to include the phrase _identity theft_ in your overall main idea sentence.

_____

_____

_____

_____

_____

_____

_____

_____

_____

_____

Internet Resources

Read More about This Topic on the World Wide Web

Directions: For further information about the topic of the selection, visit these websites:

www.idtheftcenter.org/index.shtml
This is a nonprofit resource center that helps people prevent and recover from identity theft.

www.oag.state.ny.us/consumer/tips/identity_theft.html
This website offers suggestions for protecting yourself from various forms of identity theft.

www.privacyrights.org
This is the Privacy Rights Clearinghouse website sponsored by the Nonprofit Consumer Information and Advocacy Organization. Click on the "Identity Theft" link.

www.onguardonline.gov/quiz/idtheft_quiz.html
Choose your character in this fun "ID Theft Faceoff," then click to play (take the quiz). If you answer enough questions correctly, your character's identity is restored. This website is sponsored by the federal government and the technology industry.

You can also use your favorite search engine such as Google, Yahoo!, or Alta-Vista (www.google.com, www.yahoo.com, www.altavista.com) to discover more about this topic. To locate additional information, type in combinations of keywords such as:

identity theft

or

avoiding identity theft

or

protection from identity theft

Keep in mind that whenever you go to *any* website, it is a good idea to evaluate the website and the information it contains. Ask yourself questions such as:

"Who sponsors this website?"

"Is the information contained in this website up-to-date?"

"What type of information is presented?"

"Is the information objective and complete?"

"How easy is it to use the features of this website?"

SELECTION **5-2**

Psychology

Violence in Television and Video Games: Does the Media's Message Matter?

From *Essentials of Understanding Psychology,* 6th ed.
By Robert S. Feldman

Prepare Yourself to Read

Directions: Do these exercises *before* you read Selection 5-2.

1. First, read and think about the title. What do you know about the effect of media (television and video game) violence on people who are exposed to it constantly?

   _____

   _____

2. Next, complete your preview by reading the following:

   Introduction (in *italics*)

   First sentence of paragraphs 1–7

   All of the last paragraph

   Now that you have previewed the selection, what point do you think the author is making about media violence?

   _____

   _____

   _____

   _____

   _____

Apply Comprehension Skills

Directions: Do the Annotation Practice Exercises *as* you read Selection 5-2. Apply the skills from this chapter.

Formulate implied main ideas. Follow these general steps: First determine the topic; then as what the author's most important point about the topic is; then create a sentence that expresses the author's most important point. Use the appropriate formula to "formulate" an implied main idea sentence based on information in the paragraph.

Check your formulated main idea sentences. Be sure each of your main idea sentences meets the requirements on page 267.

Complete the Annotation Practice Exercises. In these exercises you will work only with paragraphs that have implied main ideas.

299

VIOLENCE IN TELEVISION AND VIDEO GAMES: DOES THE MEDIA'S MESSAGE MATTER?

Do you play video games or computer games? If so, you are among millions of other Americans. According to Kevin Maney of USA Today, *"If you're under 35, games are a major entertainment and a part of life. . . . They are similar to what rock 'n roll meant to boomers."*

If you are a gamer, how do you compare with the profile of game players? The average game player is 30 years old and has been playing for 9.5 years. Among gamers, 35% are under 18, 43% are 18 to 49 years old, and 19% are 50+ years. With regard to gender, 55% are male and 45% female. Obe Hostetter (www.game-research.com) reports that "On average, American teens spend 1.5 hours per day playing video games. By the time they enter the workforce, they will have played 10,000 hours of computer or video games." Adult gamers have been playing an average of 12 years. Moreover, gamers spend an average of 6.8 hours per week playing games. In 2004, approximately 239 million computer and video games were sold, almost two games per household. Even cell phone users can choose games from their phone menu, download them, and play them on the phone.

How much television do you watch each week? The average American has the TV turned on nearly 8 hours a day and actually watches it for 4 of those hours.

Do you watch violent television shows? Play violent computer and video games? If so, what effect do you think exposure to this violence might be having on you? Read the following excerpt from a psychology textbook to learn about the likely effects.

1   In an episode of HBO's "The Sopranos," fictional mobster Tony Soprano murdered one of this associates. To make identification of the victim's body difficult, Soprano, along with one of this henchmen, dismembered the body and dumped the body parts.

2   A few months later, two real-life half brothers in Riverside, California, strangled their mother and then cut her head and hands from her body. Victor Bautista, 20, and Matthew Montejo, 15, who were caught by police after a security guard noticed that the bundle they were attempting to throw in a dumpster had a foot sticking out of it, told police that the plan to dismember their mother was inspired by "The Sopranos" episode.

Annotation Practice Exercises

Directions: For each exercise below,

• Write the topic of the paragraph on the lines provided.

• Formulate the implied main idea of the paragraph and write it on the lines provided.

This will help you remember the topic and the main idea.

3   Like other "media copycat" killings, the brothers' cold-blooded brutality raises a critical issue: Does observing violent and antisocial acts in the media lead viewers to behave in similar ways? Because research on modeling shows that people frequently learn and imitate the aggression that they observe, this question is among the most important being addressed by psychologists.

4   Certainly, the amount of violence in the mass media is enormous. By the time of elementary school graduation, the average child in the United States will have viewed more than 8,000 murders and more than 800,000 violent acts on network television. Adult television shows also contain significant violence, with cable television leading the way with such shows as "When Animals Attack" and "World's Scariest Police Shootouts."

5   Most experts agree that watching high levels of media violence makes viewers more susceptible to acting aggressively, and recent research supports this claim. For example, a recent survey of serious and violent young male offenders incarcerated in Florida showed that one-fourth of them had attempted to commit a media-inspired copycat crime. A significant proportion of those teenage offenders noted that they paid close attention to the media.

6   Research using video games has also linked violent media with actual aggression. According to a recent series of studies by psychologist Craig Anderson and colleagues, playing violent video games is associated with later aggressive behavior. In one study, for example, they found that college students who frequently played violent video games such as *Postal* or *Doom,* were more likely to have been involved in delinquent behavior and aggression. Furthermore, college students—particularly men—also were more apt to act aggressively toward another student if they'd played a violent video game. Frequent players also had lower academic achievement.

Practice Exercise

- Topic of paragraph 3:

  _____

  _____

  _____

- Formulate the implied main idea of paragraph 3:

  _____

  _____

  _____

  _____

  _____

  _____

  _____

  _____

  _____

  _____

  _____

Does violence in television shows like "The Sopranos" lead to real-life violence? Most research suggests that watching high levels of violence makes viewers more susceptible to acting aggressively.

7   Such results do not show that playing violent games *causes* delinquency, aggression, and lower academic performance; the research only found that the various variables were *associated with* one another. To explore the question of whether violent game play actually caused aggression, researchers conducted a laboratory study. In it, they had participants play either a violent video game (*Wolfenstein 3D*) or one that was nonviolent (*Myst*). The results were clear: Exposure to the graphically violent video game increased aggressive thoughts and actual aggression.

Practice Exercise

• Topic of paragraph 7:

_____

_____

• Formulate the implied main idea of paragraph 7

_____

_____

_____

_____

_____

_____

_____

_____

_____

8   Experiencing media violence may contribute to real-life aggressive behavior because it seems to lower inhibitions against carrying out aggression. Watching television portrayals of violence or using violence to win a video game makes aggression seem a legitimate response to particular situations. In addition, exposure to media violence may distort our understanding of the meaning of others' behavior, predisposing us to view even nonaggressive acts by others as aggressive. Finally, a continuous diet of aggression may leave us desensitized to violence, and what previously would have repelled us now produces little emotional response. Our sense of the pain and suffering brought about by aggression may be diminished.

Practice Exercise

• Topic of paragraph 8:

_____

_____

_____

• Formulate the implied main idea of paragraph 8:

_____

_____

_____

_____

Source: Adapted from Robert S. Feldman, *Essentials of Understanding Psychology,* 6th ed., p. 205. Copyright © 2005 by The McGraw-Hill Companies, Inc. Reprinted by permission of The McGraw-Hill Companies.

SELECTION **5-2**

Psychology
(continued)

Collaboration Option

Respond in Writing

Directions: Refer to Selection 5-2 as needed to answer the essay-type questions below.

Option for collaboration: Your instructor may direct you to work with other students on one or more of these items, or in other words, to work *collaboratively.* In that case, you should form groups of three or four students, as directed by your instructor, and work together to complete the exercises. After your group discusses an item and agrees on the answer, have a group member record it. Each member of your group should be able to explain all of your group's answers.

1. In your opinion, why do you think people find computer and video games so appealing? Why do you think violent television shows are so popular?

   _____   _____

   _____   _____

   _____   _____

2. Young children have difficulty separating fantasy from the real world. In video games, the gamer takes part in the violence and even gets rewards (such as points) for doing so. In many games, the only solution is violence; the gamer can't choose a nonviolent solution and stay alive (continue to play). Authorities say that watching violent television shows and playing violent video games causes the most harm before the age of nine. In light of this information, should children be prohibited from these activities? Why or why not?

   _____

   _____

   _____

3. Millions of Americans begin playing these games at an early age and then continue to play them throughout their adult life. In video games, approximately three-fourths of the perpetrators of violence go unpunished. In other words, the characters who commit violent crimes have no consequences. What are the implications of this for our society as a whole?

   _____

   _____

   _____

4. If parents allow their children access to violent television and video games and those children commit copycat crimes, what responsibility do the parents bear? Should they be held responsible for their children's actions? Why or why not? If parents should be held responsible, what punishment should they be given? When the source of a copycat crime is an extremely violent television show

and video game, what responsibility should be borne by the companies who produced them?

_____

_____

_____

_____

5. Are there *advantages* to playing computer and video games? List at least two.

_____

_____

_____

6. Overall main idea. What is the overall main idea the author wants you to understand about violent television shows and video games on those who play them? Answer this question in one sentence. Be sure that your overall main idea sentence includes the topic *violent television shows and video games* and tells the overall most important point about it. Do *not* begin your sentence with "The overall main idea is . . ." or "The author wants us to understand . . ." Just *state* the overall main idea.

_____

_____

_____

_____

Read More about This Topic on the World Wide Web

Directions: For further information about the topic of the selection, visit these websites:

Internet Resources

www.theesa.com
Entertainment Software Association website that covers "the art, science, and business of computer games." Among other things, it includes statistics about games, who plays them, sales, etc; a dictionary of game-related terms; information about the history and types of computer and video games.

www.nytimes.com/2003/12/21/magazine/21GAMES.html
This article, "Video Game Takeover: Playing Mogul" by Jonathan Dee, appeared in the December 21, 2003, *New York Times.* It focuses on Bruno Bonnell, the French C.E.O. of Atari, but contains a wealth of interesting infor-

mation about the video game industry. (The article is also available as a pdf file at www.urich.edu/~bmayes/pdf/Playing%20Mogul_video%20games.pdf.)

www.csmonitor.com/2003/1112/p09s02-cojh.html
The article, "Video Violence Isn't Harmless Fun" by John Hughes, *Christian Science Monitor,* November 12, 2003.

You can also use your favorite search engine such as Google, Yahoo!, or AltaVista (www.google.com, www.yahoo.com, www.altavista.com) to discover more about this topic. To locate additional information, type in combinations of keywords such as:

violence and television

or

violence in video games

Keep in mind that whenever you go to *any* website, it is a good idea to evaluate the website and the information it contains. Ask yourself questions such as:

"Who sponsors this website?"

"Is the information contained in this website up-to-date?"

"What type of information is presented?"

"Is the information objective and complete?"

"How easy is it to use the features of this website?"

SELECTION **5-3**

Sociology

Demography, the Study of Population

From *Sociology: An Introduction*

By Richard J. Gelles and Ann Levine

Prepare Yourself to Read

Directions: Do these exercises *before* you read Selection 5-3.

1. First, read and think about the title. What do you already know about demography?

_____

_____

_____

2. Next, complete your preview by reading the following:

  Introduction (in *italics*)

  Headings

  All of the first paragraph (paragraph 1)

  First sentence of each of the other paragraphs

  Charts

On the basis of your preview, what does the selection now seem to be about?

_____

_____

_____

_____

_____

Apply Comprehension Skills

Directions: Do the Annotation Practice Exercises *as* you read Selection 5-3. Apply the skills from this chapter:

Formulate implied main ideas. Follow these general steps: First determine the topic; then ask what the author's most important point about the topic is; then create a sentence that expresses the author's most important point. Use the appropriate formula to "formulate" an implied main idea sentence based on information in the paragraph.

Check your formulated main idea sentences. Be sure each of your main idea sentences meets the requirements on page 276.

Complete the Annotation Practice Exercises. In these exercises, you will work only with paragraphs that have implied main ideas.

315

DEMOGRAPHY, THE STUDY OF POPULATION

By the end of 2000, the world's population had climbed to more than 6 billion. Experts estimate that worldwide, 370,000 babies are born daily. In 1900, the world's population stood at 2 billion. Between 1900 and 1999—only 100 years—the human population tripled. There is great concern that humans are quickly consuming natural resources and are ruining the environment and the planet. And nearly half of the babies born will be born into poverty. If the overall rate of population growth in the developing countries remains stable, their populations will double in only 40 years.

There were 100 million people in the United States in 1915. By 2006, our population had risen to 300 million. The U.S. population is expected to reach 400 million by 2046. The state of California alone is expected to increase its population by 18 million by the year 2025, raising its population to 50 million. That means that California will be adding one resident every 45 seconds—the biggest population explosion in the nation's history. The other most populous states also face significant population increases. (Those states, in order, are: Texas, New York, Florida, Pennsylvania, Illinois, Ohio, Michigan, New Jersey, and North Carolina.) Also, the U.S. population is getting older and more Hispanic. (See Reading Selection 4-2.) The problems raised by population growth and by the rapid increases in certain segments of the population—problems such as health care, poverty, education, traffic, streets and road repair, housing, utilities, city services, and pollution, to name a few—will affect all of us. The goal of the United States census in the year 2000 was to count every person in this country: Without reliable figures, it is difficult to plan for the future. It is easy to see why the work of demographers is so important. The selection below, from a sociology textbook, explains what demography is and the population changes that occurred as Western nations shifted from being agricultural nations to industrialized nations.

Demography: The Study of Population

1   The scientific study of population is known as *demography.* The word comes from the Greek for "measuring people." But counting heads is only a small part of what demographers do. They also attempt to calculate the growth rate of a population and to assess the impact of such things as the marriage rate and life expectancy, the sex ratio (the proportion of males to females), and the age structure (the proportions of young, middle-aged, and older people) on human behavior and the structure of society. They are interested in the distribution of population and in movements of people (migration). Put another way, demographers study the effects of such numbers on social trends.

2   Demographers use a number of standard measures in translating a locality's raw totals—births, deaths, the number of those moving in and out—into general statistics that allow them to identify trends. The birthrate is the number of births per 1,000 people in a given year. Suppose there were 900 births in a city of 50,000 in a specific year. Demographers calculate the birthrate for the city by dividing the number of births (900) by the population (50,000) and multiplying the result

Annotation Practice Exercises

Directions: For each exercise below,

• Write the topic of the paragraph on the lines provided.

• Formulate the implied main idea of the paragraph and write it on the lines provided.

This will help you remember the topic and the main idea.

(0.018) by 1,000 to get 18. The birthrate in developed countries is 1.6; in less developed countries (excluding China) it is 4.0. The death rate is the number of deaths per 1,000 people in a given year. (The death rate is calculated in the same way as the birthrate.) The fertility rate is the number of live births per 1,000 women of the world. As mentioned earlier, population and population growth rates are highest in developing nations and lower in Western nations. These rates are also complicated by mass movements of refugees to and from certain countries. By 1994 the population of refugees was over 23 million, up from about 10 million refugees worldwide in 1983. Mass movements of people into and out of Afghanistan, Somalia, Bosnia, and Mozambique have contributed to this sharp increase. Famine and political upheaval are usually behind these mass exoduses. (See Table 1 and Figure 1.)

The Demographic Transition

3   The term *demographic transition* refers to a pattern of major population changes that accompanied the transformation of Western nations from agricultural into industrial societies. The demographic transition occurred in three stages. (See Figure 2.)

4   In *Stage I,* birthrates were high, but death rates were also high. As a result, the population growth rate was low. Thus in eighteenth-century Europe, birthrates were high, but many infants did not survive childhood and many adults did not reach old age. High infant mortality, epidemics, famines, and wars kept the population growth rate low.

5   In *Stage II,* which began in Europe in the late eighteenth century, birthrates remained high, but death rates began to fall. Why? Improvements in agricultural technology, the spread of new and hardier crops (such as the potato), and increased food production. Improvements in transportation facilitated food distribution: people were no longer dependent on local supplies or devastated by local crop failures. Better nutrition meant that people were more able to resist and survive disease. During the nineteenth century, improvements in public

In the United States, demographers analyze data gathered by the census.

Practice Exercise

•   Topic of paragraph 4:

_____

•   Formulate the implied main idea of paragraph 4:

_____

_____

_____

_____

_____

TABLE 1
WORLD POPULATION CLOCK, 1997

Measure	World	Developed Countries	Developing Countries	Developing Countries (Excluding China)
Population:	5,840,433,000	1,174,792,000	4,665,641,000	3,428,948,000
Births per:				
Year	139,366,897	13,450,155	125,916,742	104,917,695
Month	11,613,908	1,120,846	10,493,062	8,743,141
Week	2,680,133	258,657	2,421,476	2,017,648
Day	381,827	36,850	344,977	287,446
Hour	15,909	1,535	14,374	11,977
Minute	265	26	240	200
Second	4.4	0.4	4.0	3.3
Deaths per:				
Year	53,353,684	12,006,985	41,346,699	33,233,993
Month	4,446,140	1,000,582	3,445,558	2,769,499
Week	1,026,032	230,904	795,129	639,115
Day	146,174	32,896	113,279	91,052
Hour	6,091	1,371	4,720	3,794
Minute	102	23	79	63
Second	1.7	0.4	1.3	1.1
Natural increase per:				
Year	86,013,213	1,443,170	84,570,043	71,683,702
Month	7,167,768	120,264	7,047,504	5,973,642
Week	1,654,100	27,753	1,626,347	1,378,533
Day	235,653	3,954	231,699	196,394
Hour	9,819	165	9,654	8,183
Minute	163	3	161	137
Second	2.7	0.0	2.7	2.3
Infant deaths per:				
Year	8,166,650	116,131	8,050,519	7,391,149
Month	680,534	9,678	670,877	615,929
Week	157,051	2,233	154,818	142,137
Day	22,374	318	22,056	20,250
Hour	932	13	919	844
Minute	16	0.2	15	14
Second	0.3	0.0	0.3	0.2

Source: Population Today, May 1997, p. 2. Reprinted by permission of Population Reference Bureau, Washington, DC.

Figure 1
World Population Growth
Through most of human history, the population was more or less stable. In modern times, however, world population has skyrocketed.

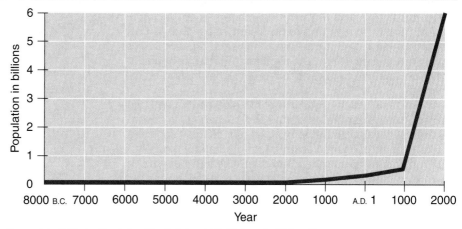

Source: John R. Weeks, *Population,* 5th ed., Belmont, CA: Wadsworth, 1992, p. 30.

Figure 2
Demographic Transition in Western Nations
In Stage I, birthrates and death rates were both high, population growth (the purple line) was slow. In Stage II, death rates declined faster than birthrates, so population growth continued to climb. Only when birthrates and deaths rates are both low, Stage III, does population growth slow down.

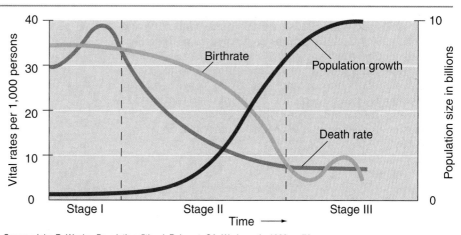

Source: John R. Weeks. *Population,* 5th ed. Belmont, CA: Wadsworth, 1992, p. 76.

health and sanitation (cleaner water, better sewage disposal, pasteurized milk) and advances in modern medicine contributed further to the decline in death rates. Many more women survived into their childbearing years. The population growth rate soared. (*Note:* The eighteenth-century population explosion was due to lower death rates rather than to higher birthrates.)

6   In *Stage III,* which began in the mid-nineteenth century in Western nations, birthrates started to fall. Stage III is associated with industrial development. In agricultural societies, children are an economic asset: the more hands, the better. In urban, industrial societies, however, children become an "economic burden." They are financially dependent on their parents for an extended period. Large families mean crowded living quarters, additional household expenses, and a lower family standard of living. Four additional factors that contributed to falling birthrates in the West in the twentieth century were the decline in infant mortality (which meant that a couple did not have to produce five or six children to ensure that three or four would live), government-sponsored Social Security programs in the 1930s and 1940s (which meant that parents did not have to depend on their children to support them in old age), access to modern birth control devices in the late 1950s and early 1960s, and postponement of the age of marriage. By the 1960s families with only two or three children had become the norm. Today birthrates in most Western nations have stabilized at replacement levels, while death rates have continued to decline. (Half of the Americans now alive would have been dead if the death rate had remained at 1900 levels.) Thus the balance between birthrates and death rates has been restored; as in Stage I the population growth rate is low.

Practice Exercise

• Topic of paragraph 5:

_____

• Formulate the implied main idea of paragraph 5:

_____

_____

_____

_____

Practice Exercise

• Topic of paragraph 6:

_____

• Formulate the implied main idea of paragraph 6:

_____

_____

_____

_____

_____

_____

Source: Richard J. Gelles and Ann Levine, *Sociology: An Introduction,* 6th ed. Boston: McGraw-Hill, 1999, pp. 594–97. Permission granted by Richard J. Gelles and Ann Levine.

SELECTION **5-3**

Sociology
(Continued)

**Student Online
Learning Center (OLC)**
Go to Chapter 5.
Choose Reading
Selection Quiz.

Reading Selection Quiz

This quiz has three parts. Your instructor may assign some or all of them.

Comprehension

Directions: Items 1–10 test your comprehension (understanding) of the material of this selection. These questions are the type a content area instructor (such as a sociology professor) would ask on a test over this material. You should be able to answer these questions after studying this selection. For each comprehension question below, use information from the selection to determine the correct answer. Refer to the selection as you answer each question. Write your answer in the space provided.

True or False

_____ **1.** The scientific study of population trends is known as the *fertility* rate.

_____ **2.** *Life expectancy* is the potential life span of the average member of any given population.

_____ **3.** Population growth rates are highest in Western nations and lower in developing nations.

_____ **4.** According to the Population Reference Bureau, in 1997 there were 381,827 births each day worldwide.

Multiple-Choice

_____ **5.** Demographers:
    a. are interested in the distribution of population and in movements of people.
    b. assess the impact of such things as life expectancy and the marriage rate.
    c. count people and calculate the growth rate of a population.
    d. all of the above

_____ **6.** In a given year, the birthrate in less developed countries (excluding China) is:
    a. 18 per 1,000 people.
    b. 4.0 per 1,000 people.
    c. 1.6 per 1,000 people.
    d. 0.018 per 1,000 people.

_____ **7.** Population growth is slowed when:
    a. birth rates are high.
    b. death rates are low.
    c. both birth rates and death rates are low.
    d. birth rates are high and death rates are low.

_____ **8.** World population skyrocketed in about:

    a. 2000 B.C.

    b. 1000 B.C.

    c. A.D. 1000

    d. A.D. 2000

_____ **9.** During Stage III of the demographic transition in Western nations, birthrates declined because:

    a. infant mortality increased.

    b. access to modern birth control devices became available in the late 1950s and early 1960s.

    c. fewer people postponed marriage.

    d. couples began having children earlier.

_____ **10.** In 1997 there were 26 births per minute in developed countries, while in developing countries the number of births per minute was:

    a. 240.

    b. 265.

    c. 932.

    d. 4,720.

SELECTION **5-3**   *Vocabulary in Context*

Sociology
(Continued)

Directions: Items 11–20 test your ability to determine the meaning of a word by using context clues. *Context clues* are words in a sentence that allow the reader to deduce (reason out) the meaning of an unfamiliar word in that sentence. Context clues also enable the reader to determine which meaning the author intends when a word has more than one meaning. For each vocabulary item below, a sentence from the selection containing an important word (*italicized, like this*) is quoted first. Next, there is an additional sentence using the word in the same sense and providing another context clue. Use the context clues from *both* sentences to deduce the meaning of the italicized word. *Be sure the answer you choose makes sense in both sentences.* If you discover that you need to use a dictionary to confirm an answer choice, remember that the meaning you select must still fit the context of *both* sentences. Write your answer in the space provided.

Pronunciation Key: ă pat   ā pay   âr care   ä father   ě pet   ē be   ĭ pit
ī tie   îr pier   ŏ pot   ō toe   ô paw   oi noise   ou out   ŏŏ took
ōō boot   ŭ cut   yōō abuse   ûr urge   th thin   *th* this   hw which
zh vision   ə about   *Stress mark:* ˈ

_____ **11.** They also attempt to calculate the growth rate of a population and to assess the impact of such things as the marriage rate and life *expectancy.*

Insurance rates are based on life *expectancy:* The younger the person, the lower the rate.

expectancy (ĭk spĕk′ tən sē) means:

a. length

b. a known quantity or amount

c. an expected amount calculated on the basis of statistical data

d. a quantity or amount that cannot be determined or estimated

_____ **12.** They are interested in the *distribution* of population and in movements of people (migration).

The *distribution* of saguaro cactus is limited to the southwestern part of the United States and northern Mexico.

distribution (dĭ strĭ byōō′ shən) means:

a. disappearance; extinction

b. planting

c. geographic occurrence or range

d. destruction

_____ **13.** Demographers use a number of *standard* measures in translating a locality's raw totals—births, deaths, the number of those moving in and out—into general statistics that allow them to identify trends.

Nutritionists have established the *standard* amount of fats, carbohydrates, and protein adults need in their diet.

standard (stăn′ dərd) means:

a. acknowledged measure

b. imprecise

c. incomplete

d. ambiguous

_____ **14.** Demographers use a number of standard measures in translating a *locality's* raw totals—births, deaths, the number of those moving in and out—into general statistics that allow them to identify trends.

Because the population in our suburb is increasing, there are many new businesses moving into our *locality.*

locality (lō kăl′ ĭ tē) means:

a. voting precinct

b. school district

c. state

d. a particular place

15. *Mass* movements of people into and out of Afghanistan, Somalia, Bosnia, and Mozambique have contributed to this sharp increase.

Most large cities have subway systems, bus systems, or other forms of *mass* transit.

mass (măs) means:

a.   pertaining to religion

b.   related to a large number of people

c.   pertaining to citizens of a country

d.   related to high speed

16. Famine and political *upheaval* are usually behind these mass exoduses.

The earthquake caused a complete *upheaval* of life in the peaceful mountain village.

upheaval (üp hē′ vəl) means:

a.   improvement

b.   elevation

c.   sudden, violent disruption

d.   gradual change

17. Famine and political upheaval are usually behind these mass *exoduses*.

Historians report that seeking refuge from war, religious persecution, and epidemics are three major reasons for *exoduses*.

exoduses (ēk′ sə dəs əz) means:

a.   trips or journeys

b.   departures of large numbers of people

c.   refusals to leave

d.   planned absences

18. High infant *mortality,* epidemics, famines, and wars kept the population growth rate low.

Child *mortality* is higher in poor countries because health care for children is so inadequate.

mortality (môr tăl′ ĭ tē) means:

a.   correct behavior

b.   heart attacks

c.   death rate

d.   protection

_____ **19.** Improvements in transportation *facilitated* food distribution: people were no longer dependent on local supplies or devastated by local crop failures.

The new, computerized traffic signals *facilitated* the smooth flow of traffic during rush hour.

facilitated (fə sĭl′ ĭ tāt ĕd) means:

a. made easier

b. slowed down

c. directed

d. authorized

_____ **20.** Today birthrates in most Western nations have *stabilized* at replacement levels, while death rates have continued to decline.

Once the paramedics *stabilized* the victim's erratic breathing and heart rate, they rushed her to the emergency room for treatment.

stabilized (stā′ bə līzd) means:

a. resuscitated

b. decreased

c. stopped

d. became steady or stable

SELECTION **5-3**   *Reading Skills Application*

Sociology
(Continued)

Directions: Items 21–25 test your ability to *apply* certain reading skills to information in this selection. These types of questions provide valuable practice for all students, especially those who must take standardized reading tests and state-mandated basic skills tests (such as the Florida CLAST Test and the Texas THEA Test). You may not have studied all of the skills at this point, so these items will serve as a helpful preview. The comprehension and critical reading skills in this section are presented in Chapters 4 through 9 of *Opening Doors;* vocabulary and figurative language skills are presented in Chapter 2. As you work through *Opening Doors,* you will practice and develop these skills. Write your answer for each question in the space provided.

_____ **21.** In paragraph 1 *counting heads* means:

a. people who are demographers and mathematicians.

b. determining the number of people in a population.

c. the work that statisticians do.

d. measuring the size of people's heads.

_____   **22.** Which of the following statements from the paragraph expresses the main idea of paragraph 2?

    a. Demographers use a number of standard measures in translating a locality's raw totals—births, deaths, the numbers of those moving in and out—into general statistics that allow them to identify trends.

    b. The birthrate is the number of births per 1,000 people in a given year.

    c. The death rate is the number of deaths per 1,000 people in a given year.

    d. These rates are also complicated by mass movements of refugees to and from certain countries.

_____   **23.** The authors organize the information in paragraphs 3–6 using which of the following patterns?

    a. list

    b. problem-solution

    c. sequence

    d. comparison

_____   **24.** Which of the following statements from the selection represents an opinion rather than a fact?

    a. The population growth rate soared.

    b. Improvements in transportation facilitated food distribution.

    c. Better nutrition meant that people were more able to resist and survive disease.

    d. During the nineteenth century, improvements in public health and sanitation and advances in modern science contributed further to the decline in death rates.

_____   **25.** From information in the selection it can be inferred that the size of a population is influenced by:

    a. the ratio between the birthrate and the death rate.

    b. the birthrate only.

    c. the death rate only.

    d. neither the birthrate nor the death rate.

SELECTION **5-3**

Sociology
(Continued)

Collaboration Option

Respond in Writing

Directions: Refer to Selection 5-3 as needed to answer the essay-type questions below.

Option for collaboration: Your instructor may direct you to work with other students on one or more of these items, or in other words, to work *collaboratively.* In that case, you should form groups of three or four students, as directed by your instructor, and work together to complete the exercises. After your group discusses an item and agrees on the answer, have a group member record it. Each member of your group should be able to explain all of your group's answers.

1. The world's population growth is not expected to slow down for the next 50 years. What are the implications of this for you and your family (or your future family)?

   _____

   _____

   _____

   _____

   _____

2. In China, the government enforces a policy that restricts most couples to only one child. Given the overpopulation problem the world is facing, do you think all countries should limit the number of children couples are allowed to have? Explain why or why not.

   _____

   _____

   _____

   _____

3. If the number of children couples could have were restricted by law, should couples be allowed to have an additional child if they can pay the government a special fee? Why or why not?

   _____

   _____

   _____

   _____

   _____

4. Are there any *advantages* to having so many more people in the world today? Try to think of at least two.

_____

_____

_____

_____

_____

_____

5. If there were a birth control pill for men, do you think the worldwide birthrate would decline? Explain why or why not.

_____

_____

_____

_____

6. Use the information from the table in the selection to complete this summary chart of population change per minute in 1997:

WORLD POPULATION CLOCK, 1997 PER MINUTE			
	World	Developed Countries	Developing Countries	Developing Countries (excluding China)
Births				
Deaths				
Natural increase				
Infant deaths				

7. Based on your chart above, what conclusion can you draw about where world population is increasing most rapidly?

    _____

    _____

8. **Overall main idea.** What is the overall main idea the authors want the reader to understand about demography? Answer this question in one sentence. Be sure that your overall main idea sentence includes the topic (*demography*) and tells the overall most important point about it.

    _____

    _____

    _____

    _____

Internet Resources

Read More about This Topic on the World Wide Web

Directions: For further information about the topic of the selection, visit these websites:

www.census.gov
This is the U.S. Census Bureau website. The goal of the Census Bureau is to provide the best mix of timelines, relevance, quality, and cost for the data it collects and the services it provides.

www.census.gov/main/www/popclock.html
This site, sponsored by the U.S. Census Bureau, gives daily estimates of United States and world population. Click on the *U.S. POPClock* or *World POPClock* links.

www.ssc.wisc.edu/cde/
The Center for Demography and Ecology (CDE) at the University of Wisconsin at Madison is one of the world's leading centers of social science.

www.demographics.com
American Demographics, a monthly magazine with a circulation of 22,000, covers human population patterns and consumer trends in behavior and attitude.

You can also use your favorite search engine such as Google, Yahoo!, or Alta-Vista (www.google.com, www.yahoo.com, www.altavista.com) to discover more about this topic. To locate additional information, type in combinations of key-words such as:

demography

or

demographics United States

or

demographics _____ **(your state or city)**

Keep in mind that whenever you go to *any* website, it is a good idea to evaluate the website and the information it contains. Ask yourself questions such as:

"Who sponsors this website?"

"Is the information contained in this website up-to-date?"

"What type of information is presented?"

"Is the information objective and complete?"

"How easy is it to use the features of this website?"

CHAPTER 6

Identifying Supporting Details

CHAPTER OBJECTIVES

In this chapter you will learn the answers to these questions:

- What are supporting details in a paragraph?

- Why is it useful to understand supporting details?

- How can I identify supporting details in paragraphs?

- How can I list supporting details clearly?

- What are major and minor details, and what is the difference between them?

SKILLS

Supporting Details in Paragraphs

- What Are Supporting Details?
- Why Are Supporting Details Important?

Identifying and Listing Supporting Details

Major and Minor Details, and How to Tell the Difference

A Word about Standardized Reading Tests: Supporting Details

CREATING YOUR SUMMARY

Developing Chapter Review Cards

READINGS

Selection 6-1   *(Health)*
"Diabetes: An Alarming Epidemic"
from *Core Concepts in Health*
by Paul Insel and Walton Roth

Selection 6-2   *(Health)*
"America's Most Popular Drug: Caffeine"
from *Understanding Your Health*
by Wayne Payne, Dale Hahn, and Ellen Mauer

Selection 6-3   *(Economics)*
"What Can Be Done to Help Third World Countries?"
from *A Beginner's Guide to the World Economy*
by Randy Charles Epping

When we read too fast or too slowly, we understand nothing.

Blaise Pascal

Knowledge is happiness.

Thomas Jefferson

SUPPORTING DETAILS IN PARAGRAPHS

What Are Supporting Details?

A paragraph consists of more than just a topic and a main idea. Other sentences in a paragraph present supporting details. The topic and the main idea are essential to understanding the paragraph, but the **supporting details** provide additional information that helps you understand the main idea *completely*. In other words, supporting details explain, illustrate, or prove the main idea of a paragraph.

Supporting details typically consist of:

- Examples
- Descriptions
- Characteristics
- Steps
- Places
- Names
- Dates
- Statistics
- Reasons
- Results
- Other information explaining, illustrating, or proving the main idea

Student Online Learning Center (OLC)
Go to **Chapter 6.**
Select **Video.**

Be careful not to confuse the main idea with the supporting details. Details pertain to the main idea, but they are not the same thing. The main idea expresses an important *general* point that is based on the supporting details or is explained by them.

Why Are Supporting Details Important?

As noted above, the supporting details in a paragraph have an important connection with the main idea. First, they help explain the main idea. Second, supporting details often lead you to the stated main idea. Similarly, supporting details contain important information that can help you formulate the main idea when it is implied. Third, it is useful to identify and understand supporting details because they can help you grasp the *organization* of a paragraph. And if you understand *how* the supporting details are organized to explain, illustrate, or prove the main idea of the paragraph, that makes it easier to remember the material, to take notes, and to mark your

Supporting details are important to include on study cards because the details explain, illustrate, or prove main ideas.

textbooks effectively. As you will learn in Chapter 7, details are usually organized according to one of several common writing patterns. Specific types of supporting details that authors use to organize ideas into paragraphs include lists of characteristics, things, places, etc. (called a *list pattern*); items in a series or steps in a process (called a *sequence pattern*); similarities, differences, or both (called a *comparison-contrast pattern*), or reasons and results (called a *cause-effect pattern*). Lastly, listing the supporting details on paper after you finish reading can help you find all of them. Therefore, when you are studying, there will be many instances when you will want to list supporting details in order to learn and remember them. For example, you might want to list important supporting details from a paragraph in a history textbook on chapter review cards. Instructors often ask test questions based on supporting details—examples, reasons, steps, names, dates, places, and other important information. Along with determining the topic and the main idea, then, identifying supporting details will help you become a more successful reader and student.

The following diagram shows the relationship between a main idea and its supporting details:

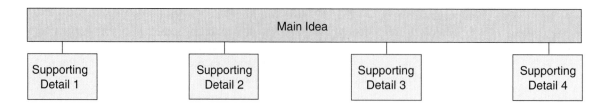

IDENTIFYING AND LISTING SUPPORTING DETAILS

Comprehension Monitoring Question for Identifying Supporting Details

What additional information does the author provide to help me understand the main idea completely?

Student Online Learning Center (OLC)
Go to Chapter 6.
Select Video.

To identify the supporting details of a paragraph, ask yourself, "*What additional information* does the author provide to help me understand the main idea completely?" One way to approach this is by turning the main idea sentence into a question by using the word *who, what, where, when, why,* or *how,* and then seeking the information that answers this question. For example, suppose that the stated main idea of a paragraph is: *In a corporation, the chief financial officer is responsible for four basic functions.* You could change this sentence into the question, "*What* are the four basic functions of a chief financial officer?" That question would lead you to the four details that describe the basic functions and, therefore, explain the main idea.

Often, you will find that supporting details are introduced by signal words such as *first, second, next, also, and, another, in addition,* and *moreover.* Watch for numbers (1, 2, 3) and letters (*a, b, c*) that signal lists of details. Watch for information introduced by the phrases *for example* and *to illustrate,* since examples are always details.

Here is an excerpt from a music appreciation textbook. Its topic is *the role of American colleges and universities in our musical culture.* The first sentence is the stated main idea: *American colleges and universities have played an unusually vital role in our musical culture.* Turn this main idea into the question, "*What* role have American colleges and universities played in our musical culture?" After you have read the paragraph, identify the details that answer this question.

> American colleges and universities have played an unusually vital role in our musical culture. They have trained and employed many of our leading composers, performers, and scholars. Music courses have expanded the horizons and interests of countless students. And since the 1950s, many universities have sponsored performing groups specializing in twentieth-century music. In addition, they have housed most of the electronic music studios.
>
> *Source:* Adapted from Roger Kamien, *Music: An Appreciation,* 5th ed., p. 444. Copyright © 1992 by The McGraw-Hill Companies, Inc. Reprinted by permission of The McGraw-Hill Companies.

Listed below are the four details that answer the question, "*What* role have American colleges and universities played in our musical culture?" As you can see, listing the supporting details below a question is an ideal format for study cards.

What role have American colleges and universities played in our musical culture?

1. They trained and employed many leading composers, performers, and scholars.
2. They expanded the horizons and interests of students through music courses.
3. Since the 1950s, they have sponsored performing groups specializing in twentieth-century music.
4. They have housed most of the electronic music studios.

The following diagram (also called a study map) shows the relationship between the main idea and the supporting details in this paragraph. This is also a good format for study cards.

Main Idea
American colleges and universities have played an unusually vital role in our musical culture.

Supporting Detail 1	**Supporting Detail 2**	**Supporting Detail 3**	**Supporting Detail 4**
They trained and employed many leading composers, performers, and scholars.	They expanded the horizons and interests of students through music courses.	Since the 1950s, they have sponsored performing groups specializing in twentieth-century music.	They have housed most of the electronic music studios.

KEY TERM

paraphrasing

Restating an author's material in your own words.

Notice that in this example, the supporting details are written out exactly as they appear in the paragraph. When *you* are listing supporting details, however, you will often want to use some of your own words and abbreviations in order to keep them brief. Restating an author's material in your own words is called **paraphrasing.** Notice also, in this excerpt, the words *And* and *In addition* in the last two sentences. These words signal to the reader that two separate details are being given. However, notice that not every detail is introduced by a signal word.

Because you are responsible for understanding the supporting details in a textbook paragraph, you will also find it helpful after you have read the paragraph to go back and insert a *number* next to each detail. Numbering the supporting details is helpful for at least three reasons. First, it helps you locate all the details. Second, it helps you remember how many details there were in the paragraph. Third, it prevents you from overmarking the paragraph by underlining or highlighting too much. (You may also find it helpful to number the details when you list them in your notes or on chapter review cards.)

Stop and Annotate

Go back to the excerpt on page 335. Locate the four supporting details and number them with a small ①, ②, ③, and ④. Underline or highlight the signal words *And* and *In addition* that helped you identify the last two details.

In the next excerpt, the topic is *Richard Feynman* (fīn′ mən), an American physicist and writer. Feynman was a Nobel laureate who worked on the atomic bomb, reinvented quantum mechanics (the mathematics describing atomic processes), and exposed the fatal error by NASA that caused the explosion of the first space shuttle, *Challenger,* in 1985. The first sentence of the paragraph is the stated main idea: *Mr. Feynman was one of the great characters of modern physics.* Change this main idea sentence into the question, "*Why* was Feynman considered a 'character'?" (As it is used in this paragraph, the word *character* refers to an unusual or eccentric person.) Then read the paragraph to identify the details that answer this question.

Richard Feynman was one of the great characters of modern physics. He was a jokester who figured out how to crack safes in Los Alamos offices while working on atomic bomb research in World War II. He was a computational genius, once beating early computers in a contest to track a rocket launch. He could demolish other physicists whose presentation contained an error or humiliate them by producing in minutes a complicated calculation that took them weeks or months.

Source: Adapted from Tom Siegfried, "Exploring the Mind of a Genius," *Dallas Morning News,* October 25, 1992, sec. J, by permission of *Dallas Morning News.*

Listed below are the two details that answer the question, "*Why* was Richard Feynman considered a 'character'?" Again, notice how listing the supporting details below a question makes an easy-to-read study card.

Stop and Annotate

Go back to the excerpt above. Locate the two supporting details and number them with a small ① and ②.

Why was Richard Feynman considered a "character"?

1. He was a jokester.
2. He was a computational genius.

Notice how briefly and succinctly these supporting details can be paraphrased and how clearly they stand out when they are listed on separate lines. Listing the supporting details this way makes it easy to see the information that explains why Feynman was considered a "character." (The contest with the computer and his "demolishing" other physicists are minor details that give proof of his computational ability.) As mentioned above, when you are listing supporting details, it is not necessary to use the exact words of the paragraph, and it is not necessary to use complete sentences. Did you notice that no signal words were used in this paragraph to identify the two supporting details? Instead, the author presents two details about Feynman that are quite different from each other: that he was a computational genius and, surprisingly, that he was also a jokester. The unusual combination of these two characteristics supports the author's main point that Feynman was a "character."

The next excerpt is from a well-known book on writing. The excerpt contains a number of important details. The topic of this paragraph is *careless writing and ways readers get lost,* and its stated main idea is the second sentence: *If the reader is lost, it's usually because the writer hasn't been careful enough.* Turn the main idea into the question, "*How* do careless writers cause readers to get lost?" Now read the paragraph to find the supporting details that answer this question.

It won't do to say that the reader is too dumb or too lazy to keep pace with the train of thought. If the reader is lost, it's usually because the writer hasn't been careful enough. The carelessness can take any number of forms. Perhaps a sentence is so excessively cluttered that the reader, hacking through the verbiage, simply doesn't know what it means. Perhaps a sentence has been so shoddily constructed that the reader could read it in several ways. Perhaps the writer has switched pronouns in mid-sentence, or has switched tenses, so the reader loses track of who is talking or when the action took place. Perhaps Sentence B is not a logical sequel to Sentence A—the writer, in whose head the connection is clear, has not bothered to provide the missing link. Perhaps the writer has used an important word incorrectly by not taking the trouble to look it up.

Source: Adapted from William K. Zinsser, *On Writing Well*, 5th ed., New York: Harper and Row, 1994, pp. 9, 12.

Here is a list of the five details that answer the question, "*How* do careless writers cause readers to get lost?"

How do careless writers cause readers to get lost?

1. Careless writers clutter sentences with too many words.
2. They write sentences that can be read in several ways.
3. They switch pronouns or tenses.
4. They don't supply links between sentences.
5. They use words incorrectly.

Stop and Annotate

Go back to the excerpt above. Locate the five supporting details and number them with a small ①, ②, ③, and ④, an ⑤. Underline or highlight the signal words *perhaps* that helped you identify all five details.

Notice that some of the details listed above have been paraphrased to make them briefer and easier to understand and remember. Notice also that none of the common signal words (such as *also, and,* and *another*) were used in this paragraph. Instead, repeated use of the word *perhaps* signals each supporting detail in the paragraph. Inserting small numbers next to the details would make them easy to locate, even though the details are spread throughout the paragraph.

The next sample paragraph is from a health textbook. As the heading indicates, its topic is *water.* Its implied main idea is: *Water serves many important functions in the body.* Turn this main idea into the question "*What* important functions does water serve in the body?" Then read the paragraph to find the details that answer this question.

Water

Water has no nutritional value, yet is a very important food component. It is used to transport nutrients to the cells and to remove cellular waste products. In addition, it acts as a medium for digestion, regulates body temperature, and helps cushion the vital organs. An inadequate water intake will restrict the function of all body systems. Finally, water and some of the chemicals it carries are responsible for bodily structure, since, on average, 60 percent of the body is water.

Source: Adapted from Marvin Levy, Mark Dignan, and Janet Shirreffs, *Targeting Wellness: The Core,* p. 52. Copyright © 1992 by The McGraw-Hill Companies. Reprinted by permission of The McGraw-Hill Companies.

Here is a list of the eight paraphrased details that answer the question, "*What important functions does water serve in the body?*"

What important functions does water serve in the body?

1. an important food component
2. transports nutrients to cells
3. removes cellular waste
4. acts as a medium for digestion
5. regulates body temperature
6. helps cushion vital organs
7. inadequate intake restricts functions of all body systems
8. partly responsible for body structure because the body is 60 percent water

Stop and Annotate

Go back to the excerpt above. Locate the eight supporting details and number each with a small number. Underline or highlight the signal words *In addition* and *Finally,* which helped you identify two of the details.

Be aware that a single sentence can contain more than one supporting detail. In this paragraph, although there are five sentences, there are eight supporting details. The second sentence contains two details, and the third sentence contains three. There are two signals in the paragraph, *In addition* and *Finally.* (There are other ways besides listing to organize supporting details you want to study and learn. These techniques are called annotation, outlining, and mapping. They are presented in Chapter 10.)

MAJOR AND MINOR DETAILS, AND HOW TO TELL THE DIFFERENCE

KEY TERM

major details

Details that directly support the main idea.

Major details are also known as *primary details.*

All the details in a paragraph ultimately support the main idea by explaining, illustrating, or proving it in some way. In each of the examples presented earlier, all the details *directly* supported (explained) the main idea. Details that directly support the main idea are called **major details** (these are also known as *primary details*). However, there are paragraphs in which some details support or explain *other details.* These are called **minor details** (they are also known as *secondary details*).

The following diagram shows the relationship between the main idea, major details, and minor details.

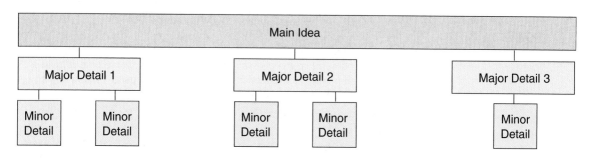

KEY TERM
minor details

Details that support
other details.

Minor details are also
known as *secondary
details.*

Here is a simple paragraph that has been created to illustrate major and minor details. Its topic is *uses of pepper.* Its stated main idea is the first sentence, *Throughout history, pepper had many other uses besides as a way to season food.* There are three major details that explain those other uses of pepper. The other sentences are minor details that explain the major details.

> Throughout history, pepper has had many other uses besides as a way to season food. Pepper was also one of the first ways of preserving meat. During the Crusades pepper was used to preserve sausages. Pepper is still used to preserve meat today. Pepper has also been used as a medicine. In medieval times peppercorns were prescribed to cure aches and pains. Native Americans today use pepper to cure toothaches. Today, pepper is also used to control insects. For example, the French and Dutch use pepper to kill moths and to repel other insects.

The following diagram shows the relationship between the main idea and the major and minor details for this paragraph.

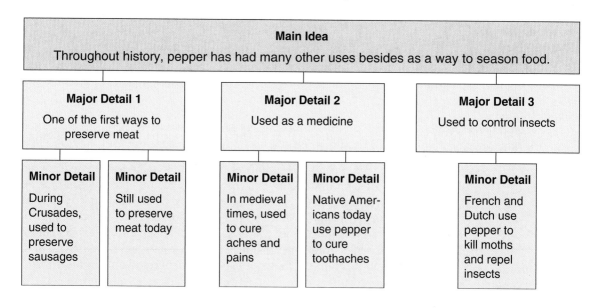

Stop and Annotate

Go back to the excerpt on page 340. Locate the three major details and number them with a small ①, ②, and ③. Underline the signal word *also*, which helped you identify the last two major details.

Again, notice that only three details directly answer the main idea question, "How has pepper been used in different ways throughout history besides as a way to season food?" Therefore, these three details are major details. The passage would make sense with only the main idea and those details. However, the author explains even more fully by giving examples of the three ways. Therefore, those details, which explain other details, are minor details.

Remember, to identify the supporting details of a paragraph, ask yourself, "What *additional information* does the author provide to help me understand the main idea completely?" Change the main idea into a question; then look for the major details that answer the question. Be aware that the author might also include minor details to increase your understanding even more. Don't spend too much time worrying about whether a detail is major or minor. The important thing is simply that you distinguish between the main idea and the details.

A WORD ABOUT STANDARDIZED READING TESTS: SUPPORTING DETAILS

Many college students are required to take standardized reading tests as part of an overall assessment program, in a reading course, or as part of a state-mandated basic skills test. A standardized reading test typically consists of a series of passages followed by multiple-choice reading skill application questions to be completed within a specified time limit.

Standardized reading tests always include questions about supporting details. The purpose of such questions is to see if you can locate and comprehend specific information stated in a passage.

Test questions about supporting details often begin with phrases such as:

According to the passage . . .

According to the information in the passage . . .

The author states . . .

The author states that . . .

Questions may also refer to specific information in a passage, as in the following examples:

One function of water in the body is . . .

The museum mentioned in the passage is located in . . .

World War I began in the year . . .

The height of the tower was . . .

To answer an item about supporting details, read the question carefully to determine exactly what information you need (for instance, a place, a person's name, or a date). Then *skim* the passage, looking for that information. When you come to the part of the passage that has what you are looking for, slow down and read it more carefully.

Don't overlook a correct answer simply because it is worded differently from the way the information appears in the passage. For instance, a passage might state that a child was rescued by a "police officer," but the correct answer choice might say "an officer of the law." Or a passage might specifically mention Bill Gates and Donald Trump, but the correct answer might be worded "two of America's wealthiest businessmen." Remember, you need to look for information in the answer choices that *means the same thing* as the information in the passage, even if the words themselves are different.

SELECTION **6-1**

Health

Diabetes: An Alarming Epidemic

From *Core Concepts in Health*

By Paul Insel and Walton Roth

Prepare Yourself to Read

Directions: Do these exercises *before* you read Selection 6-1.

1. Read and think about the title. What do you already know about diabetes?

   _____

   _____

   _____

   _____

2. Next, complete your preview by reading the following:

   Introduction (in *italics*)

   Headings

   All of the first paragraph (paragraph 1)

   First sentence of each of the other paragraphs

   Now that you have previewed the selection, write a definition of diabetes.

   _____

   _____

   _____

   _____

   _____

   _____

Apply Comprehension Skills

Directions: Do the Annotation Practice Exercises *as* you read Selection 6-1. Apply the skills from this chapter:

Determine the topic.   When you read a paragraph, ask yourself, "Who or what is this about?"

Locate or formulate the main idea.   As you read, ask yourself, "What is the most important point the author wants me to understand about the topic?"

Identify and list supporting details.   As you read, ask yourself, "What additional information does the author provide to help me understand the main idea completely?" Then list the supporting details.

DIABETES: AN ALARMING EPIDEMIC

Metabolic disorders are caused by the body's inability to control certain chemical processes that regulate tissue growth and repair. Perhaps the most well-known metabolic disorder is diabetes, a disease that can cause serious damage to the body. Diabetes kills more people each year than AIDS and breast cancer combined. Among all those in whom diabetes is diagnosed at age 40, men will lose 11.6 years of life and 18.6 years of quality life, and women will lose 14.3 years of life and 22 years of quality life as a result of the disease.

In 2005, more than 1.5 million new cases were diagnosed. There are currently 20.8 million Americans who are diabetic. One-third of them do not know they have the disease. Another 41 million are pre-diabetic. Diabetes is deadly, but in most cases, it can be prevented.

If not properly monitored and managed, diabetes can cause cataracts, glaucoma, and even blindness. It can cause dental caries (tooth decay), cardiovascular disease, heart attacks, kidney disease, gangrene of the extremities, and impotence. Diabetes can also cause stillbirths, miscarriages, neonatal deaths, and birth defects. If diabetes is not managed properly, it can lead to premature death.

As the selection below explains, there are two types of diabetes, Type 1 (insulin-dependent) and Type 2 (non-insulin-dependent). Insulin is a pancreatic hormone that the body must have in order to metabolize glucose effectively. Symptoms of Type 1 diabetes, which usually develop quickly, include extreme hunger and thirst, frequent urination, extreme weight loss, irritability, weakness and fatigue, and nausea and vomiting. In addition to any of the Type 1 symptoms, Type 2 symptoms include blurred vision or a change in eyesight, itchy skin, and tingling or numbness in the arms or legs. If these symptoms are occurring in you, it is important that you tell your doctor.

In the United States, obesity has reached epidemic proportions: 65 percent of the population is now obese. One of the most alarming side effects is the growing incidence of Type 2 (late-onset) diabetes in children, something unheard of a decade ago. This trend can be reversed, however, as the selection below suggests. The selection also tells more about the types of diabetes, treatment, prevention, warning signs, and testing for this potentially damaging disorder.

Types of Diabetes

1   Approximately 21 million Americans—7% of the population—have one of two major forms of diabetes. Five to 10 percent of people with diabetes have the more serious form, known as Type 1 diabetes. In this type of diabetes, the pancreas produces little or no insulin, so daily doses of insulin are required. (Without insulin, a person with Type 1 can lapse into a coma.) Type 1 diabetes usually strikes before age 30, most often in childhood.

2   Ninety percent of Americans with diabetes have Type 2 diabetes. This condition can develop slowly, and about half of affected individuals are unaware of their condition. In Type 2 diabetes, the pancreas doesn't produce enough insulin, cells are resistant to insulin, or both. This condition is usually diagnosed in people over age 40, although it is becoming more common at earlier ages. About one-third of people with Type 2 diabetes must take insulin; others may take medications

Annotation Practice Exercises

Directions: For each paragraph indicated, in the spaces provided:

- Write the main idea sentence.
- List the supporting details on separate lines.

Doing this will help you remember the main idea and supporting details.

that increase insulin production or stimulate cells to take up glucose.

3   A third type of diabetes occurs in 2–3 percent of women during pregnancy. So-called gestational diabetes usually disappears after pregnancy, but more than half of women who experience it eventually develop Type 2 diabetes.

4   The major factors involved in the development of diabetes are age, obesity, physical inactivity, a family history of diabetes, and lifestyle. Excess body fat reduces cell sensitivity to insulin, and it is a major risk factor for Type 2 diabetes. Ethnic background also plays a role. Thirteen percent of African Americans have diabetes, and African Americans and people of Hispanic background are 55 percent more likely than non-Hispanic whites to develop Type 2 diabetes. Over 20 percent of Hispanics over age 65 have diabetes. Native Americans also have a higher than average incidence of diabetes. American Indians and Alaska Natives are more than twice as likely to have diabetes as non-Hispanic whites. Data on the total prevalence of diabetes is not available for Asian Americans, but Asian Americans in Hawaii and California are 1.5 to 2 times as likely to have diagnosed diabetes as non-Hispanic whites.

Treatment

5   There is no cure for diabetes, but it can be successfully managed. Treatment involves keeping blood sugar levels within safe limits through diet, exercise, and, if necessary, medication. Blood sugar levels can be monitored using a home test. Nearly 90 percent of people with Type 2 diabetes are overweight when diagnosed, and an important step in treatment is to lose weight. Even a small amount of weight loss can be beneficial. People with diabetes should eat regular meals with an emphasis on complex carbohydrates and ample dietary fiber. Regular exercise and a healthy diet are often sufficient to control Type 2 diabetes.

Practice Exercise

- Main idea sentence of paragraph 3:

  _____

  _____

  _____

- Supporting details:

  _____

  _____

  _____

  _____

Practice Exercise

- Main idea sentence of paragraph 5:

  _____

  _____

  _____

- Supporting details:

  _____

  _____

  _____

  _____

  _____

  _____

  _____

  _____

  _____

  _____

  _____

Prevention

6   Exercise can help prevent the development of Type 2 diabetes, a benefit especially important in individuals with one or more risk factors for the disease. Exercise makes cells more sensitive to insulin and helps stabilize blood glucose levels. Exercise also helps keep body fat at healthy levels.

7   Eating a healthy diet to help control body fat is perhaps the most important dietary recommendation for the prevention of diabetes. However, there is some evidence that the composition of the diet may also be important. In a long-term study of over 65,000 nurses, a diet low in fiber and high in sugar and refined carbohydrates was found to increase risk for Type 2 diabetes. The foods most closely linked to higher diabetes risk were regular (nondiet) cola beverages, white bread, white rice, french fries, and potatoes; consumption of cereal fibers such as those found in cold breakfast cereals was associated with lower risk.

Warning Signs and Testing

8   A wellness lifestyle that includes a healthy diet and regular exercise is the best strategy for preventing diabetes. If you do develop diabetes, the best way to avoid complications is to recognize the symptoms and get early diagnosis and treatment.

9   Type 2 diabetes is often asymptomatic in the early stages, and routine screening is recommended for people over age 45 and anyone younger who is at high risk, including anyone who is obese. If you are concerned about your risk for diabetes, talk with your physician about being tested.

Practice Exercise

• Main idea sentence of paragraph 6:

_____

_____

_____

_____

_____

• Supporting Details:

_____

_____

_____

Source: Adapted from Paul Insel and Walton Roth, *Core Concepts in Health,* Brief, 9th ed., p. 241. Copyright © 2002 by The McGraw-Hill Companies, Inc. Reprinted by permission of The McGraw-Hill Companies.

_____ **18.** The foods most closely linked to higher diabetes risk were regular (nondiet) cola beverages, white bread, white rice, french fries, and potatoes; *consumption* of certain fibers such as those found in cold breakfast cereals was associated with lower risk.

The *consumption* of alcoholic beverages by minors is illegal.

consumption (kən sŭmp′ shən) means:

a. destruction of

b. eating or drinking, especially in large quantities

c. wasteful, careless, or extravagant use of

d. excessive spending

_____ **19.** If you do develop diabetes, the best way to avoid *complications* is to recognize the symptoms and get early diagnosis and treatment.

Unfortunately, the patient developed *complications* after surgery and died a week later.

complications (kŏm plĭ kā′ shənz) means:

a. medical problems that can be treated with antibiotics

b. undetected medical problems that develop very gradually

c. secondary medical problems that develop as a result of a primary medical condition

d. medical conditions that occur primarily in children

_____ **20.** Type 2 diabetes is often *asymptomatic* in the early stages, and routine screening is recommended for people over 45 and anyone younger who is at high risk, including anyone who is obese.

Because sexually active people who are diagnosed "HIV positive without symptoms" can feel well and be *asymptomatic* for years, they can unknowingly spread the disease to their partners.

asymptomatic (ā sĭmp tə măt′ ĭk) means:

a. showing no symptoms of disease

b. responsive to medical treatment

c. highly contagious

d. resistant to medication

SELECTION **6-1**

Health
(continued)

Reading Skills Application

Directions: Items 21–25 test your ability to *apply* certain reading skills to information in this selection. These types of questions provide valuable practice for all students, especially those who must take standardized reading tests and state-mandated basic skills tests (such as the Florida CLAST Test and the Texas THEA Test). You may not have studied all of the skills at this point, so these items will serve as a helpful preview. The comprehension and critical reading skills in this section are presented in Chapters 4 through 9 of *Opening Doors;* vocabulary and figurative language skills are presented in Chapter 2. As you work through *Opening Doors,* you will practice and develop these skills. Write your answer for each question in the space provided.

_____ 21. Which of the following best expresses the main idea of paragraph 4?

    a.   There are several factors involved in the development of diabetes.

    b.   Excess body fat is a major risk factor for Type 2 diabetes.

    c.   Ethnic background also plays a role.

    d.   Some ethnic groups have a higher incidence of diabetes than other groups.

_____ 22. The pattern used to organize the information in paragraph 6 is:

    a.   list.

    b.   sequence.

    c.   comparison-contrast.

    d.   cause-effect.

_____ 23. The author's primary purpose for writing this selection is to:

    a.   persuade people to be tested for diabetes.

    b.   instruct readers how to avoid developing diabetes as they approach middle age.

    c.   inform readers about the types of diabetes, treatment, prevention, warning signs, and testing.

    d.   persuade diabetics to lose weight and monitor their blood glucose level.

_____ 24. The authors include information about a long-term study of more than 65,000 nurses:

    a.   to support the idea that a high-fiber, high-sugar, high refined-carbohydrate diet contributes to the development of Type 2 diabetes.

    b.   to prove that white foods cause diabetes.

    c.   to provide evidence that the composition of a person's diet can be important in preventing diabetes.

    d.   to show that even many nurses do not have healthy eating habits.

_____ 25. Based on the information in the selection, which of the following represents a logical conclusion?

    a.   With a healthy lifestyle, there is no reason anyone should ever develop diabetes.

    b.   The incidence of Type 2 diabetes in the United States should decrease in coming years as medical researchers and nutritionists learn more about the disease.

    c.   Because Type 2 diabetes develops gradually and many people who have it are unaware of it, the disease can do a great deal of damage before it is detected.

    d.   Physical activity is likely to turn out to be the single most important preventive factor in diabetes.

SELECTION **6-1**

Health
(continued)

Collaboration Option

Respond in Writing

Directions: Refer to Selection 6-1 as needed to answer the questions below.

Option for collaboration: Your instructor may direct you to work with other students on one or more of these items, or in other words, to work *collaboratively.* In that case, you should form groups of three or four students, as directed by your instructor, and work together to complete the exercises. After your group discusses an item and agrees on the answer, have a group member record it. Each member of your group should be able to explain all of your group's answers.

1. Use the information in the selection to complete the comparison chart below.

	Type 1 Diabetes	Type 2 Diabetes
Requires daily doses of insulin?		
Develops slowly or quickly?		
Point in life at which the disorder usually appears?		
Best techniques for managing and/or preventing?		

2. More and more American children and teenagers are becoming obese. They eat high-sugar, high-fat, junk food diets. They spend more time watching television, sitting at the computer, and playing video games. They spend less time exercising, participating in sports, and engaging in physical activities than in the past. As a result, they are more likely to develop Type 2 diabetes and at an earlier age. What are the long-term implications of a growing percentage of the population developing diabetes? List at least three negative consequences that are likely to result.

_____

_____

_____

_____

_____

_____

_____

3. Using the information on risk factors in paragraph 4, write a profile of (describe) the type of person who would have the highest probability of developing Type 2 diabetes.

_____

4. **Overall main idea.** What is the overall main idea the authors want the reader to understand about diabetes? Answer this question in one sentence. Be sure to include the word *diabetes* in your overall main idea sentence.

_____

_____

_____

_____

Internet Resources

Read More about This Topic on the World Wide Web

Directions: For further information about the topic of the selection, visit these websites:

www.diabetes.org
Website of the American Diabetes Association. Includes a quick diabetes risk assessment, as well as information on the prevalence of diabetes and how it affects different races/ethnicities.

www.childrenwithdiabetes.com
This website is an "online community" for children, families, and adults with diabetes.

You can also use your favorite search engine such as Google, Yahoo!, or Alta-Vista (www.google.com, www.yahoo.com, www.altavista.com) to discover more about this topic. To locate additional information, type in combinations of key-words such as:

diabetes

or

type 2 diabetes

or

risk factors for diabetes

or

controlling diabetes

Keep in mind that whenever you go to *any* website, it is a good idea to evaluate the website and the information it contains. Ask yourself questions such as:

"Who sponsors this website?"

"Is the information contained in this website up-to-date?"

"What type of information is presented?"

"Is the information objective and complete?"

"How easy is it to use the features of this website?"

SELECTION **6-2**

Health

America's Most Popular Drug: Caffeine

From *Understanding Your Health*

By Wayne A. Payne, Dale B. Hahn, and Ellen B. Mauer

Prepare Yourself to Read

Directions: Do these exercises *before* you read Selection 6-2.

1. First, read and think about the title. Have you ever thought of coffee as a drug? What do you already know about the effects of *caffeine*?

    _____

    _____

2. Are you part of the coffee drinking craze? Is there a certain beverage you consume in order to become fully awake? What is your routine for waking up and "getting your motor running" each morning?

    _____

    _____

    _____

3. Many people say they experience a "caffeine withdrawal" if they don't follow their routine of coffee, tea, or soda breaks. If you have ever experienced caffeine withdrawal, describe what happened.

    _____

    _____

    _____

    _____

4. Next, complete your preview by reading the following:
    Introduction (in *italics*)
    Headings
    Caption accompanying the photo

    Now that you have completed your preview, what does this selection seem to be about?

    _____

    _____

    _____

    _____

Apply Comprehension Skills

Directions: Do the Annotation Practice Exercises *as* you read Selection 6-2. Apply the skills from this chapter:

Determine the topic.   When you read a paragraph, ask yourself, "Who or what is this about?"

Locate or formulate the main idea.   As you read, ask yourself, "What is the most important point these authors want me to understand about the topic?"

Identify and list supporting details.   As you read, ask yourself, "What additional information do the authors provide to help me understand the main idea completely?" Then list the supporting details.

AMERICA'S MOST POPULAR DRUG: CAFFEINE

Do you have to have that cup of coffee, cappuccino, chai tea, or can of Diet Coke, Dr. Pepper, or Mountain Dew to jump-start your mornings or to stay awake at work or school? If you do, you are using America's most popular drug, caffeine. This selection from a health textbook presents information about the use of the stimulant that is famous for the artificial and temporary boost that it provides.

1   Coffee is definitely hip again. On two popular television sitcoms, "Friends" hung out at Central Perk and Drs. Frasier and Niles Crane solved many of life's problems over cups of gourmet brew at Café Nervosa. Starbucks, a coffeehouse chain based in Seattle, has swept the West Coast and is becoming an international phenomenon. They're not the only ones jumping at the chance to serve you your favorite cup of espresso, cappuccino, or latte. Bookstores, fast-food restaurants, college cafeterias, and even gas stations are beginning to offer these specialty brews. This is just the latest twist on a very old habit.

2   As the story goes, tea was discovered in 2737 B.C. by Chinese emperor Shen Nung when leaves from a local plant fell into water he was boiling. More than three thousand years later, around A.D. 600, coffee berries were discovered by a goat herder in Ethiopia after the goats consumed the red berries and stayed up all night. From there, coffee consumption spread to the Middle East and then to Europe in 1615. Soft drinks and over-the-counter (OTC) medications such as No Doz are part of caffeine's more recent history, and the latest caffeinated product is caffeinated water, marketed under the brand name Water Joe. David Marcheschi, a 29-year-old Chicago mortgage banker, invented Water Joe while trying to stay awake in college. A 16.9-ounce bottle has the caffeine equivalent of an 8-ounce cup of coffee and retails for 99 cents. It's coffee without the bitterness and a soft drink without the sweetness.

Annotation Practice Exercises

Directions: For each paragraph indicated, in the spaces provided:

•   Write the main idea sentence.

•   List the supporting details on separate lines.

Doing this will help you remember main ideas and supporting details.

3   Coffee is one of the most widely consumed beverages in the world. An estimated 400 billion cups of coffee are consumed worldwide every year. The coffee trade compares with wheat in global importance. Five million tons are produced annually in fifty countries. South American countries lead production, followed by Africa, Asia, and North and Central America. The larger producers ship most of their crop abroad to countries like the United States and Europe. The United States consumes one-third of the world's coffee production.

Social Issues

4   Coffee breaks are a time to socialize. Mid-morning or mid-afternoon caffeine, conversation, and company improve the rest of the workday for many people. Whether it's at work, a high-style downtown brasserie, a homey neighborhood café, or a college hangout, coffee consumption is a social activity.

Practice Exercise

- Main idea sentence of paragraph 3:

_____

_____

_____

- Supporting details:

_____

_____

_____

_____

_____

_____

_____

_____

_____

_____

_____

_____

Combining coffee drinking and cigarette smoking may make it more difficult to decrease or eliminate either habit.

5   Historically, leaders in many countries have tried to ban coffeehouses for this very reason: being the meeting places that they are, coffeehouses tended to breed revolutionary political ideas. There may be a few revolutionaries who frequent today's coffeehouses in the United States, but by and large the clientele is more mainstream. On a typical day at a Washington, D.C. coffeehouse, mothers and their babies gather after dropping older children at school. Later in the morning, retirees come in. In the afternoon, people who work at home stop in. After school, the same coffeehouse becomes a high school hangout. After dark, young professionals and couples on dates arrive. This is evidence that today, coffeehouses are popular nongenerational meeting places that everyone can enjoy.

6   The draw of the coffeehouse is varied. It provides a relaxing atmosphere, a refuge from unpaid bills and unmade beds, a place to work where you're not entirely alone, a place to engage in conversation, a place to watch the world go by, and a familiar place where you'll probably run into someone you know in the next 15 minutes.

Health Effects

7   Of course, caffeine does have pharmacological effects on the function of cardiovascular, respiratory, renal, and nervous systems. However, at the low, fixed pattern of consumption that most people enjoy, caffeine is merely a mild stimulant. But, withdrawal from even a mild caffeine habit may cause headaches, fatigue, and difficulty concentrating. These symptoms peak in 18 to 24 hours, causing many weekday coffee drinkers to experience weekend withdrawal headaches. In high doses, caffeine can cause acute effects such as restlessness, agitation, and tremors. Excessive caffeine consumption can also cause cardiac dysrhythmias (irregular heartbeat), gastric disturbance, and diarrhea.

8   Results of studies conducted on caffeine's effects on the cardiovascular system have not proved that it does damage to the heart or circulatory system directly. It seems, though, that caffeine does trigger a rise in blood pressure and a lowering of heart rate. These effects last only for a matter of hours when a person has just started using caffeine. After a few days of consumption, caffeine tolerance sets in, and these conditions no longer occur. It seems that the only permanent toll that coffee takes on the cardiovascular system is not even related to caffeine. If the coffee is unfiltered, fats from the coffee beans can raise cholesterol levels. Suspicion that caffeine causes cancer is undeserved as well. Research suggests no meaningful association of coffee with most common cancers, including those of the digestive tract, breast, and genital tract. There is also no evidence of a relationship between caffeine consumption and delayed conception or persistent infertility.

Practice Exercise

• Main idea sentence of paragraph 6:

_____

_____

• Supporting details:

_____

_____

_____

_____

_____

_____

Practice Exercise

• Main idea sentence of paragraph 8:

_____

_____

_____

• Supporting details:

_____

_____

_____

_____

9   In children, caffeine causes inattentiveness, distraction, and impulsivity. Parents are wise to monitor the caffeine intake of their children. Pregnant women should avoid caffeine use. Three or more cups of coffee or tea a day during the first 4 months of pregnancy seems to increase the risk of miscarriage. This finding may not be entirely attributable to caffeine because coffee consumption increases with age, and aging itself is a risk factor in pregnancy.

Breaking the Habit

10   You may want to break the caffeine habit because it generates dependence and you don't like the headache you get when you can't find a vending machine or when nobody at the office made coffee. You may want to set a good example for your children to avoid caffeine, or you may simply want to live as drug-free as possible. Whatever your reasons, you can attain your goal of breaking a caffeine habit. Following these suggestions will result in reduced caffeine consumption:

1. Keep a log of where, when, how much, and with whom you consume coffee, tea, caffeinated soda, or caffeinated pills.

2. To avoid withdrawal symptoms such as headaches, don't quit cold turkey. Instead, reduce your consumption slowly, by one cup, can, or pill per day.

3. If you are a coffee drinker, gradually switch from regular to decaffeinated coffee by mixing them before brewing, or substitute decaffeinated instant coffee for some of the caffeinated instant you drink. Increase the decaffeinated proportion each day. Choose a premium decaf to reward yourself and to keep your coffee routine enjoyable.

4. Substitute decaffeinated tea for your regular caffeinated tea, and replace caffeinated soda with a caffeine-free drink.

5. Drink from smaller cups or glasses instead of large mugs or tumblers. Avoid the huge mugs made popular by the television show "Friends," huge "car cups," and the enormous beverage containers available from convenience stores and fast-food chains. If your favorite mug or tumbler is a comfort to you, don't discard it, but fill it with a caffeine-free beverage. If, on the other hand, you find your coffee paraphernalia to be a temptation, get rid of those mugs, pots, filters, and grinders.

6. Change your daily routine by taking a walk instead of your usual coffee break.

7. Use more low-fat milk in your coffee or tea to reduce the amount of caffeinated beverage you consume while increasing your calcium consumption.

8.   Consider an alternative to a caffeinated beverage, such as bouillon, cider, herbal tea, or a grain-based beverage such as Postum.

9.   Do not restructure your home and work routines to avoid caffeine so much that you lose the healthful aspects of a coffee break or an evening at your favorite hangout. Remember that noncaffeinated beverages are available; simply plan ahead.

10.   When you find yourself getting sleepy while studying, driving, or working and feel tempted to drink a caffeinated beverage, take a break, open a window, breathe deeply and stretch, jog in place, go for a walk, get a cold drink of water—or take a very short nap!

11   If you get enough sleep, exercise regularly, and follow a healthy diet, you'll be less reliant on the artificial "pep" that caffeine provides. Furthermore, you'll be less likely to develop a dependence on America's most popular drug.

Source: Adapted from Wayne A. Payne, Dale B. Hahn, and Ellen B. Mauer, *Understanding Your Health,* 8th ed., pp. 251–53. Copyright © 2005 by The McGraw-Hill Companies, Inc. Reprinted by permission of The McGraw-Hill Companies.

Reading Selection Quiz

This quiz has three parts. Your instructor may assign some or all of them.

Comprehension

Directions: Items 1–10 test your comprehension (understanding) of the material of this selection. These questions are the type a content area instructor (such as a health professor) would ask on a test over this material. You should be able to answer these questions after studying this selection. For each comprehension question below, use information from the selection to determine the correct answer. Refer to the selection as you answer each question. Write your answer in the space provided.

True or False

_____ **1.** An estimated 400 million cups of coffee are consumed worldwide every year.

_____ **2.** The United States consumes one-third of the world's coffee production.

_____ **3.** One reason caffeine consumption is so popular is the appeal and availability of coffeehouses.

_____ **4.** Research has suggested a meaningful connection between coffee consumption and the most common cancers, including those of the digestive tract, breast, and genital tract.

Multiple-Choice

_____ **5.** Coffee was discovered about A.D. 600 in:
  a. China.
  b. The Middle East.
  c. Ethiopia.
  d. Europe.

_____ **6.** Economically, the worldwide production of coffee is as important as the worldwide production of:
  a. wheat.
  b. tea.
  c. rice.
  d. fast food.

_____ **7.** Water Joe is:
  a. bottled decaffeinated water that retails for 99 cents.
  b. a coffee-flavored soft drink.
  c. a water drink containing the caffeine equivalent of an 8-ounce cup of coffee.
  d. a nickname for decaffeinated coffee.

_____ **8.** At a low, fixed pattern of consumption, caffeine:

   a. is merely a mild stimulant.

   b. can cause headaches and fatigue.

   c. can damage the cardiovascular system.

   d. is responsible for cardiovascular and circulatory disease in millions of people.

_____ **9.** If caffeine is unfiltered, fats from the coffee beans can:

   a. lower heart rate.

   b. raise blood pressure.

   c. cause dysrhythmia.

   d. raise cholesterol levels.

_____ **10.** One way to be less reliant on the artificial and temporary boost that caffeine provides is to:

   a. get enough sleep on a regular basis.

   b. follow a consistent exercise routine.

   c. develop a habit of healthy eating.

   d. all of the above

SELECTION **6-2**

Health

(continued)

Vocabulary in Context

Directions: Items 11–20 test your ability to determine the meaning of a word by using context clues. *Context clues* are words in a sentence that allow the reader to deduce (reason out) the meaning of an unfamiliar word in that sentence. Context clues also enable the reader to determine which meaning the author intends when a word has more than one meaning. For each vocabulary item below, a sentence from the selection containing an important word (*italicized, like this*) is quoted first. Next, there is an additional sentence using the word in the same sense and providing another context clue. Use the context clues from *both* sentences to deduce the meaning of the italicized word. *Be sure the answer you choose makes sense in both sentences.* If you discover that you need to use a dictionary to confirm an answer choice, remember that the meaning you select must still fit the context of *both* sentences. Write your answer in the space provided.

Pronunciation Key: ă **pat**   ā **pay**   âr **care**   ä **father**   ĕ **pet**   ē **be**   ĭ **pit**
ī **tie**   îr **pier**   ŏ **pot**   ō **toe**   ô **paw**   oi **noise**   ou **out**   ŏŏ **took**
ōō **boot**   ŭ **cut**   yōō **abuse**   ûr **urge**   th **thin**   *th* **this**   hw **which**
zh **vision**   ə **about**   *Stress mark:* ´

_____ **11.** Starbucks, a coffeehouse chain based in Seattle, has swept the West Coast and is becoming an international *phenomenon.*

Although track and field athlete Wilma Rudolph's early career was hindered by injuries and other difficulties, she went on to become an Olympic *phenomenon.*

phenomenon (fǐ nŏm′ ə nŏn) means:

a. moneymaker

b. ongoing problem

c. extraordinary success

d. mystery

_____ **12.** From there, coffee *consumption* spread to the Middle East and then to Europe in 1615.

In the future, oil *consumption* in the United States may decrease dramatically if more people buy and use hybrid automobiles that use a combination of electric power and gasoline.

consumption (kən sŭmp′ shən) means:

a. dependence

b. use of a product

c. prices of goods

d. reduction of waste

_____ **13.** There may be a few revolutionaries who frequent today's coffeehouses in the United States, but by and large the *clientele* is more mainstream.

Restaurants and fast-food companies value their *clientele* who return to their establishments week after week, month after month.

clientele (klī ən tĕl′) means:

a. atmosphere

b. young professionals and retirees

c. management

d. group of customers

_____ **14.** Historically, leaders in many countries have tried to *ban* coffeehouses for this very reason: being the meeting places that they are, coffeehouses tended to breed revolutionary political ideas.

Throughout history there have been governments, political parties, and religious groups that attempted to *ban* books that contradict their beliefs or positions.

ban (băn) means:

a. prohibit

b. close

c. destroy

d. promote

_____ **15.** This evidence that today, coffeehouses are popular *nongenerational* meeting places that everyone can enjoy.

Visit any community college campus today and the first thing you will notice is the *nongenerational* student body ranging in ages from 17 to 77!

nongenerational (nŏn jĕn ə rā′ shən əl) means:

a. unusual

b. nondenominational

c. suggesting a nontraditional collection of students

d. representing a variety of ages and generations

_____ **16.** In high doses, caffeine can cause *acute* effects such as restlessness, agitation, and tremors.

For two weeks after his automobile accident, Raymond required around-the-clock *acute* care in the hospital.

acute (ə kyo͞ot′) means:

a. sharp

b. alert

c. severe

d. expensive

_____ **17.** It seems that the only permanent *toll* that coffee takes on the cardiovascular system is not even related to caffeine.

Melody's job as a sales representative required her to travel to other cities and work on weekends, and this took a considerable *toll* on her personal life.

toll (tōl) means:

a. fee paid for a privilege or service

b. the sounding of a bell

c. cost of loss or suffering

d. permanent change

_____ **18.** This finding may not be entirely *attributable* to caffeine because coffee consumption increases with age, and aging itself is a risk factor in pregnancy.

Gilbert felt that, without a doubt, his success as a journalist was *attributable* to three extraordinary professors he had when he was in college.

attributable (ə trĭb′ yo͞o tə bəl) means:

a. regarded as having caused

b. viewed as a reason for success

c. related to overcoming a difficulty

d. pertaining to an increase in risk

_____ **19.** If on the other hand, you find your coffee *paraphernalia* to be a temptation, get rid of those mugs, pots, filters, and grinders.

Andrea played on the softball and soccer teams and enjoyed running and aerobics, so her enormous gym bag was packed with a variety of *paraphernalia.*

paraphernalia (păr ə fər nāl′ yə) means:

a. equipment

b. temptations

c. high energy snacks and sports drinks

d. mugs, cups, glasses, or bottles

_____ **20.** If you get enough sleep, exercise regularly, and follow a healthy diet, you'll be less *reliant* on the artificial "pep" that caffeine provides.

Some students have become so *reliant* on the spell-check feature of their word processing programs that they do not bother to learn the spelling of many common words.

reliant (rē lī′ ənt) means:

a. careless

b. addicted to

c. dependent on for support

d. likely to use or consume

SELECTION **6-2**   *Reading Skills Application*

Health
(continued)

Directions: Items 21–25 test your ability to *apply* certain reading skills to information in this selection. These types of questions provide valuable practice for all students, especially those who must take standardized reading tests and state-mandated basic skills tests (such as the Florida CLAST Test and the Texas THEA Test). You may not have studied all of the skills at this point, so these items will serve as a helpful preview. The comprehension and critical reading skills in this section are presented in Chapters 4 through 9 of *Opening Doors;* vocabulary and figurative language skills are presented in Chapter 2. As you work through *Opening Doors,* you will practice and develop these skills. Write your answer for each question in the space provided.

_____ **21.** The meaning of the phrase *cold turkey* as it is used in paragraph 11 is:

a. to use according to a plan or schedule.

b. to reduce consumption gradually.

c. to avoid or stop using something suddenly and completely.

d. to break a habit by changing one's diet and exercise routine.

_____ **22.** Which of the following best expresses the main idea of paragraph 5?

    a. Today, coffehouses are usually frequented by older, more affluent customers.

    b. Many countries once tried to ban coffeehouses because they were meeting places for people with revolutionary ideas.

    c. Coffeehouses contribute to our nation's health problems by promoting the use of caffeine consumption.

    d. Today, coffeehouses are popular meeting places with mainstream clientele.

_____ **23.** Which of the following represents the authors' point of view?

    a. Caffeine should be banned from use because of its dangerous effects.

    b. Excessive consumption of caffeine can be dangerous, but there are things that one can do to reduce one's caffeine intake or break the caffeine habit.

    c. It is very difficult for all users of caffeine to break their habit.

    d. Withdrawal from a caffeine habit can last from 24 to 48 hours.

_____ **24.** Which pattern did the authors use to organize the main idea and the supporting details in paragraph 10?

    a. definition

    b. sequence

    c. comparison-contrast

    d. cause-effect

_____ **25.** The authors' tone in this selection can best be described as:

    a. unemotional.

    b. alarmed.

    c. critical.

    d. arrogant.

SELECTION **6-2**

Health
(continued)

Collaboration Option

Respond in Writing

Directions: Refer to Selection 6-2 as needed to answer the essay-type questions below.

Option for collaboration: Your instructor may direct you to work with other students on one or more of these items, or in other words, to work *collaboratively.* In that case, you should form groups of three or four students, as directed by your instructor, and work together to complete the exercises. After your group discusses an item and agrees on the answer, have a group member record it. Each member of your group should be able to explain all of your group's answers.

1. As explained in paragraph 4, coffeehouses have become popular for many reasons besides being a place to get a good cup of coffee or cappuccino. Can you think of *additional* reasons people like to go to coffeehouses that were not mentioned in the selection?

   _____

   _____

   _____

   _____

   _____

   _____

   _____

2. In this selection the authors explain that in a pleasant environment such as a coffeehouse, caffeine consumption can be a relaxing and social activity. They also state that "in a low, fixed pattern of consumption, caffeine is only a mild stimulant." However, the authors identify many of caffeine's potentially dangerous effects. List at least four of them in the spaces below.

   _____

   _____

   _____

   _____

   _____

   _____

   _____

   _____

   _____

   _____

   _____

3. Paraphrase the information listed following paragraph 10. Paraphrase each item *briefly*.

_____

_____

_____

_____

_____

_____

_____

_____

_____

_____

_____

_____

4. **Overall main idea.** What is the overall main idea the author wants the reader to understand about excessive caffeine consumption? Answer this question in one sentence. Be sure to include the word *caffeine* and the phrase *excessive consumption* or *when consumed in excessive amounts* in your overall main idea sentence.

_____

_____

_____

_____

_____

_____

_____

_____

_____

_____

Internet Resources

Read More about This Topic on the World Wide Web

Directions: For further information about the topic of the selection, visit these websites:

www.gardfoods.com/coffee/index.htm
This website contains general information about coffee, a history of coffee, and an "A to Z" glossary of coffee-related terms.

www.waterjoe.com
This is the commercial website for Water Joe, the caffeine drink mentioned in the selection.

You can also use your favorite search engine such as Google, Yahoo!, or Alta-Vista (www.google.com, www.yahoo.com, www.altavista.com) to discover more about this topic. To locate additional information, type in combinations of key-words such as:

caffeine consumption

or

coffee consumption

or

coffeehouses

Keep in mind that whenever you go to *any* website, it is a good idea to evaluate the website and the information it contains. Ask yourself questions such as:

"Who sponsors this website?"

"Is the information contained in this website up-to-date?"

"What type of information is presented?"

"Is the information objective and complete?"

"How easy is it to use the features of this website?"

SELECTION **6-3**

Economics

What Can Be Done to Help Third World Countries?

From *A Beginner's Guide to the World Economy*

By Randy Charles Epping

Prepare Yourself to Read

Directions: Do these exercises *before* you read Selection 6-3.

1. First, read and think about the title. What knowledge do you have about the "world economy"? What approach do you think a "beginner's guide" might take?

    _____

    _____

2. Why do you think it is important or useful for the average person to know something about the world economy?

    _____

    _____

3. Next, complete your preview by reading the following:

    Introduction (in *italics*)
    First paragraph (paragraph 1)
    Section headings
    Last paragraph (paragraph 17)
    Diagrams

    On the basis of your preview, what three aspects of the Third World will be discussed?

    _____

    _____

Apply Comprehension Skills

Directions: Do the Annotation Practice Exercises *as* you read Selection 6-3. Apply the skills from this chapter:

Determine the topic.   When you read a paragraph, ask yourself, "Who or what is this about?"

Locate or formulate the main idea.   As you read, ask yourself, "What is the most important point this author wants me to understand about the topic?"

Identify and list supporting details.   As you read, ask yourself, "What additional information does the author provide to help me understand the main idea completely?" Then list the supporting details.

WHAT CAN BE DONE TO HELP THIRD WORLD COUNTRIES?

Poverty in Third World countries is exacerbated by natural disasters. In 2000, the worst flooding in 50 years occurred in Mozambique, Africa. Nearly a million people in this poor country were left homeless, and much of the country's crops, roads, and bridges were washed away. In the Horn of Africa (Ethiopia, Eritrea, Somalia, and Kenya) as many as 16 million people are at risk of starving because of the most severe drought since the mid-1980s. In all these countries the disasters have also caused widespread disease. More recently, on December 26, 2004, an undersea earthquake in the Indian Ocean triggered a tsunami that killed more than 283,000 people, making it one of the deadliest disasters in modern history. It devastated the shores of Indonesia, Sri Lanka, South India, Thailand, and other countries with waves up to 30 meters (100 feet) and caused serious damage and deaths as far as the east coast of Africa. What will be the ultimate fate of these and other "Third World" countries? How can the poorest of the poor countries survive? This selection will give you a basic understanding of the economic concept of "Third World," the roots of Third World poverty, and what can be done to improve the situation.

What Is the Third World?

1   The term *Third World* was based on the idea that the "first" and "second" worlds were made up of the free-market and centrally planned countries with advanced industrial economies. This developed world was seen to include most of the countries of Eastern and Western Europe as well as Australia, New Zealand, Japan, the United States, and Canada.

2   The developing and relatively poor countries that are said to make up the Third World can be divided into three groups: those developing rapidly, those developing moderately, and the poorest few whose economies are not developing at all.

3   At the top of the list of Third World nations are the rapidly developing countries called Newly Industrialized Countries (NIC). Most lists of NICs include Brazil, Argentina, Hong Kong, Israel, Singapore, South Africa, South Korea, Taiwan, and Thailand. These "lucky few" are seen to be on their way to joining the ranks of the advanced economies of the world.

4   The bulk of the Third World consists of a large group of moderately developing economies that includes most of the countries in Africa, Asia, and Latin America. The most populous countries in this group are India, China, Indonesia, and Malaysia, which together comprise more than half of the world's population.

5   At the bottom of this list are the world's poorest countries, found mainly in sub-Saharan Africa, which have so few resources and so little money that it is virtually impossible for them to develop at all. In Somalia and Sudan, for example, there are essentially no natural resources on which to base economic growth. This group is sometimes called the "Fourth World."

Annotation Practice Exercises

Directions: For each paragraph indicated, in the spaces provided:

•   Write the main idea sentence.
•   List the supporting details on separate lines.

Doing this will help you remember main ideas and supporting details.

Practice Exercise

•   Main idea sentence of paragraph 1:

_____

_____

_____

_____

_____

_____

_____

6   Although the Third World comprises three quarters of the world's population and 90 percent of the world's population growth, it provides only 20 percent of the world's economic production. And even though the Third World holds much of the world's natural resources—including vast petroleum reserves in Latin America, Asia, and the Middle East—many raw materials from the Third World are shipped abroad for consumption in the world's wealthier and more developed countries.

What Are the Roots of Third World Poverty?

7   Economic and political misjudgment can be blamed for much of the Third World's poverty, but an important factor has also been the population explosion. This caused many developing countries to see their populations double in as little as twenty years. The growth was due mainly to lack of birth control, to improved medical care, and to declining mortality rates.

8   Extreme poverty in the Third World has led many parents to create ever larger families, hoping that their children could work and increase family income. But the economic opportunities were often not available, and unemployed children and their parents ended up moving into already overcrowded Third World cities in a fruitless search for work.

9   By the end of the 1980s, most Third World nations found themselves in a vicious circle of poverty and overpopulation, with no hope in sight. The flood of poor families into major Third World cities put additional strains on the economic infrastructure. Growing urban areas like Bombay, São Paulo, and Shanghai became centers of glaring poverty and unemployment with extensive slums and squatter settlements ringing overgrown and polluted city centers.

10   Saddled with enormous debt payments, hyperinflation, surging populations, and mounting unemployment, many Third World countries in the late 1980s struggled just to keep their economies afloat. In many cases, with no money available for investment, even the infrastructure, such as roads and water systems, literally began to fall apart. The solution for many overburdened Third World governments was to simply increase debt in order to keep money flowing. But rampant inflation often ends up eroding most of these efforts, creating an ever-widening gap between the Third World's poorest and richest nations.

- Supporting details in paragraph 1:

_____

_____

_____

_____

_____

_____

_____

_____

Practice Exercise

- Main idea sentence of paragraph 7:

_____

_____

_____

_____

- Supporting details in paragraph 7:

_____

_____

_____

_____

_____

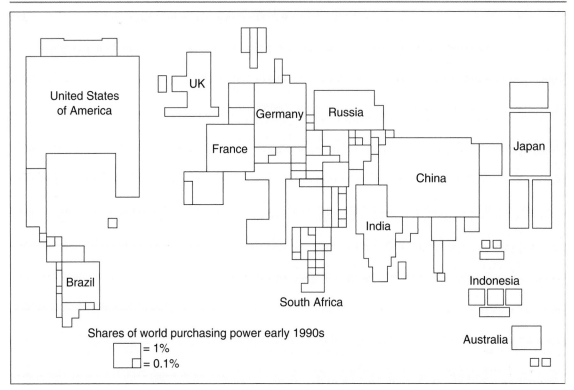

Shares of world purchasing power early 1990s

□ = 1%
□ = 0.1%

Purchasing power

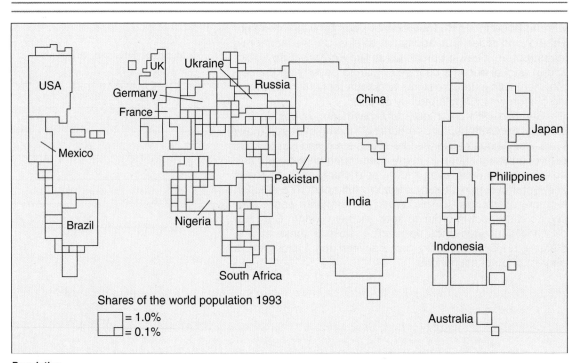

Shares of the world population 1993

□ = 1.0%
□ = 0.1%

Population

Source: From *A Beginner's Guide to the World Economy,* by Randy Charles Epping, p. xix. Copyright © 1992 by Randy Charles Epping. Copyright © 1992, 1995, 2001 by Randy Charles Epping (new Vintage ed.). Used by permission of Vintage Books, a division of Random House, Inc.

11   While many economies in Latin America, Africa, and Asia stagnated, the economies of the elite developing countries of the Pacific Rim rose to levels that rivaled Japan's in the 1960s. The success of many Third World countries in growing their way out of poverty can be traced largely to effective economic policy. By efficiently producing and exporting manufactured goods, countries such as Taiwan and Korea earned enormous amounts of money that they have been able to reinvest in their growing economies.

What Can Be Done to Promote Third World Development?

12   Economic growth cannot possibly solve all the problems facing the billions of poor and undernourished people in the Third World, but because of rapid population growth, their problems would almost certainly get worse without it.

13   In order to provide the basic food, clothing, and shelter for their citizens, the underdeveloped Third World countries need to stimulate their stagnating economies caught in a vicious circle of low growth and declining export earnings. One of the first steps in encouraging development would be to reduce the Third World nations' debt and supply additional funds to revive their moribund economies. One such plan was formulated in the 1980s by U.S. Treasury Secretary Nicholas Brady, who called for the commercial banks to forgive part of the debt owed to them and to increase new lending. The basic goal of the Brady plan was to encourage economic growth in the Third World.

14   The Brady Plan also called upon the world's major development banks and funds, such as the World Bank and the International Monetary Fund, to provide substantial "project loans" to rebuild the infrastructure in the Third World. In addition, continued bank lending in the form of "adjustment loans" would help with the payment of interest and principal on previous loans. Basically, the Brady Plan called for a net transfer of funds back to the developing countries.

15   Another way to promote Third World development is to increase development funds provided by regional development banks with the backing of the developed countries. The Inter-American Development Bank, for example, was set up to provide low-interest loans to developing countries in the Western Hemisphere. In this way, funds from wealthy countries can be channeled to less-developed nations in the form of "development loans."

16   Wealthy creditor governments also have the option of writing off their debt, accepting that it will never be repaid. France, for example, decided in the 1980s that most of its development loans to African countries need not be repaid, in an effort to encourage further economic growth in the region.

Practice Exercise

• Main idea sentence of paragraph 11:

_____

_____

_____

_____

_____

_____

_____

• Supporting details in paragraph 11:

_____

_____

_____

_____

_____

_____

17   In order to provide further assistance to Third World debtors, the world's wealthy countries can also work through specialized organizations such as the Lomé Convention, which channels development aid from the European Community to poor Third World countries, and the Paris Club, which helps governments of debtor nations "reschedule" or delay repayment of their loans until their economies are in better shape.

SELECTION **6-3**

Economics
(continued)

**Student Online
Learning Center (OLC)**
Go to **Chapter 6.**
Select **Reading
Selection Quiz.**

Reading Selection Quiz

This quiz has three parts. Your instructor may assign some or all of them.

Comprehension

Directions: Items 1–10 test your comprehension (understanding) of the material of this selection. These questions are the type a content area instructor (such as an economics professor) would ask on a test over this material. You should be able to answer these questions after studying this selection. For each comprehension question below, use information from the selection to determine the correct answer. Refer to the selection as you answer each question. Write your answer in the space provided.

True or False

_____   **1.** The *first* and *second worlds* are defined as the free-market countries and the centrally planned countries with advanced industrial economies.

_____   **2.** The first and second worlds were considered to include most of the countries of Eastern and Western Europe, Australia, New Zealand, Japan, the United States, and Canada.

_____   **3.** Some experts believe that the economic problems of Third World countries cannot be solved.

_____   **4.** The Third World can be divided into three groups: countries with rapidly developing economies, countries with moderately developing economies, and countries whose economies are not developing at all.

_____   **5.** The bulk of the Third World consists of a large group of moderately developing economies.

_____   **6.** Economic growth cannot solve all the problems faced by billions of undernourished people in the Third World.

Multiple-Choice

_____   **7.** Newly Industrialized Countries (NIC) that seem to be on their way to joining the rank of advanced economies include:
   a. Somalia and Sudan.
   b. India, China, Indonesia, and Malaysia.
   c. South Africa, South Korea, Taiwan, and Thailand.
   d. all of the above

_____ **8.** Third World poverty is caused by:

    a. economic and political misjudgment.

    b. enormous debt payments.

    c. overpopulation.

    d. all of the above

_____ **9.** According to the author, Third World development will require that:

    a. Third World countries pay off their debts completely.

    b. commercial banks press hard for debt payment from Third World countries.

    c. wealthy countries discontinue making development loans to Third World countries.

    d. none of the above

_____ **10.** The author believes that wealthy creditor nations can aid Third World development by:

    a. agreeing to follow the Brady Plan.

    b. channeling funds in the form of development loans.

    c. writing off the debt owed by Third World countries.

    d. all of the above

SELECTION **6-3**

Economics
(continued)

Vocabulary in Context

Directions: Items 11–20 test your ability to determine the meaning of a word by using context clues. *Context clues* are words in a sentence that allow the reader to deduce (reason out) the meaning of an unfamiliar word in that sentence. Context clues also enable the reader to determine which meaning the author intends when a word has more than one meaning. For each vocabulary item below, a sentence from the selection containing an important word (*italicized, like this*) is quoted first. Next, there is an additional sentence using the word in the same sense and providing another context clue. Use the context clues from *both* sentences to deduce the meaning of the italicized word. *Be sure the answer you choose makes sense in both sentences.* If you discover that you need to use a dictionary to confirm an answer choice, remember that the meaning you select must still fit the context of *both* sentences. Write your answer in the space provided.

Pronunciation Key: ă **pat**   ā **pay**   âr **care**   ä **father**   ĕ **pet**   ē **be**   ĭ **pit**
ī **tie**   îr **pier**   ŏ **pot**   ō **toe**   ô **paw**   oi **noise**   ou **out**   ŏŏ **took**
ōō **boot**   ŭ **cut**   yōō **abuse**   ûr **urge**   th **thin**   *th* **this**   hw **which**
zh **vision**   ə **about**   *Stress mark:* ʹ

_____ **11.** The term Third World was based on the idea that the "first" and "second" worlds were made up of the *free-market* and centrally planned countries with advanced industrial economies.

Currently, several countries are struggling to shift from a planned economy which the government controlled to a competitive *free-market* economy.

free market (frē mär′ kĭt) means:

a. pertaining to a market in which everything is free
b. pertaining to an economic system in which resources are allocated by corporations rather than by the government
c. pertaining to a completely unregulated economy
d. pertaining to an economic system in which the government is free to do whatever it pleases

_____ **12.** At the top of the list of Third World nations are the rapidly developing countries called Newly *Industrialized* Countries (NIC).

Advanced technology is characteristic of highly *industrialized* countries such as Japan and Germany.

industrialized (ĭn dŭs′ trē ə līzd) means:

a. having highly developed industries that produce goods and services
b. struggling
c. controlled by industries
d. busy or hardworking

_____ **13.** And even though the Third World holds much of the world's natural resources, many raw materials from the Third World are shipped abroad for *consumption* in the world's wealthier and more developed countries.

The level of energy *consumption* in the United States has risen dramatically during the twentieth century.

consumption (kən sŭmp′ shən) means:

a. use of consumer goods or services
b. spending
c. ingestion of food
d. debilitating illness

_____ **14.** The flood of poor families into major Third World cities put additional strains on the economic *infrastructure.*

The president pledged to improve two parts of the nation's *infrastructure:* public transportation and health care.

infrastructure (ĭn′ frə strŭk chər) means:

a. government buildings
b. hospitals
c. construction in rural areas
d. basic services and facilities needed by a society

_____ **15.** Saddled with enormous debt payments, *hyperinflation,* surging populations, and mounting unemployment, many Third World countries in the late 1980s struggled just to keep their economies afloat.

When Germany experienced *hyperinflation* in the 1920s, it took a wheelbarrow full of money to buy a single loaf of bread.

hyperinflation (hī pər ĭn flā′ shən) means:

   a. decrease in inflation

   b. rapid input of air

   c. excessive rate of increase in consumer prices

   d. rapid accumulation of debt

_____ **16.** Saddled with enormous debt payments, hyperinflation, *surging* populations, and mounting unemployment, many Third World countries in the late 1980s struggled just to keep their economies afloat.

When the storm hit, the *surging* sea water flooded the beaches and low-lying areas of the city.

surging (sûrj′ ĭng) means:

   a. decreasing

   b. angry

   c. increasing suddenly

   d. poor

_____ **17.** But *rampant* inflation often ends up eroding most of these efforts, creating an ever-widening gap between the Third World's poorest and richest nations.

In poverty-stricken areas of many large cities, crime is *rampant.*

rampant (răm′ pənt) means:

   a. tolerated or accepted

   b. decreasing

   c. controlled

   d. growing or spreading unchecked

_____ **18.** While many economies in Latin America, Africa, and Asia *stagnated,* the economies of the elite developing countries of the Pacific Rim rose to levels that rivaled Japan's in the 1960s.

The actor's career had *stagnated* for several years, but after he starred in a blockbuster movie, he received many offers for leading roles.

stagnated (stăg′ nā təd) means:

   a. rotted

   b. improved

   c. smelled bad

   d. failed to change or develop

_____ **19.** One of the first steps in encouraging development would be to reduce the Third World nations' debt and supply additional funds to revive their *moribund* economies.

The doctor summoned the family to the bedside of the *moribund* woman when she had only moments to live.

moribund (môr′ ə bŭnd) means:
a. abundant
b. dead
c. almost at the point of death
d. ill

_____ **20.** Wealthy *creditor* governments also have the option of writing off their debt, accepting that it will never be repaid.

Because the Newtons charged too many purchases on their credit cards and were unable to pay their debts, they were hounded by countless *creditor* calls and letters.

creditor (krĕd′ ĭ tər) means:
a. one to whom money is owed
b. one who deserves financial credit
c. one who is trustworthy
d. one who owes money

SELECTION **6-3**   *Reading Skills Application*

Economics
(continued)

Directions: Items 21–25 test your ability to *apply* certain reading skills to information in this selection. These types of questions provide valuable practice for all students, especially those who must take standardized reading tests and state-mandated basic skills tests (such as the Florida CLAST Test and the Texas THEA Test). You may not have studied all of the skills at this point, so these items will serve as a helpful preview. The comprehension and critical reading skills in this section are presented in Chapters 4 through 9 of *Opening Doors;* vocabulary and figurative language skills are presented in Chapter 2. As you work through *Opening Doors,* you will practice and develop these skills. Write your answer for each question in the space provided.

_____ **21.** As used in paragraph 8 of this selection, *fruitless* means:
a. half-hearted.
b. unrelated to fruit.
c. bearing no fruit.
d. yielding no productive results.

_____ **22.** Which of the following is the main idea of paragraph 5 of this selection?

    a. At the bottom of this list are the world's poorest countries, found mainly in sub-Suharan Africa, which have so few resources and so little money that it is virtually impossible for them to develop at all.

    b. The "Fourth World" is at the bottom of this list.

    c. The "Fourth World" consists of the world's poorest countries.

    d. In Somalia and Sudan, for example, there are essentially no natural resources on which to base economic growth.

_____ **23.** The information in paragraph 7 of this selection is organized according to which of the following patterns?

    a. cause-effect

    b. comparison-contrast

    c. problem-solution

    d. list

_____ **24.** Which of the following assumptions underlies the author's point of view that Third World countries should be helped economically?

    a. Basic food, clothing, and shelter should be made available to all underdeveloped Third World countries.

    b. Overpopulation is at the root of Third World countries' problems.

    c. Wealthy countries should help Third World countries since the economies of all countries are to some extent linked.

    d. Fixing the infrastructure of Third World countries would solve their economic problems.

_____ **25.** The author mentions the Lomé Convention and the Paris Club as examples of:

    a. regional development banks backed by wealthy countries.

    b. specialized organizations designed to help wealthy countries assist Third World countries with their economic problems.

    c. organizations created by the World Bank and the International Monetary Fund.

    d. agencies created by the Brady Plan to make "project loans" and "adjustment loans."

Economics
(continued)

Collaboration Option

Respond in Writing

Directions: Refer to Selection 6-3 as needed to answer the essay-type questions below.

Option for collaboration: Your instructor may direct you to work with other students on one or more of these items, or in other words, to work *collaboratively.* In that case, you should form groups of three or four students, as directed by your instructor, and work together to complete the exercises. After your group discusses an item and agrees on the answer, have a group member record it. Each member of your group should be able to explain all of your group's answers.

1. The author presents three essential questions that he expects you to be able to answer after you have read this selection. In the spaces below, write a complete answer to each question.

    What is the Third World?

    (Note: Before reading this selection, you may not have known exactly what the *Third World* is. Now that you have read the selection, define this term in your own words.)

    _____

    _____

    _____

    _____

    _____

    What are the roots (causes, origins) of Third World poverty?

    _____

    _____

    _____

    _____

    _____

    What can be done to promote Third World development?

    _____

    _____

    _____

    _____

    _____

2. Could the United States ever become a Third World country? (In other words, are there circumstances that could cause a "first" or "second" world country to become a Third World country?) Explain your answer.

_____

_____

_____

_____

_____

3. Third World countries fall into three categories (newly industrialized countries, moderately developed countries, and the world's poorest countries—"fourth world" countries). What would a Third World country have to do to become a "first" or "second" world country? Is there anything a "fourth world" country could do to improve its situation?

_____

_____

_____

_____

_____

4. Which two countries have the greatest purchasing power? (Use the diagram on page 380 to answer this question.)

_____

5. **Overall main idea.** What is the overall main idea the author wants the reader to understand about the Third World and its economy? Answer this question in one sentence. Be sure that your overall main idea sentence includes the phrases *the Third World* and *economic growth.*

_____

_____

_____

_____

Internet Resources

Read More about This Topic on the World Wide Web

Directions: For further information about the topic of the selection, visit these websites:

www.usaid.gov/
This is the website for the United States Agency for International Development, a federal agency providing U.S. economic and humanitarian assistance throughout the world.

You can also use your favorite search engine such as Google, Yahoo!, or Alta-Vista (www.google.com, www.yahoo.com, www.altavista.com) to discover more about this topic. To locate additional information, type in combinations of keywords such as:

third world countries

or

promoting development third world

or

newly industrialized countries

or

Paris club

Keep in mind that whenever you go to *any* website, it is a good idea to evaluate the website and the information it contains. Ask yourself questions such as:

"Who sponsors this website?"
"Is the information contained in this website up-to-date?"
"What type of information is presented?"
"Is the information objective and complete?"
"How easy is it to use the features of this website?"

CHAPTER **7**

Recognizing Authors' Writing Patterns

SKILLS

Patterns of Writing

- What Are Authors' Writing Patterns?
- Why Is Recognizing Writing Patterns Important?

Recognizing Authors' Writing Patterns

- List Pattern
- Sequence Pattern
- Definition Pattern
- Comparison-Contrast Pattern
- Cause-Effect Pattern
- Spatial Order Pattern
- Avoid Seeing Everything as a List

A Word about Mixed Patterns and Other Writing Patterns

- Mixed Patterns
- Relationships within and between Sentences

    Clarification • Example • Addition • Sequence • Comparison •
    Contrast • Cause-Effect • Problem-Solution • Spatial Order • Summary

A Word about Standardized Reading Tests: Authors' Writing Patterns

CREATING YOUR SUMMARY

Developing Chapter Review Cards

READINGS

Selection 7-1   *(Business)*
"E-Commerce? It's E-Normous!" from *Understanding Business,*
by William Nickels, James McHugh, and Susan McHugh

Selection 7-2   *(Health)*
"The Decision to Marry" from *Targeting Wellness: The Core*
by Marvin Levy, Mark Dignan, and Janet Shirreffs

Selection 7-3   *(Psychology)*
"Reactions to Impending Death" from *Essentials of Psychology*
by Dennis Coon

Good order is the foundation of all things.

Edmund Burke

If you don't know where you're going, you may end up somewhere else.

Yogi Berra

PATTERNS OF WRITING

Student Online Learning Center (OLC)
Go to **Chapter 7.**
Select **Video.**

In this chapter you will learn another skill to help you improve your reading comprehension: recognizing authors' patterns of writing. **Writing patterns** are authors' ways of organizing information they present. You may hear writing patterns referred to as *organizational patterns, patterns of development, rhetorical patterns,* and *thinking patterns.* These are all names for the same thing.

What Are Authors' Writing Patterns?

All of us use certain patterns to organize our thoughts in ways that seem logical to us. When people write, they use these same patterns to organize information in ways that seem logical to them. If you can identify the pattern a writer is using and "think along" with the author as you read, you will find it easier to comprehend what he or she is saying. Recognizing the pattern may also enable you to predict where the author is going.

The specific pattern an author uses depends on the relationship among the ideas he or she wants to emphasize. In this chapter you will be introduced to several writing patterns commonly used by textbook authors. Variations and other names for the patterns are given in parentheses.

- List
- Sequence
- Definition
- Comparison-contrast
- Cause-effect
- Spatial order

At the end of this chapter you will also be introduced to what are called *mixed patterns,* a combination of two or more patterns in the same paragraph or passage.

It is important for you to understand that, as mentioned above, the patterns that authors use are the same thinking patterns that you use every day. The box on page 396 gives examples of how college students use these patterns in typical comments they make. You use these patterns yourself when you speak or write, but you still may not be aware of them when you read. This chapter will show you how to recognize the patterns as you read. Notice that some patterns have common variations: division/classification (list), time order/process (sequence), and definition with example (definition).

EXAMPLES OF THINKING PATTERNS IN EVERYDAY COMMENTS

- "I'm taking four courses this semester: art, psychology, reading, and math." **(list)**
- "The university has several different colleges: the college of fine arts, which includes music, dance, drama, and painting; the college of social sciences, which includes history, psychology, sociology, and anthropology; and the business college, which includes marketing, finance, accounting, and international business." **(division/classification)**
- "I have a psychology paper due on Monday, a math quiz on Wednesday, a vocabulary quiz in reading on Thursday morning, and an art test Thursday afternoon!" **(sequence)**
- "To write a research paper, you must first determine your topic, then gather information, write a draft, and finally, edit it to produce a correct, polished paper." **(process)**
- "To me, success means always giving your best effort, even if the results aren't perfect." **(definition)**
- "The baccalaureate, or bachelor's, degree is awarded to students who successfully complete a college or university's undergraduate course of study; for example, a student might earn a Bachelor of Arts degree or a Bachelor of Science degree." **(definition with example)**
- "Psychology focuses on the behavior of the individual, but sociology focuses on human behavior in groups." **(comparison-contrast)**
- "When I stick to my study schedule, I learn more, do better on tests, and feel less stress." **(cause-effect)**
- "The student center is just south of the library, between the fine arts building and the science complex." **(spatial order)**

Why Is Recognizing Writing Patterns Important?

Recognizing authors' writing patterns provides several advantages:

- **Improved comprehension.**   You will comprehend more because you will be able to follow the writer's ideas more accurately and more efficiently.
- **More accurate predictions.**   As soon as you identify a pattern, you can make predictions about what is likely to come next in a paragraph. As you learned in Chapter 2, effective readers are active readers who make logical predictions.
- **Easier memorization.**   You can memorize information more efficiently when you understand the way it is organized. If you can grasp an author's pattern of organization, you will not only learn the information more quickly but also retain it more easily.
- **Improvement in your writing.**   Using these patterns yourself will enable you to write clearer, more organized paragraphs. For example, you can write better answers on essay tests when you use appropriate patterns to organize the information. Using these patterns when you prepare a presentation or a speech will help you organize your ideas logically, and this will make it easier for your listeners to follow your train of thought.

List pattern.
Three sources of information.

RECOGNIZING AUTHORS' WRITING PATTERNS

Comprehension Monitoring Question for Recognizing Authors' Writing Patterns

Which pattern did the author use to organize the main idea and the supporting details?

Six common writing patterns are described below, accompanied by textbook excerpts that illustrate each pattern. As you may already know, every writing pattern has certain signal words and phrases that are associated with it and convey to the reader which pattern is being used. The paragraph pattern signals and clue words associated with each pattern are explained after each sample excerpt. They are summarized in the table on pages 412–414. Often, the main idea sentence contains clue words that signal which pattern is being used. As you read, ask yourself, "Which pattern did the author use to organize the main idea and supporting details?"

List Pattern

KEY TERM
list pattern

A group of items presented in no specific order, since the order is unimportant.

A list pattern is also known as a *listing pattern*.

As its name indicates, the **list pattern** (sometimes called a *listing pattern*) presents a list of items in no specific order. The order of the items is not important. If the items listed in the paragraph were presented in a different order or rearranged, it would not matter.

Clue words in a paragraph that typically signal a listing pattern are *and, also, another, moreover, in addition,* and words such as *first, second, third, fourth, last,* and *finally.* Watch for words or numbers in the main idea that announce *categories (two types, five ways, several kinds).* Sometimes bullets (•) or asterisks (*) are used to set off individual items in a list. Their purpose is to ensure that the reader will notice each separate item. Sometimes authors use numbers (1, 2, 3) or letters (*a, b, c*) to set off individual items in a list even though their order is not important. Their purpose is to ensure that the reader will notice each item and the total number of items. It is important to remember that your task is to identify *all* the items in the list, even when not all of them (or perhaps any of them) are "signaled."

Here is a paragraph from an economics textbook. The topic is *the financing of corporate activity.* The first sentence states the main idea: *Generally speaking, corporations finance their activity in three different ways.* The authors have listed three details that help you understand more about this main idea. Notice that these details are in no special order. As you read this paragraph, ask yourself, "What are the *three different ways* that corporations finance their activity?"

Generally speaking, corporations finance their activity in three different ways. First, a very large portion of a corporation's activities is financed internally out of undistributed corporate profits. Second, as do individuals or unincorporated businesses, corporations may borrow from financial institutions. For example, a small corporation planning to build a new plant may obtain the needed funds from a commercial bank, a savings and loan association, or an insurance company. Third, unique to corporations, they can issue common stocks and bonds.

Source: Campbell McConnell and Stanley Brue, *Economics: Principles, Problems, and Policies,* 15th ed., p. 89. Copyright © 2002 by McGraw-Hill Companies, Inc. Reprinted by permission of McGraw-Hill Companies.

Stop and Annotate

Go back to the textbook excerpt above. Underline or highlight the words that signal the items in the list. Then number each supporting detail. Mark the words in the main idea sentence that signal a list, too.

In this paragraph, the authors use the phrase *three different ways* and the clue words *first, second,* and *third* to signal a list of three major supporting details: three ways of financing corporate activities. The order in which the items are listed is not particularly important. What is important is that there are three different ways, and what those three ways are. Notice that a minor supporting detail signaled by the phrase "for example" follows the second major detail. This sentence merely gives examples of financial institutions, a term mentioned in the second major detail. (Major and minor details are defined and explained on pages 339–341.)

The next excerpt is from a health and fitness textbook. It illustrates the listing pattern in a very obvious way: the items in the list are numbered. The topic of the paragraph is *signs of alcoholism,* and its implied main idea (which must be formulated by the reader) is: *The diagnosis of alcoholism is often imprecise and difficult for nonprofessionals to make, but there are certain changes in behavior that can warn of possible alcoholism.* On the basis of the topic and the main idea, what do you predict will be listed?

Signs of Alcoholism

The diagnosis of alcoholism is not something that can be precise, and it is often difficult for nonprofessionals to make. The disease carries such a stigma that the alcoholic, friends, and family often postpone seeking treatment. Meanwhile, it is not unusual for the alcoholic to deny the problem and rationalize continued drinking. Certain signs in a person's behavior that warn of possible alcoholism include :

1. Surreptitious, secretive drinking
2. Morning drinking (unless that behavior is not unusual in the person's peer group)
3. Repeated, conscious attempts at abstinence
4. Blatant, indiscriminate use of alcohol
5. Changing beverages in an attempt to control drinking
6. Having five or more drinks daily
7. Having two or more blackouts while drinking

Source: Adapted from Marvin Levy, Mark Dignan, and Janet Shirreffs, *Targeting Wellness: The Core,* p. 251. Copyright © 1992 by The McGraw-Hill Companies, Inc. Reprinted by permission of The McGraw-Hill Companies.

Stop and Annotate

Go back to the textbook excerpt above. Underline or highlight the clues that signal a list.

KEY TERM

division/classification pattern

Groups or categories of items that are named, and the parts in each group are explained. (This is a variation of the list pattern.)

The list of warning signs of possible alcoholism is actually set off from the text, indicated by a colon (:), and announced by the phrase *Certain signs in a person's behavior that warn of possible alcoholism include.* The topic *signs of alcoholism* in the heading and the words *certain signs* in a person's behavior in the main idea sentence help readers predict that a list will be given. The authors list seven supporting details (signs) and number these details even though they are not in any particular order. The numbers are included to make sure that the reader notices each separate detail and so that the reader understands that, indeed, there are *several different* signs in a person's behavior—not just one or two—that can warn of possible alcoholism. (Numbering items in a list is referred to as *enumeration.*)

A variation of the list pattern is the division or classification pattern. In the **division** or **classification pattern,** items are divided into groups or categories that are named, and the parts in each group are explained. In the main idea sentence watch for clue words such as *two categories, four kinds, three types, five elements, six classes, three kinds,* etc. The paragraph below, from a nutrition textbook, uses the division or classification pattern.

Lipids

Lipids (mostly fats and oils) can be separated into two basic types—saturated fat and unsaturated fat—based on the chemical structure of their dominant fatty acids. *Saturated fats* are rich in saturated fatty acids. These fatty acids do not contain carbon-carbon-double bonds. *Unsaturated fats* are rich in unsaturated fatty acids. These fatty acids contain one or more carbon-carbon double bonds. The presence of carbon-carbon double bonds determines whether the lipid is solid or liquid at room temperature. Plant oils tend to contain many unsaturated fatty acids—this makes them liquid. Animal fats are often rich in saturated fatty acids— this makes them solid.

Source: Adapted from Gordon Wardlaw and Anne Smith, *Contemporary Nutrition,* 6th ed. Boston: McGraw-Hill, 2006, p. 7. Copyright © 2006 The McGraw-Hill Companies.

Stop and Annotate

Go back to the textbook excerpt on page 399. Underline or highlight the cues that signal the division or classification form of the list pattern.

In the first sentence of the paragraph (the stated main idea sentence), the phrase *two basic types* alerts readers that a classification will follow. The two classifications are the two types of fats: saturated and unsaturated. The authors italicize the terms. They explain the two types and then tell the types of oils and fats (plant and animal) that belong in each category. Notice that it would not make any difference if the authors had presented the two categories in the reverse order because order is not important. What is important is for the reader to understand is that there are two types of fats and the distinguishing characteristics of each type.

Sequence Pattern

The **sequence pattern** presents a list of items *in a specific order* because the order is important. The sequence pattern is a type of list, but it differs from a simple list because the order of the items is significant. A very common type of sequence is the occurrence of events in time, and therefore a sequence pattern is often called *time order* or *chronological order.* The sequence pattern is also known as a *process* or a *series.* Sets of directions are examples of sequences that students encounter daily.

Clue words in a paragraph that signal a sequence pattern include *first, second, third, then, next,* and *finally.* Words that refer to time, such as dates and phrases like *during the twenty-first century* or *in the last decade,* may also signal sequences. Watch also for enumeration (1, 2, 3, etc.), letters (*a, b, c,* etc.), and signal words such as *sequence, steps, stages, phases, progression, process,* and *series.* When numbers are used in a sequence, they indicate the order, and not just how many items there are.

KEY TERMS

sequence pattern

A list of items presented in a specific order because the order is important.

The sequence pattern is also known as *time order, chronological order, a process,* or *a series.*

process

A series of actions or changes that bring about a result. (This is a variation of the sequence pattern.)

Sequence pattern. The seasons follow a predictable sequence.

Following is an excerpt in which authors use a sequence pattern to show the order in which certain events occur. This excerpt is from the same health and fitness textbook, but this time the topic is *the alcohol continuum.* (A "continuum" is what it sounds like: a gradual progression from one stage to the next.) Read the paragraph and notice the list of details and the order in which they are given.

The Alcohol Continuum

Alcoholism is a progressive disease that develops as a series of stages through which any drinker may pass. At one end of the spectrum is occasional and moderate social drinking with family or friends on special occasions. At the other end is long-term, frequent, uncontrollable drinking with severe physical, psychological, and social complications. The full continuum can be summarized as follows :

1. **Occasional drinker** drinks in small quantities only on special occasions.
2. **Light drinker** drinks regularly in small and nonintoxicating quantities.
3. **Social drinker** drinks regularly in moderate and nonintoxicating quantities.
4. **Problem drinker** drinks to intoxication with no pattern to episodes, gets drunk without intending to or realizing it.
5. **Binge drinker** drinks heavily in recurrent episodes, often brought on by disturbances in work, home, or social life.
6. **Excessive drinker** experiences frequent episodes of uncontrollable drinking affecting work, family, and social relationships.
7. **Chronic alcoholic** is in serious trouble from long-term, frequent, and uncontrollable drinking; experiences physical complications including organic dysfunction, tolerance, and dependence; and develops severe work, home, and social problems.

Source: From Marvin Levy, Mark Dignan, and Janet Shirreffs, *Targeting Wellness: The Core,* pp. 250–56. Copyright © 1992 by The McGraw-Hill Companies, Inc. Reprinted by permission of The McGraw-Hill Companies.

Stop and Annotate

Go back to the textbook excerpt above. Underline or highlight the clues that signal a sequence.

The details in this paragraph are numbered, announced by a colon, and clearly listed after the phrase *can be summarized as follows.* But there are other clues indicating that a sequence pattern is being used: the words *progressive, continuum, series of stages,* and *spectrum.* In this paragraph, the order of the supporting details is obviously important. Students would be expected to learn them in this order.

Now read this excerpt from a music textbook, in which the author also uses the sequence pattern. Notice the dates that are associated with important events in the Beatles' career.

The Beatles

The Beatles—the singer-guitarists Paul McCartney, John Lennon, and George Harrison, and the drummer Ringo Starr—have been the most influential performing group in the history of rock. Their music, hairstyle, dress, and lifestyle were imitated all over the world, resulting in a phenomenon known as Beatlemania. All four Beatles were born during the early 1940s in Liverpool, England, and dropped out of school in their teens to devote themselves to rock. Lennon and McCartney, the main songwriters of the group, began working together in 1956 and were joined by Harrison about two years later. In 1962 Ringo Starr became their new drummer. The group gained experience by performing in Hamburg, Germany, and in Liverpool, a port to which sailors brought the latest American rock, rhythm-and-blues, and country-and-western records. In 1961, the Beatles made their first record, and by 1963 they were England's top rock group. In 1964, they triumphed in the United States, breaking attendance records everywhere and dominating the record market. Audiences often became hysterical, and the police had to protect the Beatles from their fans. Beatle dolls, wigs, sweatshirts, and jackets flooded the market. Along with a steady flow of successful records, the Beatles made several hit movies: *A Hard Day's Night, Help!* and *Yellow Submarine.*

Source: Roger Kamien, *Music: An Appreciation,* 5th ed., p. 608. Copyright © 1992 by The McGraw-Hill Companies, Inc. Reprinted by permission of The McGraw-Hill Companies.

Stop and Annotate

Go back to the textbook excerpt above. Underline or highlight the clues that signal a sequence.

The details in this paragraph support the author's main idea: the Beatles have been the most influential performing group in the history of rock. The supporting details are given in chronological order: the order in which they occurred. The author uses dates throughout the paragraph to tell when each important event occurred. In addition, the phrases *were born during the early 1940s* and *dropped out of school in their teens* indicate the sequence of events in the Beatles' history.

Here is a passage from a business textbook in which the authors use the process pattern, a form of the sequence pattern. As defined earlier, a process is a series of actions or changes that lead to bring a specific result, such as the process of obtaining a driver's license or the process of digestion. This paragraph presents seven steps managers can use in order to make sound decisions.

All management functions involve some kind of decision making. Decision making is choosing among two or more alternatives. It sounds easier here than it is in practice. In fact decision making is at the heart of all the management functions. The rational decision-making process is a series of steps managers often follow to make logical, intelligent, and well-founded decisions. The steps can be thought of as the seven Ds of decision making:

1. Define the situation.
2. Describe and collect needed information.
3. Develop alternatives.
4. Develop agreement among those involved.

5. Decide which alternative is best.

6. Do what is indicated (begin implementation).

7. Determine whether the decision was a good one and follow up.

Source: William Nickels, James McHugh, and Susan McHugh *Understanding Business,* 7th ed., pp. 218–29. Copyright © 2005 by The McGraw-Hill Companies, Inc. Reprinted by permission of The McGraw-Hill Companies.

Stop and Annotate

Go back to the textbook excerpt above. Underline or highlight the cues that signal the process form of the sequence pattern.

The details of the paragraph support the implied main idea: All management functions involve decision making, and the seven Ds of decision making are the steps managers often follow to make good decisions. The details present in order the specific steps of the process. Notice that the authors use the words *process, series of steps,* and *steps.* Furthermore, they number the steps in the process because the steps must be done in that order. These clue words and signals are characteristic of any sequence pattern, including processes.

Definition Pattern

KEY TERM

definition pattern

Pattern presenting the meaning of an important term discussed throughout a passage. The definition may be followed by examples that illustrate or clarify the meaning.

The **definition pattern** presents the meaning of an important term that is discussed throughout the passage. The definition itself is the main idea. The details in the rest of the paragraph discuss or illustrate the term that is being defined.

Definitions are easy to identify because the terms being defined often appear in **bold print,** *italics,* or color. Moreover, they are typically introduced by signal words such as *the term, refers to, is called, is defined as, means,* and so forth. Even the simple verb *is* can be a signal to the reader that a definition is being given.

Sometimes an author will use a synonym (a word or a phrase with a similar meaning) in order to define a term. The synonym will be signaled by words such as *or, in other words,* or *that is.* Take, for example, this sentence:

Many women encounter what is termed a *glass ceiling,* or barrier of subtle discrimination, that keeps them from the top positions in business.

The term that is being defined (glass ceiling) appears in italics. Notice that the word *or* introduces a phrase that is set off by commas and that defines the term: a barrier of subtle discrimination. The term "glass ceiling" is a metaphor, a type of figurative language introduced in Chapter 2. The term, of course, does not refer to a real ceiling made of glass but, rather, the invisible barrier of discrimination that many women encounter in the workplace.

Definitions can also be signaled by punctuation marks. All the examples below define the term *anorexia nervosa.* Notice how the different punctuation marks in each of the examples indicate the definition.

• **Commas (,)**

Anorexia nervosa, an eating disorder that can lead to starvation, occurs most often in teenage girls.

Teenage girls are the most common victims of anorexia nervosa, an eating disorder that can lead to starvation.

* **Parentheses ( )**

Anorexia nervosa (an eating disorder that can lead to starvation) occurs most often in teenage girls.

* **Brackets [ ]**

Anorexia nervosa [an eating disorder than can lead to starvation] occurs most often in teenage girls.

* **Dashes (—)**

Anorexia nervosa—an eating disorder that can lead to starvation—occurs most often in teenage girls.

* **Colon (:)**

An illness affecting primarily teenage girls is anorexia nervosa: an eating disorder that can lead to starvation.

Below is an excerpt from a psychology textbook in which the author presents a definition as the stated main idea in the second sentence and then goes on to explain it more fully by giving an example. The term the author is defining is the *foot-in-the-door principle.*

Foot-in-the-Door Principle

People who sell door-to-door have long recognized that once they "get a foot in the door," a sale is almost a sure thing. To state the **foot-in-the-door principle** more formally, a person who agrees to a small request is later more likely to comply with a larger demand. Evidence suggests, for instance, that if someone asked you to put a large sign in your front yard to support the police department you might refuse. If, however, you had first agreed to put a small sign in your window, you would later be much more likely to allow the big sign to be placed in your yard.

Source: Essentials of Psychology, 5th ed., by Dennis Coon, p. 627. © 1991. Reprinted with permission of Wadsworth, a division of Thomson Learning: www.thomsonrights.com. Fax: 800-730-2215.

Stop and Annotate

Go back to the textbook excerpt above. Underline or highlight the clues that signal a definition and example.

In this paragraph the author gives the definition of the foot-in-the-door principle within the main idea sentence: *a person who agrees to a small request is later more likely to comply with a larger demand.* To announce to the reader that the foot-in-the-door effect is being defined precisely, the author uses the phrase *To state the* **foot-in-the-door principle** *more formally.* Did you notice that the definition is set off by a comma, and that the important term appears in the heading and in bold print within the paragraph? To help readers understand the meaning of the foot-in-the-door principle, the author includes a specific example. In the third sentence, he says *for instance,* and then gives the example of a small sign placed in a window and then a large one placed in the yard.

Here is a paragraph from a business textbook in which the authors define two forms of *sexual harassment* in the workplace. Notice that the entire paragraph defines sexual harassment.

Another sensitive issue concerning primarily women in the workplace is **sexual harassment.** As defined by the Equal Employment Opportunity Commission, sexual harassment takes two forms : the obvious request for sexual favors with an implicit reward or punishment related to work, and the more subtle creation of a sexist environment in which employees are made to feel uncomfortable by off-color jokes, lewd remarks, and posturing.

Source: David Rachman, Michael Mescon, Courtland Bovée, and John Thill, *Business Today,* p. 110. Copyright © 1993 by The McGraw-Hill Companies, Inc. Reprinted by permission of The McGraw-Hill Companies.

Stop and Annotate

Go back to the textbook excerpt above. Underline or highlight the clues that signal a definition.

KEY TERM

comparison-contrast pattern

Similarities (comparisons) between two or more things are presented, differences (contrasts) between two or more things are presented, or both similarities and differences are presented.

The comparison-contrast pattern is also known as *ideas in opposition.*

In this paragraph, the phrases *as defined by* and *takes two forms* signal to the reader that there are two distinct definitions of sexual harassment in the workplace. Notice that a colon (:) announces the two definitions. Notice also that although the term *sexual harassment* appears in the first sentence, it is actually defined in the following sentence.

Comparison-Contrast Pattern

Often writers want to emphasize comparisons and contrasts. A *comparison* shows how two or more things are similar or alike. A *contrast* points out the differences between them. The **comparison-contrast pattern** presents similarities (comparisons) between two or more things, differences (contrasts) between two or more things, or both. The comparison-contrast pattern is also known as *ideas in opposition.*

To signal comparisons, authors use the words *similarly, likewise, both, same,* and *also.* To signal contrasts, authors use clues such as *on the other hand, in contrast, however, while, whereas, although, nevertheless, different, unlike,* and *some . . . while others.* Contrasts are also signaled by words in a paragraph that have opposite meanings, such as *advantages* and *disadvantages, strengths* and *weaknesses, plusses* and *minuses,* or *assets* and *liabilities.*

Comparison-contrast pattern.
The size of these two dogs presents a startling contrast. How are these two animals alike? How are they different?

In the following excerpt from an art appreciation textbook, the author presents important information about the advantages and disadvantages of the very slow rate at which oil paint dries. Read the paragraph to determine what the author says about the positive and negative aspects of this characteristic.

> The outstanding characteristic of oil paint is that it dries very slowly. This creates both advantages and disadvantages for the artist. On the plus side, it means that colors can be blended very subtly, layers of paint can be applied on top of other layers with little danger of separating or cracking, and the artist can rework sections of the painting almost indefinitely. This same asset becomes a liability when the artist is pressed for time—perhaps when an exhibition has been scheduled. Oil paint dries so very slowly that it may be weeks or months before the painting has truly "set."
>
> *Source:* Mark Getlein, *Gilbert's Living with Art,* 7th ed., pp. 169, 171. Copyright © 2005 by The McGraw-Hill Companies, Inc. Reprinted by permission of The McGraw-Hill Companies.

Stop and Annotate

Go back to the textbook excerpt above. Underline or highlight the clues that signal a comparison-contrast pattern.

In this paragraph, *advantages, disadvantages, on the plus side, asset,* and *liability* are clues or signals that the author is presenting both the positive and the negative aspects of the slow rate at which oil paint dries.

Here is another paragraph from the same art appreciation textbook, which also uses the comparison-contrast pattern. Notice that the author presents similarities and differences between a Buddhist shrine and a medieval Christian cathedral.

> Buddhist shrines—the word stupa means "shrine"—often housed relics of the Buddha, and worship rituals called for circumambulation ("walking around") of the stupa. Thus, on the outside of the Great Stupa of Sanchi, in India, we see a railed pathway, where pilgrims could take the ritual clockwise walk following the Path of Life around the World Mountain. Elsewhere the stupa is embellished richly with carvings and sculpture evoking scenes from the Buddha's life. Every part of the stupa is geared to the pursuit of personal enlightenment and transcendence. But if the Buddhist temple is dedicated to private worship, then its extreme opposite can be found in the total encompassment of a community religious experience: the medieval Christian cathedral. And the supreme example of that ideal is the Cathedral of Notre Dame de Chartres, in France. Chartres Cathedral was built, rebuilt, and modified over a period of several hundred years, but the basic structure, which is in the Gothic style, was established in the thirteenth century. A cathedral is the bishop's domain and therefore is always in a town or a city. This one fact is crucial to understanding the nature of Chartres and the communal role it played in the people's lives.
>
> *Source:* Adapted from Rita Gilbert, *Living with Art,* 3rd ed., pp. 64–65. Copyright © 1992 by The McGraw-Hill Companies, Inc. Reprinted by permission of The McGraw-Hill Companies.

In the middle of this passage, the author signals the major difference she is presenting between the Great Stupa of Sanchi and Chartres Cathedral by the words *extreme opposite.* She wants the reader to understand that these two structures were built to serve different religious purposes. More specifically, she wants the reader to understand that Buddhist stupas were designed for *personal enlightenment* and *private worship,* whereas Christian cathedrals were designed for a *community religious experience.* In this passage, the words *personal* and *private* are used in contrast to *community.*

Stop and Annotate

Go back to the textbook excerpt on page 406. Underline or highlight the clues that signal a comparison-contrast pattern.

When information is presented in comparison-contrast pattern, take notes by creating a chart of the information. A chart makes it easy to see similarities and differences. Below is a chart of the information in the preceding excerpt about the similarities and differences between the Great Stupa of Sanchi and Chartres Cathedral.

When you list the differences, use one column for each item. Be sure to write the contrasting information on the same lines. For example, the first line contrasts the religions, the second the location of the building, the third the buildings' shapes, etc. Organizing comparison-contrast information in chart form makes it easier to memorize.

	Great Stupa of Sanchi & Chartres Cathedral	
Similarities:	• Places of worship	
	• Large and elaborate stone structures	
(Comparisons)	• Centuries old	
	• Embellished with carvings and sculpture	
	• Designed for specific religious purposes	
	Great Stupa of Sanchi	*Chartres Cathedral*
	• Buddhist	• Christian
Differences:	• Sanchi, India	• Chartres, France
	• Round structure	• Cruciform structure (cross-shaped)
(Contrasts)	• Domed roof (symbol of World Mountain)	• Gothic style
	• Housed relics of Buddha	
	• Circumambulation	
	• Geared to private worship	• Geared to community religious experience
	• Geared to the pursuit of personal enlightenment	• Played a communal role in people's lives

Cause-Effect Pattern

KEY TERM

cause-effect pattern

Reasons (causes) and results (effects) of events or conditions are presented.

The **cause-effect pattern** presents *reasons* (causes) and *results* (effects) of events or conditions. Authors often use these words to indicate a cause: *because, the reasons, causes, is due to,* and *is caused by.* These words are often used to indicate an effect: *therefore, consequently, thus, as a consequence, led to, the results, as a result, the effect was,* and *resulted in.*

The following excerpt from a health textbook uses the cause-effect pattern. Its topic is *lung cancer and the way an individual smokes*. The verb *affects* and the phrase *depending on* signal to the reader that the cause-effect pattern is being used. The first sentence of this paragraph is its stated main idea.

> The way an individual smokes affects the chances of developing lung cancer. The risk increases depending on how many cigarettes are smoked each day, how deeply the smoker inhales, and how much tar and nicotine are contained in the cigarettes. People who started smoking early in their lives are also at greater risk than those who have only smoked for a few years.
>
> *Source:* Adapted from Marvin Levy, Mark Dignan, and Janet Shirreffs, *Targeting Wellness: The Core*, p. 261.
> Copyright © 1992 by The McGraw-Hill Companies, Inc. Reprinted by permission of The McGraw-Hill Companies.

Stop and Annotate

Go back to the textbook excerpt above. Underline or highlight the clues that signal a cause-effect pattern. Number the causes with a small ①, ②, ③, and ④. to make each cause stand out clearly.

In this paragraph, the authors present four supporting details that are *causes* that contribute to one *effect,* the smoker's increased risk of lung cancer: (1) how many cigarettes are smoked daily, (2) how deeply the smoker inhales, (3) the amount of tar and nicotine in the cigarettes, and (4) the age at which a person starts smoking. (Notice that three causes are mentioned in a single sentence.)

Arranging information presented in a cause-effect pattern by mapping is also an ideal format for study notes or review cards. (Mapping is an informal way of organizing main ideas and supporting details by using boxes, circles, lines, arrows, and so on. Guidelines for mapping are presented in Chapter 10.) The study map below presents information from the excerpt above. It shows the four causes that have an effect on a person's chances of developing lung cancer.

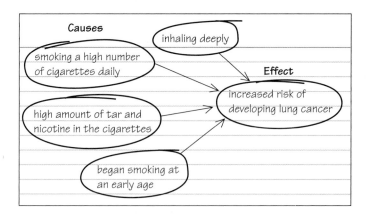

Here is an excerpt from a physics textbook that uses the cause-effect pattern. It explains *why* many people enjoy physics.

Many People Enjoy Physics. Why?

There are several reasons physicists and many of those who study physics find it enjoyable. First, it is a joy to find out how the world behaves. Knowledge of the laws of nature allows us to look on the world with a fuller appreciation of its beauty and wonder. Second, we all enjoy discovering something new. Scientists take great satisfaction in exposing a facet of nature that was previously not seen or perhaps not understood. Imagine how Columbus must have felt when he sighted America. Scientists share a similar excitement when their work results in the discovery of a new aspect of nature. Fortunately, it seems that the more we discover about nature, the more there is to discover. The excitement of discovery drives science forward. Third, most of us enjoy the successful completion of a demanding task. That is why people of all ages work puzzles. Each question or problem in science is a new puzzle to be solved. We enjoy the satisfaction of success. Fourth, science benefits humanity. A substantial fraction of those who embark on scientific work do so because they wish to contribute to the progress of civilization. Call it idealistic, perhaps, but ask yourself what medical tools we would have today without the work of countless scientists in physics, chemistry, biology, and the related sciences. Our present civilization is heavily indebted not only to those in science but also to those in the general populace who know enough about science to support its progress.

Source: Frederick J. Bueche, *Principles of Physics,* 5th ed., p. 3. Copyright © 1988 by The McGraw-Hill Companies, Inc. Reprinted by permission of The McGraw-Hill Companies.

Stop and Annotate

Go back to the textbook excerpt above. Underline or highlight the clues that signal a cause-effect pattern.

In the stated main idea sentence (the first sentence), this author uses the clue words *several reasons.* Then he uses *first, second, third,* and *fourth* to announce the four reasons that explain his main idea: *There are several reasons physicists and many of those who study physics find it enjoyable.* Even the word *Why?* in the title tells readers to expect a list of reasons (causes).

In the excerpt from a business textbook on page 410, the authors present several effects (results) of employee assistance programs. This paragraph does not contain signal words such as *results* or *effects.* Instead, the authors assume that the reader will understand the relationship between these programs and their results. The phrase *Such programs have been reported to reduce* implies that employee assistance programs have certain effects. Read the paragraph and notice the four effects the authors present.

Cause-effect pattern.
Cause: a bowling ball
Effect: a strike

A number of companies have also instituted **employee assistance programs** (EAPs) for employees with personal problems, especially drug or alcohol dependence. Such programs have been reported (on the average) to reduce absenteeism by 66 percent, to reduce health-care costs by 86 percent, to reduce sickness benefits by 33 percent, and to reduce work-related accidents by 65 percent. Participation in EAPs is voluntary and confidential. Employees are given in-house counseling or are referred to outside therapists or treatment programs.

Source: David Rachman, Michael Mescon, Courtland Bovée, and John Thill, *Business Today,* pp. 283–84. Copyright © 1993 by The McGraw-Hill Companies, Inc. Reprinted by permission of The McGraw-Hill Companies.

Stop and Annotate

Go back to the textbook excerpt above. Underline or highlight the phrase that signals a cause-effect pattern. Number the effects with a small ①, ②, ③, and ④ to make each effect stand out clearly.

In a single sentence, these authors present four beneficial *effects* of employee assistance programs: reductions in (1) absenteeism, (2) costs of health care, (3) costs of sickness benefits, and (4) work-related accidents. (Notice that all four effects are given in a single sentence.)

Here is another informal study map that presents the information from the preceding excerpt. The study card shows the four positive effects of an employee assistance program.

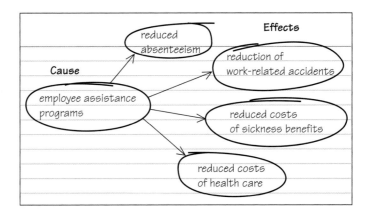

Spatial Order Pattern

KEY TERM

spatial order pattern

The location or layout of something or someplace is described.

A spatial order pattern is also known as a *place order pattern.*

The **spatial order pattern,** also known as *place order,* describes the location or layout of something or someplace. For example, authors would use this pattern to describe the location of troops in an important battle, the elements of a painting, the location of a country, or the floor plan of a medieval church. To do this, they use clue words such as *beside, near, adjacent to, next to, close to, below, beneath, above, over, opposite, facing, to the right or left, north, south, east, west, within, outside of,* and so forth. Also watch for clues such as *site, location, is located, is situated, placed, positioned,* and other such words.

The passage below describes the location of the state of Kansas. As you read it, watch for clues that indicate a spatial order pattern.

Kansas is situated at the geographic center of the United States. It is halfway between the East and West coasts. It is bounded by four states: Nebraska to the north, Oklahoma to the south, Missouri to the east, and Colorado on the west.

Stop and Annotate

Go back to the excerpt above. Underline or highlight the words that signal the spatial order pattern.

Did you notice the words *situated at* in the first sentence, the stated main idea? The other sentences contains additional place words: *halfway between, east,* and *west* in the second sentence, and *north, south, east,* and *west* in the last sentence.

Now read this art history textbook's description of a famous painting that hangs in the Galleria degli Uffizi in Florence, Italy.

Madonna Enthroned, painted by the 13th-century Italian master Cimabue, depicts Mary, mother of Christ, with her son. Mary sits tranquilly on her throne, her hand a classic gesture indicating the Christ child on her lap, who is the hope of the earth's salvation. On both sides of her are figures of angels, heavenly beings who assist humankind in its quest for Paradise. Again, all these wear halos symbolizing their holiness. Yet again, the Virgin, being the most important figure in this painting, dominates the composition, is the largest, and holds the most serenely frontal posture.

Source: Adapted from Mark Getlein, *Gilbert's Living with Art,* 7th ed., p. 54. Copyright © 2005 by The McGraw-Hill Companies, Inc. Reprinted by permission of The McGraw-Hill Companies.

Stop and Annotate

Go back to the textbook excerpt above. Underline or highlight the words that signal the spatial order pattern.

The author describes the position of Mary in the painting: she sits *on her throne.* She is holding her child *on her lap,* and angels appear *on both sides* of her. Mary has a *frontal posture,* meaning that she faces directly out at the viewer. The author presents the picture with words.

In this chapter so far, you have learned about forms of six common paragraph patterns textbook authors use: list, sequence, definition, comparison-contrast, cause-effect, and spatial order. The following chart summarizes the signals and clue words for each of these patterns.

SUMMARY OF PARAGRAPH PATTERN SIGNALS AND CLUE WORDS

1. List Pattern (Division/Classification)

and	a, b, c . . .
also	bullets (•)
another	asterisks (*)
moreover	words that announce lists
in addition	(such as *categories, kinds, types, ways, examples,*
first, second, third	*classes, groups, parts, elements, features,*
finally	*characteristics,* etc.)
1, 2, 3 . . .	

2. Sequence Pattern (Time Order/Process)

first, second, third	*series*
now, then, next, finally	*stages*
dates	*when*
1, 2, 3 . . .	*before, during, after*
a, b, c . . .	*at last*
steps	*process, spectrum, continuum*
phases	*hierarchy*
progression	instructions and directions
words that refer to time	

3. Definition Pattern (Definition with Example)

words in bold print	*in other words*
words in italics	*that is* (also abbreviated as *i.e.,* for *id est,* Latin for "that is")
words in color	
is defined as	*by this we mean*
means	*or* (preceding a synonym)
refers to, is referred to as	punctuation that sets off a definition
the term	or synonym , : ( ) [ ] —
is called	examples that illustrate the definition or meaning of a term
in other words	
is, is known as	

4. Comparison-Contrast Pattern

Comparisons:

similarly

likewise

both

same

also

resembles

parallels

in the same manner

in the same way

words that compare

(adjectives that describe

comparisons, such as *safer,*

slower, lighter, more

valuable, less toxic, etc.)

Contrasts:

in contrast

however

on the other hand

whereas

while

although

nevertheless

instead (of)

different

unlike

conversely

rather than

as opposed to

some . . . others

opposite words

5. Cause-Effect Pattern

Causes:

the reason(s)

the cause(s)

because

is due to (cause)

was caused by (cause)

(cause) *led to*

resulted from (cause)

since

Effects:

the result(s)

the effect(s)

the outcome

the final product

therefore

thus

consequently

as a consequence

hence

on that account

resulted in, results in (effect)

(effect) *was caused by*

(effect) *is due to*

led to (effect)

(effect) *resulted from*

Both the cause and the effect:

- (effect) *is due to* (cause)
- (effect) *resulted from* (cause)
- (effect) *was caused by* (cause)
- (cause) *led to* (effect)
- (cause) *results in* (effect)

Some questions that indicate cause-effect:

- *What causes* (effect)? (Answer will be the cause.)
- *Why does* (effect) *occur?* (Answer will be the cause.)
- *What is the reason for* (effect)? (Answer will be the cause.)
- *How can* (effect) *be explained?* (Answer will be the cause.)
- *What does* (cause) *lead to?* (Answer will be the effect.)

(Continued on next page)

(Continued from previous page)

6. Spatial Order Pattern (Place Order)

over, above	*north, south, east, west*
below, beneath	*right, left*
beside	*situated*
near, close to	*positioned*
adjacent to	*located*
opposite	*placed*
facing	*site*

Avoid Seeing Everything as a List

When you are first learning to identify authors' writing patterns, you may mistakenly view every paragraph as having a list pattern, since the same clue words can signal more than one pattern. For example, you may have noticed that some of the cause-effect clue words in the excerpt on physics (page 409) are the same clue words that could signal a sequence or a simple list. The passage about physics, however, uses the clue words *first, second, third,* and *fourth* to present a list of *reasons* (causes). Because these reasons demonstrate the cause-effect relationship that the author wants to emphasize, this paragraph should be viewed as having a cause-effect pattern, and not a list pattern.

Whenever you encounter what at first glance appears to be a list, ask yourself, "A list of *what?*" Your answer should help you realize if the author is using one of the other common patterns instead. For instance,

- If your answer is "a list of *events in a particular order,*" then the paragraph has a *sequence* pattern.
- If your answer is "a list of *similarities* or *differences,*" the paragraph has a *comparison-contrast* pattern.
- If your answer is "a list of *causes, reasons,* or *results,*" then the paragraph has a *cause-effect* pattern.

View a paragraph as having a list pattern only when you are certain that no other pattern can be used to describe the way the supporting details are organized.

A WORD ABOUT MIXED PATTERNS AND OTHER WRITING PATTERNS

The six writing patterns in this chapter are the most common patterns authors use to organize their writing. Of course, there are other writing patterns that are less common but serve useful purposes. Keep in mind that the reason authors use any pattern is always the same: to organize main ideas and supporting details so that they will be as logical and clear to readers as possible.

Mixed Patterns

Each of the textbook excerpts presented so far in this chapter has illustrated one particular writing pattern, but you should be aware that authors frequently use two or more of the patterns in the *same* paragraph or a longer passage. Such a combination of two or more writing patterns in the same paragraph or passage is called a **mixed pattern.**

Below is an example of a *mixed pattern in a single paragraph.* This excerpt, from a health and fitness textbook, uses both the definition pattern and the cause-effect pattern. The paragraph presents a definition of passive smoking, and it also presents the effects of passive smoking.

KEY TERM
mixed pattern

Combination of two or more writing patterns in the same paragraph or passage.

Passive Smoking and the Rights of Nonsmokers

Reports from the U.S. surgeon general's office suggest that tobacco smoke in enclosed indoor areas is an important air pollution problem. This has led to the controversy about **passive smoking**—the breathing in of air polluted by the secondhand tobacco smoke of others. Carbon monoxide levels of sidestream smoke (smoke from the burning end of a cigarette) reach a dangerously high level. True, the smoke can be greatly diluted in freely circulating air, but the 1 to 5 percent carbon monoxide levels attained in smoke-filled rooms can cause health problems in people with chronic bronchitis, other lung disease, or cardiovascular disease. As a result, nicotine also builds up in the blood of nonsmokers exposed to cigarette smoke hour after hour. It has been estimated that passive smoking can give nonsmokers the equivalent in carbon monoxide and nicotine of one to ten cigarettes per day.

Source: Adapted from Marvin Levy, Mark Dignan, and Janet Shirreffs, *Targeting Wellness: The Core,* pp. 262–63. Copyright © 1992 by The McGraw-Hill Companies, Inc. Reprinted by permission of The McGraw-Hill Companies.

Stop and Annotate

Go back to the textbook excerpt above. Underline or highlight the clues that signal the definition pattern and the cause-effect pattern.

In this paragraph, the bold print and the dash (**passive smoking**—) are clues that the authors are defining a term. The clue words that signal cause-effect are *cause* and *as a result.* Therefore, this paragraph can be described as a mixed pattern because it includes both a definition *and* a cause-effect relationship.

Here is an excerpt from a textbook on American government that is an example of a *mixed pattern in a longer passage.* It consists of four paragraphs in which the author uses three patterns. The overall topic of the passage is *regionalism.* In the first paragraph, the author presents a *definition* of regionalism (the tendency of people in a particular geographic area to defend their interests against those of people in other geographic areas). In the second paragraph, the author uses the *comparison-contrast* pattern to emphasize differences between two regions of the United States, the "Sunbelt" and the "Frostbelt." In the third paragraph, the author uses the *cause-effect* pattern to explain the conflict over federal aid that resulted from a shift of economic influence to the Sunbelt. In the fourth paragraph, the author again uses a *cause-effect* pattern to explain a shift of political influence (an increased number of seats in Congress) from the northeastern and midwestern (Frostbelt) to the southern and western states (Sunbelt). (Although the passage includes several references to time—*past two decades, in the first half of the 1980s,* etc.—the author is not emphasizing a sequence relationship.)

Regionalism

An important characteristic of intergovernmental politics is **regionalism,** the tendency of people in a particular geographic area to defend their interests against those of people in other geographic areas. One central regional issue is the competition between Sunbelt and Frostbelt for federal moneys.

The so-called **Sunbelt** region (the states of the South and Southwest) experienced significant increases in population and economic development during the 1970s and 1980s. During that same time, the Northeastern and Midwestern states of the so-called **Frostbelt** saw both their population and their economic growth lag behind that of the nation at large. In the first half of the 1980s, the North Central region actually lost more jobs than it gained. Southwestern oil states such as Texas and Oklahoma were also hit hard in the middle 1980s by the collapse of the oil boom. Nevertheless, the Sunbelt grew in economic influence relative to the rest of the nation.

This shift of economic influence from the Frostbelt to the Sunbelt has led to a sharp conflict between these regions in seeking greater amounts of federal aid. Frostbelt leaders have charged that their region pays more income taxes into the federal treasury than comes back in the form of grants-in-aid, and they subsequently have pressured Congress to rewrite funding formulas so that they will be more favorable to the Frostbelt. Faced with this challenge, Sunbelt leaders also began to lobby Washington for their version of how federal aid ought to be distributed.

The rise of the South and the West is seen not only in economic influence but in political influence as well. The reapportionment of congressional seats after the 1990 census resulted in a dramatic shift of congressional seats from the Northeast and Midwest to fast-growing Southern and Western states such as Florida and California.

Source: Adapted from John J. Harrigan, *Politics and the American Future,* 3rd ed. New York: McGraw-Hill, pp. 72–73. Copyright © 1992 by John J. Harrigan. Reprinted by permission of the author.

Stop and Annotate

Underline or highlight the clues that signal the three patterns used in this passage.

Here is another excerpt, from a business textbook, that illustrates the use of a mixed pattern in a longer passage. In this excerpt, which discusses *crisis management,* the authors have used four patterns: *definition, cause-effect, comparison-contrast,* and *sequence.* As you read this excerpt, look for clue words that indicate which pattern is being used in each paragraph.

Crisis Management

The most important goal of any business is to survive. But any number of problems may arise, some threatening the very existence of the company. An ugly fight for control of a company, a product failure, breakdowns in an organization's routine operations (as a result of fire, for example)—any surprising event may develop into a serious and crippling crisis. **Crisis management,** the handling of such unusual and serious problems, goes a long way toward determining the company's future. For example, Johnson & Johnson is widely thought to have done a good job of coping with the two Tylenol poisoning scares, moving quickly to remove capsules from the shelves and to publicize the problem. As a result, the effects of the first scare had been almost completely overcome by the time the second hit.

In contrast, H.J. Heinz handled a crisis so badly that the future of its Canadian subsidiary of StarKist Foods was in doubt. StarKist was accused of shipping a million cans of "rancid and decomposing" tuna, which were first rejected by Canadian inspectors but later passed by a high government official. Under the prodding of Canadian news media, the prime minister finally had the tainted tuna seized. All along, Heinz and StarKist maintained a stony silence over "Tunagate," and their mishandling of the crisis cost plenty: The company that once controlled half of the Canadian tuna market watched its revenues fall 90 percent.

Companies that experience a crisis for which they are ill prepared seem to make a series of mistakes. First, warnings about possible problems are ignored at one or several management levels. Then the crisis hits. Under pressure, the company does the worst thing it could do: It denies the severity of the problem or it denies its own role in the problem. Finally, when the company is forced to face reality, it takes hasty, poorly conceived action.

A better way does exist. Management experts caution that the first 24 hours of a crisis are critical. The first move is to explain the problem—both to the public and to the company's employees. Immediately after, the offending product is removed from store shelves. Finally, the offending action is stopped, or the source of the problem (whatever it is) is brought under control to the extent possible.

Source: Adapted from David Rachman, Michael Mescon, Courtland Bovée, and John Thill, *Business Today,* pp. 169–170. Copyright © 1993 by The McGraw-Hill Companies, Inc. Reprinted by permission of The McGraw-Hill Companies.

Stop and Annotate

Underline or highlight the clues that signal the four patterns used in this mixed pattern.

Relationships within and between Sentences

Authors also use many of the same clue words to indicate the relationship between information in a single sentence, or to show the connection between information in two consecutive sentences. Because you use these same transition words every day of your life, you may not be consciously aware of them. Although there seem to be many types of relationships described in this section, you will be pleased to discover that you are already familiar with them and that they are simply common sense.

On a standardized reading test or state-mandated basic skills test, you may be asked about the relationship of ideas in two parts of the *same* sentence or between two *different* sentences. Such questions are usually worded, "What is the relationship between . . ." or "Identify the relationship between . . . ." You will be asked to identify the way in which two ideas relate to each other, or in other words, how the ideas are connected to each other. Watch for clue words and transition words since they will help you determine the connection. If there are two sentences, the transition word often appears at the beginning of the second sentence, such as the word *therefore* in *It takes time to review for a test. Therefore, you should start early.* Sometimes, though, you may have to supply the transition word. For example, in the sentence, *It takes times to review for a test; start early,* you would mentally supply the word *so: It takes time to review for a test, so start early.*

Now read about various types of relationships and the transition words authors use to signal them. Two examples are given for each type. The first example illustrates the relationship in the context of a *single* sentence; the second one illustrates the relationship in the context of two *or more* sentences. You have already met sequence, comparison-contrast, cause-effect, and spatial order as paragraph patterns. In this section, you will see them illustrated in single sentences relationships as well.

1. Clarification

Authors use certain words to indicate that they are trying to make information in a sentence clearer or easier to understand. These include *in other words, clearly, it is obvious, that is, as a matter of fact, evidently,* and *of course.* Often a general or potentially confusing statement is followed by a clarification.

Examples:

- The most common form of marriage is monogamy, *that is,* a marriage consisting of one husband and one wife.
- A form of marriage that has been widely practiced throughout the world is polygyny. *In other words,* marriage that consists of one husband and several wives is widespread throughout the world.

2. Example

Authors use examples, specific incidences, or illustrations to help explain other, more general information in a sentence or paragraph. For this reason, the relationship is also referred to as "generalization and example." (The second example, below, illustrates this.) To introduce examples, authors use *for example, to illustrate, such as, are examples of,* and *for instance.*

Examples:

- Dogs, cats, lions, and bears are *examples* of carnivores, flesh-eating animals.
- Some animals are herbivores. Cows, goats, giraffes, and elephants, *for instance,* belong to this category of plant-eating animals.

3. Addition

Authors use the clue words for lists to signal that information is being added. That is, they use words such as *and, also, further, in addition, equally, besides, next, moreover, furthermore,* and *finally.* This pattern or relationship is also referred to as *elaboration.*

Examples:

- Computer science is a popular major; business is *also* popular, *and* so is psychology.
- Driving a hybrid car is one way to reduce fuel costs. *Another* is to carpool or use public transportation. *Finally,* there are motorcycles, bicycling, *and* even walking.

4. Sequence

Authors use a sequence to present information in a specific order because the order is important. Events are given in the order in which they occurred or in order of importance. Clue words are those that refer to time, such as *during the last century, next year, in the 1990s, at the start of the Middle Ages;* specific dates, words such as *first, second, then, next, last, before, after, at that time, during, formerly, now, soon, while, presently, when, later, followed by;* and words such as *sequence, process, steps, procedure, ranking, series, progression,* etc. Authors may also use numbers, letters, or bullets when sequencing or ranking items. Narratives follow a sequence pattern since they tell a story.

Examples:

- In higher education, an associate's degree is *followed by* a bachelor's degree, *then* a master's degree, and *finally,* a doctorate.
- The Richter scale is used to *rank* the effects of earthquakes that occur near the earth's surface. Earthquakes with a *magnitude of 0, 1,* or *2* are not felt at all; at *level 3,* some people feel it. At *levels 4 and 5,* windows rattle and break. *At magnitudes of 6 through 8* there is increasingly severe damage to structures. *Finally,* at *9,* the *highest magnitude,* there is total destruction.

A special type of sequence is *climactic order.* When writers want to end a paragraph with the high point, the climax, they deliberately arrange the information from least to most important (or to a *conclusion*). (Logical conclusions are discussed, along with inductive and deductive reasoning, in Chapter 9.) Literary writers often use the climactic pattern because it is a way to build suspense. Non-fiction writers use it to emphasize their most important point, as well as to provide readers with information needed to understand or the reasoning to be convinced of it. There are no clue words for this pattern, but watch for increasing importance or intensity.

Examples:

- The proposed city budget will lead our community into financial difficulty, increasing debt, total bankruptcy!

- The proposed city budget is based on inaccurate numbers. It is based on unrealistic estimates of future costs. It can only lead to increasing, unsustainable debt. In short, it will plunge the entire city into bankruptcy!

5. Comparison

Comparisons show similarities or likenesses. Clue words are *as, like, similarly, likewise, same, similar,* and *in the same manner.* Also watch for comparative forms of words, such as *lesser, greater, highest,* etc.

Examples:

- Reading, *like* writing, is a form of the thinking process.
- Paintings reflect an artist's culture and values. *Similarly,* musical compositions reflect a composer's culture and values.

6. Contrast

Contrasts focus on differences or opposites. Clue words include pairs of words that have opposite meanings (such as *rich* and *poor*), and words such as *in contrast, but, although, however, yet, nevertheless, on the contrary, on the one hand,* and *on the other hand.*

Examples:

- *Although* only a small percentage of pregnant women choose home birth, the number is increasing.
- It was assumed that with the increased use of computers, the amount of paper used in business would decrease. *However,* that has not proved to be the case.

7. Cause-Effect

Authors use words such as *because, due to, since,* and *causes* to indicate reasons, and words such as *thus, therefore, as a result, consequently, result, outcome, lead to, resulted in,* and *hence* to indicate results.

Examples:

- *Because* of Hurricane Katrina, millions of people were displaced from their homes.
- The number of years of school a person completes is correlated with the amount of money that person will make during a lifetime. *Therefore,* it is an advantage to complete as many years of school as possible.

8. Problem-Solution

The problem-solution pattern is actually just a variation of the cause-effect pattern. Authors use it when they want to present a problem and its solutions. They typically include the factors that led to the problem and explain the significance of the problem so that readers understand why the problem is important. Solutions or recommendations for solving the problem may be tied to each of the specific causes. (The *solution* itself may be a sequence pattern, in which the author spells out a certain procedure or steps that must be followed to remedy a situation.) Watch for words such as *problem* (the *cause* of the difficulty), the *significance* (the *effects* of the problem; why it matters), and *solutions.*

Examples:

- To address the *problem* of homelessness, the city must join with local organizations and churches to develop comprehensive, cost-effective *solutions.*

- A major *problem* in our country is drivers running red lights. The *consequences* include increased insurance premiums for all of us, but more importantly injury and death. Besides maiming or killing themselves, these reckless drivers hurt thousands of innocent victims each year. What can be done? Possible *solutions* include installing traffic cameras at high-risk intersections, imposing more stringent fines for violators, and suspending driving privileges of repeat offenders.

9. Spatial Order

Authors use words such as *above, beyond, within, near, facing, next to, north, south, to the right, site, location,* and so forth to describe the placement or location of one or more things. (A variation of this pattern is the *description pattern.* For example, in a film history textbook, the author might describe Judy Garland's costume as Dorothy in *The Wizard of Oz* or certain lighting that was used in a famous movie scene.)

Examples:

- The floor plan of many Christian churches *forms the shape of* a cross: the large, open area called the nave intersects with the transept, a *lengthwise* section *perpendicular to* it.

- The *site of* central Chicago is on a lake plain. More important, however, is its *situation* astride the Great Lakes-Mississippi waterways, and *near* the *western margin* of the manufacturing belt, the *northern boundary* of the Corn Belt, and the southeastern reaches of a major dairy region.

10. Summary

Some paragraphs simply review the important points presented earlier. The author condenses or consolidates them in a sentence or paragraph at the end of a longer paragraph or selection. Sometimes the author draws an overall conclusion based on those major points, as well. To signal a summary or conclusion, authors use words such as *in summary, in conclusion, in brief, thus, therefore, to summarize, to sum up, in short,* and *the point is.*

Examples:

- The *point is,* movement is a characteristic of all living things.

- Water helps digestion and circulation. It helps regulate body temperature and flushes toxins from the body. It also cushions the internal organs. *In short, water serves a variety of important functions in the body.*

A WORD ABOUT STANDARDIZED READING TESTS: AUTHORS' WRITING PATTERNS

Many college students are required to take standardized reading tests as part of an overall assessment program, in a reading course, or as part of a state-mandated basic skills test. A standardized reading test typically consists of a series of passages followed by multiple-choice reading skill application questions, to be completed within a specified time limit.

Questions about the organization of material in a passage may be worded several ways. Sometimes you are asked to identify the *type* of pattern; sometimes you are asked about specific *information* that has been listed, presented in a sequence, defined, compared or contrasted, or discussed in terms of causes and effects.

Here are some examples of typical wording of questions about authors' writing patterns:

Which of the following organizational patterns does the author use to present information in the passage?

In this passage the author presents . . . (*a comparison, a sequence of events,* etc.)

How is the information in the selection organized?

In this passage, what is compared with . . . ?

According to this passage, what are effects of . . . ?

This passage explains (*two, three, four*) similarities between . . .

Which of the following is an effect of . . . ?

Paragraph 3 contrasts childhood aggression with . . .

The second step in the process of carbon filtration is . . .

To answer questions about organization, watch for clue words that signal each pattern. When you find clue words in a passage, *circle them* so that you can clearly see relationships among the ideas presented. You will also find it helpful to *number items* in lists and sequences, causes and effects, and similarities and differences so that you do not overlook any of them. Remember, too, that words in a stated main idea sentence often suggest the pattern (for example, words such as *ways, factors, causes, reasons, series, stages, differences, similarities,* etc.).

SELECTION **7-1**

Business

E-Commerce? It's E-Normous!

From *Understanding Business*

By William Nickels, James McHugh, and Susan McHugh

Prepare Yourself to Read

Directions: Do these exercises *before* you read Selection 7-1.

1. First, read and think about the title. What do you know about e-commerce?

_____

_____

2. Next, complete your preview by reading the following:

Introduction (in *italics*)

The headings

The first paragraph

The photo and caption

Figure 1

First sentence of paragraphs 1–11

Now that you have previewed the selection, what point do you think the author is making about e-commerce?

_____

_____

_____

_____

_____

_____

Apply Comprehension Skills

Directions: Do the Annotation Practice Exercises *as* you read Selection 7-1.

Determine topics and main ideas. When you read a paragraph, ask yourself what it is about (the topic) and the most important point the author wants you to understand about the topic (the main idea).

Identify supporting details. As you read, ask yourself what else the author wants you to know so that you can understand the main idea.

Recognize the authors' writing patterns. As you read, ask yourself, "What pattern did the authors use to organize the main idea and the supporting details?" Watch for clue words that signal the pattern.

425

E-COMMERCE? IT'S E-NORMOUS!

Do you do your banking online? Have you ever purchased airline tickets, booked hotel reservations, or made other travel arrangements online? Are you among the millions of Americans who shop online? If so, have your experiences been positive ones?

In his article, "Online Shoppers Wary of Online Shopping" (www.e-commerce-guide.com/ solutions/customer_relations/article.php/3566676, November 28, 2005), Tim Gray reports that "nearly 90 percent of those making online purchases, at least some of the time, become frustrated with the process." Hardly a surprise! He continues, "More than 80 percent of shoppers polled said they are unwilling to accept lower levels of customer service online than they would offline." Moreover, a third said they would move to a competitor's website if they experienced a problem with online shopping, banking, travel, or insurance websites. Clearly, e-commerce businesses face many challenges.

Despite these findings, an October 2005 Yahoo! poll of more than 1,800 U.S. online adults revealed that 83 percent of holiday shoppers planned to buy online. ("Cyber Monday," the Monday after Thanksgiving, is the official kickoff day for online holiday shopping.) Nearly a third of those polled planned to do at least half *of their holiday shopping online!*

Read this business textbook selection to learn more about e-commerce, its appeal, and what will distinguish the e-commerce companies that succeed from those that don't.

The Growth of E-Commerce

1   The business environment is rapidly changing and businesses need to adjust to these changes. One of the more important changes of recent years is the growth of **e-commerce,** the buying and selling of goods over the Internet. There are two major types of e-commerce transactions: business-to-consumer (B2C) and business-to-business (B2B).

2   As important as the Internet has been in the consumer market, it has become even more important in the B2B market, which consists of selling goods and services from one business to another. For example, IBM sells consulting services to banks. B2B e-commerce is already at least five times as big as B2C e-commerce. While the potential of the B2C e-commerce market is measured in billions, B2B e-commerce is said to be measured in trillions of dollars.

3   The rise of Internet marketing came so fast and furious that it drew hundreds of competitors into the fray. Many of the new Internet companies failed. Companies such as Pets.com, CDnow, Internet Capital Group, Peapod, eToys, and Drkoop .com have failed entirely or seen their stock prices drop dramatically. Many B2B stocks experienced similar failures. There is no question that some Internet businesses will grow and prosper, but along the way there will continue to be lots of failures, just as there have been in traditional businesses. Traditional businesses will have to learn how to deal with the new competition from B2B and B2C firms.

Annotation Practice Exercises

Directions: For each exercise, use the spaces provided to write:

•   Main idea sentence of the paragraph

•   Author's pattern for organizing the supporting details (writing pattern)

4   There once were dozens of automobile companies. Almost all of them failed, and only a few large companies now dominate the auto industry. Just as a few companies now dominate the auto industry, success will come to those e-commerce businesses that offer quality products at good prices with great service. Many of those successful companies, such as Sears and General Electric, combined their traditional brick-and-mortar operations with new Internet sites that make them more competitive.

Using Technology to Be Responsive to Customers

5   Businesses succeed or fail largely because of the way they treat their customers. The businesses that are most responsive to customer wants and needs will succeed, and those that do not respond to customers will not be as successful. One way traditional retailers can respond to the Internet revolution is to use technology to become much more responsive to customers. For example, businesses mark goods with Universal Product Codes (bar codes)—those series of lines and numbers that you see on most consumer packaged goods. Bar codes can be used to tell retailers what product you bought, in what size and color, and at what price. A scanner at the checkout counter can read that information and put it into a database.

6   Businesses use databases, electronic storage files where information is kept, several ways. One use of databases is to store vast amounts of information about consumers. For example, a retailer may ask for your name, address, and telephone number so that it can put you on its mailing list. The information you give the retailer is added to the database. Because companies routinely trade database information, many retailers know what you buy and from whom you buy it. Using that information, companies can send you catalogs and other direct mail advertising that offers the kind of products you might want, as indicated by your past purchases. Another use of databases is that they enable stores to carry only the merchandise that the local population wants. Finally, they enable stores to carry less inventory saving them money.

The Competitive Environment

7   Competition among businesses has never been greater than it is today. Some companies have found a competitive edge by focusing on quality. The goal for many companies is zero defects—no mistakes in making the product. Some companies, such as Motorola in the United States and Toyota in Japan, have come close to meeting that standard. However, simply making a high-quality product is not enough to allow a company to stay competitive in world markets. Companies

Practice Exercise

• Main idea sentence of paragraph 4:

_____

_____

_____

_____

_____

• Writing pattern:

_____

_____

_____

_____

Practice Exercise

• Main idea sentence of paragraph 6:

_____

_____

• Writing pattern:

_____

_____

_____

now have to offer both high-quality products and outstanding service at competitive prices (value). That is why General Motors (GM) is building automobile plants in Argentina, Poland, China, and Thailand. The strategies of combining excellence with low-cost labor and minimizing distribution costs have resulted in larger markets and potential long-term growth for GM. Figure 1 shows how competition has changed businesses from the traditional model to a new, world-class model.

Figure 1 How Competition Has Changed Business

Traditional Businesses	World-Class Businesses
Customer satisfaction	Delighting the customer
Customer orientation	Customer and stakeholder orientation
Profit orientation	Profit and social orientation
Reactive ethics	Proactive ethics
Productive orientation	Quality and service orientation
Managerial focus	Customer focus

Competing by Exceeding Customer Expectations

8   Manufacturers and service organizations throughout the world have learned that today's customers are very demanding. Not only do they want good quality at low prices, but they want great service as well. In fact, some products in the 21st century will be designed to fascinate, bewitch, and delight customers, exceeding their expectations. Every manufacturing and service organization in the world should have a sign over its door telling its workers that the customer is king. Business is becoming customer-driven, not management-driven as in the past. This means that customers' wants and needs must come first.

9   Customer-driven organizations include Nordstrom department stores (they have a very generous return policy, for example) and Disney amusement park (the parks are kept clean and appeal to all ages). Moto Photo does its best to please customers with fast, friendly service. Such companies can successfully compete against Internet firms if they continue to offer better and friendlier service. Successful organizations must now listen more closely to customers to determine their wants and needs, then adjust the firm's products, policies, and practices to meet those demands.

Adjusting to the E-Commerce Era

10   One of the more significant changes occurring today is the movement toward doing business on the Internet. Many businesses are finding the new competition overwhelming. That includes, for example, traditional bookstores that now have to compete with eBay and Amazon.com.

11   Who would have thought that garage sales would be done over the Internet? Or that cars or homes could be sold online? What is this e-commerce revolution and why is it happening now? That is, what are the advantages of e-commerce that other businesses have to accept and incorporate into their long-term strategies? Businesses are lured to e-commerce for a number of reasons, including, but not limited to:

- *Less investment in land, buildings and equipment.* E-commerce firms can usually sell things for less be-cause they don't have to invest as much in buildings (bricks), and can reach people inexpensively over the Internet (clicks).

- *Low transaction costs.* The automation of customer service lowers costs, which may make it possible for a company to offer products at a lower price. Also, there are no sales taxes (yet) on the Internet so everything is a little less expensive than in stores.

- *Large purchases per transaction.* Online stores like Amazon.com often make personalized recommenda-tions to customers that increase their order size.

- *Integration of business processes.* The Internet offers companies the ability to make more information available to customers than ever before. For example, a computer company that tracks each unit through the manufactur-ing and shipping process can allow customers to see exactly where the order is at any time. This is what over-night package delivery company Federal Express did when it introduced online package tracking.

- *Larger catalogs.* Amazon.com offers a catalog of 3 mil-lion books on the Internet. Imagine fitting a paper catalog that size in your mailbox!

- *Flexibility.* Successful websites are not just glorified mail-order catalogs. The Internet offers companies the ability to configure products and build custom orders, to compare prices between multiple vendors easily, and to search large catalogs quickly.

- *Improved customer interactions.* Online tools allow busi-nesses to interact with customers in ways unheard of before, and at almost instant speeds. For example, cus-tomers can receive automatic e-mails to confirm orders and to notify them when orders are shipped. Despite these many benefits, Internet-based companies have

---

Practice Exercise

- Main idea sentence of paragraph 11:

  _____

  _____

  _____

- Writing pattern:

  _____

not captured the retail market as expected. Instead, traditional retail stores have adapted to the changing environment and have used the Internet to supplement their traditional stores. The combination of e-commerce with traditional stores is called click-and-brick retailing, for obvious reasons. The top 20 online sellers are names that are quite familiar to most students. They include Dell, Sears, Best Buy, Office Depot, QVC, JCPenney, Staples, and Victoria's Secret. Four years after going online, Victoria's Secret sold about a third of its goods on the Internet.

12   Two companies have done quite well as Web-only firms: eBay and Amazon.com.

Webvan, like many other Internet firms, failed during the dot-com explosion in 2000–2002. It's not that the Internet does not provide an excellent opportunity to sell things. It does. But the cost of setting up distribution centers and delivery systems and satisfying customer concerns of not being able to see, touch, and examine products has proven too difficult for some businesses to overcome.

SELECTION **7-1**
Business
(continued)

Reading Selection Quiz

This quiz has three parts. Your instructor may assign some or all of them.

Comprehension

Directions: Items 1–10 test your comprehension (understanding) of the material of this selection. These questions are the type a content area instructor (such as a business professor) would ask on a test over this material. You should be able to answer these questions after studying this selection. For each comprehension question below, use information from the selection to determine the correct answer. Refer to the selection as you answer the questions. Write your answer in the space provided.

True or False

_____ **1.** E-commerce refers to the buying and selling of goods over the Internet.

_____ **2.** "B2B" refers to business-to-consumer e-commerce transactions.

_____ **3.** In order to become more competitive, many businesses that sell through stores are adding Internet sites.

_____ **4.** Since only a few companies dominate each industry, business today is less competitive than it has been in the past.

_____ **5.** "Zero defects" refers to no mistakes in marketing a product.

_____ **6.** Amazon.com and Pets.com are cited as two companies that have done quite well as Web-only firms.

Multiple-Choice

_____ **7.** In terms of sales, B2B e-commerce is:
  a. at least 5 times less than B2C e-commerce.
  b. approximately the same as B2C e-commerce.
  c. slightly greater than B2C e-commerce.
  d. at least 5 times greater than B2C e-commerce.

_____ **8.** Whether businesses succeed or fail will depend mostly on:
  a. the types of products they sell.
  b. whether they have websites.
  c. how they treat their customers.
  d. whether they use bar codes in their products.

_____ **9.** Which of the following is not mentioned as an example of what is likely to be included in a database?

   a. customers' names, addresses, and telephone numbers

   b. customers' past purchases

   c. customers' jobs and income levels

   d. companies from which customers have made past purchases

_____ **10.** Many e-commerce firms are able to offer lower prices because:

   a. they do not have to invest as much money in land.

   b. they do not have to invest as much money in buildings.

   c. they have automated customer service.

   d. all of the above

SELECTION **7-1**   *Vocabulary in Context*

Business
(continued)

Directions: Items 11–20 test your ability to determine the meaning of a word by using context clues. *Context clues* are words in a sentence that allow the reader to deduce (reason out) the meaning of an unfamiliar word in that sentence. Context clues also enable the reader to determine which meaning the author intends when a word has more than one meaning. For each vocabulary item below, a sentence from the selection containing an important word (*italicized, like this*) is quoted first. Next, there is an additional sentence using the word in the same sense and providing another context clue. Use the context clues from *both* sentences to deduce the meaning of the italicized word. *Be sure the answer you choose makes sense in both sentences.* If you discover that you need to use a dictionary to confirm an answer choice, remember that the meaning you select must still fit the context of *both* sentences. Write your answer in the space provided.

Pronunciation Key: ă pat   ā pay   âr care   ä father   ĕ pet   ē be   ĭ pit
ī tie   îr pier   ŏ pot   ō toe   ô paw   oi noise   ou out   ŏŏ took
ōō boot   ŭ cut   yōō abuse   ûr urge   th thin   *th* this   hw which
zh vision   ə about   *Stress mark:* '

_____ **11.** As important as the Internet has been in the *consumer* market, it has become even more important in the B2B market, which consists of selling goods and services from one business to another.

Companies spend billions of dollars on *consumer* research in order to determine products their customers want, how much they are willing to spend, and so forth.

consumer (kən sōō' mər) means:

   a. pertaining to people who buy things in order to resell them

   b. pertaining to people who buy things to use in producing or manufacturing other items *c.* pertaining to people who prefer to save money rather than spend it

    d. pertaining to people who acquire goods for the direct purpose of owning or using them

_____ **12.** The rise of Internet marketing came so fast and furious that it drew hundreds of competitors into the *fray*.

During the debate, the two political opponents began shouting at each other, and then their supporters joined the *fray*.

fray (frā) means:

    a. heated contest or competition

    b. search for new opportunities

    c. orderly discussion

    d. a series of websites

_____ **13.** There is no question that some Internet businesses will grow and *prosper*, but along the way there will continue to be lots of failures, just as there have been in traditional businesses.

Many immigrants come to this country with little or no money, but are able to *prosper* because of their talent and hard work.

prosper (prŏs′ pər) means:

    a. to merge with other businesses

    b. to remain the same

    c. to be successful; thrive

    d. to become well known

_____ **14.** Almost all of them failed, and only a few large companies now *dominate* the auto industry.

A few major television networks used to *dominate* the airways, but with the rise of cable television, there are hundreds of channels viewers can choose from.

dominate (dŏm′ ə nāt) means:

    a. to have a commanding, controlling position in

    b. to treat in a harsh, cruel manner

    c. to block or shut out

    d. to govern by using superior power or force

_____ **15.** Bar codes can be used to tell *retailers* what product you bought, in what size and color, and at what price.

Sears, Roebuck & Company, now called Sears, was one of the first great *retailers* in the United States, and for millions of people, it was their main source for clothes, tools, equipment, home furnishings, appliances, etc.

retailers (rə′ tāl ərz) means:

a. those who advertise in magazines and newspapers

b. those who sell goods in small quantities directly to consumers

c. those who manufacture goods

d. those who take items in trade

_____ **16.** Manufacturers and service organizations throughout the world have learned that today's customers are very *demanding*.

Perfectionists are highly *demanding* people who never seem satisfied, no matter how good something is or how well it has been done.

demanding (dĭ măn′ dĭng) means:

a. requiring great strength and endurance

b. irritating; annoying

c. weighing down; burdensome

d. making severe and uncompromising demands

_____ **17.** That is, what are the advantages of e-commerce that other businesses have to accept and *incorporate* into their long-term strategies?

The college is considering ways to *incorporate* actual work experience into their career training courses.

incorporate (ĭn kôr′ pə rāt) means:

a. to review

b. to legally form a corporation

c. to replace

d. to unite something with something else already in existence

_____ **18.** Successful websites are not just *glorified* mail-order catalogs.

Because of the *glorified* description of the house in the ad, we were very disappointed when we saw how small and rundown it was.

glorified (glôr′ ə fīd) means:

a. made to seem more wonderful than is actually the case

b. made to seem more expensive than is actually the case

c. made to seem more religious than is actually the case

d. made to seem more time-saving than is actually the case

_____ **19.** The Internet offers companies the ability to *configure* products and build custom orders, to compare prices between multiple vendors easily, and to search large catalogs quickly.

By modifying the engine, tires, and other features, manufacturers can *configure* trucks for different types of purposes and terrains.

configure (kən fĭg′ yər) means:
a. to change the appearance of
b. to improve the value of
c. to lower the cost of
d. to design for specific uses

_____ **20.** The Internet offers companies the ability to configure products and build custom orders, to compare prices between multiple *vendors* easily, and to search large catalogs quickly.

Bill Gates is a billionaire; his company, Microsoft, is one of the most successful software *vendors* in the world.

vendors (vĕn′ dərz) means:
a. people and companies that shop on the Internet
b. people and companies that buy things
c. people and companies that sell things
d. people and companies that advertise on the Internet

SELECTION **7-1**

Business
(continued)

Reading Skills Application

Directions: Items 21–25 test your ability to *apply* certain reading skills to information in this selection. These types of questions provide valuable practice for all students, especially those who must take standardized reading tests and state-mandated basic skills tests (such as the Florida CLAST Test and the Texas THEA Test). You may not have studied all of the skills at this point, so these items will serve as a helpful preview. The comprehension and critical reading skills in this section are presented in Chapters 4 through 9 of *Opening Doors;* vocabulary and figurative language skills are presented in Chapter 2. As you work through *Opening Doors,* you will practice and develop these skills. Write your answer for each question in the space provided.

_____ **21.** In paragraph 5, the term "brick-and-mortar operations" is used to describe companies:
a. actual stores.
b. sales personnel.
c. marketing strategies.
d. headquarters.

_____ **22.** The selection cites which of the following as examples of successful customer-driven organizations?

    a. Internet Capital Group, Peapod, and eToys.

    b. Motorola, General Motors, and Sears.

    c. Nordstrom, Disney, and Moto Photo.

    d. Amazon.com and eBay.com.

_____ **23.** Information in Figure 1 about traditional businesses and world-class businesses indicates that:

    a. neither focuses on customers.

    b. profit is the most important concern, whether a business is traditional or world class

    c. both focus on long-range company goals.

    d. world-class businesses try to do the right thing ethically instead of responding only when there is criticism.

_____ **24.** The authors would be most likely to agree with which of the following statements?

    a. Internet-only firms will eventually replace actual stores.

    b. Customers prefer companies' printed paper catalogs to online catalogs.

    c. Databases should not be used since they violate customers' privacy.

    d. E-commerce is likely to do nothing but increase in the future.

_____ **25.** Which of the following represents an opinion rather than a fact?

    a. Amazon.com offers a catalog of 3 million books on the Internet.

    b. Another use of databases is that they enable stores to carry only the merchandise that the local population wants.

    c. Every manufacturing and service organization in the world should have a sign over its door telling its workers that the customer is king.

    d. The Internet offers companies the ability to make more information available to customers than ever before.

SELECTION **7-1**

Business
(continued)

Respond in Writing

Directions: Refer to Selection 7-1 as needed to answer the essay-type questions below.

Collaboration Option

Option for collaboration: Your instructor may direct you to work with other students on one or more of these items, or in other words, to work *collaboratively.* In that case, you should form groups of three or four students, as directed by your instructor, and work together to complete the exercises. After your group discusses an item and agrees on the answer, have a group member record it. Each member of your group should be able to explain all of your group's answers.

1. Do you shop online? If so, what types of products have you ordered? Has your experience been a positive one? If you do not shop online, why not? If you have never purchased anything online, would you be likely to in the future? Why or why not?

   _____

   _____

   _____

   _____

2. List at least four reasons you think consumers might rather shop online than go to a store.

   _____

   _____

   _____

   _____

   _____

   _____

3. List at least four reasons you think consumers might rather shop at an actual store than to shop online.

   _____

   _____

   _____

   _____

   _____

   _____

   _____

   _____

4. Do you think the combination of stores ("bricks") and a website ("clicks") is the best option for most companies? Why or why not?

   _____

   _____

   _____

   _____

   _____

5. Based on the information in the selection, what types of things would a new e-commerce company need to do in order to become highly successful?

_____

_____

_____

_____

6. **Overall main idea.** What is the overall main idea the author wants you to understand about e-commerce? Answer this question in one sentence. Be sure that your overall main idea sentence includes the topic (*e-commerce*) and tells the overall most important point about it. Do *not* begin your sentence with "The overall main idea is . . . " or "The author wants us to understand . . . " Just *state* the overall main idea.

_____

_____

_____

_____

_____

Internet Resources

Read More about This Topic on the World Wide Web

Directions: For further information about the topic of the selection, visit these websites:

www.ecommerce-guide.com
"News, reviews and practical solutions for your online business." In the right column is the "Ecommerce Guide Essentials," where you can click on information about starting a successful e-business, selling on eBay, PayPal payments, and more.

http://e-comm.webopedia.com/
Webopedia describes itself as "the #1 online encyclopedia dedicated to computer technology." This website gives the definitions of 20 key e-commerce terms, from "cookies" to "digital wallet" to "shopping cart."

www.ecommercetimes.com/
Established in 1999, ECT New Network is one of the largest e-business and technology news publishers in the United States. The targeted audience of their network of business and technology news publications is buyers and decision-makers who need timely industry news and reliable analysis.

You can also use your favorite search engine such as Google, Yahoo!, or Alta-Vista (www.google.com, www.yahoo.com, www.altavista.com) to discover more about this topic. To locate additional information, type in combinations of keywords such as:

e-commerce

or

B2B commerce

or

B2C commerce

Keep in mind that whenever you go to *any* website, it is a good idea to evaluate the website and the information it contains. Ask yourself questions such as:

"Who sponsors this website?"

"Is the information contained in this website up-to-date?"

"What type of information is presented?"

"Is the information objective and complete?"

"How easy is it to use the features of this website?"

SELECTION **7-2**

Health

The Decision to Marry

From *Targeting Wellness: The Core*

By Marvin Levy, Mark Dignan, and Janet Shirreffs

Prepare Yourself to Read

Directions: Do these exercises *before* you read Selection 7-2.

1. First, read and think about the title. In your opinion, why do most people decide to marry?

   _____

   _____

   _____

   _____

2. How much consideration do you think most people really give to their reasons for marrying?

   _____

   _____

   _____

   _____

3. Next, complete your preview by reading the following:

   > Introduction (in *italics*)
   > First paragraph (paragraph 1)
   > Headings in *italics*
   > First sentence of each paragraph
   > Words in *italics*
   > Last paragraph (paragraph 9)

   On the basis of your preview, what three aspects of the decision to marry does this selection seem to be about?

   _____

   _____

   _____

   _____

   _____

Apply Comprehension Skills

Directions: Do the Annotation Practice Exercises *as* you read Selection 7-2.

Determine topics and main ideas. When you read a paragraph, ask yourself what it is about (the topic) and the most important point the author wants you to understand about the topic (the main idea).

Identify supporting details. As you read, ask yourself what else the author want you to know so that you can understand the main idea.

Recognize the authors' writing pattern. As you read, ask yourself, "What pattern did the author use to organize the main idea and supporting details?" Watch for clue words that signal the pattern.

THE DECISION TO MARRY

Today, an estimated 40 to 50 percent of all marriages fail. Part of this can be attributed to getting married for the wrong reasons or marriage between people who are incompatible. What are poor reasons for getting married? What characterizes a successful, high-quality marriage? What determines a couple's compatibility? This textbook selection answers these questions.

1   Marriage is an institution that is changing. Traditionally, marriage has been an economic arrangement in which husbands have worked outside the home to provide financial security for their families, while wives have cared for the children and run the home. Today, however, this arrangement is changing. The roles of husband and wife are not as clearly defined as in the past, especially when both partners work and earn money for the family. Many people today expect and get more from marriage than economic benefits. They look to their spouses for sharing, emotional support, and intimacy. Happily married people often identify the spouse as their best friend.

Why Do People Marry?

2   The pressures for a couple to marry can be enormous. This pressure often comes from parents and other relatives as well as from the media. Sometimes the members of a family, ethnic group, or religious group may pressure individuals to marry so that a new generation can be raised in the teaching and values of the group.

3   Aside from these pressures, people marry for a variety of reasons. Some still marry for economic reasons. For others, marriage is viewed as the only acceptable framework in which to enjoy sex freely. Some people marry to escape from an unhappy home life, on the rebound from another relationship, or to avoid loneliness.

4   Researchers have identified several patterns in "high-quality," or well-balanced marriages. Some of these married people tend to focus their energies on joint activities. Their strongest wish is to spend time together, yet they also strike a balance between privacy and togetherness. Other couples focus their energies on being parents and on raising their children. Some dual-career couples, although they spend much of their energy on their individual careers, develop intimacy by sharing what is going on in their work. It thus seems that the desire to spend time together, raise children, and share other aspects of life and career are all healthy reasons for marrying.

Annotation Practice Exercises

Directions: For each exercise, use the spaces provided to write:

- Main idea sentence of the paragraph
- Author's pattern for organizing the supporting details (writing pattern)

Practice Exercise

- Main idea sentence of paragraph 2:

_____

_____

_____

- Writing pattern:

_____

_____

_____

Practice Exercise

- Main idea sentence of paragraph 4:

_____

_____

_____

_____

- Writing pattern:

_____

Love and Romance

5   A basic element in most marriages is the love one person feels for another. There are many different types of love between persons, including parental love, fraternal love, and romantic love. Each requires caring and respect. Romantic love includes the qualities of deep intimacy and passion and begins with a feeling of intense attraction between two people.

6   Although most marriages are based on romantic love, few couples sustain that romance as the years go by. Romantic love often develops into a less intense, less all-consuming type of love known as companionate love. A companionate love relationship is steadier than romantic love and is based on trust, sharing, affection, and togetherness. Maintaining the love in a marriage requires considerable effort and commitment. Married partners who succeed in communicating, giving physical warmth, and sharing interests and responsibilities are more likely to remain in love.

> **Practice Exercise**
>
> • Main idea sentence of paragraph 6:
>
> _____
>
> _____
>
> _____
>
> _____
>
> • Writing pattern:
>
> _____
>
> _____

Assessing Compatibility

7   When people are looking for a mate, they tend to be attracted to potential partners whose ethnic, religious, economic, and educational background is similar to their own. Certain physical attributes are also significant factors. They are least likely to match up with a similar person in the area of compatibility of personality. Personality factors are not always easy to observe. Sometimes people do not reveal their true selves during courtship. Moreover, people with opposite personality types often attract each other, perhaps because one personality rounds out the other.

8   Unfortunately, great differences in personality can often lead to conflict later on. One study found that a source of marital dissatisfaction among husbands was a feeling that their wives were too possessive, neglectful, and openly admiring of other men. Dissatisfied wives complained that their husbands were possessive, moody, and openly attracted to other women. The study also found that sex is a source of great difficulties for unhappy married men and women. It found that women see sex as following from emotional intimacy, while men see it as a road to intimacy. As a result, men complain that their wives withhold sex from them and women complain that their husbands are too sexually aggressive.

9   How can people be sure they are marrying people with whom they are truly compatible? One way is by taking plenty of time to get to know the other person. Researchers have found that couples seem to go through three stages in this process. First, each person tries to measure his or her good and bad qualities against those of the other person. People tend to be drawn to others who seem to have about the same assets and liabilities they themselves possess. Second, people look for compatible beliefs, attitudes, and interests to support the initial attraction. It is not until the third stage that people reveal to each other how they handle responsibility, react to disappointment, and cope with a wide variety of situations. The key to compatibility is for the couple to be sure that they have arrived at this last stage before they think seriously about marriage. Such people are less likely to be unpleasantly surprised than are those who marry quickly.

Since antiquity, the marriage ceremony has provided a formal setting in which a couple can publicly affirm their love for and commitment to each other.

Reading Selection Quiz

This quiz has three parts. Your instructor may assign some or all of them.

Comprehension

Directions: Items 1–10 test your comprehension (understanding) of the material of this selection. These questions are the type a content area instructor (such as a health professor) would ask on a test over this material. You should be able to answer these questions after studying this selection. For each comprehension question below, use information from the selection to determine the correct answer. Refer to the selection as you answer the question. Write your answer in the space provided.

True or False

_____   **1.** Marriage is an unchanging institution.

_____   **2.** People can experience enormous pressure to marry.

_____   **3.** Pressure to marry can come from many sources.

_____   **4.** Sometimes people do not reveal their true selves during courtship.

_____   **5.** As years go by in a marriage, most couples are able to sustain the intense attraction of romantic love.

_____   **6.** People with opposite personality types do not attract each other.

Multiple-Choice

_____   **7.** Which of the following is *not* a characteristic of companionate love?
   a. steadiness
   b. all-consuming intensity of feeling
   c. mutual trustworthiness
   d. shared areas of responsibility

_____   **8.** Which of the following is *not* a characteristic of "high-quality" marriages?
   a. Energy is focused on the economic benefits of marriage.
   b. Energy is focused on joint activities.
   c. Energy is focused on being parents and raising children.
   d. A balance is struck between privacy and togetherness.

_____ **9.** Which of these is a source of marital dissatisfaction?

    a. husbands' feeling that wives are too possessive, neglectful, and openly admiring of other men

    b. wives' feeling that husbands are possessive, moody, and openly attracted to other women

    c. conflicts over sex

    d. all of the above

_____ **10.** Researchers have found that people seem to go through three stages in the process of selecting a mate. Which of the following is *not* a stage?

    a. A person measures his or her good and bad qualities against those of the other person.

    b. People evaluate the physical attractiveness of a possible partner.

    c. People look for compatible beliefs, attitudes, and interests in the other person.

    d. People reveal how they handle responsibility and disappointment.

SELECTION **7-2**

Health
(Continued)

Vocabulary in Context

Directions: Items 11–20 test your ability to determine the meaning of a word by using context clues. *Context clues* are words in a sentence that allow the reader to deduce (reason out) the meaning of an unfamiliar word in that sentence. Context clues also enable the reader to determine which meaning the author intends when a word has more than one meaning. For each vocabulary item below, a sentence from the selection containing an important word (*italicized, like this*) is quoted first. Next, there is an additional sentence using the word in the same sense and providing another context clue. Use the context clues from *both* sentences to deduce the meaning of the italicized word. *Be sure the answer you choose makes sense in both sentences.* If you discover that you need to use a dictionary to confirm an answer choice, remember that the meaning you select must still fit the context of *both* sentences. Write your answer in the space provided.

Pronunciation Key: ă pat ā pay âr care ä father ĕ pet ē be ĭ pit
ī tie îr pier ŏ pot ō toe ô paw oi noise ou out ŏŏ took
ōō boot ŭ cut yōō abuse ûr urge th thin *th* this hw which
zh vision ə about *Stress mark:* ʹ

_____ **11.** Marriage is an *institution* that is changing.

The family is an *institution* that has been studied extensively by researchers.

institution (ĭn stĭ tōō′ shən) means:

a. building
b. written agreement
c. political decision
d. established custom or practice

_____ **12.** Some people marry to escape from an unhappy home life, on the *rebound* from another relationship, or to avoid loneliness.

The senator was quickly on the *rebound* after losing the election, and soon began making plans to enter a new career.

rebound (rē′ bound) means:

a. recovery from disappointment
b. capture of something
c. sideways movement
d. ground

_____ **13.** There are many different types of love between persons, including parental love, *fraternal* love, and romantic love.

He joined a *fraternal* organization to make new friends and enjoy social activities.

fraternal (frə tûr′ nəl) means:

a. pertaining to friendship
b. pertaining to business
c. pertaining to hobbies
d. none of the above

_____ **14.** Although most marriages are based on romantic love, few couples *sustain* that romance as the years go by.

Although he was in an irreversible coma, his family asked the doctors to do everything possible to *sustain* his life.

sustain (sə stān′) means:

a. prevent
b. alter
c. end
d. maintain

_____ **15.** Romantic love often develops into a less intense, less all-*consuming* type of love known as companionate love.

Sailing has become such a time-*consuming* hobby for Bob that he never has time for anything else on weekends.

consuming (kən sōōm′ ĭng) means:

a. engrossing; absorbing

b. confusing

c. wasting

d. saving

_____ **16.** Sometimes people do not reveal their true selves during *courtship.*

Lynn and Pat's *courtship* lasted for six years before they decided to marry.

courtship (kôrt′ shĭp) means:

a. court case

b. extended voyage at sea

c. legal separation

d. seeking someone's affection with the hope of marrying him or her

_____ **17.** One study found that a source of *marital* dissatisfaction among husbands was a feeling that their wives were too possessive, neglectful, and openly admiring of other men.

Please indicate your *marital* status: single, married, divorced, or widowed.

marital (măr′ ĭ təl) means:

a. pertaining to fighting

b. pertaining to marriage

c. pertaining to divorce

d. pertaining to a wedding

_____ **18.** People tend to be drawn to others who seem to have about the same assets and *liabilities* they themselves possess.

Not knowing how to use computers and lack of rapport with others are *liabilities* for anyone who plans to enter the business world.

liabilities (lĭ ə bĭl′ ĭ tēz) means:

a. handicap; something that holds one back

b. advantages; benefits

c. business skills

d. lies; deceptions

_____ **19.** Second, people look for compatible beliefs, attitudes, and interests to support the *initial* attraction.

The doctor changed her *initial* diagnosis after she received the patient's test results.

initial (ĭ nĭsh′ əl) means:

a. professional

b. inappropriate

c. first

d. puzzling

_____ **20.** The key to *compatibility* is for the couple to be sure that they have arrived at this last stage before they think seriously about marriage.

In families with stepchildren, psychological counseling can promote *compatibility* and make family life more pleasant.

compatibility (kəm păt ə bĭl′ ə tē) means:

a. an interesting marriage

b. financial security

c. a harmonious or agreeable combining

d. achievement of career goals

SELECTION **7-2**   *Reading Skills Application*

Health
(Continued)

Directions: Items 21–25 test your ability to *apply* certain reading skills to information in this selection. These types of questions provide valuable practice for all students, especially those who must take standardized reading tests and state-mandated basic skills tests (such as the Florida CLAST Test and the Texas THEA Test). You may not have studied all of the skills at this point, so these items will serve as a helpful preview. The comprehension and critical reading skills in this section are presented in Chapters 4 through 9 of *Opening Doors;* vocabulary and figurative language skills are presented in Chapter 2. As you work through *Opening Doors,* you will practice and develop these skills. Write your answer for each question in the space provided.

_____ **21.** Which of the following statements best expresses the main idea of paragraph 8?

a. One study found that unhappily married men and women often have great differences in personality, and that they report that sex is a source of significant difficulties in their marriages.

b. One study found that, unfortunately, marital conflict often arises from large differences in the couple's personalities.

c. One study found that many unhappy men feel that their wives are too possessive, neglectful, and openly admiring of other men.

d. One study found that wives often express dissatisfaction about husbands who are possessive, moody, and openly attracted to other women.

_____ **22.** The meaning of *road* as it is used in paragraph 8 is:

    a. result of.

    b. unknown source.

    c. way of achieving.

    d. destination.

_____ **23.** The authors' primary purpose for writing this selection is to:

    a. describe how marriage has changed from previous times.

    b. convince parents not to pressure their adult children into marriage.

    c. persuade couples not to get married without first seeking premarital counseling.

    d. provide readers with information that will help them understand marriage and compatibility.

_____ **24.** The information in paragraph 9 is organized as a:

    a. comparison of three stages.

    b. list of results.

    c. list of causes of a problem.

    d. sequence of stages.

_____ **25.** The authors would be most likely to agree with which of the following statements?

    a. It is not unreasonable for a person to marry in order to escape from an unhappy home life.

    b. A couple is more likely to have a successful marriage if they consider carefully the reasons they are getting married, the type of love they feel for each other, and their compatibility.

    c. The main cause of marital conflict is couples not revealing their true selves to each other during courtship.

    d. Marriage today is essentially an economic arrangement between men and women.

SELECTION **7-2**

Health

(Continued)

Collaboration Option

Respond in Writing

Directions: Refer to Selection 7-2 as needed to answer the essay-type questions below.

Option for collaboration: Your instructor may direct you to work with other students on one or more of these items, or in other words, to work *collaboratively.* In that case, you should form groups of three or four students, as directed by your instructor, and work together to complete the exercises. After your group discusses an item and agrees on the answer, have a group member record it. Each member of your group should be able to explain all of your group's answers.

1. List several reasons mentioned in paragraphs 2 and 3 of the selection that are *inappropriate* reasons for marrying.

   _____

   _____

   _____

   _____

   _____

   _____

2. In paragraph 4, what three reasons do the authors say are *healthy* reasons for marrying?

   First healthy reason:

   _____

   _____

   Second healthy reason:

   _____

   _____

   Third healthy reason:

   _____

   _____

3. In addition to the inappropriate reasons for marrying that are discussed in the selection, describe at least one other reason that can cause marriages to fail.

   _____

   _____

   _____

4. Suppose that two people are attracted to each other, and they share similar ethnic, religious, economic, and educational backgrounds. However, because their personalities are quite different, they are not sure they are compatible. According to the selection, what three stages should they go through to determine whether their personalities are truly compatible?

   _____

   _____

   _____

   _____

_____

_____

_____

_____

5. **Overall main idea.** What is the overall main idea the author wants the reader to understand about the decision to marry? Answer this question in one sentence. Be sure that your overall main idea sentence includes the topic (*the decision to marry*) and tells the overall most important point about it.

_____

_____

_____

_____

_____

_____

Internet Resources

Read More about This Topic on the World Wide Web

Directions: For further information about the topic of the selection, visit this website:

www.family.org/married/
This is part of a magazine-format website that contains articles and links to websites about various aspects of marriage.

You can also use your favorite search engine such as Google, Yahoo!, or Alta-Vista (www.google.com, www.yahoo.com, www.altavista.com) to discover more about this topic. To locate additional information, type in combinations of keywords such as:

marriage compatibility

or

decision to marry

or

marriage

Keep in mind that whenever you go to *any* website, it is a good idea to evaluate the website and the information it contains. Ask yourself questions such as:

"Who sponsors this website?"

"Is the information contained in this website up-to-date?"

"What type of information is presented?"

"Is the information objective and complete?"

"How easy is it to use the features of this website?"

SELECTION **7-3**

Psychology

Reactions to Impending Death

From *Essentials of Psychology*

By Dennis Coon

Prepare Yourself to Read

Directions: Do these exercises *before* you read Selection 7-3.

1. First, read and think about the title. What do you already know about dying people's reactions to impending death?

_____

_____

_____

_____

2. Next, complete your preview by reading the following:

> Introduction (in *italics*)
> First paragraph (paragraph 1)
> Headings
> First sentence of each paragraph
> Words in **bold print** and *italics*
> Last paragraph (paragraph 16)

On the basis of your preview, what does this selection seem to be about?

_____

_____

_____

_____

Apply Comprehension Skills

Directions: Do the Annotation Practice Exercises *as* you read Selection 7-3.

Determine topics and main ideas. When you read a paragraph, ask yourself what it is about (the topic) and the most important point the author wants you to understand about the topic (the main idea).

Identify supporting details. As you read, ask yourself what else the author wants you to know so that you can understand the main idea.

Recognize the author's writing pattern. As you read, ask yourself, "What pattern did the author use to organize the main idea and supporting details?" Watch for clue words that signal the pattern.

455

REACTIONS TO IMPENDING DEATH

"It's not that I'm afraid to die; I just don't want to be there when it happens," Woody Allen once quipped. Although he was making a joke, his comment reflects our culture's squeamish attitude towards death. Kahlil Gibran, author of The Prophet, had a very different view: "For life and death are one, even as the river and the sea are one."

Because the topic of death makes many people in our society uncomfortable, it tends not to be discussed. Yet death is a reality, the natural, inevitable end of life, and not talking about it only makes death more difficult for those who are dying and for the survivors who will grieve for them. Fortunately, extensive, thorough, and thoughtful research on terminally ill patients' reactions to their impending deaths was done by Dr. Elisabeth Kübler-Ross. We now know that certain reactions are normal and predictable. Kübler-Ross's findings have proved extraordinarily helpful to the terminally ill, to those who love them, to others who provide them emotional support, and to those who provide their health care.

In this selection from a psychology textbook, the author presents Kübler-Ross's findings, as well as helpful information on hospices and bereavement. This selection will provide you with valuable insights that will benefit you in a variety of ways.

1　　A direct account of emotional responses to death comes from the work of Elisabeth Kübler-Ross (1975). Kübler-Ross is a **thanatologist** (one who studies death) who spent hundreds of hours at the bedsides of the terminally ill. She found that dying persons tend to display several emotional reactions as they prepare for death. Five basic reactions are described here:

1. **Denial and isolation.** A typical first reaction to impending death is an attempt to deny its reality and to isolate oneself from information confirming that death is really going to occur. Initially the person may be sure that "It's all a mistake," that lab reports or X-rays have been mixed up, or that a physician is in error. This may proceed to attempts to ignore or avoid any reminder of the situation.

2. **Anger.** Many dying individuals feel anger and ask, "Why me?" As they face the ultimate threat of having everything they value stripped away, their anger can spill over into rage or envy toward those who will continue living. Even good friends may temporarily evoke anger because their health is envied.

3. **Bargaining.** In another common reaction the terminally ill bargain with themselves or with God. The dying person thinks, "Just let me live a little longer and I'll do anything to earn it." Individuals may bargain for time by trying to be "good" ("I'll never smoke again"), by righting past wrongs, or by praying that if they are granted more time they will dedicate themselves to their religion.

Annotation Practice Exercises

Directions: For each exercise, use the spaces provided to write:

- Main idea sentence of the paragraph
- Author's pattern for organizing supporting details (writing pattern)

Practice Exercise

- Main idea sentence of paragraph 1:

_____

_____

_____

- Writing pattern:

_____

4. **Depression.** As death draws near and the person begins to recognize that it cannot be prevented, feelings of futility, exhaustion, and deep depression may set in. The person recognizes that he or she will be separated from friends, loved ones, and the familiar routines of life, and this causes a profound sadness.

5. **Acceptance.** If death is not sudden, many people manage to come to terms with dying and accept it calmly. The person who accepts death is neither happy nor sad, but at peace with the inevitable. Acceptance usually signals that the struggle with death has been resolved. The need to talk about death ends, and silent companionship from others is frequently all that is desired.

As cultural rituals, funerals encourage a release of emotion and provide a sense of closure for survivors, who must come to terms with the death of a loved one.

2   Not all terminally ill persons display all these reactions, nor do they always occur in this order. Individual styles of dying vary greatly, according to emotional maturity, religious beliefs, age, education, the attitudes of relatives, and so forth. Generally, there does tend to be a movement from initial shock, denial, and anger toward eventual acceptance of the situation. However, some people who seem to have accepted death may die angry and raging against the inevitable. Conversely, the angry fighter may let go of the struggle and die peacefully. In general, one's approach to dying will mirror his or her style of living.

3   It is best not to think of Kübler-Ross's list as a fixed series of stages to go through in order. It is an even bigger mistake to assume that someone who does not show all the listed emotional reactions is somehow deviant or immature. Rather, the list describes typical and appropriate reactions to impending death. It is also interesting to note that many of the same reactions accompany any major loss, be it divorce, loss of a home due to fire, death of a pet, or loss of a job.

Question: How can I make use of this information?

4   First, it can help both the dying individual and survivors to recognize and cope with periods of depression, anger, denial, and bargaining. Second, it helps to realize that close friends or relatives of the dying person may feel many of the same emotions before or after the person's death because they, too, are facing a loss.

5   Perhaps the most important thing to recognize is that the dying person may have a need to share feelings with others and to discuss death openly. Too often, the dying person feels isolated and separated from others by the wall of silence erected by doctors, nurses, and family members. Adults tend to "freeze up" with a dying person, saying things such as, "I don't know how to deal with this."

6   Understanding what the dying person is going through may make it easier to offer support at this important time. A simple willingness to be with the person and to honestly share his or her feelings can help bring dignity, acceptance, and meaning to death. In many communities these goals have been aided by the hospice movement.

Hospice

7   A **hospice** is basically a hospital for the terminally ill. The goal of the hospice movement is to improve the quality of life in the person's final days. Hospices typically offer support, guidance, and companionship from volunteers, other patients, staff, clergy, and counselors. Pleasant surroundings, an atmosphere of informality, and a sense of continued living help patients cope with their illnesses. Unlimited around-the-clock visits are permitted by relatives, friends, children, and even pets. Patients receive constant attention, play games, make day trips, have predinner cocktails if they choose, and enjoy entertainment. In short, life goes on for them.

8   At present most larger cities in the United States have hospices. They have been so successful that they are likely to be added to many more communities. At the same time, treatment for the terminally ill has dramatically improved in hospitals—largely as a result of pioneering efforts in the hospice movement.

Bereavement

9   After a friend or relative has died, a period of grief typically follows. Grief is a natural and normal reaction to death as survivors adjust to loss.

10   Grief tends to follow a predictable pattern. Grief usually begins with a period of **shock** or numbness. For a brief time the bereaved remain in a dazed state in which they may show little emotion. Most find it extremely difficult to accept the reality of their loss. This phase usually ends by the time of the funeral, which unleashes tears and bottled-up feelings of despair.

11   Initial shock is followed by sharp **pangs of grief.** These are episodes of painful yearning for the dead person and, sometimes, anguished outbursts of anger. During this period the wish to have the dead person back is intense. Often, mourners continue to think of the dead person as alive. They may hear his or her voice and see the deceased vividly in dreams. During this period, agitated distress alternates with silent despair, and suffering is acute.

12   The first powerful reactions of grief gradually give way to weeks or months of **apathy, dejection,** and **depression.** The person faces a new emotional landscape with a large gap that cannot be filled. Life seems to lose much of its meaning, and a sense of futility dominates the person's outlook. The

mourner is usually able to resume work or other activities after 2 or 3 weeks. However, insomnia, loss of energy and appetite, and similar signs of depression may continue.

13   Little by little, the bereaved person accepts what cannot be changed and makes a new beginning. Pangs of grief may still occur, but they are less severe and less frequent. Memories of the dead person, though still painful, now include positive images and nostalgic pleasure. At this point, the person can be said to be moving toward **resolution.**

14   As was true of approaching death, individual reactions to grief vary considerably. In general, however, a month or two typically passes before the more intense stages of grief have run their course. As you can see, grief allows survivors to discharge their anguish and to prepare to go on living.

Question: Is it true that suppressing grief leads to more problems later?

15   It has long been assumed that suppressing grief may later lead to more severe and lasting depression. However, there is little evidence to support this idea. A lack of intense grief does not usually predict later problems. Bereaved persons should work through their grief at their own pace and in their own way—without worrying about whether they are grieving too much or too little. Some additional suggestions for coping with grief follow.

Coping with Grief

- Face the loss directly and do not isolate yourself.
- Discuss your feelings with relatives and friends.
- Do not block out your feelings with drugs or alcohol.
- Allow grief to progress naturally; neither hurry nor suppress it.

16   The subject of death brings us full circle in the cycle of life.

Source: Adapted from *Essentials of Psychology: Exploration and Application,* 5th ed., by Dennis Coon, pp. 136–38. Copyright ©1991. Reprinted with permission of Wadsworth, a division of Thomson Learning: www.thomsonrights.com. Fax: 800-730-2215.

SELECTION **7-3**

Psychology
(Continued)

Student Online
Learning Center (OLC)
Go to Chapter 7.
Select Reading
Selection Quiz.

Reading Selection Quiz

This quiz has three parts. Your instructor may assign some or all of them.

Comprehension

Directions: Items 1–10 test your comprehension (understanding) of the material of this selection. These questions are the type a content area instructor (such as a psychology professor) would ask on a test over this material. You should be able to answer these questions after studying this selection. For each comprehension question below, use information from the selection to determine the correct answer. Refer to the selection as you answer each question. Write your answer in the space provided.

True or False

_____   **1.**   Elisabeth Kübler-Ross found that every terminally ill patient displays five basic reactions to dying.

_____   **2.**   Kübler-Ross's list of reactions represents a fixed series of stages.

_____   **3.**   Many of the reactions outlined by Kübler-Ross also accompany major losses such as divorce, loss of a job, and loss of a home in a fire.

_____   **4.**   The primary goal of the hospice movement is to provide advanced medical treatment for the dying person.

_____   **5.**   The hospice movement has had no effect on the quality of care that terminally ill patients receive in hospitals.

_____   **6.**   Patients in a hospice may have a predinner cocktail if they choose to.

Multiple-Choice

_____   **7.**   A thanatologist is one who studies:
   a.   hospital care.
   b.   diseases.
   c.   death.
   d.   psychology.

_____   **8.**   The author states that individual styles of dying are influenced by all the following factors *except* the:
   a.   attitude of relatives.
   b.   gender of the dying person.
   c.   age of the dying person.
   d.   emotional maturity of the dying person.

_____ **9.** Which of the following does *not* illustrate the value of Kübler-Ross's findings?

　　a. We can assume that someone who does not exhibit all the emotional reactions described by Kübler-Ross is immature.

　　b. The dying person who is familiar with Kübler-Ross's theory may be able to recognize, cope with, and discuss the various stages.

　　c. As survivors, we can better understand and support the terminally ill person.

　　d. Doctors and nurses may have a better understanding of the feelings of the terminally ill person.

_____ **10.** Hospice care is characterized by:

　　a. restricted visits.

　　b. a hospital-like environment.

　　c. day trips, entertainment, and visits by the family (even pets), if the patient is able.

　　d. care, guidance, and support by doctors and staff only.

SELECTION **7-3**

Psychology
(Continued)

Vocabulary in Context

Directions: Items 11–20 test your ability to determine the meaning of the word by using context clues. *Context clues* are words in a sentence that allow the reader to deduce (reason out) the meaning of an unfamiliar word in that sentence. Context clues also enable the reader to determine which meaning the author intends when a word has more than one meaning. For each vocabulary item below, a sentence from the selection containing an important word (*italicized, like this*) is quoted first. Next, there is an additional sentence using the word in the same sense and providing another context clue. Use the context clues from *both* sentences to deduce the meaning of the italicized word. *Be sure the answer you choose makes sense in both sentences.* If you discover that you need to use a dictionary to confirm an answer choice, remember that the meaning you select must still fit the context of *both* sentences. Write your answer in the space provided.

Pronunciation Key:　ă **pat**　ā **pay**　âr **care**　ä **father**　ĕ **pet**　ē **be**　ĭ **pit**
ī **tie**　îr **pier**　ŏ **pot**　ō **toe**　ô **paw**　oi **noise**　ou **out**　ŏŏ **took**
ōō **boot**　ŭ **cut**　yōō **abuse**　ûr **urge**　th **thin**　*th* **this**　hw **which**
zh **vision**　ə **about**　*Stress mark:* ʹ

_____ **11.** As death draws near and the person begins to recognize that it cannot be prevented, feelings of *futility,* exhaustion, and deep depression may set in.

When they saw how vast the forest fire was, the firefighters realized the *futility* of their efforts to put it out and simply tried instead to prevent it from spreading.

futility (fyo͞o tĭl′ ĭ tē) means:

a.   reasonableness; sensibleness

b.   uselessness; lack of useful results

c.   cheerfulness

d.   helpfulness

_____ **12.** Acceptance usually signals that the struggle with death has been *resolved.*

My parents always *resolved* their problems by discussing them.

resolved (rĭ zōlvd′) means:

a.   found a solution to; settled

b.   ignored; paid no attention to

c.   made known publicly

d.   kept secret

_____ **13.** It is an even bigger mistake to assume that someone who does not show all the listed emotional reactions is somehow *deviant* or immature.

Children who are abused often exhibit *deviant* behavior later in their lives.

deviant (dē′ vē ənt) means:

a.   kind; gentle

b.   illegal; against the law

c.   difficult to diagnose

d.   differing from accepted standards

_____ **14.** Rather, the list describes typical and appropriate reactions to *impending* death.

We knew from the dark clouds that the *impending* storm could hit at any minute.

impending (ĭm pĕn′ dĭng) means:

a.   about to take place

b.   severe; harsh

c.   delayed; later than expected

d.   soothing

15. For a brief time the *bereaved* remain in a dazed state in which they may show little emotion.

The *bereaved* widow of the police officer received hundreds of letters expressing sympathy over the loss of her courageous husband.

bereaved (bǐ rēvd′) means:

a. peaceful; serene

b. young; childlike

c. suffering the loss of a loved one

d. suffering from a serious illness

16. This phase usually ends by the time of the funeral, which *unleashes* tears and bottled-up feelings of despair.

When a hurricane *unleashes* its fury, it can cause millions of dollars of damage.

unleashes (ŭn lēsh′ əz) means:

a. releases

c. controls

c. calms; soothes

d. prevents

17. Initial shock is followed by sharp *pangs* of grief.

We had not eaten since morning, and our hunger *pangs* increased when we smelled the delicious aroma coming from the campfire that night.

pangs (păngz) means:

a. strong desires

b. strong, sudden sensations

c. sad, despondent feelings

d. strong dislikes

18. During this period, agitated distress alternates with silent despair, and suffering is *acute*.

Everyone in the search party felt *acute* relief when the missing child was found.

acute (ə kyo͞ot′) means:

a. intense

b. mild

c. moderate

d. not noticeable

19. The first powerful reactions of grief gradually give way to weeks or months of apathy, *dejection,* and depression.

We could tell from their *dejection* that they had lost the final game of the baseball playoffs.

dejection (dĭ jĕkt′ shən) means:

a. agitation; nervousness

b. energy; liveliness

c. discouragement or low spirits

d. happiness; elation

20. Life seems to lose much of its meaning, and a sense of futility *dominates* the person's outlook.

The rumor of the president's resignation *dominates* the media this week.

dominates (dŏm′ ə nāts) means:

a. controls or occupies

b. treats harshly

c. treats as unimportant

d. is excluded from

SELECTION **7-3**   *Reading Skills Application*

Psychology
(Continued)

Directions: Items 21–25 test your ability to *apply* certain reading skills to information in this selection. These types of questions provide valuable practice for all students, especially those who must take standardized reading tests and state-mandated basic skills tests (such as the Florida CLAST Test and the Texas THEA Test). You may not have studied all of the skills at this point, so these items will serve as a helpful preview. The comprehension and critical reading skills in this section are presented in Chapters 4 through 9 of *Opening Doors;* vocabulary and figurative language skills are presented in Chapter 2. As you work through *Opening Doors,* you will practice and develop these skills. Write your answer for each question in the space provided.

21. The main idea of paragraph 6 is best expressed by which of the following sentences from this selection?

a. A simple willingness to be with a dying person and to honestly share his feelings can help bring dignity, acceptance, and meaning to death.

b. In many communities, these goals have been aided by the hospice movement.

c. Understanding what the dying person is going through may make it easier for you to offer support at this important time.

d. The hospice movement was created to help terminally ill people die with dignity.

_____ **22.** Which of the following is an accurate assessment of the author's credibility?

    a. The author has little credibility because he presents only his personal experience.

    b. The author has limited credibility because he presents only theories, not facts.

    c. The author has credibility because he is a renowned thanatologist.

    d. The author has credibility because he presents the results of research studies.

_____ **23.** What is the meaning of *discharge* as it is used in paragraph 14?

    a. to dismiss

    b. to empty

    c. to survive

    d. to be relieved of

_____ **24.** Which of the following does the author intend as his primary audience?

    a. anyone who is going through bereavement

    b. anyone who might at some point become terminally ill or deal with someone who is terminally ill

    c. anyone who is in denial after being diagnosed with a terminal illness

    d. anyone who works in a hospice

_____ **25.** Which of the following assumptions underlies the author's main argument?

    a. The process of grieving can be speeded up if a person understands the process.

    b. Knowing the typical reactions to impending death allows those who deal with the terminally ill to assess whether they are going through the appropriate stages.

    c. The more people understand about impending death, loss, and bereavement, the more likely they are to be able to cope and to help others.

    d. All people eventually die, so it is important to reassure the terminally ill that they are not unique or alone in what they are feeling.

S E L E C T I O N **7-3**

Psychology
(Continued)

Collaboration Option

Respond in Writing

Directions: Refer to Selection 7-3 as needed to answer the essay-type questions below.

Option for collaboration: Your instructor may direct you to work with other students on one or more of these items, or in other words, to work *collaboratively.* In that case, you should form groups of three or four students, as directed by your instructor, and work together to complete the exercises. After your group discusses an item and agrees on the answer, have a group member record it. Each member of your group should be able to explain all of your group's answers.

1. The thanatologist Elisabeth Kübler-Ross found five basic reactions to death (or any major loss). Give examples of how each of these reactions might manifest itself in a person's behavior. You may add examples of your own to any the author gives. (For instance, one possible behavior accompanying the first emotional reaction is avoiding calling to get results of medical tests.)

Emotional reaction	Possible behaviors accompanying the reaction
Denial and isolation	
Anger	
Bargaining	
Depression	
Acceptance	

2. What are at least two important ways a person could benefit from knowing about the five reactions Kübler-Ross describes?

_____

_____

_____

_____

_____

_____

_____

_____

_____

3. How does a hospice differ from a hospital? In your answer, use words that signal contrasts (see page 413 for these words).

_____

_____

_____

_____

_____

_____

_____

_____

_____

_____

_____

_____

4. With the exception of the "bargaining stage," there is a predictable pattern of grief, just as there is a predictable pattern of reactions to impending death. Review this comparison (presented at the end of the selection) and complete the table below. (To get you started, the answers to be inserted opposite *Denial and isolation* are "shock or numbness" and "difficulty accepting the reality of the loss." Write them on the first two lines provided.)

Reactions to death or loss	Reactions to grief
Denial and isolation	_____
	_____
Anger	_____
	_____
Bargaining	(No equivalent reaction)
Depression	_____
Acceptance	_____

5. Think of a situation in which you or someone you know experienced a significant loss (such as the loss of a valued job, divorce, loss of a home through fire or a natural disaster, or the death of a pet). Describe any of the reactions mentioned in the selection that you or the person who experienced the loss went through.

_____

_____

6. In his best-selling book *Tuesdays with Morrie,* the journalist Mitch Albom chronicles the final months of his favorite college professor's life. Morrie Schwartz, a sociology professor, was dying from amyotrophic lateral sclerosis (ALS), a terminal illness that gradually moves up the body, destroying the nerves and eventually rendering a person unable to move, swallow, or breathe. Morrie tells Mitch, "Death ends a life, not a relationship" and "Learn how to die and you learn how to live." Take one of these "lessons" of Morrie's and explain why you agree or disagree with it.

_____

_____

7. **Overall main idea.** What is the overall main idea the author wants the reader to understand about reactions to impending death? Answer this question in one sentence. Be sure that your overall main idea sentence includes the topic (*reactions to impending death*) and tells the overall most important point about it.

_____

_____

_____

_____

_____

Internet Resources

Read More about This Topic on the World Wide Web

Directions: For further information about the topic of the selection, visit these websites:

www.elisabethkublerross.com
This website is sponsored by the Elisabeth Kübler-Ross Foundation (EKR Foundation). The mission of the EKR Foundation is to continue Kübler-Ross's life work by educating caregivers on the intricacies of compassionate bereavement care and to provide bereavement care to all families affected by death worldwide.

www.wic.org/bio/eross.htm
This website contains a concise educational and professional profile of Dr. Elisabeth Kübler-Ross's accomplishments. This site is sponsored by the Women's Educational Center, a nonprofit and service foundation.

www.amazon.com
In the search box, select "Books," then type in, *"Tuesdays with Morrie."* This website will give you information on the book *Tuesdays with Morrie,* a story about important lessons learned from a dying college professor by one of his former students.

You can also use your favorite search engine such as Google, Yahoo!, or Alta-Vista (www.google.com, www.yahoo.com, www.altavista.com) to discover more about this topic. To locate additional information, type in combinations of keywords such as:

reactions to impending death

or

Elisabeth Kübler-Ross

or

stages of grief

or

hospice care

Keep in mind that whenever you go to *any* website, it is a good idea to evaluate the website and the information it contains. Ask yourself questions such as:

"Who sponsors this website?"

"Is the information contained in this website up-to-date?"

"What type of information is presented?"

"Is the information objective and complete?"

"How easy is it to use the features of this website?"

CHAPTER 8

Reading Critically

In this chapter you will learn the answers to these questions:

- What is critical reading?

- How can I determine an author's purpose?

- How can I determine an author's intended audience?

- How can I determine an author's point of view or bias?

- How can I determine an author's tone and intended meaning?

SKILLS

What Is Critical Reading?

Critical Reading Skills

* Determining an Author's Purpose and Intended Audience
* Determining an Author's Point of View, Tone, and Intended Meaning

A Word about Standardized Reading Tests: Critical Reading

CREATING YOUR SUMMARY

Developing Chapter Review Cards

READINGS

What we see depends mainly on what we look for.

John Lubbock

The end of reading is not more books, but more life.

Holbrook Jackson

WHAT IS CRITICAL READING?

Going *beyond* basic comprehension to gain insights as you read is called **critical reading.** Whenever you read, of course, you should identify basic information: topic, main idea, and supporting details. However, to gain greater understanding, you will need to go beyond these basic elements.

Reading critically requires you to ask certain questions *after* you read a passage and to think carefully about what you have read. Critical reading requires you to understand implied (suggested) and figurative (nonliteral) meanings in addition to literal (stated) meanings. As you will learn in Chapter 9, this also means taking time to reread and reconsider an author's message so that you can make careful evaluations and judgments about what you are reading.

CRITICAL READING SKILLS

Student Online Learning Center (OLC)
Go to Chapter 8.
Select Video.

The important, interrelated critical reading skills presented in this chapter are:

- Determining an author's purpose (the author's reason for writing).
- Determining an author's intended audience (whom the author had in mind as his or her readers).
- Determining an author's point of view (the author's position on an issue).
- Determining an author's tone and intended meaning (a way an author reveals his or her attitude toward the topic).

Because these skills are *interrelated,* they are presented together in this chapter. As you will soon discover, an author's *purpose* causes him or her to present certain facts and opinions, and to use a certain *tone* to convey a *point of view* and an *intended meaning* to an *intended audience.*

Determining an Author's Purpose and Intended Audience

Authors write for specific purposes. An author's **purpose** is simply his or her reason for writing. The author's purpose may be to *inform,* to *instruct,* to *entertain,* or to *persuade* the reader to believe something or take a certain action. Most textbook authors write for the purpose of informing (giving information, explaining) or instructing (teaching the reader how to do something). However, some authors, such as movie critics, newspaper editors, and political writers, write to give their opinion and to persuade the reader to accept this opinion. Finally, other writers, such as humorists or certain newspaper columnists, write for the purpose of entertaining. They may entertain readers, for example, with humorous stories or with enjoyable descriptions.

473

Reading critically involves asking yourself certain questions *after* you read a passage and thinking carefully about what you have read.

Sometimes an author will state his or her purpose. For example, the author of a biology textbook might simply tell readers, "The purpose of this section is to define and explain the two types of cell division." At other times, the author may feel that the purpose is obvious and assume that the reader can infer it. Understanding an author's purpose means that you are aware of his or her motive for writing.

To determine an author's purpose, think carefully about the words he or she has used. Authors often choose certain words precisely because those words can direct or influence the reader's thinking.

For example, when authors want to *inform* you of important information or *explain* something, they use phrases such as:

The important point is . . .

Be sure you know . . .

It is important to understand . . .

Remember that . . .

When authors want to *instruct,* or *teach* you how to do something, they often use phrases such as:

Follow these directions to . . .

The steps below will enable you to . . .

These instructions tell how to . . .

This is the procedure for . . .

When authors want to *persuade* you to do something or *convince* you to believe something, they may use phrases such as:

The only intelligent choice, then, is . . .

Any reasonable person will agree that . . .

Only an uninformed person would believe that . . .

Those who understand the issue will certainly agree . . .

When authors are writing to *entertain* or *amuse* readers, they may use phrases such as:

You'll never believe what happened to me when I . . .

The funny thing about . . .

And then the oddest thing happened . . .

I'll never forget the day I . . .

Comprehension Monitoring Question for Determining an Author's Purpose

Why did the author write this?

Noticing certain words and phrases the author has used is one way to determine the author's purpose. Another way to determine an author's purpose is to examine whether or not both sides of a controversial issue have been presented. That is, check to see whether important information has been left out. Authors frequently choose to leave out information that does not support their point of view. Keep in mind that although an author may appear to be neutral on an issue, his or her real purpose may be to persuade you to support one side. It is important to understand an author's purpose for writing so that you can prevent yourself from being unknowingly influenced by the author.

Remember, then: To read critically, you must determine the author's purpose by asking yourself, "Why did the author write this?"

KEY TERM
intended audience

People an author has in mind as his or her readers.

Authors also have specific audiences in mind when they write. An author's **intended audience** consists of the people the author has in mind as readers; that is, the people he or she is writing for. The intended audience will be a particular individual, a specific group, or the general public. For instance, a psychologist writing a textbook may assume that his or her audience will be students taking an introductory psychology course. The psychologist will have these students in mind while writing, and this will shape decisions about the material to be included and about the level of difficulty. "Who did the author intend to read this?" is a question critical readers always ask themselves.

Comprehension Monitoring Question for Determining an Author's Intended Audience

Who did the author intend to read this?

Sometimes, of course, an author will tell you who the intended audience is. However, when you must determine an author's intended audience, examine these three things: the topic being discussed (Is it of *technical* or of *general interest?*), the level of language used (Is it *simple, sophisticated,* or *specialized?*), and the purpose for writing (Is it to *instruct, inform, persuade,* or *entertain?*). These three things should help you answer the question "Who did the author intend to read this?"

Following is a paragraph about using humor to deal with stress. After you read this paragraph, ask yourself, "Why did the author write this?" and "Who did the author intend to read this?"

It's true. You really can laugh your stress away. In fact, humor is one of the best stress busters around. You can't belly laugh and feel bad at the same time. So, if you're caught in a situation you can't escape or change (a traffic jam, a slow line at the bank, a long wait at the doctor's office, or a crying baby at the table next to you at a restaurant, for example), then humor may be the healthiest form of temporary stress release possible.

What is the author's purpose?

_____

_____

_____

Who is the author's intended audience?

_____

_____

Stop and Annotate

Go back to the excerpt above. Determine the author's purpose and intended audience, and write your responses in the spaces provided.

In this paragraph, the author's purpose is simply to *inform* the reader that humor can be an effective way to temporarily reduce stress. You can see that the author uses simple language and short sentences. Notice that he uses informal language: *stress busters* and *belly laugh*. He also includes several everyday examples of potentially stressful situations. Because his topic requires no special prior knowledge and because his approach is uncomplicated, you can assume that the author's intended audience is *the general public*. Practically anyone could understand and benefit from the information he presents.

Now read this passage from a business communication textbook to determine the authors' purpose and the audience they had in mind.

Think about the people you know. Which of them would you call successful communicators? What do these people have in common? Chances are, the individuals on your list share five qualities:

- **Perception.** They are able to predict how their message will be received. They anticipate your reaction and shape the message accordingly. They read your response correctly and constantly adjust to correct any misunderstanding.
- **Precision.** They include specific definitions and helpful examples. They create a "meeting of the minds." When they finish expressing themselves, you share the same mental picture.

What is the authors' purpose?

_____

_____

Who is the authors' intended audience?

_____

_____

_____

_____

_____

- **Credibility.** They are believable. You have faith in the substance of their message. You trust their information and their intentions.
- **Control.** They shape your response. Depending on their purpose, they can make you laugh or cry, calm down, change your mind, or take action.
- **Congeniality.** They maintain friendly, pleasant relations with the audience. Regardless of whether you agree with them, good communicators command your respect and goodwill. You are willing to work with them again, despite your differences.

Source: Adapted from Courtland Bovée and John Thill, *Business Communication Today,* 4th ed., Upper Saddle River, NJ: Prentice Hall, 1995, p. 44.

Stop and Annotate

Go back to the preceding excerpt. Determine the authors' purpose and intended audience, and write your responses in the spaces provided.

In this excerpt, the authors' purpose is also to *inform.* The authors list specific elements that characterize good communicators and describe how these people interact with others. The authors' intended audience is a particular group of people: *students in a business communications course* or *adults who want to know about characteristics of effective communication.*

Here is a passage from a health textbook whose purpose and audience are easy to determine. In this passage, the authors use simple, factual language to describe the Heimlich maneuver, the procedure to use when someone is choking.

The Heimlich Maneuver

If a person who seems to be choking on food or a foreign object can speak, do not interfere with that individual's attempt to cough up the object. If the person is unable to speak, it is appropriate to provide emergency care by using the Heimlich maneuver. Stand behind the victim and place both arms around his or her waist. Grasp one fist with the other hand and place the thumb side of the fist against the victim's abdomen, slightly above the navel and below the rib cage. Press your fist into the victim's abdomen with a quick inward and upward thrust. Repeat this procedure until the object is dislodged. The Heimlich maneuver should not be used with infants under one year of age.

What is the authors' purpose?

_____

_____

Who is the authors' intended audience?

_____

_____

_____

_____

_____

Source: Marvin R. Levy, Mark Dignan, and Janet H. Shirreffs, *Targeting Wellness: The Core,* pp. 284–85.
Copyright © 1992 by The McGraw-Hill Companies, Inc. Reprinted by permission of The McGraw-Hill Companies.

Stop and Annotate

Go back to the excerpt on page 477. Determine the authors' purpose and intended audience, and write your responses in the spaces provided.

The purpose of the passage is to *instruct*. The paragraph describes the steps necessary for performing the Heimlich maneuver. The intended audience is *students in a health course* or *people who are interested in learning how to perform the Heimlich maneuver.* (In Chapter 7 you learned that sets of instructions are sequences. When the author's purpose is to instruct, watch for a sequence.)

Here is a short paragraph from an article entitled "The Time Message." After you have read it, ask yourself, "Why did the author write this?" and "Who did the author intend to read this?"

Time is dangerous. If you don't control it, it will control you! If you don't make it work for you, it will work against you. You must become the master of time, not the servant. In other words, as a college student, time management will be your number-one problem.

What is the author's purpose?

_____

_____

Who is the author's intended audience?

_____

Source: E. N. Chapman, "The Time Message," in Frank Christ, ed., *SR/SE Resource Book,* Chicago: SRA, 1969, p. 3.

Stop and Annotate

Go back to the excerpt above. Determine the author's purpose and intended audience, and write your responses in the spaces provided.

Although the author of this paragraph informs the reader about the importance of controlling time, his primary purpose is to *persuade* the reader to deal with this potentially "dangerous" problem. The author also used an exclamation point in the second sentence to emphasize the importance of dealing with time so that you are not "controlled" by it. The author's intended audience is clearly stated in the last sentence of the paragraph: the *college student,* especially one who has not yet mastered time management.

Here is a paragraph written for a completely different purpose. It is from the best-selling memoir *Having Our Say: The Delany Sisters' First 100 Years* (Selection 8-2). In this excerpt, 103-year-old Bessie Delany describes her nearly fatal bout with typhoid fever when she was 15 years old.

When I got out of the hospital, I looked like death. They had cut off my hair, real short, and I weighed next to nothing. I could not get enough to eat. Mama was so worried that she fixed a small basket of fruit each morning for me to carry with me all day, so I could eat whenever I wanted. For a long time I was on crutches, and I was not expected to recover fully. They used to say that typhoid fever left its mark on people. Well, nothing has shown up yet, so I guess I'm in the clear!

What is the authors' purpose?

_____

_____

Who is the authors' intended audience?

_____

Source: From Sarah Delany, Elizabeth Delany with Amy Hill Hearth, *Having Our Say: The Delany Sisters' First 100 Years,* Kodansha America, Inc., 1993, p. 83. Reprinted by permission of Kodansha America, Inc.

As the humor in the last sentence suggests, the purpose of this paragraph is to *entertain* the reader. At 103 years of age Bessie Delany "guesses" she's "in the clear" and no longer needs to worry that any aftereffects of her bout with typhoid fever will show up. The intended audience of this passage is *the general public* who would enjoy reading about a centenarian's recollection of her childhood.

Remember, part of critical reading involves asking yourself these two questions in order to determine the author's purpose and intended audience: "Why did the author write this?" and "Who did the author intend to read this?"

Determining an Author's Point of View, Tone, and Intended Meaning

Point of view refers to an author's position on an issue. In other words, an author's point of view is his or her opinion about that topic. It is the position he or she hopes to convince the reader to accept or believe. An author's point of view is also known as the *author's argument* or the *author's bias.*

Even though authors are generally experts in their fields, they do not always agree on every topic and issue. Because authors may have different points of view and may disagree with other experts, it is important that you recognize what each author's point of view is. For example, one author's point of view might be, "Gun control is necessary if we are to have a safe society." The point of view of an author with the opposite bias would be, "Gun control would only make society less safe." A neutral point of view would be, "Gun control has both advantages and disadvantages."

Notice the use of the word *bias* in the preceding paragraph. In everyday conversation, people often use the word *bias* to mean *prejudice;* that is, they mean that a biased person has taken a position without thinking it through and without examining the evidence. In this context, the word *bias* has a negative connotation. However, with regard to written material, an **author's bias** simply represents his or her *preference* for one side of an issue over the other—his or her point of view. (For example, one writer might have a bias for yearround school, while another writer has the opposite bias.) There is nothing wrong with an author having a bias; many thoughtful writers weigh the evidence carefully, then adopt the point of view that makes the most sense to them. When you read, you must try to determine whether the author has a bias. In some cases, a bias may cause an author to slant the facts and not be objective.

Sometimes the author states his or her bias or point of view directly. For example, an author might state that he or she has a bias against home schooling. At other times, authors expect the reader to recognize their bias, on the basis of the information they include (or leave out) and the way they present the information. Consider the following paragraph, in which the author clearly expresses a bias about using a cell phone while driving.

Stop and Annotate

Go back to the excerpt on page 478. Determine the authors' purpose and intended audience, and write your responses in the spaces provided.

KEY TERM
point of view

An author's position (opinion) on an issue.

Point of view is also known as the *author's argument* or the *author's bias.*

KEY TERM
author's bias

The side of an issue an author favors; an author's preference for one side of an issue over the other.

> There should be a law against using a cell phone when driving. In spite of what they say, drivers become distracted reaching for the phone, dialing it, or answering it. The conversation itself can also take their attention away from the road. Suppose a driver having a conversation gets upset or angry with the caller. In that case, is the driver's full concentration really on the road? Drivers who are busy with their cell phones are involved in more accidents than drivers who do not use cell phones. They cause more accidents that kill and injure not only themselves, but other innocent, unsuspecting drivers. The bumper sticker says it all: "Hang up and drive!"

What is the author's point of view (bias)?

_____

_____

_____

Stop and Annotate

Go back to the excerpt above. Determine the author's point of view (bias), and write your response in the spaces provided.

Comprehension Monitoring Question for Determining an Author's Point of View

What is the author's position on this issue?

KEY TERM
tone

Manner of writing (choice of words and style) that reveals an author's attitude toward a topic.

Clearly, this author has a bias against people using cell phones while driving. This author's point of view is that using cell phones when driving is dangerous and that there should be a law that forbids this. (Incidentally, the author's purpose here is to persuade anyone who uses a cell phone when driving to stop doing so and to persuade everyone to support laws against using cell phones when driving. The author's intended audience is the general public, but especially anyone who uses a cell phone when driving.)

By the way, you should be aware of your *own* biases whenever you are reading about a controversial issue. If you have a strong bias on a subject and an author has the opposite bias, you might be tempted to reject the author's point of view without giving it serious consideration. (For example, readers who favor being able to use cell phones while driving might immediately close their minds after reading the first sentence of the paragraph above.) Do not let your own bias cause you to automatically close your mind to an author's point of view just because it is different from yours.

To determine the author's point of view, critical readers ask, "What is the author's position on this issue?" Look for words that reveal the author's point of view:

Supporting this new policy is *essential* because . . .

The proposed legislation *will benefit* all the citizens of Dallas county because . . .

It is *not in the best interest* of the country to . . .

Voters *should oppose* the state lottery because . . .

An author's **tone** is a manner of writing that reveals or reflects his or her attitude toward a topic, just as tone of voice reveals a speaker's attitude. When someone is speaking, you can generally tell by the tone whether he or she is serious,

Comprehension Monitoring Question for Determining an Author's Tone

What do the author's choice of words and style of writing reveal about his or her attitude toward the topic?

sarcastic, sympathetic, enthusiastic, and so forth. To convey a tone, a speaker relies on pitch, volume, and inflection, along with choice of words. For example, if someone says, "I made a C on my biology test," you would need to know the speaker's tone to know whether he or she was excited, relieved, or disappointed.

Authors use tone just as speakers do. Authors, however, must rely on style of writing and choice of words to reveal their tone. They select words and writing styles that fit their purposes for writing (to inform, instruct, persuade, or entertain) and their point of view (for example, in favor of or opposed to something). In other words, they use a certain tone (informal, serious, sincere, humorous, etc.) to help convey their intended meaning. You can determine an author's tone by carefully examining his or her choice of words and style of writing. To determine an author's tone, ask yourself, "What do the author's choice of words and style of writing reveal about his or her attitude toward the topic?"

As just noted, choice of words—or *word choice*—is one way authors reveal their tone. For example, when describing a politician who did not tell the truth, one writer might use the word *lied* to convey a critical, disapproving, or bitter tone; another author might choose the word *exaggerated* instead to convey a tolerant or even an amused tone. Compare the following two sentences; they contain the same message (taxpayers' money will be used to help the unemployed), but the word choice makes their tone very different:

Once again, the American taxpayers have to foot the bill for those who are too lazy or unmotivated to work.

Once again, American taxpayers are showing their generosity by helping those who are unable to find employment.

Note the disapproving tone conveyed by the word choice in the first sentence (*foot the bill* and *too lazy or unmotivated to work*). A more positive, compassionate tone is conveyed by the choice of words in the second sentence (*showing their generosity by helping* and *unable to find employment*).

Now consider how an author's *writing style* also conveys a tone. Compare these two sentences; they contain the same message (computer science majors should consider a career in multimedia), but the writing style makes their tone quite different:

Since there will be a significant increase in employment opportunities in the field of multimedia, computer science majors would be wise to investigate this fast-growing area.

Video game design is becoming a really hot career option, so all computer science majors should check it out!

These two sentences present essentially the same information, but the first sentence has a more formal, factual tone. It is the type of sentence you might find in a career brochure or a computer science textbook. In the second sentence, however, the use of the phrase *really hot career option* and the expression *check it out!* convey an informal and enthusiastic tone. This kind of sentence might appear in a computer magazine or in an advertisement for computer job training.

Although an author's tone is often obvious, there may be times when the tone is less clear and requires careful thought on your part. If you misunderstand an author's tone, you may misinterpret his or her entire message. For example, if you read a short story and you miss the author's ironic or sarcastic tone, you will mistakenly think his or her meaning is the opposite of what it actually is. When authors use **irony,** they create a deliberate contrast between their apparent meaning and their intended meaning: their words say one thing but mean the opposite. That is, the words are intended to express something different from their literal meaning. You use irony every day in conversation. For example, you might say, "Well, that test was a breeze!" but your ironic tone makes it clear how difficult the test actually was. Another form of irony occurs when there is incongruity between what might be expected and what actually occurs. For example, it would be ironic if you won a new car in a contest on the same day that you bought a new one. Students sometimes confuse irony with sarcasm. **Sarcasm** is a remark, often ironic, that is intended to convey contempt or ridicule. Sarcasm is always meant to hurt; irony is not intended to be hurtful.

If you overlook irony or sarcasm you may think authors are being serious when they are actually joking; that they are calm when, in fact, they are angry; or that they are in favor of something when, in reality, they oppose it. Author's **intended meaning** is what an author wants readers to understand even when his or her words seem to be saying something different. Determining the author's tone correctly will enable you to grasp the author's intended meaning, even when the author's words appear on the surface to be saying something different. Critical readers ask themselves, "What is the author's *real* meaning?"

For many students, especially those for whom English is a second language, it can be challenging to detect sarcasm in written material and therefore understand the author's intended meaning. When you are reading, you can concentrate so much on following what the author is saying that you forget to think about how sensible it is and whether the author really expects you to take the words literally. It is often helpful to "step back" and think about whether the author is being sarcastic. If the author is using sarcasm, his or her true message will be the opposite of what the words appear to be saying. For example, suppose you read this letter from a high school principal to a newspaper editor about students who cheat in school:

KEY TERMS

irony

A deliberate contrast between an author's apparent meaning and his or her intended meaning.

sarcasm

A remark, often ironic, that is intended to convey contempt or ridicule.

intended meaning

What an author wants readers to understand even when his or her words seem to be saying something different.

Comprehension Monitoring Question for Determining an Author's Intended Meaning

"What is the author's *real* meaning?"

As a high school principal, I strongly believe that there shouldn't be any penalties for students who are caught cheating. After all, everyone does it. Besides, cheating in school will help prepare these same students to cheat their employers later on, to cheat on their spouses when they marry, and to cheat on their income taxes. In fact, we could help students even more if we offered a course on how to cheat.

What is the author's intended meaning?

_____

_____

_____

What is the author's tone?

_____

_____

The fact that you feel surprised, shocked, or confused at what the writer is saying should alert you to the fact that he or she is being sarcastic. Does the writer, a high school principal, really mean that it is fine for students to cheat in school? No, of course not. To make his point, the writer sarcastically says the *opposite* of what he or she actually means. Sometimes an author is deliberately ridiculous. The author's words are so absurd, in fact, that their absurdity makes it clear that the author does not mean at all what the words appear to be saying. In the preceding example, the author's intended meaning is that students who are caught cheating in school *should* be punished. Otherwise, those who cheat in school without any consequences will turn out to be dishonorable adults who continue to cheat in a variety of ways and think that there is nothing wrong with it. Would it really make sense that a school principal, the writer of the letter, would advocate cheating? Of course not. However, if you are not reading critically and you fail to notice the writer's sarcasm and intended meaning, you might go away feeling puzzled and mistakenly believing that the high school principal who wrote the letter thinks it is all right for students to cheat.

There are additional clues that can help you detect sarcasm in written material. First, pay attention when authors use words that seem inappropriate for what they are describing, such as an obvious exaggeration or an obvious understatement. For example, an author might exaggerate by saying that if the city's baseball team ever won a single game, the entire population would turn out on the streets for a week-long celebration. Or in describing a bitter legal case over property rights that has gone on for years, the writer might deliberately understate and describe it as "that unfriendly little property dispute." A second way to detect sarcasm is to think about how a passage would sound if the author *spoke* the words rather than wrote them. You may even want to read the passage aloud yourself and listen to your tone of voice. Can you hear any sarcasm in it?

As noted earlier, irony involves using words that seem straightforward but that actually contain a different, hidden meaning. For example, in the year 2000, just before the Academy Awards, there were many complaints that the program the preceding year had lasted entirely too long—four hours. In spite of this, the 2000 Academy Awards lasted even longer—four and a half hours! The emcee, Billy Crystal, made an ironic comment when he said he didn't understand why anyone was complaining because "the 2000 Academy Awards ceremony was the shortest one of the millennium." His comment was ironic because technically he was right, since that evening's ceremony was the *only* ceremony in this millennium. Therefore, regardless of how long the ceremony was, it was automatically the "shortest one of the millennium."

Another form of irony occurs when there is incongruity or difference between what is expected and what actually occurs. For example, it would be ironic if you took a trip to surprise a friend in another city, and your friend was not there because he was making a trip to pay a surprise visit to you in your city! The cartoon on page 484 is another example of this form of irony.

Satire is a type of writing in which the author sometimes uses sarcasm or irony for a specific purpose. To be precise, **satire** is a style of writing in which the author uses sarcasm, irony, or ridicule to attack or expose human foolishness, corruption, or stupidity. When authors are being satirical (using satire), they expect readers to

---

Stop and Annotate

Go back to the preceding excerpt. Determine the author's intended meaning and tone, and write your responses in the spaces provided.

KEY TERM

satire

A style of writing in which the author uses sarcasm, irony, or ridicule to attack or expose human foolishness, corruption, or stupidity.

This cartoon illustrates situational irony since it is the *mosquito* that is being bitten.

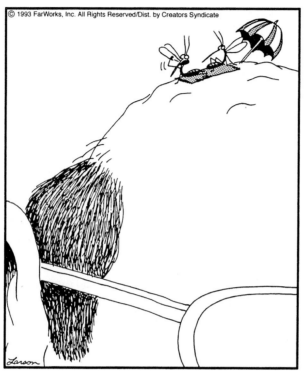

THE FAR SIDE® BY GARY LARSON

© 1993 FarWorks, Inc. All Rights Reserved/Dist. by Creators Syndicate

"Wow. ... That's ironic. I think something bit me."

pick up on it and understand their real message. Many famous writers have used satire to expose weaknesses in human society and morals. When you read a selection, ask yourself if the writer is trying to expose some problem by making fun of it. Here is an example of a passage in which the author uses satire to expose a politician's corrupt nature:

Would our distinguished state senator ever accept bribes from large corporations in exchange for his vote on important issues? Certainly not! He was never convicted when those charges were brought against him in the past. Is he a corrupt man who would accept illegal campaign contributions? Absolutely not. When it was

What is the author's intended meaning?

_____

_____

_____

revealed that he had accepted several questionable donations, he eventually returned all of them. Would the noble senator ever fail to report income on his tax form? Ridiculous. Although he has refused to release any of his tax returns, he obviously has nothing to hide. Would this fine man ever accept trips or other expensive gifts from lobbyists? Definitely not. Even though he cannot afford them on his salary, he shouldn't have to explain how he paid for all those expensive golf and ski vacations or how he is able to afford a second home in the country. After all, he's told us he hasn't done anything wrong, and as we all know, the senator is an honorable man.

> **What is the author's tone?**
>
> _____
>
> _____

You can almost hear the writer's voice drip with sarcasm. To show how "honorable" the senator is, the writer reveals that the senator:

Has previously had charges brought against him of selling his votes for bribes.

Returned certain campaign contributions once it was revealed to the public that they might be illegal.

Refuses to make his income tax returns available to the public.

Refuses to explain how he can afford certain very expensive luxuries on his salary.

Stop and Annotate

Go back to the preceding excerpt. Determine the author's intended meaning and tone, and write your responses in the spaces provided.

By mentioning one questionable matter after another that the senator has been involved in or accused of, and pretending to discount them, the writer reveals the senator's dishonest nature. The writer refers to the senator as "distinguished," "noble," and "honorable," although the sarcasm makes it clear that the writer believes the senator is none of these. In response to accusations about the senator's behavior, the writer vigorously declares, "Certainly not," "Absolutely not," "Ridiculous," and "Definitely not." Again, though, these overly strong denials make it clear the writer thinks the senator is guilty of the charges. If readers fail to recognize that the writer is satirizing the senator, they will completely misunderstand the writer's intended meaning: the senator is corrupt.

It is not so important that you be able to distinguish among sarcasm, irony, and satire. What is important is that you pick up on clues that authors use to signal that their intended meaning is different from what their words *appear* to be saying.

WORDS THAT DESCRIBE TONE

There are many words that can be used to describe tone, and you already know lots of them, such as *happy, sad,* and *angry.* There are many other words that can describe tone, and you may not be familiar with all of them. Here is a list of several. (Incidentally, these are valuable words to have in your own vocabulary.) To make it easier for you to learn the words, they are grouped into general categories.

Words That Describe a *Neutral* Tone

(typically used in textbooks, reference material, sets of directions, instructional manuals, most newspaper and magazine articles, and other factual, objective material that is presented in a straightforward manner)

unemotional	involving little or no emotion or feeling
dispassionate	devoid or unaffected by passion, emotion, or bias
indifferent	appearing to have no preference or concern

Words That Describe a *Serious* Tone

(typically used in important formal announcements and obituaries, for example)

solemn	deeply earnest, serious, and sober
serious	grave, earnest, not trifling or jesting; deeply interested or involved
reserved	marked by self-restraint and reticence

Words That Describe an *Emotional* Tone

(typically found in personal articles, political writing, and some persuasive writing, such as editorials)

compassionate	showing kindness, mercy, or compassion; sympathetic
concerned	caring deeply about a person or issue
impassioned	characterized by passion or zeal
nostalgic	feeling bittersweet longing for things, persons, or situations in the past
sentimental	based on emotion rather than reason
remorseful	feeling regret
self-pitying	feeling sorry for oneself
urgent	calling for immediate attention; instantly important
defiant	intentionally contemptuous; resisting authority or force

Words That Describe a *Critical, Disapproving* Tone

(typically found in movie and book reviews, editorials, some magazine articles)

critical	inclined to criticize or find fault
disapproving	passing unfavorable judgment upon; condemning
pessimistic	expecting the worst; having a negative attitude or gloomy outlook
intolerant	not allowing a difference of opinion or sentiment
indignant	angered by something unjust, mean, or unworthy; irate

Words That Describe a *Humorous, Sarcastic, Ironic,* or *Satiric* Tone

(can appear in writing of many sorts, including literature and social criticism and some newspaper and magazine columns and articles)

lighthearted	not being burdened by trouble, worry, or care; happy and carefree
irreverent	disrespectful; critical of what is generally accepted or respected; showing a lack of reverence
cynical	scornful of the motives, virtue, or integrity of others; expressing scorn and bitter mockery
scornful	treating someone or something as despicable or unworthy; showing utter contempt
contemptuous	showing open disrespect or haughty disdain
mocking	treating with scorn or contempt
malicious	intended to cause harm or suffering; having wicked or mischievous intentions or motives
ironic	humorously sarcastic or mocking
sarcastic	characterized by the desire to show scorn or contempt
bitter	characterized by sharpness, severity, or cruelty
skeptical	reluctant to believe; doubting or questioning everything
disbelieving	not believing; refusing to believe

Words That Describe a *Supportive* Tone

(found in writing of many types, such as certain textbooks, inspirational writing, some magazine articles, and personal correspondence)

encouraging	showing support
supportive	showing support or assistance
enthusiastic	showing excitement
optimistic	expecting the best; having a positive outlook
approving	expressing approval or agreement
positive	being in favor of; supportive; optimistic
sympathetic	inclined to sympathy; showing pity
tolerant	showing respect for the rights or opinions or practices of others

Some *Other* Words That Can Describe Tone

authoritative	speaking in a definite and confident manner
ambivalent	having opposite feelings or attitudes at the same time
conciliatory	willing to give in on some matters
cautious	careful; not wanting to take chances; wary
arrogant	giving oneself an undue degree of importance; haughty
grim	gloomy; dismal; forbidding
humble	marked by meekness or modesty; not arrogant or prideful
apologetic	self-deprecating; humble; offering or expressing an apology or excuse

To be sure you understand an author's intended meaning, you must understand the author's tone. Ask yourself the questions critical readers ask: "What do the author's choice of words and style of writing reveal about his or her attitude toward the topic?" and "What is the author's *real* meaning?"

Here is an excerpt from an essay by George Will, a well-known political commentator and columnist. The topic of this excerpt is legal gambling (state lotteries and betting on the sport of jai alai). As you read, notice that his disapproving tone helps convey his negative point of view toward legal forms of gambling.

Each year Americans legally wager billions of dollars. Stiffening resistance to taxes is encouraging states to seek revenues from gambling, and thus to encourage gambling. There are three rationalizations for this:

- State-run gambling controls illegal gambling.
- Gambling is a painless way to raise revenues.
- Gambling is a "victimless" recreation, and thus is a matter of moral indifference.

Actually, there is evidence that legal gambling increases the respectability of gambling, and increases public interest in gambling. This creates new gamblers, some of whom move on to illegal gambling, which generally offers better odds. And as a revenue-raising device, gambling is severely regressive.

Gamblers are drawn disproportionately from minority and poor populations that can ill afford to gamble, that are especially susceptible to the lure of gambling, and that especially need a government that will not collaborate with gambling entrepreneurs, as in jai alai, and that will not become a gambling entrepreneur through a state lottery.

A depressing number of gamblers have no margin for economic losses and little understanding of the probability of losses. During the 1970s there was an enormous increase in spending to advertise lotteries—lotteries in which more than 99.9 percent of all

What is the author's point of view (bias)?

_____

_____

_____

What is the author's tone?

_____

_____

_____

players are losers. Such advertising is apt to be especially effective, and cruel, among people whose tribulations make them susceptible to dreams of sudden relief.

Grocery money is risked for such relief. Some grocers in Hartford's poorer neighborhoods report that receipts decline during jai alai season. Aside from the injury gamblers do to their dependents, there is a more subtle but more comprehensive injury done by gambling. It is the injury done to society's sense of elemental equities. Gambling blurs the distinction between well-earned and "ill-gotten" gains.

State-sanctioned gambling institutionalizes windfalls, whets the public appetite for them, and encourages the delusion that they are more frequent than they really are. Thus do states simultaneously cheat and corrupt their citizens.

Source: Adapted from George F. Will, "Lotteries Cheat, Corrupt the People," *The Washington Post.* Copyright © 1994, The Washington Post Writers' Group. Reprinted with permission.

This passage clearly shows George Will's point of view: *he opposes legal gambling* because he believes it cheats and corrupts citizens. His tone is *disapproving.* His disapproval of legal gambling is revealed by his deliberate choice of these words:

rationalizations (instead of *reasons*)
collaborating with (which suggests helping someone do something wrong)
the *lure* of gambling
a *depressing* number of gamblers
cruel
dreams of sudden relief (which probably will not happen)
injury
ill-gotten gains
encourages the *delusion*
cheat and corrupt their citizens

Stop and Annotate

Go back to the preceding excerpt. Determine the author's point of view and tone, and write your responses in the spaces provided.

In addition, George Will's style of writing conveys his tone and point of view. He appears extremely knowledgeable about his subject. He uses factual support and presents a convincing, well-reasoned argument against gambling. There is no intended meaning beyond what he has stated. His meaning is exactly as he presents it: states cheat and corrupt their citizens when they allow legal gambling.

In the passage below from a study skills textbook, the authors' tone is completely different. Its purpose is to define concentration and explain why it is a complex process. After you read this paragraph, ask yourself, "What is the authors' position on this issue?" and "What do the authors' choice of words and style of writing reveal about their attitude toward the topic?"

Psychologically defined, concentration is the process of centering one's attention over a period of time. In practical application, however, concentration is not as simple to cope with as the definition may imply. For this reason, it is important to keep the following points in mind:

- Your attention span varies.
- Your attention span is short.
- When you truly concentrate, you are paying attention to only one thing at a time.
- Distractors to concentration can be both physical and psychological.
- Emotions are the most powerful psychological distractors.

What is the authors' point of view (bias)?

_____

_____

_____

What is the authors' tone?

_____

_____

_____

Source: Adapted from William Farquar, John Krumboltz, and Gilbert Wrenn, "Controlling Your Concentration," in Frank Christ, ed., *SR/SE Resource Book,* Chicago: SRA, 1969, p. 119.

Stop and Annotate

Go back to the excerpt above. Determine the authors' point of view (bias) and tone, and write your responses in the spaces provided.

In this paragraph, the authors' tone is *unemotional and straightforward* rather than emotional and persuasive. The authors' point of view is that *concentration is not as simple a process as it might seem.* Since this is factual material presented in a straightforward manner, the authors' intended meaning is exactly what it appears to be.

Remember, part of reading critically involves asking yourself, "What is the author's position on this issue?" "What do the author's choice of words and style of writing reveal about his or her attitude toward the topic?" and "What is the author's *intended* meaning?"

It is obvious from the two examples above that an author's tone is related to his or her purpose for writing and his or her point of view: being aware of the author's tone will help you determine that purpose and point of view. The chart on page 491 shows the *interrelationship* among author's purpose, tone, point of view, intended meaning, and intended audience.

HOW THE CRITICAL READING SKILLS ARE INTERRELATED

The author's purpose causes him or her to use a certain tone to convey a point of view to an intended audience.

- *The author decides on a **purpose** (reason) for writing:*

    to inform   to instruct   to persuade   to entertain

    - *To accomplish this purpose, the author uses an appropriate **tone,** such as:*

serious	formal	sincere	enthusiastic
disapproving	sympathetic	informal	humorous
ironic	lighthearted	ambivalent	encouraging

        - *To convey his or her main idea or **point of view** (position on an issue):*

            expresses *support* for an issue or *opposition* to an issue

            - *To an **intended** audience:*

                the general public   a specific group   a particular person

The chart below illustrates the application of critical reading skills to a piece of writing, a make-believe movie critic's review of an imaginary movie. It is also designed to show that critical reading skills are related and that they can be applied to reading tasks that you encounter daily.

EXAMPLE OF CRITICAL READING APPLIED TO A CRITIC'S REVIEW OF A MOVIE

Here is an imaginary critic's review of *Cyberpunk*, a new science fiction movie:

Another movie from Extreme Studios has just been released, *Cyberpunk*. Is it worth seeing? That depends: Do you enjoy violence? Do you like vulgar language? Do you appreciate painfully loud sound effects? What about watching unknown actors embarrass themselves? Or sitting for three hours and ten minutes without a break? If so, and you've got $8.50 to burn, then *Cyberpunk* is the movie you must see!

Critical Reading Questions	Answers
What is the author's purpose?	To persuade readers to skip this movie
Who is the author's intended audience?	The moviegoing public
What is the author's point of view?	*Cyberpunk* is a terrible movie.*
What is the author's tone?	Sarcastic
What is the author's intended meaning?	Don't waste your money or your time on this movie. (*Not* "This is a movie you must see.")

*Notice that this is also the author's main idea or argument.

A WORD ABOUT STANDARDIZED READING TESTS: CRITICAL READING

Many college students are required to take standardized reading tests as part of an overall assessment program, in a reading course, or as part of a state-mandated basic skills test. A standardized reading test typically consists of a series of passages followed by multiple-choice reading skill application questions, to be completed within a specified time limit.

Here are some examples of typical wording about critical reading:

Questions about the author's purpose *may be worded:*

The author's purpose for writing this passage is to . . .

The reason the author wrote this passage is to . . .

It is likely that the author wrote this in order to . . .

The reason the author wrote this selection is primarily to . . .

The author wrote this passage in order to . . .

Questions about the author's intended audience *may be worded:*

The author intended this passage to be read by . . .

The author's intended audience is . . .

The author expects this passage to be read by . . .

Questions about the author's point of view *may be worded:*

The passage suggests that the author's point of view is . . .

The author's opinion about . . . is . . .

It is clear that the author believes that . . .

The passage suggests that the author's opinion about . . . is . . .

Questions about the author's tone *may be worded:*

The tone of this passage is . . .

The tone of this passage can be described as . . .

Which of the following words best describes the tone of this passage?

Questions about the author's intended meaning *may be worded:*

The author wants the reader to understand that . . .

The author's use of sarcasm suggests that . . .

The author's meaning is . . .

The author's use of irony indicates . . .

In this passage, the author intended the reader to understand that . . .

Although the author states that . . . , she means that . . .

Although the author appears to be supporting . . . , he actually wants the reader to . . .

DEVELOPING CHAPTER REVIEW CARDS

Student Online Learning Center (OLC)
Go to **Chapter 8.**
Select **Flashcards**
or **Chapter Test.**

Review cards, or *summary cards,* are an excellent study tool. They are a way to select, organize, and review the most important information in a textbook chapter. The process of creating review cards helps you organize information in a meaningful way and, at the same time, transfer it into long-term memory. The cards can also be used to prepare for tests (see Part Three). The review card activities in this book give you structured practice in creating these valuable study tools. Once you have learned how to make review cards, you can create them for textbook material in your other courses.

Now complete the five review cards for Chapter 8 by answering the questions or following the directions on each card. When you have completed them, you will have summarized (1) what critical reading is, (2) author's purpose, (3) author's intended audience, (4) author's point of view, and (5) author's tone and intended meaning. Use the type of handwriting that is clearest for you to reread (printing or cursive) and write legibly.

Critical Reading
Define *critical reading.*
List *and define* the skills of critical reading.
1.
2.
3.
4.
Card 1   Chapter 8: Reading Critically

Author's Purpose

Define the *author's purpose.*

List four common purposes for writing.

1.

2.

3.

4.

What are two ways to determine an author's purpose?

1.

2.

To determine an author's purpose, what question should you ask yourself?

Card 2 Chapter 8: Reading Critically

Author's Intended Audience

Define *intended audience.*

To determine an author's intended audience, what question should you ask yourself?

What are three things you can examine in order to determine the author's intended audience?

1.

2.

3.

Card 3 Chapter 8: Reading Critically

Author's Point of View

Define *point of view.*

Give some examples of words that reveal an author's point of view.

Define *author's bias.*

To determine an author's point of view, what question should you ask yourself?

Card 4   Chapter 8: Reading Critically

Author's Tone and Intended Meaning

Define *tone.*

What are two things you can examine in order to determine an author's tone?

1.

2.

To determine an author's tone, what question should you ask yourself?

Define *intended meaning.*

To determine an author's intended meaning, what question should you ask yourself?

Card 5   Chapter 8: Reading Critically

SELECTION **8-1**

Speech Communication

Think Before You Speak: Public Speaking in a Multicultural World
From *The Art of Public Speaking*
By Stephen Lucas

Prepare Yourself to Read

Directions: Do these exercises *before* you read Selection 8-1.

1. First, read and think about the title. What do you already know about public speaking?

_____

_____

_____

_____

_____

2. Next, complete your preview by reading the following:

Introduction (in *italics*)

Headings

All of the first paragraph (paragraph 1)

First sentence of each of the other paragraphs

The last paragraph (paragraph 30)

Now that you have previewed the selection, what aspects of public speaking does the selection seem to be about?

_____

_____

_____

_____

_____

_____

_____

_____

_____

Apply Comprehension Skills

Directions: Do the Annotation Practice Exercises *as* you read Selection 8-1.

Apply the critical reading skills presented in this chapter:

Determine the author's purpose. To identify an author's purpose, ask yourself, "Why did the author write this?"

Determine the author's intended audience. To identify an author's intended audience, ask yourself, "Who did the author intend to read this?"

Determine the author's point of view. To identify an author's point of view, ask yourself, "What is the author's position on this issue?"

Determine the author's tone. To identify an author's tone, ask yourself, "What do the author's choice of words and style of writing reveal about his or her attitude toward the topic?"

Determine the author's intended meaning. To identify an author's intended meaning, ask yourself, "What is the author's *real* meaning?"

THINK BEFORE YOU SPEAK: PUBLIC SPEAKING IN A MULTICULTURAL WORLD

This selection from a speech communication textbook explains how cultural diversity in our society affects the way we should communicate. Adjusting your delivery to the diversity and multiculturalism of your audience will play a role in almost any speech you give. Many—perhaps most—of the audiences you address will include people of different cultural backgrounds. The need for effective public speaking can affect you as a college student, a business person, a traveler, or a member of a civic, social, or religious organization. This selection gives you pointers on how to effectively address a diverse, multicultural audience.

Cultural Diversity in the Modern World

1   The United States has always been a diverse society. In 1673, more than three centuries ago, a visitor to what is now New York City was astonished to find that 18 languages were spoken among the city's 8,000 inhabitants. By the middle of the nineteenth century, so many people from so many lands had come to the United States that novelist Herman Melville exclaimed, "You cannot spill a drop of American blood without spilling the blood of the whole world."

2   One can only imagine what Melville would say today! The United States has become the most diverse society on the face of the earth. For more than a century, most immigrants to the United States were Europeans—Irish, Germans, English, Scandinavians, Greeks, Poles, Italians, and others. Together with African-Americans, they made America the "melting pot" of the world. Today another great wave of immigration—mostly from Asia and Latin America—is transforming the United States into what one writer has called "the first universal nation," a multicultural society of unmatched diversity.

3   The diversity of life in the United States can be seen in cities and towns, schools and businesses, community groups and houses of worship all across the land. Consider the following:

- There are 215 nations in the world, and every one of them has someone living in the United States.
- New York City has over 170 distinct ethnic communities.
- Houston has two radio stations that broadcast in Chinese and a daily newspaper that prints in Chinese.
- Nearly 61 percent of the people of Miami were born outside the United States.
- More than 32 million people in the United States speak a language other than English at home.
- Asian Americans make up 45 percent of first-year students at the University of California, Berkeley.

Annotation Practice Exercises

Directions: For each of the exercises below, read critically to answer the questions. This will help you gain additional insights as you read.

4   These kinds of changes are not limited to the United States. We are living in an age of international multiculturalism. The Internet allows for instant communication almost everywhere around the world. CNN is broadcast in more than 200 countries. International air travel has made national boundaries almost meaningless. The new global economy is redefining the nature of business and commerce. All nations, all people, all cultures are becoming part of a vast global village. For example:

- There are 60,000 transnational corporations around the world, and they account for more than a quarter of the world's economic output.
- Restaurants in coastal towns of Queensland, Australia, print their menus in both Japanese and English.
- McDonald's sells more hamburgers and French fries abroad than it does in the United States; Gillette makes 70 percent of its sales through exports.
- In Geneva, Switzerland, there are so many people from around the world that nearly 60 percent of the school population is non-Swiss.
- France has more Muslims than practicing Catholics; radio CHIN in Toronto, Canada, broadcasts in 32 languages.
- Four out of every five new jobs in the United States are generated as a direct result of international trade.

Cultural Diversity and Public Speaking

5   "That's all very interesting," you may be saying to yourself, "but what does it have to do with my speeches?" The answer is that diversity and multiculturalism are such basic facts of life that they can play a role in almost any speech you give. Consider the following situations:

- A business manager briefing employees of a multinational corporation.
- A lawyer presenting her closing argument to an ethnically mixed jury.
- A minister sermonizing to a culturally diverse congregation.
- An international student explaining the customs of his land to students at a U.S. university.
- A teacher addressing parents at a multiethnic urban school.

These are only a few of the countless speaking situations affected by the cultural diversity of modern life.

6   As experts in intercultural communication have long known, speech-making becomes more complex as cultural

Today, speakers should be prepared for the multicultural audiences they are likely to encounter.

diversity increases. Part of the complexity stems from the differences in language from culture to culture. But language and thought are closely linked. So, too, are language and culture. Nothing separates one culture from another more than language. Not only do words change from language to language, but so do ways of thinking and of seeing the world. Language and culture are so closely bound that we communicate the way we do because we are raised in a particular culture and learn its language, rules, and norms.

7   The meanings attached to gestures, facial expressions, and other nonverbal signals also vary from culture to culture. Even the gestures for such basic messages as "yes" and "no," "hello" and "goodbye" are culturally based. In the United States people nod their heads up and down to signal "yes" and shake them back and forth to signal "no." In Thailand the same actions have exactly the opposite meaning! To take another example, the North American "goodbye" wave is interpreted in many parts of Europe and South America as the motion for "no," while the Italian and Greek gesture for "goodbye" is the same as the U.S. signal for "come here."

8   Many stories have been told about the fate of public speakers who fail to take into account cultural differences between themselves and their audiences. Consider the following scenario:

9   The sales manager of a U.S. electronics firm is in Brazil to negotiate a large purchase of computers by a South American corporation. After three days of negotiations, the sales manager holds a gala reception for all the major executives to build goodwill between the companies.

10   As is the custom on such occasions, time is set aside during the reception for an exchange of toasts. When it is the sales manager's turn to speak, she praises the Brazilian firm for its many achievements and talks eloquently of her respect for its president and other executives. The words are perfect, and the sales manager can see her audience smiling in approval.

11   And then—disaster. As the sales manager closes her speech, she raises her hand and flashes the classic U.S. "OK" sign to signal her pleasure at the progress of the negotiations. Instantly the festive mood is replaced with stony silence; smiles turn to icy stares. The sales manager has given her Brazilian audience a gesture with roughly the same meaning as an extended middle finger in the United States.

12   The next day the Brazilian firm announces it will buy its computers from another company.

13   As this scenario illustrates, public speakers can ill afford to overlook their listeners' cultural values and customs. This is true whether you are speaking at home or abroad, in Atlanta or Rio de Janeiro, in a college classroom or at a meeting of community volunteers. Because of the increasing diversity of modern life, many—perhaps most—of the audiences you address will include people of different cultural backgrounds.

14   With that in mind, let us turn now to the importance of avoiding ethnocentrism. Ethnocentrism, which is explained below, often blocks communication between speakers and listeners of different cultural, racial, and ethnic backgrounds.

Avoiding Ethnocentrism

15   *Ethnocentrism* is the belief that our own group or culture—whatever it may be—is superior to all other groups or cultures. Because of ethnocentrism, we identify with our group or culture and see its values, beliefs, and customs as "right" or "natural"—in comparison to the values, beliefs, and customs of other groups or cultures, which we tend to think of as "wrong" or "unnatural."

16   Ethnocentrism is part of every culture. If you were born and raised in the United States, you may find it strange that most people in India regard the cow as a sacred animal and forgo using it as a source for food. On the other hand, if you were born and raised in India, you might well be shocked at the use of cows in the United States for food, clothing, and other consumer goods. If you are Christian, you most likely think of Sunday as the "normal" day of worship. But if you are Jewish, you probably regard Saturday as the "correct" Sabbath. And if you are Muslim, you doubtless see both Saturday and Sunday as unusual times for worship. For you, Friday is the "right" day.

Practice Exercise

What is the author's *purpose* in paragraphs 5–13?

_____

_____

_____

_____

_____

_____

_____

_____

_____

17   Ethnocentrism can play a positive role in creating group pride and loyalty. But it can also be a destructive force—especially when it leads to prejudice and hostility toward different racial, ethnic, or cultural groups. To be an effective public speaker in a multicultural world, you need to keep in mind that all people have their special beliefs and customs.

18   Avoiding ethnocentrism does not mean you must agree with the values and practices of all groups and cultures. At times you might try to convince people of different cultures to change their traditional ways of doing things—as speakers from the United Nations seek to persuade farmers in Africa to adopt more productive methods of agriculture, as Muslim parents in the United States urge public school officials to accommodate Muslim customs for children who adhere to Islam, or as delegates from the United States and Japan attempt to influence the other country's trade policies.

19   If such speakers are to be successful, however, they must show respect for the cultures of the people they address. They cannot assume that their cultural assumptions and practices will be shared—or even understood—by all members of their audience. They need to adapt their message to the cultural values and expectations of their listeners.

20   When you work on your speeches, keep in mind the growing diversity of life in the modern world and be alert to how cultural factors might affect the way listeners respond to your speeches. For classroom speeches, you can use audience-analysis questionnaires to learn about the backgrounds and opinions of your classmates in regard to specific speech topics. For speeches outside the classroom, the person who invites you to speak can usually provide information about the audience.

21   Once you know about any cultural factors that might affect the audience's response to your speech, you can work on adapting the speech to make it as effective and appropriate as possible. As you prepare the speech, try to put yourself in the place of your listeners and to hear your message through their ears. If there is a language difference between you and your audience, avoid any words or phrases that might cause misunderstanding. When researching the speech, keep an eye out for examples, comparisons, and other supporting materials that will relate to a wide range of listeners. Also consider using visual aids in your speech. They can be especially helpful in bridging a gap in language or cultural background.

22   When delivering your speech, be alert to feedback that might indicate the audience is having trouble grasping your ideas. If you see puzzled expressions on the faces of your listeners, restate your point to make sure it is understood. With some audiences, you can encourage feedback by asking, "Am I making myself clear?" or "Did I explain this point fully enough?"

23   If you pose such questions, however, be aware that listeners from different cultures may respond quite differently. Most Arabs, North Americans, and Europeans will give you fairly direct feedback if you ask for it. Listeners from Asian and Caribbean countries, on the other hand, may not respond, out of concern that doing so will show disrespect for the speaker.

24   Finally, we should note the importance of avoiding ethnocentrism when *listening* to speeches. Speech audiences have a responsibility to listen courteously and attentively. When you listen to a speaker from a different cultural background, be on guard against the temptation to judge that speaker on the basis of his or her appearance or manner of delivery. Too often we form opinions about people by the way they look or speak rather than by listening closely to what they say. No matter what the cultural background of the speaker, you should listen to her or him as attentively as you would want your audience to listen to you.

Some Final Thoughts

25   The need for effective public speaking will almost certainly touch you sometime in your life. When it does, you want to be ready. But even if you never give another speech in your life, you still have much to gain from studying public speaking. A speech class will give you training in researching topics, organizing your ideas, and presenting yourself skillfully. This training is invaluable for every type of communication.

26   There are many similarities between public speaking and daily conversation. The three major goals of public speaking—to inform, to persuade, to entertain—are also the three major goals of everyday conversation. In conversation, almost without thinking about it, you employ a wide range of skills. You tell a story for maximum impact. You adapt to feedback from your listener. These are among the most important skills you will need for public speaking.

27   Public speaking is also different from conversation. First, public speaking is more highly structured than conversation. It usually imposes strict time limitations on the speaker, and it requires more detailed preparation than does ordinary conversation. Second, public speaking requires more formal language. Listeners react negatively to speeches loaded with slang, jargon, and bad grammar. Third, public speaking demands a different method of delivery. Effective speakers adjust their voices to the larger audience and work at avoiding distracting physical mannerisms and verbal habits.

Practice Exercise

What is the author's *purpose* in paragraphs 15–23?

_____

_____

_____

_____

_____

Practice Exercise

What is the author's *purpose* in paragraph 24?

_____

_____

_____

_____

_____

28   One of the major concerns of students in any speech class is stage fright. Actually, most successful speakers are nervous before making a speech. A speech class will give you an opportunity to gain confidence and make your nervousness work for you rather than against you. You will take a big step toward overcoming stage fright if you think positively, prepare thoroughly, visualize yourself giving a successful speech, and think of your speech as communication rather than as performance in which you must do everything perfectly. Like other students over the years, you too can develop confidence in your speech-making abilities.

29   Besides building your confidence, a course in public speaking can help you develop your skills as a critical thinker. Critical thinking is the ability to perceive relationships among ideas. It can help you spot weaknesses in other people's reasoning and avoid them in your own. Critical thinking can make a difference in many areas of your life, from your schoolwork to your activities as a consumer to your responsibilities as a citizen.

30   Because of the growing diversity of modern life, many—perhaps most—of the audiences you address will include people of different cultural, racial, and ethnic backgrounds. When you work on your speeches, be alert to how such factors might affect the responses of your listeners and take steps to adapt your message accordingly. Above all, avoid the ethnocentric belief that your own culture or group—whatever it may be—is superior to every other culture or group. Also keep in mind the importance of avoiding ethnocentrism when listening to speeches. Accord every speaker the same courtesy and attentiveness you would want from your listeners.

Practice Exercise

Who is the author's *intended audience* for this selection?

_____

_____

_____

Practice Exercise

What is the author's *point of view* throughout this selection?

_____

_____

_____

_____

Practice Exercise

What is the author's *tone* throughout this selection?

_____

_____

_____

Source: Adapted from Stephen E. Lucas, *The Art of Public Speaking,* 8th ed., pp. 22–28. Copyright © 2004 by The McGraw-Hill Companies, Inc. Reprinted by permission of The McGraw-Hill Companies.

Reading Selection Quiz

This quiz has three parts. Your instructor may assign some or all of them.

Comprehension

Directions: Items 1–10 test your comprehension (understanding) of the material of this selection. These questions are the type a content area instructor (such as a speech communication professor) would ask on a test over this material. You should be able to answer these questions after studying this selection. For each comprehension question below, use information from the selection to determine the correct answer. Refer to the selection as you answer the questions. Write your answer in the space provided.

_____ **1.** How many people in the United States speak a language other than English at home?

 a. more than 32 million

 b. more than 170 million

 c. more than 215 million

 d. more than 320 million

_____ **2.** If current trends in the United States continue:

 a. immigration from Latin America and Asia will decline.

 b. immigration from Europe will increase.

 c. people of European descent will become a minority of U.S. citizens by 2050.

 d. America will become the "melting pot" of the world.

_____ **3.** International multiculturalism is on the rise as a result of:

 a. worldwide communication available via the Internet.

 b. the new global economy and the redefining of the nature of worldwide business and commerce.

 c. international air travel becoming more popular and more convenient.

 d. all of the above

_____ **4.** Ethnocentrism is the belief that:

 a. our own group's culture is different from all other groups' cultures.

 b. our own group or culture is superior to all other groups or cultures.

 c. cultural diversity is at the center of every society.

 d. ethnic groups are the most important part of our cultural heritage.

_____ **5.** Once you have learned about any cultural factors that might affect the audience's response to your speech, you should:

     a. work on adapting the speech to make it as effective and appropriate as possible.

     b. restate your point to make sure it is clear.

     c. agree with the values and practices of the audience.

     d. select a topic that will be understood by everyone in the audience.

_____ **6.** The goals of public speaking are:

     a. to build confidence and to conquer nervousness.

     b. to treat all audiences the same.

     c. to persuade, to inform, and to entertain.

     d. to create group pride and loyalty.

_____ **7.** One way that public speaking is different from everyday conversation is that you must:

     a. organize your ideas logically.

     b. use more formal language.

     c. tailor your message to your audience.

     d. adapt to feedback from your listeners.

_____ **8.** When giving a speech, you should remember that:

     a. your audience will very likely include people of different cultural backgrounds.

     b. audiences react well to informal communication and jargon.

     c. your audience will identify with only one particular group or culture.

     d. audiences expect you to maintain your composure.

_____ **9.** One way to help overcome nervousness when giving a speech is to:

     a. encourage feedback by asking, "Am I making myself clear?" or "Did I explain this point fully enough?"

     b. adapt your message to each person in the audience.

     c. think of your speech as communication rather than as a performance in which you must do everything perfectly.

     d. memorize as much of the speech as possible and rehearse the speech several times in private.

_____ **10.** To be successful, speakers must:

     a. adapt their message to the cultural values of their audience.

     b. show respect for the cultures of the people they address.

     c. not assume that their cultural practices will be understood by all members of their audience.

     d. all of the above

Vocabulary in Context

Directions: Items 11–20 test your ability to determine the meaning of a word by using context clues. *Context clues* are words in a sentence that allow the reader to deduce (reason out) the meaning of an unfamiliar word in that sentence. Context clues also enable the reader to determine which meaning the author intends when a word has more than one meaning. For each vocabulary item below, a sentence from the selection containing an important word (*italicized, like this*) is quoted first. Next, there is an additional sentence using the word in the same sense and providing another context clue. Use the context clues from *both* sentences to deduce the meaning of the italicized word. *Be sure the answer you choose makes sense in both sentences.* If you discover that you need to use a dictionary to confirm an answer choice, remember that the meaning you select must still fit the context of *both* sentences. Write your answer in the space provided.

Pronunciation Key: ă pat   ā pay   âr care   ä father   ĕ pet   ē be   ĭ pit
ī tie   îr **pier**   ŏ pot   ō toe   ô paw   oi **noise**   ou **out**   ŏŏ **took**
ōō **boot**   ŭ **cut**   yōō abuse   ûr **urge**   th **thin**   *th* **this**   hw **which**
zh vision   ə **about**   *Stress mark:* ′

---

11. Today another great wave of immigration—mostly from Asia and Latin America—is *transforming* the United States into what one writer has called "the first universal nation," a multicultural society of unmatched diversity.

Computer technology is *transforming* American businesses into high-tech, "networked" work environments.

transforming (trăns fôrm′ ĭng) means:
a. modernizing; renovating
b. changing the nature of; converting
c. forming improved environments
d. limiting the nature of; stifling

12. There are 60,000 *transnational* corporations around the world, and they account for more than a quarter of the world's economic output.

Worldwide, the governments of free countries are working to deal with the *transnational* effects of terror networks.

transnational (trănz năsh′ ə nəl) means:
a. within the boundaries of a single country
b. reaching beyond the boundaries of states within the United States
c. reaching beyond national boundaries
d. reaching across the boundaries of oceans

_____ **13.** All nations, all people, all cultures are becoming part of a *vast* global village.

Our thirteen-hour flight from Los Angeles to Sydney over the *vast* Pacific Ocean transported us from the North American continent to the Australian continent.

vast (văst) means:

a. having extensive variety; diverse

b. extremely long

c. complicated

d. very great in size or extent

_____ **14.** Four of every five new jobs in the United States are *generated* as a direct result of international trade.

The worldwide demand for cell phones has *generated* a new kind of retail store, the phone "boutique," where customers can buy, rent, or upgrade cell phones.

generated (jĕn′ ə rā təd) means:

a. brought into being; produced

b. forfeited; lost

c. ended; stopped

d. changed the shape of; transformed

_____ **15.** As experts in *intercultural* communication have long known, speech-making becomes more complex as cultural diversity increases.

Robert and Madhu have a truly *intercultural* marriage; he was born and reared in Canada, and she lived the first nineteen years of her life in India.

intercultural (ĭn tər kŭl′ chər əl) means:

a. complex

b. representing different cultures

c. a bond between two cultures

d. difficult to communicate or comprehend

_____ **16.** After three days of negotiations, the sales manager holds a gala reception for all the major executives to build *goodwill* between the companies.

Many of our city's restaurants and shops contribute financial support to youth athletic teams in order to promote *goodwill* throughout the community.

goodwill (good wĭl′) means:

a. a financial relationship; a contract

b. a cheerful willingness to help the less fortunate

c. a good relationship, as between a business enterprise with its customers

d. a negotiation between two parties for profit

_____ **17.** If you were born and raised in the United States, you may find it strange that most people in India regard the cow as a sacred animal and *forgo* using it as a source for food.

We ate so much during dinner that everyone at our table decided to *forgo* dessert.

forgo (fôr gō′) means:

a. to consume; eat

b. to choose not to do something

c. to feast on; devour

d. to give away or contribute something of value

_____ **18.** They cannot *assume* that their cultural assumptions and practices will be shared—or even understood—by all members of their audience.

Most people *assume* that the price of most of the things we buy will rise each year.

assume (ə soॊom′) means:

a. to take responsibility for; adopt

b. to take for granted; suppose

c. to understand; comprehend

d. to think; ponder

_____ **19.** They need to *adapt* their message to the cultural values and expectations of their listeners.

When a person moves from one city to another, it can often take several months to *adapt* to his or her new surroundings.

adapt (ə dăpt′) means:

a. to create

b. to match

c. to adjust

d. to change

_____ **20.** In conversation, almost without thinking about it, you employ a wide *range* of skills.

We had difficulty finding an apartment that was within our price *range*.

range (rānj) means:

a. a collection of useful skills

b. amount required for ownership; price

c. suitable style; preference

d. an amount of variation; variation within limits

Reading Skills Application

Directions: Items 21–25 test your ability to *apply* certain reading skills to information in this selection. These types of questions provide valuable practice for all students, especially those who must take standardized reading tests and state-mandated basic skills tests (such as the Florida CLAST Test and the Texas THEA Test). You may not have studied all of the skills at this point, so these items will serve as a helpful preview. The comprehension and critical reading skills in this section are presented in Chapters 4 through 9 of *Opening Doors;* vocabulary and figurative language skills are presented in Chapter 2. As you work through *Opening Doors,* you will practice and develop these skills. Write your answer for each question in the space provided.

_____ **21.** The information in paragraph 16 is organized using which of the following patterns?

a. list

b. sequence

c. comparison-contrast

d. cause-effect

_____ **22.** Which of the following represents a fact rather than an opinion?

a. The new global economy is redefining the nature of business and commerce.

b. All nations, all people, all cultures are becoming part of a vast global village.

c. Asian Americans make up 45 percent of first-year students at the University of California, Berkeley.

d. International air travel has made national boundaries almost meaningless.

_____ **23.** The author's purpose for including the story about the U.S. sales manager who spoke to a group of executives in Brazil is to:

a. inform readers about the cultural values and customs of Brazil.

b. instruct readers how to avoid ethnocentrism.

c. convince readers that an inappropriate gesture or remark to an audience with different cultural backgrounds can have a disastrous effect.

d. persuade readers not to take into account the cultural differences between themselves and their audiences.

_____ **24.** The author mentions the use of audience analysis questionnaires and contacting the person who has invited you to speak in order to:

a. suggest ways that you can learn about your audience's backgrounds, opinions, and cultural differences.

b. demonstrate the challenges of public speaking in today's world.

c. prove that diversity and multiculturalism are basic facts of life.

d. show that ethnocentrism is part of every culture.

_____ **25.** Which of the following best expresses the main idea of paragraph 2?

    a. Today a great wave of immigrants from Asia and Latin America is transforming the United States.

    b. For more than a century, most immigrants to the United States were Europeans.

    c. The United States is now the most diverse society in the world.

    d. African Americans and Europeans made America a "melting pot."

SELECTION **8-1**

Speech Communication

(Continued)

Collaboration Option

Respond in Writing

Directions: These essay-type exercises will help you bring your thoughts into the open. Refer to Selection 8-1 as needed to answer them.

Option for collaboration: Your instructor may direct you to work with other students on one or more of these items, or in other words, to work *collaboratively.* In that case, you should form groups of three or four students, as directed by your instructor, and work together to complete the exercises. After your group discusses an item and agrees on the answer, have a group member record it. Each member of your group should be able to explain all of your group's answers.

1. Describe at least three situations in which you have addressed a group of people who have had diverse, multicultural backgrounds. If you have not yet had this type of experience, describe at least three situations when you might have to address a diverse, multicultural group in the future.

    _____

    _____

    _____

    _____

    _____

2. List at least three ways that you can find out about your audience in order to prepare an appropriate speech.

    _____

    _____

    _____

    _____

    _____

    _____

3. **Overall main idea.** What is the overall main idea the author wants the reader to understand about public speaking in a multicultural world? Answer this question in one sentence. Be sure to include the topic (*public speaking in a multicultural world*) in your overall main idea sentence.

_____

_____

_____

_____

Internet Resources

Read More about This Topic on the World Wide Web

Directions: For further information about the topic of the selection, visit these websites:

www.news.wisc.edu/misc/speeches
This website lists the best 100 speeches of the twentieth century as determined by a survey of speech communication professors.

www.nsaspeaker.org
The website of the National Speakers Association describes the activities of thousands of people who earn their living as professional speakers.

dir.yahoo.com/Regional/Countries
Yahoo's Society and Culture website provides a good starting point for accessing links to websites dealing with countries and cultures around the world.

You can also use your favorite search engine such as Google, Yahoo!, or AltaVista (www.google.com, www.yahoo.com, www.altavista.com) to discover more about this topic. To locate additional information, type in combinations of keywords such as:

effective public speaking

or

public speaking diverse audiences

or

avoiding ethnocentrism

Keep in mind that whenever you go to *any* website, it is a good idea to evaluate the website and the information it contains. Ask yourself questions such as:

"Who sponsors this website?"

"Is the information contained in this website up-to-date?"

"What type of information is presented?"

"Is the information objective and complete?"

"How easy is it to use the features of this website?"

From *Having Our Say: The Delany Sisters' First 100 Years*

By Sarah Delany and Elizabeth Delany with Amy Hill Hearth

Prepare Yourself to Read

Directions: Do these exercises *before* you read Selection 8-2.

1. First, read *only* the title, the introduction, and the first three paragraphs of this autobiography.

   What comes to your mind when you read the title *Having Our Say: The Delany Sisters' First 100 Years?*

   _____

   _____

   _____

   _____

   _____

   _____

2. Do you personally know or have you met anyone who is 100 years (or more) of age? When you think of him or her, what comes to mind?

   _____

   _____

   _____

   _____

   _____

   _____

   _____

   _____

   _____

   _____

   _____

   _____

   _____

3. As you read the rest of the selection, keep in mind which sister is speaking.

SELECTION **8-2**

Literature
(Continued)

Apply Comprehension Skills

Directions: Do the Annotation Practice Exercises *as* you read Selection 8-2.

Apply the critical reading skills presented in this chapter:

Determine the author's purpose. To identify an author's purpose, ask yourself, "Why did the author write this?"

Determine the author's intended audience. To identify an author's intended audience, ask yourself, "Who did the author intend to read this?"

Determine the author's point of view. To identify an author's point of view, ask yourself, "What is the author's position on this issue?"

Determine the author's tone. To identify an author's tone, ask yourself, "What do the author's choice of words and style of writing reveal about his or her attitude toward the topic?"

Determine the author's intended meaning. To identify an author's intended meaning, ask yourself, "What is the author's *real* meaning?"

FROM *HAVING OUR SAY: THE DELANY SISTERS' FIRST HUNDRED YEARS*

What would it be like to live for more than 100 years? To be nearly half as old as the United States itself? Sarah ("Sadie") Delany was born in 1889; her sister Elizabeth ("Bessie") was born in 1891. Neither sister ever married, and the two lived together nearly all of their lives. Sadie Delany said that she and her sister probably know each other "better than any two human beings on this Earth." Their book, Having Our Say, *was published in 1993 and quickly went onto the* New York Times *best-seller list. In their book, they are described this way: "Sarah Delany and Dr. Elizabeth Delany were born in Raleigh, North Carolina, on the campus of St. Augustine's College. Their father, born into slavery, and freed by the Emancipation, was an administrator at the college and America's first elected black Episcopal bishop. Sarah received her bachelor's and master's degrees from Teachers College at Columbia University and was New York City's first appointed black home economics teacher on the high school level. Elizabeth received her degree in dentistry from Columbia University and was the second black woman licensed to practice dentistry in New York City. The sisters retired to Mount Vernon, New York." Bessie Delany died in 1996 at the age of 104. Sadie died in 1999 at the age of 109.*

1   Both more than one hundred years old, Sarah ("Sadie") Delany and her sister, Annie Elizabeth ("Bessie") Delany, are among the oldest living witnesses to American history. They are also the oldest surviving members of one of the nation's preeminent black families, which rose to prominence just one generation after the Civil War.

2   Few families have ever achieved so much so quickly. Henry Beard Delany, the sisters' father, was born into slavery but eventually became the first elected "Negro" bishop of the Episcopal Church, U.S.A. All ten of his children were college-educated professionals at a time when few Americans—black or white—ever went beyond high school.

3   The Delany creed centered on self-improvement through education, civic-mindedness, and ethical living, along with a strong belief in God. The family motto was, "Your job is to help somebody." According to Bessie and Sadie Delany, this code applied to anyone who needed help, regardless of color. Their accomplishments could not shield them from discrimination and the pain of racism, but they held themselves to high standards of fair-minded idealism.

Sadie

4   One thing I've noticed since I got this old is that I have started to dream in color. I'll remember that someone was wearing a red dress or a pink sweater, something like that. I also dream more than I used to, and when I wake up I feel tired. I'll say to Bessie, "I sure am tired this morning. I was teaching all night in my dreams!"

Annotation Practice Exercises

Directions: For each of the exercises below, read critically to answer the questions. This will help you gain additional insights as you read.

5   Bessie was always the big dreamer. She was always talking about what she dreamed the night before. She has this same dream over and over again, about a party she went to on Cotton Street in Raleigh, way back when. Nothing special happens; she just keeps dreaming she's there. In our dreams, we are always young.

6   Truth is, we both forget we're old. This happens all the time. I'll reach for something real quick, just like a young person. And realize my reflexes are not what they once were. It surprises me, but I can't complain. I still do what I want, pretty much.

7   These days, I am usually the first one awake in the morning. I wake up at six-thirty. And the first thing I do when I open my eyes is smile, and then I say, "Thank you, Lord, for another day!"

8   If I don't hear Bessie get up, I'll go into her room and wake her. Sometimes I have to knock on her headboard. And she opens her eyes and says, "Oh, Lord, another day?" I don't think Bessie would get up at all sometimes, if it weren't for me. She stays up late in her room and listens to these talk-radio shows, and she doesn't get enough sleep.

9   In the mornings, Monday through Friday, we do our yoga exercises. I started doing yoga exercises with Mama about forty years ago. Mama was starting to shrink up and get bent down, and I started exercising with her to straighten her up again. Only I didn't know at that time that what we were actually doing was "yoga." We just thought we were exercising.

10   I kept doing my yoga exercises, even after Mama died. Well, when Bessie turned eighty she decided that I looked better than her. So she decided she would start doing yoga, too. So we've been doing our exercises together ever since. We follow a yoga exercise program on the TV. Sometimes, Bessie cheats. I'll be doing an exercise and look over at her, and she's just lying there! She's a naughty old gal.

11   Exercise is very important. A lot of older people don't exercise at all. Another thing that is terribly important is diet. I keep up with the latest news about nutrition. About thirty years ago, Bessie and I started eating much more healthy foods. We don't eat that fatty Southern food very often. When we do, we feel like we can't move!

12   We eat as many as seven different vegetables a day. Plus lots of fresh fruits. And we take vitamin supplements: Vitamin A, B complex, C, D, E, and minerals, too, like zinc. And Bessie takes tyrosine when she's a little blue.

13   Every morning, after we do our yoga, we each take a clove of garlic, chop it up, and swallow it whole. If you swallow it all at once, there is no odor. We also take a teaspoon of cod liver oil. Bessie thinks it's disgusting, but one day I said,

Bessie and Sadie Delany at home in Mount Vernon, New York.

Practice Exercise

In paragraph 7, what is the author's (Sadie's) *point of view* about being alive?

_____

_____

_____

Practice Exercise

In paragraph 8, what is the author's (Sadie's) *point of view* regarding Bessie?

_____

_____

_____

"Now, dear little sister, if you want to keep up with me, you're going to have to start taking it, every day, and stop complainin'." And she's been good ever since.

14   As soon as we moved to our house in 1957, we began boiling the tap water we use for our drinking water. Folks keep telling us that it's not necessary, that the City of Mount Vernon purifies the water. But it's a habit and at our age, child, we're not about to change our routine.

15   These days, I do most of the cooking, and Bessie does the serving. We eat our big meal of the day at noon. In the evening, we usually have a milkshake for dinner, and then we go upstairs and watch "MacNeil/Lehrer" on the TV.

16   After that, we say our prayers. We say prayers in the morning and before we go to bed. It takes a long time to pray for everyone, because it's a very big family—we have fifteen nieces and nephews still living, plus all their children and grandchildren. We pray for each one, living and dead. The ones that Bessie doesn't approve of get extra prayers. Bessie can be very critical and she holds things against people forever. I always have to say to her, "Everybody has to be themselves, Bessie. Live and let live."

Bessie

17   I wonder what Mr. Miliam would think of his granddaughters living this long. Why, I suppose he'd get a kick out of it. I know he'd have lived longer if Grandma hadn't died and it broke his heart. Sometimes, you need a reason to keep living.

18   Tell you the truth, I wouldn't be here without sister Sadie. We are companions. But I'll tell you something else. Sadie has taken on this business of getting old like it's a big *project.* She has it all figured out, about diet and exercise. Sometimes, I just don't want to do it, but she is my big sister and I really don't want to disappoint her. Funny thing about Sadie is she rarely gets—what's the word?—depressed. She is an easygoing type of gal.

19   Now, honey, I get the blues sometimes. It's a shock to me, to be this old. Sometimes, when I realize I am 101 years old, it hits me right between the eyes. I say, "Oh Lord, how did this happen?" Turning one hundred was the worst birthday of my life. I wouldn't wish it on my worst enemy. Turning 101 was not so bad. Once you're past that century mark, it's just not as shocking.

20   There's a few things I have had to give up. I gave up driving a while back. I guess I was in my late eighties. That was terrible. Another thing I gave up on was cutting back my trees so we have a view of the New York City skyline to the south. Until I was ninety-eight years old, I would climb up on the ladder

---

Practice Exercise

What is the author's (Sadie's) *tone* in paragraph 14?

_____

_____

_____

Practice Exercise

In paragraph 19, what is the author's (Bessie's) *point of view* about growing old?

_____

_____

_____

_____

_____

and saw those tree branches off so we had a view. I could do it perfectly well; why pay somebody to do it? Then Sadie talked some sense into me, and I gave up doing it.

21   Some days I feel as old as Moses and other days I feel like a young girl. I tell you what: I have only a little bit of arthritis in my pinky finger, and my eyes aren't bad so I know I could still be practicing dentistry. Yes, I am sure I could still do it.

22   But it's hard being old, because you can't always do everything you want, exactly as *you* want it done. When you get old as we are, you have to struggle to hang onto your freedom, your independence. We have a lot of family and friends keeping an eye on us, but we try not to be dependent on any one person. We try to pay people, even relatives, for whatever they buy for us, and for gasoline for their car, things like that, so that we do not feel beholden to them.

23   Longevity runs in the family. I'm sure that's part of why we are still here. As a matter of fact, until recently there were still five of us, of the original ten children. Then, Hubert went to Glory on December 28, 1990, and Hap, a few weeks later, in February 1991. Laura, our dear baby sister, passed on in August 1993. That leaves just me and Sadie.

24   Now, when Hubert died, that really hurt. He was just shy of ninety years old. It never made a bit of difference to me that Hubert became an assistant United States attorney, a judge, and all that. He was still my little brother.

25   Same way with Hap. You know what? Even when he was ninety-five years old, Sadie and I still spoiled him. When he didn't like what they were cooking for dinner at his house, he would get up and leave the table and come over here and we'd fix him what he liked to eat.

26   Good ol' Hap knew he was going to Glory and he was content. He said, "I've had a good life. I've done everything I wanted to do. I think I've done right by people." We Delanys can usually say that when our time comes.

> **Practice Exercise**
>
> What is the author's (Bessie's) *intended meaning* when she says, "Hubert went to Glory?"
>
> _____

> **Practice Exercise**
>
> What is the authors' (the Delany sisters') *purpose* in telling their story?
>
> _____
> _____
> _____
> _____

> **Practice Exercise**
>
> Who is the *intended audience* of this selection?
>
> _____
> _____
> _____
> _____

Source: Sarah Delany and A. Elizabeth Delany with Amy Hill Hearth, *Having Our Say: The Delany Sisters' First 100 Years,* Kodansha America Inc., 1993, pp. 3, 5, 287–90, 296–98. Reprinted by permission of Kodansha America, Inc.

Literature
(Continued)

Reading Selection Quiz

This quiz has three parts. Your instructor may assign some or all of them.

Comprehension

Directions: Items 1–10 test your comprehension (understanding) of the material of this selection. These questions are the type a content area instructor (such as an English professor) would ask on a test over this material. You should be able to answer these questions after studying this selection. For each comprehension question below, use information from the selection to determine the correct answer. Refer to the selection as you answer each question. Write your answer in the space provided.

True or False

_____ **1.** The Delany sisters have similar outlooks on living and growing older.

_____ **2.** Bessie can be pessimistic at times.

_____ **3.** The Delany sisters attribute their longevity to hard work and luck.

_____ **4.** Sadie is more optimistic and easygoing than Bessie.

_____ **5.** The Delany sisters pray twice each day.

Multiple-Choice

_____ **6.** Bessie Delany believes that one reason for her longevity is:
  a. determination.
  b. genetics.
  c. independence.
  d. assistance from family members.

_____ **7.** Bessie Delany started doing yoga exercises when she was:
  a. a young girl.
  b. a teenager.
  c. in her forties.
  d. quite old.

_____ **8.** In addition to exercise and eating healthy foods, the Delany sisters also:
  a. take vitamin supplements.
  b. eat a clove of garlic every day.
  c. take a teaspoon of cod liver oil each day.
  d. all of the above

_____ 9. The reason the Delany sisters still boiled the tap water they used for drinking was that:

    a. it had simply become a habit.

    b. their city did not have a water purification system.

    c. it was cheaper than buying bottled water.

    d. all of the above

_____ 10. For Bessie Delany, one difficult part of old age was:

    a. fighting boredom.

    b. worrying about financial security.

    c. struggling to maintain independence.

    d. staying in contact with other family members.

SELECTION **8-2**

Literature
(Continued)

Vocabulary in Context

Directions: Items 11–20 test your ability to determine the meaning of a word by using context clues. *Context clues* are words in a sentence that allow the reader to deduce (reason out) the meaning of an unfamiliar word in that sentence. Context clues also enable the reader to determine which meaning the author intends when a word has more than one meaning. For each vocabulary item below, a sentence from the selection containing an important word (*italicized, like this*) is quoted first. Next, there is an additional sentence using the word in the same sense and providing another context clue. Use the context clues from *both* sentences to deduce the meaning of the italicized word. *Be sure the answer you choose makes sense in both sentences.* If you discover that you need to use a dictionary to confirm an answer choice, remember that the meaning you select must still fit the context of *both* sentences. Write your answer in the space provided.

Pronunciation Key: ă **pat**   ā **pay**   âr **care**   ä **father**   ĕ **pet**   ē **be**   ĭ **pit**
ī **tie**   îr **pier**   ŏ **pot**   ō **toe**   ô **paw**   oi **noise**   ou **out**   ŏŏ **took**
ōō **boot**   ŭ **cut**   yōō **abuse**   ûr **urge**   th **thin**   *th* **this**   hw **which**
zh **vision**   ə **about**   *Stress mark:* '

_____ 11. They are also the oldest surviving members of one of the nation's *preeminent* black families, which rose to prominence just one generation after the Civil War.

Pearl Buck, William Faulkner, John Steinbeck, Ernest Hemingway, and Saul Bellow are *preeminent* 20th-century American writers who have each won both the Pulitzer Prize and the Nobel Prize for literature.

preeminent (prē ĕm′ ə nənt) means:

a. possessing unusual academic skills

b. college-educated

c. unknown by the general public

d. outstanding; superior

_____ **12.** They are also the oldest surviving members of one of the nation's preeminent black families, which rose to *prominence* just one generation after the Civil War.

A former California governor, Earl Warren gained national *prominence* as Chief Justice of the Supreme Court and as the leader of a government commission that investigated the assassination of President John F. Kennedy.

prominence (prŏm′ ə nəns) means:

a. limited power or influence

b. vast wealth

c. being superior and widely known

d. great popularity

_____ **13.** The Delany *creed* centered on self-improvement through education, civic-mindedness, and ethical living, along with a strong belief in God.

Two important aspects of the architect Frank Lloyd Wright's innovative *creed* were uniting buildings with their surroundings and integrating technology into his structures.

creed (krēd) means:

a. slogan or motto

b. quotation whose source is unknown

c. selfishness and greed

d. system of beliefs, principles, or opinions

_____ **14.** The Delany creed centered on self-improvement through education, civic-mindedness, and *ethical* living, along with a strong belief in God.

Because of their honesty and integrity, George Washington and Abraham Lincoln are considered two of the most *ethical* men ever to serve as president of the United States.

ethical (ĕth′ ĭ kəl) means:

a. exceedingly popular

b. in accordance with other people's beliefs

c. plain; not fancy

d. in accordance with the accepted principles of right and wrong; moral

_____ **15.** Their accomplishments could not shield them from discrimination and the pain of racism, but they held themselves to high standards of fair-minded *idealism*.

The ruthlessness of the corporate world quickly destroyed the young employee's *idealism*.

idealism (ī dē′ ə lĭz əm) means:
a. pursuit of honorable or worthy principles or goals
b. enthusiasm; excitement
c. racial prejudice or bigotry
d. misguided beliefs

_____ **16.** We have a lot of family and friends keeping an eye on us, but we try not to be *dependent* on any one person.

If you have *dependent* children for whom you provide the primary financial support, you must indicate this when you file your income tax.

dependent (dĭ pĕn′ dənt) means:
a. unreasonable
b. grateful; appreciative
c. relying on or requiring the aid of another for support
d. dependable; reliable

_____ **17.** We try to pay people, even relatives, for whatever they buy for us, and for gasoline for their car, things like that, so that we do not feel *beholden* to them.

Because my wonderful parents helped pay for my college education, I will always be *beholden* to them.

beholden (bĭ hōl′ dən) means:
a. holding tightly to someone or something
b. owing something, such as gratitude, to another; indebted
c. feeling guilty; guilt-ridden
d. hostile

_____ **18.** *Longevity* runs in the family.

My 90-year-old grandmother attributes her *longevity* to a healthy lifestyle and positive attitude.

longevity (lŏn jĕv′ ĭ tē) means:
a. long life; great duration of life
b. being unusually tall
c. illness characterized by weakened muscles
d. addiction to harmful substances

_____   **19.** As a matter of fact, until recently, there were still five of us, of the *original* ten children.

Were you able to locate the *original* documents or only the later versions of them?

original (ə rĭj′ ə nəl) means:

a.   creative or unusual in nature

b.   new

c.   there at the beginning

d.   fresh

_____   **20.** Good ol' Hap knew he was going to Glory and he was *content.*

After serving twelve years as her company's chief executive, she was *content* to turn the role over to her capable vice president.

content (kən tĕnt′) means:

a.   full; complete

b.   dissatisfied

c.   angry; resistant

d.   willing; ready to accept

SELECTION **8-2**   *Reading Skills Application*

Literature
(Continued)

Directions: Items 21–25 test your ability to *apply* certain reading skills to information in this selection. These types of questions provide valuable practice for all students, especially those who must take standardized reading tests and state-mandated basic skills tests (such as the Florida CLAST Test and the Texas THEA Test). You may not have studied all of the skills at this point, so these items will serve as a helpful preview. The comprehension and critical reading skills in this section are presented in Chapters 4 through 9 of *Opening Doors;* vocabulary and figurative language skills are presented in Chapter 2. As you work through *Opening Doors,* you will practice and develop these skills. Write your answer for each question in the space provided.

_____   **21.** The main idea of paragraph 2 is best expressed by which of the following?

a.   The Delany family not only achieved much more than most other families, they did it quickly.

b.   Henry Beard Delany was a remarkable man to have produced such outstanding children.

c.   Few families have ever achieved so much so quickly.

d.   All ten children were college-educated professionals at a time when few Americans went beyond high school.

22. In paragraph 19, the author (Bessie) uses the phrase "hits me right between the eyes" to mean:

    a. insults her.

    b. makes her head ache.

    c. shocks her.

    d. impairs her vision.

23. The tone of the author (Sadie) in paragraph 10 is:

    a. playful.

    b. bitter.

    c. reproachful.

    d. respectful.

24. Which of the following represents a logical inference about the Delany sisters?

    a. Because of their devotion to each other, neither sister ever married.

    b. The sole reason for their long lives is that longevity runs in the family.

    c. They exemplified with their lives the family motto, "Your job is to help somebody."

    d. Because of their unusually high levels of education, neither sister ever experienced discrimination or the pain of racism.

25. Which of the following statements accurately describes Bessie's point of view with regard to growing old?

    a. She accepts it and is grateful for each day.

    b. Because of the problems associated with growing old, she is tired of living and has little interest in life.

    c. She is cheerful about it and actively seeks ways to improve her quality of life.

    d. She finds it difficult and frustrating, but Sadie's optimism and efforts help her keep going.

SELECTION **8-2**

Literature
(Continued)

Collaboration Option

Respond in Writing

Directions: Refer to Selection 8-2 as needed to answer the essay-type questions below.

Option for collaboration: Your instructor may direct you to work with other students on one or more of these items, or in other words, to work *collaboratively.* In that case, you should form groups of three or four students, as directed by your instructor, and work together to complete the exercises. After your group discusses an item and agrees on the answer, have a group member record it. Each member of your group should be able to explain all of your group's answers.

1. What was the most surprising or interesting thing you learned about either or both of the Delany sisters?

    _____

    _____

    _____

    _____

2. In what ways are Sadie and Bessie Delany alike? In what ways are they different?

    _____

    _____

    _____

    _____

    _____

3. Bessie states that "longevity runs in the family." In addition to heredity, what else do you think contributed to the Delanys' long lives?

    _____

    _____

    _____

    _____

    _____

    _____

    _____

4. Being educated made a significant difference in the Delanys' lives. How do you think *you* will look back on the time you spent in college? What difference do you think it might make in your life?

_____

_____

_____

_____

_____

_____

_____

_____

5. Assuming that you were able to maintain good health, what do you think would be some of the *best* things about being 100 years old?

_____

_____

_____

_____

_____

_____

6. **Overall main idea.** What is the overall main idea the author wants the reader to understand about the Delany sisters and their lives? Answer this question in one sentence. Be sure that your overall main idea sentence includes the topic (*the Delany sisters*) and tells the most important point about it.

_____

_____

_____

_____

_____

_____

Internet Resources

Read More about This Topic on the World Wide Web

Directions: For further information about the topic of the selection, visit this website:

www.havingoursay.com/History.htm
This website gives the chronology of the Delany family and presents information about both the book and the stage play about the Delany family members' lives.

You can also use your favorite search engine such as Google, Yahoo!, or AltaVista (www.google.com, www.yahoo.com, www.altavista.com) to discover more about this topic. To locate additional information, type in combinations of keywords such as:

Bessie Delany

or

Sadie Delany

or

Delany family

or

centenarians

Keep in mind that whenever you go to *any* website, it is a good idea to evaluate the website and the information it contains. Ask yourself questions such as:

"Who sponsors this website?"

"Is the information contained in this website up-to-date?"

"What type of information is presented?"

"Is the information objective and complete?"

"How easy is it to use the features of this website?"

SELECTION **8-3**

Literature

From *The Joy Luck Club*

By Amy Tan

Prepare Yourself to Read

Directions: Do these exercises *before* you read Selection 8-3.

1. First, read and think about the title. What kind of a club do you think the Joy Luck Club might be?

_____

_____

_____

_____

2. Next, complete your preview by reading the following:

Introduction (in *italics*)

All of the first and second paragraphs (paragraphs 1 and 2)

All of the last paragraph (paragraph 9)

On the basis of your preview, what does the selection now seem to be about?

_____

_____

_____

_____

Apply Comprehension Skills

Directions: Do the Annotation Practice Exercises *as* you read Selection 8-3.

Apply the critical reading skills presented in this chapter:

Determine the author's purpose. To identify an author's purpose, ask yourself, "Why did the author write this?"

Determine the author's intended audience. To identify an author's intended audience, ask yourself, "Who did the author intend to read this?"

Determine the author's point of view. To identify an author's point of view, ask yourself, "What is the author's position on this issue?"

Determine the author's tone. To identify an author's tone, ask yourself, "What do the author's choice of words and style of writing reveal about his or her attitude toward the topic?"

Determine the author's intended meaning. To identify an author's intended meaning, ask yourself, "What is the author's *real* meaning?"

531

THE JOY LUCK CLUB

In The Joy Luck Club, *the novelist Amy Tan tells the story of four Chinese women who have immigrated to the United States after the Second World War. In the novel, the narrator's mother starts a "club" with three other recent immigrant women. They meet once a week to play a game called mah jong, eat special Chinese foods, "say" stories, and keep each others' spirits up. In the selection below, the narrator's mother explains how she first created a "Joy Luck Club" many years ago in China during a time when conditions were awful and how it helped them have hope that things would get better.*

Amy Tan was born in California two and a half years after her own parents immigrated to the United States from China. The Joy Luck Club, *Tan's first novel, was an immediate best seller and a finalist for both the prestigious National Book Award and the National Book Critics Circle Award. Tan is also the author of three other novels,* The Kitchen God's Wife, The Hundred Secret Senses, *and* The Bonesetter's Daughter. *Her work is characterized by insight into family relationships and into the challenges facing those who come to a new country and their children. Her essays and fiction have been published in many well-known magazines.*

1   "My idea was to have a gathering of four women, one for each corner of my mah jong table. I knew which women I wanted to ask. They were all young like me, with wishful faces. One was an army officer's wife, like myself. Another was a girl with very fine manners from a rich family in Shanghai. She had escaped with only a little money. And there was a girl from Nanking who had the blackest hair I have ever seen. She came from a low-class family, but she was pretty and pleasant and had married well, to an old man who died and left her with a better life.

2   "Each week one of us would host a party to raise money and to raise our spirits. The hostess had to serve special *dyansyin* foods to bring good fortune of all kinds—dumplings shaped like silver money ingots, long rice noodles for long life, boiled peanuts for conceiving sons, and of course, many good-luck oranges for a plentiful, sweet life.

3   "What fine food we treated ourselves to with our meager allowances! We didn't notice that the dumplings were stuffed mostly with stringy squash and that the oranges were spotted with wormy holes. We ate sparingly, not as if we didn't have enough, but to protest how we could not eat another bite, we had already bloated ourselves from earlier in the day. We knew we had luxuries few people could afford. We were the lucky ones.

4   "After filling our stomachs, we would then fill a bowl with money and put it where everyone could see. Then we would sit down at the mah jong table. My table was from my family and was of a very fragrant red wood, not what you call rosewood, but *hong mu,* which is so fine there's no English word for it. The table had a very thick pad, so that when the mah

Annotation Practice Exercises

Directions: For each of the exercises below, read critically to answer the questions. This will help you gain additional insights as you read.

Practice Exercise

In paragraph 3, what is the author's *intended meaning* when she describes the food as "fine" and then mentions it was "stringy" and "wormy"?

_____

_____

_____

_____

_____

jong *pai* were spilled onto the table the only sound was of ivory tiles washing against one another.

5   "Once we started to play, nobody could speak, except to say 'Pung!' or 'Chr!' when taking a tile. We had to play with seriousness and think of nothing else but adding to our happiness through winning. But after sixteen rounds, we would again feast, this time to celebrate our good fortune. And then we would talk into the night until the morning, saying stories about good times in the past and good times yet to come.

6   "Oh, what good stories! Stories spilling out all over the place! We almost laughed to death. A rooster that ran into the house screeching on top of dinner bowls, the same bowls that held him quietly in pieces the next day! And one about a girl who wrote love letters for two friends who loved the same man. And a silly foreign lady who fainted on a toilet when firecrackers went off next to her.

7   "People thought we were wrong to serve banquets every week while many people in the city were starving, eating rats and, later, the garbage that the poorest rats used to feed on. Others thought we were possessed by demons—to celebrate when even within our own families we had lost generations, had lost homes and fortunes, and were separated, husband from wife, brother from sister, daughter from mother. Hnnnh! How could we laugh, people asked.

8   "It's not that we had no heart or eyes for pain. We were all afraid. We all had our miseries. But to despair was to wish back for something already lost. Or to prolong what was already unbearable. How much can you wish for a favorite warm coat that hangs in the closet of a house that burned down with your mother and father inside of it? How long can you see in your mind arms and legs hanging from telephone wires and starving dogs running down the streets with half-chewed hands dangling from their jaws? What was worse, we asked among ourselves, to sit and wait for our own deaths with proper somber faces? Or to choose our own happiness?

9   "So we decided to hold parties and pretend each week had become the new year. Each week we could forget past wrongs done to us. We weren't allowed to think a bad thought. We feasted, we laughed, we played games, lost and won, we told the best stories. And each week, we could hope to be lucky. That hope was our only joy. And that's how we came to call our little parties Joy Luck."

Award-winning writer Amy Tan, the author of *The Joy Luck Club*.

Practice Exercise

What is the author's *purpose* in writing this selection?

_____

_____

_____

Practice Exercise

Who is the author's (not the narrator's) *intended audience* in this selection?

_____

_____

_____

Practice Exercise

In paragraph 9, how does the author describe her mother's *point of view* about finding happiness in life in the United States?

_____

_____

_____

_____

Source: From Amy Tan, *The Joy Luck Club,* pp. 23–25. Copyright © 1989 by Amy Tan. Used by permission of G. P. Putnam's Sons, a division of Penguin Group (USA) Inc.

SELECTION **8-3**
Literature
(Continued)

Reading Selection Quiz

This quiz has three parts. Your instructor may assign some or all of them.

Comprehension

Student Online
Learning Center (OLC)
Go to Chapter 8.
Select Reading
Selection Quiz.

Directions: Items 1–10 test your comprehension (understanding) of the material of this selection. These questions are the type a content area instructor (such as an English professor) would ask on a test over this material. You should be able to answer these questions after studying this selection. For each comprehension question below, use information from the selection to determine the correct answer. Refer to the selection as you answer each question. Write your answer in the space provided.

True or False

_____ **1.** The Joy Luck Club got its name because hoping to be lucky was the only joy of the four women in the club.

_____ **2.** The four women in the club enjoyed telling stories and eating while they played mah jong.

_____ **3.** At meetings of the Joy Luck Club, *dyansyin* foods were served to remind the women of all their misfortunes.

Multiple-Choice

_____ **4.** There were four members of the Joy Luck Club because:
   a. that is how many people are needed to play mah jong.
   b. the speaker wanted one player for each corner of her mah jong table.
   c. the speaker only wanted to include her very best friends.
   d. several women refused to join the club.

_____ **5.** The hostess of the Joy Luck Club served all of the following except:
   a. dumplings.
   b. oranges.
   c. roast duck.
   d. long rice noodles.

_____ **6.** The speaker started the Joy Luck Club:
   a. to raise money for her family and the families of her friends.
   b. to be sure she and her friends could eat a nice meal at least once a week.
   c. to make the most of her new mah jong table.
   d. to provide herself and her friends with a distraction from the terrible conditions in which they lived.

_____ **7.** The members of the Joy Luck Club did all of the following except:

        a.   play mah jong.

        b.   sing traditional songs.

        c.   tell stories.

        d.   raise money.

_____ **8.** The speaker's mah jong table is made of:

        a.   glass.

        b.   ivory.

        c.   red wood.

        d.   marble.

_____ **9.** All of the Joy Luck Club members:

        a.   had great sadness in their lives in China.

        b.   learned to speak fluent English.

        c.   were elderly women when the club began.

        d.   came from upper-class families.

_____ **10.** The Joy Luck Club held its parties:

        a.   daily.

        b.   weekly.

        c.   monthly.

        d.   twice a year.

SELECTION **8-3**

Literature

(Continued)

Vocabulary in Context

Directions: Items 11–20 test your ability to determine the meaning of a word by using context clues. *Context clues* are words in a sentence that allow the reader to deduce (reason out) the meaning of an unfamiliar word in that sentence. Context clues also enable the reader to determine which meaning the author intends when a word has more than one meaning. For each vocabulary item below, a sentence from the selection containing an important word (*italicized, like this*) is quoted first. Next, there is an additional sentence using the word in the same sense and providing another context clue. Use the context clues from *both* sentences to deduce the meaning of the italicized word. *Be sure the answer you choose makes sense in both sentences.* If you discover that you need to use a dictionary to confirm an answer choice, remember that the meaning you select must still fit the context of *both* sentences. Write your answer in the space provided.

Pronunciation Key: ă **pat**   ā **pay**   âr **care**   ä **father**   ĕ **pet**   ē **be**   ĭ **pit**
ī **tie**   îr **pier**   ŏ **pot**   ō **toe**   ô **paw**   oi **noise**   ou **out**   ŏŏ **took**
ŏŏ **boot**   ŭ **cut**   yŏŏ **abuse**   ûr **urge**   th **thin**   *th* **this**   hw **which**
zh **vision**   ə **about**   *Stress mark:* ʹ

---

11. What fine food we treated ourselves to with our *meager* allowances!

In spite of a *meager* salary, John managed to save enough money to buy a car.

meager (mēʹ gər) means:

a. large or excessive

b. generous

c. increased

d. insufficient in quantity

12. We ate *sparingly,* not as if we didn't have enough, but to protest how we could not eat another bite, we had already bloated ourselves from earlier in the day.

During the drought, citizens were encouraged to use water *sparingly.*

sparingly (spârʹ ĭng lē) means:

a. with enthusiasm

b. often, but in small amounts

c. whenever possible

d. in small amounts

13. We ate sparingly, not as if we didn't have enough, but to protest how we could not eat another bite, we had already *bloated* ourselves from earlier in the day.

I wasn't used to eating such a large dinner, and afterwards, I felt so *bloated* that I had to loosen my belt.

bloated (blōtʹ əd) means:

a. made abnormally large

b. obliged to eat excessive amounts

c. starved

d. embarrassed

14. My table was from my family and was of a very *fragrant* red wood, not what you call rosewood, but hong mu, which is so fine there's no English word for it.

The corsage was beautiful, but it was a little too *fragrant,* and Sally found herself sneezing all evening.

fragrant (frā′ grənt) means:

a. moldy

b. having an odor

c. cracked or rotting

d. likely to decay

_____ **15.** But to *despair* was to wish back for something already lost.

Our team was behind by fifteen points in the fourth quarter, but the coach told us not to *despair.*

despair (dĭ spâr′) means:

a. to lose hope

b. to win

c. to quit

d. to try harder

_____ **16.** What was worse, we asked among ourselves, to sit and wait for our own deaths with proper *somber* faces? Or to choose our own happiness?

My younger brother looked particularly *somber* on the last day of his summer vacation.

somber (sŏm′ bər) means:

a. unlikely to change

b. excited

c. gloomy or depressed

d. pale

_____ **17.** People thought we were wrong to serve *banquets* every week while many people in the city were starving, eating rats and, later, the garbage that the poorest rats used to feed on.

It took my mother and grandmother three days to prepare the food for my sister's wedding *banquet.*

banquet (ban′ kwət) means:

a. an informal party with no host

b. any family gathering

c. a long and involved performance

d. an elaborate meal, often in honor of a person (or people)

_____ **18.** The hostess had to serve special *dyansyin* foods to bring good luck of all kinds—dumplings shaped like silver money *ingots,* long rice noodles for long life, boiled peanuts for conceiving sons, and of course, many goodluck oranges for a plentiful, sweet life.

When we toured the United States Mint in Philadelphia, we saw row after row of stacked silver *ingots* that would eventually be melted and used to make certain coins.

ingots (ĭng′ gəts) means:
a. metal that is cast into bars for storage or shipment
b. flat, irregular-shaped blocks
c. ancient coins
d. molds used to shape metal

_____ **19.** The hostess had to serve special *dyansyin* foods to bring good luck of all kinds—dumplings shaped like silver money ingots, long rice noodles for long life, boiled peanuts for conceiving sons, and of course, many goodluck oranges for a *plentiful,* sweet life.

The survivors of the shipwreck did not starve on the island because of the *plentiful* coconuts and tropical fruits.

plentiful (plĕn′ tĭ fəl) means:
a. lucky; filled with good fortune
b. fully as much as one needs or desires
c. excessive
d. easy to obtain

_____ **20.** We *feasted,* we laughed, we played games, lost and won, we told the best stories.

At the dinner following the wedding ceremony, guests *feasted* on chicken cordon bleu, asparagus in hollandaise sauce, chocolate mousse, and champagne.

feasted (fēs′ təd) means:
a. heartily ate a large, elaborately prepared meal
b. prepared a large, elaborate meal
c. delighted in
d. greedily gulped down a large meal

SELECTION **8-3** *Reading Skills Application*

Literature
(Continued)

Directions: Items 21–25 test your ability to *apply* certain reading skills to information in this selection. These types of questions provide valuable practice for all students, especially those who must take standardized reading tests and state-mandated basic skills tests (such as the Florida CLAST Test and the Texas THEA Test). You may not have studied all of the skills at this point, so these items will serve as a helpful preview. The comprehension and critical reading skills in this section are presented in Chapters 4 through 9 of *Opening Doors;* vocabulary and figurative language skills are presented in Chapter 2. As you work through *Opening Doors,* you will practice and develop these skills. Write your answer for each question in the space provided.

_____ **21.** Which is the meaning of the word *washing* as it is used in paragraph 4 of the selection?

    a. leaning

    b. scrubbing

    c. breaking

    d. bumping gently

_____ **22.** Which of the following best expresses the main idea of the first paragraph?

    a. My idea was to have a gathering of our women, one for each corner of my mah jong table.

    b. I knew which women I wanted to ask.

    c. They were all young like me, with wishful faces.

    d. One was an army officer's wife, like myself.

_____ **23.** Which pattern has been used to organize the information in paragraph 4?

    a. problem-solution

    b. comparison-contrast

    c. sequence

    d. cause-effect

_____ **24.** From information in the selection, it can be inferred that members of the Joy Luck Club

    a. helped each other get through a difficult time of war and poverty.

    b. planned to disband the club after a few months.

    c. vowed to immigrate to the United States as soon as possible.

    d. encouraged other Chinese women to start Joy Luck Clubs of their own.

_____ **25.** According to information in the selection,

    a. one member of the Joy Luck Club was married to an army officer.

    b. two members of the Joy Luck Club were married to army officers.

    c. three members of the Joy Luck Club were married to army officers.

    d. all of the members of the Joy Luck Club were married to army officers.

Respond in Writing

Directions: Refer to Selection 8-3 as needed to answer the essay-type questions below.

Collaboration Option

Option for collaboration: Your instructor may direct you to work with other students on one or more of these items, or in other words, to work *collaboratively.* In that case, you should form groups of three or four students, as directed by your instructor, and work together to complete the exercises. After your group discusses an item and agrees on the answer, have a group member record it. Each member of your group should be able to explain all of your group's answers.

1. People of all ages join clubs. Children often form neighborhood clubs or join church groups, athletic clubs, or organizations such as Boy Scouts and Girl Scouts. Teenagers often join organizations at their schools; some join gangs. College students join school clubs and social organizations such as fraternities and sororities. Adults belong to many kinds of clubs and organizations, such as country clubs, hobby clubs, and civic groups such as the Lions Club or Rotary Club. Why is it people are drawn to join clubs? List at least three reasons people are inclined to join clubs and organizations.

   _____

   _____

   _____

   _____

2. There can be disadvantages to joining clubs and organizations. List at least three negative aspects of joining or belonging to a club.

   _____

   _____

   _____

   _____

   _____

   _____

   _____

   _____

   _____

3. What clubs and organizations have you been a member of or do you currently belong to? Have you belonged to any of them for a long time? Have your experiences been positive? If so, why? If not, why not?

_____

_____

_____

_____

_____

_____

_____

_____

4. In this selection the narrator's mother recounts to her daughter the story of how she created the Joy Luck Club. Describe briefly a story that one of your parents or grandparents told you about an important event in his or her early life (or his or her life before you were born).

_____

_____

_____

_____

_____

_____

5. **Overall main idea.** What is the overall main idea the author wants the reader to understand about her mother's creating the Joy Luck Club? Answer this question in one sentence. Be sure that your overall main idea sentence includes the topic (*the Joy Luck Club*) and tells the most important point about it.

_____

_____

_____

_____

_____

_____

Internet Resources

Read More about This Topic on the World Wide Web

Directions: For further information about the topic of the selection, visit this website:

www.luminarium.org/contemporary/amytan
Contains links to bibliographical information, interviews, essays, reviews, synopses, excerpts from Tan's writings, and more. Interestingly, this page was created by someone who is "just a fan" of Amy Tan's work.

You can also use your favorite search engine such as Google, Yahoo!, or Alta-Vista (www.google.com, www.yahoo.com, www.altavista.com) to discover more about this topic. To locate additional information, type in combinations of key-words such as:

Amy Tan

or

Joy Luck Club

or

Asian American culture

or

mah jong

or

dyansyin

Keep in mind that whenever you go to *any* website, it is a good idea to evaluate the website and the information it contains. Ask yourself questions such as:

"Who sponsors this website?"
"Is the information contained in this website up-to-date?"
"What type of information is presented?"
"Is the information objective and complete?"
"How easy is it to use the features of this website?"

CHAPTER 9

Thinking Critically

In this chapter you will learn the answers to these questions:

- What is critical thinking?

- How can I distinguish between facts and opinions?

- How can I make inferences and draw logical conclusions?

- What is the difference between deductive and inductive reasoning?

- How can I evaluate an author's argument?

- What are propaganda devices?

SKILLS

What Is Critical Thinking and Why Is It Important?

Critical Thinking Skills

- Why Readers Fail to Think Critically
- Distinguishing Facts from Opinions and Determining Whether Opinions Are Well Supported
- Making Inferences and Drawing Logical Conclusions
- Distinguishing between Deductive and Inductive Reasoning
- Evaluating an Author's Argument
- Identifying Propaganda Devices

A Word about Standardized Reading Tests: Critical Thinking

CREATING YOUR SUMMARY

Developing Chapter Review Cards

READINGS

Selection 9-1   *(Government)*
"Poverty in America and Improving Social Welfare
through Public Education"
from *The American Democracy*
by Thomas E. Patterson

Selection 9-2   *(Editorial)*
"Sport Utility Vehicles: How Do I Hate Thee?
Let Me Count the Ways"
from *The Washington Post*
by Geneva Overholser

Selection 9-3   *(Magazine Article)*
"Take Out the Trash, and Put It . . . Where?"
from *Parade Magazine*
by Bernard Gavzer

People see only what they are prepared to see.

Ralph Waldo Emerson

It is not enough to have a good mind. The main thing is to use it well.

René Descartes

WHAT IS CRITICAL THINKING, AND WHY IS IT IMPORTANT?

KEY TERM

critical thinking

Thinking in an organized way about material you have read in order to evaluate it accurately.

Critical thinking is also referred to as *critical reasoning* or *critical analysis*.

Student Online Learning Center (OLC)
Go to **Chapter 9.**
Select **Video.**

Critical thinking means thinking in an organized way about material that you have read in order to evaluate it accurately. Before you can think critically about material that you have read, you must first understand the main idea, the supporting details, and the pattern of organization. Only when you understand this basic information are you ready to think critically about what you have read.

You may be wondering why it is necessary to think critically rather than just accept the author's information and leave it at that. After all, thinking critically about information you have read can, quite frankly, be hard work. However, the consequences of *not* thinking critically and of *not* evaluating ideas for yourself can be costly. Failing to think critically can result, for example, in your choosing a college major that does not really suit you, accepting a job that you are ill-suited for, signing a contract or credit agreement you do not fully understand, making the wrong decision as a member of a jury, being misled or defrauded, supporting a cause that later turns out to be an embarrassment, and even marrying the wrong person! Most professors would agree that learning to think critically, along with learning how to learn, is one of the most important skills any college student can acquire.

Rather than accept everything you read as true, you should question it to see if it stands up to the test of critical thinking: thinking critically can help you avoid the kinds of problems mentioned above and other painful, unpleasant experiences. Moreover, thinking critically will not only help you when you read, but it will also help you when you write. This is because reading and writing are both forms of the thinking process. To improve the quality of your reading and writing, you must improve the quality of your *thinking*. Although thinking critically may seem difficult at times, it simply means applying certain reading and thinking skills in a systematic, thorough fashion. In other words, critical thinking means consistently asking certain additional questions and applying logic when you read.

CRITICAL THINKING SKILLS

You must apply these three skills in a systematic, careful manner in order to think critically when you read:

- Distinguishing facts from opinions, and determining how well supported the opinions are.
- Making inferences and drawing logical conclusions.
- Evaluating an author's argument accurately.

545

Thinking critically involves thinking in an organized way about material you have read in order to evaluate it accurately.

In this chapter, each of these three important skills will be explained and demonstrated. These skills can also be applied to things you hear, but our focus in this chapter is on applying them to material that you read.

Why Readers Fail to Think Critically

If critical thinking simply means applying thinking skills in a systematic, careful manner, why do people not do it more often when they read? Actually, besides mental laziness, there are at least five reasons:

1. **We let "experts" and "authorities" do our thinking for us.** Rather than think through a complex issue, we just accept the information or judgment of someone or something we perceive as an authority. This might be a parent or other relative; a college adviser; a doctor or therapist; a minister, priest, or rabbi. We may accept the beliefs or positions of a political entity (such as a political party or the government itself) or the beliefs and rules of a religious or social institution without thinking critically about them. (This is not to say that all experts and authorities are wrong, only that you should think through what they have written or said, rather than accepting their words without question.) For example, you might be tempted to accept the advice of a favorite uncle who is a highly successful real estate agent that you should also become a real estate agent—even though you may prefer to work by yourself at a computer rather than sell to the public.

2. **We want things to be different from the way they are.** In other words, we deny reality and refuse to see what is really there. Denial is based on emotion, not on reason. Perhaps a person you have just begun dating is attractive, yet has a serious drinking problem. But because you like dating someone who is so attractive, you ignore obvious facts and deny to yourself that the person is an alcoholic. Or, for example, you are not making any systematic effort to save money each month, yet you are hoping that you will somehow have enough money by the time you graduate to pay for a new car and a trip to Europe.

3. **We mentally put things into one of two mutually exclusive categories.** This means that we mistakenly view things as "either-or." Another way of putting this is "seeing everything as either black or white." Needless to say, very few things in life are simple enough to fall into one of only two categories. Thinking of everything in terms of good or bad, beautiful or ugly, fair or unfair, generous or selfish, conservative or liberal, immature or mature, and so forth, prevents us from thinking critically about issues.

4. **We view things too much in light of our culture and our experience.** We are all ethnocentric, which can cause us to accept that whatever our cultural group believes or does is the proper way. Whether it is encouraging large or small families, eating with a fork or chopsticks or one's fingers, or celebrating events and holidays in certain ways, we consider anything different from what we do to be odd or even wrong. Viewing things only in light of our culture and past experience prevents us from looking at new ideas and considering them objectively. With regard to personal experience, for example, someone who had a happy experience being a stepchild would have a very different view of stepparents from someone who had an unhappy experience as a stepchild.

5. **We stereotype and label.** The world can be overwhelming and confusing. One way we try to make sense of it is to put things and people into categories. While this is helpful, it also has some negative effects. It prevents us from seeing situations and individuals as unique because we assume things about them that may not be true. For example, on the first day of the semester, suppose you notice a classmate who is very physically fit and is wearing a baseball cap. You might be inclined to make an automatic judgment (stereotype) about him and what he is like as a person: that he is a "jock" (or even a "dumb jock"). Consequently, you decide he is not worth taking the time to get to know. Perhaps he is a straight-A student who has a full academic scholarship, and whose goal is to become a dentist. You will never know unless you think critically enough to question your assumptions and the stereotypes you hold.

Which of these reasons prevent you from thinking critically when you read? (Think critically about this! You may find it helpful to mark the items in the preceding list that pertain to you.) Becoming aware of these tendencies in yourself is essential in order for you to think critically. Let's look now at three critical thinking skills.

Distinguishing Facts from Opinions and Determining Whether Opinions Are Well Supported

Many students mistakenly believe that anything that appears in print, especially in textbooks, must be a fact. Although most college textbooks do consist primarily of facts, textbooks typically include many useful and valuable opinions as well.

What is the difference between a fact and an opinion? A **fact** is something that can be proved to exist or to have happened. An example would be: *In 1620 the Pilgrims landed in what is now Plymouth, Massachusetts.* In addition, a fact can be something that is generally assumed to exist or to have happened. An example would be: *Thousands of years ago, early people migrated from Asia to the North American continent*

KEY TERM
fact

Something that can be proved to exist or to have happened.

by walking from Siberia to Alaska across the frozen Bering Strait. The process of proving that something is a fact (that it is true) is called *verification.* Verification requires experimentation and research or direct experience and observation.

An **opinion,** on the other hand, is a judgment or belief that cannot be proved or disproved. When information in a statement cannot be proved to be either factual or false, it represents an opinion. It is important to realize, however, that not all opinions are equally valuable. Although opinions cannot be proved, they are valuable when they are supported by valid reasons and plausible evidence. Therefore, well-supported opinions are useful, since they are based on facts or on the ideas of knowledgeable people. Opinions in textbooks typically represent this type of valuable opinion, since they are the well-reasoned beliefs of the author or other experts. Scientific theories are also examples of "expert opinions." (If a theory could be proved, then it would no longer be a theory, of course. It would become a fact.) Needless to say, poorly supported or unsupported opinions are not useful.

Students sometimes mistake incorrect information for an opinion because they assume if something is not a fact, it must automatically be an opinion. However, information can be one of three things: it can be a fact (it is correct information); it can be an opinion (it represents someone's belief); or it can be a *false statement of fact* (it is simply incorrect information). *January follows February* and *Water freezes at 212°F* are examples of false statements of fact. Since they can be *proved incorrect,* they are not opinions.

How can you tell when you are reading an opinion rather than a fact? Because opinions represent judgments, beliefs, or interpretations, authors often use certain words or phrases to indicate that they are presenting an opinion. The following words and phrases are typical of those that signal an opinion:

perhaps	many experts believe
apparently	many people think that
presumably	it seems likely
one possibility is	this suggests
one interpretation is	in our view
in our opinion	in the opinion of

In addition, words that indicate value judgments can signal opinions. These include descriptive words such as:

better	interesting
more	outdated
less	beautiful
safer	wealthy
most	incompetent
greatest	successful
worst	irresponsible
best	dangerous
excellent	fascinating
harmful	effective

KEY TERM
opinion

Something that cannot be proved or disproved; a judgment or a belief.

These words signal opinions because people will often disagree about what is considered "successful," "fascinating," etc. For example, in the sentence *Adults must have a college degree in order to be successful,* the word *successful* could mean successful financially, personally, socially, or in all these ways. Because there are different interpretations of what *successful* means, it would be impossible to prove a statement like this (although it could be supported with certain facts about college graduates). Consequently, the statement expresses an opinion. (Even though this may be a widely held opinion, it is still an opinion.) As you read, then, watch for value judgment—words that can be interpreted in different ways by different people.

Critical readers ask themselves, "Can the information the author presents be proved, or does it represent a judgment?" When an author includes opinions, it is important for you to evaluate them, because not all opinions are valid or useful. An opinion is of little value if it is poorly supported (that is, if the author does not give good reasons for it). A well-supported opinion, on the other hand, can be as important and as useful as a fact. To repeat: Even though opinions cannot be proved, they are valuable when supported by facts and other well-reasoned opinions; poorly supported opinions are of little value, even if the author writes persuasively. For example, consider the following two sets of support for this statement: *Anna Garcia has excellent qualifications for serving as governor.* (This statement is an opinion, of course, because of the use of the word *excellent.*) Note how both facts and opinions are used to support the statement. Also, note the important difference between the quality of the two sets of facts and opinions given as support for the statement.

> *Opinion:* Anna Garcia has excellent qualifications for serving as governor.

Well-reasoned support:

> She has a law degree from Harvard. (fact)
> She was chief legal counsel of a *Fortune* 500 company for six years. (fact)
> She served 12 years as a state senator. (fact)
> She is extremely ethical. (opinion)
> She is strongly committed to family values. (opinion)
> She is an effective problem-solver. (opinion)

Poor support:

> Her father served as an ambassador. (fact)
> Her brother is a millionaire. (fact)
> She has been married to the same man for 20 years. (fact)
> She has smart, beautiful children. (opinion)
> She is attractive. (opinion)
> She comes across well on TV. (opinion)

A critical reader would be much more likely to accept the opinion that "Anna Garcia has excellent qualifications for serving as governor" if it were supported with good reasons (the first set of support) rather than with poor reasons (the second set). Critical readers know that support is convincing if it consists of relevant facts and well-reasoned opinions. Don't discount a statement simply because it is an opinion or is supported with other opinions. They may all be valuable, pertinent opinions.

Comprehension Monitoring Question for Thinking Critically to Evaluate Whether Statements Are Facts or Opinions

Can the information the author presents be proved, or does it represent a judgment?

Student Online Learning Center (OLC) *Go to* **Chapter 9.** *Select* **Video.**

The flowchart below summarizes the process for determining whether statements are facts, false statements of fact, or opinions. Use this process to distinguish between facts, false statements of fact, well-supported opinions (which are valuable), and unsupported or poorly supported opinions (which are of no value).

DETERMINING WHETHER A STATEMENT REPRESENTS A FACT, A FALSE STATEMENT OF FACT, OR AN OPINION

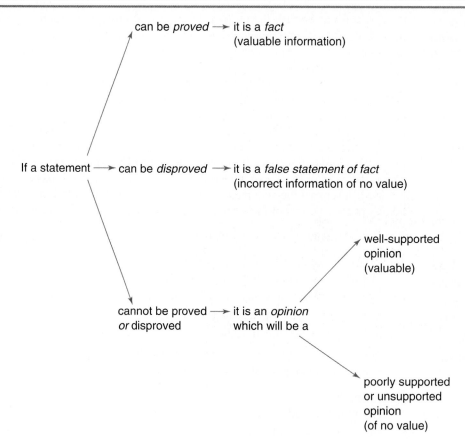

To distinguish between facts and opinions by thinking critically, ask yourself these questions in this order:

1. *Can the information in the statement be proved?*
If so, it is a fact (correct information).

2. *Can the information in the statement be disproved?*
If so, it is a false statement of fact (incorrect information).

3. *Is the information in the statement something that cannot be proved or disproved?*
If so, it is an opinion.

When the statement is an opinion, ask yourself these additional questions:

- *Is the opinion well-supported?* (That is, is it based on valid reasons and plausible evidence?)
If so, it is a valuable opinion.

- *Is the opinion poorly supported or unsupported?*
If so, it is of little or no value.

Following are two excerpts from *The Autobiography of Malcolm X* (Selection 1-3, "Saved"). The first contains *facts* that can be verified about the prison in which Malcolm X served time.

The Norfolk Prison Colony's library was in the school building. A variety of classes was taught there by instructors who came from such places as Harvard and Boston universities. The weekly debates between inmate teams were also held in the school building.

List the facts in this excerpt.

_____

_____

_____

_____

_____

Source: From Malcolm X and Alex Haley, *The Autobiography of Malcolm X,* p. 173. Copyright © 1964 by Alex Haley and Malcolm X. Copyright © 1965 by Alex Haley and Betty Shabazz. Used by permission of Random House, Inc.

Stop and Annotate

Go back to the excerpt above. In the space provided, list on separate lines the facts contained in the excerpt.

Notice that this passage contains information that can be verified by objective proof: the location of the prison library, some of the universities the instructors came from, and that weekly debates were held in the school building.

In the next passage, Malcolm X states his *opinions* about the new vistas that reading opened to him:

Reading had changed forever the course of my life. The ability to read awoke inside me some long dormant craving to be mentally alive.

List the opinions in this excerpt.

_____

_____

_____

_____

_____

Source: From Malcolm X and Alex Haley, *The Autobiography of Malcolm X,* p. 179. Copyright © 1964 by Alex Haley and Malcolm X. Copyright © 1965 by Alex Haley and Betty Shabazz. Used by permission of Random House, Inc.

Stop and Annotate

Go back to the excerpt above. In the space provided, list on separate lines the opinions contained in the excerpt.

Malcolm X's opinions are that reading changed the course of his life forever and that it awoke in him a craving to be mentally alive. These are statements that reflect Malcolm X's judgment about reading; they cannot be proved or disproved.

The next excerpt, from an American government textbook, discusses how historians and political scientists rank the first 39 presidents of the United States. The excerpt includes four lists that summarize the results of several surveys. As this passage shows, experts often agree in their opinions. When such agreement exists, the opinions are especially valuable.

Scholars Rank the Presidents

Several surveys have asked American historians and political scientists to rank the presidents from best to worst. Although some presidential reputations rise or fall with the passage of time, there has been remarkable consistency in whom the scholars rank as the best and worst presidents. The consistency of these results suggests that scholars use some unspoken criteria when assessing the presidents. At least four criteria stand out: the effectiveness of presidential policy, the president's vision of the office, the president's handling of crises, and the president's personality.

In three surveys conducted in the 1980s, scholars were asked to rank the presidents. The results below show only those presidents who clearly and consistently ranked near the top or bottom. The surveys included all presidents except Reagan (who was still in office and thus could not be assessed dispassionately), George H. W. Bush, Bill Clinton, and George W. Bush (who had not yet served at the time these surveys were conducted); and William Harrison and James Garfield (whose terms were too short to be realistically assessed).

Greatest presidents
(in top five on all three surveys)
- Abraham Lincoln
- George Washington
- Franklin Delano Roosevelt
- Thomas Jefferson
- Theodore Roosevelt

> **What is the opinion of these historians and political scientists as to which presidents have been the greatest?**
>
> _____
>
> _____
>
> _____
>
> _____
>
> _____

Near-greats

(in top ten on all three surveys)

- Woodrow Wilson
- Andrew Jackson
- Harry S. Truman

Near-failures

(in bottom ten on all three surveys)

- Calvin Coolidge
- Millard Fillmore
- Andrew Johnson
- John Tyler
- Franklin Pierce

Failures

(in bottom five in all three surveys)

- James Buchanan
- U. S. Grant
- Warren G. Harding
- Richard M. Nixon

Source: John J. Harrigan, *Politics and the American Future,* 3rd ed., New York: McGraw-Hill, pp. 282–83. Copyright © 1992 by John J. Harrigan. Reprinted by permission of the author. Data in table from: 1982 poll of forty-nine scholars in *Chicago Tribune Magazine,* January 10, 1982, pp. 8–13, 15, 18; poll of forty-one scholars by David L. Porter in 1981, reprinted in Robert K. Murray and Tim H. Blessing, "The Presidential Performance Study: A Progress Report," *Journal of American History* 70, No. 3 (December 1983: 535–55.

Stop and Annotate

Go back to the preceding excerpt. In the space provided, list the presidents who have been the greatest, in the opinion of the scholars surveyed.

As you can see from the information listed in the selection, five presidents have been judged, in the opinion of all the scholars surveyed, to be the greatest: Abraham Lincoln, George Washington, Franklin Delano Roosevelt, Thomas Jefferson, and Theodore Roosevelt.

Here are two additional points about facts and opinions: First, you should remember that although some paragraphs contain only facts or only opinions, a paragraph may contain *both* facts and opinions (it may even present both facts and opinions in the same sentence). Second, you should realize that it may seem difficult at times to distinguish opinions from facts. This is because authors sometimes present opinions in ways that make them seem like facts. For example, a writer might introduce his or her opinion by stating, "The fact is . . ." (For example, "The fact is, Hawaii's weather makes it the perfect place for your winter vacation." This statement is really an opinion about winter vacations and Hawaii's weather.) Stating that something is a fact, however, does not make it a fact. (Hawaii certainly isn't the perfect place for your winter vacation if you want to go snow skiing.) Ideally, of course, an author would always express an opinion in a way that makes it clear that it *is* an opinion. ("In this writer's opinion, Hawaii's weather makes it the perfect place for your winter vacation.") But authors do not always do this, and it is your job to *think critically* as you read, being alert for opinions. When you identify an opinion, continue reading to determine whether or not the opinion is well supported. Although you should not accept an opinion unless it is well supported, you should be open to accepting opinions that *are* well supported.

Making Inferences and Drawing Logical Conclusions

KEY TERMS

inference

A logical conclusion based on what an author has stated.

conclusion

A decision that is reached after thoughtful consideration of information the author presents.

Thinking critically as you read also entails understanding not only what the author states directly, but also what the author *suggests*. In other words, it is the responsibility of critical readers to make inferences and draw conclusions about what they have read. An **inference** is a logical conclusion based on what an author has stated. A **conclusion** is a decision that is reached after thoughtful consideration of information the author presents. The information that is given will lead you to the conclusion that should be drawn. Needless to say, any inferences or conclusions you draw will be affected by your experience, your prior knowledge (or lack of it), and your own biases.

Making inferences is not new to you. In fact, you make inferences continually in your daily life. You draw conclusions based on descriptions, facts, opinions, experiences, and observations. Assume, for example, that a woman in your class arrives late. She seems frustrated and upset, and her hands are covered with grease and grime. It would be logical to infer that she has had a flat tire or some other trouble with her car and that she had to fix the problem herself. Your inference would be based on your observations. Similarly, you make inferences every day about things you read. For instance, suppose that your roommate leaves you a note saying, "Hope you didn't need your iPod this afternoon. I wanted to listen to music while I worked out." You would infer that your roommate has borrowed—and is using— your iPod. This is your roommate's *intended meaning* ("I borrowed your iPod, and I'm using it"), even though this information does not appear in the message. Making logical inferences will help you understand an author's intended meaning, just as the author's tone can (Chapter 8).

In fact, jokes and cartoons (including editorial and political cartoons) are funny only if the listener or reader makes the correct inference. Take, for example, the editorial cartoon below. It comes from *BusinessWeek* magazine. What inferences does the cartoonist expect readers to make about the fuel efficiency and size of the SUV (sport utility vehicle)? What inference could be made about the cartoonist's (and the publication's) position regarding SUVs?

You have already had many opportunities to make inferences earlier in this book. The skill in Chapter 5, "Formulating Implied Main Ideas," involves making inferences. You learned that when authors *suggest* a main idea but do not state it directly, they are *implying* it. When readers comprehend an implied main idea, they are *inferring* it (making an inference about it). The writer implies the main idea; the reader infers it. Some of the skills in Chapter 8, "Reading Critically," also involve making inferences. In that chapter you learned, for example, how an author's tone can help you infer his or her intended meaning. You learned that after determining the author's purpose, you can conclude who the intended audience was.

Critical thinking routinely involves making inferences and drawing logical conclusions, although there are times when an author simply states his or her conclusion. When the author does state the conclusion, it typically appears at the end of the passage, and it is often the main idea of a paragraph or the overall main idea of the entire selection. Authors use phrases such as these to announce a conclusion: *in conclusion, consequently, thus,* and *therefore.* Stated conclusions are important, so pay careful attention to them.

When the author states the conclusion, you do not need to infer it, of course. The author has done the work for you. However, when there is a conclusion to be drawn—that is, when the author does not state it—then it is up to you to infer it.

An inference goes beyond what the author states but must always be *based on* what the author has said. That is, your inferences are conclusions you have made on the basis of what is stated in the passage. Remember that you cannot use as an inference anything *stated* in the paragraph. For example, if the author states that "The *Titanic* sank because it hit an iceberg," you cannot give as an inference, "The *Titanic* sank because it hit an iceberg," because this information has been directly stated. This is logical: if the author has already stated it, there is no reason for you to infer it. Nor are you making an inference if you merely paraphrase (restate) information that is presented in the paragraph. For example, you cannot give as an inference, "An iceberg caused the *Titanic* to sink," because it is merely a paraphrase of information that was given by the author. You could, however, make this inference: "The water in which the *Titanic* sank was extremely cold." This is a logical inference, since the author states that there were icebergs in the water, and their presence indicates that the water was extremely cold.

Comprehension Monitoring Question for Making Inferences

What logical inference (conclusion) can I make, based on what the author has stated?

When you read, you should ask yourself, "What logical inference (conclusion) can I make, based on what the author has stated?" To draw a conclusion, the reader must deduce (reason out) the author's meaning. That is, readers must use the "evidence" and facts the author presents in order to arrive at the conclusion or inference the author wants them to make. Readers must make a connection between what an author says and what the author wants them to conclude. For example, a writer might describe the benefits of regular exercise but not state directly that you should exercise. The writer expects you to make the inference (draw the conclusion) that you should exercise regularly because he or she has presented the facts needed in order for you to conclude that exercise is beneficial.

You can understand more about how to make logical inferences by studying examples of correct inferences. An excerpt from a business communications textbook about a well-known ice cream company, Ben & Jerry's Homemade, appears

Down at the factory in Waterbury, Vermont, they're known as "the boys." They are Ben Cohen and Jerry Greenfield, arguably America's most famous purveyors of ice cream and certainly two of America's most colorful entrepreneurs. They've been friends since seventh grade and business partners since 1978 when they opened their first scoop shop, using techniques gleaned from a $5 correspondence course on how to make ice cream. Their firm, Ben & Jerry's Homemade, sold more than $76 million worth of super premium ice cream in 1990 and employs around 300 people, give or take a few, depending on the season.

Ben and Jerry have strong personalities and strong opinions. They believe that work should be fun, or else it isn't worth doing. They also believe in helping the unfortunate, protecting the environment, and treating people fairly. They want their company to be a happy, humanitarian place where everybody feels good about coming to work and producing a top-notch product.

Actions also telegraph Ben & Jerry's commitment to an egalitarian work environment: the open office arrangement, the bright colors, the pictures of cows and fields hanging on warehouse walls, the employee committees, the casual clothes, the first-name relationships, the compressed pay scale that keeps executive salaries in balance with lower-level compensation, the free health club memberships for everyone, the upcoming on-site day-care facility. And the free ice cream. Three pints a day per person. Now that's communication at its best!

What logical conclusions can you make about the employees at Ben and Jerry's Homemade?

_____

_____

_____

_____

_____

_____

_____

_____

_____

_____

Source: Courtland Bovée and John Thill, "Communication Close-Up at Ben & Jerry's Homemade," _Business Communication Today,_ 4th ed. Upper Saddle River, NJ: Prentice Hall, 1995, pp. 26–28.

on p. 556. After reading the excerpt, you can see that you can draw logical inferences about how employees feel about working at Ben & Jerry's.

Because the owners of Ben & Jerry's Homemade provide their employees with a fair, supportive, informal, and comfortable work environment, it is logical to conclude that:

> Employees are happy to work there.
>
> They appreciate the company's philosophy.
>
> They do not feel a high level of stress.
>
> They are likely to remain employees of Ben & Jerry's.

The following details from the passage are the ones on which these inferences are based:

> Employees call Ben and Jerry "the boys."
>
> Ben and Jerry believe that work should be fun.
>
> Ben and Jerry are interested in protecting the environment.
>
> They believe in treating people fairly.
>
> They want their company to be a happy, humanitarian place.
>
> They have an open office arrangement.
>
> They use bright colors.
>
> There are pictures on warehouse walls.
>
> Employees wear casual clothes.
>
> First names are used.
>
> There is a compressed pay scale.
>
> There is a free health club.
>
> There will soon be an on-site day-care facility.
>
> Employees receive free ice cream daily.

Stop and Annotate

Go back to the preceding excerpt. In the space provided, write the logical conclusions that can be made about the employees at Ben and Jerry's Homemade.

You could draw other logical conclusions from these details as well. For example, you could conclude that companies can be humane and humanitarian yet still be extremely profitable. You could conclude that the public appreciates a high-quality product and is willing to pay for it. You might even conclude that you would like to work at Ben & Jerry's.

Here is another textbook excerpt in which conclusions must be inferred by reading and thinking critically. The passage is from a health textbook, and its topic is *passive smoking*.

Passive Smoking

Reports from the U.S. surgeon general's office suggest that tobacco smoke in enclosed indoor areas is an important air pollution problem. This has led to the controversy about **pas-sive smoking**—the breathing in of air polluted by the secondhand tobacco smoke of others. Carbon monoxide levels of sidestream smoke (smoke from the burning end of a cigarette) reach a dangerously high level. True, the smoke can be greatly diluted in freely circulating air, but the 1 to 5 percent carbon monoxide levels attained in smoke-filled rooms can be suffi-cient to harm the health of people with chronic bronchitis, other lung disease, or cardiovascular disease.

What logical conclusions can you make about nonsmokers and smokers?

_____

_____

_____

_____

_____

_____

_____

Source: Marvin R. Levy, Mark Dignan, and Janet H. Shirreffs, *Targeting Wellness: The Core,* pp. 262–63.
Copyright © 1992 by The McGraw-Hill Companies, Inc. Reprinted by permission of The McGraw-Hill Companies.

Stop and Annotate

Go back to the excerpt above. In the space provided, write the logical conclusions that can be made about both non-smokers and smokers.

The authors want the reader to conclude that nonsmokers, especially those with certain health conditions, should avoid enclosed indoor areas in which there is cig-arette smoke. Smokers should also conclude that they ought to refrain from smok-ing around others in an enclosed area. These are conclusions the authors want the reader to infer, even though they do not state them. These inferences are based on the statements that "carbon monoxide levels of side-stream smoke reach danger-ously high levels" and that these levels "can be sufficient to harm the health of peo-ple with chronic bronchitis, other lung disease, or other cardiovascular disease."

When you read, remember to ask yourself, "What logical conclusion can I draw, based on what the author has stated?"

The chart below illustrates the application of critical thinking skills to a review of an imaginary movie. (This is the same movie review that appeared in Chapter 8, "Reading Critically.") It is designed to show that critical thinking skills are related and that they are applicable to reading tasks that you encounter daily.

Distinguishing between Deductive and Inductive Reasoning

KEY TERM
deductive reasoning

A process of reasoning in which a general principle is applied to a specific situation.

No discussion of critical thinking would be complete without explaining the dif-ference between deductive reasoning and inductive reasoning. As a college student, you should know the difference between the two. **Deductive reasoning** refers to rea-soning by taking a generalization and seeing how it applies to a specific situation. It is often called "reasoning from the general to the specific." This is the type of reason-ing that is used when a judge or an attorney applies a general law or legal precedent to a particular, specific legal case. It is also the type of reasoning that is used when a general theorem in geometry is applied to a specific problem, or a general algebraic formula is applied to a specific problem. It is the kind of reasoning you apply when you take a general principle or value you hold, such as being honest, and apply it in a particular situation ("I need to find the owner of this billfold and return it").

EXAMPLE OF CRITICAL THINKING APPLIED TO CRITIC'S REVIEW OF A MOVIE

Here is a critic's imaginary review of *Cyberpunk,* a new science fiction movie:

Another movie from Extreme Studios has just been released, *Cyberpunk.* Is it worth seeing? That depends: Do you enjoy violence? Do you like vulgar language? Do you appreciate painfully loud sound effects? What about watching unknown actors embarrass themselves? Or sitting for three hours and ten minutes without a break? If so, and you've got $8.50 to burn, then *Cyberpunk* is the movie you must see!

Critical Reading Questions	Answers
What is the author's purpose?	To persuade readers to skip this movie
Who is the author's intended audience?	The moviegoing public
What is the author's point of view?	*Cyberpunk* is a terrible movie.*
What is the author's tone?	Sarcastic
What is the author's intended meaning?	You shouldn't waste your money or your time on this movie.
Does the author include facts, opinions, or both?	Both
What logical inference (conclusion) does the author expect you to make?	This movie isn't worth seeing.

*Notice that this is also the author's main idea or argument.

KEY TERM
inductive reasoning

A process of reasoning in which a general principle is developed from a set of specific instances.

The opposite of deductive reasoning is inductive reasoning. **Inductive reasoning** refers to drawing a general conclusion that is based on specific details or facts. It is also called "reasoning from the specific to the general." You use inductive reasoning whenever you read a paragraph that consists only of details, and on the basis of these details, you reason out the general point the author is making (the implied main idea). Or a doctor might examine specific case histories of several patients with similar symptoms and draw the general conclusion that a certain toxic chemical is the common factor that caused their illness.

Students sometimes get deductive and inductive reasoning mixed up. Here is a memory peg that may help you avoid this problem:

- With *de*ductive reasoning, you are going *down* or *away* from something larger and more general to smaller, more specific things (deduct = take away).

- With *in*ductive reasoning, the smaller parts or specific details lead *in* to the larger generalization (induct = lead into).

The chart on pages 560–561 presents three examples of deductive and inductive reasoning in textbook paragraphs.

DEDUCTIVE AND INDUCTIVE REASONING IN TEXTBOOK PARAGRAPHS

Deductive Reasoning

Here is an example of a paragraph that opens with a general statement (which also happens to be the main idea). The rest of the paragraph, the details, explains specific ways reading can enrich a person's life.

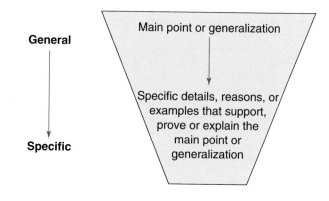

General

Specific

Main point or generalization

Specific details, reasons, or examples that support, prove or explain the main point or generalization

Example:

Being a good reader can enrich your life in many ways. Of course, reading is a key to doing well in college. But once you leave college, reading allows you to continue learning throughout your life. Moreover, many satisfying, high-paying careers, such as law and medicine, require the ability to read and comprehend large amounts of information. And reading is a wonderful pastime, an enjoyable way to relax and escape from the stresses of everyday life.

Main idea
(general statement that presents the author's main point about reading)

Supporting details
(examples of ways that reading can be enriching)

In this example of deductive writing, the author begins with a general principle, then presents specific examples to illustrate it.

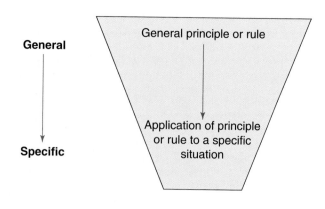

General

Specific

General principle or rule

Application of principle or rule to a specific situation

Example:

According to the Miranda ruling, if a person is not informed of his or her legal rights at the time of an arrest, the charges may be dropped. A woman charged of shoplifting may have the charges against her dropped if she is not informed when she is arrested, "You have the right to remain silent" and "Anything you say can be used against you in court." Or someone accused of assault may have the charges dismissed if the arresting officers fail to inform him, "You have the right to talk to an attorney before we ask you any questions and to have an attorney with you during questioning." A homeless person could have legal charges against her dismissed if the arresting officer neglects to tell her, "If you cannot afford an attorney, one will be provided for you before any questioning, if you wish."

Main idea
(general statement that presents the author's main point about being informed at the time of arrest about legal rights according to the Miranda ruling)

Supporting details
(specific examples of Miranda violations)

Inductive Reasoning

In this example of inductive writing, the author presents specific examples that lead to a general statement that sums them up.

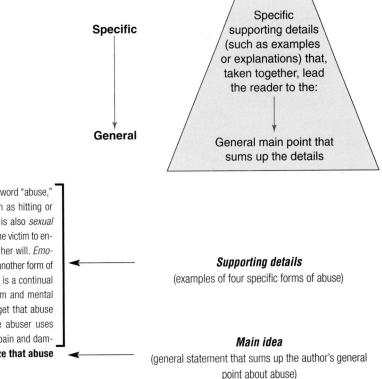

Specific

General

Specific supporting details (such as examples or explanations) that, taken together, lead the reader to the:

General main point that sums up the details

Example:

When most people hear the word "abuse," they think of *physical abuse,* such as hitting or kicking someone. However, there is also *sexual abuse,* in which the abuser forces the victim to engage in sexual acts against his or her will. *Emotional (psychological) abuse* is still another form of abuse. In this form of abuse there is a continual eroding of the victim's self-esteem and mental well-being. And many people forget that abuse can also be *verbal,* in which the abuser uses words to inflict severe emotional pain and damage. **It is important to recognize that abuse can take many forms.**

Supporting details
(examples of four specific forms of abuse)

Main idea
(general statement that sums up the author's general point about abuse)

Evaluating an Author's Argument

You now know that critical thinking includes the skills of distinguishing between facts and opinions and making logical inferences. Now you will learn how to use these two skills (along with the critical reading skills you learned in Chapter 8) to *evaluate* material you read. The steps below describe the process for evaluating an author's argument.

Step 1: Identify the Issue

The first step, of course, is to identify the issue. An *issue* is simply a controversial topic. In other words, an issue is a topic that people have differing opinions about. To identify the issue, ask yourself: "What controversial topic is this passage about?" Examples of issues are: *whether there should be regulation of pornographic websites, whether government-subsidized health care should be provided for all Americans,* and *whether U.S. corporations should outsource jobs to workers in foreign countries.*

Step 2: Determine the Author's Argument

The second step is to determine the author's argument. An **author's argument** is the author's position on an issue. That is, an author's argument is his or her opinion on an issue. (An author's argument is simply an overall main idea that is an opinion.) The author's argument is what the author believes and wants to persuade the reader to believe or do. You may also hear an author's argument referred to as his or her *point of view.*

An author's argument is not the same as an argument that is verbal disagreement or dispute. The author's purpose in a written argument is to persuade the reader to believe or do something by "arguing" (presenting) a case for it. An author "argues" for it in the same way an attorney "argues" his or her client's side of a case during a trial. For example, an author might argue that *All college students should be required to take at least one computer science course.* To persuade the reader to accept (believe) his or her argument, the author typically presents support or evidence that backs it up. An author does this in the same way that an attorney presents evidence to support his or her case. To determine the author's argument, ask yourself, "What is the author's position on this issue?"

Part of understanding an author's argument is recognizing the **author's bias** in favor of one side of an issue. For example, if the author's argument is *All college students should be required to take at least one computer science course,* then the author's bias is that he or she *favors* computer literacy for college students. If an author's argument is *Our government should not impose any restrictions on gun ownership,* then the author's bias is that he or she *opposes* gun control.

Authors who have a bias in favor of one side of a controversial issue support that side: they are *for* it. For example, the term *pro-environmental* would describe an author who favors legislation to protect the environment. Authors who have an opposing bias take the opposite position: they are *against* it. For example, the term *anti-environmental* would describe an author who opposes efforts or legislation to protect the environment. As you can see, the prefixes *pro-* and *anti-* can be helpful in describing an author's bias on an issue.

Critical Thinking Question for Determining the Author's Bias

Which side of the issue does the author support?

How can you tell whether an author has a bias when the author does not directly state his or her position? The best way is to examine the support the author gives. Ask yourself, "Does the author present support and information about both sides of the issue?" If not, ask yourself, "Which side of the issue does the author present support for?" This will reveal the author's bias.

By the way, part of thinking critically involves asking yourself whether *you* have a bias about an issue. If you do, you will have to make an extra effort to be open-minded and objective when you evaluate an author's argument. Otherwise, you may reject the author's argument without seriously considering it or without considering it objectively.

Of course, there will be times when an author chooses not to take a position on an issue. That is, the author remains *neutral* on an issue. The author does not take a position on one side of an issue because his or her purpose is to present *both* sides of the issue objectively. The author wants to present relevant support for both sides of an issue so that readers can make their own informed decision about the matter. Most of the time, however, authors *do* have a point of view.

Step 3: Identify the Assumptions on Which the Author Bases His or Her Argument

KEY TERM
author's assumption

Something the author takes for granted without proof.

Critical Thinking Question for Identifying the Author's Assumptions

What does the author take for granted?

When authors present an argument, they typically base it on certain assumptions. An **author's assumption** is something that he or she takes for granted or assumes to be true. That is, it is something the author does not state directly but that he or she accepts as true, without offering any proof that it is true. To identify an author's assumptions, ask yourself, "What does the author take for granted?" To illustrate, suppose an author's argument is, "Society must do more to protect young children from abuse." To make this argument, the author would have to have made these assumptions:

- Young children are worth protecting.
- Young children are not being protected adequately at present.
- Young children are not able to protect themselves.
- There are things society can and should do to protect young children.

These are all valid assumptions because they are reasonable and logical. Sometimes, though, an author bases an argument on illogical, unreasonable, or even incorrect assumptions. Incorrect assumptions weaken an argument. For example, an author's argument might be, *The minimum age for obtaining a driver's license should be 20.* In this case, the author's assumptions might be:

- Teenagers are irresponsible.
- If people are older when they begin driving, they will be better drivers.

It is incorrect to assume that all teenagers are irresponsible, or that if people are older when they begin driving, they will automatically be better drivers.

When you read an author's argument, you must think critically about assumptions the author makes to be sure that they are not incorrect assumptions and so that you are not manipulated by the author. Let's say that an author's argument is, "We should hire Margaret Jones as our city manager because only a woman cares enough about the city's historic district to preserve it." Two of the assumptions this argument is based on are:

A man would not care about the city's historic district.

A man is not capable of saving the city's historic district.

The author also assumes that saving the city's historic district is the sole or most important issue upon which the selection of the city manager should be based. These are illogical and incorrect assumptions, of course. Readers who do not question the author's assumptions might be manipulated into believing the author's argument.

Step 4: Identify the Types of Support the Author Presents

Critical Thinking Question for Identifying Support

What types of support does the author present?

Examine the supporting details to see if the author gives facts, examples, case studies, research results, or expert opinions. Is the author himself or herself an expert? Does he or she cite personal experience or observations, make comparisons, give reasons or evidence? Ask yourself, "What types of support does the author present?"

Step 5: Decide Whether the Support Is Relevant

Critical Thinking Question for Deciding Whether an Author's Support Is Relevant

Does the support pertain directly to the argument?

Support is *relevant* when it pertains directly to the argument. In other words, the support is meaningful and appropriate, and it relates directly to the argument. Ask yourself, "Does the support pertain directly to the argument?" For example, the author might argue that *All states should lower the blood alcohol level used to determine when drivers are legally drunk.* Statistics that show a decrease in traffic accidents and deaths in the states that already have a lower blood alcohol level would be relevant support. Sometimes, however, an author will try to persuade readers by using support that is irrelevant. If the author mentions that many drivers damage their own vehicles after drinking a large amount of alcohol, it would not be relevant support for this argument.

Step 6: Determine Whether the Author's Argument Is Objective and Complete

Critical Thinking Questions for Evaluating Whether an Author's Argument Is Objective and Complete

Is the argument based on facts and other appropriate evidence?

Did the author leave out information that might weaken or disprove the argument?

The term *objective* means that an argument is based on facts and evidence instead of on the author's feelings or unsupported opinions. Suppose the author who is arguing that *All states should lower the blood alcohol level used to determine when drivers are legally drunk* knows someone who was injured by a drunk driver and is angry because the inebriated driver was not penalized. As support for his argument, the author talks about how angry drunk drivers make him. This would not be objective support; it would be *subjective* support (support based on emotion). Ask yourself, "Is the author's argument based on facts and other appropriate evidence?" An author's support should be objective, not merely personal or emotional.

The term *complete* means that an author has not left out information simply because it might weaken or even disprove his or her argument. Suppose an author's argument is *Our city would benefit from a new sports arena.* Perhaps the author mentions that a new arena would boost the city's image and increase civic pride, but does not mention that a special bond would have to be passed by voters in order to pay for the arena, or that the new arena would cause major traffic congestion whenever sporting events were held. Particularly when an author has a bias, he or she may deliberately leave out important information that would weaken the argument. When evaluating the completeness of an author's argument, ask yourself, "Did the author leave out information that might weaken or disprove the argument?" To be fully convincing, an author should *present and overcome* opposing points.

Step 7: Evaluate the Overall Validity and Credibility of the Author's Argument

The term *valid* means that an argument was correctly reasoned and its conclusions follow logically from the information, evidence, or reasons that were presented. You must evaluate the author's logic, the quality of his or her thinking. To evaluate the validity of an author's argument, ask yourself, "Is the author's argument logical?" You should not accept an author's argument if it is not valid. Before you can determine whether an argument is valid, you must consider your answers to the questions mentioned in the previous steps:

* "What does the author take for granted?"
* "What type of support does the author present?"
* "Does the support pertain directly to the argument?"
* "Is the argument objective and complete?"

Critical Thinking Question for Evaluating Whether an Author's Argument Is Valid and Credible

Is the author's argument logical and believable?

Finally, you must evaluate the credibility of the author's argument. The term *credibility* refers to how believable an author's argument is. To be believable, the author's argument must be based on logic or relevant evidence. You must once again consider the author's assumptions, the types and relevance of the support, objectivity, completeness, and validity to determine the believability of the author's argument. To evaluate the credibility of an author's argument, ask yourself, "Is the argument believable?" An argument that has credibility is a convincing one. You must think critically about an author's argument in order to evaluate it. Just as you should reject any argument that lacks validity and credibility, you should be open to accepting one that is valid and credible.

Let's look at an example of how an author's argument could be evaluated critically. Consider the argument *All college students should be required to take at least one computer science course.* To evaluate its credibility, you would first examine the assumptions the author has made. For example, he or she obviously assumes that it is valuable to know about computers, that computers will continue to be important in people's personal and professional lives, and so on. The types of support the author gives might include facts and research findings about the growing use of computers, several examples of ways college students could benefit from computer skills, and his or her personal experience with computers. As a reader, you would then have to decide whether or not the support is relevant (directly supports the argument), whether it is complete (whether information that might support the other side of the issue was omitted), whether it is objective (based on facts and other appropriate evidence), and whether it is valid (logical). Consideration of these elements would enable you to evaluate whether or not the author's argument has validity and credibility.

Now read and evaluate an excerpt from a wellness textbook. This excerpt (from Selection 7-2, "The Decision to Marry") discusses the compatibility of married couples who have great differences in personality. After you have read this passage, apply the seven steps above to evaluate it critically.

Unfortunately, great differences in personality can often lead to marital conflict later on. For example, one study found that a source of marital dissatisfaction among husbands was a feeling that their wives were too possessive, neglectful, and openly admiring of other men. Dissatisfied wives complained that their husbands were possessive, moody, and openly attracted to other women. The study also found that sex is a source of great difficulties for unhappy married men and women. It found that women see sex as following from emotional intimacy, while men see it as a road to intimacy. As a result, men complain that their wives withhold sex from them and women complain that their husbands are too sexually aggressive.

Evaluating an Author's Argument

Issue: "*What controversial topic is this passage about?*"

_____

_____

_____

Authors' argument: "*What is the authors' position on the issue?*"

_____

_____

_____

Authors' assumptions: "*What do the authors take for granted?*"

_____

_____

_____

_____

_____

_____

Type of support: "*What type of support do the authors present?*"

_____

_____

_____

_____

Relevance of support: *"Does the support pertain directly to the argument?"*

_____

_____

_____

_____

_____

Objectivity and completeness: *"Is the argument based on facts and other appropriate evidence?"* and *"Did the authors leave out information that might weaken or disprove the argument?"*

_____

_____

_____

Validity and credibility: *"Is the argument logical and believable?"*

_____

_____

Source: Adapted from Marvin R. Levy, Mark Dignan, and Janet H. Shirreffs, "The Decision to Marry," in *Targeting Wellness: The Core,* p. 123. Copyright © 1992 by The McGraw-Hill Companies, Inc. Reprinted by permission of The McGraw-Hill Companies.

The issue in this passage is *personality differences and marital conflict.* The authors' argument is stated in the first sentence: *Unfortunately, great differences in personality can often lead to marital conflict later on.*

The authors assume that personality traits can be accurately measured and that they remain consistent throughout people's lives. Also, the authors would not bother to present the information unless they assume that people can make better decisions in selecting a spouse if they are aware of the effects of personality differences on relationships. Their assumptions seem reasonable and logical.

The support the authors present is the result of a research study that compares husbands' and wives' sources of dissatisfaction with each other.

Some of the support is relevant; some of it is not. The first finding of the study *does* support the argument that personality differences can lead to conflict later on (since possessiveness, moodiness, and aggressiveness can be viewed as personality traits). On the other hand, the second finding of the study (regarding sex as a source of difficulties for unhappy married couples) does *not* directly support the authors' argument (since it is differences in attitudes toward sex rather than personality differences that appear to cause the problems). Moreover, the differing attitudes of husbands and wives appear to be related to gender rather than to personality. Therefore, this second finding of the study is not as relevant to the authors' argument.

The argument is objective, but it is not complete. It is objective because the authors present research rather than merely giving their own unsupported opinions. Although the authors do present the findings from one study, their argument would have been more complete had they presented several sets of research findings or other types of support, such as case studies or interviews of couples.

Although the argument could have been made stronger had the authors included additional relevant support, their argument nevertheless appears to have some validity and, therefore, some credibility as well.

An evaluation of the authors' argument could be summed up as follows: The authors' argument (that great differences in personalities can lead to conflict between a married couple) does have some validity and credibility. This is because the authors' argument is based on logical assumptions and is supported with a relevant finding from a research study.

Now look at two short selections that both address the issue of legalizing drugs that are currently illegal. As you read, think about which side presents the better argument. (Before you begin reading, think about whether *you* already have a bias on this issue.)

Stop and Annotate

Go back to the preceding excerpt. In the spaces provided, answer the critical thinking questions for evaluating an author's argument.

Pro-legalization: Weighing the Costs of Drug Use

For over 100 years this society has made the use of certain drugs illegal and has penalized illegal drug use. But during that time the use of marijuana, heroin and other opiates, and cocaine has become an epidemic. Most recently, Americans have spent billions of dollars on arresting and imprisoning sellers and importers of crack cocaine, with almost no effect on the supply or street price of the drug.

The societal costs of illegal drugs are immense. They include the costs of law enforcement, criminal proceedings against those arrested, and jails and prisons. They also include the spread of deadly diseases such as AIDS and hepatitis through the use of shared needles; the cost to society of raising "crack babies," children poisoned by drugs even before

Evaluating an Author's Argument

Issue: "*What controversial topic is this passage about?*"

_____

_____

Authors' argument: "*What is the authors' position on the issue?*"

_____

_____

Authors' assumptions: "*What do the authors take for granted?*"

_____

_____

_____

_____

birth; and the cost of raising a generation of young people who see illegal drug selling and violence as their only escape from poverty and desperation. Finally, the societal costs include the emotional cost of the violence that no one can now escape.

Legalizing drug use in this country would eliminate many of these costs. Billions of dollars would be saved. This money could be spent on treatment of addicts, job training, and education programs to help many disadvantaged young people assume valuable roles in society. The government could make drug use legal for adults but impose severe penalties on anyone who sells drugs to young people. Drug sales could be heavily taxed, thus deterring drug purchases and giving society the benefit of tax revenues that could be used for drug treatment and education.

Type of support: *"What type of support do the authors present?"*

_____

_____

_____

_____

Relevance of support: *"Does the support pertain directly to the argument?"*

_____

_____

Objectivity and completeness: *"Is the argument based on facts and other appropriate evidence?"* and *"Did the authors leave out information that might weaken or disprove the argument?"*

_____

_____

_____

_____

Validity and credibility: *"Is the argument logical and believable?"*

_____

_____

_____

_____

_____

Source: Richard Schlaad and Peter Shannon, "Legalizing Drugs," in Marvin R. Levy, Mark Dignan, and Janet H. Shirreffs, *Targeting Wellness: The Core,* p. 235. Copyright © 1992 by The McGraw-Hill Companies, Inc. Reprinted by permission of The McGraw-Hill Companies.

Anti-legalization: Providing a Positive Role Model

Certain drugs are illegal because they are dangerous and deadly and provide no societal value. To make their possession or use legal would send a message to young people that using drugs is acceptable and that drugs are not treacherous or life-destroying.

Making drugs illegal has not increased the number of drug users or sellers, just as making alcohol legal after Prohibition did not reduce the number of people who drank. Recent law enforcement efforts have indeed made a difference. Over the past few years, as law enforcement efforts have sent more and more people to jail, the number of young people who use illegal drugs has steadily declined. Furthermore, education about the ill effects of drug use has begun to deter people from buying and using illegal drugs.

Recently, the incidence of drug-related deaths and violence has begun to level off even in the areas of the most hard-core drug use. This is proof that strict law enforcement is working. This country has begun to turn the corner on this drug epidemic.

Evaluating an Author's Argument

Issue: "*What controversial topic is this passage about?*"

_____

_____

_____

_____

Authors' argument: "*What is the authors' position on the issue?*"

_____

_____

_____

_____

Authors' assumptions: "*What do the authors take for granted?*"

_____

_____

_____

_____

Type of support: "*What type of support do the authors present?*"

_____

_____

_____

_____

Relevance of support: "*Does the support pertain directly to the argument?*"

_____

_____

_____

Objectivity and completeness: "*Is the argument based on facts and other appropriate evidence?*" and "*Did the authors leave out information that might weaken or disprove the argument?*"

_____

_____

_____

_____

_____

Validity and credibility: "*Is the argument logical and believable?*"

_____

_____

_____

_____

_____

_____

_____

_____

_____

Source: Richard Schlaad and Peter Shannon, "Legalizing Drugs," in Marvin R. Levy, Mark Dignan, and Janet H. Shirreffs, *Targeting Wellness: The Core,* p. 235. Copyright © 1992 by The McGraw-Hill Companies, Inc. Reprinted by permission of The McGraw-Hill Companies.

Stop and Annotate

Go back to the two selections above. In the spaces provided, answer the two sets of critical thinking questions for evaluating an author's argument.

Of the two selections, the pro-legalization argument (the first argument) is stronger. The authors give five distinct "costs" of illegal drugs and then explain how legalizing drugs (and the revenue from taxing them) could be directed at treating the problem. Further, the authors make it clear that there could still be strong penalties for any adults who sell drugs to young people. The anti-legalization argument is very general and is less convincing. Of course, the issue of drug legalization is a complex one, and this is not to say that these two short passages address all the issues. Still, of the two selections, the stronger argument was made in the pro-legalization selection.

Identifying Propaganda Devices

Examining support is a crucial element in evaluating an author's argument. Readers must be aware that authors sometimes use unfair techniques in order to persuade readers to believe their argument. Authors with a bias may use what are known as **propaganda devices** to try to unduly influence the reader to accept their point of view. This means that the "support" they present is in some way inadequate, misleading, or flawed. You are more likely to encounter propaganda in editorials, advertisements, and certain other types of writing than in textbooks, of course. Still, you must think critically to detect whether propaganda is offered as support. If you are not alert to propaganda devices, you may find yourself being manipulated by them.

There are too many types of propaganda to describe all of them, but here are brief descriptions and examples of several of the most common ones. Although speakers often use these same propaganda techniques, our focus is on authors' use of them. In either case, and as the explanations show, each propaganda device is based either on emotion or on flawed reasoning. To think critically and detect propaganda devices, ask yourself, "Has the author tried to unfairly influence me to accept his or her point of view?"

Authors often try to appeal to readers' emotions, such as appeals to fear, sympathy, and vanity, rather than to reason. Examples of appeals to these emotions are:

- **Appeal to fear.**　The author tries to manipulate readers by frightening them into accepting his or her point of view.

  Examples

  "If you don't know how to use a computer, you might as well give up any hope of having a good career."

  "Afraid to smile? Embarrassed by dingy yellow teeth? Don't let yellow teeth stand between you and an active social life. Brush with Gleam-Brite twice daily and in just three weeks, you'll no longer be afraid to smile."

  Volvo: "Pay more for a car and live to see why."

- **Appeal to sympathy.**　The author tries to manipulate readers by making them feel sorry for someone or something.

  Examples

  "Adopt a pet today. There's nothing more heartbreaking than a sad, lonely kitten or puppy in need of a loving home."

  "Thousands of innocent children will die if our readers do not donate at least half a million more dollars to our fund by the end of the year."

  "Yes, some athletes and scholarship students cheat on tests, but they are under tremendous pressure to maintain a certain GPA. If they do not maintain their average, they will lose their eligibility or their scholarships. They will have to drop out of college, and after that, they will have no chance of getting a good job or being successful in life."

- **Appeal to vanity.**   The author tries to manipulate readers by making them feel that they are special or superior to other people.

Examples

"Discriminating buyers insist on a Lexus."

"Connoisseurs of fine wine insist on Grape Arbor Chardonnay."

"You'll be the envy of everyone when you glide down the street in your sleek, new Mercedes-Benz. Your refined sense of taste and elegance will be obvious to all. Move up to a Mercedes-Benz and drive the car you deserve."

Army: "Be all you can be."

Marines: "The few. The proud. The Marines."

L'Oréal: "L'Oréal . . . because I'm worth it."

Other types of propaganda devices include the following:

- **Appeal to tradition.**   The author tries to manipulate readers by telling them that they should do or believe something because that is the way it has always been done in the past, or that they can create a new tradition.

Examples

"In this part of the country, we've always voted for conservative candidates."

DeBeers: "A diamond is forever."

- **Bandwagon.**   The author says, in effect, that everyone believes, accepts, or does what he is describing and therefore the reader should "get on the band-wagon" too. In other words, the author says you should believe something just because "everyone else" believes it. The author knows that this strategy appeals to people's desire to be part of the crowd and not feel different or left out.

Examples

"We all want to be in great shape nowadays, so join the millions of Americans who have bought the home Exer-Gym. Everyone agrees that it's the only piece of exercise equipment you'll ever need, that it's the world's best, and that it's the most enjoyable way to get in shape. Join the Exer-Gym crowd now!"

- **Appeal to authority.**   The author tries to influence the reader to accept his or her argument or point of view by citing some authority who believes it.

Examples

"Dr. Doe, my psychology teacher, believes that there was once life on Mars. If he believes it, it must be right. He is well-educated and has read dozens of books about extraterrestrial life."

"Three out of four dentists who recommend mouthwash recommend Rinse-O-Dent to their patients."

- **Testimonial.**   This is similar to the appeal to authority. In this case, a famous person endorses an idea or product in order to influence others to believe or buy it. Many times, however, the person endorsing the product has no special knowledge about it or experience with it, so the testimonial is not worth very much. Testimonial is also called *endorsement*.

Examples

A celebrity such as an actor, model, sports figure, or entertainer endorses a certain brand of automobile or a particular line of clothing.

Many celebrities have participated in the American Dairy Association's "Got Milk?" campaign.

"Golf pros like Tiger Woods know that Nike athletic products are the best money can buy!"

- **Straw man.**   The author misrepresents what an opponent believes, then attacks that belief.

Example

"Our college cafeteria has awful food. Obviously, the cafeteria's manager doesn't care at all about students' preferences or their health. The college administration needs to replace the current cafeteria manager with someone who actually cares about cafeteria customers."

- **Either-or.**   The author puts everything into one of two mutually exclusive categories and acts as if there are no other possibilities besides one category or the other.

Examples

"Either install a Blammo Home Security System or pay the consequences."

"There are cultivated people who like opera and there are uncultivated ones who don't."

"Yes, there is an alternative to calcium supplements. It's called osteoporosis."

- **False analogy.**   The author makes a comparison that is either inaccurate or inappropriate.

Examples

"Taking a shower with Spring Burst soap is like a refreshing romp in the surf."

"Everyone knows that professional athletes are just overgrown, spoiled children."

- **Circular reasoning.**   The author merely restates the argument or conclusion rather than providing any real support. This is also called *begging the question.*

Examples

"Vote for Bob Griggs for senator. He's the best person for the job because there is no one else who's better!"

"Fourth World countries could improve their economic situation by making their economies better."

- **Transfer.**   The author transfers the good or bad qualities of one person or thing to another in order to influence the reader's perception of it.

Examples

"Mother Teresa would have supported the legislation we are proposing to help the country's homeless."

"Our candidate is another JFK!"

"Our competitor's car gets the same gas mileage as an army tank!"

- **Sweeping generalization.** The author presents a broad general statement that goes far beyond the evidence. (*Stereotyping* is one form of sweeping generalization.)

Examples

BMW: "The best-handling car in America. The ultimate driving machine."

"All women are bad drivers."

"No man will ever admit he's lost."

"All jocks are dumb."

"The homeless are lazy, unmotivated people who would rather ask for a handout than work for a living."

- **Hasty generalization.** The author jumps to a conclusion that is based on insufficient proof or evidence.

Examples

"Sudzo made all my clothes spotless and bright again. It'll work on all of your laundry, too!"

"My brother was a Boy Scout and loved it. Any boy would find that becoming a Boy Scout is one of the best decisions he could ever make!"

"If you care at all about animals, you'll make a generous donation to the Ferret Fund."

- **Plain folks.** The author appeals to readers by presenting himself or herself as someone who is just like the readers.

Examples

Shimano fishing reels: "For the rich, there's therapy. For the rest of us, there's bass. The Cariolus reel is built with care and precision by people who, just like you, would go crazy if they couldn't fish."

"Why should we hardworking, middle-class folks have to carry the tax burden in this country? We work hard, but we never get ahead. It's time Congress gave us middle-class citizens the tax break we deserve."

- **Ad hominem.** The author attacks the person rather than the views or ideas the person presents.

Example

"My opponent once lied about serving in the military when he was a young man. Why should you believe him now when he says he will reduce taxes if you elect him? He's a liar, and every campaign promise he makes is just another lie."

PROPAGANDA TECHNIQUES EXERCISE

Directions: Here is a list of propaganda techniques. Decide which type of propaganda technique is used in each of the examples that follow. Each propaganda device is used only once. The first item has been completed for you.

appeal to authority	ad hominem	hasty generalization
appeal to fear	bandwagon	plain folks
appeal to sympathy	circular reasoning	straw man
appeal to tradition	either-or	sweeping generalization
appeal to vanity	false analogy	testimonial
		transfer

1. Insist on Best Brand Turkeys—because Thanksgiving Day is too important to ruin. *appeal to fear*

2. The victims of the devastating tornado need more than your pity. They need you to roll up your sleeve and donate blood.

3. Gold Star Butter—it's not for just anyone.

4. Christmas just wouldn't be Christmas without Creamy Smooth Eggnog! It's been America's number one choice for more than half a century.

5. Each year more than one million Americans trust Nationwide Realty to sell their homes. Shouldn't you?

6. Parents are justified in doing whatever it takes to keep themselves informed about their child if they think their child is doing something wrong. Dr. Laura says it's OK for parents to search their teenagers' rooms, read their diaries, and even make them take drug tests.

7. I've been a radio talk show host for fifteen years now, and I've never found an arthritis pain reliever more effective than Salvo.

8. The governor opposes legislation that mandates safety locks on guns. Obviously, he has no problem with innocent children being killed from playing with guns. It's time to vote the governor out of office!

9. You can either buy a Health Trip exercise bicycle or continue to be overweight and out of shape.

10. Having a career in real estate is like being able to print money!

11. America will have better-educated citizens when fewer students drop out of school.

12. Princess Diana would have donated her time and energy to this worthy cause.

13. All of today's youth are self-centered and irresponsible. _____

14. Blue Label Beer—the working man's brew! _____

15. Senator Bledsoe is opposed to campaign funding reform. _____
He's just the type of person who would solicit illegal
contributions! I'll bet that during the last decade he's
taken in hundreds of thousands of dollars illegally.

16. If you like being near the beach, you'll love living in Hawaii. _____

A WORD ABOUT STANDARDIZED READING TESTS: CRITICAL THINKING

Many college students are required to take standardized reading tests as part of an overall assessment program, in a reading course, or as part of a state-mandated basic skills test. A standardized reading test typically consists of a series of passages followed by multiple-choice reading skill application questions, to be completed within a specified time limit.

Here are some examples of typical wording of questions about critical thinking:

Questions about fact and opinion *may be phrased:*

Which of the following statements expresses an opinion rather than a fact?

Which of the following sentences from the passage represents a fact?

Which of the following sentences from the passage represents an opinion?

In dealing with questions about fact and opinion, watch for words (such as *perhaps, apparently, it seems, experts believe*) that signal opinions. Watch also for judgmental words (such as *best, worst,* or *beautiful*), which also indicate opinions.

Questions about inferences and logical conclusions *may be worded:*

Which of the following conclusions could be made about . . . ?

On the basis of information in this passage, the reader could conclude . . .

It can be inferred from the passage that . . .

The passage implies that . . .

In dealing with questions on inferences and logical conclusions, remember that an inference must be logical and must be based on information in the passage.

Questions about the author's argument *may be worded:*

In this selection, the author argues that . . .

The author's position on this issue is . . .

The author's point of view is . . .

The passage suggests that the author believes . . .

(Continued on next page)

(Continued from previous page)

Questions about the author's credibility *may be worded:*

    The author has credibility because . . .

    The author establishes his credibility by . . . (by presenting data, giving examples, etc.)

    The author's argument is believable because . . .

    The author is believable because . . .

Questions about the author's assumptions *may be worded:*

    The author bases his (or her) argument on which of the following assumptions?

    Which of the following assumptions underlies the author's argument?

    The author's argument is based on which of the following assumptions?

Questions about types of support *the author presents may be worded:*

    The author presents which of the following types of support?

    The author includes all of the following types of support except . . .

DEVELOPING CHAPTER REVIEW CARDS

Student Online Learning Center (OLC)
Go to Chapter 9.
Select Flashcards
or Chapter Test.

Review cards, or *summary cards,* are an excellent study tool. They are a way to select, organize, and review the most important information in a textbook chapter. The process of creating review cards helps you organize information in a meaningful way and, at the same time, transfer it into long-term memory. The cards can also be used to prepare for tests (see Part Three). The review card activities in this book give you structured practice in creating these valuable study tools. Once you have learned how to make review cards, you can create them for textbook material in your other courses.

Now complete the eight review cards for Chapter 9 by answering the questions or following the directions on each card. When you have completed them, you will have summarized (1) what critical thinking is, (2) distinguishing facts from opinions, (3) making logical inferences and drawing logical conclusions, (4) deductive and inductive reasoning, (5) the steps in evaluating an author's argument, (6) the definition of author's argument, author's bias and author's assumptions, (7) critical thinking questions to ask yourself, and (8) propaganda devices. Use the type of handwriting that is clearest for you to reread (printing or cursive) and write legibly.

Critical Thinking
Define *critical thinking*.
List the skills of critical thinking.
1.
2.
3.
Card 1   Chapter 9: Thinking Critically

Distinguishing Facts and Opinions

What is a *fact?*

What is an *opinion?*

List several clue words and phrases that typically signal an opinion.

To distinguish facts from opinions, what question should you ask yourself?

What makes an opinion "valuable"?

Card 2   Chapter 9: Thinking Critically

Making Inferences and Drawing Logical Conclusions

What is an *inference?*

What is a *conclusion?*

When reading, what question should you ask yourself about making an inference?

Card 3   Chapter 9: Thinking Critically

Deductive and Inductive Reasoning

Define *deductive reasoning*.

Define *inductive reasoning*.

Card 4   Chapter 9: Thinking Critically

Steps in Evaluating an Author's Argument

List the seven steps you must take to evaluate an author's argument.

1.

2.

3.

4.

5.

6.

7.

Card 5   Chapter 9: Thinking Critically

Author's Argument, Bias, and Assumptions

Define *author's argument*.

Define *author's bias*.

Define *author's assumption*.

Card 6   Chapter 9: Thinking Critically

Critical Thinking Questions for Evaluating an Author's Argument

What are the questions you should ask yourself in order to complete the seven steps for evaluating an author's argument?

1.

2.

3.

4.

5.

6.

7.

Card 7   Chapter 9: Thinking Critically

Identifying Propaganda Devices

What are propaganda devices?

List 16 types of propaganda devices.

Card 8 Chapter 9: Thinking Critically

SELECTION **9-1**

Government

Poverty in America and Improving Social Welfare Through Public Education

From *The American Democracy*

By Thomas E. Patterson

Prepare Yourself to Read

Directions: Do these exercises *before* you read Selection 9-1.

1. First, read and think about the title. What comes to mind when you think about the term *social welfare?*

   _____

   _____

   _____

2.   Next, complete your preview by reading the following:

   Introduction (in *italics*)

   All of the first paragraph (paragraph 1)

   Headings

   Terms in bold print

   Now that you have completed your preview, what does this selection seem to be about?

   _____

   _____

   _____

   _____

Apply Comprehension Skills

Directions: Do the Annotation Practice Exercises *as* you read Selection 9-1.

Apply the critical thinking skills presented in this chapter:

Distinguish facts from opinions. To determine whether statements in written material are facts or opinions, ask yourself, "Can the information the author presents be proved, or does it represent a judgment?"

Make inferences and draw logical conclusions. After you read, you should ask yourself, "What logical inference (conclusion) can I make, based on what the author has stated?"

Identify the controversial issues the author presents. As yourself, "What controversial topic is this paragraph about?"

585

POVERTY IN AMERICA AND IMPROVING SOCIAL WELFARE THROUGH PUBLIC EDUCATION

How is it that the wealthiest country in the world has so many of its citizens living in poverty? What should be done to improve the economic condition of millions of American families, and why are there such strong disagreements about ways to remedy this situation? This selection from a U.S. government textbook examines the problem of poverty in our nation and describes how our public education system was created to provide "equality of opportunity" and, ultimately, to improve the welfare of its citizens.

Social Welfare Policy

1   In the broadest sense, social welfare policy includes any effort by government to improve social conditions. In a narrower sense, however, social welfare policy refers to those efforts by government to help individuals meet basic human needs, including food, clothing and shelter.

The Poor: Who and How Many?

2   Americans' social welfare needs are substantial. Although Americans are far better off economically than most of the world's peoples, poverty is a significant and persistent problem in the United States. The government defines the **poverty line** as the annual cost of a thrifty food budget for an urban family of four, multiplied by three to include the cost of housing, clothes, and other necessities. Families whose incomes fall below that line are officially considered poor. In 2005, the poverty line was set at an annual income of roughly $19,000 for a family of four. One in nine Americans—roughly thirty million people, including more than ten million children—lives below the poverty line. If they could all join hands, they would form a line stretching from New York to Los Angeles and back again.

3   America's poor include individuals of all ages, races, religions, and regions, but poverty is concentrated among certain groups. Children are one of the largest groups of poor Americans. One in every five children lives in poverty. Most poor children live in single-parent families, usually with the mother. In fact, a high proportion of Americans residing in families headed by divorced, separated, or unmarried women live below the poverty line. *(See Figure 1.)* These families are at a disadvantage because most women earn less than men for comparable work, especially in nonprofessional fields. Women without higher education or special skills often cannot find jobs that pay significantly more than the child-care expenses they incur if they work outside the home. Single-parent, female-headed families are roughly five times as likely as two-

Directions: For each of the exercises below, think critically to answer the questions. This will help you gain additional insights as you read.

Practice Exercise

Does the author present a statement of *fact* or *opinion* in the first sentence of paragraph 2?

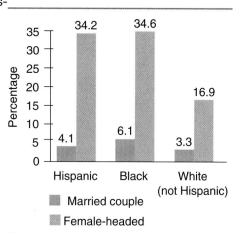

Figure 1

Percentage of Families Living in Poverty, by Family Composition and Race/Ethnicity

Poverty is far more prevalent among female-headed households and African American and Hispanic households.

Source: U.S. Bureau of the Census, 2004.

income families to fall below the poverty line, a situation referred to as "the feminization of poverty."

4   Poverty is also widespread among minority-group members. More than 20 percent of African Americans and Hispanics live below the poverty line, compared with 10 percent of whites.

5   Poverty is also geographically concentrated. Although poverty is often portrayed as an urban problem, it is somewhat more prevalent in rural areas. About one in seven rural residents—compared with one in nine urban residents—lives in a family with income below the poverty line. The urban figure is misleading, however, in that the poverty rate is very high in some inner-city areas. Suburbs are the safe haven from poverty. Because suburbanites are far removed from it, many of them have no sense of the impoverished condition of what Michael Harrington called "the other America."

6   The "invisibility" of poverty in America is evident in polls showing that most Americans greatly underestimate the number of poor in their country. Certainly nothing in the daily lives of many Americans or in what they see on television would lead them to think that poverty rates are uncommonly high. Yet the United States has the highest level of poverty among the advanced industrialized nations, and its rate of child poverty is roughly twice the average rate of the others. *(See Figure 2.)*

Practice Exercise

Does the author present a statement of *fact* or *opinion* in the last sentence of paragraph 4?

_____

_____

Practice Exercise

What logical *conclusion* does the author want you to draw about the number of Americans living in poverty?

_____

_____

_____

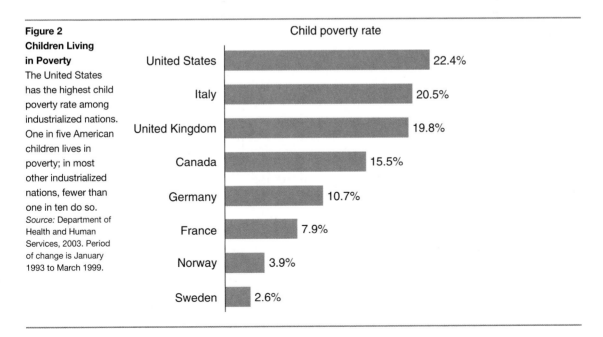

Figure 2
Children Living in Poverty
The United States has the highest child poverty rate among industrialized nations. One in five American children lives in poverty; in most other industrialized nations, fewer than one in ten do so.
Source: Department of Health and Human Services, 2003. Period of change is January 1993 to March 1999.

Child poverty rate

Country	Rate
United States	22.4%
Italy	20.5%
United Kingdom	19.8%
Canada	15.5%
Germany	10.7%
France	7.9%
Norway	3.9%
Sweden	2.6%

Living in Poverty: By Choice or Chance?

7   Many Americans hold to the idea that poverty is largely a matter of choice—that most low-income Americans are unwilling to make the effort to hold a responsible job and get ahead in life. In his book *Losing Ground,* Charles Murray argues that America has a permanent underclass of unproductive citizens who prefer to live on welfare and whose children receive little educational encouragement at home and grow up to be copies of their parents. There are, indeed, many such people in America. They number in the millions. They are the toughest challenge for policymakers because almost nothing about their lives equips them to escape from poverty and its attendant ills.

8   Yet most poor Americans are in their situations as a result of circumstance rather than choice. A ten-year study of American families by a University of Michigan research team found that most of the poor are poor only for a while and that they are poor for temporary reasons such as the loss of a job or desertion by the father. When the U.S. economy goes into a tailspin, the impact devastates many families. The U.S. Department of Labor reported that three million jobs were lost in the manufacturing sector alone during the recessionary period that began in 2000.

9   It is also true that a full-time job does not guarantee that a family will rise above the poverty line. A family of four with one employed adult who works forty hours a week at six dollars an hour (roughly the minimum wage level) has an annual income of about $12,000, which is well below the poverty line. Millions of Americans—mostly household workers, service workers, unskilled laborers, and farm workers—are in this position. The U.S. Bureau of Labor Statistics estimates that roughly 7 percent of full-time workers do not earn enough to lift their family above the poverty line.

Education as Equality of Opportunity: The American Way

10   Economic security has a higher priority in European democracies than in the United States. European democracies have instituted programs such as government-paid health care for all citizens, compensation for all unemployed workers, and retirement benefits for all elderly citizens. The United States provides these benefits only to some citizens in each category. For example, not all elderly Americans are entitled to social security benefits. If they paid social security taxes for a long enough period when they were employed, they (and their spouses) receive benefits. Otherwise they do not, even if they are in dire economic need.

Practice Exercise

What *controversial topic* does the author present in paragraph 7?

Practice Exercise

Does the author present a statement of *fact* or *opinion* in the last sentence of paragraph 9?

Practice Exercise

Does the author present *facts, opinions,* or both in paragraph 10?

11 Such policy differences between Europe and the United States stem from cultural and historical differences. Democracy developed in Europe in reaction to centuries of aristocratic rule, which brought the issue of economic privilege to the forefront. When strong labor and socialist parties then emerged as a result of industrialization, European democracies initiated sweeping social welfare programs that brought about greater economic equality. In contrast, American democracy emerged out of a tradition of limited government that emphasized personal freedom. Equality was a lesser issue, and class consciousness was weak. No major labor or socialist party emerged in America during industrialization to represent the working class, and there was no persistent and strong demand for welfare policies that would bring about a widespread sharing of wealth.

12 Americans look upon jobs and the personal income that comes from work as the proper basis of economic security. Rather than giving welfare payments to the poor, Americans prefer that the poor be given training and education so that they can learn to help themselves. This attitude is consistent with Americans' preference for **equality of opportunity,** the belief that individuals should have an equal chance to succeed on their own. The concept embodies *equality* in its emphasis on giving everyone a fair chance to get ahead. Yet equality of opportunity also embodies *liberty* because it allows people to succeed or fail on their own as a result of what they do with their opportunities. The expectation is that people will end up differently—some will be rich, some poor. It is sometimes said that equality of opportunity offers individuals an equal chance to become unequal.

13 In practice, equality of opportunity works itself out primarily in the private sector, where Americans compete for jobs, promotions, and other advantages. However, a few public policies have the purpose of enhancing equality of opportunity. The most significant of these policies is public education.

Public Education:
Enhancing Equality of Opportunity

14 During the first hundred years of our nation's existence, the concept of a free education for all children was a controversial and divisive issue. Wealthy interests feared that an educated public would challenge their power. The proponents of a more equal society wanted to use education as a means of enabling ordinary people to get ahead. This second view won out. Public schools sprang up in nearly every community and were open free of charge to all children who could attend.

15 Today, the United States invests more heavily in public education at all levels than does any other country. The curriculum in American schools is also relatively standardized.

Practice Exercise

What logical *conclusion* does the author want you to draw about the concept of "equality of opportunity" and economic success or security?

_____

_____

Practice Exercise

What *controversial topic* does the author present in paragraph 14?

_____

_____

_____

Unlike those countries that divide children even at the grade school level into different tracks that lead ultimately to different occupations, the United States aims to educate all children in essentially the same way. Of course, public education is not a uniform experience for American children. The quality of education depends significantly on the wealth of the community in which a child resides.

16   Nevertheless, the United States through its public schools educates a broad segment of the population. Arguably, no country in the world has made an equivalent effort to give children, whatever their parents' background, an equal opportunity in life through education. Per pupil spending on public elementary and secondary schools is roughly twice as high in the Untied States as it is in Western Europe. America's commitment to broad-based education extends to college. The United States is far and away the world leader in terms of the proportion of adults receiving a college education.

17   The nation's education system preserves both the myth and the reality of the American dream. The belief that success can be had by anyone who works for it could not be sustained if the education system were tailored for a privileged few. And educational attainment is related to personal success, at least as measured by annual incomes. In fact, annual incomes of college graduates consistently exceed the incomes of those with only a high school diploma.

18   In part because the public schools play such a large role in creating an equal-opportunity society, they have been heavily criticized in recent years. Violence in public elementary and secondary schools is a major parental concern. So too is student performance on standardized tests. American students are not even in the top ten internationally in terms of their test scores in science or math.

19   Disgruntled parents have demanded changes in public schools, and these demands have led some communities to allow parents to choose the public school their children will attend. Under this policy, the schools compete for students, and those that attract the most students are rewarded with the largest budgets. A majority of Americans favor such a policy. Advocates of this policy contend that it compels school administrators and teachers to do a better job and gives students the option of rejecting a school that is performing poorly. Opponents of the policy say that it creates a few well-funded schools and a lot of poorly funded ones, yielding no net gain in educational quality. Critics also claim that the policy discriminates against poor and minority-group children, whose parents are less likely to be in a position to steer them toward the better schools.

20   An even more contentious issue than school choice is the voucher system issue. The voucher system allows parents to use tax dollars to send their children to private or parochial

Practice Exercise

What *controversial topic* does the author present in paragraph 19?

_____

_____

_____

schools instead of public schools. The recipient school receives a voucher redeemable from the government, and the student receives a corresponding reduction in his or her tuition. Advocates claim that vouchers force failing schools to improve their instructional programs. Opponents argue that vouchers weaken the public schools by siphoning off both revenue and students. They also note that vouchers are of little value to students from poor families because they cover only part of the cost of attending a private or parochial school. *(See Figure 3.)*

21   The issue of school choice reflects the tensions inherent in the concept of equal opportunity. On one hand, competition between schools expands the number of alternatives available to students. On the other hand, not all students have a realistic opportunity to choose among the alternatives.

Practice Exercise

What *controversial topic* does the author present in paragraph 20?

_____

_____

_____

"**Last year's Supreme Court decision says that the U.S. Constitution does not prevent a state from offering vouchers that parents can use to send their students to private schools at public expense. Do you favor or oppose your state making such vouchers available?**

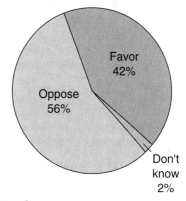

Favor
42%

Oppose
56%

Don't
know
2%

Figure 3
Opinions on School Vouchers
Americans are divided in their opinions on school vouchers.
Source: Lowell C. Rose and Alec M. Gallup, The 35th Annual Phi Delta Kappa/Gallup Poll of the Public's Attitudes Toward the Public Schools. Phi Delta Kappa, September, 2003, pp. 29, 56. Reprinted by permission of Phi Delta Kappa International, Inc.

Reading Selection Quiz

This quiz has three parts. Your instructor may assign some or all of them.

Comprehension

Directions: Items 1–10 test your comprehension (understanding) of the material of this selection. These questions are the type a content area instructor (such as a government professor) would ask on a test over this material. You should be able to answer these questions after studying this selection. For each comprehension question below, use information from the selection to determine the correct answer. Refer to the selection as you answer the questions. Write your answer in the space provided.

1. In a specific sense, social welfare policy refers to the efforts of our government to:

   a. improve the conditions in our society.

   b. help people meet basic human needs, including shelter, clothing, and food.

   c. eliminate poverty.

   d. provide Americans with equal opportunities.

2. In 2005, the poverty line annual income for a family of four was set at about:

   a. $9,000.

   b. $12,000.

   c. $19,000.

   d. $24,000.

3. Which of the following is an *incorrect* statement about poverty in America today?

   a. One in every five children lives in poverty.

   b. Single-parent, female-headed families are more likely to fall below the poverty line than two-income families.

   c. More than 40 percent of Hispanics and African Americans live below the poverty line.

   d. Poverty is somewhat more prevalent in rural areas.

4. According to the information presented in the bar graph and accompanying caption in Figure 1, poverty is:

   a. more prevalent in married-couple households.

   b. the most urgent problem facing the United States.

   c. more prevalent in female-headed households.

   d. likely to affect most minority-group families.

_____ **5.** According to information in the selection, the child poverty rate in the United States is:
   a. more than 50 percent.
   b. about 22 percent.
   c. 7 percent.
   d. less than 3 percent.

_____ **6.** The American concept of *equality of opportunity* is the belief that:
   a. all people are basically the same.
   b. everyone in the United States deserves economic equality.
   c. individuals should have an equal chance to succeed on their own.
   d. no one in the United States should live in poverty.

_____ **7.** An example of evidence that supports the United States' commitment to providing public education for the purpose of enhancing equality of opportunity would be:
   a. The United States invests more heavily in public education at all levels than does any other country.
   b. The public education system in the United States is tailored for children and young adults, regardless of their parents' background.
   c. Per pupil spending on public elementary and secondary schools is roughly twice as high in the United States as it is in Western Europe.
   d. all of the above

_____ **8.** Today a majority of Americans support:
   a. a voucher system.
   b. public school choice.
   c. standardized tests.
   d. a tracking system.

_____ **9.** Opponents of the voucher system claim that the system:
   a. weakens public schools by reducing revenues.
   b. reduces the number of alternatives available to students.
   c. forces failing schools to change their instructional programs.
   d. creates a few well-funded schools and many poorly funded ones.

_____ **10.** The author believes that public education in the United States:
   a. can lift people out of poverty.
   b. benefits a broad segment of the population.
   c. enhances equality of opportunity.
   d. all of the above

Vocabulary in Context

Directions: Items 11–20 test your ability to determine the meaning of the word by using context clues. *Context clues* are words in a sentence that allow the reader to deduce (reason out) the meaning of an unfamiliar word in that sentence. Context clues also enable the reader to determine which meaning the author intends when a word has more than one meaning. For each vocabulary item below, a sentence from the selection containing an important word (*italicized, like this*) is quoted first. Next, there is an additional sentence using the word in the same sense and providing another context clue. Use the context clues from *both* sentences to deduce the meaning of the italicized word. *Be sure the answer you choose makes sense in both sentences.* If you discover that you need to use a dictionary to confirm an answer choice, remember that the meaning you select must still fit the context of *both* sentences. Write your answer in the space provided.

Pronunciation Key: ă pat ā pay âr care ä father ĕ pet ē be ĭ pit
ī tie îr **pier** ŏ pot ō toe ô paw oi **noise** ou **out** ŏŏ took
ōō boot ŭ cut yōō abuse ûr **urge** th **thin** *th* **this** hw **which**
zh vision ə about *Stress mark:* ′

_____ **11.** Americans' social welfare needs are *substantial.*

When Ryan began college, he was surprised to discover that each one of his courses required a *substantial* amount of reading and notetaking.

substantial (səb stăn′ shəl) means:

a. having substance; material

b. possessing wealth or poverty

c. solidly built; strong

d. large in amount or degree

_____ **12.** Although Americans are far better off economically than most of the world's peoples, poverty is a significant and *persistent* problem in the United States.

Throughout her childhood, Carmen was annoyed by *persistent* rumors about her parents' lifestyle.

persistent (pər sĭs′ tənt) means:

a. existing for a long time; continuing

b. important; significant

c. cruel; unkind

d. bothered; troubled

_____ **13.** These families are at a disadvantage because most women earn less than men for *comparable* work, especially in nonprofessional fields.

The cost of living in Boston is *comparable* to the cost of living in Chicago; both cities are expensive places to live.

comparable (kŏm′ pər ə bəl) means:

a. different; opposite

b. difficult; challenging

c. similar; equivalent

d. expensive; costly

_____ **14.** Although poverty is often portrayed as an urban problem, it is somewhat more *prevalent* in rural areas.

Today, violence is *prevalent* in movies and on network television.

prevalent (prĕv′ ə lənt) means:

a. concentrated in urban and rural areas

b. widely or commonly occurring or existing

c. gradually increasing

d. accepted

_____ **15.** In his book *Losing Ground,* Charles Murray *argues* that America has a permanent underclass of unproductive citizens who prefer to live on welfare and whose children receive little educational encouragement at home and grow up to be copies of their parents.

Our father routinely *argues* that without a good education, it will be difficult for us to obtain satisfying jobs and earn substantial incomes.

argues (är′ gyo͞oz) means:

a. quarrels constantly; disputes

b. pesters; nags

c. attempts to prove by reasoning; claims

d. explains in writing

_____ **16.** If they paid social security taxes for a long enough period when they were employed, they (and their spouses) receive benefits. Otherwise they do not, even if they are in *dire* economic need.

Following a disastrous hurricane, residents found themselves in *dire* need of basic necessities such as water, food, clothing, and shelter.

dire (dīr) means:

a. urgent; desperate

b. expensive; difficult to obtain

c. basic; essential

d. deserving; entitled

_____ **17.** The *proponents* of a more equal society wanted to use education as a means of enabling ordinary people to get ahead.

Recycling *proponents* want everyone to get into the habit of properly recycling all bottles, glass, paper, and plastic containers.

proponents (prə pō′ nənts) means:
- *a.* officials; authorities
- *b.* opponents; detractors
- *c.* supporters; advocates
- *d.* manufacturers; producers

_____ **18.** Of course, public education is not a *uniform* experience for American children.

All McDonalds cheeseburgers have a *uniform* taste and appearance because they are made with the same ingredients and in the exact same way.

uniform (yo͞o′ nə fôrm) means:
- *a.* always the same; unvarying
- *b.* similar in color and texture
- *c.* satisfying; fulfilling
- *d.* successful; productive

_____ **19.** *Advocates* of this policy contend that it compels school administrators and teachers to do a better job and gives students the option of rejecting a school that is performing poorly.

Fitness *advocates* remind us to maintain a healthy diet and exercise regularly.

advocates (ăd′ və kĭts) means:
- *a.* those who argue against a cause; opponents
- *b.* those who argue for a cause; supporters
- *c.* those who reject an idea
- *d.* those who debate an issue

_____ **20.** An even more *contentious* issue than school choice is the voucher system issue.

Human cloning, stem cell research, alternative medicine, and abortion are all examples of *contentious* topics.

contentious (kən tĕn′ shəs) means:
- *a.* controversial
- *b.* important
- *c.* confusing
- *d.* difficult

SELECTION **9-1**   *Reading Skills Application*

Government
(continued)

Directions: Items 21–25 test your ability to *apply* certain reading skills to information in this selection. These types of questions provide valuable practice for all students, especially those who must take standardized reading tests and state-mandated basic skills tests (such as the Florida CLAST Test and the Texas THEA Test). You may not have studied all of the skills at this point, so these items will serve as a helpful preview. The comprehension and critical reading skills in this section are presented in Chapters 4 through 9 of *Opening Doors;* vocabulary and figurative language skills are presented in Chapter 2. As you work through *Opening Doors,* you will practice and develop these skills. Write your answer for each question in the space provided.

_____ **21.** Which of the following sentences expresses the main idea of the second paragraph of this selection?

    a. If all the people living in poverty in the United States could join hands, they would form a line stretching from New York City to Los Angeles and back again.

    b. The United States will never be able to eliminate poverty completely.

    c. Americans' social welfare needs are substantial, and poverty is a significant and persistent problem in our nation.

    d. The poverty line is the annual cost of basic human needs for a family of four.

_____ **22.** Which writing pattern did the author use to organize the main idea and supporting details in paragraph 8?

    a. listing

    b. comparison-contrast

    c. sequence

    d. cause-effect

_____ **23.** Which of the following best describes the author's purpose for writing this selection?

    a. to persuade readers that poverty is largely a matter of choice and to inform readers about ways to alleviate it

    b. to explain the nature of the problem of poverty in the United States and to illustrate how public education policy is designed to improve social welfare

    c. to instruct readers how to combat social inequity in the United States and how to reduce the number of children living in poverty

    d. to inform readers about the educational opportunities that exist in the United States today

_____ **24.** Our nation has the highest child poverty rate among the advanced industrialized nations, but two countries that have child poverty rates almost as high as the United States are:

   a. France and Germany.

   b. Italy and the United Kingdom.

   c. Sweden and Norway.

   d. China and Japan.

_____ **25.** Which of the following expresses an opinion rather than a fact?

   a. All individuals should have an equal chance to succeed on their own.

   b. If individuals paid social security for a long enough period when they were employed, they (and their spouses) receive benefits.

   c. Spending on public schools is roughly twice as high in the United States as it is in Europe.

   d. America's poor include individuals of all ages, races, religions, and regions.

SELECTION **9-1**

Government
(continued)

Collaboration Option

Respond in Writing

Directions: Refer to Selection 9-1 as needed to answer the essay-type questions below.

Option for collaboration: Your instructor may direct you to work with other students on one or more of these items, or in other words, to work *collaboratively.* In that case, you should form groups of three or four students, as directed by your instructor, and work together to complete the exercises. After your group discusses an item and agrees on the answer, have a group member record it. Each member of your group should be able to explain all of your group's answers.

1. The author explains that our system of public education was designed to benefit individuals in many ways. List at least four of these ways.

_____

_____

_____

_____

_____

_____

_____

_____

_____

_____

2. In paragraph 19 the author presents what both the advocates and the opponents have to say about the issue of public school choice, the policy that allows parents to choose the public school that their children will attend. What is your position on this issue? Explain why you support or oppose public school choice.

    _____

    _____

    _____

    _____

    _____

    _____

3. In paragraph 20 the author presents what both the supporters and detractors have to say about the issue of school vouchers, the policy that allows parents to use tax dollars to send their children to private or parochial schools instead of public schools. What is your position on this issue? Explain why you support or oppose the voucher system.

    _____

    _____

    _____

    _____

    _____

    _____

4. **Overall main idea.** What is the overall main idea the author wants the reader to understand about the relationship between poverty and public education? Answer this question in one sentence. Be sure to include the words *poverty* and *public education* in your overall main idea sentence.

    _____

    _____

    _____

    _____

    _____

    _____

Internet Resources

Read More about This Topic on the World Wide Web

Directions: For further information about the topic of the selection, visit these websites:

www.census.gov/hhes/www/poverty/poverty.html
This is the "poverty" link for the U.S. Census Bureau. This site presents a variety of current poverty data and definitions. For further information on poverty statistics visit **www.ask.census.gov**.

www.npc.umich.edu/poverty
This is the site for the National Poverty Center, a service provided by The University of Michigan and the Gerald R. Ford School of Public Policy. The site contains a section of Frequently Asked Questions (FAQs) about poverty in the United States.

You can also use your favorite search engine such as Google, Yahoo!, or Alta-Vista (www.google.com, www.yahoo.com, www.altavista.com) to discover more about this topic. To locate additional information, type in combinations of key-words such as:

poverty United States

or

public education United States

Keep in mind that whenever you go to *any* website, it is a good idea to evaluate the website and the information it contains. Ask yourself questions such as:

"Who sponsors this website?"

"Is the information contained in this website up-to-date?"

"What type of information is presented?"

"Is the information objective and complete?"

"How easy is it to use the features of this website?"

SELECTION **9-2**

Editorial

Sport Utility Vehicles: How Do I Hate Thee? Let Me Count the Ways

From *The Washington Post*

By Geneva Overholser

Prepare Yourself to Read

Directions: Do these exercises *before* you read Selection 9-2.

1. First, read and think about the title. Do you own an SUV or have you had an unpleasant experience with an SUV someone else was driving? How do you feel about SUVs?

   _____

   _____

   _____

   _____

2. Next, complete your preview by reading the following:

   Introduction (in *italics*)

   Skim the entire editorial

   On the basis of your preview, what does the editorial seem to be about?

   _____

   _____

   _____

   _____

   _____

Apply Comprehension Skills

Directions: Do the Annotation Practice Exercises *as* you read Selection 9-2.

Apply the critical thinking skills presented in this chapter:

Distinguish facts from opinions. To determine whether statements in written material are facts or opinions, ask yourself, "Can the information the author presents be proved, or does it represent a judgment?"

Make inferences and draw logical conclusions. After you read, you should ask yourself, "What logical inference (conclusion) can I make, based on what the author has stated?"

Apply the step-by-step process for evaluating an author's argument. Begin by asking yourself, "What controversial topic is this passage about?"

SPORT UTILITY VEHICLES: HOW DO I HATE THEE? LET ME COUNT THE WAYS

In the past few years, sales of sport utility vehicles (SUVs) have exceeded other car sales. Today, SUVs are ubiquitous—they're in every parking lot and on every highway. In fact, you could say that SUVs are more popular than ever. However, just as there are millions of Americans who have fallen in love with these vehicles, there are perhaps just as many who are outraged by these "land barges." There have even been arson attacks on SUV dealerships, including one that destroyed 30 SUVs at a Eugene, Oregon, dealership. Environmentalists, safety experts, economists, carpooling parents, off-road enthusiasts, and commuters all have their own opinions of SUVs. The emergence of "hybrid" cars (powered by both electricity and gasoline) reflects the continuing concern about gas-guzzling SUVs. What is your opinion of SUVs? As the title suggests, this author has a strong opinion on this issue. Read the selection to see why she feels the way she does.

1   Let me say out front that sport utility vehicles drive me nuts. No one need waste time writing to tell me I sound like a raving lunatic about this. I feel like a lunatic about SUVs, and I hereby invite you to join me in raving.

2   Of course, you already may be among the hordes of Americans who have purchased one of these inexplicably popular extravagances. Or you may be among what surely must be the equally fast-growing numbers who seethe over the idiocy of buying mammoth, highly engineered off-road vehicles in order to go to the drugstore. But on the off chance you remain uncommitted, I offer three reasons that SUVs' growing popularity should alarm and infuriate you.

3   First, gasoline. Anyone of age in the 1970s will remember when our great nation was brought to its knees by something called OPEC. This international oil cartel—the Organization of Petroleum Exporting Countries—was able to cripple our economy because of our then-shameful reliance on others for 36 percent of our oil.

4   Once OPEC put the fear of the Lord into us, we admirably changed our ways. We began insulating our homes and businesses, turning out lights, buying energy-efficient appliances and—most important—switching to smaller cars that burned less gasoline.

5   What a difference a quarter-century makes. Now, our cars' gas mileage no longer is improving. We are driving more. Fuel consumption keeps rising. And these nonsensical, gas-guzzling behemoths are one of the fastest-growing segment of the vehicle market. Depending on driving conditions, the six most popular SUVs get as low as 13 miles to the gallon.

6   In case you thought nothing like what happened in the 1970s could happen again, you should recall that OPEC's members, concerned about low oil costs, got together in March, 1999, in Vienna and decreed a cut in production of

about 3 percent. And guess how much of our oil we import nowadays? It is more than 50 percent.

7   The good news here is that in 1999 Vice President Al Gore proposed that automakers triple SUV fuel efficiency by 2007. More power to him.

8   If energy dependence doesn't concern you, how about safety? Ford Motor Co. introduced a design change to make its SUVs a little safer in crashes. Its SUV, the Excursion, has steel bars below its bumpers so it won't ride over other cars during collisions.

9   The Excursion, please note, is nearly 7 feet tall and weighs more than three tons. Ford tested it with its own Taurus and found that in a head-on collision, the SUV would ride over the normal car's hood and strike the base of the Taurus windshield, causing "tremendous damage to the passenger compartment," as the *New York Times* delicately put it.

Source: John Branch. © NAS. North American Syndicate. Reprinted by permission.

10   The National Highway Traffic Safety Administration says the size of SUVs makes them responsible for 2,000 deaths a year more than conventional cars would have caused in the same collisions.

11   Not concerned about gasoline or accidents? Perhaps you worry about the environment or like to breathe. Carbon dioxide emissions from cars and trucks make up about a third of this country's generous contribution to global warming. And SUVs are the carbon-dioxide-spewing champs: The new SUVs send out 70 tons per year, compared with the average car's 50 tons.

12   There is modest good news here, too. The Clinton administration proposed rules that would force most SUVs to meet the same emissions standards as cars. The new standards would be phased in over five years, beginning in 2004—a reasonable enough expectation.

13   Opponents began weighing in immediately. The often sensible Sen. Dick Lugar of Indiana, for example, complained about "cracking down on automobiles that are popular with the American people."

14   Heaven forbid we would seek to do anything to control America's appetite for vehicles that spew pollution and guzzle gas, weigh twice as much as normal cars, shine their headlights directly into everyone's rearview mirrors, and run over hoods in collisions.

15   If a nation increasingly full of SUV drivers who never even go off-road is sane, I am proud to sound otherwise. I only hope you will join me.

> **Practice Exercise**
>
> Does the author present a *fact* or an *opinion* in paragraph 10?
>
> _____
>
> _____

> **Practice Exercise**
>
> In paragraph 13, what *conclusion* can you draw about Senator Lugar's position on SUVs?
>
> _____
>
> _____
>
> _____

Source: Geneva Overholser, "Three Things I Hate About SUVs," *The Washington Post,* May 28, 1999, p. A35. Copyright © 1999 The Washington Post Writers Group. Reprinted with permission.

Evaluating the Author's Argument

Issue:
"What controversial topic is this passage about?"

_____

_____

_____

_____

Author's argument:
"What is the author's position on the issue?"

_____

_____

_____

_____

Author's assumptions:
"What does the author take for granted?"

_____

_____

_____

_____

Type of support:
"What type of support does the author present?"

_____

_____

_____

_____

Relevance of support:
"Does the support pertain directly to the argument?"

_____

_____

_____

_____

Objectivity and completeness:
"Is the argument based on facts and other appropriate evidence?" and *"Did the author leave out information that might weaken or disprove the argument?"*

_____

_____

_____

_____

_____

Validity and credibility:
"Is the argument logical and believable?"

_____

_____

_____

_____

SELECTION **9-2**

Editorial
(Continued)

Reading Selection Quiz

This quiz has three parts. Your instructor may assign some or all of them.

Comprehension

Directions: Items 1–10 test your comprehension (understanding) of the material of this selection. These questions are the type a college professor would ask on a test over this material. You should be able to answer these questions after studying this selection. For each comprehension question below, use information from the selection to determine the correct answer. Refer to the selection as you answer each question. Write your answer in the space provided.

True or False

_____ **1.** One-third of all carbon dioxide emissions released into the atmosphere comes from cars and trucks.

_____ **2.** United States oil imports are not affected by OPEC's oil production.

_____ **3.** Sport utility vehicles are one of the fastest-growing segments of the vehicle market.

_____ **4.** Because of the size of sport utility vehicles, 2,000 more people die in collisions with them each year than would have died in collisions with conventional cars.

Multiple-Choice

_____ **5.** According to the author, sport utility vehicles are:
a. acceptable.
b. extravagances.
c. becoming less popular.
d. a help to large families.

_____ **6.** In response to the OPEC cartel in 1970, many people in the United States:
a. switched to smaller cars.
b. bought energy-efficient appliances.
c. turned off unnecessary lights and began insulating their homes.
d. all of the above

_____ **7.** How much carbon dioxide does a new sports utility vehicle send out into the atmosphere each year?
a. 3 tons
b. 7 tons
c. 50 tons
d. 70 tons

_____ **8.** The author hopes that:

   a. sports utility vehicle owners will use their vehicles only for off-road driving.

   b. the government will force cars to have the same emission standards as sports utility vehicles.

   c. more people will oppose sports utility vehicles.

   d. raving lunatics will stay off our roads.

_____ **9.** Many sports utility vehicles cause unnecessary deaths in collisions because they:

   a. run over normal cars' hoods.

   b. shine their headlights directly into everyone else's rearview mirrors.

   c. are engineered to go off-road.

   d. send out so much carbon dioxide into the atmosphere.

_____ **10.** The author believes that the growing popularity of sports utility vehicles should alarm and infuriate everyone because:

   a. sports utility vehicles cause more deaths in collisions than conventional cars.

   b. the most popular sports utility vehicles get as low as 13 miles to the gallon.

   c. sports utility vehicles pollute more than ordinary cars.

   d. all of the above

SELECTION **9-2**   *Vocabulary in Context*

Editorial
(Continued)

Directions: Items 11–20 test your ability to determine the meaning of a word by using context clues. *Context clues* are words in a sentence that allow the reader to deduce (reason out) the meaning of an unfamiliar word in that sentence. Context clues also enable the reader to determine which meaning the author intends when a word has more than one meaning. For each vocabulary item below, a sentence from the selection containing an important word *(italicized, like this)* is quoted first. Next, there is an additional sentence using the word in the same sense and providing another context clue. Use the context clues from *both* sentences to deduce the meaning of the italicized word. *Be sure the answer you choose makes sense in both sentences.* If you discover that you need to use a dictionary to confirm an answer choice, remember that the meaning you select must still fit the context of *both* sentences. Write your answer in the space provided.

Pronunciation Key: ă **pat**   ā **pay**   âr **care**   ä **father**   ĕ **pet**   ē **be**   ĭ **pit**
ī **tie**   îr **pier**   ŏ **pot**   ō **toe**   ô **paw**   oi **noise**   ou **out**   ŏŏ **took**
ōō **boot**   ŭ **cut**   yōō **abuse**   ûr **urge**   th **thin**   *th* **this**   hw **which**
zh **vision**   ə **about**   *Stress mark:* '

_____ **11.** Let me say out front that sport *utility* vehicles drive me nuts.

Besides blades, a Swiss Army knife has a screwdriver, scissors, and other features that enhance its *utility*.

utility (yo͞o tĭl′ ĭ tē) means:

a. fashion

b. low price

c. usefulness

d. difficulty of use

_____ **12.** No one need waste time writing to tell me I sound like a raving *lunatic* about this.

The man was standing naked in the middle of the busy intersection singing, hopping around, and flapping his arms like a *lunatic*.

lunatic (lo͞o′ nə tĭk) means:

a. person who is insane

b. traffic officer

c. athletic person

d. ballet dancer

_____ **13.** Of course, you already may be among the *hordes* of Americans who have purchased one of these inexplicably popular extravagances.

Hordes of last-minute shoppers jammed the mall on Christmas Eve.

hordes (hôrdz) means:

a. a smattering

b. large groups or crowds

c. small but steady number

d. troops

_____ **14.** Of course, you already may be among the hordes of Americans who have purchased one of these *inexplicably* popular extravagances.

Everyone thought the company president was satisfied with his job, so we were shocked when he *inexplicably* resigned last week and joined the Peace Corps.

inexplicably (ĭn ĕk splĭ′ kəb lē) means:

a. difficult or impossible to explain

b. understandably

c. predictably

d. without any warning

_____ **15.** Or you may be among what surely must be the equally fast-growing numbers who *seethe* over the idiocy of buying mammoth, highly engineered off-road vehicles in order to go to the drugstore.

It makes me *seethe* when reckless drivers endanger others by running red lights.

seethe (sē*th*) means:

  a. feel unhappy

  b. feel pleasure or enjoyment

  c. feel violently agitated

  d. feel deep sadness

_____ **16.** Or you may be among what surely must be the equally fast-growing numbers who seethe over the idiocy of buying *mammoth,* highly engineered off-road vehicles in order to go to the drugstore.

Mammoth Caves, the largest caves in the state, are a popular tourist attraction.

mammoth (măm′ əth) means:

  a. dark; gloomy

  b. having a distinctive shape

  c. brightly colored

  d. of enormous size; huge

_____ **17.** This international oil *cartel*—the Organization of Petroleum Exporting Countries—was able to cripple our economy because of our then-shameful reliance on others for 36 percent of our oil.

The Colombian drug *cartel* controls most of the heroin and cocaine traffic from South America to the United States.

cartel (kär tĕl′) means:

  a. organizations working together to regulate the production, pricing, and marketing of goods

  b. police

  c. processing company

  d. a group of victims

_____ **18.** You should know that OPEC's members, concerned about low oil costs, got together in March in Vienna and *decreed* a cut in production of about 3 percent.

The mayor *decreed* that until the water shortage was over, homeowners would be allowed to water their lawns only once a week.

decreed (dĭ krēd′) means:

  a. worried intensely

  b. hoped fervently

  c. was unable to comprehend

  d. issued an order that has the force of law

_____ **19.** And SUVs are the carbon-dioxide-*spewing* champs: The new SUVs send out 70 tons per year, compared with the average car's 50 tons.

The radiator hose suddenly broke, *spewing* boiling water like a fountain.

spewing (spyōō′ ĭng) means:

a. sending out in a stream; ejecting forcefully

b. soaking up

c. trickling down and melting

d. releasing

_____ **20.** Heaven forbid we would seek to do anything to control America's *appetite* for vehicles that spew pollution and guzzle gas, weigh twice as much as normal cars, shine their headlights directly into everyone else's rearview mirrors, and run over hoods in collisions.

The public's *appetite* for violence is reflected in the popularity of violent movies and video games.

appetite (ăp′ ĭ tīt) means:

a. hostility toward

b. a strong wish or desire for

c. tolerance for

d. disgust with

SELECTION **9-2**   *Reading Skills Application*

Editorial
(Continued)

Directions: Items 21–25 test your ability to *apply* certain reading skills to information in this selection. These types of questions provide valuable practice for all students, especially those who must take standardized reading tests and state-mandated basic skills tests (such as the Florida CLAST Test and the Texas THEA Test). You may not have studied all of the skills at this point, so these items will serve as a helpful preview. The comprehension and critical reading skills in this section are presented in Chapters 4 through 9 of *Opening Doors;* vocabulary and figurative language skills are presented in Chapter 2. As you work through *Opening Doors,* you will practice and develop these skills. Write your answer for each question in the space provided.

_____ **21.** The author would be likely to agree with which of the following statements?

a. All cars should be banned.

b. All fuel-inefficient cars should be prohibited.

c. The OPEC cartel should be broken up.

d. SUVs would be acceptable if they could be made safer.

_____ **22.** The meaning of *conventional* in paragraph 10 is:
　　a. traditional.
　　b. imported.
　　c. economy.
　　d. used.

_____ **23.** The overall organization of the selection is:
　　a. cause and effect.
　　b. sequence.
　　c. contrast.
　　d. comparison.

_____ **24.** The author argues that people should avoid buying or driving SUVs because:
　　a. OPEC cannot restrict the availability of gasoline.
　　b. SUVs can be made more environmentally friendly.
　　c. car makers are producing other cars that are safer.
　　d. SUVs waste gas, cause pollution, and are not safe.

_____ **25.** The author's tone in this selection can be described as:
　　a. sentimental.
　　b. ambivalent.
　　c. disgusted.
　　d. tolerant.

S E L E C T I O N　**9-2**

Editorial
(Continued)

Collaboration Option

Respond in Writing

Directions: Refer to Selection 9-2 as needed to answer the essay-type questions below.

Option for collaboration: Your instructor may direct you to work with other students on one or more of these items, or in other words, to work *collaboratively*. In that case, you should form groups of three or four students, as directed by your instructor, and work together to complete the exercises. After your group discusses an item and agrees on the answer, have a group member record it. Each member of your group should be able to explain all of your group's answers.

1. The author presents three reasons not to own or drive an SUV. On the other side of the issue, what are at least three *advantages* of owning or driving a sport utility vehicle?

_____

_____

_____

_____

_____

2. Besides the drawbacks mentioned in the article, what are some *other* problems associated with sport utility vehicles? (The drawbacks can be either for the owners or for other drivers.)

_____

_____

_____

_____

_____

_____

_____

3. Males between the ages of 16 and 25 tend to be involved in more accidents than other drivers, and collisions between sport utility vehicles and conventional cars tend to result in an increased number of deaths to drivers of the conventional cars. On the basis of these statistics, should these young male drivers be prohibited from driving SUVs? Explain your position.

_____

_____

_____

_____

_____

_____

_____

4. **Overall main idea.** What is the overall main idea the author wants the reader to understand about SUVs? Answer this question in one sentence. Be sure that your overall main idea sentence includes the topic *(SUVs)* and tells the most important point about it.

_____

_____

_____

_____

_____

Internet Resources

Read More about This Topic on the World Wide Web

Directions: For further information about the topic of the selection, visit these websites:

www.sierraclub.org/globalwarming/SUVreport
This website contains a report from the Sierra Club about SUV pollution, safety, and energy consumption.

www.cars.com/go/index.jsp
This commercial website contains links that list reviews, services, auto shows, and news about all types of vehicles. Click on the link for *SUVs*.

You can also use your favorite search engine such as Google, Yahoo!, or Alta-Vista (www.google.com, www.yahoo.com, www.altavista.com) to discover more about this topic. To locate additional information, type in combinations of key-words such as:

SUVs

or

SUV safety

or

SUV fuel efficiency

or

SUV hybrids

Keep in mind that whenever you go to *any* website, it is a good idea to evaluate the website and the information it contains. Ask yourself questions such as:

"Who sponsors this website?"

"Is the information contained in this website up-to-date?"

"What type of information is presented?"

"Is the information objective and complete?"

"How easy is it to use the features of this website?"

SELECTION **9-3**

Magazine Article

Take Out the Trash, and Put It . . . Where?

From *Parade Magazine*
By Bernard Gavzer

Prepare Yourself to Read

Directions: Do these exercises *before* you read Selection 9-3.

1. First, read and think about the title. What do you think this article will be about?

   _____

   _____

   _____

   _____

2. Next, complete your preview by reading the following:
   Introduction (in *italics)*
   Skim the entire article
   Charts and graphs

   On the basis of your preview, what problem do you think will be discussed in this article?

   _____

   _____

   _____

   _____

Apply Comprehension Skills

Directions: Do the Annotation Practice Exercises *as* you read Selection 9-3.

Apply the critical thinking skills presented in this chapter:

Distinguish facts from opinions. To determine whether statements in written material are facts or opinions, ask yourself, "Can the information the author presents be proved, or does it represent a judgment?"

Make inferences and draw logical conclusions. After you read, you should ask yourself, "What logical inference (conclusion) can I make, based on what the author has stated?"

Apply the step-by-step process for evaluating an author's argument. Begin by asking yourself, "What controversial topic is this passage about?"

TAKE OUT THE TRASH, AND PUT IT . . . WHERE?

Perhaps you had to take out the garbage when you were younger. Did you ever wonder where the garbage went after it was picked up? Did you ever wonder whether we might eventually run out of places to put garbage? Read this magazine article to find the answers to the troubling questions of where garbage goes and whether there is enough space for it.

1   "Dealing with America's cascade of garbage is as vital an issue as Social Security, or Medicare, or maintaining a defense structure," says Denis Hayes, president of Seattle's nonprofit Bullitt Foundation and one of the founders of Earth Day in 1970, "We need to be an Heirloom Society instead of a Throw-Away Society."

2   Governor George E. Pataki of New York says, "Americans have to be made more aware of the value of recycling and pass that knowledge on to our children."

3   From Maine to California, from Seattle to Miami, increasingly Americans are confronted by our remarkable capacity to create *garbage.* Fresh Kills Landfill, on New York City's Staten Island, is one of the largest man-made constructions in the world (and one of the highest points of land on the eastern seaboard). The Environmental Protection Agency estimates that, on average, we each produce 4.4 pounds of garbage a day, for a total of 217 million tons in 1997. The cost of handling garbage is the fourth biggest item—after education, police, and fire protection—in many city budgets.

4   But where does each of our 4.4 pounds per day go? Some is recycled, some is incinerated, but the majority of it is laid to rest in the more than 2,300 landfills in operation in the United States today. And that's where the problem starts.

5   In examining garbage in America, *Parade* found these unsettling facts:

- Landfills produce leachate, which is runoff that can contaminate ground water.

- Incinerators, no matter how sophisticated, have risky emissions.

Landfills: Are They Safe?

6   "We have learned that it is only a matter of time until even the best engineered landfill with state-of-the-art design will leak," says Stephen Lester, science director of the Center for Health, Environment, and Justice in Falls Church, Virginia. "Even the very best landfill liners made with tough high-density polyethylene are vulnerable to chemicals found in most household garbage."

Annotation Practice Exercises

Directions: For each of the exercises below, think critically to answer the questions. This will help you gain additional insights as you read.

Practice Exercise

Does the first statement by Denis Hayes in paragraph 1 represent a *fact* or an *opinion?*

Our Garbage Problem Is Growing and Growing

The annual production of municipal solid waste in the United States has more than doubled since 1960.
Source: Office of Solid Waste/Environmental Protection Agency, 1997.

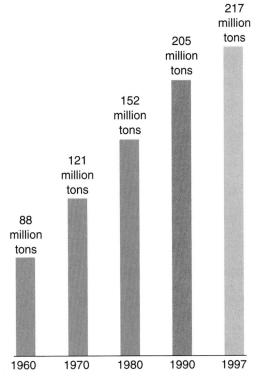

88 million tons — 1960
121 million tons — 1970
152 million tons — 1980
205 million tons — 1990
217 million tons — 1997

What's in our garbage?

Paper and paperboard........................38.6%

Yard waste 12.8%

Food waste........................10.1%

Plastics 9.9%

Metals................................. 7.7%

Glass.................................. 5.5%

Wood.................................. 5.3%

Other materials such as rubber, leather, textiles, etc. 10.1%

Who makes the most garbage?

California makes more garbage than any other state, according to *BioCycle* magazine. It generated 56 million tons in 1998. Texas made 33.8 million tons, followed by New York (30.2 million), Florida (23.8 million), Michigan (19.5 million), Illinois (13.3 million), North Carolina (12.6 million) and Ohio (12.3 million).

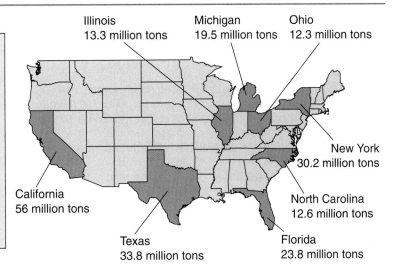

Illinois 13.3 million tons
Michigan 19.5 million tons
Ohio 12.3 million tons
New York 30.2 million tons
North Carolina 12.6 million tons
California 56 million tons
Texas 33.8 million tons
Florida 23.8 million tons

7   Toxic elements can be carried into ground-water by leachate, which is water that becomes contaminated when it seeps through waste. It's often called "garbage juice." Environmental advocates estimate that New York's Fresh Kills Landfill produces 1 million gallons per day of leachate. Even after the landfill closing on December 31, 2001, New York City must treat the leachate to stop it from leaking into New York Harbor.

What Is Garbage?

8   "It certainly isn't just food scraps and stuff you throw in a garbage pail," says William Rathje, an archeologist at the University of Arizona and coauthor of *Rubbish!* and *Use Less Stuff.* "Garbage, in order of its volume, consists mainly of cardboard, paper, yard trimmings, and food waste."

9   There is also commercial garbage, mainly from construction and demolition, as well as hazardous, radioactive, medical, and nuclear waste. Sludge from sewage treatment plants and toxic waste may end up in some municipal solid waste landfills, but generally they require special disposal.

10   Rathje, who is known as "the garbology professor" because of his exploration of landfills, says his studies have put an end to the notion that things decompose and degenerate in the landfill. "The thought that after 30 or so years newspapers and food would disintegrate is offtrack," Rathje says. "Things become mummified. We found hot dogs that could be recooked and perfectly legible newspapers." Gerald Backhaus, a waste management director in Chandler, Arizona, says, "Landfills are like giant Tupperware bowls, preserving the trash."

Not in My Backyard!

11   Communities have an almost universal resistance to having a landfill nearby. But the fact is that nearly every state engages in exporting and importing garbage. The landfills receive "tipping" fees—$10 a ton in Wyoming to $65 a ton and higher in Vermont—for the waste they handle. The tipping fees are used by communities to reduce taxes on the people who live near where the garbage is buried.

12   New York has to find a place for garbage, since it must shut down its 50-year-old Fresh Kills Landfill soon. Every day, 18 Sanitation Department barges, each carrying 700 tons of garbage, go from the city's marine transfer stations to Fresh Kills. Trucks then haul the trash to the landfill site, accompanied by an estimated 40,000 seagulls that swoop perilously close to bulldozers to snatch food scraps. In all, Fresh Kills gets the bulk of the city's daily generation of 13,200 tons of municipal waste. The city's businesses, using private carters,

Practice Exercise

What logical *conclusion* can you draw about whether landfills are safe?

_____

_____

_____

dispose of another 13,000 tons a day. This waste goes to private landfills or incinerators outside the city.

Can We Burn It?

13   The idea of burning waste to create energy seemed to make a lot of sense. But in practice it hasn't turned out that way because of the very high cost and problems of environmental pollution.

14   According to the EPA, there are 110 plants in the United States that burn municipal waste to get rid of it or use it as fuel to generate power. The word "incinerator" dismays industry representatives at the Integrated Waste Services Association, in Washington, D.C., who prefer the label "waste-to-energy plants." Maria Zannes, the association president, says the plants that burn municipal garbage to create steam and electricity are "one of the cleanest sources of power in the world. The process destroys bacteria, pathogens, and other harmful elements usually found in garbage, and burning cuts its volume by about 90 percent." Incinerators now dispose of 16 percent of the waste stream, with tipping fees ranging from $80 a ton in Alaska to $34 a ton in California and $27 in Indiana.

15   But incinerators produce bottom ash, which sifts through the grate at the bottom of the furnace; and fly ash, which is collected by air-pollution-control devices. Inevitably, some fly ash escapes.

16   "The fly ash is very toxic," says Paul Connett, a professor of chemistry at St. Lawrence University in Canton, New York. He adds that although ash by-products pass toxicity tests, the way such tests are conducted can invalidate the results.

Reduce, Reuse, Recycle

17   The most practical solution to our waste problem, says Professor Connett, "is not to perfect the destruction of our waste, but to find ways to avoid making it in the first place."

18   The Bullitt Foundation's Denis Hayes, an environmentalist who studies waste problems, agrees. "Think of how much could be saved just by cutting down the vast amount of cardboard and paper that goes into packaging," he says.

19   "The fact is, you use 96 percent less energy when you make aluminum from aluminum cans rather than bauxite; you save half the amount of energy when you recycle paper as opposed to using virgin timber," says Allen Hershkowitz, senior scientist of the Natural Resources Defense Council in New York.

20   One of the most optimistic views of the future of garbage in America comes from Jerome Goldstein, publisher and editor of *BioCycle* magazine in Emmaus, Pennsylvania, which has conducted annual reports on America's garbage for 11 years.

Practice Exercise

What logical *conclusion* can you make about what New York will do with its garbage?

_____

_____

_____

Practice Exercise

Does Allen Hershkowitz's statement in paragraph 19 represent a *fact* or an *opinion?*

_____

_____

He says: "Many places in North America have come up with a new way of thinking about garbage—creating systems that sort trash into recyclables, compostables, and disposables. These systems can keep 60 to 70 percent of what was trash out of landfills and incinerators."

Evaluating the Author's Argument

Issue:
"What controversial topic is this passage about?"

_____

_____

_____

_____

Author's argument:
"What is the author's position on the issue?"

_____

_____

_____

Author's assumptions:
"What does the author take for granted?"

_____

_____

_____

Type of support:
"What type of support does the author present?"

_____

_____

_____

Relevance of support:
"Does the support pertain directly to the argument?"

_____

_____

_____

Objectivity and completeness:
"Is the argument based on facts and other appropriate evidence?" and *"Did the author leave out information that might weaken or disprove the argument?"*

_____

_____

_____

Validity and credibility:
"Is the argument logical and believable?"

_____

_____

_____

_____

SELECTION **9-3**

Magazine Article
(Continued)

**Student Online
Learning Center (OLC)**
Go to **Chapter 9.**
Select **Reading
Selection Quiz.**

Reading Selection Quiz

This quiz has three parts. Your instructor may assign some or all of them.

Comprehension

Directions: Items 1–10 test your comprehension (understanding) of the material of this selection. These questions are the type a content area instructor (such as an ecology professor) would ask on a test over this material. You should be able to answer these questions after studying this selection. For each comprehension question below, use information from the selection to determine the correct answer. Refer to the selection as you answer each question. Write your answer in the space provided.

True or False

_____ **1.** Since 1960, the yearly production of municipal solid waste has more than doubled.

_____ **2.** The cost of handling garbage is the biggest item in many city budgets.

_____ **3.** Newspapers and food dumped into a landfill will decompose in less than ten years.

Multiple-Choice

_____ **4.** On average, each person in the United States produces how many pounds of garbage each day?
   a. 44 pounds
   b. 14 pounds
   c. 4.4 pounds
   d. less than 3 pounds

_____ **5.** Most of our garbage consists of:
   a. food waste.
   b. plastics.
   c. materials such as rubber, leather, and textiles.
   d. paper and paperboard.

_____ **6.** Which two states generate the most garbage?
   a. New York and Texas
   b. New York and Florida
   c. New York and California
   d. Texas and California

_____ **7.** What is "garbage juice"?

    a. water that has become contaminated as it seeps through waste in a landfill

    b. toxic substances found in most household garbage

    c. fuel made from recycled garbage

    d. purified water

_____ **8.** The majority of the garbage in the United States ends up in:

    a. open dumps.

    b. state-of-the-art incinerators.

    c. modern landfills.

    d. recycling plants.

_____ **9.** The problem with landfills is that:

    a. we are running out of land for them.

    b. eventually they leak.

    c. they release toxic emissions.

    d. they cause tipping fees to rise.

_____ **10.** According to Jerome Goldstein of *BioCycle* magazine, we could reduce the amount of garbage sent to landfills and incinerators by 60 to 70 percent by:

    a. sorting trash and then processing recyclables and compostables.

    b. lining landfills with leak-proof polyethylene.

    c. increasing landfill tipping fees.

    d. incinerating only those materials that do not produce fly ash.

S E L E C T I O N **9-3**   *Vocabulary in Context*

Magazine Article
(Continued)

Directions: Items 11–20 test your ability to determine the meaning of a word by using context clues. *Context clues* are words in a sentence that allow the reader to deduce (reason out) the meaning of an unfamiliar word in that sentence. Context clues also enable the reader to determine which meaning the author intends when a word has more than one meaning. For each vocabulary item below, a sentence from the selection containing an important word (*italicized, like this*) is quoted first. Next, there is an additional sentence using the word in the same sense and providing another context clue. Use the context clues from *both* sentences to deduce the meaning of the italicized word. *Be sure the answer you choose makes sense in both sentences.* If you discover that you need to use a dictionary to confirm an answer choice, remember that the meaning you select must still fit the context of *both* sentences. Write your answer in the space provided.

Pronunciation Key: ă pat ā pay âr care ä father ĕ pet ē be ĭ pit
ī tie îr pier ŏ pot ō toe ô paw oi noise ou out ŏŏ took
ōō boot ŭ cut yōō abuse ûr urge th thin *th* this hw which
zh vision ə about *Stress mark:* ′

_____ **11.** Dealing with America's *cascade* of garbage is as vital an issue as Social Security or Medicare or maintaining a defense structure.

When we opened an upper storage cabinet in my grandfather's garage, a *cascade* of 40 years' worth of *National Geographic* magazines came tumbling down on us.

cascade (kă skād′) means:

a. small, steady trickle

b. large, compacted block of material

c. limited amount

d. something that resembles a waterfall

_____ **12.** We need to be an *Heirloom* Society instead of a Throw-Away Society.

I treasure this *heirloom* baby crib because it was hand-carved by my great-great-grandfather.

heirloom (ār′ lōōm) means:

a. a possession that belongs to a relative

b. valued possession passed down in a family through succeeding generations

c. property specified in a will

d. furniture that has been restored

_____ **13.** Some is recycled, some is *incinerated,* but the majority of it is laid to rest in the more than 2,300 landfills in operation in the United States today.

The passengers' baggage was *incinerated* by the explosion and fire that raged in the plane's cargo hold.

incinerated (ĭn sĭn′ ə rā təd) means:

a. burned slightly

b. burned completely

c. damaged

d. scorched

_____ **14.** Even the very best landfill liners made with tough high-density polyethylene are *vulnerable* to chemicals found in most household garbage.

People with weakened immune systems are more *vulnerable* to infections.

vulnerable (vŭl′ nər ə bəl) means:

a. susceptible to

b. unaffected by

c. resistant to

d. killed by

_____ **15.** Environmental *advocates* estimate that New York's Fresh Kills Landfill produces 1 million gallons per day of leachate.

Advocates of free speech believe that nothing on the Internet should be regulated or censored.

advocates (ăd′ və kətz) means:
a.   supporters of something
b.   those who oppose something
c.   protestors
d.   terrorists

_____ **16.** Things become *mummified.*

When excavated from the pyramid after nearly 3,000 years, the *mummified* body of the Egyptian pharaoh was still remarkably intact.

mummified (mŭm′ mĭ fīd) means:
a.   disintegrated
b.   badly damaged
c.   destroyed
d.   dried up and preserved

_____ **17.** In all, Fresh Kills gets the bulk of the city's daily *generation* of 13,200 tons of municipal waste.

Both solar and nuclear energy can be used for the *generation* of electricity.

generation (jĕn ə rā′ shən) means:
a.   destruction
b.   conversion
c.   production
d.   reduction

_____ **18.** According to the EPA, there are 110 plants in the United States that burn *municipal* waste to get rid of it or use it as fuel to generate power.

Our *municipal* government consists of a mayor and a 12-member city council.

municipal (myo͞o nĭs′ ə pəl) means:
a.   uncontrollable
b.   pertaining to a city
c.   unspecified
d.   pertaining to a state

_____ **19.** The fly ash is very *toxic.*

Botulism is a form of severe, sometimes fatal, food poisoning caused by *toxic* bacteria.

toxic (tŏk′ sĭk) means:
a. difficult to detect
b. easy to identify
c. having a distinct odor
d. capable of causing injury or death

_____ **20.** Although ash by-products pass toxicity tests, the way such tests are conducted can *invalidate* the results.

When the private investigator discovered new evidence, he was able to *invalidate* the police officer's theory about the murder.

invalidate (ĭn văl′ ĭ dāt) means:
a. make unnecessary
b. improve the quality of; enhance
c. publicize widely
d. cancel the value of; nullify

SELECTION **9-3**

Magazine Article
(Continued)

Reading Skills Application

Directions: Items 21–25 test your ability to *apply* certain reading skills to information in this selection. These types of questions provide valuable practice for all students, especially those who must take standardized reading tests and state-mandated basic skills tests (such as the Florida CLAST Test and the Texas THEA Test). You may not have studied all of the skills at this point, so these items will serve as a helpful preview. The comprehension and critical reading skills in this section are presented in Chapters 4 through 9 of *Opening Doors;* vocabulary and figurative language skills are presented in Chapter 2. As you work through *Opening Doors,* you will practice and develop these skills. Write your answer for each question in the space provided.

_____ **21.** Which of the following is the meaning of *garbology* as it is used in paragraph 10?
a. the study of leachates in landfills
b. the study of trash in landfills
c. the study of commercial garbage
d. the study of garbage incinerators

_____ **22.** According to the information in the graph, "Who Makes the Most Garbage?", the state that generates the most garbage is:

    a. Texas

    b. New York

    c. Florida

    d. California

_____ **23.** The overall organization of the selection is:

    a. sequence.

    b. cause and effect.

    c. comparison and contrast.

    d. problem-solution.

_____ **24.** The author's point of view is:

    a. Paper should not be permitted in landfills since paper is the largest component in trash.

    b. There is an ever-increasing amount of garbage produced, and therefore we need to find ways to avoid making it in the first place.

    c. By studying landfills, scientists will be able to come up with ways to deal with the excessive trash we produce.

    d. There should be legislation that reduces the amount of commercial trash that is produced.

_____ **25.** Which of the following assumptions underlies the author's argument?

    a. Americans cannot be persuaded to care about the excessive garbage they produce.

    b. Only scientists can comprehend the magnitude of the trash problem in America.

    c. Working together, scientists and government officials can solve the problem of excessive garbage.

    d. If Americans understand the severity of the trash problem, they will be willing to help solve it.

S E L E C T I O N **9-3**

Magazine Article
(Continued)

Respond in Writing

Directions: Refer to Selection 9-3 as needed to answer the essay-type questions below.

Collaboration Option

Option for collaboration: Your instructor may direct you to work with other students on one or more of these items, or in other words, to work *collaboratively.* In that case, you should form groups of three or four students, as directed by your instructor, and work together to complete the exercises. After your group discusses an item and agrees on the answer, have a group member record it. Each member of your group should be able to explain all of your group's answers.

1. What recycling efforts does your college currently make? If your college does not participate in recycling at present, what recycling measures could it implement?

   _____

   _____

   _____

2. How does your city dispose of its garbage after it is collected? Does your city have a recycling program? (You may need to do some research to answer these questions.)

   _____

   _____

   _____

3. Give at least three examples of materials or products that can be recycled. Tell what the material is and the products into which it could be recycled.

   _____

   _____

   _____

   _____

   _____

4. Describe at least four uses for old tires or old telephone poles that would allow them to be recycled into something "new." Be creative!

   _____

   _____

   _____

   _____

   _____

5. **Overall main idea.** What is the overall main idea the author wants the reader to understand about dealing with our garbage? Answer this question in one sentence. Be sure that your overall main idea sentence includes the topic (_dealing with our garbage_) and tells the most important point about it.

   _____

   _____

   _____

Internet Resources

Read More about This Topic on the World Wide Web

Directions: For further information about the topic of the selection, visit these websites:

www.envirolink.org
This website is sponsored by EnviroLink, an online environmental community. Click on the links for *waste management* and *ground pollution.*

http://people.howstuffworks.com/landfill.htm
Read the interesting selections "How Landfills Work" and "How Much Trash Is Generated." The latter has an excellent pie chart and bar graph.

www.kab.org
This is the Keep America Beautiful Inc. website. Its mission is to empower individuals to take greater responsibility for enhancing their community's environment.

You can also use your favorite search engine such as Google, Yahoo!, or Alta-Vista (www.google.com, www.yahoo.com, www.altavista.com) to discover more about this topic. To locate additional information, type in combinations of keywords such as:

waste management

or

U.S. landfills

or

landfill efficiency

or

recycling

or

garbology

Keep in mind that whenever you go to *any* website, it is a good idea to evaluate the website and the information it contains. Ask yourself questions such as:

"Who sponsors this website?"
"Is the information contained in this website up-to-date?"
"What type of information is presented?"
"Is the information objective and complete?"
"How easy is it to use the features of this website?"

Systems for Studying Textbooks

*Developing a System
That Works for You*

CHAPTERS IN PART THREE

10 Selecting and Organizing Textbook Information

11 Rehearsing Textbook Information and Preparing
for Tests

CHAPTER 10

Selecting and Organizing Textbook Information

CHAPTER OBJECTIVES

In this chapter you will learn the answers to these questions:

- How can I select important textbook information?

- Why should I organize textbook information as I read?

- How can I use textbook features to make my studying more efficient?

- What are effective ways to mark textbooks?

- How can I take notes from textbooks by outlining, mapping, and summarizing?

- How can I interpret graphic material correctly?

SKILLS

Studying Better Rather Than Harder

Three Keys to Studying College Textbooks

- Key 1: Selectivity
- Key 2: Organization
- Key 3: Rehearsal

Using Textbook Features

- Prefaces • Tables of Contents • Part Openings • Chapter Outlines • Chapter Objectives and Introductions • Boxes • Tables • Graphic Aids • Vocabulary Aids • Study Questions and Activities • Chapter Summaries • Glossaries and Appendixes • Bibliographies, Suggested Readings, and Webliographies • Indexes • Additional Features and Supplements

Marking Textbooks: Underlining, Highlighting, and Annotating

Taking Notes from Textbooks: Outlining, Mapping, and Summarizing

- Guidelines for Outlining
- Guidelines for the Cornell Method of Note-Taking
- Guidelines for Mapping
- Guidelines for Summarizing

Guidelines for Interpreting Graphic Material

- Bar Graphs
- Line Graphs
- Pie Charts
- Flowcharts
- Tables

CREATING YOUR SUMMARY

Developing Chapter Review Cards

READING

Selection 10-1 *(History)*
"The Age of Globalization" from *American History: A Survey*
by Alan Brinkley

*One of the toughest things to learn is the ability to make yourself
do the thing you have to do, when it ought to be done, whether you like it or not.*

Thomas Huxley

Good order is the foundation of all things.

Edmund Burke

STUDYING BETTER RATHER THAN HARDER

Chapter 1 of this book emphasized that it can take considerable time to learn the information in your textbooks. Although experienced college students know this, new students sometimes do not. Beginning students often have unrealistic expectations about the amount of time it will take to read and study textbooks and prepare for tests. In fact, they may be shocked to discover just how much time studying requires; and they may also conclude, mistakenly, that *they* are the only ones who have to spend so much time.

You already know, then, that one of the things it takes to be successful is allowing sufficient study time. However, you also need to recognize that simply spending large amounts of time studying will not by itself guarantee success: what you *do* during your study times is equally important.

Staring at a book is not the same as reading, and sitting at a desk is not the same as studying. Some students who claim they are studying are in reality daydreaming. (Studying a little and daydreaming a lot do not add up to studying.) Other students really do invest many hours in studying, yet are disappointed in the results. Still other students are successful at studying, but feel discouraged because it seems to take them too much time. You yourself have undoubtedly had the experience of finishing an assignment, realizing that you did it the "hard way," and feeling frustrated because you know you worked harder and longer than you needed to. You are probably wondering, "Isn't there a better, more efficient way?"

The answer is yes, there *is* a better, more efficient way to study. This chapter and the next one describe specific techniques to help you read your textbooks more efficiently and learn to study *better,* rather than harder or longer. Often, what makes the difference between a successful student and a less successful one is *applying these study skills in a systematic way.*

You may already be familiar with some of these study techniques, or you may be learning them for the first time. In either case, by mastering and using these skills you can become a more effective student. These skills will serve you well in all your courses, adding new techniques to your study repertoire. They will also help you in a variety of other learning situations. There will always be situations in college and in the workplace in which you must organize, learn, and remember information.

Keep in mind, however, that these study skills are not "magic." They simply allow you to study better rather than harder. The truth is that being a successful student demands time, effort, skill, and dedication. You can become a better and better student each semester, but only if you are willing to invest enough time and effort, and if you bring enough skill and dedication to the task.

631

Effective students learn to select, organize, and rehearse information as they read and study their college textbook assignments.

THREE KEYS TO STUDYING COLLEGE TEXTBOOKS

The strategies in this chapter and Chapter 11 are based on three essential skills of studying: three *keys* to studying better. The three keys are *selecting* essential information to study, *organizing* that information in a meaningful way, and *rehearsing* it in order to remember it. As you will see, the skills of selectivity, organization, and rehearsal are interrelated and interdependent.

Key 1: Selectivity

KEY TERM
selectivity

Identifying main ideas and important supporting details. First of three essential study strategies.

Selectivity is the first essential key to understanding and remembering what you read. Too many students think that they can (and must) learn and remember everything in their textbooks, but this is a mistaken idea that leads only to frustration. Generally, *it is necessary to identify and remember only main ideas and major supporting details.* Therefore, you must be selective as you read and study.

Chapters 4 through 9 (Part Two, the "comprehension core") explained how to read selectively by focusing on main ideas and major supporting details. The techniques in the present chapter will further increase your ability to be selective: You will learn about textbook features, textbook marking, and textbook notes.

Key 2: Organization

KEY TERM
organization

Arranging main ideas and supporting details in a meaningful way. Second of three essential study strategies.

Organization is the second key to learning and remembering what you read. The reason is simple: *Organized material is easier to learn, memorize, and recall* than unorganized material.

Chapter 7 explained how to see relationships between main ideas and supporting details by identifying authors' patterns of writing, a skill that makes learning and remembering easier. In this chapter, you will learn additional organization skills. Using textbook features, along with your own textbook marking and note-taking, will help you to organize material more effectively.

Key 3: Rehearsal

Rehearsal, a concept introduced in Chapter 3, is the third key to learning and remembering textbook material. Rehearsal involves saying aloud or writing down material you want to memorize. It is *not* merely rereading, nor is it a casual overview. Rehearsal is a way of reviewing material that puts the material into your memory. Particularly with complex material, it is necessary to *rehearse information to transfer it to long-term (permanent) memory.*

It is important to understand that comprehending and remembering are two separate tasks. The fact that you comprehend textbook material does not necessarily mean that you will remember it. To *remember* material as well as understand it, you must take additional steps; that is, you must rehearse. Just as actors begin to memorize their lines long before a performance, students need to rehearse textbook material frequently, long before a test. (Rehearsal is discussed in detail in Chapter 11.)

Selectivity, organization, and rehearsal are the foundation for the study techniques in this chapter and in Chapter 11. At this point, however, it will be useful to look back at the three-step process for reading and studying textbooks presented in Chapter 3, since we will now be adding specific study skills to that general approach. The three-step process is shown again in the box below.

SUMMARY OF THE THREE-STEP PROCESS FOR STUDYING COLLEGE TEXTBOOKS

Step 1: Prepare to Read

- Preview to see what the selection contains and how it is organized.
- Assess your prior knowledge.
- Plan your reading and study time.

Step 2: Ask and Answer Questions to Guide Your Reading

- Use questions to guide your reading.
- Read actively, looking for answers.
- Record the answers to your questions.

Step 3: Review by Rehearsing Your Answers

- Review the material by *rehearsing,* to transfer it to long-term memory.

USING TEXTBOOK FEATURES

Using textbook features will help you locate, select, and organize material you want to learn. Taking advantage of textbook features is one way to study better rather than harder.

KEY TERM

textbook feature

Device used by an author to emphasize important material and show how it is organized.

A **textbook feature** is a device an author uses to emphasize important material or to show how material is organized. It is a way authors help readers get the most out of a textbook. Another term for *textbook feature* is *learning aid*.

There are many kinds of textbook features, and in this section you will look at some of the most important. Though no single college textbook is likely to include all of these features, most of your textbooks will have several of them.

Keep in mind that different authors may call the same feature by different names. For example, what one author may call a *chapter summary*, another may call a *chapter review, chapter highlights, key points, points to remember, a look back,* or *summing up.*

Be sure to take advantage of textbook features as you study; they are there to help you locate, select, and organize the material you must learn.

Prefaces

KEY TERM

preface

Introductory section in which authors tell readers about the text.

At the beginning of a textbook, you will usually find one or more kinds of introductory material. A **preface** is a section in which the author tells readers about the text. It is an important message from the author. Whether a preface is addressed to students, to instructors, or to both, it is likely to provide helpful information. It typically describes the author's approach to the subject, explains how the book is

Preface

"The first purpose of education," the American essayist Norman Cousins once said, *"is to enable a person to speak clearly and confidently."* [1]

The primary goal of this book is to show students how to achieve clarity and confidence during the speeches they must give in college classes, in career settings, and in their communities.

To reach this goal, I cover the basic principles of speech communication, drawn from contemporary research and from the accumulated wisdom of over 2,000 years of rhetorical theory. At the same time, I try to show students the real-life applicability of those principles by providing many examples and models from both student and professional speeches.

Source: Hamilton Gregory, *Public Speaking for College and Career,* 7th ed., p. xvi. Copyright © 2005 by The McGraw-Hill Companies, Inc. Reprinted by permission of the McGraw-Hill Companies.

organized, and mentions special features the book contains. The author may also explain how the current edition of a book improves on the previous edition.

Regardless of what a preface is called (*Preface, To the Student, A Word to Students*), you should read it before you read anything else because it gives important information and advice. For instance, in the excerpt from the sample preface (on page 634), from a speech communication text, the author explains his primary goal and his approach to teaching speech communication.

Today, many textbooks contain as part of the preface, or in addition to it, a "visual preview" of the book's features. This consists of mini-pages from the book that illustrate its special features, along with an explanation of each. Visual previews may be called exactly that, or they may also be labeled *Visual Walkthrough, Preface: A Guided Tour,* etc. Take time to study visual previews that appear in any text. They are designed to help you to use the text fully and efficiently. In *Opening Doors,* the section "To the Student" is a visual preface; it appears on pages xx–xxvi. Did you read it? If not, you should do so now.

Tables of Contents

Another feature at the beginning of a textbook is a **table of contents.** This may simply be a list of chapter titles, or it may be more detailed, including major chapter headings. Some tables of contents show chapter subheadings as well. The table of contents is your first chance to get an overview of the organization of the textbook as a whole: the "big picture."

The table of contents for *Opening Doors* appears on pages vi–xii. This table of contents contains chapter headings and subheadings and also includes information about the 29 reading selections in this text. Did you preview it when you first obtained this book? If not, take a look at it now. On page v you'll find a short version of the table of contents, titled *Brief Contents.* This feature lists only this text's part titles, chapter titles, and appendixes. As explained above, this type of table of contents gives you an overview of the text, a brief look at the text's overall scope.

In addition to the main table of contents at the beginning of a textbook, there may also be a separate listing of some special sections or features. The example on page 636, from a criminal justice text, lists "boxes" (a feature that will be discussed on page 641).

Part Openings

Chapters in a textbook may be grouped into larger sections or parts. *Opening Doors,* for example, has three major parts. **Part openings** are often useful features. A part opening may list the chapters contained in that part (as in *Opening Doors*), or it may present an opening statement or briefly describe each of its chapters. This gives you a quick overview of the material that will be covered by all chapters in the part and also suggests how those chapters are connected or interrelated.

Sometimes, important text material is given in the part opening, as in the example on page 637 from a biology textbook. (Note the definition of *microbiology.*) Information mentioned in a part opening may actually appear in several different

List of Boxes

part four

IV

Microbiology and Evolution

Microbiology is the study of viruses, bacteria, archaea, protists (such as algae and protozoans), and fungi. From the fossil record we know that microorganisms have existed on Earth for 3.5 to 3.8 billion years. Most (aside from fungi) are unicellular, and from these single cells came multicellular forms such as plants and animals—they are our ancestors. Even though microorganisms are usually too small to be seen without a microscope, they are extremely plentiful, being present on everything we touch, including ourselves.

Although they seem relatively simple, microorganisms are extraordinarily complex. They are diverse in appearance, metabolism, physiology, and genetics. Their metabolic complexity gives them the ability to grow in a wide variety of different environments and to interact with all other forms of life, including human beings. Although they may cause diseases, they also perform services that make life on Earth possible.

chapters; by consolidating this information at the beginning of the part, the authors clarify it and make it easier to remember. In the example above, the author also lists the three chapters continued in Part Four of that text.

Chapter Outlines

KEY TERM

chapter outline

Textbook feature at the beginning of a chapter, listing the topics or headings in their order of appearance.

A **chapter outline** is a list of chapter topics or headings in their order of appearance in the chapter. It provides a preliminary overview of the chapter. This feature helps you see the content and organization of the entire chapter. It lets you know in advance not only what topics the chapter will cover, but how they fit together. Trying to read or study a chapter without first seeing its outline is like trying to solve a jigsaw puzzle without looking at the picture on the box. It can be done, certainly, but it takes longer and is much more difficult!

Chapter outlines may be called by various names, such as *Chapter Contents, Chapter Topics, Preview, Overview,* or *In This Chapter;* or they may have no title at all. They can also take various forms. They may or may not actually be set up in outline style, and they may be general or detailed.

Chapter outlines in *Opening Doors,* for instance, appear on separate pages at the beginning of each chapter, include headings and subheadings, and also list reading selections. The example shown below (from a text on human sexuality) lists the major headings and subtitles of the chapter.

Chapter Objectives and Introductions

Authors often use a list of **chapter objectives** at the beginning of a chapter to tell you what you should know or be able to do after studying the chapter. Objectives appear in various forms and may also be called *Preview Questions, What You'll Learn, Goals,* and so on. In the example on page 640 (from a speech communication text), the authors list the objectives. Note the directions *explain, describe* and *identify.* In the example from the business textbook on page 639, the authors state directly, "After you have read and studied this chapter, you should be able to . . ." In *Opening Doors,* chapter objectives are written as questions.

Chapter 5

Developmental and Social Perspectives on Gender

Chapter Outline

How Many Sexes Are There?
Intersexuality
The Biological Levels of Sex
Gender Identity and Role

Sexual Differentiation
Prenatal Factors
What Abnormalities of Sexual Differentiation Can Tell Us
Hormones and Behavior
Factors of Infancy and Childhood
Factors at Puberty
Adult Gender Identity and Role

Interpretations of Gender
Models of Masculinity and Femininity
Lessons from Transgenderism
Gender as a Social Construction
Biological and Evolutionary Foundations of Gender Roles
Differences Between Females and Males

Theories of Gender Role Development
Psychodynamic Perspectives
Social Learning Theory

Cognitive-Developmental Theory
Gender Schema Theory
Behavioral Genetics
Multifactorial "Web"

Gender in Society and Culture
Growing Up Female and Male
Gender in the Workplace
Feminism
The Men's Movement
Gender Across Cultures
Gender Aware Therapy

Self-Evaluation
Masculinity and Femininity in Your Life

Chapter Summary

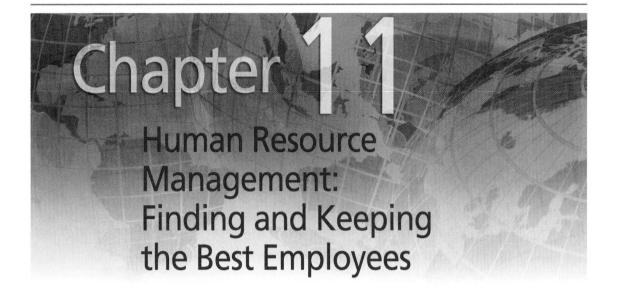

Chapter 11

Human Resource Management: Finding and Keeping the Best Employees

Learning Goals

After you have read and studied this chapter, you should be able to

1 Explain the importance of human resource management, and describe current issues in managing human resources.

2 Summarize the five steps in human resource planning.

3 Describe methods that companies use to recruit new employees, and explain some of the issues that make recruitment challenging.

4 Outline the six steps in selecting employees.

5 Illustrate the use of various types of employee training and development methods.

6 Trace the six steps in appraising employee performance.

7 Summarize the objectives of employee compensation programs, and describe various pay systems and fringe benefits.

8 Explain scheduling plans managers use to adjust to workers' needs.

9 Describe the ways employees can move through a company: promotion, reassignment, termination, and retirement.

10 Illustrate the effects of legislation on human resource management.

Source: William G. Nickels, James M. McHugh, and Susan M. McHugh, *Understanding Business,* 7th ed., p. 328. Copyright © 2005 by The McGraw-Hill Companies, Inc. Reprinted by permission of The McGraw-Hill Companies.

Intercultural Communication

What will you learn?

When you have read and thought about this chapter, you will be able to:

1. Explain why you should study intercultural communication.
2. Distinguish between cultures and co-cultures.
3. Provide examples of co-cultural strategies.
4. Explain potential intercultural communication problems.
5. Identify broad cultural characteristics.
6. Practice strategies for improving communication with people from other cultures and co-cultures.

This chapter introduces you to communication between cultures and co-cultures. Being an effective communicator means interacting positively with people from various racial, ethnic, and cultural backgrounds. The goal of this chapter is to increase your confidence in your ability to communicate with people of other cultures and co-cultures. The chapter stresses the importance of communicating effectively in an ever-changing world. The chapter explains cultures and co-cultures, reveals strategies used by co-cultures to interact with dominant cultures, identifies broad characteristics of several cultures, and provides strategies for improving intercultural communication. When you have completed this chapter you should know more about people outside your own group and you should feel more confident about communicating successfully with others.

Source: Judy C. Pearson, Paul E. Nelson, Scott Titsworth, and Lynn Harter, *Human Communication,* 2nd ed., p. 167. Copyright © 2006 by The McGraw-Hill Companies, Inc. Reprinted by permission of The McGraw-Hill Companies.

KEY TERM

chapter introduction

Textbook feature at the beginning of a chapter, describing the overall purpose and major topics.

A **chapter introduction** is an opening passage that describes the chapter's overall purpose, major topics and their sequence, or how the chapter is linked to preceding chapters. Or it may "set the scene" by giving, for instance, a case study or an anecdote. A chapter introduction may actually be called *Introduction,* or it may be indicated by special type or a large ornamental letter at the beginning of the first word. Read chapter introductions carefully; they are a helpful guide to what lies ahead.

Boxes

A **box,** or *sidebar,* is a supplementary feature that is separated from the regular text. It may appear at the bottom or top of a page of text (like the example below) or on one or more pages by itself. "Box" material may or may not be in an actual box; it may be set off in columns, in a different typeface, or by color.

Boxes can contain a variety of information: case studies, research studies, biographical sketches, interviews, excerpts from other works, controversial issues, practical applications—the possibilities are almost endless. Boxes may be numbered, and authors often create box titles to fit the subject matter: for example *Points to Ponder, Issues and Debate, Close-Up, Speaking Out, Current Research,* and *What Do You Think?*

Pay close attention to boxes: They clarify important points, provide vivid examples, and broaden and deepen your understanding of the material.

CURRENT CONTROVERSIES

DO THE REVENUES GENERATED BY GAMBLING OUTWEIGH THE COSTS?

States and localities are in an inherently competitive position with regard to raising revenues. People and firms faced with state or local tax increases can move to another state or locality where taxes are lower. Accordingly, states and localities have looked for revenue sources, such as license fees, that seem somewhat less onerous than income or sales taxes. In recent decades, gambling in one form or another has become a prime source of direct and indirect new revenues. Most states today conduct lotteries, with the revenues going either into a general fund or for a special purpose, such as the public schools. A few states, such as New Jersey, have also legalized casino gambling. At one time, Nevada was the only state with legalized gambling. The trend toward legalized gambling is heralded by some as a net benefit in terms of jobs and tax revenues. Others claim that the long-term costs of gambling far outweigh its short-term benefits.

YES: The gaming industry is helping the economy grow by creating jobs, paying taxes, and providing economic stability to hundreds of communities across the United States. Today the industry directly and indirectly employs more than one million people, from card dealers, construction workers, and carpet makers to ranchers, dancers, and cooks. In 1995, the casino gaming industry alone reported $25 billion in total revenues (double the revenues from 1990). . . . While gaming opponents may offer vague economic theories about gaming revenues, the facts show empirically that when gaming-entertainment is introduced into a region, it creates jobs and generates tax revenues.
—American Gaming Association

NO: Gambling costs far more than it benefits. Studies show that for every dollar gambling produces for a regional economy, three dollars are lost because of the economic and social costs of gambling. When government legalizes more gambling, taxpayers lose—whether they gamble or not. Gambling cannibalizes local businesses. A hundred dollars spent in a slot machine is a hundred dollars that is not spent in a local restaurant, theatre, or retail store. . . . Gambling victimizes the poor. The poorest citizens spend the largest percentage of their incomes on gambling. Those who can afford it the least gamble the most.
—National Coalition Against Legalized Gambling

Source: Thomas E. Patterson, *The American Democracy,* 5th ed., Election ed., p. 612. Copyright © 2001 by The McGraw-Hill Companies, Inc. Reprinted by permission of The McGraw-Hill Companies.

Tables

A **table** consists of material arranged in rows and columns. Tables contain words, numbers, or both. They may also include symbols, calculations, diagrams, and other types of information.

A table is an important textbook feature because it summarizes a great deal of information in a clear, concise, and organized way, as you can see from the example here. To understand a table, it is necessary to read its title and the headings of the rows and columns. (A section on interpreting tables and other graphic aids is included on pages 672–77 of this chapter.)

TABLE 13.1
Percent of State and Federal Prisoners with Minor Children

By sex of prisoners, United States, 1997

	State Prisoners			Federal Prisoners		
	Total	Male	Female	Total	Male	Female
Have minor children						
No	44.6%	45.3%	34.7%	37.0%	36.6%	41.2%
Yes	55.4	54.7	65.3	63.0	63.4	58.8
Number of minor children						
1	23.8	24.0	20.5	24.0	24.0	24.5
2	15.8	15.6	18.7	18.5	18.7	17.1
3	8.7	8.4	13.7	11.1	11.3	9.7
4	4.1	3.9	7.3	5.0	5.1	4.1
5	1.7	1.6	3.6	2.3	2.2	2.7
6 or more	1.3	1.3	1.6	2.1	2.2	0.7
Lived with children at time of admission	45.3	43.8	64.3	57.2	55.2	84.0

Source: U.S. Department of Justice, Bureau of Justice Statistics, *Incarcerated Parents and Their Children*, Special Report NCJ 182335 (Washington, DC: U.S. Department of Justice, August 2000), p. 2, Table 1; p. 3, Table 4. Table adapted by SOURCEBOOK staff.

Source: *Sourcebook of Criminal Justice Statistics 2000*, p. 521

Source: Freda Adler, Gerhard O. W. Mueller, and William S. Laufer, *Criminal Justice*, 3rd ed. Boston: McGraw-Hill, 2003, p. 394.

Graphic Aids

Graphic aids, or *illustrations,* consolidate information and present it more clearly than would be possible with words alone. Graphic aids include figures, cartoons, and photographs.

Figures include maps, charts, diagrams, graphs, and "how-to" processes. They also include anatomical drawings (like the example on page 643) and drawings of laboratory apparatus.

Textbook figures are often numbered for reference (for example, "Figure 6a," "Figure 10-2"). They typically have *legends:* titles, descriptions, and explanations that appear above, below, or alongside the illustration. To understand a figure, you must read the legend and any labels within the figure. To understand a graph, be sure to read the *axis labels* (the labels that appear on the sides and bottom of the graph).

FIGURE 5-5
Hierarchy of needs

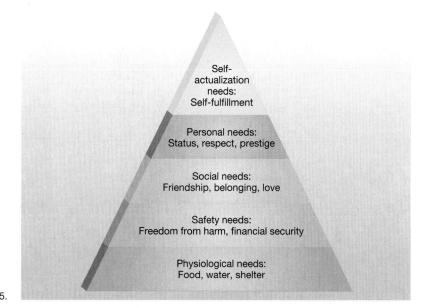

Self-
actualization
needs:
Self-fulfillment

Personal needs:
Status, respect, prestige

Social needs:
Friendship, belonging, love

Safety needs:
Freedom from harm, financial security

Physiological needs:
Food, water, shelter

Source: Roger Kerin, Steven
Hartley, and William Rudelius,
Marketing: The Core. Boston:
McGraw-Hill-Irwin, 2004, p. 105.

Source: Charles Corbin, Ruth Lindsey,
Gregory Welk, and William Corbin, *Funda-
mental Concepts of Fitness and Wellness,*
Figure 2, p. 170. Copyright © 2001 by The
McGraw-Hill Companies, Inc. Reprinted by
permission of The McGraw-Hill Companies.

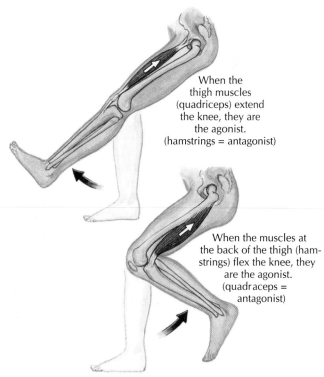

When the
thigh muscles
(quadriceps) extend
the knee, they are
the agonist.
(hamstrings = antagonist)

When the muscles at
the back of the thigh (hamstrings) flex the knee, they
are the agonist.
(quadraceps =
antagonist)

Figure 2
Agonist and antagonist muscles

"HERE WE ARE, CONWAY — THE FINANCIAL DISTRICT
KEEP YOUR EYES OPEN FOR ANY SHADY DEALS
AND VIOLATIONS OF THE SECURITIES BUSINESS."

Source: ScienceCartoonsPlus.com.
Reprinted with permission.

Developmental tests are designed to chart
the progress of infants and toddlers.

Cartoons are a popular feature because they can make a point quickly and humorously. To be sure the reader will understand how a cartoon relates to the chapter material, the author may provide a legend (a comment or explanation) in addition to the caption (as in the example above left). Often, however, a cartoon is simply allowed to "speak for itself," and the reader must infer its relationship to the text.

Some *photographs* in textbooks (like the example above right) are included to enrich the text, to provide an example of a concept or situation, or to give the "flavor" of a time or place. Other photographs are informational and should be studied as carefully as the text itself: photos of paintings, statues, and buildings in an art appreciation text (like Selection 3-3 in *Opening Doors*) are good examples. Of course, photos often fall somewhere between these two categories. Be sure to read photo captions, the words accompanying the photograph.

Vocabulary Aids

Among the most common and most helpful textbook features are **vocabulary aids,** devices that highlight important terms and definitions. Authors highlight vocabulary in a variety of ways. Important terms may be set in **boldface,** *italic,* or color. They may also be printed in the margins (like *Key Terms* in *Opening Doors,*

KEY WORDS

absolute direction 10	earth science tradition 20	relative distance 11
absolute distance 11	formal region 17	relative location 9
absolute location 9	functional region 17	scale 11
accessibility 14	globalization 15	site 9
area analysis tradition 21	locational tradition 20	situation 9
connectivity 14	natural landscape 13	spatial diffusion 15
cultural landscape 13	region 16	spatial interaction 14
culture–environment tradition 20	relative direction 10	

Source: Arthur Getis, Judith Getis, and Jerome Fellmann, *Introduction to Geography,* 10th ed., p. 21. Copyright © 2006 by The McGraw-Hill Companies, Inc. Reprinted by permission of The McGraw-Hill Companies.

one of which appears beside this paragraph). There may be a list of terms, perhaps without definitions (like the example at the top of this page) or a list of terms with definitions (like the example below). These lists can appear at the beginning of a chapter or reading or they can appear at the end of a chapter or reading. They may be called *Key Terms, Basic Terms, Terms to Know, Vocabulary, Terms to Remember,* and so on.

A list of important terms and definitions from the entire textbook may appear near the end of the book in a mini-dictionary, the *glossary. Opening Doors* includes a *Glossary of Key Reading and Study Skills Terms* on pages 749–54.

It is important to pay attention to vocabulary aids, because instructors expect you to know important terms, and often include them on tests.

Key Terms

Dominant ideology   A set of cultural beliefs and practices that help to maintain powerful social, economic, and political interests. (page 154)

Gatekeeping   The process by which a relatively small number of people control what material eventually reaches the audience. (154)

Mass media   Print and electronic instruments of communication that carry messages to often widespread audiences. (149)

Narcotizing dysfunction   The phenomenon in which the media provide such massive amounts of information that the audience becomes numb and generally fails to act on the information, regardless of how compelling the issue. (153)

Opinion leader   Someone who, through day-to-day personal contacts and communication, influences the opinions and decisions of others. (160)

Stereotype   An unreliable generalization about all members of a group that does not recognize individual differences within the group. (154)

Surveillance function   The collection and distribution of information concerning events in the social environment. (153)

Source: Richard Schaefer, *Sociology,* 9th ed., p. 167. Copyright © 2005 by The McGraw-Hill Companies, Inc. Reprinted by permission of The McGraw-Hill Companies.

Chapter Review

"I can recognize and recall information."

Self-Test Questions

1. Today's data transmission speeds are measured in _____, _____, _____, and _____.

2. A(n) _____ connects a personal computer to a cable-TV system that offers an internet connection.

3. A space station that transmits data as microwaves is a _____.

4. A company that connects you through your communications line to its server, which connects you to the internet, is a(n) _____.

5. A small rectangular area on the computer screen that contains a document or displays an activity is called a(n) _____.

6. _____ is writing an online message that uses derogatory, obscene, or inappropriate language.

7. A(n) _____ is software that enables users to view web pages and to jump from one page to another.

8. A computer with a domain name is called a(n) _____.

9. _____ comprises the communications rules that allow browsers to connect with web servers.

10. A(n) _____ is a program that adds a specific feature to a browser, allowing it to play or view certain files.

11. Unsolicited email in the form of advertising or chain letters is known as _____.

12. The expression of how much data—text, voice, video, and so on—can be sent through a communications channel in a given amount of time is known as _____.

Multiple-Choice Questions

1. Kbps means _____ bits per second.
   a. 1 billion
   b. 1 thousand
   c. 1 million
   d. 1 hundred
   e. 1 trillion

2. A location on the internet is called a(n):
   a. network
   b. user ID
   c. domain
   d. browser
   e. web

3. In the email address *Kim_Lee@earthlink.net.us*, Kim_Lee is the:
   a. domain
   b. URL
   c. site
   d. user ID
   e. location

4. Which of the following is *not* one of the four components of a URL?
   a. web protocol
   b. name of the web server
   c. name of the browser
   d. name of the directory on the web server
   e. name of the file within the directory

5. Which of the following is the fastest method of data transmission?
   a. ISDN
   b. DSL
   c. modem
   d. T1 line
   e. cable modem

6. Which of the following is *not* a netiquette rule?
   a. Consult FAQs.
   b. Flame only when necessary.
   c. Don't shout.
   d. Avoid huge file attachments.
   e. Avoid sloppiness and errors.

7. Which protocol is used to retrieve email messages from the server to your computer?
   a. HTTP (Hypertext Transport Protocol)
   b. SMTP (Simple Mail Transfer Protocol)
   c. POP3 (Post Office Protocol version 3)
   d. POP (point of presence)

8. Who owns the internet?
   a. Microsoft
   b. IBM
   c. Apple
   d. U.S. government
   e. No one owns the internet; the components that make up the Internet are owned and shared by thousands of public and private entities.

The Internet & the World Wide Web

⸮ Questions for Discussion

1. Discuss public attitudes toward the poor. How have these attitudes changed over time?

2. How have the income differences between social classes been changing in America? What are the social and political consequences of these disparities?

3. Contrast the differences between income and wealth. Which is more important in the upper class and why?

4. Most Americans say they are middle class. Are they? What does it mean to be middle class in American society?

5. The chapter states that there are roughly 10 million working poor. What is life like for them? What does the future hold?

6. What is meant by the term "American Dream"? Has it changed? Is it a reasonable expectation in contemporary America?

7. Discuss structural mobility in America. Is it increasing or decreasing?

8. Millions of immigrants have come to America hoping to make their fortune. Is it possible today? What field(s) would you recommend to someone seeking economic success?

9. How does the government calculate poverty? Who are the poor? As a group what are the characteristics of the poor?

10. Welfare reform has become a major political topic. Why is this? What changes in welfare programs are occurring nationally and in your state?

Source: J. John Palen, *Social Problems for the Twenty-First Century,* p. 57. Copyright © 2001 by The McGraw-Hill Companies, Inc. Reprinted by permission of The McGraw-Hill Companies.

Study Questions and Activities

KEY TERM

study questions and activities

Textbook features such as exercises, drills, and practice sections that direct readers to essential information.

Many textbooks include **study questions and activities,** such as *exercises, drills,* and *practice sections.* These can be among the most important features you use, because they direct you to essential information you will be expected to know. Generally, if you are able to answer study questions and exercises, you will be able to do well on an actual test.

Study questions and activities may appear at the beginning or end of a chapter, a reading, or other subdivisions of the text. In *Opening Doors,* for instance, questions appear preceding and following each reading selection. In addition to the terms noted above, questions or activities may be called *Questions for Study and Review, Review, Ask Yourself, Self-Test, Check Your Mastery, Mastery Test, Learning Check, Check Your Understanding, Topics for Discussion, Problems,* and so forth. The examples shown here are typical. Today, most textbooks also include Web-based activities. These may be called by names such as *WebReview, Internet Connection, Taking It to the Net,* and *Internet Exercises.*

Don't neglect study questions and activities; take the time to work on them. They provide valuable practice and give you a way to monitor your learning. Also, instructors often use these same items, or similar items, on tests.

Chapter Summaries

A **chapter summary** is one of the most helpful textbook features because in it the author collects and condenses the essential ideas of the chapter. Many students find it useful to read a chapter summary both before and after studying a chapter. Of course, when you read a summary before you read the chapter, you may not understand it completely, but you will have a general idea of the most important material in the chapter. Therefore, you will know to pay special attention to it as you read.

Summaries can be short (like the example below, from a public speaking text) or a full page or more in length. A summary may also be called *Conclusion, Recapitulation, Looking Back, Summing Up, Key Points, Key Concepts,* and so on. Chapter summaries in textbooks may be written as paragraphs or lists, and they may contain special graphic aids. One that also contains graphics may be referred to as a *Visual Summary.* The second example on page 649, from a marketing text, highlights main points and key terms.

■ Summary

The nervousness engendered by stage fright is a normal, understandable emotion experienced by most public speakers. The major reasons for speakers' nervousness are (1) fear of being stared at, (2) fear of failure, (3) fear of rejection, and (4) fear of the unknown.

Instead of trying to eliminate nervousness, welcome it as a source of energy. Properly channeled, it can help you give a better speech than you would deliver if you were completely relaxed.

The best way to avoid excessive, crippling nervousness is to pour time and energy into preparing and practicing your speech. Then, when you stand up to speak, deal rationally with your nervous symptoms (such as trembling knees and dry throat); remind yourself that the symptoms are not a prelude to disaster, but instead are evidence that you are keyed up enough to give a good speech. Never call attention to your nervousness and never apologize for it; the listeners don't care about your emotional state—they just want to hear your message. Concentrate on getting your ideas across to the audience; this will get your mind where it belongs—on your listeners and not on yourself—and it will help you move your nervousness to a back burner, where it can still simmer and energize you without hindering your effectiveness.

SUMMARY

1 Marketing is the process of planning and executing the conception, pricing, promotion, and distribution of goods, services, and ideas to create exchanges that satisfy individual and organizational objectives. This definition relates to two primary goals of marketing: (a) discovering the needs of consumers and (b) satisfying them.

2 Because an organization doesn't have the resources to satisfy the needs of all consumers, it selects a target market of potential customers — a subset of the entire market — on which to focus its marketing program.

3 Four elements in a marketing program designed to satisfy customer needs are product, price, promotion, and place. These elements are called the *marketing mix,* the *four Ps,* or the *controllable variables* because they are under the general control of the marketing department.

4 Environmental factors, also called *uncontrollable variables,* are largely beyond the organization's control. These in-

clude social, technological, economic, competitive, and regulatory forces.

5 Building on customer value and relationship marketing concepts, successful firms develop mutually beneficial long-term relationships with their customers.

6 In marketing terms, U.S. business history is divided into four periods: the production era, the sales era, the marketing concept era, and the current market orientation era.

7 Marketing managers must balance consumer, organizational, and societal interests. This involves issues of ethics and social responsibility.

8 Profit-making and nonprofit organizations perform marketing activities. They market goods, services, and ideas that benefit consumers, organizations, and countries. Marketing creates utilities that give benefits, or customer value, to users.

Source: Roger Kerin, Steven Hartley, and William Rudelius, *Marketing: The Core,* p. 19. Copyright © 2004 by The McGraw-Hill Companies, Inc. Reprinted by permission of The McGraw-Hill Companies.

Glossaries and Appendixes

glossary

Mini-dictionary at the end of a textbook that lists important terms and definitions from the entire text.

appendix

Section at the end of a book that includes supplemental material or specialized information.

A **glossary** is a mini-dictionary at the end of a textbook that lists important terms and definitions from the entire text. It is a feature you should refer to often especially as you prepare for tests. Some glossaries, such as the one in *Opening Doors,* indicate where each term was introduced in the book.

An **appendix** is a section at the end of a book that includes supplemental material or specialized information. (Information may be presented as an appendix so that it can be referred to conveniently, or because it is too long to be included in any single chapter, or because it relates to more than one chapter.) The appendix is a useful textbook feature because it presents additional information that you may need to refer to repeatedly.

In an American history or American government text, the Declaration of Independence and the Constitution may appear as appendixes. Physics and chemistry texts may have formulas in appendixes. In texts with self-tests, an answer key may appear as an appendix. A very helpful appendix in some history texts is a chronology or "time line." The first page of an appendix from a text on effective group discussion is shown on page 651. It describes formats that groups can use to present information to the public.

Opening Doors has four appendixes: a "Glossary of Reading and Study Skills Key Terms," a "List of Word Parts," "A United States Map, World Map, and List of World Capitals," and a "Master Vocabulary List."

Source: Gary Kelly, *Sexuality Today,* updated 7th ed., p. G-1. Copyright © 2004 by The McGraw-Hill Companies, Inc. Reprinted by permission of The McGraw-Hill Companies.

Glossary

A

abnormal   anything considered not to be normal, that is, not conforming to the subjective standards a social group has established as the norm. 198

abortifacients   substances that cause termination of pregnancy. 329

acquaintance (date) rape   a sexual encounter forced by someone who is known to the victim. 461

acquired dysfunction   a difficulty with sexual functioning that develops after some period of normal sexual functioning. 538

acquired immunodeficiency syndrome (AIDS)   fatal disease caused by a virus that is transmitted through the exchange of bodily fluids, primarily in sexual activity and intravenous drug use. 508

activating effect   the direct influence some hormones can have on activating or deactivating sexual behavior. 109

acute urethral syndrome   infection or irritation of the urethra. 50

adolescence   period of emotional, social, and physical transition from childhood to adulthood. 166

affectional   relating to feelings or emotions, such as romantic attachments. 204

afterbirth   the tissues expelled after childbirth, including the placenta, the remains of the umbilical cord, and fetal membranes. 295

agenesis (absence) of the penis (ae-JEN-a-ses)   a congenital condition in which the penis is undersized and nonfunctional. 82

AIDS   acquired immunodeficiency syndrome. 508

amniocentesis (am-nee-oh-sen-TEE-sis)   a process whereby medical problems with a fetus can be determined while it is still in the womb; a needle is inserted into the amniotic sac, amniotic fluid is withdrawn, and fetal cells are examined. 289

amnion (AM-nee-on)   a thin membrane that forms a closed sac around the embryo; the sac is filled with amniotic fluid, which protects and cushions the embryo. 272

anal intercourse   insertion of the penis into the rectum of a partner. 356

androgen (ANN-dra-gin)   a male hormone, such as testosterone, that affects physical development, sexual desire, and behavior. Testosterone is produced by both male and female sex glands

and influences each sex in varying degrees. 109

androgen insensitivity syndrome   a developmental condition in which cells do not respond to fetal androgen, so that chromosomally male (XY) fetuses develop external female genitals. There also is a feminization of later behavioral patterns. 125

androgyny (an-DROJ-a-nee)   the presence of high frequencies of both masculine and feminine behaviors and traits in the same individual. 130

anejaculation   lack of ejaculation at the time of orgasm. 85

anodyspareunia   pain associated with anal intercourse. 543

anorchism (a-NOR-kiz-um)   rare birth defect in which both testes are lacking. 75

anti-Müllerian hormone (AMH)   secretion of the fetal testes that prevents further development of female structures from the Müllerian ducts. 120

aphrodisiacs (af-ro-DEE-zee-aks)   foods or chemicals purported to foster sexual arousal; they are believed to be more myth than fact. 357

areola (a-REE-a-la)   darkened, circular area of skin surrounding the nipple of the breast. 55

artificial embryonation   a process in which the developing embryo is flushed from the uterus of the donor woman 5 days after fertilization and placed in another woman's uterus. 283

artificial insemination   injection of the sperm cells of a male into a woman's vagina, with the intention of conceiving a child. 278

asceticism (a-SET-a-siz-um)   usually characterized by celibacy, this philosophy emphasizes spiritual purity through self-denial and self-discipline. 213

asexuality   a condition characterized by a low interest in sex. 401

autoerotic asphyxiation   accidental death from pressure placed around the neck during masturbatory behavior. 418

autofellatio (aw-toh-fe-LAY-she-o)   a male providing oral stimulation to his own penis, an act most males do not have the physical agility to perform. 348

B

Bartholin's glands (BAR-tha-lenz)   small glands located in the opening through the minor lips that produce some secretion during sexual arousal. 45

behavior therapy   therapy that uses techniques to change patterns of behavior; often employed in sex therapy. 552

benign prostatic hyperplasia (BPH)   enlargement of the prostate gland that is not caused by malignancy. 83

bestiality (beest-ee-AL-i-tee)   a human being's having sexual contact with an animal. 419

biological essentialism   a theory that holds that human traits and behaviors are primarily formed by inborn biological determinants such as genes and hormonal secretions, rather than by environmental influences. 14

biphobia   prejudice, negative attitudes, and misconceptions relating to bisexual people and their lifestyles. 211

birth canal   term applied to the vagina during the birth process. 294

birthing rooms   special areas in the hospital, decorated and furnished in a nonhospital way, set aside for giving birth; the woman remains here to give birth rather than being taken to a separate delivery room. 297

bisexual   refers to some degree of sexual activity with or attraction to members of both sexes. 204

blastocyst   the ball of cells, after 5 days of cell division, that has developed a fluid-filled cavity in its interior; it has entered the uterine cavity. 272

bond   the emotional link between parent and child created by cuddling, cooing, and physical and eye contact early in the newborn's life. 297

bondage   tying, restraining, or applying pressure to body parts as part of sexual arousal. 417

brachioproctic activity   a sexual activity, sometimes called "fisting" in slang, involving insertion of the hand into a partner's rectum. 358

brothels   houses of prostitution. 413

bulbourethral glands   another term for Cowper's glands. 82

C

call boys   highly paid male prostitutes. 413

call girls   highly paid female prostitutes who work by appointment with an exclusive clientele. 413

cantharides (kan-THAR-a-deez)   a chemical extracted from a beetle that, when taken internally, creates irritation of blood vessels in the genital region; it can cause physical harm. 357

Source: John Brilhart, Gloria Galanes, and Katherine Adams, *Effective Group Discussion,* 10th ed., p. 391. Copyright © 2001 by The McGraw-Hill Companies, Inc. Reprinted by permission of The McGraw-Hill Companies.

APPENDIX A   **MAKING PUBLIC PRESENTATIONS OF THE GROUP'S OUTPUT**

Often groups must make public presentations of their output, which may take the form of a report, a set of findings or recommendations, and so forth. The group's leader or selected representatives may present a report from the group to the parent organization, a political body, an open meeting of interested community representatives, or another type of public gathering. The members of the audience at such public gatherings may themselves become participants who will discuss the report of the group. The following information presents formats for a variety of public discussion sessions in which group members may find themselves participating.

PANEL DISCUSSIONS

A **panel discussion** is a public presentation in which a small group of people representing varying perspectives informally discusses issues relevant to an important question in front of a listening audience. For example, a panel might discuss abortion laws, solutions to congested parking on campus, what might be done to solve a community's solid waste problem, or the responsibility of society to the victims of crimes. A panel format is sometimes used with a group of aspirants for political office.

Groups may participate in panel discussions in a variety of ways. A group may be asked to plan and conduct an entire panel discussion, in which case the entire group must research and present fairly all relevant points of view about the issue. More typically, a group known to support a particular point of view will be asked to supply a representative to serve as a panelist with other panelists who represent different viewpoints. The **moderator** of a panel coordinates the discussion so it does not ramble and so all viewpoints are represented. Participants need to be both knowledgeable about the question under discussion and articulate in expressing their, or the group's, opinions. Panelists generally have an outline of questions to follow, but their speaking is relatively impromptu. Panelists need not agree on anything except which issues to discuss; the lively argument that often ensues can make for an intellectually stimulating program. The panel format is excellent for presenting an overview of different points of view on an issue of public concern. CNN and C-SPAN often include such discussions in their programming.

KEY TERM
bibliography

List of sources from which the author of the text has drawn information.

Bibliographies, Suggested Readings, and Webliographies

A **bibliography** (which usually appears near the end of a textbook) is a list of sources: books, articles, and other works from which the author of the text has drawn information. A bibliography may also be called *References, Works Cited,* or *Sources.* A bibliography sometimes lists works the author recommends for further (supplemental) reading, such as the one on page 652. Or it may be titled *Annotated Bibliography* and include comments about the attributes of each work listed. Of course, some bibliographies serve both functions and are called *Bibliography and Selected Readings* or *References and Bibliography.*

KEY TERM
suggested readings

Textbook feature listing
the author's recommen-
dations for supplemental
reading or research,
sometimes with
annotations.

A list of **suggested readings** often appears at the end of chapters (or parts), where it may be called *Additional Readings, Suggestions for Further Reading, Supplementary Readings,* and so on. Like the humanities textbook example below, suggested readings may be annotated. That is, the textbook author may provide brief descriptions and explain why each work is listed. (Notice that this example also includes *Suggestions for Listening.*)

■ SUGGESTIONS FOR FURTHER READING

Bryant, Jennings, and Dolf Zillmann. *Media Effects.* Hillsdale, NJ: Erlbaum, 1994.

Comstock, George, and Erica Scharrer. *Television: What's On, Who's Watching, and What It Means.* New York: Academic Press, 1999.

Harris, Richard. *A Cognitive Psychology of Mass Communication.* Hillsdale, NJ: Erlbaum, 1999.

Heibert, Ray. *Impact of Mass Media.* New York: Longman, 1995.

Jeffres, Leo, and Richard Perloff. *Mass Media Effects.* Prospect Heights, IL: Waveland Press, 1997.

Lowery, Shearon, and Melvin DeFleur. *Milestones in Mass Communication Research.* New York: Longman, 1994.

National Television Study. Thousand Oaks, CA: Sage, 1997.

Reeves, Byron. *The Media Equation: How People Treat Computers, Television and New Media Like Real People and Places.* Stanford, CA: Center for the Study of Language, 1996.

Van Evra, Judith. *Television and Child Development.* Hillsdale, NJ: Erlbaum, 1990.

Zillmann, Dolf. *Media, Children and the Family.* Hillsdale, NJ: Erlbaum, 1994.

Source: Joseph Dominick, *The Dynamics of Mass Communication: Media in the Digital Age*, 7th ed., p. 515. Copyright © 2002 by The McGraw-Hill Companies, Inc. Reprinted by permission of The McGraw-Hill Companies.

SUGGESTIONS FOR FURTHER READING

Primary Sources

CASTIGLIONE, B. *The Book of the Courtier.* Translated by G. Bull. New York: Penguin, 1967. A flowing translation; includes a helpful introduction and descriptions of characters who participate in the conversations recorded by Castiglione; first published in 1528.

MACHIAVELLI, N. *The Prince.* Translated by G. Bull. New York: Penguin, 1971. The introduction covers Machiavelli's life and other writings to set the stage for this important political work; written in 1513.

SUGGESTIONS FOR LISTENING

WILLAERT, ADRIAN (about 1490–1562). Willaert is particularly noted for his motets, such as *Sub tuum praesidium,* which reflect the Renaissance humanist ideal of setting the words precisely to the music. His *Musica nova,* published in 1559 and including motets, madrigals, and instrumental music, illustrates the complex polyphony and sensuous sounds that made him a widely imitated composer in the second half of the sixteenth century.

Source: Roy Matthews and F. DeWitt Platt, *The Western Humanities*, 4th ed., p. 343. Copyright © 2001 by The McGraw-Hill Companies, Inc. Reprinted by permission of The McGraw-Hill Companies.

KEY TERM
webliography

List of websites that
feature material related
to a topic.

A **webliography** is a list of websites that feature material related to a topic. A webliography gives a list of Web "addresses" where pertinent material is located. Some webliographies (such as the ones that accompany the reading selections in *Opening Doors*) are annotated. This means that there is a brief description of the type of material found at each website. Websites usually contain "links," which allow users to go directly to additional, related websites. In textbooks, webliographies may

Annotated Bibliography

Prologue   An Introduction to Integrated Humanities

Bennett, William J. *To Reclaim a Legacy: A Report on the Humanities in Higher Education.* Washington, D.C.: Government Printing Office, 1984. Bennett bewails the current lack of emphasis on our past cultural creations and argues for their centrality in education and for understanding our own civilization.

Boorstein, Daniel J. *The Discoverers: A History of Man's Search to Know His World and Himself.* New York: Random House, 1983. An exciting introduction to cultural and intellectual history. Very highly recommended.

Hassan, Ihab, and Sally Hassan, eds. *Innovation/ Renovation: New Perspectives on the Humanities.* Madison: The University of Wisconsin Press, 1982. Innovative approaches to furthering our understanding of the humanities.

Munro, Thomas. *The Arts—Their Interrelations.* Western Reserve University Press, 1967. An unusual and fascinating approach to comparative aesthetics by a man who is both a professor of philosophy and professor of art.

Post, Gaines, Jr. *The Humanities in American Life.* Berkeley: University of California Press, 1980. Supported by the Rockefeller Foundation, this report of a special commission notes deficiencies in current education and recommends a better integration of the humanities into the curriculum.

Rader, Melvin, and Bertram Jessup. *Art and Human Values.* Englewood Cliffs, N.J.: Prentice Hall, 1976. The role of art in formulating and communicating values.

Read, Herbert. *Education Through Art.* New York: Pantheon Books, 1974. The author bases his approach to aesthetic education on Plato's thesis that art should be the basis of education.

Toynbee, Arnold. *A Study of History.* In several editions (preferably the one-volume abridgement). This classic study articulates and documents one of the most impressive culture-epoch theories of the rise and fall of civilizations.

Chapter 1   The Emergence of Early Culture

Amiet, Pierre. *Art of the Ancient Near East.* Trans. John Shepley and Claude Choquet. New York: Harry N. Abrams, 1980. Probably the best illustrated text on this subject now available.

Kostof, Spiro. *A History of Architecture: Settings and Rituals.* New York: Oxford University Press, 1985. From the first prehistoric environments on record to the most recent examples of architecture and urban design. A splendid one-volume survey.

Moorthat, Anton. *The Art of Mesopotamia: The Classical Art of the Near East.* New York: Phaidon, 1969. Richly illustrated.

Wagner, Roy. *The Invention of Culture.* Revised and expanded edition. Chicago: University of Chicago Press, 1981. The basic idea that humans invent their own realities, culture, society, and so forth.

Chapter 2   Egypt: Land of the Pharaohs

Aldred, Cyril. *The Egyptians.* New York: Thames & Hudson, 1984. An overview of cultural and political history.

Edwards, I. E. S. *The Pyramids of Egypt.* Baltimore: Penguin, 1975. The development of the pyramids with speculation on their meaning.

Osman, Ahmed. *Stranger in the Valley of the Kings: Solving the Mystery of an Ancient Egyptian Mummy.* San Francisco: Harper & Row, 1987. A well-documented thesis that the biblical Joseph was the father-in-law of Amenhotep III and grandfather of Akhenaton, thus implying that the latter's monotheism was derived from the Hebrew religion.

Romer, John. *Ancient Lives: Daily Life in Egypt of the Pharaohs.* New York: Holt, Rinehart & Winston, 1984. Fascinating study of a New Kingdom village based on recent excavations.

Samson, Julia. *Amarna: City of Akhenaton and Nefertiti.* London: Biddles, 1972. Discussion, with many illustrations, of one of the finest collections of Amarna art.

Source: Robert C. Lamm, *The Humanities in Western Culture*, 10th ed., Volume 1, p. 469. Copyright © 1996 by The McGraw-Hill Companies, Inc. Reprinted by permission of The McGraw-Hill Companies.

be called by various names, such as *Read More about It on the World Wide Web, Related Websites, Net Search,* and *On the Web* (such as in the example below, which comes from a fitness and wellness textbook).

Bibliographies, suggested readings, and Webliographies can be especially helpful for research assignments, such as papers and reports, or when you want or need to read other material to improve your understanding of the text.

Source: Charles Corbin, Ruth Lindsey, Gregory Welk, and William Corbin, *Fundamental Concepts of Fitness and Wellness,* p. 138. Copyright © 2001 by The McGraw-Hill Companies, Inc. Reprinted by permission of The McGraw-Hill Companies.

 Web Review

Web review materials for Concept 9 are available at *www.mhhe.com/hper/physed/clw/student/.*

American Council on Exercise
   www.acefitness.org
**American Association
   for Active Lifestyles and Fitness**
   www.aahperd.org/aaalf/aaalf-main.html
**National Association for Sport
   and Physical Education**
   www.aahperd.org/naspe/naspe-main.html
**President's Council on Physical
   Fitness and Sports**
   *http://www.whitehouse.gov/WH/PCPFS/
   html/fitnet.html*
American Running Association
   www.americanrunning.org
Disabled Sports USA
   www.dsusa.org
Special Olympics International
   www.specialolympics.org
Women's Sports Foundation
   www.lifetimetv.com/wosport/index_.htm

Indexes

At the end of a textbook you will usually find one or more indexes. An **index** is an alphabetical listing of topics and names in the text, giving the specific pages on which you can find information about them. The index is a useful textbook feature because it helps you locate information quickly.

On page 656 is an example of a general index, from a biology text. Some textbooks have a separate *subject index* and *name index,* like the examples on page 655 from a business text. Anthologies and other textbooks with reading selections often have an *index of authors and titles.*

Indexes sometimes include special features. For instance, in the example from the biology textbook, the notations *f* and *t* tell readers where they will find figures (photos, etc.) and tables. The index for *Opening Doors* begins on page I-1.

Additional Features and Supplements

There are numerous other types of textbook features. Many texts (such as *Opening Doors*) include *epigraphs,* quotations at the opening of chapters (or other

Name Index

Subject Index

Source: William G. Nickels, James M. McHugh, and Susan M. McHugh, *Understanding Business,* 7th ed., p. I-13. Copyright © 2005 by The McGraw-Hill Companies, Inc. Reprinted by permission of The McGraw-Hill Companies.

sections) that suggest overall themes or concerns. Some texts put vivid or provocative quotations in the margins.

Depending on the subject matter, a text may include special *exhibits* or *examples* such as student papers, plot summaries, profit-and-loss statements, documents, forms, and printouts. Useful material (such as the periodic table of the elements in a chemistry text) may even appear on the inside of the cover. Sometimes a textbook has a unique feature, such as the chapter review cards in *Opening Doors.*

Finally, many textbooks have *supplements,* separate aids that accompany the text. These might include *study guides, supplemental readings, student workbooks,* and *CD-ROMs* (computer diskettes). Supplements are a good investment: They have been developed to help you guide your own learning, test yourself, and check your progress. (In addition, many texts have online learning centers, websites that contain such things as supplemental exercises and activities, practice quizzes, key term flashcards, Web links to related information, and video clips. The *Opening Doors* OLC is an example.)

Index

All these textbook features can help you use your study time effectively and efficiently. Students often remark that in college textbooks "everything seems important." They find it hard to get a sense of how the facts and concepts add up to a coherent whole. Taking advantage of textbook features as you read can enable you to identify the essential information in a chapter and to understand its organization. Remember that authors and publishers want to help you study and learn from your textbooks. For this reason, they put a great deal of time, effort, and thought into designing textbook features.

STUDY TIPS FOR USING TEXTBOOK FEATURES

Prefaces

Read the preface to see what the book contains, how it is organized, and what its special features are.

Tables of Contents

Use the table of contents, particularly if no chapter outlines are given. Your chapter study notes should cover each item listed in the table of contents. Pay attention to the size and type style, which indicate major and minor headings.

Part Openings

Reading a part opening will help you understand the scope of what is contained in the section, how the section is organized, and how its chapters are interrelated.

Chapter Outlines

Pay attention to major topics in a chapter outline. Your notes should also include all subtopics. The author has done some of your selecting for you, so take advantage of it.

Chapter Objectives and Introductions

Use objectives and introductions to test yourself on the chapter material. Try to write out the answers from memory.

Boxes

Pay attention to boxed information. It helps you understand the text. Also, you may be tested on boxed material.

Tables

Pay attention to tables. They consolidate important information and help you understand relationships among ideas. Instructors may base test questions on them.

Graphic Aids

Watch for graphic aids. Figures, cartoons, and photographs may present or reinforce important information or may explain the text.

Vocabulary Aids

Write out the definition for each term included in a vocabulary aid. If your book includes a glossary, use it. It is your responsibility to learn the special vocabulary of each subject you study. Expect to be asked these terms on tests.

Study Questions and Activities

Take the time to answer study questions and work on exercises, especially if your instructor

(Continued on next page)

has not provided study questions. Think carefully about discussion topics. Items like these may appear on tests.

Chapter Summaries

Read the chapter summary both *before and after* you read the chapter itself. This will help you to read thoughtfully and to consolidate your learning.

Appendixes

Use appendixes for reference and as a source of additional information.

Bibliographies, Suggested Readings, and Webliographies

Use source lists when you are doing papers, reports, and other research assignments. You can also use supplementary readings to improve your understanding of the textbook.

Indexes

Indexes will help you quickly locate specific material in textbooks.

Additional Features

Look for epigraphs (quotations), exhibits, and examples in the text. Don't neglect special reference material that may appear on the inside of the cover.

Supplements

Study guides, study guides with supplemental readings, workbooks, and software accompanying your textbooks usually prove to be good investments. Use supplements like these to direct and focus your study, to test yourself, and to evaluate your learning.

MARKING TEXTBOOKS: UNDERLINING, HIGHLIGHTING, AND ANNOTATING

KEY TERMS

underlining and highlighting

Techniques for marking topics, main ideas, and definitions.

annotation

Explanatory notes you write in the margins of a textbook to organize and remember information.

It has been estimated that as much as 80 percent of the material on college tests comes from textbooks. For this reason alone, you need to be able to underline, highlight, and annotate your textbooks effectively.

Underlining and **highlighting** are techniques for marking topics, main ideas, and important definitions in reading materials. **Annotation** refers to explanatory notes you write *in the margins of your textbook* to help you organize and remember important information that appears within paragraphs. Taking a moment to annotate information (write or jot it down) also helps you concentrate. When you are reading a difficult textbook, you need to concentrate on one paragraph at a time. Effective students mark their textbooks by both underlining or highlighting *and* annotating.

Here are some guidelines for *underlining and highlighting*. First, you need to avoid the most typical mistake students make in marking textbooks: *overmarking* (underlining or highlighting too much). Students often make this mistake because they try to underline or highlight *while* they are reading the material instead of *after* they have read it. The process of underlining and highlighting a textbook is very selective. Further, you cannot know what is important in a paragraph or section until you have *finished* reading it. Remember, for example, that the main idea sometimes does not appear until the end of a paragraph. Remember, too, that you may not be able to understand some paragraphs until you have read an entire section. The rule, then, is this: *Read first, and underline only after you have identified the important ideas.* A word of caution: Some students substitute underlining and highlighting for *thinking.* They mistakenly believe that if they have marked a lot in a chapter, they must have read it carefully and found the important information. To avoid this error, follow these steps: Read and *think; then* underline or highlight *selectively.*

Second, you need to know the kinds of things you *should* underline or highlight. As mentioned above, underline or highlight the *topic* of a paragraph. Underline or highlight the *main idea* of a paragraph if it is stated directly. Keep in mind that often you will not need to underline every word of a main idea sentence to capture the idea it is expressing. Underline or highlight important *definitions.* You may find it helpful to mark important *terms* as well.

Third, you need to know the kinds of things you should *not* underline or highlight. Do *not* underline or highlight supporting details, since this results in over-marking. (As you will see below, annotation can be used effectively to indicate supporting details.)

Once you have underlined and highlighted topics, main ideas, and important terms, you will want to *annotate,* that is, write explanatory notes and symbols in the margins. If a textbook has narrow margins, you may prefer to use notebook paper or even stick-on notes for your annotations, to give yourself more room.

The following box shows how a passage from a human development textbook (about different forms of marriage) could be underlined and annotated. Notice how relatively little is underlined and how helpful the annotations would be in preparing for a test on this material.

AN EXAMPLE OF UNDERLINING AND ANNOTATION

A lifestyle practice that apparently exists in all societies is marriage—a socially and/or religiously sanctioned union between a woman and a man with the expectation that they will perform the mutually supportive roles of wife and husband. After studying extensive cross-cultural data, anthropologist George P. Murdock (1949) concluded that reproduction, sexual relations, economic cooperation, and the socialization of offspring are functions of families throughout the world. We now recognize that Murdock overstated the matter, because in some societies, such as Israeli kibbutz communities, the family does not perform all four of these functions (Spiro, 1954; Gough, 1960). What Murdock describes are commonly encountered tendencies in family functioning in most cultures.

(def) marriage: socially and/or religiously sanctioned union of a woman and a man with the expectation they will play the mutually supportive roles of wife and husband

*4 tendencies in functions of families:
—reproduction
—sexual relations
—economic cooperation
—socialization of offspring

(Continued on next page)

Societies differ in how they structure marriage relationships. Four patterns are found: monogamy, one husband and one wife; polygyny, one husband and two or more wives; polyandry, two or more husbands and one wife; and group marriage, two or more husbands and two or more wives. Although monogamy exists in all societies, Murdock discovered that other forms are not only allowed but preferred. Of 238 societies in his sample, only about one-fifth were strictly monogamous.

Polygyny has been widely practiced throughout the world. The Old Testament reports that both King David and King Solomon had several wives. In his cross-cultural sample of 238 societies, Murdock found that 193 (an overwhelming majority) permitted husbands to take several wives. In one-third of these polygynous societies, however, less than one-fifth of the married men had more than one wife. Usually only the rich men in a society can afford to support more than one family.

In contrast with polygyny, polyandry is rare among the world's societies. And in practice, polyandry has not usually allowed freedom of mate selection for women—it has often meant simply that younger brothers have sexual access to the wife of an older brother. For example, if a father is unable to afford wives for each of his sons, he may secure a wife for only his oldest son.

(def) Four patterns of marriage:
—*monogamy: 1 husband/1 wife*
—*polygyny: 1 husband/2+ wives*
—*polyandry: 2+ husbands/1 wife*
—*group marriage: 2+ husbands/2+ wives*

Polygyny: widely practiced
Old Testament kings with several wives:
—*Solomon* ⎱ *ex.*
—*David* ⎰
—*Murdock study: 193/238 societies permitted polygyny*
—*Usually only rich were polygynous*

Polyandry: rare
—*women not usually allowed to choose mates*
—*often simply means younger brothers have sexual access to wife of older brother.*

Source: James Vander Zanden, revised by Thomas Crandell and Corinne Crandell, *Human Development*, Updated 7th ed., p. 476. Copyright © 2003 by The McGraw-Hill Companies, Inc. Reprinted by permission of The McGraw-Hill Companies.

You may be wondering what types of annotations are helpful and why it is necessary to annotate as well as to underline or highlight. First, you may want to list the topics of certain paragraphs in the margin. This can help you grasp the sequence of the author's ideas.

Writing out an *important term* and a brief *definition* in the margin is also helpful. When your instructor uses these terms in class, you will recognize them and be able to record them more easily in your lecture notes. And, of course, you will remember the terms and definitions more clearly. Obviously, you will need to know the meaning of these terms for tests.

Also, you may choose to list major *supporting details* in shortened form in the margin. Annotating is an effective, convenient, and concise way to organize supporting details; also, jotting details down in the margin will help you connect them with the main ideas they support.

Formulated main ideas are another type of helpful annotation. Your formulated main idea sentence can be written in the margin next to the paragraph.

Symbols and *abbreviations* are still another helpful form of annotation. Your symbols and abbreviations will enable you to locate important material quickly and

Wouldn't it be convenient if a computer software program could automatically find and highlight main ideas in college textbooks?

CLOSE TO HOME   JOHN McPHERSON

Source: CLOSE TO HOME © 2000 John McPherson. Reprinted with permission of UNIVERSAL PRESS SYNDICATE. All rights reserved.

(if necessary) return to passages that need further study. Here are a few examples of abbreviations and symbols you can use in the margins of your textbooks:

def *Definition.* Use *def* when an important term is defined.

? *Question mark.* Use this when you do not understand something and need to study it further or get help with it.

1, 2, 3 . . . *Numbers.* Use numbers when an author gives items in a list or series.

* *Asterisk.* Use an asterisk to mark important information.

ex *Example.* Use *ex* to identify helpful examples.

TAKING NOTES FROM TEXTBOOKS: OUTLINING, MAPPING, AND SUMMARIZING

In addition to underlining, highlighting, and marginal annotations, *taking notes from textbooks* is another important study skill. Students who take notes and review them are four to five times more likely to recall important information during a test. In fact, you are much more likely to recall *any* idea that you have written out. Note-taking is your single greatest aid to successful test preparation later on. (Note-taking during a lecture is also your single greatest aid to concentration.) Three very useful forms of textbook note-taking are outlining, mapping, and summarizing.

Guidelines for Outlining

Outlining is a formal way of organizing main ideas and the supporting details that go with them. Even if you underline main ideas in your textbook and annotate supporting details in the margin, there may be times when it is helpful to outline a section or chapter. Outlines are especially useful for organizing complex material. Outlining is best done on separate paper rather than written in the textbook.

When should you outline? Obviously, you will not need to outline every section or every chapter. As mentioned above, outlining can be very helpful for complex material. It is also useful when you need to condense a lengthy section or chapter in order to give yourself an overview. Because outlining condenses information and lets you see and understand how an entire section or chapter is organized, an outline makes the material easier to study and remember.

How do you create an outline of textbook material? To outline a paragraph, you need to write its main idea. Then, on separate, indented lines below the main idea, write the supporting details that go with it, like this:

I. Main idea sentence
  A. Supporting detail
  B. Supporting detail
  C. Supporting detail
  D. Supporting detail

For longer passages consisting of several paragraphs, continue your outline in the same way:

I. First main idea sentence
  A. Supporting detail for main idea I
  B. Supporting detail for main idea I
  C. Supporting detail for main idea I
  D. Supporting detail for main idea I

II. Second main idea sentence
  A. Supporting detail for main idea II
  B. Supporting detail for main idea II

III. Third main idea sentence
  A. Supporting detail for main idea III
  B. Supporting detail for main idea III
  C. Supporting detail for main idea III

The purpose of your study outline is to show you how ideas are related. Making your outline look perfect is not as important as making sure that the relationships are clear to *you*. Main ideas should stand out, and it should be obvious which details go with each main idea. Roman numerals (I, II, III) are often used for main ideas, and uppercase letters (A, B, C, D) are used for supporting details. This notation helps you see how ideas are related. When the information you are writing for a main idea or a detail is longer than a single line, be sure to indent the second line beneath the first word in the line above it. Do not go any farther to the left. The goal is to make the numbers and letters stand out clearly.

An outline can consist of phrases or sentences. However, when you have complex material, a sentence outline works well because it gives complete thoughts.

Use the same title for your outline as the one that appears in the original material. Do not entitle your outline "Outline." It will be obvious that it is an outline!

The box below shows a sentence outline of a passage from Selection 7-3. Notice also the identifying title: *Reactions to Impending Death.*

SAMPLE OUTLINE

Reactions to Impending Death

I. Elisabeth Kübler-Ross, a thanatologist, found in her research on the terminally ill that they tend to have certain basic emotional reactions as they prepare for death.

    A.   There are five types of reactions: denial and isolation, anger, bargaining, depression, and acceptance.

    B.   Different patients display different emotions.

    C.   Reactions may occur in various orders, although the general pattern is shock, denial, anger, and acceptance.

    D.   Several factors influence a person's type and sequence of emotional reactions.

    E.   Overall, a person's approach to dying reflects his or her approach to living.

    F.   These same emotions are characteristic of anyone who has experienced a major loss.

II. There are several uses of Kübler-Ross's research.

    A.   It can be used to help the dying cope with their emotions by enabling them to discuss these emotions.

    B.   It can be used to help survivors cope with the dying person's emotions as well as their own.

III. A hospice is a special hospital for the terminally ill.

    A.   A hospice can enhance a dying person's final days.

    B.   Life goes on more normally in this pleasant, informal environment.

    C.   There are many supportive people, including personnel and family members.

IV. Survivors normally go through a period of grieving or bereavement following an ill person's death.

    A.   Grief follows the pattern of shock or numbness; pangs of grief; apathy, dejection, and depression; and resolution.

    B.   Survivors' reactions vary, but survivors are usually able to discharge their anguish by grieving, and thus prepare to go on living.

    C.   Each person must grieve at his or her own pace and in his or her own way.

Guidelines for the Cornell Method of Note-Taking

The Cornell Method of note-taking is an organized way of taking notes that includes a built-in review column. Sheets of loose-leaf notebook paper are marked ahead of time with a line to rule off a review column on the left side of the page. (See the examples on pages 665–66.) You record information on the main part of the page using outline form to organize main ideas and the supporting details that go with each of them. Read over your notes to make sure you will be able to understand them weeks from now. Write out words that are unclear and be sure you understand all your abbreviations. Add any words or information needed to clarify your notes, such as a detail, an example, or a definition. Underline, circle, or star key points. (To evaluate your current note-taking skills, complete the "Checklist for Good Note-Taking" on page 668.)

When you have finished taking notes from your book or from a lecture, fill in the review column by writing clue words or questions. When you are ready to review, cover your notes so that only the review column shows. Try to answer the review column questions by reciting the information aloud. If you cannot remember, uncover the material, look at the answer, re-cover it, and try it again until you can recite it successfully. (An example of the information in Selection 7-3, "Reactions to Impending Death," in Cornell format is provided on page 666.)

The Cornell format for taking notes.

(Rule Review Column off ahead of time.)

Date/Course	Topic of Notes
Reduce to clues to Recite from when Reviewing	Record information in outline form (at a minimum, put topics on separate lines and indent details on separate lines beneath the points they go with).
After class, fill in this column with either clue words or questions to help you recite the material in your notes.	Write notes in your own words. Use abbreviations and sketches. To review, cover the portion of your notes to the right of the line. Try to recite information in this part out loud, from memory. If you need help, uncover the material, look at the answer, re-cover it, and try it again until you can recite it successfully from memory. *If you can't say it from memory, you don't know it!*

Review Column   Note-Taking Area

Review Column	**Record Section**
↓	↓
Nov. 14-PSY/1301	Reactions to Impending Death
What are 5 general reactions of dying persons?	1. Thanatologist Elisabeth Kübler-Ross found terminally-ill patients have certain reactions as they prepare for death: • denial and isolation ("test results are wrong!") • anger (at God, at those who are healthy, etc.) • bargaining ("If you let me live, I'll be a better person.") • depression • acceptance (uses time left as well as possible)
Is there one specific sequence of reactions?	−not everyone has all 5 reactions or has them in that order
Uses of findings?	−helps both the dying and the survivors understand and cope with their reactions
What is a hospice?	2. Hospice = hospital for the terminally ill that seeks to improve the quality of life their final days: • supportive staff, clergy, counselors • pleasant surroundings • round-the-clock visits from everyone, including pets • constant attention, flexible rules
What is bereavement?	3. Bereavement = natural, normal period of grief after a death
What are the stages of grief?	Grief follows predictable pattern: • shock or numbness (dazed; ends by time of funeral) • pangs of grief (painful yearning for person; suffering acute; may think person is still alive, see them in dreams) • apathy, dejection and depression (lasts weeks or months; person feels futility, but resumes activities) • resolution (acceptance; memories now include positive images and nostalgic pleasure)
Purpose of grief?	−Allows survivors to discharge anguish and prepare to go on living
Does suppressing grief lead to problems later on?	−Suppressing grief does not lead to depression later on; lack of intense grief does not predict problems later on; each person must grieve in his or her own way and at own pace.
↑ **Fill in questions after writing information in the Record Section. Cover Record Section so you can test yourself aloud.**	↑ **Record information here in an organized fashion.**

Because of its built-in "Review Column," the Cornell Format is an effective way to take notes. The review column is especially helpful when studying for tests.

CREATING A REVIEW SHEET USING THE CORNELL NOTE-TAKING FORMAT

- You should take your notes on loose-leaf notebook paper in Cornell format. Remove your notes and spread them out on a desk or table top so that only the review column of each page is visible.

- Overlap the review columns so that you create a continuous review column for the material you want to review.

- Use this built-in review aid when you review for tests. Prepare by reciting the answers to questions you have written in the review column.

- As you answer each question in the review column, lift up the page to check whether your answer is complete and correct.

- When you can say the information from memory—without looking at it—you *know* it.

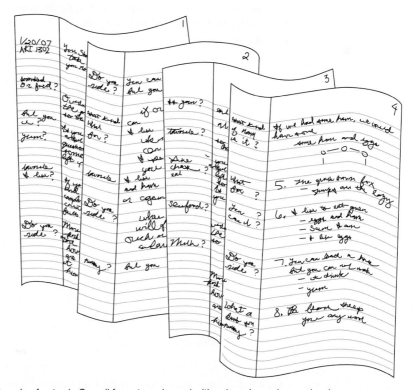

Sample of notes in Cornell format overlapped with only review columns showing.

CHECKLIST FOR GOOD NOTE-TAKING

Here are guidelines for evaluating notes you take from classroom lectures or from your textbooks. Answer **yes** or **no** for each question.

Which of the following do you currently do when you take notes?

Yes   No

___ ___ **1.** Use standard-sized loose-leaf notebook paper rather than a spiral notebook?

___ ___ **2.** Rule off your paper ahead of time so that you can use the Cornell format for clear, organized notes?

___ ___ **3.** Always label your notes with the name of the course and the date (for lecture notes) or the chapter and pages (for material from your text)?

___ ___ **4.** Write the title or general topic of the notes at the top of the page?

___ ___ **5.** Wait until a point shapes up before you write it down?

___ ___ **6.** Write each major point on a separate line and skip a line or two before writing another major point?

___ ___ **7.** Set off details and examples by indenting them beneath the main point they go with?

___ ___ **8.** Add quick sketches or diagrams whenever they can help illustrate a point or aid recall later on?

___ ___ **9.** Invent your own abbreviations to save time?

___ ___ **10.** Strive for brief yet complete notes?

___ ___ **11.** Edit your notes for readability, clarity, and completeness as soon as possible after you take them, and then review your notes within 24 hours?

___ ___ **12.** Review again within a week to strengthen your recall later on?

Circle items to which you answered **No.** Consider ways to change or improve your note-taking skills by following the strategy listed in the items you circled.

Guidelines for Mapping

Another form of textbook note-taking is mapping. **Mapping** is an informal way of organizing main ideas and supporting details by using boxes, circles, lines, arrows, and the like. The idea is to show information in a way that clarifies relationships among ideas. Like outlining, mapping is done on separate paper rather than in the margins of the textbook.

One simple type of map consists of the topic or main idea in a circle or box in the middle of the sheet of paper, with supporting details radiating out from it. Another type of map has the main idea in a box at the top of the paper, with supporting ideas in smaller boxes below it and connected to it by arrows or "leader lines." If the information is sequential (for instance, significant events in World War I), a map can take the form of a flowchart. Samples of these kinds of maps are shown on page 669.

TYPES OF MAPS

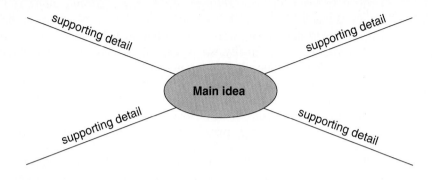

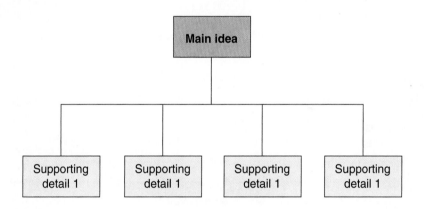

Significant events in World War I:

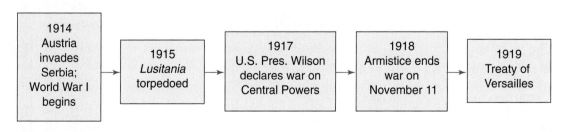

There is no one right way to make maps. They are personal records of information you want to understand and remember. However, research on study maps (which are also called *concept maps, study maps, learning maps,* and *idea maps*) indicates that using different colors helps many students remember the material. It also seems to help if key words are written in bold capital letters and if simple sketches are included. Finally, when you make a map, you may find it helps to turn the page sideways, since this gives you more room.

A study map for the passage on reactions of dying patients is shown below. It condenses all the important information onto a single page. A complete study map such as this requires considerable thought and effort.

Since outlines and study maps both show relationships among important ideas in a passage, how can you decide which to use for a particular passage? Your decision will depend on how familiar you are with each technique and on how the passage itself is written. Keep in mind that mapping is an informal study technique, whereas outlining can be formal or informal. When you are asked to prepare a formal outline in a college course, do not assume that you can substitute a study map.

SAMPLE STUDY MAP

Reactions to Impending Death

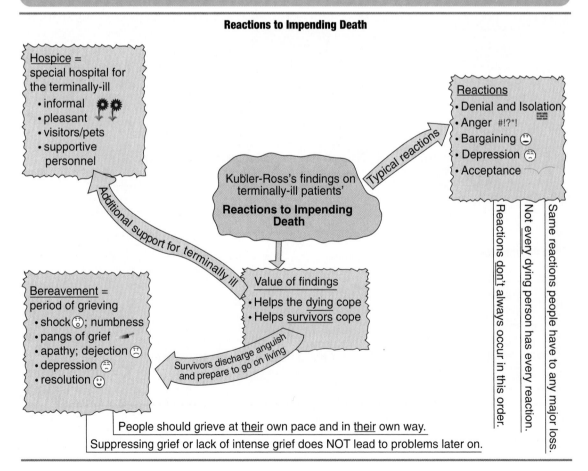

Guidelines for Summarizing

A third technique of textbook note-taking is summarizing. A **summary** is a way of condensing into one paragraph all the main ideas an author has presented in a longer selection (such as an essay or article) or a section of a chapter. When you have correctly identified the main ideas in a passage, you have identified the information necessary to prepare your summary.

Summarizing is an effective way to check your comprehension. Writing a summary also helps you transfer the material into your long-term memory. You will find summarizing particularly helpful if you will be answering essay questions on a test. Summarizing allows you to "rehearse" an answer you may have to write on the test.

Here are some things to keep in mind when you are preparing a summary:

- **Include all the main ideas.** You must include *all* the main ideas the author presents in the section. Include a supporting detail (such as the definition of an important term) only if a main idea cannot be understood without it.

- **Do not add anything.** You must not add anything beyond the author's ideas (such as information from other sources or your own opinions).

- **Keep the original sequence.** Present the ideas in the same order that the author has used. In other words, keep the same sequence in which the author presented the information.

- **Reword as necessary, providing connections.** You should reword (paraphrase) the main ideas and supply clear connections among these ideas.

- **Give your summary a title.** Use the same title that the original material has. Do not entitle your summary "Summary."

The box below shows a sample summary of the passage about the reactions of people who are terminally ill.

SAMPLE SUMMARY

Reactions to Impending Death

Elisabeth Kübler-Ross is a thanatologist whose research with terminally ill patients revealed that they tend to display several emotional reactions as they prepare for death. The five basic responses she found were *(1) denial and isolation, (2) anger, (3) bargaining, (4) depression,* and *(5) acceptance.* Different patients display different emotions. These may occur in various orders, although the general pattern is shock, denial, anger, and acceptance. Several factors influence a person's types and sequence of emotions. Overall, the individual's approach to dying reflects his or her approach to living. Emotions displayed by a dying person are the typical, appropriate ones that accompany any major loss. This information can be used to help dying persons and survivors cope with their emotional reactions. Most important, knowledge of these emotions can enable others to be supportive of dying people and help them discuss death and their feelings. The hospice, a hospital for the terminally ill, can enhance a dying person's last days. The ill person is offered emotional support and guidance from family as well as from other people. Life

(Continued on next page)

goes on more nearly as normal in this informal, pleasant environment. A period of bereavement (grieving) by survivors normally follows the death of the ill person. Grief also follows a pattern: *shock or numbness; pangs of grief; apathy, dejection, and depression;* and *resolution.* Survivors' reactions vary, but survivors are usually able to discharge their anguish by grieving, and thus they prepare to go on living. Each person must grieve at his or her own pace and in his or her own way.

GUIDELINES FOR INTERPRETING GRAPHIC MATERIAL

KEY TERMS

graphic aids

Visual explanations of concepts and relationships, for example, bar graphs, line graphs, pie charts, flowcharts, and tables.

Nearly every textbook contains graphic aids: tables, graphs (such as bar graphs, pie charts, and line graphs), time lines, diagrams, charts, maps, cartoons, photographs, flowcharts, and so forth. **Graphic aids** provide visual explanations of concepts and relationships in ways that are often more concise and easier to understand than words alone. For example, graphic aids can be used to illustrate numerical relationships (such as profits and losses), sequences (such as stages of cognitive development), processes (such as how a bill becomes a law), and spatial relationships (such as a floor plan). Writers include graphic aids precisely because they enable students to grasp and recall information more easily. When an author directs you to a graphic aid ("See Figure 1-3"), you should stop and look at it *at that very moment* and then resume reading. Authors mention graphic aids at the point where they think the graphic aids will help readers the most.

In the past, graphic aids in texts served mainly to illustrate information discussed in paragraphs. Today, though, graphic material is also used to present additional information that does *not* appear in the written portion. Instead, the graphics often add to or complement the written material. If you don't pay attention to them, you may miss information that doesn't appear anywhere else. **Visual literacy,** the ability to "read" (interpret) images, graphs, diagrams, and other visual symbols, is becoming a crucial skill in today's world. (Think about the thousands of symbols and images you see in print or on screen every day of your life.)

visual literacy

The ability to "read" (interpret) images, graphs, diagrams, and other visual symbols.

Although graphic aids contain important information, they can appear difficult unless you know how to interpret them. The following strategies will enable you to interpret graphic material more effectively and efficiently.

- Read the *title* and any *explanation* that accompanies the graphic aid. The title tells you what aspect of the writer's topic is being clarified or illustrated.

- Check the *source* of the information presented in the graphic aid to see if it seems current and reliable.

- Read all the *headings* in a table and all the *labels* that appear in a chart or a graph (such as those on the bottom and side of a graph) to determine what is being presented or measured. For example, the side of a bar graph may be labeled "Annual Income in Thousands of Dollars" and the bottom may be labeled "Level of Education."

- Examine the *units of measurement* in a graphic aid (for example, decades, percents, thousands of dollars, per hour, kilograms, per capita, milliseconds).

• Finally, use the information provided by the title and explanation (if any), the source, the headings and labels, and the units of measurement to help you determine the *important points or conclusions* that the author is conveying. Try to understand how the information in the graphic aid clarifies or exemplifies the written explanation. See if there are patterns or trends that allow you to draw a general conclusion. A *trend* is a steady, overall increase or decrease.

Here are explanations and examples of five commonly used graphic aids: bar graphs, line graphs, pie charts, flowcharts, and tables. With bar graphs, line graphs, and tables, look for trends. Along with each graphic aid is a summary of its important elements as well as the conclusions that can be drawn from the graph.

Bar Graphs

A *bar graph* is a chart in which the length of parallel rectangular bars is used to indicate relative amounts of the items being compared. The bars in a bar graph may be vertical or horizontal. The bar graph below is from a textbook on human development.

• *Title or explanation.* Population of the United States Aged 65 and Over, 1900–2030 (projected).
• *Source.* U.S. Bureau of the Census.
• *Headings and labels.* Millions (of people), years (1900–2030; bars for 2000 to 2030 differ from the other bars to indicate that all of these figures were projections at the time the data were compiled).
• *Units of measurement.* Millions (increments of 10 million), years (20-year increments from 1900 to 1980; 10-year increments from 1980 to 2030), percents (of population aged 65 and over).

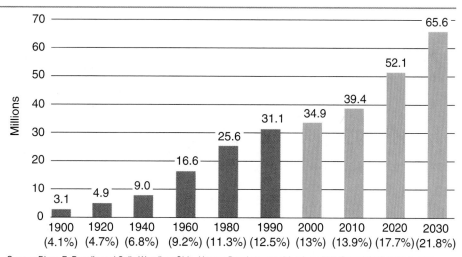

Population of the United States Aged 65 and Over
Source: U.S. Bureau of the Census

Source: Diane E. Papalia and Sally Wendkos Olds, *Human Development,* 6th ed., p. 528. Copyright © 1995 by The McGraw-Hill Companies, Inc. Reprinted by permission of The McGraw-Hill Companies.

- *Important points or conclusions.* Since the beginning of the 20th century, the number of people aged 65 and over has continued to increase. This trend is expected to continue through the aging of the "baby boom" generation. The number of people 65 and over will nearly double by 2030.

Line Graphs

A *line graph* is a diagram whose points are connected to show a relationship between two or more variables. There may be one line or several lines, depending on what the author wishes to convey.

- *Title or explanation.* Juvenile Homicides by Weapon.
- *Source.* FBI, *Supplementary Homicide Reports.*
- *Headings and labels.* Number of homicides; year; handgun, other/weapon, other gun.
- *Units of measurement.* Number, in increments of 500; year, from 1976 to 1994, in 2-year increments.
- *Important points and conclusions.* Since approximately 1981, handguns have accounted for the greatest number of juvenile homicides. Deaths from handguns began to increase sharply around 1988, and they had nearly quadrupled by the mid-1990s. Although other weapons have consistently accounted for about 500 homicides per year, handguns and other guns together have been responsible for the majority of deaths.

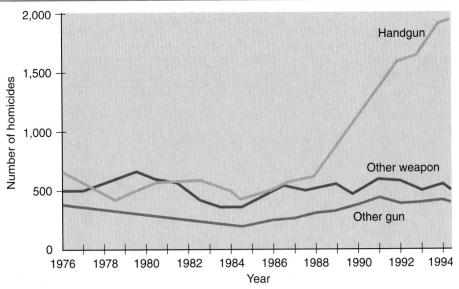

Figure 12.3
Juvenile Homicides
by Weapon
(*Source:* FBI,
Supplementary
Homicide Reports)

Source: J. John Palen, *Social Problems for the Twenty-First Century*, p. 334. Copyright © 2001 by The McGraw-Hill Companies, Inc. Reprinted with permission of The McGraw-Hill Companies.

**Figure 23-1
Language Use
on the Internet,
1996 and 2005**
(*Source:* Global
Reach 2003)

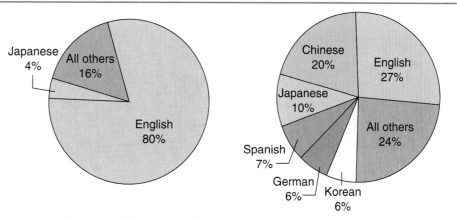

Source: Richard Schaefer, *Sociology,* 9th ed., p. 538. Copyright © 2005 by The McGraw-Hill Companies, Inc. Reprinted by permission of The McGraw-Hill Companies.

Pie Charts

A *pie chart,* as its name suggests, is a circle graph in which the sizes of the "slices" represent parts of the whole. Pie charts are a convenient way to show the relationship among component parts as well as the relationship of each part to the whole. The example above is from a sociology textbook.

● *Title or explanation.* Language Use on the Internet 1996 and 2005.
● *Source.* Global Reach 2003.
● *Headings and labels.* 1996; 2005 (Projected).
● *Units of measurement.* Percentage.
● *Important points and conclusions.* Since 1996 the use of English on the Internet has decreased sharply while Chinese has increased dramatically. By 2005, Asian languages represented at least 36 percent of the language used on the Internet.

Flowcharts

A *flowchart* shows steps in procedures or processes by using boxes, circles, and other shapes that are connected with lines or arrows. The example on the next page is from the *Dictionary of Cultural Literacy* and presents the legislative process (how a bill becomes a law).

● *Title or explanation.* How a Bill Becomes a Law.
● *Source.* Hirsch, Kett, and Trefil, *The Dictionary of Cultural Literacy,* 1988.
● *Headings and labels.* Introduction, Committee Action, Floor Action, Enactment into Law.
● *Units of measurement.* None.

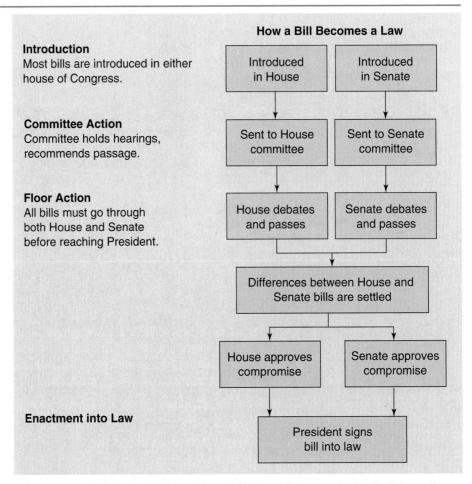

How a Bill Becomes a Law

Introduction
Most bills are introduced in either house of Congress.

Introduced in House | Introduced in Senate

Committee Action
Committee holds hearings, recommends passage.

Sent to House committee | Sent to Senate committee

Floor Action
All bills must go through both House and Senate before reaching President.

House debates and passes | Senate debates and passes

Differences between House and Senate bills are settled

House approves compromise | Senate approves compromise

Enactment into Law

President signs bill into law

Source: From E. D. Hirsch Jr., Joseph F. Kett, and James Trefil, "How a Bill Becomes a Law," in *The Dictionary of Cultural Literacy,* p. 319. Copyright © 1988 by Houghton Mifflin Company. Reprinted by permission of Houghton Mifflin Company. All rights reserved.

- *Important points and conclusions.* Although bills can be introduced in either the House or the Senate, all bills must go through committee hearings and through floor action in both the House and Senate, before the bill is submitted to the president for enactment into law.

Tables

A *table* is a systematic listing of data in rows and columns. The example on page 677, from a textbook on human development, presents data about how school-age children spend their time. (Textbook features, including tables, are discussed earlier in this chapter.)

- *Title or explanation.* Male-Female Involvement in Crime.
- *Source.* Federal Bureau of Investigation, *Crime in the United States, 1993.*

- *Headings or labels.* UCR Index Crimes; Percentage of Arrests by Gender (Males, Females).
- *Units of measurement.* Percentage.
- *Important points and conclusions.* In every category of crime, the vast majority of those arrested are males, who on average account for approximately 80 percent of all arrests. In four major categories, more than 90 percent of those arrested were male. The only category of crime in which females accounted for more than approximately 16 percent of the arrests was larceny-theft. Approximately one-third of all arrests in that category were female.

Table 12.2 Male-Female Involvement in Crime

	Percentage of Arrests by Gender	
UCR Index Crimes	**Males**	**Females**
Murder and nonnegligent manslaughter	90.6%	9.4%
Rape	98.7	1.3
Robbery	91.3	8.7
Aggravated assault	84.3	15.7
Burglary	90.1	9.9
Larceny-theft	67.3	32.7
Motor vehicle theft	88.2	11.8
Arson	85.3	14.7
Average, all major crimes	80.5	19.5

Source: Federal Bureau of Investigation, *Crime in the United States, 1993* (Washington, DC: U.S. Government Printing Office, 1994).

Source: J. John Palen, *Social Problems for the Twenty-First Century.* Boston: McGraw-Hill, 2001, p. 341.

Directions: The four graphic aids in this exercise come from marketing, psychology, advertising, and human development textbooks. Identify each type of graphic aid and answer the questions that follow.

Figure 18.3
Online consumer sales by product/service category: 2001 and 2005
Source: Roger Kerin, Steven Hartley, and William Rudelius, *Marketing: The Core,* p. 394. Copyright © 2004 by The McGraw-Hill Companies, Inc. Reprinted by permission of The McGraw-Hill Companies.

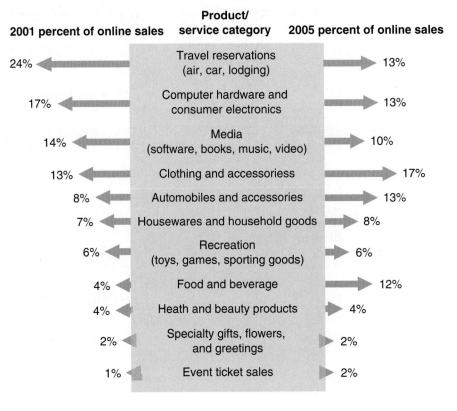

2001 percent of online sales	Product/service category	2005 percent of online sales
24%	Travel reservations (air, car, lodging)	13%
17%	Computer hardware and consumer electronics	13%
14%	Media (software, books, music, video)	10%
13%	Clothing and accessoriess	17%
8%	Automobiles and accessories	13%
7%	Housewares and household goods	8%
6%	Recreation (toys, games, sporting goods)	6%
4%	Food and beverage	12%
4%	Heath and beauty products	4%
2%	Specialty gifts, flowers, and greetings	2%
1%	Event ticket sales	2%

1. What type of graphic aid is this? _____

2. What is the topic of this graphic? _____

3. Sales in which categories decreased between 2001 and 2005? _____

_____

4. What important points or conclusions can be drawn about online consumer sales?_____

_____

_____

_____

_____

Table 4–1 Now Hear This

Various sounds, their decibel levels, and the amount of exposure that results in hearing damage

Sound	Decibel Level	Exposure Time Leading to Damage
Whispering	25 dB	
Library	30 dB	
Average home	50 dB	
Normal conversation	60 dB	
Washing machine	65 dB	
Car	70 dB	
Vacuum cleaner	70 dB	
Busy traffic	75 dB	
Alarm clock	80 dB	
Noisy restaurant	80 dB	
Average factory	85 dB	16 hours
Live rock music (moderately loud)	90 dB	8 hours
Screaming child	90 dB	8 hours
Subway train	100 dB	2 hours
Jackhammer	100 dB	2 hours
Helicopter	105 dB	1 hour
Sandblasting	110 dB	30 minutes
Auto horn	120 dB	7.5 minutes
Live rock music (loud)	130 dB	3.75 minutes
Air raid siren	130 dB	3.75 minutes
THRESHOLD OF PAIN	140 dB	Immediate damage
Jet engine	140 dB	Immediate damage
Rocket launching	180 dB	Immediate damage

5. What type of graphic aid is this? _____

6. What is the topic of this graphic aid? _____

_____

7. What are the three column headings? _____

8. Assuming they did not take precautions to protect their hearing, would an average factory worker or a helicopter pilot be more likely to experience job-related hearing damage? _____

_____

9. At what decibel level do sounds become painful to humans? _____

10. What important points or conclusions can be drawn about the decibel level of sounds and damage to hearing? _____

_____

_____

_____

**Percentage of Total Sales of
Online Product Mix in 2000**
Note: Computer products
(which total $2.1 billion), travel
($1.58 billion), and entertainment
($1.3 billion) account for the
lion's share.

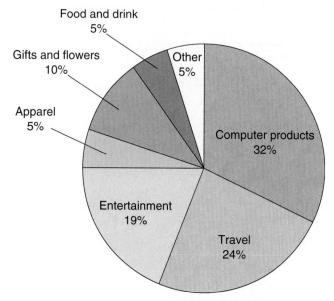

Source: William F. Arens, *Contemporary Advertising,* 7th ed., p. 512. Copyright © 1999 by The McGraw-Hill Companies, Inc. Reprinted by permission of The McGraw-Hill Companies.

11. What type of graphic aid is this? _____

12. What is the topic of this graphic aid? _____

13. What category represents the third highest percentage of online sales? _____

14. Which is greater: online sales of food and drink or online sales of gifts and flowers? _____

15. What important point or conclusion can be drawn about types of online sales? _____

_____

_____

_____

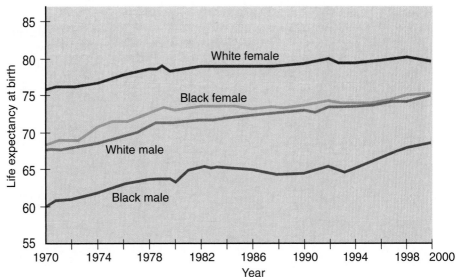

Life expectancy by sex and race, 1970–2000.
(*Source:* Anderson, 2001b; data for 2000 from Miniño et. al., 2002)

Source: Diane E. Papalia, Sally Wendkos Olds, and Ruth Duskin Feldman, *Human Development,* 9th ed., p. 467. Copyright © 2004 by The McGraw-Hill Companies, Inc. Reprinted by permission of The McGraw-Hill Companies.

16. What type of graphic aid is this? _____

17. What is the topic of this graphic aid? _____

18. What is being represented on the *X* and *Y* axes (bottom and side) of the graph? _____

_____

19. What is the unit of measurement on the *Y* axis (the side of the graph)? _____

20. What important points or conclusions can be drawn about life expectancy with regard to sex and race? _____

_____   _____

_____

_____

_____

_____

The reading selection in this chapter (Selection 10-1, beginning on page 687) is itself a chapter-length selection from a history textbook. It will give you an opportunity to try out the study skills in Chapter 10, and it will also help you gain a realistic idea of how much time is needed to master a textbook chapter. Then, whenever a course involves mastering textbook information, you will know *how* to master it and will feel confident that you *can* master it.

DEVELOPING CHAPTER REVIEW CARDS

Student Online Learning Center (OLC)
Go to Chapter 10.
Select Flashcards
or Chapter Test.

Review cards, or *summary cards,* are an excellent study tool. They are a way to select, organize, and review the most important information in a textbook chapter. The process of creating review cards helps you organize information in a meaningful way and, at the same time, transfer it into long-term memory. The cards can also be used to prepare for tests (see Chapter 11). The review card activities in this book give you structured practice in creating these valuable study tools. Once you have learned how to make review cards, you can create them for textbook material in your other courses.

Now complete the seven review cards for Chapter 10 by supplying the important information about each topic. When you have completed them, you will have summarized important information about the skills in this chapter.

Three Keys to Studying College Textbooks
1.
2.
3.
Card 1 Chapter 10: Selecting and Organizing Textbook Information

Guidelines for Underlining and Highlighting Textbook Material

Card 2 Chapter 10: Selecting and Organizing Textbook Information

Guidelines for Annotating Textbooks

Card 3 Chapter 10: Selecting and Organizing Textbook Information

Guidelines for Outlining

Card 4   Chapter 10: Selecting and Organizing Textbook Information

Guidelines for Mapping

Card 5   Chapter 10: Selecting and Organizing Textbook Information

Guidelines for Summarizing Textbook Information

Card 6   Chapter 10: Selecting and Organizing Textbook Information

Guidelines for Interpreting Graphic Material

Card 7   Chapter 10: Selecting and Organizing Textbook Information

SELECTION **10-1**   **The Age of Globalization**

History   From *American History: A Survey*
By Alan Brinkley

Prepare Yourself to Read

Directions: Do these exercises *before* you read Selection 10-1.

1. First, read and think about the title. What do you already know about globalization?

   _____

   _____

   _____

   _____

2. Next, complete your preview by reading the following:

   Introduction: "September 11, 2001"

   "Timeline of Significant Events"

   Section headings and subheadings

   First sentence of each paragraph

   Photos and graphs

   Conclusion

   On the basis of your preview, what aspects of globalization does this chapter seem to be about?

   _____

   _____

   _____

   _____

   _____

Apply Comprehension Skills

Directions: Do these exercises *as* you read Selection 10-1.

- Budget your time for reading this selection. It has five sections. If you wish, divide the selection into shorter reading sessions.

- As you read, apply the skills of selectivity and organization you have learned in this chapter. To remember essential information, underline, highlight, annotate, and take notes.

THE AGE OF GLOBALIZATION

September 11, 2001

At 8:45 A.M. on the bright, sunny morning of September 11, 2001, as tens of thousands of workers—executives and financiers, secretaries and clerks, security guards and maintenance workers, chefs and waiters, citizens of dozens of nations—were beginning a day's work in lower Manhattan, a commercial airliner crashed into the side of one of the two towers of the World Trade Center, the tallest buildings in New York. The collision created a huge explosion and a great fire of extraordinary intensity. Less than half an hour later, as thousands of workers fled the burning building, another commercial airliner rammed into the companion tower, creating a second fireball. Within an hour after that, both towers, their steel girders buckling in response to the tremendous heat, collapsed. The burning floors gave way and fell onto the floors below them, pulling one of New York's (and America's) most famous symbols to the ground. At about the same time, in Virginia, another commercial airliner crashed into a side of the Pentagon, the headquarters of the nation's military, turning part of the building's facade into rubble. And several hundred miles away, still another airplane crashed in a field not far from Pittsburgh.

These four almost simultaneous catastrophes were the result of a single orchestrated plan by Islamic militants to bring terrorism—for years the bane of such nations as Israel, Turkey, Italy, Germany, Britain, Japan, and Ireland—into the United States, which had previously had relatively little recent experience of it. Similarly committed Middle Eastern terrorists had previously attacked American targets overseas—military barracks, a naval vessel, embassies, and consulates. And they had staged a less cataclysmic attack on the World Trade Center in 1993.

On September 11, groups of terrorists boarded each of the four planes armed with nothing more than box cutters and set out to use the aircraft as weapons against important buildings. In three cases, they succeeded. In the fourth, passengers—alerted by cell phone conversations to the intentions of the hijackers—apparently took over the plane and forced it down before it could reach its target. More than 3,000 people died as a result of the September 11 disasters.

The events of September 11 produced great changes in American life. They also seemed to bring to a close an extraordinary period in modern American history—a time of heady prosperity, bitter partisanship, cultural frivolity and excess, and tremendous social and economic change. And yet there was also at least one great continuity between the world of the 1990s and the world that seemed to begin on September 11, 2001. The United States, more than at any other time in its history, was becoming deeply entwined in a new age of globalism, an age that combined great promise with great peril.

Timeline of Significant Events

1977 • Apple introduces first personal computer.

1979 • Nuclear accident at Three Mile Island.

1981 • Existence of AIDS first reported in United States.

1985 • Crack cocaine appears in American cities.

1989 • Human genome project launched.

1991 • Controversy surrounds confirmation of Clarence Thomas to Supreme Court.

1992 • Major race riot in Los Angeles.
• Bill Clinton elected president.

1993 • Congress approves tax increase as part of deficit reduction.
• Congress ratifies North American Free Trade Agreement.
• Clinton proposes national health-care system.

1994 • Congress rejects health-care reform.
• Republicans win control of both houses of Congress.

1995 • New Republican Congress attempts to enact "Contract with America."
• Showdown between president and Congress leads to shutdown of federal government.

• National crime rates show dramatic decline.
• O.J. Simpson trial.

1996 • Congress passes and president signs major welfare reform bill, minimum wage increase, and health-insurance reform.
• Clinton reelected president; Republicans retain control of Congress.

1997 • President and Congress agree on plan to balance budget.
• Justice Department files antitrust suits against Microsoft.

1998 • Lewinsky scandal rocks Clinton presidency.
• Democrats gain in congressional elections.
• Clinton impeached by House.

1999 • Senate acquits Clinton in impeachment trial.

2000 • George W. Bush wins contested presidential election.

2001 • Terrorists destroy World Trade Center and damage Pentagon.
• United States begins military action against Afghanistan.

2003 • U.S. military forces depose Iraqi dictator Saddam Hussein.

September 11, 2001
One great American symbol, the Statue of Liberty, stands against a sky filled with the thick smoke from the destruction of another American symbol, New York City's World Trade Center towers, a few hours after terrorists crashed two planes into them.

Globalization of the Economy

1   Perhaps the most important economic change toward the end of the 20th century, and certainly the one whose impact was the most difficult to gauge, was what became known as the "globalization" of the economy. The great prosperity of the 1950s and 1960s had rested on, among other things, the relative insulation of the United States from the pressures of international competition. As late as 1970, international trade still played a relatively small role in the American economy as a whole, which thrived on the basis of the huge domestic market in North America.

2   By the end of the 1970s, however, the world had intruded on the American economy in pro-found ways, and that intrusion increased unabated for the next twenty years. Exports rose from just under $43 billion in 1970 to over $789 billion in 2000. But imports rose even more dramatically: from just over $40 billion in 1970 to over $1.2 trillion in 2000. Most American products, in other words, now faced foreign competition inside the United States. America had made 76 percent of the world's automobiles in 1950 and 48 percent in 1960. By 1990, that share had dropped to 20 percent; in 2000, even after a substantial revival of the automobile industry, the American share had risen only to 21.5 percent. The first American trade imbalance in the postwar era occurred in 1971; only twice since then, in 1973 and 1975, has the balance been favorable.

3 Globalization brought many benefits for the American consumer: new and more varied products, and lower prices for many of them. Most economists, and most national leaders, welcomed the process and worked to encourage it through lowering trade barriers. The North American Free Trade Agreement (NAFTA) and the General Agreement on Trade and Tariffs (GATT) were the boldest of a long series of treaties designed to lower trade barriers stretching back to the 1960s. But globalization had many costs as well. It was particularly hard on industrial workers, who saw industrial jobs disappear as American companies lost market share to foreign competitors. American workers also lost jobs as American companies began exporting work—building plants in Mexico, Asia, and other lower-wage countries to avoid having to pay the high wages workers had won in America.

Science and Technology in the New Economy

4 The "new economy" that emerged in the last decades of the twentieth century was driven by, and in turn helped to drive, dramatic new scientific and technological discoveries. Much as in the late nineteenth century—when such technological innovations as modern manufacturing, the railroad, the telegraph, the telephone, electricity, and automobiles—transformed both society and the economy; so in the late twentieth century, new technologies had profound effects on the way Americans—and peoples throughout the world—lived.

The Personal Computer

5 The most visible element of the technological revolution to most Americans was the dramatic growth in the use of computers in almost every area of life. Computers had been important to government and to many businesses since World War II. But their reach expanded with extraordinary speed in the 1980s and beyond. By the end of the 1990s, most Americans were doing their banking by computer. Most retail transactions were conducted by computerized credit mechanisms. Most businesses, schools, and other institutions were using computerized record-keeping. Many areas of manufacturing were revolutionized by computer-driven product design and factory robotics. Scientific and technological research in almost all areas was transformed by computerized methods.

6 Among the most significant innovations was the development of the microprocessor, first introduced in 1971 by Intel, which represented a notable advance in the technology of integrated circuitry. A microprocessor miniaturized the central processing unit of a computer, making it possible for a small machine to perform calculations that in the past only very large machines could do. Personal computers quickly established a presence in many areas of American life: homes, schools, businesses, universities, hospitals, government agencies, newsrooms. Computerized word processing programs replaced typewriters. Computerized spreadsheets revolutionized bookkeeping. Computerized data processing made obsolete much traditional information storage, such as filing. Some computer enthusiasts talked about the imminent coming of a "paperless" office, in which all information or communication would be stored and distributed through computers, a prediction that failed to materialize. But the emergence of ever smaller and more powerful computers—laptops, notebooks, and palm-sized devices—greatly extended the reach of computer-related technology. At the same time, however, computer scientists were creating extraordinary powerful new forms of networking; and many were predicting that before long the stand-alone personal computer would be obsolete, that the future lay in linking many computers together into powerful networks.

7 The computer revolution created thousands of new, lucrative businesses: computer manufacturers themselves (IBM, Apple, Compaq, Dell, Gateway, Sun, Digital and many others); makers of the tiny silicon chips that ran the computers and allowed smaller and smaller machines to become more and more powerful (most notably Intel); and makers of software—chief among them Microsoft, the most powerful new corporation to arise in American life in generations.

8 But if Microsoft was the most conspicuous success story of the computer age, it was only one of many. Whole regions—the so-called Silicon Valley in northern California; areas around Boston, Austin, Texas, and Seattle, even areas in

downtown New York City—became centers of booming economic activity servicing the new computer age.

The Internet

9   Out of the computer revolution emerged another dramatic source of information and communication: the Internet. The Internet is, in essence, a vast, geographically far-flung network of computers that allows people connected to the network to communicate with others all over the world.

10   In the early 1980s, the Defense Department, an early partner in the development of the Arpanet, the predecessor of the Internet, withdrew from the project for security reasons. The network, soon renamed the Internet, was then free to develop independently. It did so rapidly, especially after the invention of technologies that made possible electronic mail (or e-mail) and the emergence of the personal computer, which vastly increased the number of potential users of the Internet. As late as 1984, there remained fewer than a thousand host computers connected to the Internet. A decade later, there were over 6 million. And in 2001, an estimated 400 million people around the world were using the Internet, including 130 million in the United States.

11   As the amount of information on the Internet unexpectedly proliferated, without any central direction, new forms of software emerged to make it possible for individual users to navigate through the vast number of Internet sites. In 1989, a laboratory in Geneva introduced the World Wide Web, through which individual users could publish information for the Internet, which helped establish an orderly system for both the distribution and retrieval of electronic information.

12   The Internet is still a relatively young communications medium, and its likely impact on society is not yet fully understood. Already, however, it has revolutionized many areas of life. E-mail has replaced conventional mail, telephone calls, and even face-to-face conversation for millions of people. Newspapers, magazines, and other publications have begun to publish on the Internet. It has become a powerful marketing tool, through which people can purchase items as small as books and as large as automobiles. It

is a site for vast amounts of documentary material for researchers, reporters, students, and others. And it is, finally, a highly democratic medium through which virtually anyone with access to a personal computer can establish a website and present information in a form that is available to virtually anyone in the world who chooses to look at it. New technologies that make it easier to transmit moving images over the Internet—and new forms of "broadband" access that give more users high-speed connections to the Web—promise to expand greatly the functions that the Internet can perform.

Breakthroughs in Genetics

13   Aided in part by computer technology, there was explosive growth in another area of scientific research: genetics. Early discoveries in genetics by Gregor Mendel, Thomas Hunt Morgan, and others laid the groundwork for more dramatic breakthroughs—the discovery of DNA by the British scientists Oswald Avery, Cohn MacLeod, and Maclyn McCarty in 1944; and in 1953, the dramatic discovery by the American biochemist James Watson and the British biophysicist Francis Crick of the double-helix structure of DNA, and thus of the key to identifying genetic codes. From these discoveries emerged the new science—and ultimately the new industry—of genetic engineering, through which new medical treatments and new techniques for hybridization of plants and animals have already become possible.

14   Little by little, scientists began to identify specific genes in humans and other living things that determine particular traits and to learn how to alter or reproduce them. But the identification of genes was painfully slow, and in 1989, the federal government appropriated $3 billion to fund the National Center for the Human Genome to accelerate the mapping of human genes. The Human Genome Project set out to identify all of the more than 100,000 genes by 2005. But new technologies for research and competition from other projects (some of them funded by pharmaceutical companies) drove the project forward faster than expected. In 1998, the genome project announced that it would finish its work in 2003. In the meantime, in 2000, other researchers produced a list of all the genes in the human

body, even if their relationship to one another remained unmapped.

15 In the meantime, DNA research had already attracted considerable public attention. In 1997, scientists in Scotland announced that they had cloned a sheep—which they named Dolly—using a cell from an adult ewe; in other words, the genetic structure of the newborn Dolly was identical to that of the sheep from which the cell was taken. The DNA structure of an individual, scientists have discovered, is as unique and as identifiable as a fingerprint. DNA testing, therefore, makes it possible to identify individuals through their blood, semen, skin, or even hair. It played a major role first in the O.J. Simpson trial in 1995 and then in the 1998 investigation into President Clinton's relationship with Monica Lewinsky. Also in 1998, DNA testing appeared to establish with certainty that Thomas Jefferson had fathered a child with his slave Sally Hemings, by finding genetic similarities between descendants of both, thus resolving a political and scholarly dispute stretching back nearly two hundred years. Genetic research has already spawned important new areas of medical treatment and has helped the relatively new biotechnology industry to grow into one of the nation's most important economic sectors. Eventually, scientists expect the research to open up vast new areas for medical treatment—and also controversial new possibilities for genetically designing foods, animals, and even humans.

16 But genetic research was also the source of great controversy. Many people grew uneasy about the predictions that the new science might give scientists the ability to alter aspects of life that had previously seemed outside the reach of human control. Some critics feared genetic research on religious grounds, seeing it as an interference with God's plan. Others used moral arguments and expressed fears that it would allow parents, for example, to choose what kinds of children they would have. And a particularly heated controversy emerged over the way in which scientists obtained genetic material. One of the most promising areas of medical research involved the use of stem cells, genetic material obtained in large part from undeveloped fetuses, mostly fetuses created by couples attempting *in vitro* fertilization. (*In vitro*

fertilization is the process by which couples unable to conceive a child have a fetus conceived outside the womb using their eggs and sperm and then implanted in the mother.)

17 Supporters of stem-cell research—which showed promising signs of offering cures for Parkinson's disease, Alzheimer's disease, ALS, and other previously incurable illnesses—argued that the stem cells they used came from fetuses that would otherwise be discarded, since *in vitro* fertilization always produces many more fetuses than can be used. The controversy over stem-cell research became an issue in the 2000 presidential campaign. George W. Bush, once president, kept his promise to antiabortion advocates and in the summer of 2001 issued a ruling barring the use of federal funds to support research using any stem cells that scientists were not already using at the time of his decision.

A Changing Society

18 The changes in the economy were one of many factors producing major changes in the character of American society. By the end of the twentieth century, the American population was growing larger, older, and more racially and geographically diverse.

The Graying of America

19 One of the most important, if often unnoticed, features of American life in the late twentieth century was the aging of the American population. After decades of steady growth, the nation's birthrate began to decline in the 1970s and remained low through the 1980s and 1990s. In 1970, there were 18.4 births for every 1,000 people in the population. By 1996, the rate had dropped to 14.8 births. The declining birthrate and a significant rise in life expectancy produced a substantial increase in the proportion of elderly citizens. Almost 13 percent of the population was more than sixty-five years old in 2000, as compared with 8 percent in 1970. The median age in 2000 was 35.3, the highest in the nation's history. In 1970, it was 28.0.

20 The aging of the population had important, if not entirely predictable, implications. It was, for example, a cause of the increasing costliness of Social Security pensions. It meant rapidly

The American Birthrate, 1960–2000

This chart shows the sharp decline of the nation's birthrate during the period between 1960 and 1975. This was a striking change in the pattern of the nation's birthrate from the twenty years after 1940, which produced the great "baby boom."

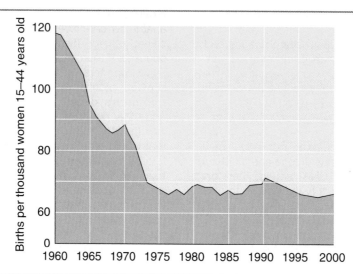

increasing health costs, both for the federal Medicare system and for private hospitals and insurance companies, and was one of the principal reasons for the anxiety about health-care costs that played such a crucial role in the politics of the early 1990s. It ensured that the elderly, who already formed one of the most powerful interest groups in America, would remain politically formidable well into the twenty-first century.

21   It also had important implications for the nature of the workforce in the twenty-first century. In the last twenty years of the twentieth century, the number of people aged 25 to 54 in the native-born workforce in the United States grew by over 26 million. In the first ten years of the twenty-first century, the number of workers in that age group will not grow at all. That will put increasing pressure on the economy to employ more older workers. It will also create a greater demand for immigrant workers.

New Patterns of Immigration and Ethnicity

22   The enormous change in both the extent and the character of immigration was one of the most dramatic social developments of the last decades of the twentieth century. The nation's immigration quotas expanded significantly in those years (partly to accommodate refugees from Southeast Asia and other nations), allowing more newcomers to enter the United States legally than at any point since the beginning of the twentieth century. In 2000, over 28 million Americans—over 10 percent of the total population—consisted of immigrants (people born outside the United States).

23   Equally striking was the character of the new immigration. The Immigration Reform Act of 1965 had eliminated quotas based on national origin; from then on, newcomers from regions other than Latin America were generally admitted on a first-come, first-served basis. In 1965, 90 percent of the immigrants to the United States came from Europe. By the mid-1980s, only 10 percent of the new arrivals were Europeans, although that figure rose slightly in the 1990s as emigrants from Russia and eastern Europe—now free to leave their countries—came in increasing numbers. The extent and character of the new immigration were causing a dramatic change in the composition of the American population. By the end of the twentieth century, people of white European background constituted under 80 percent of the population (as opposed to 90 percent a half-century before).

24   Particularly important to the new immigration were two groups: Latinos (people from Spanish-speaking nations, particularly Mexico) and Asians. Both had been significant segments of the American population for many decades—

Naturalization, 1996 On September 17, 1996, ten thousand people, representing 113 different countries, were sworn in as U.S. citizens in Texas Stadium near Dallas, the largest naturalization ceremony in the nation's history. They were part of over 1 million immigrants who became American citizens in 1996, which was also a record (and was more than twice the number naturalized in any previous year). The high number of new citizens was a result of the dramatic increase in immigration over the previous two decades. It was also a result of fears among many immigrants that restrictive new laws would deny them important benefits (including education for their children) if they did not become citizens.

Latinos since the beginning of the nation's history, Asians since the waves of Chinese and Japanese immigration in the nineteenth century. But both groups experienced enormous, indeed unprecedented, growth after 1965. People from Latin America constituted more than a third of the total number of legal immigrants to the United States in every year after 1965—and a much larger proportion of the total number of illegal immigrants. Mexico alone accounted for over one-fourth of all the immigrants living in the United States in 2000. In California and the Southwest, in particular, Mexicans became an increasingly important presence. There were also substantial Latino populations in Illinois, New York, and Florida. High birthrates within Latino communities already in the United States further increased their numbers. In the 1980 census, 6 percent of the population (about 14 million) was listed as being of Hispanic origin.

By 1997, census figures showed an increase to 11 percent, or 29 million people. In the 1980s and 1990s, Asian immigrants arrived in even greater numbers than Latinos, constituting more than 40 percent of the total of legal newcomers. They swelled the already substantial Chinese and Japanese communities in California and elsewhere. And they created substantial new communities of immigrants from Vietnam, Thailand, Cambodia, Laos, the Philippines, Korea, and India. By 2000, there were more than 10 million Asian Americans in the United States (4 percent of the population), more than twice the number of fifteen years before. Like Latinos they were concentrated mainly in large cities and in the West. Many of the new Asian immigrants were refugees, including Vietnamese driven from their homes in the aftermath of the disastrous war in which the United States had so long been involved.

**Total Immigration,
1961–2000**

This chart shows the tremendous increase in immigration to the United States in the decades since the Immigration Reform Act of 1965. The immigration of the 1980s and 1990s was the highest since the late nineteenth century.

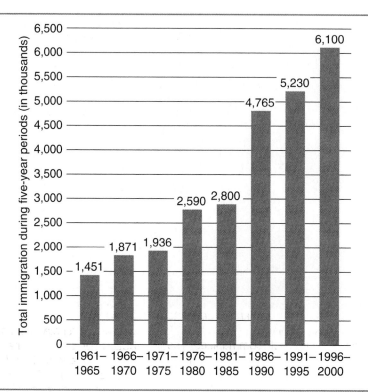

**Sources of Immigration,
1960–1990**

The Immigration Reform Act of 1965 lifted the national quotas imposed on immigration policy in 1924 and opened immigration to large areas of the world that had previously been restricted. In 1965, 90 percent of the immigrants to the United States came from Europe. As this chart shows, by 1990 almost the reverse was true. Over 80 percent of all immigrants came from non-European sources.

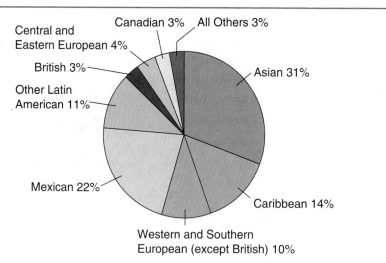

The Black Middle Class

25   The civil rights movement and the other liberal efforts of the 1960s had two very different effects on African Americans. On the one hand, there were increased opportunities for advancement available to those in a position to take advantage of them. On the other hand, as the industrial economy declined and government services dwindled, there was a growing sense of helplessness and despair among the large groups of nonwhites who continued to find themselves barred from upward mobility.

26   For the black middle class, which by the end of the twentieth century constituted over half of the African American population of America, progress was remarkable in the thirty years since the high point of the civil rights movement. Disparities between black and white professionals did not vanish, but they diminished substantially. African American families moved into more affluent urban communities and, in many cases, into suburbs—at times as neighbors of whites, more often into predominantly black communities. The number of African Americans attending college rose by 350 percent in the decade following the passage of the civil rights acts (in contrast to a 150 percent increase among whites); African Americans made up 12 percent of the college population in the 1990s (up from 5 percent twenty-five years earlier). The percentage of black high school graduates going on to college was virtually the same as that of white high school graduates by the end of the twentieth century (although a far smaller proportion of blacks than whites managed to complete high school). And African Americans were making rapid strides in many professions from which, a generation earlier, they had been barred or within which they had been segregated. In increasing numbers, they were becoming partners in major law firms and joining the staffs of major hospitals and the faculties of major universities. Nearly half of all employed blacks in the United States had skilled white-collar jobs. There were few areas of American life from which blacks were any longer entirely excluded. Middle-class blacks, in other words, had realized great gains from the legislation of the 1960s, from the changing national mood on race, from the creation of controversial affirmative action programs, and from their own strenuous efforts.

Poor and Working-Class African Americans

But the rise of the black middle class also 27 accentuated (and perhaps even helped cause) the increasingly desperate plight of other African Americans, whom the economic growth and the liberal programs of the 1960s and beyond had never reached. These impoverished people—sometimes described as the "underclass"—made up as much as a third of the nation's black population. Many of them lived in isolated, decaying, and desperately poor inner-city neighborhoods. As more successful blacks moved out of the inner cities, the poor were left virtually alone in their decaying neighborhoods. Fewer than half of young inner-city blacks finished high school; more than 60 percent were unemployed. The black family structure suffered as well from the dislocations of urban poverty. There was a radical increase in the number of single-parent, female-headed black households. In 1970, 59 percent of all black children under 18 lived with both their parents (already down from 70 percent a decade earlier). In 2000, only 38 percent of black children lived in such households, while 75 percent of white children did.

Nonwhites were disadvantaged by many fac- 28 tors in the changing social and economic climate of the 1980s and 1990s. Among them was a growing impatience with affirmative action and other programs designed to advance their fortunes. They suffered as well from a steady decline in the number of unskilled jobs in the economy, the departure of businesses from their neighborhoods, the absence of adequate transportation to areas where jobs were more plentiful, and failing schools that did not prepare them adequately for employment. And they suffered, in some cases, from a sense of futility and despair, born of years of entrapment in brutal urban ghettoes.

Modern Plagues: Drugs and AIDS

The new immigrants of the 1980s and 1990s 29 arrived in cities being ravaged by two new and deadly epidemics. One was a dramatic increase in drug use, which penetrated nearly every community in the nation. The enormous demand for drugs, and particularly for "crack" cocaine, spawned what was in effect a multibillion-dollar industry, and those reaping the enormous profits of the illegal trade fought strenuously and often savagely to protect their positions. Political figures of both parties spoke heatedly about the need for a "war on drugs," but in the absence of significant funding for such programs, government efforts appeared to be having little effect. Drug use declined significantly among middle-class people beginning in the late 1980s, but the epidemic showed no signs of abating in the poor urban neighborhoods where it was doing the most severe damage.

30   The drug epidemic was directly related to another scourge of the 1980s and 1990s: the epidemic spread of a new and lethal disease first documented in 1981 and soon named AIDS (acquired immune deficiency syndrome). AIDS is the product of the HIV virus, which is transmitted by the exchange of bodily fluids (blood or semen). The virus gradually destroys the body's immune system and makes its victims highly vulnerable to a number of diseases (particularly to various forms of cancer and pneumonia) to which they would otherwise have a natural resistance. Those infected with the virus (i.e., HIV positive) can live for a long time without developing AIDS, but for many years those who became ill were virtually certain to die.

31   The first American victims of AIDS (and for many years the group among whom cases remained the most numerous) were homosexual men. But by the late 1980s, as the gay community began to take preventive measures, the most rapid increase in the spread of the disease occurred among heterosexuals, many of them intravenous drug users who spread the virus by sharing contaminated hypodermic needles. In 2000, U.S. government agencies estimated that about 780,000 Americans were infected with the HIV virus and that another 427,000 had already died from the disease. But the United States represented only a tiny proportion of the worldwide total of people afflicted with AIDS, an estimated 36.1 million people at the end of 2000. Seventy percent (over 25 million) of those cases were concentrated in Africa. Governments and private groups, in the meantime, began promoting AIDS awareness in increasingly visible and graphic ways—urging young people, in particular, to avoid "unsafe sex" through abstinence or the use of latex condoms. The success of that

effort in the United States was suggested by the drop in new cases from 70,000 in 1995 to approximately 40,000 in 2000.

In the mid-1990s, AIDS researchers, after 32 years of frustration, began discovering effective treatments for the disease. By taking a combination of powerful drugs on a rigorous schedule, among them a group known as protease inhibitors, even people with relatively advanced cases of AIDS experienced dramatic improvement—so much so that in many cases there were no measurable quantities of the virus left in their bloodstreams. The new drugs gave promise for the first time of dramatically extending the lives of people with AIDS, perhaps to normal life spans. The drugs were not a cure for AIDS; people who stopped taking them experienced a rapid return of the disease. And the effectiveness of the drugs varied from person to person. In addition, the drugs were very expensive and difficult to administer; poorer AIDS patients often could not obtain access to them, and they remained very scarce in Africa and other less affluent parts of the world where the epidemic was rampant. Nevertheless, the new medications restored hundreds of thousands of desperately ill people to health and gave them realistic hopes of long and relatively normal lives.

The Decline in Crime

One of the most striking social develop- 33 ments of the late 1990s was also one of the least expected: a dramatic reduction in crime rates across most of the United States. The rising incidence of violent crime had been one of the most disturbing facts of American life for two generations—and a central fact of national politics since at least the 1960s. But beginning in the early 1990s, crime began to fall—in many cities, quite dramatically. The government's crime index—which measures the incidence of seven serious crimes—fell by 19.5 percent between 1992 and 2000, with some of the most dramatic reductions occurring in murder and other violent crimes.

There was no agreement about the causes 34 of this unexpected reduction. Prosperity and declining unemployment were certainly factors. So were new, sophisticated police techniques that helped deter many crimes and that led to the arrest of many criminals who would previously have escaped capture. New incarceration policies—longer, tougher sentences and fewer paroles and early releases for violent criminals—led to a radical increase in the prison population and, consequently, a reduction in the number of criminals at liberty to commit crimes. Whatever the reason, the decline in crime—when combined with the booming prosperity of the 1990s, which (however unequally distributed) affected most Americans at least to some degree—helped produce an unusual level of social contentment, as recorded in public opinion surveys, in the late 1990s and in 2000. In stark contrast to the late 1970s, and even the 1980s, most Americans expressed general contentment with the state of their society and optimism about the future until at least September 2001.

The Perils of Globalization

35   The celebration of the beginning of a new millennium on January 1, 2000, was a notable moment not just because of the dramatic change in the calendar. It was notable above all as a global event—a shared and for the most part joyous experience that united the world in its exuberance. Television viewers around the world followed the dawn of the new millennium from Australia, through Asia, Africa, and Europe, and on into the Americas. Never had the world seemed more united. But if the millennium celebrations suggested the bright promise of globalization, other events at the dawn of the new century suggested its dark perils.

Opposing the "New World Order"

36   In the United States and other industrial nations, opposition to globalization—or to what President George H. W. Bush once called the "new world order"—took several forms. To many Americans on both the left and the right, the nation's increasingly interventionist foreign policy was deeply troubling. Critics on the left charged that the United States was using military action to advance its economic interests, most notably in the 1991 Gulf War. Critics on the right claimed that the nation was allowing itself to be swayed by the interests of other nations; they opposed such supposedly humanitarian interventions as the 1993 invasion of Somalia and the American

interventions in the Balkans in the late 1990s—both because they insisted no vital American interests were at stake and because they feared that the United States was ceding its sovereignty in these actions to international organizations. But the most impassioned opposition to globalization in the West came from an array of groups that challenged the claim that the "new world order" was economically beneficial. Environmentalists argued that globalization, in exporting industry to low-wage countries, also exported industrial pollution and toxic waste into nations that had no effective laws to control them. And still others opposed global economic arrangements on the grounds that they enriched and empowered large multinational corporations and threatened the freedom and autonomy of individuals and communities.

37   The varied opponents of globalization may have had different reasons for their hostility. However, they were agreed on the targets of their discontent: not just free-trade agreements, but also the multinational institutions that policed and advanced the global economy.

The Rise of Islamic Fundamentalism

38   Outside the industrialized West, the impact of globalization created other concerns. Many citizens of nonindustrialized nations resented the way the world economy had left them in poverty and, in their view, exploited and oppressed. But in some parts of the nonindustrialized world—and particularly in some of the Islamic nations of the Middle East—the increasing reach of globalization created additional grievances, less rooted in economics than in religion and culture.

39   The Iranian Revolution of 1979, in which orthodox Muslims ousted a despotic government whose leaders had embraced many aspects of modern Western culture, was one of the first large and visible manifestations of a phenomenon that would eventually reach across much of the Islamic world and threaten the stability of the globe. In one Islamic nation after another, waves of fundamentalist orthodoxy emerged to defend traditional culture against incursions from the West. The new fundamentalism met considerable resistance within Islam—from established governments, from affluent middle classes that had made their peace with the modern industrial world, from

women who feared the antifeminist agenda of many of these movements. But it emerged nevertheless as a powerful force—and in a few nations, among them Iran after 1979 and Afghanistan in the late 1990s—the dominant force.

40   Islamic fundamentalism is a complex phenomenon and takes many different forms, but among some particularly militant fundamentalists, the battle to preserve orthodoxy came to be defined as a battle against the West generally and the United States in particular. Resentment of the West was rooted in the incursion of new and, in their view, threatening cultural norms into traditional societies. It was rooted as well in resentment of the support Western nations gave to corrupt and tyrannical regimes in some Islamic countries and in opposition to Western (and particularly American) economic and military incursions into the region. The continuing struggle between Palestinians and Israelis—a struggle defined in the eyes of many Muslims by American support for Israel—added further to their contempt.

41   One product of this combination of resentments was individuals and groups committed to using violence to fight the influence of the West. No fundamentalist movement had any advanced military capabilities. Militants resorted instead to isolated incidents of violence and mayhem, designed to disrupt societies and governments and to create fear among their peoples. Such tactics became known to the world as terrorism.

The Rise of Terrorism

42   The United States has experienced terrorism for many years, much of it against American targets abroad. These included the bombing of the Marine barracks in Beirut in 1983, the explosion that brought down an American airliner over Lockerbie, Scotland, in 1988, the bombing of American embassies in 1998, the assault on the U.S. naval vessel *Cole* in 2000, and other events around the world. Terrorist incidents were relatively rare, but not unknown, within the United States itself prior to September 11, 2001. Militants on the American left performed various acts of terror in the 1960s and early 1970s. In February 1993, a bomb exploded in the parking garage of the World Trade Center in New York, killing six people and causing serious, but no irreparable,

structural damage to the towers. Several men connected with militant Islamic organizations were convicted of the crime. In April 1995, a van containing explosives blew up in front of a federal building in Oklahoma City, killing 168 people. Timothy McVeigh, a former Marine who had become part of a militant antigovernment movement of the American right, was convicted of the crime and eventually executed in 2001.

43   Most Americans, however, considered terrorism a problem that mainly plagued other nations. Few thought about it as an important concern in their own country. One of the many results of the terrible events of September 11, 2001, was to jolt the American people out of complacency and alert them to the presence of continuing danger. That awareness increased in the weeks after September 11. New security measures began to change the way in which Americans traveled. New government regulations began to alter immigration policies and to affect the character of international banking. Warnings of possible new terrorist attacks created widespread tension and uneasiness. A puzzling and frightening epidemic of anthrax—a potent bacterial agent that can cause illness and death if not properly treated—began in the weeks after September 11 and spread through the mail to media outlets, members of Congress, and seemingly random others.

44   In the meantime, the United States government launched what President George W. Bush called a "war against terrorism." The attacks on the World Trade Center and the Pentagon, government intelligence indicated, had been planned and orchestrated by Middle Eastern agents of a powerful terrorist network known as Al Qaeda. Its leader, Osama Bin Laden—until 2001 little known outside the Arab world—quickly became one of the best known and most notorious figures in the world. Fighting a shadowy terrorist network spread out among many nations of the world was a difficult task, and the administration made clear from the beginning that the battle would be waged in many ways, not just militarily. But the first visible act of the war against terrorism was, in fact, a military one. Convinced that the militant "Taliban" government of Afghanistan had sheltered and supported Bin Laden and his organization, the United States began a sustained campaign of

bombing against the regime and sent in small numbers of ground troops to help a resistance organization overthrow the Afghan government. This first battle in the struggle against terrorism produced a surprisingly quick military victory. Afghanistan's Taliban regime collapsed, and its leaders—along with the Al Qaeda fighters allied with them—fled the capital, Kabul. American and anti-Taliban Afghan troops pursued them into the mountains, but were, at least at first, unable to find Bin Laden and the other leaders of his organization. In the aftermath of this speedy victory, however, American forces found themselves caught up in the instability of factionalized Afghanistan. While continuing to pursue terrorists, they also had to deal with infighting among the new leaders of the nation.

45   In his State of the Union Address to Congress in January 2002, President Bush spoke of an "axis of evil," which included the nations of Iraq, Iran, and North Korea—all nations with anti-American regimes, all nations that either possessed or were thought to be trying to acquire nuclear weapons. Although Bush did not say so, many people—both in America and elsewhere—took his words to mean that the United States would soon try to topple the government of Saddam Hussein in Iraq. In 2003, U.S. military forces did, in fact, invade Iraq and depose Iraqi dictator Saddam Hussein.

A New Era?

46   In the immediate aftermath of September 11, 2001, many Americans came to believe that they had entered a new era in their history. The instability that had plagued so much of the rest of the world for years seemed suddenly to have arrived in the United States, shattering long-standing assumptions about safety and security and opening a period of uncertainty and fear. Prospects for the future were clouded further by a significant weakening of the economy that was already well advanced before September 11 and that the events of that day helped to increase.

47   But fear and uncertainty were not the only results of the September 11 attacks. The reaction to the catastrophe—in New York, in Washington, and in much of the rest of the country—exposed a side of American life and culture that had always

existed but that had not always been visible during the booming, self-indulgent years of the 1980s and 1990s. Americans responded to the tragedies with countless acts of courage and generosity, large and small, and with a sense of national unity and commitment that seemed, at least for a time, to resemble the unity and commitment at the beginning of World War II. The displays of courage began with the heroism of firefighters and rescue workers in New York City, who unhesitatingly plunged into the burning towers of the World Trade Center in an effort to save the people inside. Over 300 such workers died when the towers collapsed. In the weeks after the disaster, New York was flooded with volunteers—welders, metal workers, police, firefighters, medical personnel, and many others—who flocked to the city from around the country and the world to assist with rescue and recovery. Charitable donations to help the victims of the disasters exceeded $1 billion, the largest amount ever raised for a single purpose in such a short time in American history. Open and unembarrassed displays of patriotism and national pride—things that many Americans had once scorned—suddenly became fashionable again. Faith in government and its leaders, in decline for decades, suddenly surged. "Nothing has changed. . . . Everything has changed," wrote one prominent journalist in the weeks after September 11. In fact, no one could reliably predict whether the catastrophe would prove to be a fundamental turning point in the course of American and world history or simply another in the countless changes and adjustments, great and small, that have characterized the nation's experience for centuries.

Conclusion

Americans entered the twenty-first century 48 afflicted with many anxieties, doubts, and resentments. Faith in the nation's institutions—most notably, government—was at its lowest point in many decades. Vague resentments over the increasingly unequal patterns of income and wealth in the new economy, which few Americans seemed able to translate into a coherent economic agenda, increased the nation's unease.

But the United States at the end of the twen- 49 tieth century was, despite its many problems, a remarkably successful society. It had made dramatic strides in improving the lives of its citizens and in dealing with many of its social problems since the end of World War II. It entered the new century with the strongest economy in the world, with violent crime—one of its most corrosive problems for more than a generation—in a marked decline, and with its international power and stature unrivaled.

50   The traumatic events of September 11, 2001, changed many aspects of American life, not least the nation's sense of its isolation, and insulation, from the problems of the rest of the world. But both the many longstanding problems and the many long-standing strengths of the United States survived the attacks. It seemed safe to predict that the American people would go forward into their suddenly uncertain future not simply burdened by difficult challenges, but also armed with great wealth, great power, and perhaps most of all with the extraordinary energy and resilience that has allowed the nation—throughout its long and often turbulent history—to endure, to flourish, and to strive continually for a better future.

SELECTION **10-1**
History
(Continued)

Collaboration Option

Selecting and Organizing Textbook Information: Chapter-Length Selection

Directions: Refer to Selection 10-1 as necessary to complete the following activities.

Option for collaboration: Your instructor may direct you to work with other students on one or more of these items, or in other words, to work collaboratively. In that case, you should form groups of three of four students, as directed by your instructor, and work together to complete the exercises. After your group discusses an item and agrees on the answer, have a group member record it. Each member of your group should be able to explain all of your group's answers.

The chapter-length selection, "The Age of Globalization," contains the following sections and subsections:

September 11, 2001	Introduction
Timeline of Significant Events	Table
Globalization of the Economy	Paragraphs 1–3
Science and Technology in the New Economy	Paragraphs 4–17
The Personal Computer	
The Internet	
Breakthroughs in Genetics	
A Changing Society	Paragraphs 18–34
The Graying of America	
New Patterns of Immigration and Ethnicity	
The Black Middle Class	
Poor and Working-Class African Americans	
Modern Plagues: Drugs and AIDS	
The Decline in Crime	
The Perils of Globalization	Paragraphs 35–45
Opposing the "New World Order"	
The Rise of Islamic Fundamentalism	
The Rise of Terrorism	
A New Era	Paragraphs 46–47
Conclusion	Paragraphs 48–50

1. Your instructor will give you specific instructions for completing one or more of the following activities in order to apply the skills that you learned in this chapter:

   - Reread the section "Globalization of the Economy" (paragraphs 1–3), and then **mark** (underline or highlight) and **annotate** it. You should underline or highlight only stated main ideas. If a paragraph has an implied main idea, formulate the main idea and write it in the margin. Number the major details in each paragraph. *See pages 658–61 for guidelines for marking and annotating textbooks.*

   - Create a detailed **formal outline** of the three paragraphs in the section "Globalization of the Economy" (paragraphs 1–3). Your outline should be entitled "Globalization of the Economy." Your outline should consist of the main idea for each of the three paragraphs and the major details for each main idea. *See pages 662–63 for guidelines for outlining.*

   - Write a one-paragraph **summary** of the section "Globalization of the Economy" (paragraphs 1–3). Your summary should be entitled "Globalization of the Economy," and it should consist of the three main ideas in this section. *See pages 671–72 for guidelines for summarizing.*

   - Create a **study map** of the section "Science and Technology in the New Economy" (paragraphs 4–17). Your study map should contain the three major topics indicated in the three subheadings and also include some of the major details. *See pages 668–70 for guidelines for mapping.*

   - Create a **topic outline** of the section "A Changing Society" (paragraphs 18–34). Your topic outline should contain *only* the six subheadings of this section and no main ideas or details. Use the Roman numerals I, II, III, IV, V, and VI for your topic outline.

   - Take **Cornell notes** for the subsection "Modern Plagues: Drugs and AIDS" (paragraphs 29–32). Use the subheading, "Modern Plagues: Drugs and AIDS" as the title for your notes. Your notes, which will appear to the right of the review column, should list the four main points (the main idea of each of the four paragraphs) and their major details. The review column should contain the topics of the four paragraphs:

     - The drug epidemic
     - The disease of AIDS
     - AIDS in America and worldwide
     - AIDS treatment

   See pages 664–68 for guidelines for using the Cornell note-taking method.

2. Your instructor may distribute a practice quiz on one or more sections of the selection, "The Age of Globalization." Use any outlines, maps, notes, and summaries you have created to review (study) for this quiz. (Your instructor may also allow you to use your summaries, outlines, notes, and study maps when you take the quiz.)

Read More about This Topic on the World Wide Web

Directions: To discover more information about the topics mentioned in this selection, use your favorite search engine such as Google, Yahoo!, or AltaVista (www.google.com, www.yahoo.com, www.altavista.com). Type in combinations of keywords such as:

globalization

or

economic globalization

or

technological revolution

or

history of the Internet

or

genetic breakthroughs

or

graying of America

or

U.S. immigration patterns

or

black middle class

or

rise of terrorism

or

21st century globalization

CHAPTER 11

Rehearsing Textbook Information and Preparing for Tests

In this chapter you will learn the answers to these questions:

- Why is rehearsal important to memory?

- What are the important guidelines for test preparation?

- What is the five-day test review plan?

- How can I use review cards to prepare for a test?

- How can I consolidate important information on test review sheets?

SKILLS

Rehearsal and Memory

Studying for Tests

- General Guidelines
- Five-Day Test Review Plan
- Creating Review Cards to Prepare for a Test
- Creating Test Review Sheets

CREATING YOUR SUMMARY

Developing Chapter Review Cards

READING

Selection 11-1 *(Marriage and Family)*
"Cultural Diversity: Family Strengths and Challenges"
from *Marriages and Families: Intimacy, Diversity, and Strengths*
by David Olson and John DeFrain

Little strokes fell great oaks.

Benjamin Franklin

No great thing is created suddenly.

Epictetus

REHEARSAL AND MEMORY

As you may have discovered, it is difficult to memorize information that you do not understand. This is why you must focus on understanding material before attempting to memorize it. Understanding what you read does not mean you will automatically remember it. Thorough comprehension, however, enables you to memorize the material more efficiently.

Even when you understand material, however, you should not underestimate the time or effort needed to memorize it. To do well on tests, you must study information effectively enough to store it in **long-term memory,** or permanent memory. One serious mistake students make is leaving too little study time before a test to transfer material into long-term memory. Instead, they try to rely on **short-term memory.** However, as the term implies, material remains in short-term memory only temporarily. If you rely only on short-term memory (this kind of studying is called *cramming*), the information you need may not be there later when you try to recall it during a test.

To understand the difference between long-term and short-term memory, consider a telephone number that you have just heard on the radio. The number is only in your short-term memory and will be forgotten in a matter of minutes or even seconds *unless you do something to transfer it into long-term memory.* In other words, you will forget the number unless you "rehearse" it in some way.

Rehearsal refers to taking specific steps to transfer information into long-term memory. Typical steps include writing information down and repeatedly reciting it aloud. In the example above, for instance, rehearsing the telephone number would probably involve writing it, saying it aloud several times, or both. Consider how much information you already have stored in long-term memory: the alphabet; the multiplication tables; names of thousands of people, places, and things; meanings and spellings of thousands of words. You have successfully stored these in your long-term memory because you rehearsed them again and again.

As noted in Chapter 10, rehearsal is the third key to effective studying. When you are preparing for a test, you should study over several days, enough time to enable you to transfer information from short-term memory into long-term memory. Psychologists who study how people learn emphasize that both sufficient time and ample repetition are needed to accomplish this transfer.

Before you can rehearse the information in a textbook chapter efficiently, you need to *organize* it. Obviously, the better you organize material, the more efficiently you will be able to memorize it. If you organize the material in your assignments consistently as you study, right from the beginning of the semester, you will be prepared

709

Effective rehearsal requires taking specific steps to transfer information into long-term memory.

to rehearse and memorize material for each test. You can organize material by using any of these techniques:

- Underlining and annotating textbook material
- Outlining or mapping information
- Preparing summaries
- Making review cards
- Making test review sheets

Underlining, annotating, outlining, mapping, and summarizing are discussed in Chapter 10; review cards and test review sheets are discussed below. The very act of preparing these study tools helps you store information in long-term memory.

After you have organized material, you should *rehearse* by doing one or more of the following:

- Reciting from review cards
- Reciting from test review sheets
- Reciting from your notes
- Writing out information from memory

Too often, students try to review for a test simply by rereading their notes and their textbook over and over again. But rereading is a time-consuming process that does not automatically result in remembering. It has been estimated that 80 percent of the time spent studying for a test should be used for memorizing, that is, for transferring information into long-term memory. Here is an example of how you could apply this "80 percent rule." If you need 5 hours to study for a test, you should spend the first hour organizing the material and getting help with, or clarification of, things you do not understand. The remaining 4 hours would be spent rehearsing the material in order to memorize it.

You may be wondering, "How can I tell when I have successfully transferred information into long-term memory?" The way to find out is to test yourself. Try to write the information from memory on a blank sheet of paper. If material is in your long-term memory, you will be able to recall it and write it down. If you cannot write it, or if you are able to write only a part of it, then not all of the information is in your long-term memory yet; you need to rehearse it further.

These steps may sound like a lot of work, but they are necessary if you want to lock information into long-term memory. It is precisely this type of study effort that leads to mastery.

STUDYING FOR TESTS

General Guidelines

This chapter presents a five-day test review plan, but the day to begin studying for a test is actually the first day of the semester. That means attending all classes, reading every assignment, taking good notes, and reviewing regularly. The review plan described here is designed to complement your careful day-to-day preparation. No review plan can replace or make up for inadequate daily studying and preparation. Following are a few more points you should be aware of before you examine the review plan itself.

First, one reason for starting to review several days ahead of time is that the amount of material covered is too much to learn at the last minute. In fact, in college you are typically given new material right up to the day of a test.

Second, it is appropriate to ask your instructor what type of test will be given and what will be included on it. Usually, instructors are willing to give a fairly complete description of tests. Don't miss the opportunity to ask questions about a test. For example, you might ask:

- Will the test be based on textbook material, on class material (lectures, demonstrations, etc.), or on both?
- How many textbook chapters will the test cover?
- What will be the format of the test (multiple-choice questions, essay questions, etc.)?
- How many questions will there be?
- Should certain topics be emphasized in studying?

Third, be realistic about "test anxiety," or "freezing up," when you take a test. Students often complain that they "go blank" on tests, but what really happens is that they discover during the test that they did not rehearse and learn the material well enough. They did not actually forget; after all, a person cannot forget something he or she never knew. Good daily preparation and an effective test review plan are the best ways to prevent test anxiety. Knowing what to expect on a test can also leave you feeling calmer, and this is another reason for asking questions about tests, as noted above.

KEY TERM
distributed practice

Study sessions that are
spaced out over time; a
more efficient study
method than massed
practice.

Fourth, research studies have found that **distributed practice** is more effective than *massed practice*. This simply means that studying and reviewing sessions that are spaced out over time are more effective than a single session done all at once. Earlier in this chapter, *cramming* was described as trying to rely on short-term memory when you should be putting the information into long-term memory. Cramming can also be thought of as massed rather than distributed practice. Frantic, last-minute cramming usually results in faulty understanding, poor recall, increased anxiety, and lower grades.

Fifth, to study and review efficiently, you must be rested. Cramming typically involves going without sleep, but staying up late or all night can do more harm than good. Late-night or all-night cramming overtires you, increases stress, and contributes to test anxiety. Cramming forces you to rely on short-term memory, which can fail under the pressure of fatigue and stress. Try to get at least 8 hours of sleep the night before a test. On the day of the test, eat a good breakfast: for example, fruit or juice, whole-grain cereal or bread, yogurt, eggs, or low-fat milk. It is especially important to get enough protein. Don't rely on caffeine; avoid sugary, salty, and fatty foods. Getting enough rest and eating a nourishing breakfast will give you sustained energy and help you concentrate and think clearly.

A final word: Your attitude toward tests can make a big difference. Students often see tests as negative and threatening—even as punishment. Instead, try to think of a test as a learning experience. Try also to consider it an opportunity to demonstrate to yourself and your instructor how much you have learned. Remember that a test can tell you what you understand and how well you understand it. When you get a test back from an instructor, don't look at just the grade. Study the test carefully to see what you missed and why. A test also gives you an opportunity to evaluate the effectiveness of your test preparation techniques.

Five-Day Test Review Plan

Here is a detailed description of an effective five-day plan for preparing for a test. Although you may need more than five days, that is the least amount of time you should allow.

Five Days before the Test

Get an overview of all the material that will be on the test. This includes text material, class notes, handouts, and so on. Identify important main ideas and details and prepare review cards and one or more test review sheets for the material to be covered. (Such cards and sheets summarize all the important points you expect to encounter on the test. You will learn to construct review cards and test review sheets later in this chapter.) You might also have a study guide that accompanies your textbook, or perhaps your instructor has given you a special review guide. In any case, try to anticipate questions that may be asked on the test. This is also the time to identify questions and problem areas you need further help on. By starting five days ahead, you will have allowed yourself enough time to get any help you need. You will have time to ask the instructor or a classmate or to get help from a tutor. Plan to spend at least 2 hours studying. Take a 5- to 10-minute break after each hour.

Four Days before the Test

Briefly overview all the material that will be covered on the test; then review and rehearse the first third of the material in detail. First review all the material on your review cards and your test review sheet or sheets. Then, as you carefully study the first third of the material, use rehearsal techniques to memorize it and test yourself on it: that is, write and recite. Remember that you want to transfer the material into long-term (permanent) memory. Write the information; recite the information; test yourself by taking a blank sheet of paper and writing from memory what you have learned. Plan to spend at least 2 hours studying. If there are problem areas, get extra help or clarification from a tutor, a classmate, or your instructor.

Three Days before the Test

After a brief overview of all the material, review and rehearse the second third of the material in detail. Use the rehearsal techniques of writing and reciting to memorize and test yourself on the material. Plan to spend at least 2 hours studying. If any problem areas still remain, this is the time to clear them up. If you still don't understand, make another attempt at getting some additional help.

Two Days before the Test

After a brief overview of all the material, review and rehearse the last third of the material in detail. Use the rehearsal techniques of writing and reciting to memorize and test yourself on the material. Plan to spend at least 2 hours studying. Rehearse material in the problem areas that you cleared up earlier.

One Day before the Test

Make a final review of all of the material. Rehearse! Write! Recite! Test yourself! This is your final study session for the test, a full "dress rehearsal." Use this session to study your review cards and your test review sheet or sheets, covering all the important information in the material. At this point you should be feeling confident about the test. At the end of the day, right before you go to sleep, look through the material one last time. Then get a good night's rest. Resist any temptation to celebrate the completion of your review by watching television or going to a movie or a sports event. These activities create interference that can make it harder to recall information when you take the test the next day.

Creating Review Cards to Prepare for a Test

As suggested above, one highly effective way to prepare for a test is to make review cards. You already have some experience with such cards, since you have been completing your chapter-by-chapter review cards throughout *Opening Doors*.

Review cards, especially useful in preparing for tests, are index cards with an important question on the front and the answer on the back. The question and answer may have to do with a single main idea and its supporting details, a term and its definition, a name and an identification, a mathematical or chemical formula,

KEY TERM
test review cards

Index cards with an important question on the front and the answer on the back.

714 Systems for Studying Textbooks

PART **3** Systems for Studying Textbooks

and so on. Review cards are an efficient, effective, and convenient way to study for tests. Review cards can be prepared from textbook material or from lecture notes.

The boxes below show an example of a review card for an important concept presented in a sociology textbook. Notice how this card focuses on one main idea and its two supporting details. Notice also the format of this card: one side presents a probable test question, and the other side answers the question.

Just as outlining, mapping, and summarizing help you organize material, review cards allow you to arrange material clearly and concisely. Most students prefer to use 3 × 5 inch or 4 × 6 inch index cards. Cards of this size are convenient

SAMPLE REVIEW CARD: FRONT

Card 5

What are the two levels of sociological analysis?

SAMPLE REVIEW CARD: BACK

The two basic levels of sociological analysis are microsociology and macrosociology.

Microsociology: Small-scale analysis of data derived from the study of everyday patterns of behavior.

Macrosociology: Large-scale analysis of data in which overall social arrangements are scrutinized.

to carry and can be reviewed whenever you have spare moments. Index cards are available in several colors, and some students find it helpful to use a different color for each chapter or course. Other students use different colors for different categories of study material; for instance, vocabulary terms might be on cards of one color and key people and their accomplishments on cards of another color. You may want to number your review cards so that they can be easily rearranged and then put back in order. For instance, you may want to set aside cards with especially difficult questions so that you can give them special attention before the test.

Review cards are helpful in numerous ways. First, since preparing these cards involves writing out certain information, the very act of making them will help you rehearse material and commit it to long-term memory. Do not assume, though, that simply making the review cards is a substitute for rehearsing the information on them.

Second, review cards let you concentrate on one small, manageable part of the material at a time. Lecture and textbook material can seem overwhelming if you try to review it all at once before a test or at the end of a semester, but it can be quite manageable in small parts.

Third, review cards can be especially useful for memorizing key terms, key events, formulas, and the like. For example, a college instructor might require students to learn math or chemistry formulas or to memorize a set of important terms. Learning 10 definitions, names, or formulas a week is much easier than trying to learn 150 of them just before a final exam.

Fourth, review cards can be a good way to review material with a study partner, because one partner can "test" the other partner by asking questions based on the material on the cards. Partners can test each other in this manner, reciting the answers aloud, until the material on the cards becomes familiar. When you are studying for a test, working with a partner can be highly effective. In fact, even when you use review cards by yourself, it is helpful to say the answers out loud, as you would if you had a partner.

Fifth, effective students try to anticipate test questions, and review cards are a good way to guide this effort. Writing an anticipated test question on the front of a card, with the answer on the back, allows you to test yourself on material before the instructor tests you.

Sixth, review cards can help you monitor your learning by measuring what you know and what you still need to learn or rehearse further.

To sum up, if you prepare your review cards carefully and use them to rehearse and learn information, they can be an important key to success.

Creating Test Review Sheets

Suppose that you are going to be given a test in a sociology course. The test will cover a full chapter of your sociology textbook and the corresponding class sessions. Your instructor has announced that you will be allowed to prepare one sheet of notes (front *and* back) to use while you are taking the test. How could you consolidate an entire chapter's worth of information on one sheet of paper?

To begin with, consolidating all this information on a single test review sheet would *not* mean trying to recopy all the lecture notes, handouts, and textbook material in tiny handwriting. In other words, the question really is, "What kind of information would you include on this review sheet?" Preparing the sheet would mean being very selective; it would mean summarizing essential information from different sources, such as the chapter, your own class and textbook notes, and your instructor's handouts.

This example is imaginary, but in fact you should create a real **test review sheet** whenever you prepare for a test. You should try to restrict yourself to a single sheet (front and back), consolidating all the crucial information you would bring to the test if you could. If a test will cover several chapters, though, you might want to prepare several review sheets: one sheet for each chapter. Preparing review sheets is in itself a way of selecting, organizing, and rehearsing the material you must learn.

Obviously, you need to start by identifying major topics that you know will be on the test. Remember that you must be selective, because you cannot include everything. If you have been preparing review *cards* as you went along, then you have already taken the first step in preparing a test review *sheet,* because you have already identified most of the important information you need for the sheet. However, you will probably have to condense this information even more to create your test review sheet.

Another way to proceed with the first step in making a test review sheet is to list the major topics and the most important points about each. If your instructor does not identify the major topics for you, you should check your lecture notes. You should also refer to the main table of contents or to the chapter-opening table of contents in the textbook for an overview of the material that will be covered. The main headings and subheadings of the chapter are the major topics. If there is no detailed main table of contents or chapter-opening table of contents, you will need to check the chapter itself for titles and headings.

Your next step is to organize the material that you will include on the sheet. There is no one correct way to organize a test review sheet. However, the chapter material itself may often suggest logical ways in which the sheet can be organized. For example, a test review sheet can be as simple as a list of major topics with key words beside or beneath each topic. It could also consist of a grid of rows and columns, a set of mapped notes, a list of formulas, important terms (with or without definitions), a diagram or sketch, or some combination of these. The key is to organize the test review sheet in some way that is meaningful to *you.* Moreover, since this is your personal review sheet, you should feel free to use abbreviations, symbols, underlining, and highlighting in different colors to make this review sheet as clear and helpful to you as possible.

The boxes on pages 717–19 show entries in a table of contents for one chapter of a sociology text (note the major headings and subheadings) and the front and back of a test review sheet that could be prepared for this chapter.

EXAMPLE: CHAPTER TABLE OF CONTENTS USED TO PREPARE A TEST REVIEW SHEET

Source: Donald Light, Suzanne Keller, and Craig Calhoun, *Sociology,* 5th ed., p. xi. Copyright © 1989 by The McGraw-Hill Companies, Inc. Reprinted by permission of The McGraw-Hill Companies.

SAMPLE TEST REVIEW SHEET (FRONT OF PAGE)

CHAPTER 1—APPROACHES TO SOCIOLOGY

1. SOCIOLOGICAL PERSPECTIVE

Social Facts & Social Causes
   Sociology—systematic study of human societies & behavior in social settings
   Sociological perspective—lets us see how our background, social position, time, &
   place affect how we view world & act—also, who we interact with & how others
   see us
   Sociological facts—properties of group life that can't be explained by indiv
   traits, actions, or feelings. Soc facts emerge from social forces (e.g., concept of
   beauty, romantic love)

Sociological Imagination
   Soc imag—ability to see personal experience in world (pers exper is limited, so we
   shouldn't make hasty generalizations)

Science, Sociology, & Common Sense
   Scientific method used by sociologists—collect data (facts, statistics); develop
   theories
   Theory (th)—systematic formal explanation of how two or more phenomena are
   related
   Local th = narrow aspect; middle-range th = broader; general th = most
   comprehensive (explain how several ths fit together). (Contrast w common
   sense—from pers exper, facts not checked, no organization into ths to be tested.)

Levels of Sociological Analysis
   Microsociology—small-scale analysis of data from everyday behavior patterns
   Macrosociology—large-scale anal of data on overall social arrangements

2. BASIC SOCIOLOGICAL QUESTIONS

What Holds Society Together?
   Functional perspective—different parts of society contribute to whole
   Power perspective—those who control resources prob will shape society to their
   own advantage

What Is Relationship btwn Individuals & Society?
   Structural perspective—indiv choices explained by forces arising from social
   organization
   Action perspective—society shaped by people's actions

SAMPLE TEST REVIEW SHEET (BACK OF PAGE)

3. ORIGINS OF SOCIAL THEORY

Rational-Choice Th
    Founder—Adam Smith. People choose & decide for own advantage; soc = self-
    regulating system; all parts act in own interest; market forces mesh pts into
    whole
    Expanded by Jeremy Bentham—govt intervention needed to help soc function
    & let peo benefit from resources

Th of Karl Marx
    Economic system shapes social life, breeds conflict; proletariat (workers) should
    overcome capitalists (oppressors—owners of resources)

Th of Émile Durkheim
    Human behav explained by soc forces binding society (social solidarity); society
    held together by interrelated working of pts

Th of Max Weber
    Power comes from diff factors—education, soc connections, etc.; society produced
    by actions of indivs. Stressed politics & culture (not only econ like Marx)

Interactionist Th
    George Herbert Mead—peo interact depending on how they interpret soc situations;
    we learn our place in world thru soc interactions; th developed from
    phenomenology

4. FOUNDING THEORIES & CONTEMPORARY SOCIOLOGY

• Sociologists still influenced by ths above—have expanded orig ths to apply to
  modern issues
• Some to combine functional and power prespective; structural & action-oriented
  perspective

DEVELOPING CHAPTER REVIEW CARDS

**Student Online
Learning Center (OLC)**
Go to Chapter 11.
Select Flashcards
or Chapter Test.

Review cards, or *summary cards,* are an excellent study tool. They are a way to select, organize, and review the most important information in a textbook chapter. The process of creating review cards helps you organize information in a meaningful way and, at the same time, transfer it into long-term memory. The cards can also be used to prepare for tests. The review card activities in this book give you structured practice in creating these valuable study tools. Once you have learned how to make review cards, you can create them for textbook material in your other courses.

Now complete the five review cards for Chapter 11 by supplying the important information about each topic. When you have completed them, you will have summarized important material about the study skills in this chapter.

Rehearsal and Its Importance to Memory
Card 1   Chapter 11: Rehearsing Textbook Information and Preparing for Tests

Studying for Tests: General Guidelines

Card 2   Chapter 11: Rehearsing Textbook Information and Preparing for Tests

Five-Day Test Review Plan

Card 3   Chapter 11: Rehearsing Textbook Information and Preparing for Tests

Test Review Cards

Card 4 Chapter 11: Rehearsing Textbook Information and Preparing for Tests

Test Review Sheets

Card 5 Chapter 11: Rehearsing Textbook Information and Preparing for Tests

SELECTION **11-1**

Marriage and Family

Cultural Diversity: Family Strengths and Challenges

From *Marriages and Families: Intimacy, Diversity, and Strengths*

By David Olson and John DeFrain

Prepare Yourself to Read

Directions: Do these exercises *before* you read Selection 11-1.

1. First, read and think about the title. What do you already know about family strengths and challenges within various cultural groups in America?

_____

_____

_____

_____

2. Next, complete your preview by reading the following:

    First paragraph (chapter introduction)

    Headings and subheadings

    Key terms in **bold print**

    Graphics (boxes, figures, and photos) and any accompanying captions

    Chapter summary

    List of key terms

On the basis of your preview, what aspects of culture and families does this chapter seem to be about?

_____

_____

_____

_____

_____

Apply Comprehension Skills

Directions: Do these exercises *as* you read Selection 11-1.

- Budget your time for reading this selection. As the headings indicate, it has six major sections. If you wish, divide your reading time into several sessions.

- To remember essential information, underline or highlight and annotate or take notes on a separate sheet of paper.

CULTURAL DIVERSITY: FAMILY STRENGTHS AND CHALLENGES

The United States is a gathering place of many cultures. Each cultural group that has come here has surrendered some of its past in an effort to build a new life in a new land. But the United States is not so much a "melting pot" in which these distinct cultures meld together, as it is a "salad bowl" in which each of the ingredients retains its distinct flavor. The United States can also be likened to a symphony, and its various cultural groups to instruments. Each instrument has its distinct part to play—its distinct contribution—but all must work together to produce beautiful music.

Appreciating Diversity and Strengths

1   Our goal in this chapter is to point out some of the major strengths of various ethnic groups in the United States. One of the reasons our country has prospered is that the various cultural groups have different strengths. These strengths can be seen at the individual level, family level, and cultural level for each of these groups. Some ethnic groups place a high value on the importance of kin networks and are very group oriented; other cultures emphasize more individual achievement. Some ethnic groups value both individual achievement and group connection.

2   Diversity and strengths are also interconnected. There are strengths in diversity, and diversity helps build further strengths. The different abilities, interests, attitudes, and values of each ethnic group provide a broad range of options and ideas that can improve the ability to solve problems and create new ideas. These diverse strengths can help people at all levels of society at the personal level, at school, and at work.

3   When we see people from different ethnic groups, we typically do not focus on their strengths. The more common reaction is to notice how they are different from you. The next reaction can be that the difference is seen as interesting or it could be perceived as a potential problem. But after getting to know someone who is from a different ethnic group, you will be able to see that some of the differences can be both personal strengths and things you value about your relationship with them.

4   So one way to increase our appreciation of diversity is to seek out opportunities to talk with people who have ethnic backgrounds different from our own. Sharing feelings about one's cultural heritage with someone from another ethnic group can be a mutually rewarding experience, an opportunity to learn more about others and their unique cultures.

Cultural and Ethnic Identity

5   In order to put life in the United States into a more global perspective, Box 2.1 illustrates what the world village would be like if it contained 100 people. As you will notice, those from North and South America account for only 14 people. Over 70 percent of the people would be nonwhite and non-Christian. Most would live in substandard housing and 70 percent would be unable to read. At least half would suffer from malnutrition. Only 1 percent would have a college degree and less than 1 percent would have access to a computer. An even more dramatic indication of the power of the United States is that 50 percent of the world's wealth is controlled by 6 Americans.

6   One's cultural identity is an important aspect of being human. **Cultural identity** evolves from the shared beliefs, values, and attitudes of a group of people. It embodies standards of behavior and the ways in which beliefs, values, and attitudes are transmitted to the younger generation. Cultural identity also entails the ways in which kinship relationships and marital and sexual relationships are structured. Examples of the vast array of cultural identities in the United States include Anglo American, Italian American, African American, and Asian American—to name just a few.

7   Cultural identity transcends **ethnic identity,** or ethnicity, which refers to the geographic origin of a minority group within a country or culture. Whereas many people learn about their

BOX 2.1: GLOBAL DIVERSITY

The United States is a culturally diverse nation. To put cultural diversity in a global perspective, however, consider the following figures.

If the earth's population were shrunk to a village of 100 people, the composition of the village would be

- 57 Asians
- 21 Europeans
- 14 North and South Americans
- 8 Africans

And they would have the following characteristics

- 51% would be female; 49% would be male
- 70% would be non-Caucasian; 30% would be Caucasian
- 70% would be non-Christian; 30% would be Christian
- 80% would live in substandard housing
- 70% would be unable to read
- 50% would suffer from malnutrition
- 1% would have a college education
- Less than 1% would own a computer
- 50% of the world's wealth would be in the hands of only 6 people, and all 6 would be citizens of the United States

Source: World Citizen Update (Winter 1998).

specific ethnic identities from their parents, many more children are born with parents from several ethnic groups. As this increases in the United States, more young people are unclear about their ethnic identity and are simply calling themselves American.

8   A **cultural group** is a set of people who embrace core beliefs, behaviors, values, and norms and transmit them from generation to generation. Most cultures contain subgroups called **cocultures,** distinct cultural or social groups living within the dominant culture but also having membership in another culture, such as gay men and lesbians. An **ethnic group** is a set of people who are embedded within a larger cultural group or society and who share beliefs, behaviors, values, and norms that are also transmitted from generation to generation. Ethnicity "plays a major role in determining what we eat and how we work, re-

late, celebrate holidays and rituals, and feel about life and death and illness" (McGoldrick, Giordano, & Pearce, 1996, p. ix).

The United States today is one of the most 9 culturally diverse nations in the world. Although the dominant culture of the United States is European American or Caucasian American, this country is home to many other ethnic and cultural groups. The major ethnic minority groups that are usually distinguished in the United States are African Americans (or Blacks), Latinos (or Hispanics), Asian Americans, and American Indians (or Native Americans). When discussing ethnic and other minority groups, however, it is important to remember that tremendous diversity exists among the people who are commonly grouped together.

Race, which refers to the common physical 10 characteristics of a group, is a problematic concept that is being dropped from scientific and popular use. The concept of race originally arose as a way to explain the diversity of the human population worldwide. As such, "race is a social, cultural, and political creation, a product of human invention" (Cameron & Wycoff, 1988, p. 279). Race has often been used as a psychologically and emotionally divisive tool, such as when Hitler and the Nazis identified Jews as racial scapegoats that needed to be eliminated from society.

11   From a strictly scientific perspective, so-called racial characteristics do not exist (Root, 1992). Skin color, for example, can be defined only on a continuum, just as the colors black and white exist on a continuum, with gray in the middle and no clear-cut distinctions in between. As such, classifying people by racial groups becomes rather arbitrary. For example, consider the child of an Irish American mother and a Japanese American father. The child may have a skin color like her mother's and eyes like her father's.

12   What will the future bring? "More intermarriage will make it harder to figure out an individual's ancestry. But it can only hasten the approach of a color-blind society," according to Steve Olson (2001, p. 80). For the reasons just mentioned, we will try to avoid using the term *race;* rather, we will use the terms *culture* (or cultural group) or *ethnicity* (or ethnic group) when referring to different groups of people. Because of the great diversity within groups, however, even calling them ethnic or cultural groups can be misleading. Jews, for example, are often classified as an ethnic group, but doing so stretches the imagination considerably, for a number of reasons: (1) Jews hold a wide variety of religious views, from very conservative to very liberal—some are Orthodox believers, and others are atheists; (2) Jews speak a variety of languages, and many Jews today cannot speak Hebrew, the language of tradition; (3) Jews are of many nationalities as a result of Judaism's expanding influence worldwide over the centuries; and (4) Jews exhibit a variety of physical characteristics, ranging from dark-skinned, black-haired African Jews to light-skinned, blue-eyed, blond European Jews. From a cultural viewpoint, a nomadic Jewish shepherd in Ethiopia has much more in common with other Africans than he does with a Jewish dentist in suburban Chicago.

Perhaps the key issue in determining membership in an ethnic or cultural group is whether the individual *believes* he or she is a member of that group. Clearly, human beings are diverse. Classifications cannot be based solely on religious views, language, ancestry, or physical characteristics. 13

A Changing Picture: Demographic Trends in the United States

In the 2000 census, the United States government classified people into six racial categories as opposed to five in previous censuses. The six are White or Caucasian, Black or African American, Hispanic/Latino, American Indian and Alaska Native, Asian, Native Hawaiian and Other Pacific Islander. The sixth category was created by separating "Asian" and "Native Hawaiian and Other Pacific Islander." For the first time, the U.S. census made it possible for respondents to identify themselves as belonging to more than one race (U.S. Bureau of the Census, 2001c), and they obtained 63 different combinations of race. 14

The U.S. population increased 13.2 percent between 1990 and 2000, from 248.7 million people to 281.4 million. This was the largest population increase in American history (U.S. Bureau of the Census, 2001a). The 2000 census shows America's diversity, and the ethnic composition of the U.S. population continues to change. Census data indicate that 3 in 10 Americans now are minorities, and 6.8 million people identify themselves as multiracial (2.4 percent of the population). 15

Caucasians remain the majority group, 75.1 percent of the population. There are almost an equal number of African American and Hispanic people, with each comprising about 35 million or 12.5 percent of the population (U.S. Bureau of the Census, 2001b; "Impact of Census' Race Data Debated," March 13, 2001). There are about 30.5 million foreign-born residents comprising about 11 percent of the United States population, and about 40 percent arrived in the 1990s from Mexico and South America. Estimates are that there are 8 to 9 million illegal immigrants in the United States and about 5 million are from Mexico. African Americans, Hispanics, American Indians, and Asian Americans have increased their share of the total population, while the 16

TABLE 2.1
POPULATION BY RACE AND HISPANIC ORIGIN FOR THE UNITED STATES: 2000

Race and Hispanic or Latino	Number	Percent of total population
RACE		
Total population	**281,421,906**	**100.0**
One race	274,595,678	97.6
White	211,460,626	75.1
Black or African American	34,658,190	12.3
American Indian and Alaska Native	2,475,956	0.9
Asian	10,242,998	3.6
Native Hawaiian and Other Pacific Islander	398,835	0.1
Some other race	15,359,073	5.5
Two or more races	6,826,228	2.4
HISPANIC OR LATINO		
Total population	**281,421,906**	**100.0**
Hispanic or Latino	35,305,818	12.5
Not Hispanic or Latino	246,116,088	87.5

Source: U.S. Census Bureau, Census 2000 Redistricting (Public Law 94–171) Summary File, Tables PL1 and PL2.

Caucasian percentage has dropped (U.S. Bureau of the Census, 2001b; U.S. Bureau of the Census, 1997, p. 14).

17 As indicated in Table 2.1, Hispanics or Latinos of any race number 35.3 million and comprise 12.5 percent of the population. This group includes Mexican Americans, Puerto Rican Americans, and Cuban Americans, as well as a smaller number of individuals from Central or South American and Caribbean backgrounds. African Americans, numbering 34.7 million, make up 12.3 percent of the total population. Asian Americans number 10.2 million and represent 3.6 percent of the total population. Asian Americans comprise people of Japanese, Chinese, Vietnamese, Laotian, Cambodian, Korean, and Filipino descent. American Indians and Alaska Natives number 2.5 million and are 0.9 percent of the total. Most members of this group embrace a tribal identity, such as Navaho, Hopi, or Lakota, rather than identifying themselves as

Native Americans or American Indians. Native Hawaiians and other Pacific Islanders number almost 400,000, and are 0.1 percent of the total. (See Table 2.1 for complete details.)

Asian Americans have the highest median 18 household income as compared to Caucasians, African Americans, and Hispanics (Figure 2.1). Greater percentages of African Americans and Hispanics live below the poverty line than do Asian Americans and Caucasians. Figure 2.1 summarizes data on income level, percentage living in poverty, level of education, and percentage of married couples for these four ethnic groups. Comparable census data on American Indians and Alaska Natives do not exist. The most recent figures are from 1989. But this group historically has not fared well when compared to Caucasians, having a lower median household income, a higher percentage of families living below the poverty line, a lower percentage of people age 25 who have completed high school, and a lower

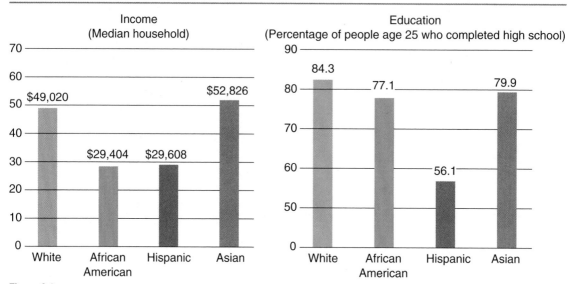

Figure 2.1

Characteristics of Families from Various Ethnic Groups

Source: U.S. Bureau of the Census (2001, table 41, p. 43; table 42, p. 44; table 44, p. 45; table 53, p. 51; table 743, p. 470; table 744, p. 470; table 760, p. 478).

percentage of families with married couples present (U.S. Bureau of the Census, 2001).

Kin Relationships across Cultures

19   Most of us learn about kinship early in our lives, with little or no theoretical explanations. We learn, for example, about brothers and sisters and about aunts, uncles, and cousins; but we identify with them as people rather than focus on specific kinship principles. We know who Uncle Jack and Aunt Libby are long before we understand the concepts of "mother's brother" or "father's sister."

20   All cultures recognize **kinship,** the relatedness of certain individuals within a group, and have norms and expectations that structure and govern kin behavior. The diversity of these norms is wide-ranging. These kinship concepts describe kinds of kinship groups and the norms that govern marital forms, family structure and organization, inheritance, authority, and residence.

21   Kinship groups range from nuclear families to various forms of extended families and may even include symbolic relationships. The **nuclear family**—the smallest, most elementary kinship unit—usually consists of two parents and their dependent children. Even in societies in which the nuclear family is embedded within a larger group, it is recognized as a distinct entity. The nuclear family is a **conjugal family system,** one that emphasizes the relationships formed through marriage. Typically, a conjugal system comprises only two generations and is relatively transitory, dissolving when the parents die or the children grow up and leave. Because nuclear families are comparatively small and short-lived, they are less likely to develop traditions that are handed down through the generations.

Many family functions are better performed 22 by composite family groups, or **consanguineal family systems,** which emphasize blood ties more than marital ties. In consanguineal systems, married couples and their children are embedded in a larger kinship group of three or more generations related by blood. Consanguineal systems can include extended families or families resulting from plural marriages. An **extended family** consists of a nuclear family and those people related to its members by blood ties, such as aunts, uncles, cousins, and grandparents.

23   A **plural marriage,** or **polygamy,** is a marriage in which a man has more than one wife **(polygyny)** or, more rarely, a marriage in which a woman has more than one husband **(polyandry).** In **monogamy,** a man or woman has only one mate. Although people from monogamous societies often perceive potential hazards in plural marriages, family patterns appear to operate smoothly in groups in which plural marriages are the norm.

24   A third kind of kinship group is a **pseudo-kin group,** in which relationships resembling kinship ties develop among unrelated individuals. Relationships with these groups range in intensity, from close friendships to godparent-godchild connections to individuals living together and caring for each other without any legal or blood relationship.

25   Although a society may have norms regarding marital and family organization and interaction, diversity is generally also evident within that society's families and kinship groups. Understanding the concept of kin relationships, however, enables observers to compare and analyze the structure and dynamics of a broad range of kinship groups.

Six Family Strengths across Various Ethnic Groups

26   There are six characteristics for describing family strengths that are very useful. Three are family system characteristics of cohesion, flexibility, and communication, and three are sociocultural characteristics of extended family, social system, and belief system.

Three Family System Characteristics

27   There has been a great deal of research looking at the characteristics of strong families, focusing on their family system. The three dimensions (clusters of concepts) of family systems that have been found are cohesion, flexibility, and communication (Gorall & Olson, 1995; Olson, 1996; Walsh, 1998). These three dimensions also relate directly to the six characteristics of strong families described by DeFrain and Stinnett in their

family strengths model (DeFrain, 1999; Stinnett & DeFrain, 1985).

- **Family cohesion** is the emotional closeness a person feels to other family members.
- **Family flexibility** is the ability to change and adapt when necessary.
- **Family communication** is the sharing of information, ideas, and feelings with each other.

28   Douglas Abbott and William Meredith (1988) studied over 500 successful families from five American ethnic groups—Native Americans, Hmong refugees, African Americans, Mexican Americans, and Caucasians—focusing on the three clusters (cohesion, flexibility, and communication) and on the family strengths items developed earlier by David Olson, Andrea Larsen, and Hamilton McCubbin (Olson, McCubbin, et al., 1989). The study revealed more similarities than differences across the five groups. In fact, there were significant similarities among all the groups, with correlations in the range of .60–85, except between the Hmong and the Native Americans and between the Hmong and the Caucasians.

29   All five groups agreed that strong families (1) use effective communication and listening skills, (2) are trusting and trustworthy, (3) are affirming and supportive, and (4) teach a sense of right and wrong behavior. Other common strengths were teaching respect for others, spending time doing things together, and feeling a sense of shared responsibility.

30   In summary, Abbott and Meredith noted that the most striking finding was the consensus among all five ethnic groups on the traits they considered most important to healthy family functioning. The researchers concluded that strong families are those that are high in family cohesion, family flexibility, and family communication. These traits of strong families, according to Abbott and Meredith, "extend beyond ethnic boundaries" (1988, p. 146).

Three Sociocultural Characteristics

31   In describing successful families, we have emphasized three important family system characteristics, but it is also important to consider

the sociocultural context in which families live. The three sociocultural characteristics that are particularly useful in describing and understanding families from diverse ethnic groups are the extended-family system, the social system, and the belief system.

- The **extended-family system** encompasses relatives, kin, and other family members connected to the family system.
- The **social system** includes the economic, educational and other related resources available.
- The **belief system** refers to a family's spiritual beliefs and values.

Family Strengths and Challenges across Five Ethnic Groups

32   This section describes some of the most salient family strengths and family challenges of the major ethnic groups in the United States. The summary lists that follow were created from reviewing several hundred publications related to the ethnic groups. Although the characteristics in each list are commonly found in a particular ethnic group, it does not mean that every family has these particular characteristics. Also, within an ethnic group, there will be families that possess many of the characteristics we have listed from other ethnic groups. So this is simply a general summary to help you more readily focus on strengths in various ethnic groups.

Strengths of White Families

Much of the early research on family strengths 33 was done with predominant focus on White or European-American families and resulted in the family strengths framework of Nick Stinnett and John DeFrain (1985). In addition, David Olson and his colleagues completed a study of 1,000 couples and families across the family life cycle and identified strengths that helped families at each stage maintain high levels of marital and family satisfaction. We will summarize these strengths here (Figure 2.2):

- *Commitment to family.* Strong White families are very committed to one another and are able to give all family members the freedom and support they need to achieve their individual goals.
- *Enjoyable time together.* Caucasian families that remain strong throughout the family life cycle find ways to spend time together and enjoy each other.
- *Ability to cope with stress and crisis.* Although all families encounter marital and family stress, strong families see stress as a challenge and deal directly with issues as they occur.
- *Spiritual well-being.* Strong Caucasian families have spiritual beliefs and values, often including religious beliefs, that help them deal with ongoing life issues.
- *Positive communication.* One of the most important characteristics of healthy Cau-

Figure 2.2 Strengths and Challenges of White Families	Strengths	Challenges
	• Commitment to the family	• Balancing work and family
	• Enjoyable time together	• Maintaining physical and emotional health
	• Ability to cope with stress and crisis	• Creating healthy relationships in a society that glorifies winning, money, and things
	• Spiritual well-being	• Learning about other cultures and being sensitive to the needs of those who are no in positions of power and authority
	• Positive communication	• Preserving the natural environment in an economic system that is fueled by consumption
	• Appreciation and affection	

casian families is that they feel good about their communication with one another.

- *Appreciation and affection.* Sharing the positive feelings they have about one another helps keep relationships positive in strong White families.

Strengths of African American Families

34   A number of family researchers have been interested in African American family strengths for more than two decades (Billingsley 1992; McAdoo, 1997, 1999). A major book, *Family Life in Black America* by Robert Taylor, James Jackson, and Linda Chatters (1997), provides an alternative to the more negative picture painted by past studies and writings about African American families. One of the earliest studies of positive aspects of African American families was conducted by Marie Peters (1981). She reviewed her own work and other African American family investigators and identified six strengths of African American families (Figure 2.3):

- *Strong kinship bonds.* The extended family is very important to many African American families, and African Americans tend to take relatives into their households (Hunter, 1997; Padgett, 1997).
- *Strong work orientation.* Dual-job households are common among strong African American families.
- *Flexibility in family roles.* Role flexibility serves as an effective coping mechanism in

healthy African American families. Because it has been necessary for many mothers to work outside the home, Black mothers tend to have considerable power in the family. The typical strong African American family is not matriarchal or patriarchal but is equalitarian in style. African American families have a longer tradition of equalitarian marriages than White families. Compared with African American couples, White couples as a group are relative newcomers to the dual-job arena (McAdoo, 1999).

- *Strong motivation to achieve.* African American parents believe education is important, and many would like to see their children go to college.
- *Strong religious orientation.* African American churches provide emotional, spiritual, and intellectual satisfaction to African American families. Church work provides meaning and purpose for many African Americans. Dr. Martin Luther King, Jr., for example, achieved "greatness . . . through the leadership developed and cultivated in the African American church" (Azubike, 1987, p. 99).
- *Caring parenting.* Researchers have studied rates of corporal punishment (slapping and spanking) across all income levels of Black and White families. Murray Straus, a nationally known family researcher who has focused on violence in families, reports that 78 percent of White parents hit their 4-year-old children in a given year as compared to

Figure 2.3 Strengths and Challenges of African American Families	Strengths	Challenges
	• Strong kinship bonds	• Being judged as a financial risk
	• Strong work orientation	• Feeling powerless
	• Flexibility in family roles	• Building self-esteem
	• Strong motivation to achieve	• Facing a high risk of being killed as a young man
	• Strong religious orientation	• Overcoming discrimination
	• Caring parenting	• Achieving higher levels of education
	• Egalitarian marriages	• Violence against each other
		• Identifying male role models

70 percent of parents of color (1994). In families with 16-year-old adolescents, 48 percent of White parents hit their teenagers as compared to 39 percent of parents of color. African American parents are apparently better than White parents at staying cool and using less punishment.

35   Researchers at Howard University (Gary, Beatty, & Berry, 1986) studied 50 strong African American families in Washington, D.C., and found that the strengths these families exhibited were similar to the strengths reported in a study of strong families who were predominantly White. One difference between healthy families in these two groups is that religious values and kinship ties are somewhat more important in African American families (Lee, Peek, & Coward, 1998).

Strengths of Latino Families

36   As mentioned earlier, Latinos encompass people from numerous Spanish-speaking cultures (Zambrana, 1995). About two-thirds are Mexican Americans, but even within this group there is diversity. Scholars Mario Garcia and Rodolfo Alvarez suggest that people of Mexican descent in the United States constitute several rather than a single demographic group (Shorris, 1992). Two such reference groups are Mexican Americans and Chicanos/Chicanas. The Mexican American group comprises people who immigrated to border states, such as California and Texas, following World War II. People who consider themselves Mexican Americans are generally older and more conservative than those who identify themselves as Chicanos or Chicanas, who are younger and more militant.

There are cultural commonalities that allow 37 us to refer, in general terms, to the Latino population of the United States. (*Hispanic* is the term most often used in studies and statistics, including those published by the U.S. government, for Latino populations.) But always keep in mind that commonalities are broad and general; every individual and every family is unique.

Latinos in the United States have managed 38 to preserve a strong family system in spite of the difficult challenges they face. Latinos place a high priority on the family as a source of identity and support. Family encompasses the immediate family unit (*la casa*), the extended family (*la familia*), and godparents (*los compadres*).

In Latino culture, the well-being of the entire 39 family system has priority over individual goals. In one extensive overview of the strengths of Hispanic families, William Vega (1995) identified the six most important characteristics, which are similar to those identified for families from other cultures in the United States (Figure 2.4):

- *Familism.* The family is a major priority; it is highly valued. There is a strong emotional commitment to the family.
- *High family cohesion.* Strong Latino families have high cohesion, or closeness, although cohesion decreases across generations somewhat among Latino families living in the United States.

Figure 2.4
Strengths and
Challenges of
Latino Families

Strengths	Challenges
• Familism	• Remaining family centered
• High family cohesion	• Maintaining traditions
• High family flexibility	• Gaining financial resources
• Supportive kin network system	• Overcoming the language barrier
• Equalitarian decision making	• Overcoming social and economic discrimination
• Strong ethnic identity	• Handling relocation issues
	• Achieving higher levels of education
	• Acculturating across generations

- *High family flexibility.* There is considerable role flexibility in Latino families, in contrast to the stereotyped view in which the male is seen as dominant.

- *Supportive kin network system.* The large kin network system of most Latino families is important as a supportive resource and is a strong tradition.

- *Equalitarian decision making.* Increasingly, families share roles more equally; decision making is equalitarian.

- *Strong ethnic identity.* The importance of the Latino culture and values binds families together and helps give them a strong ethnic identity.

40   Researchers have found that Mexican American families and Anglo families share two strengths. The researchers expected to find differences between the two groups, based not so much on culture but on social class. In short, they hypothesized that money helped family life run a bit more smoothly. They were surprised to find that even though the Mexican American families had the additional challenges that come with low income, their group scored no differently on cohesion and adaptability than the middle-income Anglo families. However, conflicts between generations are a common family problem in Hispanic families, as they are in many ethnic and cultural groups.

Strengths of Asian American Families

41   Families of Asian descent are another resilient group in this country. Although Asian Americans have faced prejudice and discrimination throughout their history in the United States, they have fared better than other ethnic minorities economically and have managed to preserve their family ties, traditions, and values (McLeod, 1986; Schwartz, Raine, & Robins, 1987). A period of disruption occurred in the 1940s. Following the bombing of Pearl Harbor, fear of further attacks by Japan led the U.S. government to resettle Japanese Americans—even those born in this country—in what were essentially prison camps until the war ended. Four decades later, the federal government agreed to modestly recompense surviving family members for the ill treatment they suffered.

Although Asian Americans probably do not 42 face the same level of discrimination that African Americans face in the workplace, a report by the Commission on Civil Rights was forced to conclude that "anti-Asian activity in the form of violence, vandalism, harassment and intimidation continues to occur across the nation" (Schwartz et al., 1987). Even today there is a degree of discrimination against Asian Americans, fueled by a fear of competition from the economies in East Asia. Many Asian immigrants have come to this country in search of economic progress, which was unachievable in their homelands. Having reached their goals through hard work, Asian Americans are sometimes seen as a threat to those who have lived in this country longer and have settled into a comfortable, more easygoing life.

Many Asian Americans share a cultural heritage that values discipline, family commitment, 43 hard work, and education (Blair & Qian, 1998). Young people reared in such an environment become challenging competitors in a society such as ours, which values competition and individual initiative. Asian American families are very diverse, but they commonly share many of the strengths of other cultural groups. Following are six major strengths of Asian American families, which are summarized in Figure 2.5:

- *Strong family orientation.* Both the nuclear and the extended family are important historically and today.

- *Filial piety.* The great respect Asian American families have for their elders is noteworthy. It helps explain the high level of mutual support each generation receives from the other generations.

- *High value on education.* Asian American families emphasize the importance of education, from nursery school through college.

- *Well-disciplined children.* Traditionally, children are expected to be quiet, well behaved, and somewhat passive.

- *Extended-family support.* Financial and emotional support is provided by the extended family when the nuclear family needs it.

- *Family loyalty.* Family members support each other and protect each other's privacy.

Figure 2.5
Strengths and
Challenges of Asian
American Families

Strengths	Challenges
• Strong family orientation • Filial piety • High value on education • Well-disciplined children • Extended-family support • Family loyalty	• A need to relax personal expectations somewhat • Maintaining ties with kin • Overcoming emotional vulnerability • Overcoming the stigma against seeking help • Trusting those outside the group • Relaxing the focus on work

Figure 2.6
Strengths and
Challenges of
American Indian
Families

Strengths	Challenges
• Extended-family system • Traditional beliefs • High family cohesion • Respect for elders • Bilingual language skills • Tribal support system	• Dealing with the conflicting values of the tribe and U.S. society • Maintaining family traditions • Staying cohesive and connected • Identifying role models • Achieving higher levels of education

44   Recent immigrants from Southeast Asia (Vietnam, Cambodia, and Laos) have had a more difficult time adjusting to American culture than earlier immigrants from Japan, China, and Korea did. Although many recent arrivals have been farmers from rural areas, these immigrants often find themselves in poor inner-city neighborhoods, where their traditional values are challenged, making the adjustment to American culture difficult.

Strengths of American Indian Families

45   American Indian families in the United States are represented by approximately 400 tribes (McCubbin, Thompson, & Fromer, 1998). About half live on reservations (Carson, Dail, Greeley, & Kenote, 1990). The tremendous degree of diversity among tribes contributes to the difficulty researchers have in studying American Indian families. In this section on the strengths of American Indian families, we are looking only at the groups living in North America.

Six important strengths of American Indian families are listed here and summarized in Figure 2.6:   46

- *Extended family system.* The extended family is strong in American Indian families.
- *Traditional beliefs.* The belief system of American Indian tribes focuses on harmony with nature and the value of contentment.
- *High family cohesion.* The connectedness of the family is important. The family is broadly defined to include the nuclear family, the extended family, and the tribal community.
- *Respect for elders.* Elders are the most respected individuals in traditional American Indian tribes, and the family reinforces this attitude.
- *Bilingual language skills.* Most American Indians work hard to maintain their native languages, but this objective is becoming more difficult because the children attend school off the reservations and are increas-

ingly exposed to television and other mass media.

- *Tribal support system.* Many American Indians rely on their tribal support system for all types of problems. Only when that is inadequate do they turn to outside support.

47   Although American Indian families are characterized by diversity (Strauss, 1986), some investigators have asserted that the family remains the basic unit of the American Indian community and that the American Indian family can be characterized as having traditional beliefs, practices, and languages and a unique history and lifestyle. American Indian families derive support from both individual family members and the clan or tribal group to which they belong.

48   Studies have found that many American Indian tribes emphasize mutual dependence among tribal members, responsibility, respect for others, courage, optimism, and contentment. This contentment comes from an identification with the cosmos (feeling one with the world), a spiritual orientation to life, and traditional religious practices. Living in harmony with nature and with other human beings is of utmost importance, nature being a powerful learning tool for family members and the tribe (J. S. Olson & Wilson, 1984).

49   The extended family is still a source of strength for many American Indians, but this is changing as more family members leave the reservation to seek opportunities elsewhere. American Indian youths may have a wider array of people to whom they are attached than do non-Indians. In times of crisis, support from both the extended family and the tribal community helps people survive (Robbins, 1987). Nuclear families are important, but the tribal community also acts as a safety net, assuming a great deal of responsibility for the welfare of its individual members. Many fathers actively care for their own children along with the mothers and serve as father substitutes for children whose fathers have died or deserted the family (Carson et al., 1990).

50   How an individual behaves, in both positive and negative ways, reflects upon the individual's family and tribe (Carson et al., 1990). The group is in part collectively liable for the transgressions of its individual members, so the group provides a collective conscience and consciousness that emphasize individual responsibility. Respect for elders is common among American Indian tribes, and grandparents often hold a unique position, passing on cultural values and beliefs to their grandchildren and educating the young about the physical, social, and spiritual world. Social shame (that is, embarrassment) is a common tool for disciplining children. In general, physical punishment is not encouraged or condoned. Parents usually praise their children only for special accomplishments. The young are not socialized to expect praise, and it is not given lightly.

    A number of tribes stress marriages based 51 not only on an attraction between two people but on the consensus of their relatives and the tribal community. This approach to marriage recognizes the fact that an individual marries not only another individual but also that person's family and cultural community. Research suggests that these officially sanctioned marriages are more stable than those not recognized by the couple's family members or the tribe (Stauss, 1986).

    The bilingual childrearing seen in some 52 tribes and families is also identified as a strength of American Indian families (Carson et al., 1990). Although most American Indians learn English for survival in a White-dominant culture, they often find strength in sharing their own common languages. The family strengths and culturally adaptive patterns of American Indians deserve more extensive study in the years ahead (Carson et al., 1990).

Cross-Cultural Family Studies

    Cross-cultural family studies tend to focus 53 on two interrelated questions. First, how are families in the United States different from those in other parts of the world? Second, how are they similar? At first glance, people are often struck by the obvious differences between family cultures. Clothing styles, food preferences, religious beliefs, housing, music, education—all these aspects of culture vary from one society to another. When visiting a new culture, people often look for the differences between it and their own culture. Eventually, they also begin to see the similarities. When learning about another culture, then, the key is to look for both similarities and differences.

American Indian families have many strengths on which they rely, including a strong extended-family system, traditional beliefs that focus on harmony with nature and the value of contentment, high family cohesion, respect for elders, bilingual language skills, and the tribal support system.

54   **Cross-cultural family studies** focus on how particular cultural contexts influence a wide variety of issues: family values and behaviors, courtship patterns and weddings, marital and parent-child communication, power and gender roles, work and the family, ethical and religious values, childrearing patterns, sexuality, the role of grandparents and the extended family, and the role people outside the immediate family play in helping families in crisis.

55   We are all ethnocentric to some extent; we see others through unique lenses that are shaped by our own culture. **Ethnocentrism** is the assumption that one's own culture is the standard by which other cultures should be judged. Our ethnocentricity influences the extent to which we judge other people, families, and cultures as similar to or different from us. Tolerance of the traditions and values of other cultural and ethnic groups is the first step in transcending our overconcern with human differences. Understanding other ways of looking at life and the world around us can lead to genuine, mutual appreciation among people of different backgrounds.

Family researchers attempt to combine 56 these two perspectives, recognizing the differences between cultures but also trying to identify similarities. Researchers from one culture can never completely discard their personal lenses. They can, however, try to become more open to new ideas and behaviors by submerging themselves in another culture, even learning that culture's language and living within that culture.

Challenges for Ethnic Families

Ethnic families in the United States face many 57 challenges. Among them are intercultural marriage, the issue of assimilation, and relationships between men and women and between parents and children. Ethnic families do not experience the "advantages of being in the majority" that European Americans in the predominant culture experience.

Assimilation, Acculturation, and Segregation

58   Newcomers to any society face a difficult set of choices: Should they swiftly reject their former life and the culture from which they came? Should they downplay their ethnic origins in an effort to fit the mainstream view? Or should they build their own ethnic enclave and try to create a safe microworld that reflects their cultural heritage? These questions are extremely difficult to answer, and minority-group members often disagree on how to proceed. Some families are torn apart by controversies of this nature.

59   There are three important processes that help explain what happens when a cultural group from another country encounters the dominant culture of the new country. **Assimilation** is *the process in which old cultural traits and values are relinquished and replaced by those of the dominant culture.* **Acculturation** is *the process whereby cultural traits and values from one ethnic group become blended with those of the dominant culture.* **Segregation** is *the process in which an ethnic group isolates itself or is forced into isolation within the dominant culture.* All three of these processes can occur in an interactive way as a family adapts to living in another culture.

60   Members of the majority culture whose families have been in the United States for two, three, or more generations sometimes do not understand why immigrants are hesitant about assimilation—adopting the values of the dominant culture. But it is clear that immigrants are in a difficult psychological position. They see and are attracted by the strengths of American culture, especially its abundance of economic resources. But they also see the weaknesses of American culture—materialism, competitiveness, wasteful exploitation of the natural world, a fast-paced and often impersonal existence. Immigrants are in some ways in a better position to see America's strengths and weaknesses than are Americans, for they have another culture with which they can compare this one.

61   Unfortunately, most of what people know about ethnic and cultural groups other than their own is based on **stereotypes**—standardized and oversimplified views. When a person from one group describes people from another, the description is often a stereotype. **Prejudice,** which liter-

ally means prejudging, is also closely linked with stereotyping; both attitudes reinforce each other. As a society we need to move beyond stereotypes and focus on each group's strengths and challenges. Recognizing others' strengths helps reduce prejudice.

62   Racism is closely related to ethnocentrism and may even be a by-product of it. All the various "isms" tend to distance human beings from each other by accentuating differences and ignoring fundamental similarities, which in turn leads to tension and conflict. **Racism** develops when the most powerful group in a society creates an elaborate mythology (a set of beliefs that grossly distort reality) about a minority group. These prejudices often endure because of the need of the dominant group to feel superior to others.

63   Racist myths focus on a wide variety of issues. The minority group may be said to lack intelligence, eat strange foods, play weird music, be extremely violent and dangerous, or take dreaded drugs. The men of the minority group are often reputed to be sex starved, lusting after the women of the majority group. These fears are powerful and can increase prejudice and discrimination against minority-group members.

64   In sheer numbers, a minority group may actually outnumber the majority. For example, African Americans outnumber European Americans in many parts of Washington, D.C. Because minority-group members are often the victims of prejudice and discrimination, they may develop prejudices against the "other" group. Unfortunately, this reduces both groups to the charge of stereotyping. In effect, "We have met the enemy, and they are us."

Marriage outside the Group

65   In many countries throughout the world, marriage is seen primarily as an agreement between two families. An alliance through marriage between two successful families can enhance the power, prestige, and well-being of all the members of both families. In this sense, one marries not just an individual but also that person's family.

66   Because American culture stresses individuality, the importance of a good "fit" between families is often overlooked, and individuals who wish to marry often purposely ignore advice from

Ethnic identity is a social construction rather than a biological fact. The children in this family are of mixed Anglo and Asian heritage; their ethnic identity depends not on their physical characteristics but on the tradition within which they are being raised.

family members. Sometimes that advice is based on ignorance of the proposed partner's personal strengths or on prejudice toward the cultural group from which the proposed partner comes. The greater the differences between the two families, the more likely the chance for conflict.

67   As our society becomes more ethnically diverse, marriage across ethnic groups has increased and, in turn, expanded ethnic diversity. Asian Americans have the highest rate of **intercultural marriage**—marriage between people from two different cultural or ethnic groups—of all U.S. groups. The rate of intercultural marriage is 34 percent among Japanese Americans, 31 percent among Korean Americans, and 16 percent among Chinese Americans. African Americans and Latinos have the lowest rates of intercultural marriage, at 2 percent and 12 percent, respectively (S. M. Lee & Yamanaka, 1990).

68   When same-culture and intercultural marriages are compared statistically, intercultural couples are somewhat more likely to divorce. Lack of support from parents and other family members probably contributes to this higher divorce rate. This is not to say that intercultural marriages cannot succeed, but couples in such marriages do need the support of their families and friends.

Black–White Marriages

69   Black–White relationships and marriages are not common among Americans. In 1999, out of a total of almost 56 million married couples in

the United States, only about 307,000 consisted of one Black partner and one White partner (U.S. Bureau of the Census, 2001).

70   One study found that Black–White couples experienced more negative reactions and discrimination than either African American couples or European American couples. To gather information about Black–White couples, Paul Rosenblatt, Tern Karis, and Richard Powell (1995) conducted a study of 21 multiracial couples (*multiracial* was the term the couples preferred). Tern Karis, a White woman, and Richard Powell, a Black man, who are themselves a couple, interviewed all the couples in the study. In 16 of the 21 couples, the man was African American; in the other 5 couples, the woman was African American. This percentage is similar to the national sample. Of the 21 couples, 19 were married, and most were between the ages of 20 and 50. The couples were generally well educated.

71   Most of the multiracial couples in the Rosenblatt, Karis, and Powell study experienced opposition from the family of the White partner. Fathers and other kin are often more opposed than mothers. These families typically will not discuss with other family members or friends that their White daughter is involved with a Black man. The White partner often grows distant from family members who are not supportive of the relationship.

72   Rosenblatt, Karis, and Powell (1995) identified six principal objections to the multiracial relationship raised by family members of the

White partner. First, they worried about disapproval from other family members, friends, and society in general. Second, they expressed concern about the safety and well-being of their adult child. Third, they pointed to the alleged clannishness of African Americans. Fourth, they worried about problems the children of the couple might have. Fifth, they expressed concern about the likelihood of a poor economic future for the couple. And sixth, they foresaw other problems that were often not specified. The White partner's reaction to the parents' opposition was often complicated; some said their feelings were a "blend of pain, anger, frustration, desperation, [and] determination" (p. 81).

73   In contrast, the African American family was often more accepting of the multiracial relationship than was the White family (Kouri & Lasswell, 1993). The mother was generally more accepting than the father and other kin. About half of the Black families did have some objections, including concerns that their child was marrying outside the group, perhaps marrying "down" in terms of education or status, or "sleeping with the enemy."

74   All the multiracial couples hoped that they would not experience racism. They hoped others would see them as any other couple and not relate to them on the basis of racial stereotypes. One person said, "I want the larger society to know that "interracial relationships or not, people are people. All races of people require the same thing . . . we all need love and affection" (Rosenblatt et al., 1995, p. 278). Another person suggested that "interracial couples aren't good or bad because of being interracial. It is what the relationship becomes that determines its goodness or badness, but it has nothing to do with the complexion of the people" (p. 281). And a third person suggested that the biggest difference between partners in a Black-White marriage was not their race but their gender—something that most couples have to deal with, no matter their skin color (pp. 294–295).

Relationships between Men and Women

75   Regardless of nationality or cultural background, friction occurs between men and women in intimate relationships. Although couples strive for mutual love and caring, different socialization processes and biological inheritances produce misunderstanding and conflict. Women in developed countries, because of greater education and more employment opportunities outside the home, tend to have more options. If they are dissatisfied with their marriages and can support themselves, they are not as likely to stay in these marriages. Women in rural areas and in developing countries have fewer options, even though they may be just as unhappy. As a result, divorce rates tend to be higher in industrialized, urban-oriented societies around the world and lower in less-developed, agrarian societies. But the lower divorce rates in the more rural societies do not necessarily indicate happier marriages.

Relationships between Parents and Children

  Children often develop into adults much like **76** their own parents. In the process of growing up, however, children and parents often experience much conflict. The younger generation strives to create a relatively independent life, and the older generation tries to maintain control of the children. These struggles are played out in countless cultures around the world. Family power structures in various cultures seem to change gradually over time, as societies move from agriculturally oriented economies to industrialized economies. In an agriculturally oriented family, the father, who is responsible for making sure the farm runs smoothly, has more control over his children. In the city, the father's influence lessens, and the influence of others (peers, school, the work place) increases. Rural societies generally emphasize respect for the authority of the dominant males. In more modern societies, the rights of the individual receive more weight because the family is more likely to succeed if all its members become well educated and find good jobs. When a family moves from one culture to another, parent-child relationships can be especially strained, because the youngsters struggle to fit into the new culture and inevitably lose touch with past traditions.

Summary

Appreciating Diversity and Strengths

- Appreciating diversity and the strengths of diversity are major goals of this chapter.
- When viewing people from different ethnic groups, it is important to look beyond their

physical qualities and get to know the person and family strengths.

Cultural and Ethnic Identity

- Cultural identity evolves from shared beliefs, values, and attitudes.
- Ethnic identity refers to the geographic origin of a particular group.
- Race is based on the physical characteristics of a group of people and is a concept that is losing value.
- The U.S. census now classifies people into six ethnic categories instead of five. The six are White or Caucasian, Black or African American, Hispanic/Latino, American Indian and Alaska Native, Asian, and Native Hawaiian and Other Pacific Islander. The sixth category was created by separating "Asian" and "Native Hawaiian and Other Pacific Islander." For the first time, the U.S. census also made it possible for respondents to identify themselves as belonging to more than one race; 63 different combinations of race were reported.
- Kin relationships—the structure of marital and family relationships—vary considerably across ethnic and cultural groups.

Six Family Strengths across Various Ethnic Groups

- Strong families share the three family system traits of cohesion, flexibility, and communication. Three sociocultural characteristics are also useful for understanding strong families: the extended family system, the social system, and belief system.

Five Family Strengths and Challenges

- The strengths of White families in the United States include commitment to the family, enjoyable time spent together, the ability to cope with stress and crisis, spiritual well-being, positive communication, and appreciation and affection for each other.
- The strengths of African American families include strong kinship bonds, strong work orientation, flexibility in family roles, strong

motivation to achieve, strong religious orientation, and caring parenting.
- The strengths of Latino families include familism, high family cohesion, high family flexibility, a supportive kin network system, equalitarian decision making, and strong ethnic identity.
- The strengths of Asian American families include strong family orientation, filial piety, a high value on education, well-disciplined children, extended-family support, and family loyalty.
- The strengths of American Indian families include an extended-family system, traditional beliefs, high family cohesion, respect for elders, bilingual language skills, and a tribal support system.

Cross-Cultural Family Studies

- Intercultural marriage can be challenging for families, but it can also be the source of considerable learning and personal growth.
- Male-female relationships and parent-child struggles are common issues in families from a variety of ethnic groups.

Challenges for Ethnic Families

- The issues of assimilation, acculturation, and segregation must be faced by any new ethnic or cultural group.

Key Terms

cultural identity
ethnic identity
cultural group
coculture
minority group
kinship
conjugal family
   system
segregation
prejudice
racism
intercultural marriage
polyandry
monogamy

pseudo-kin group
cross-cultural family
   study
ethnocentrism
nuclear family
acculturation
stereotypes
plural marriage
polygamy
family communication
extended-family
   system
social system
belief system

ethnic group
race
assimilation
consanguineal family
   system

extended family
family cohesion
family flexibility

Suggested Readings

Billingsley, A. (1992). *Climbing Jacob's ladder: The enduring legacy of African American families.* New York: Simon & Schuster. A professor of family studies at the University of Maryland, College Park, argues that African American families are amazingly "strong, enduring, adaptive, and highly resilient."

McAdoo, H. P. (Ed.). (1997). *Black families* (3rd ed.). Thousand Oaks, CA: Sage. Focuses on the diversity of Black families and balances the strengths of these families with the challenges they face.

McAdoo, H. P. (Ed.). (1999). *Family ethnicity: Strength in diversity.* Thousand Oaks, CA: Sage. Explores family ethnicity in five major cultural groups in the United States: African Americans, Latino Americans, American Indians, Asian Americans, and Muslim Americans.

McCubbin, H. I., Thompson, A. I., & Fromer, J. E. (Eds.). (1998). *Resiliency in Native American and immigrant families.* Thousand Oaks, CA: Sage. A much-needed addition to the research literature.

Rosenblatt, P. C., Karis, T., & Powell, R. D. (1995). *Multiracial couples.* Thousand Oaks, CA: Sage. Describes the experiences of interracial couples, including opposition from both African American and European American family members, racism in the workplace, and institutional racism.

Taylor, R. J., Jackson, J. S., & Chatters, L. M. (Eds.). (1997) *Family life in Black America.* Thousand Oaks, CA: Sage.

Zambrana, R. E. (1995). *Understanding Latino families: Scholarship, policy, and practice.* Thousand Oaks, CA: Sage. Focuses on the strengths of Latino/Hispanic groups, the structural processes that impede their progress, and the cultural and familial processes that enhance their intergenerational adaptation and resiliency.

Source: From David H. Olson and John DeFrain, "Cultural Diversity: Family Strengths and Challenges," Ch. 2 including figures and tables in *Marriages and Families: Intimacy, Diversity, and Strengths,* 4th ed., pp. 33–66. Copyright © 2003 by The McGraw-Hill Companies, Inc. Reprinted by permission of The McGraw-Hill Companies.

Collaboration Option

Rehearsing Textbook Information and Preparing for Tests: Chapter-Length Selection

Directions: Refer to Selection 11-1 as necessary to complete the following activities.

Option for collaboration: Your instructor may direct you to work with other students on one or more of these items, or in other words, to work *collaboratively.* In that case, you should form groups of three or four students, as directed by your instructor, and work together to complete the exercises. After your group discusses an item and agrees on the answer, have a group member record it. Each member of your group should be able to explain all of your group's answers.

The chapter-length selection, "Cultural Diversity: Family Strengths and Challenges," contains the following sections and subsections:

Introduction	
Appreciating Diversity and Strengths	Paragraphs 1–4
Cultural and Ethnic Identity	Paragraphs 5–25
A Changing Picture: Demographic Trends in the United States	
Kin Relationships across Cultures	
Six Family Strengths across Various Ethnic Groups	Paragraphs 26–31
Three Family System Characteristics	
Three Sociocultural Characteristics	
Five Family Strengths and Challenges	
across Five Ethnic Groups	Paragraphs 32–52
Strengths of White Families	
Strengths of African American Families	
Strengths of Latino Families	
Strengths of Asian American Families	
Strengths of American Indian Families	
Cross-Cultural Family Studies	Paragraphs 53–56
Challenges for Ethnic Families	Paragraphs 57–76
Assimilation, Acculturation, and Segregation	
Marriage outside the Group	
Black–White Marriages	
Relationships between Men and Women	
Relationships between Parents and Children	
Summary	
List of Key Terms and Suggested Readings	

1.   Your instructor will give you specific instructions for completing one or more of the following activities in order to apply the skills that you learned in this chapter:

- Create **test review cards** for the two sections "Cultural and Ethnic Identity" (paragraphs 5–25) and "Six Family Strengths across Various Ethnic Groups" (paragraphs 26–31). To make your review cards, look at the key points for these two sections in the chapter summary on pages 742–43. These key points will be the *answers* you write on the *back* of your review cards. Once you have written each key point on the back of a card, you should create a question about it on the front of the card. You may have more than six review cards since you may need to create more than one question for some key points. *See pages 713–14 for guidelines for making review cards.*

- On notebook paper, create a test review sheet for the section "Five Family Strengths and Challenges across Five Ethnic Groups" (paragraphs 32–52). Your test review sheet should contain the five subheadings of this section and should consist of a comparison of the strengths and challenges of each ethnic group. *See pages 715–19 for guidelines for making a test review sheet.* You may wish to organize the information in the form of a table, such as this one:

ETHNIC GROUP	STRENGTHS	CHALLENGES

Your chart will be much larger, of course.

- On small index cards, create *vocabulary cards* for the important terms listed on page 743. Write the term on one side of the card and its definition on the back. These cards are an excellent study tool for learning important terms since you must write the information. Then you can turn through the cards over and over as you recite the information and transfer it to long-term memory. The cards will enable you to "test" yourself on the terms so that you will know when you have learned them. (Vocabulary cards are just a special type of test review card for learning important terms.)

2. Your instructor may distribute a practice quiz on one or more sections of the selection, "Cultural Diversity: Family Strengths and Challenges." Use any test review cards, test review sheets, and vocabulary cards you have created to rehearse the material and transfer it into your long-term memory for this quiz. (On the other hand, your instructor may allow you to use your test review cards, test review sheets, and vocabulary cards when you take the quiz.)

Read More about This Topic on the World Wide Web

Directions: To discover more information about the topics mentioned in this selection, use your favorite search engine such as Google, Yahoo!, or AltaVista (www.google.com, www.yahoo.com, www.altavista.com). Type in combinations of keywords such as:

U.S. cultural groups

or

U.S. ethnic groups

or

21st century U.S. demographic trends

or

cultural diversity in families

or

Latino families

or

African American families

or

European American families

or

Native American families

or

Asian American families

or

cross-cultural families

or

ethnocentrism

Glossary of Key Reading and Study Skills Terms

IN THIS APPENDIX . . .

Appendix 1 lists key terms from *Opening Doors,* with definitions. This list will help you review text material and monitor your understanding of the concepts and skills you have studied. The listing is alphabetical; the numbers in parentheses indicate chapters in which the key terms are introduced.

annotation   Explanatory notes you write in the margins of a textbook to organize and remember information. (*Chapter 10*)

appendix   Section at the end of a book that includes supplemental material or specialized information. (*10*)

assessing your prior knowledge   Determining what you already know about a topic. (*3*)

auditory learner   One who prefers to hear information to be learned. (*1*)

author's argument   Point of view or position the author wants to persuade the reader to believe. (*9*)

author's assumption   Something the author takes for granted without proof. (*9*)

author's bias   An author's preference for one side of an issue over the other. (*8, 9*)

average reading rate   Rate used for textbooks and more complex material in periodicals (200–300 words per minute). (*2*)

bar graph   Chart in which the length of parallel rectangular bars is used to indicate relative amounts of the items being compared. (*10*)

bibliography   Textbook feature near the end of the book, giving a list of sources: books, articles, and other works from which the author of the text has drawn information; it may also be called *references, works cited,* or *sources.* Bibliographies sometimes include works the author recommends for further (supplemental) reading. (*10*)

box   Textbook feature consisting of supplementary material separated from the regular text; also called a *sidebar.* (*10*)

cause-effect pattern   Writing pattern presenting reasons for (causes of) events or conditions and results (effects) of events or conditions. (*7*)

chapter introduction   Textbook feature opening a chapter, describing the overall purpose and major topics or "setting the scene" with a case study, anecdote, etc. (*10*)

chapter objectives   Textbook features at the beginning of a chapter, telling you what you should know or be able to do after studying the chapter; also called *preview questions, what you'll learn, goals,* etc. (*10*)

chapter outline   Textbook feature at the beginning of a chapter, listing the chapter topics or headings in their order of appearance; also called *chapter contents, preview, overview,* etc. (*10*)

chapter review cards   A way to select, organize, and review the most important information in a chapter; a study tool and special textbook feature in *Opening Doors;* also called *summary cards.* (*1*)

chapter summary   Textbook feature at or near the end of a chapter, in which the author collects and condenses the most essential ideas. (*10*)

classification pattern   Items are divided into groups or categories that are named, and the parts in each group are explained; also called *division pattern.* (*7*)

comparison-contrast pattern   Writing pattern used to present similarities (comparisons), differences (contrasts), or both. (*7*)

comprehension monitoring   Evaluating your understanding as you read and correcting the problem whenever you realize that you are not comprehending. (*2*)

conclusion   A decision that is reached after thoughtful consideration of information the author presents. (*9*)

connotation   Additional, nonliteral meaning associated with a word. (*2*)

context clues   Words in a sentence or paragraph that help the reader deduce (reason out) the meaning of an unfamiliar word. (*2*)

credibility   Believability of an author's argument. (*9*)

critical reading   Going beyond basic comprehension to gain additional insights. (*8*)

critical thinking   Thinking in an organized way about material you read or hear in order to evaluate it accurately. (*9*)

deductive reasoning   A process of reasoning in which a general principle is applied to a specific situation. (*9*)

definition pattern   Writing pattern presenting the meaning of an important term discussed throughout a passage. The definition may be followed by examples that illustrate or clarify the meaning. (*7*)

definition with examples pattern   See *definition pattern.* (*7*)

denotation   Literal, explicit meaning of a word; its dictionary definition. (*2*)

dictionary pronunciation key   Guide to sounds of letters and combinations of letters in words. A full pronunciation key usually appears near the beginning of a dictionary; an abbreviated key, showing only vowel sounds and the more unusual consonant sounds, usually appears at or near the bottom of each page. (*2*)

distributed practice   Study sessions that are spaced out over time; a more efficient study method than massed practice. (*11*)

division pattern   See *classification pattern.* (*7*)

epigraphs   Quotations that suggest overall themes or concerns of a chapter; this kind of textbook feature is usually found at chapter openings or in the margins. (*10*)

etymology   Origin and history of a word. (*2*)

exhibits   Special textbook features such as student papers, plot summaries, profit-and-loss statements, documents, forms, and printouts. (*10*)

fact   Something that can be proved to exist or have happened or is generally assumed to exist or have happened. (*9*)

figurative language   Imagery; words that create unusual comparisons, vivid pictures, and special effects; also called *figures of speech.* (*2*)

flowchart   Diagram that shows steps in procedures or processes by using boxes, circles, and other shapes connected with lines or arrows. (*10*)

glossary   Mini-dictionary at end of a textbook, listing important terms and definitions from the entire text. (*10*)

graphic aids Illustrations that consolidate information and present it more clearly than words alone; graphic aids include figures, cartoons, and photographs. (*10*)

hyperbole Figure of speech using obvious exaggeration for emphasis. (*2*)

illustrations See *graphic aids*. (*10*)

implied main idea Main point that is not stated directly as one sentence and therefore must be inferred and formulated by the reader. (*5*)

index Alphabetical listing of topics and names in a textbook, with page numbers, usually appearing at the end of the book. (*10*)

inductive reasoning A process of reasoning in which a general principle is developed from a set of specific instances. (*9*)

inference In reading, a logical conclusion based on what an author has stated. (*9*)

intended audience People an author has in mind as readers; the people he or she is writing for. (*8*)

intended meaning What an author wants you to understand even when his or her words seem to be saying something different. (*8*)

intermediate goal Goal you want to accomplish within the next 3 to 5 years. (*1*)

irony A deliberate contrast between an author's apparent meaning and his or her intended meaning. (*8*)

kinesthetic learner One who prefers to incorporate movement when learning. (*1*)

learning style The modality through which an individual learns best. (*1*)

line graph Diagram whose points are connected to show a relationship between two or more variables. (*10*)

list pattern Series of items in no particular order, since order is unimportant. (*7*)

long-term goal Goal you want to accomplish during your lifetime. (*1*)

long-term memory Permanent memory, as contrasted with short-term (temporary) memory. (*11*)

major details Details that directly support the main idea. (*6*)

mapping Informal way of organizing main ideas and supporting details by using boxes, circles, lines, arrows, etc. (*10*)

metaphor Figure of speech implying a comparison between two essentially dissimilar things, usually by saying that one of them *is* the other. (*2*)

minor details Details that support other details. (*6*)

mixed pattern Combination of two or more writing patterns. (*7*)

monitoring your comprehension Evaluating your understanding as you read and correcting the problem whenever you realize that you are not comprehending. (*2*)

monthly assignment calendar Calendar showing test dates and due dates in all courses for each month of a semester. (*1*)

opinion Belief or judgment that cannot be proved or disproved. (*9*)

organization Arranging main ideas and supporting details in a meaningful way. Second of three essential study strategies. (*10*)

outlining Formal way of organizing main ideas and supporting details to show relationships among them. (*10*)

paraphrasing Rewriting someone else's material in your own words. (*6*)

part opening Textbook feature that introduces a section (part) consisting of several chapters. (*10*)

personification Figure of speech giving human traits to nonhuman or nonliving things. (*2*)

pie chart Circle graph in which the sizes of the "slices" represent parts of the whole. (*10*)

place order pattern See *spatial order pattern*. (*7*)

point of view An author's position (attitude, belief, or opinion) on a topic. (*8*)

predicting Anticipating what is coming next as you read. (*2*)

preface Introductory section in which authors tell readers about a text. (*10*)

prefix Word part attached to the beginning of a root that adds its meaning to the root. (*2*)

preparing to read Previewing the material, assessing your prior knowledge, and planning your time. (*3*)

previewing Examining reading material to determine its subject matter and organization. Previewing is step 1 of the three-step reading process in *Opening Doors*. (*3*)

prior knowledge What you already know about a topic; background knowledge. (*3*)

process A series of actions or changes that bring about a result. (*7*)

propaganda devices Techniques authors use in order to unfairly influence the reader to accept their point of view. (*9*)

purpose An author's reason for writing. (*8*)

rapid reading rate Rate used for easy or familiar material (300–500 words per minute). (*2*)

rehearsal Saying or writing material to transfer it into long-term memory. Third of three essential study strategies. (*10, 11*)

review See *rehearsal*. (*10*)

review card Index card with an important question on the front and the answer on the back. (*11*) Also, throughout *Opening Doors*, a technique for reviewing a chapter; *chapter review cards* summarize the most important information in the chapter and therefore are also called *summary cards*.

root Base word that has a meaning of its own. (*2*)

sarcasm A remark, often ironic, that is intended to convey contempt or ridicule. (*8*)

satire A style of writing in which the author uses sarcasm, irony, or ridicule to attack or expose human foolishness, corruption, or stupidity. (*8*)

scanning   Information-gathering technique used to locate specific information quickly and precisely. (*2*)

selectivity   Identifying main ideas and important supporting details. First of three essential study strategies. (*10*)

sequence pattern   List of items in a specific, important order. (*7*)

series   A number of objects or events arranged one after the other in succession. (*7*)

short-term goal   Goal you want to accomplish within 3 to 6 months. (*1*)

short-term memory   Temporary memory. (*11*)

sidebar   See *box*. (*10*)

simile   Figure of speech stating a comparison between two essentially dissimilar things by saying that one of them is *like* the other. (*2*)

skimming   Information-gathering technique that involves moving quickly and selectively through material to find only important material. (*2*)

spatial order pattern   The location or layout of something or someplace is described; may also be called *place order pattern*. (*7*)

stated main idea   Sentence in a paragraph that expresses the most important point about the topic. (*4*)

study questions and activities   General term for textbook features such as activities, exercises, drills, and practice sections. These features may also be called *questions for study and review, review, ask yourself, self-test, check your mastery, mastery test, learning check, check your understanding, topics for discussion, problems,* etc. (*10*)

study reading rate   Rate used for material that is complex, technical, new, demanding, or very important (50–200 words per minute). (*2*)

study schedule   Weekly schedule with specific times set aside for studying. (*1*)

suffix   Word part attached to the end of a root word. (*2*)

suggested readings   Textbook feature, often at the end of chapters (or parts), listing the author's recommendations for supplemental reading or research, sometimes with annotations (comments); may be called *additional readings, suggestions for further reading, supplementary readings,* etc. (*10*)

summary   Single-paragraph condensation of all the main ideas presented in a longer passage. (*10*)

summary cards   See *chapter review cards*. (*1*)

supplements   Separate aids accompanying a textbook; supplements include *study guides, supplemental readings, student workbooks,* and *CD-ROMs.* (*10*)

supporting details   In a paragraph, additional information necessary for understanding the main idea completely. (*6*)

table   Material arranged in rows and columns. (*10*)

table of contents   Textbook feature at the beginning of a book, listing chapter titles and sometimes including headings within chapters as well. (*10*)

tactile learner   One who prefers to touch and manipulate materials physically when learning. (*1*)

test review cards   Index cards with an important question on the front and the answer on the back. (*11*)

test review sheet   Single sheet of paper consolidating and summarizing, on its front and back, the most important information to be covered on a test. (*11*)

textbook feature   Device used by an author to emphasize important material and show how it is organized. (*10*)

To Do list   Prioritized list of items to be accomplished in a single day. (*1*)

tone   Manner of writing (choice of words and style) that reveals an author's attitude toward a topic. (*8*)

topic   Word or phrase that tells what an author is writing about. (*4*)

underlining and highlighting   Techniques for marking topics, main ideas, and definitions. (*10*)

visual learner   One who prefers to see or read information to be learned. (*1*)

visual literacy   The ability to read (interpret) images, graphs, diagrams, and other visual symbols. (*10*)

visual summary   A textbook chapter summary that contains graphic aids in addition to written informa-tion (*10*)

vocabulary aids   Textbook devices that highlight important terms and definitions. Vocabulary aids may be called *key terms, basic terms, terms to know, vocabulary, terms to remember,* etc. (*10*)

webliography   List of websites that feature material related to a topic. (*10*)

word-structure clue   Root, prefix, or suffix that helps you determine a word's meaning. Also known as *word-part clues.* (*2*)

writing patterns   Ways authors organize and present their ideas. (*7*)

A List of Word Parts: Prefixes, Roots, and Suffixes

Understanding the meaning of various word parts can help you determine the meaning of many unfamiliar words, especially in context. Most of the word parts listed in this appendix are Latin; a few are Greek, Old English, or Slavic.

The first part of this appendix presents the meaning of 215 useful roots, prefixes, and suffixes. Prefixes are followed by a hyphen (for example, *pre-*), and suffixes are preceded by a hyphen (for example, *-itis*). Try to associate each word part (left column) with its meaning (middle column) as well as with the example word (right column). Associating the word part, its definition, and an example in this way will help you remember word parts that are new to you. Also, if you can associate the word part with a word that you already know, you will strengthen your understanding and recall of the word part even more.

The second part of this appendix presents the most common suffixes. For convenience, these suffixes are presented in categories.

	Word Part	Definition	Example
1.	a-	without, not	amoral, apolitical
2.	ab-	from	abduct, abstain
3.	acou	hear	acoustic
4.	acro	high	acrobat
5.	alter	another	alternate
6.	ambi	both; around	ambidextrous, ambivalent
7.	ambul	walk; go	ambulatory
8.	andr	man (human)	android
9.	annu, anni	year	annual, anniversary
10.	ante-	before, forward	antebellum, antecedent
11.	anthrop	humankind	anthropology
12.	anti-	against	antifreeze
13.	aqua	water	aquarium
14.	arch	ruler; chief, highest	archbishop, archenemy
15.	astro	star	astronomy
16.	aud	hear	auditory
17.	auto-	self	automatic, autobiography
18.	avi	bird	aviator, aviary
19.	belli	war	belligerent
20.	bene-	well, good	beneficial
21.	bi-	two	bicycle
22.	bio	life	biology
23.	bov	cattle	bovine
24.	by-	secondarily, secondary	by-product
25.	camera	chamber	bicameral
26.	capit	head	decapitate
27.	card	heart	cardiac
28.	carn	flesh	carnivorous
29.	caust, caut	burn	caustic, cauterize
30.	cav	hollow	cavity
31.	cent-	hundred	century
32.	chromo	color	monochromatic
33.	chrono	time	chronology, chronicle
34.	cide	kill	homicide
35.	circum-	around	circumference
36.	contra-	against	contraceptive
37.	cosm	universe	microcosm, cosmology
38.	counter-	against	counteract, counter-terrorist
39.	crat, cracy	rule	democratic
40.	cred, creed	belief	credibility, creed
41.	crypt	secret, hidden	cryptography, cryptic
42.	cycl	circle	tricycle
43.	dec, deci	ten	decade, decimal
44.	dei	god	deity
45.	demo	people	democracy

	Word Part	Definition	Example
46.	dent	tooth	dentist, dental
47.	derm	skin	dermatology
48.	di-	two, double	dichotomy, divide
49.	dict	speak	diction, dictate
50.	dorm	sleep	dormitory, dormant
51.	dyna	power	dynamo
52.	dys-	bad, difficult	dysfunctional
53.	enni	year	centennial
54.	epi-	upon, outer	epidermis
55.	equ	horse	equine
56.	-esque	like, resembling	statuesque
57.	ethn	race, nation	ethnic, ethnocentric
58.	eu-	good, well	eulogy, euphemism
59.	ex-	out	exit
60.	extra-	beyond, over	extravagant, extramarital
61.	fer	carry, bear	conifer, aquifer
62.	ferr	iron	ferrous
63.	fid	faith, trust	fidelity, fiduciary
64.	fini	limit	finite
65.	flagr	burn	conflagration
66.	flect, flex	bend	reflect, flexible
67.	fore-	before	forewarn, forecast
68.	fort	strong	fortress, fortify
69.	frater	brother	fraternity
70.	gamy	marriage	monogamy
71.	gastr	stomach	gastric
72.	gene, gen	origin, race, type	genesis, genocide, genre
73.	geo	earth	geography
74.	geronto	old	gerontology
75.	grad, gress	go, step	regress, progress
76.	graph, gram	write, record	telegram, photography
77.	gyne	woman	gynecology
78.	helio	sun	heliocentric
79.	hemi-	half	hemisphere
80.	hemo	blood	hemophilia
81.	hetero-	other, different	heterosexual, heterogeneous
82.	homo	same	homosexual, homogeneous
83.	hydr	water	hydrant, hydrate
84.	hyper-	over, above	hyperactive
85.	hypo-	under, less than	hypodermic
86.	ign	fire	ignite
87.	in-, il-, im-, ir-	not	inactive, illegal, impotent
88.	inter-	between	intercept, interrupt
89.	intra-	within	intravenous, intramural
90.	-itis	inflammation	tonsillitis
91.	ject	throw	eject, reject

	Word Part	Definition	Example
92.	junct	join	junction, conjunction
93.	kilo	thousand	kilometer, kilogram
94.	later	side	lateral
95.	leg	law	legal, legislate
96.	liber	free	liberate
97.	libr	book	library
98.	lingua	tongue, language	sublingual, bilingual
99.	lith	stone	lithograph
100.	locu, loqu, log	speak	elocution, colloquial, dialogue
101.	-logy	study of	psychology
102.	luc	light, clear	lucid
103.	macro-	large	macrocosm
104.	magn	great	magnify
105.	mal-	bad, ill	malfunction
106.	mamma	breast	mammal
107.	mania	craving for	kleptomania
108.	manu	hand	manual
109.	matri, mater	mother	maternal, matriarchy
110.	mega-	large	megaphone
111.	meter, metr	measure	thermometer, metric
112.	micro-	small	microscope
113.	milli-	thousand, thousandth	millenium, millimeter
114.	mini-	less	minimal
115.	mis-	bad, wrong	mistreat, misspell
116.	miss, mit	send	dismiss, transmit
117.	mob, mov, mot	to move	mobile, movable, motion
118.	mono-	one	monotone, monopoly
119.	morph	form	amorphous, morph
120.	mort	death	mortal, mortuary
121.	multi-	many	multitude
122.	nat	born, birth	prenatal
123.	naut	sail	nautical
124.	neo-	new	neophyte, neologism
125.	nox	harmful	noxious
126.	noct	night	nocturnal
127.	ob-, oc-, of-, op-	against	object, occlude, offend, oppress
128.	oct-, octo-	eight	octopus, octagon
129.	ocul	eye	oculist
130.	-oid	resembling	humanoid
131.	omni	all	omnipotent
132.	onym	name, word	pseudonym, synonym
133.	ortho	correct, straight	orthodontist
134.	-osis	condition	psychosis
135.	osteo, ost	bone	osteopath, osteoporosis
136.	out-	better than	outrun, outdistance

	Word Part	Definition	Example
137.	pac, pax	peace	pacifist, pacific
138.	pan-	all	panorama, pandemic
139.	para-	beside	parallel, parapsychology
140.	path	feeling, illness	sympathy, pathology
141.	patri, pater	father	paternity, patriotic
142.	ped, pod	foot	pedal, tripod
143.	pel	drive	repel, impel, dispel
144.	pend	hang	pendulum, pending
145.	penta-	five	pentagon, pentathlon
146.	per-	through	perspire
147.	peri-	around	perimeter
148.	petr	rock	petrified
149.	philo	love	philosophy
150.	phobia	fear of	acrophobia
151.	phono	sound	phonics, phonograph
152.	photo	light	photograph
153.	pneum	air	pneumatic
154.	poly-	many	polygon, polyglot
155.	port	carry	portable, porter
156.	pos	place	position
157.	post-	after	postwar
158.	pre-	before	prewar
159.	primo	first	primitive, primordial
160.	pro-	forward, in favor of	progress, pro-American
161.	pseud	false	pseudoscience
162.	psych	mind	psychic
163.	pugn	fight	pugnacious
164.	punct	point	puncture
165.	purg	cleanse	purge
166.	pyre	fire	pyromania
167.	quad-, quar-	four	quadruplets, quartet
168.	quint-	five	quintet
169.	re-	back, again	return, repeat
170.	reg	guide, rule; king	regulate, regal
171.	rupt	break	rupture, disrupt
172.	scend	climb	descend, ascend
173.	scope	see; view	telescope
174.	scribe, scrip	write	scribble, prescription
175.	sequ	follow	sequence, sequel
176.	semi-	half	semicircle
177.	seni	old	senile
178.	simil	like	similar
179.	sol	sun	solar, solstice
180.	sol, soli	alone	solo, solitude
181.	somni	sleep	insomnia, somnolent

	Word Part	Definition	Example
182.	soph	wise	sophomore, sophisticated
183.	spect	see	spectator, spectacle
184.	spir	breathe	respiratory
185.	strict	tighten	constrict, restrict
186.	sub-	under	submarine
187.	super-, sur-	over	supervisor, surpass
188.	surg	rise	surge, resurgent
189.	tang, tact	touch	tangible, tactile
190.	tech	skill	technician
191.	tele-	far	telepathy, telescope
192.	tend, tens	stretch	tendon, tension, extend
193.	terri	earth	territory
194.	tert-	third	tertiary
195.	theo	god	theology
196.	therm	heat	thermometer, thermal
197.	tomy	cut	vasectomy, appendectomy
198.	tors, tort	twist	distort, torture
199.	toxi	poison	toxic
200.	tract	pull, drag	tractor, extract
201.	tri-	three	trio
202.	ultra-	beyond, over	ultramodern
203.	unct, ung	oil	unctuous, unguent
204.	uni-	one	unity, unify, uniform
205.	vacu	empty	vacuum
206.	veni, vent	come	convene, convention
207.	verd	green	verdant
208.	vers, vert	turn	reverse, vertigo, divert
209.	vid, vis	see	video, vision
210.	vinc	conquer	invincible
211.	vit, viv	life	vitality, vivacious
212.	voc, voke	voice, call	vocal, evoke
213.	voli, volunt	wish	volition, volunteer
214.	volv	roll, to turn	revolve, evolve
215.	zoo	animal	zoology

COMMON SUFFIXES

Suffix	Meaning	Examples
Suffixes That Indicate a Person:		
1. -er, -or, -ist	one who (does what the root word indicates)	banker, inventor, scientist, pacifist
Suffixes That Indicate a Noun:		
2. -ance, -ence, -tion, -sion, -ment, -ness, -ity, -ty, -tude, -hood, -age	state of, quality of, condition of, act of	tolerance, permanence, retention, vision, government, happiness, maturity, beauty, gratitude, statehood, marriage
3. -itis	inflammation of (whatever the root indicates)	sinusitis, tonsillitis
4. -ology	study or science of (whatever the root indicates)	psychology, microbiology
5. -ism	philosophy of or belief in	terrorism, Buddhism, pacifism
Suffixes That Indicate an Adjective:		
6. -al, -ic, -ish, -ical, -ive	pertaining to (whatever the root indicates)	normal, hormonal, psychic, selfish, magical, defective, pacific
7. -less	without, lacking (whatever the root indicates)	homeless, toothless
8. -ous, -ful	full of (whatever the root indicates)	harmonious, colorful
9. -able, -ible	able to do or be (whatever the root indicates)	comfortable, comprehensible
Suffixes That Indicate a Verb:		
10. -ify, -ate, -ize, -en	to do (whatever the root indicates)	pacify, meditate, criticize, enlighten
Suffixes That Indicate an Adverb:		
11. -ly	in the manner (indicated by the root)	slowly, heavily, peacefully
12. -ward	in the direction of (whatever the root indicates)	eastward, homeward, backward

World Map, United States Map, and List of World Capitals

Appendix 3 contains current maps of the world and the United States. Also included is a list of all 192 countries and the capital of each.

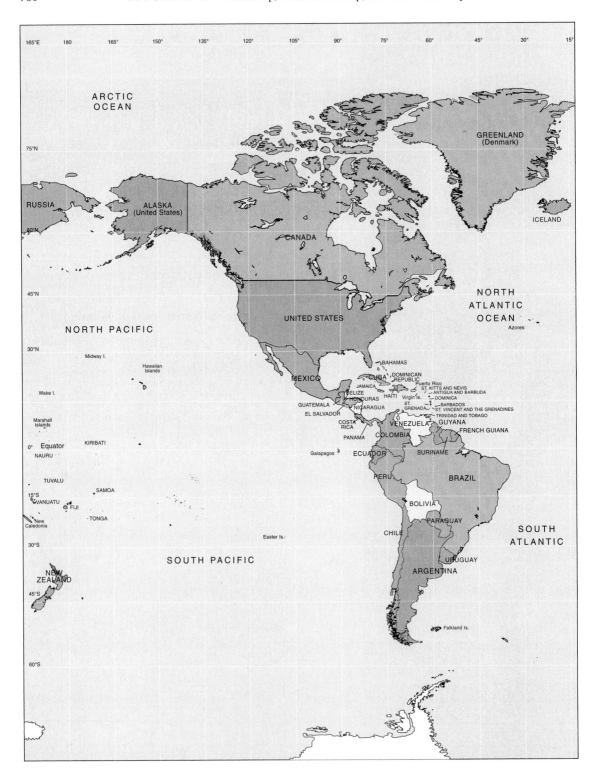

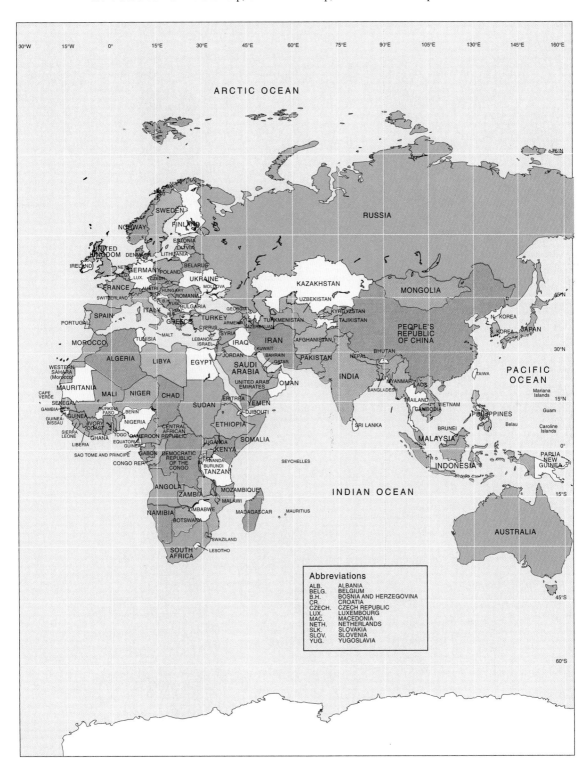

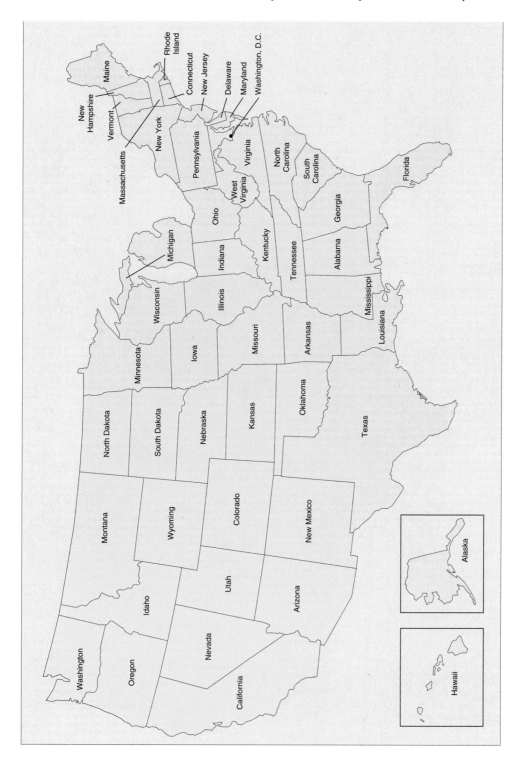

Country	Capital	Country	Capital	Country	Capital
Afghanistan	Kabul	Cuba	Havana	Kiribati	Tarawa
Albania	Tirane	Cyprus	Nicosia	Korea, North	Pyongyang
Algeria	Algiers	Czech Republic	Prague	Korea, South	Seoul
Andorra	Andorra la	Denmark	Copenhagen	Kuwait	Kuwait City
	Vella	Djibouti	Djibouti	Kyrgyzstan	Bishkek
Angola	Luanda	Dominica	Roseau	Laos	Vientiane
Antigua and		Dominican		Latvia	Riga
Barbuda	St. John's	Republic	Santo Domingo	Lebanon	Beirut
Argentina	Buenos Aires	Ecuador	Quito	Lesotho	Maseru
Armenia	Yerevan	Egypt	Cairo	Liberia	Monrovia
Australia	Canberra	El Salvador	San Salvador	Libya	Tripoli
Austria	Vienna	Equatorial		Liechtenstein	Vaduz
Azerbaijan	Baku	Guinea	Malabo	Lithuania	Vilnius
Bahamas	Nassau	Eritrea	Asmera	Luxembourg	Luxembourg
Bahrain	Manama	Estonia	Tallinn	Macedonia	Skopje
Bangladesh	Dhaka	Ethiopia	Addis Ababa	Madagascar	Antananarivo
Barbados	Bridgetown	Fiji	Suva	Malawi	Lilongwe
Belarus	Minsk	Finland	Helsinki	Malaysia	Kuala Lumpur
Belgium	Brussels	France	Paris	Maldives	Male
Belize	Belmopan	Gabon	Libreville	Mali	Bamako
Benin	Porto-Novo	The Gambia	Banjul	Malta	Valleta
Bhutan	Thimphu	Georgia	Tbilisi	Marshall Islands	Majuro
Bolivia	La Paz	Germany	Berlin	Mauritania	Nouakchott
Bosnia and		Ghana	Accra	Mauritius	Port Louis
Herzegovina	Sarajevo	Great Britain	London	Mexico	Mexico City
Botswana	Gaborone	Greece	Athens	Micronesia	Palikir
Brazil	Brasilia	Grenada	St. George's	Moldova	Chisinau
Brunei	Bandar Seri	Guatemala	Guatemala City	Monaco	Monaco
	Begawan	Guinea	Conakry	Mongolia	Ulaanbaatar
Bulgaria	Sofia	Guinea-Bissau	Bissau	Morocco	Rabat
Burkina Faso	Ougadougou	Guyana	Georgetown	Mozambique	Maputo
Burundi	Bujumbura	Haiti	Port-au-Prince	Myanmar	Yangon
Cambodia	Phnom Penh	Honduras	Tegucigalpa	Namibia	Windhoek
Cameroon	Yaounde	Hungary	Budapest	Nauru	Yaren
Canada	Ottawa	Iceland	Reykjavik	Nepal	Kathmandu
Cape Verde	Praia	India	New Delhi	The Netherlands	Amsterdam
Central African		Indonesia	Jakarta	New Zealand	Wellington
Republic	Bangul	Iran	Tehran	Nicaragua	Managua
Chad	N'Djamena	Iraq	Baghdad	Niger	Niamey
Chile	Santiago	Ireland	Dublin	Nigeria	Abuja
China	Beijing	Israel	Jerusalem	Norway	Oslo
Colombia	Bogota	Italy	Rome	Oman	Muscat
Comoros	Moroni	Jamaica	Kingston	Pakistan	Islamabad
Congo	Brazzaville	Japan	Tokyo	Palau	Koror
Costa Rica	San Jose	Jordan	Amman	Panama	Panama City
Cote d'Ivoire	Abidjan	Kazakhstan	Almaty	Papua New	
Croatia	Zagreb	Kenya	Nairobi	Guinea	Port Moresby

Country	Capital	Country	Capital	Country	Capital
Paraguay	Asuncion	Singapore	Singapore	Tunisia	Tunis
Peru	Lima	Slovakia	Bratislava	Turkey	Ankara
Philippines	Manila	Slovenia	Ljubljana	Turkmenistan	Ashgabat
Poland	Warsaw	Solomon Islands	Honiara	Tuvalu	Funafuti
Portugal	Lisbon	Somalia	Mogadishu	Uganda	Kampala
Qatar	Doha	South Africa	Pretoria	Ukraine	Kiev
Romania	Bucharest	Spain	Madrid	United Arab	
Russia	Moscow	Sri Lanka	Colombo	Emirates	Abu Dhabi
Rwanda	Kigali	Sudan	Khartoum	United States	
Saint Kitts		Suriname	Paramaribo	of America	Washington, D. C.
and Nevis	Basseterre	Swaziland	Mbabane	Uruguay	Montevideo
Saint Lucia	Castries	Sweden	Stockholm	Uzbekistan	Tashkent
Saint Vincent		Switzerland	Bern	Vanuatu	Vila
and the		Syria	Damascus	Vatican City	Vatican City
Grenadines	Kingstown	Taiwan	Taipei	Venezuela	Caracas
San Marino	San Marino	Tajikistan	Dushanbe	Vietnam	Hanoi
Sao Tome		Tanzania	Dar-es-Salaam	Western Samoa	Apia
and Principe	Sao Tome	Thailand	Bangkok	Yemen	Sanaa
Saudi Arabia	Riyadh	Togo	Lome	Yugoslavia	Belgrade
Senegal	Dakar	Tonga	Nuku'alofa	Zaire	Kinshasa
Seychelles	Victoria	Trinidad		Zambia	Lusaka
Sierra Leone	Freetown	and Tobago	Port-of-Spain	Zimbabwe	Harare

Master Vocabulary List

Appendix 4 lists vocabulary words the vocabulary in context exercises in *Opening Doors*. This list will help you locate the vocabulary in context exercise where each word appears.

In *Part One*, vocabulary words are listed by selection. In *Part Two*, vocabulary words are listed alphabetically. The numbers in parentheses indicate the reading selection in which the vocabulary word appears.

Part One

vary (1-1), 36
practical (1-1), 37
pursuing (1-1), 37
capacity (1-1), 37
intellectual (1-1), 37
anticipate (1-1), 38
diversity (1-1), 38
necessitates (1-1), 38
quest (1-1), 38
poised (1-1), 39

prime (1-2), 52
diverse (1-2), 52
strive (1-2), 53
verbal (1-2), 53
pursue (1-2), 53
composure (1-2), 53
etiquette (1-2), 54
ethical (1-2), 54
impact (1-2), 54
succinct (1-2), 54

convey (1-3), 66
articulate (1-3), 66
emulate (1-3), 66
painstaking (1-3), 66
succeeding (1-3), 67
inevitable (1-3), 67
willed (1-3), 67
rehabilitation (1-3), 67
corridor (1-3), 68
feigned (1-3), 68

peak (2-1), 108
lapse (2-1), 108
constructive (2-1), 109
duration (2-1), 109
counter (2-1), 109
sabotage (2-1), 109
legacy (2-1), 110
prestige, (2-1), 110
adversity (2-1), 110
resiliency (2-1), 110

lethal (2-2), 123
veered (2-2), 124
aptly (2-2), 124
profoundly (2-2), 124
plummeted (2-2), 124
undetected (2-2), 125
distinguished (2-2), 125
adversary (2-2), 125
haven (2-2), 125
adversity (2-2), 126

intrepid (2-3), 136
perpetually (2-3), 137

condensing (2-3), 137
frigid (2-3), 137
expelling (2-3), 138
leviathan (2-3), 138
relatively (2-3), 138
metabolic (2-3), 138
elaborate (2-3), 139
galaxy (2-3), 139

bestowed (3-1), 170
relinquish (3-1), 170
persistent (3-1), 171
plane (3-1), 171
inherently (3-1), 171
peaked (3-1), 171
enacted (3-1), 172
elusive (3-1), 172
substantial (3-1), 172
decades (3-1), 172

universal (3-2), 184
cohabitating (3-2), 185
preindustrial (3-2), 185
sole (3-2), 185
primary (3-2), 185
breadwinners (3-2), 186
predominantly (3-2), 186
plateau (3-2), 186
attrition (3-2), 186
skew (3-2), 187

profess (3-3), 198
veneration (3-3), 199
façade (3-3), 199
renounced (3-3), 199
supposition (3-3), 199
cosmos (3-3), 200
relics (3-3), 200
embellished (3-3), 200
transcendence (3-3), 200
medieval (3-3), 201

prospective (4-1), 233
quadriplegic (4-1), 233
catastrophic (4-1), 233
boon (4-1), 233
enticing (4-1), 234
exodus (4-1), 234
mandated (4-1), 234
accessible (4-1), 234
compliance (4-1), 235
advocates (4-1), 235

heritage (4-2), 247
marketable (4-2), 247
proficiency (4-2), 247
concentrated (4-2), 247
assimilate (4-2), 248
prominent (4-2), 248
en masse (4-2), 248

enclave (4-2), 249
subsequent (4-2), 249
bicultural (4-2), 249

promulgated (4-3), 259
pervasive (4-3), 259
pivotal (4-3), 259
modest (4-3), 259
Islamic (4-3), 260
secular (4-3), 260
omnipotent (4-3), 260
converts (4-3), 260
theology (4-3), 261
proselytizing (4-3), 261

hounding (5-1), 291
summons (5-1), 291
fraud (5-1), 291
elapse (5-1), 292
liable (5-1), 292
impersonating (5-1), 292
stow (5-1), 292
commercial (5-1), 293
marketing (5-1), 293
scams (5-1), 293

fictional (5-2), 306
dismember (5-2), 307
susceptible (5-2), 307
incarcerated (5-2), 307
exposure (5-2), 308
inhibitions (5-2), 308
portrayals (5-2), 308
legitimate (5-2), 308
predisposing (5-2), 309
desensitized (5-2), 309

expectancy (5-3), 323
distribution (5-3), 323
standard (5-3), 323
locality (5-3), 323
mass (5-3), 324
upheaval (5-3), 324
exoduses (5-3), 324
mortality (5-3), 324
facilitated (5-3), 325
stabilized (5-3), 325

lapse (6-1), 353
gestational (6-1), 353
family history (6-1), 353
managed (6-1), 354
sensitive (6-1), 354
stabilize (6-1), 354
composition (6-1), 354
consumption (6-1), 355
complications (6-1), 355
asymptomatic (6-1), 355

phenomenon (6-2), 370

consumption (6-2), 370
clientele (6-2), 370
ban (6-2), 370
nongenerational (6-2), 371
acute (6-2), 371
toll (6-2), 371
attributable (6-2), 371
paraphernalia (6-2), 372
reliant (6-2), 372

free market (6-3), 385
industrialized (6-3), 385
consumption (6-3), 385
infrastructure (6-3), 385
hyperinflation (6-3), 386
surging (6-3), 386
rampant (6-3), 386
stagnated (6-3), 386
moribund (6-3), 387
creditor (6-3), 387

consumer (7-1), 432
fray (7-1), 433
prosper (7-1), 433
dominate (7-1), 433
retailers (7-1), 434
demanding (7-1), 434
incorporate (7-1), 434
glorified (7-1), 434
configure (7-1), 435
vendors (7-1), 435

institution (7-2), 448
rebound (7-2), 448
fraternal (7-2), 448
sustain (7-2), 448
consuming (7-2), 449
courtship (7-2), 449
marital (7-2), 449
liabilities (7-2), 449
initial (7-2), 450
compatibility (7-2), 450

futility (7-3), 462
resolved (7-3), 462
deviant (7-3), 462
impending (7-3), 462
bereaved (7-3), 463
unleashes (7-3), 463
pangs (7-3), 463
acute (7-3), 463
dejection (7-3), 464
dominates (7-3), 464

transforming (8-1), 508
transnational (8-1), 508
vast (8-1), 509
generated (8-1), 509
intercultural (8-1), 509

goodwill (8-1), 509
forgo (8-1), 510
assume (8-1), 510
adapt (8-1), 510
range (8-1), 510

preeminent (8-2), 522
prominence (8-2), 523
creed (8-2), 523
ethical (8-2), 523
idealism (8-2), 524
dependent (8-2), 524
beholden (8-2), 524
longevity (8-2), 524
original (8-2), 525
content (8-2), 525

meager (8-3), 536
sparingly (8-3), 536
bloated (8-3), 536
fragrant (8-3), 536
despair (8-3), 537
somber (8-3), 537
banquet (8-3), 537
ingots (8-3), 538
plentiful (8-3), 538
feasted (8-3), 538

substantial (9-1), 594
persistent (9-1), 597
comparable (9-1), 595
prevalent (9-1), 595
argues (9-1), 595
dire (9-1), 595
proponents (9-1), 596
uniform (9-1), 596
advocates (9-1), 596
contentious (9-1), 596

utility (9-2), 607
lunatic (9-2), 607
hordes (9-2), 607
inexplicably (9-2), 607
seethe (9-2), 608
mammoth (9-2), 608
cartel (9-2), 608
decreed (9-2), 608
spewing (9-2), 609
appetite (9-2), 609

cascade (9-3), 621
heirloom (9-3), 621
incinerated (9-3), 621
vulnerable (9-3), 621
advocates (9-3), 622
mummified (9-3), 622
generation (9-3), 622
municipal (9-3), 622
toxic (9-3), 623
invalidate (9-3), 623

Part Two

accessible (4-1), 234
acute (6-2), 371
acute (7-3), 463
adapt (8-1), 510
adversary (2-2), 125
adversity (2-1), 110
adversity (2-2), 126
advocates (4-1), 235
advocates (9-1), 596
advocates (9-3), 622
anticipate (1-1), 38
appetite (9-2), 609
aptly (2-2), 124
argues (9-1), 595
articulate (1-3), 66
assimilate (4-2), 248
assume (8-1), 510
asymptomatic (6-1), 355
attributable (6-2), 371
attrition (3-2), 186
ban (6-2), 370
banquet (8-3), 537
beholden (8-2), 524
bereaved (7-3), 463
bestowed (3-1), 170
bicultural (4-2), 249
bloated (8-3), 536
boon (4-1), 233
breadwinners (3-2), 186
capacity (1-1), 37
cartel (9-2), 608
cascade (9-3), 621
catastrophic (4-1), 233
clientele (6-2), 370
cohabiting (3-2), 185
commercial (5-1), 293
comparable (9-1), 595
compatibility (7-2), 450
compliance (4-1), 235
complications (6-1), 355
composition (6-1), 354
composure (1-2), 53
concentrated (4-2), 247
condensing (2-3), 137
configure (7-1), 435
constructive (2-1), 109
consumer (7-1), 432
consuming (7-2), 449
consumption (6-1), 355
consumption (6-2), 370
consumption (6-3), 385
content (8-2), 525

contentious (9-1), 596
converts (4-3), 260
convey (1-3), 66
corridor (1-3), 68
cosmos (3-3), 200
counter (2-1), 109
courtship (7-2), 449
creditor (6-3), 387
creed (8-2), 523
decades (3-1), 172
decreed (9-2), 608
dejection (7-3), 464
demanding (7-1), 434
dependent (8-2), 524
desensitized (5-2), 309
despair (8-3), 537
deviant (7-3), 462
dire (9-1), 595
dismember (5-2), 307
distinguished (2-2), 125
distribution (5-3), 323
diverse (1-2), 52
diversity (1-1), 38
dominate (7-1), 433
dominates (7-3), 464
duration (2-1), 109
elaborate (2-3), 139
elapse (5-1), 292
elusive (3-1), 172
embellished (3-3), 200
emulate (1-3), 66
en masse (4-2), 248
enacted (3-1), 172
enclave (4-2), 249
enticing (4-1), 234
ethical (1-2), 54
ethical (8-2), 523
etiquette (1-2), 54
exodus (4-1), 234
exoduses (5-3), 324
expectancy (5-3), 323
expelling (2-3), 138
exposure (5-2), 308
façade (3-3), 199
facilitated (5-3), 325
family history (6-1), 353
feasted (8-3), 538
feigned (1-3), 68
fictional (5-2), 306
forgo (8-1), 510
fragrant (8-3), 536
fraternal (7-2), 448
fraud (5-1), 291
fray (7-1), 433
free market (6-3), 385

frigid (2-3), 137
futility (7-3), 462
galaxy (2-3), 139
generated (8-1), 509
generation (9-3), 622
gestational (6-1), 353
glorified (7-1), 434
goodwill (8-1), 509
haven (2-2), 125
heirloom (9-3), 621
heritage (4-2), 247
hordes (9-2), 607
hounding (5-1), 291
hyperinflation (6-3), 386
idealism (8-2), 524
impact (1-2), 54
impending (7-3), 462
impersonating (5-1), 292
incarcerated (5-2), 307
incinerated (9-3), 621
incorporate (7-1), 434
industrialized (6-3), 385
inevitable (1-3), 67
inexplicably (9-2), 607
infrastructure (6-3), 385
ingots (8-3), 538
inherently (3-1), 171
inhibitions (5-2), 308
initial (7-2), 450
institution (7-2), 448
intellectual (1-1), 37
intercultural (8-1), 509
intrepid (2-3), 136
invalidate (9-3), 623
Islamic (4-3), 260
lapse (2-1), 108
lapse (6-1), 353
legacy (2-1), 110
legitimate (5-2), 308
lethal (2-2), 123
leviathan (2-3), 138
liabilities (7-2), 449
liable (5-1), 292
locality (5-3), 323
longevity (8-2), 524
lunatic (9-2), 607
mammoth (9-2), 608
managed (6-1), 354
mandated (4-1), 234
marital (7-2), 449
marketable (4-2), 247
marketing (5-1), 293
mass (5-3), 324
meager (8-3), 536
medieval (3-3), 201

metabolic (2-3), 138
modest (4-3), 259
moribund (6-3), 387
mortality (5-3), 324
mummified (9-3), 622
municipal (9-3), 622
necessitates (1-1), 38
nongenerational (6-2), 371
omnipotent (4-3), 260
original (8-2), 525
painstaking (1-3), 66
pangs (7-3), 463
paraphernalia (6-2), 372
peak (2-1), 108
peaked (3-1), 171
perpetually (2-3), 137
persistent (3-1), 171
persistent (9-1), 597
pervasive (4-3), 259
phenomenon (6-2), 370
pivotal (4-3), 259
plane (3-1), 171
plateau (3-2), 186
plentiful (8-3), 538
plummeted (2-2), 124
poised (1-1), 39
portrayals (5-2), 308
practical (1-1), 37
predisposing (5-2), 309
predominantly (3-2), 186
preeminent (8-2), 522
preindustrial (3-2), 185
prestige, (2-1), 110
prevalent (9-1), 595
primary (3-2), 185
prime (1-2), 52
profess (3-3), 198
proficiency (4-2), 247
profoundly (2-2), 124
prominence (8-2), 523
prominent (4-2), 248
promulgated (4-3), 259
proponents (9-1), 596
proselytizing (4-3), 261
prospective (4-1), 233
prosper (7-1), 433
pursue (1-2), 53
pursuing (1-1), 37
quadriplegic (4-1), 233
quest (1-1), 38
rampant (6-3), 386
range (8-1), 510
rebound (7-2), 448
rehabilitation (1-3), 67
relatively (2-3), 138

reliant (6-2), 372
relics (3-3), 200
relinquish (3-1), 170
renounced (3-3), 199
resiliency (2-1), 110
resolved (7-3), 462
retailers (7-1), 434
sabotage (2-1), 109
scams (5-1), 293
secular (4-3), 260
seethe (9-2), 608
sensitive (6-1), 354
skew (3-2), 187
sole (3-2), 185
somber (8-3), 537
sparingly (8-3), 536
spewing (9-2), 609
stabilize (6-1), 354
stabilized (5-3), 325
stagnated (6-3), 386
standard (5-3), 323
stow (5-1), 292
strive (1-2), 53
subsequent (4-2), 249
substantial (3-1), 172
substantial (9-1), 594
succeeding (1-3), 67
succinct (1-2), 54
summons (5-1), 291
supposition (3-3), 199
surging (6-3), 386
susceptible (5-2), 307
sustain (7-2), 448
theology (4-3), 261
toll (6-2), 371
toxic (9-3), 623
transcendence (3-3), 200
transforming (8-1), 508
transnational (8-1), 508
undetected (2-2), 125
uniform (9-1), 596
universal (3-2), 184
unleashes (7-3), 463
upheaval (5-3), 324
utility (9-2), 607
vary (1-1), 36
vast (8-1), 509
veered (2-2), 124
vendors (7-1), 435
veneration (3-3), 199
verbal (1-2), 53
vulnerable (9-3), 621
willed (1-3), 67

Credits

Index

Use the space below to record words and definitions in the Vocabulary in Context Quizzes (or from any other part of this book) that were *new* to you. You should also record any words that you *missed*. You may find it helpful to indicate the page on which the word appeared in the book. This simple procedure will help you remember the words and their definitions and, thereby, increase your vocabulary.

Word	Definition	Page

Monitoring your comprehension means *evaluating your understanding as you read and correcting the problem whenever you realize that you are not comprehending.* You should monitor your comprehension whenever you read and study college textbooks. Asking yourself comprehension monitoring questions as you read will guide your reading and enhance your understanding. The comprehension monitoring questions that are presented throughout *Opening Doors* are listed below.

Reading Comprehension   Chapters 4–7

Determining the Topic: *"Who or what is this paragraph about?"*
Stated Main Idea: *"What is the single most important point the author wants me to understand about the topic of this paragraph?"*
Implied Main Idea: *"What is the single most important point the author wants me to infer about the topic of this paragraph?"*
Identifying Supporting Details: *"What additional information does the author provide to help me understand the main idea completely?"*
Recognizing Authors' Writing Patterns: *"Which pattern did the author use to organize the main idea and the supporting details?"*

Critical Reading and Thinking   Chapters 8–9

Determining an Author's Purpose: *"Why did the author write this?"*
Determining an Author's Intended Audience: *"Who did the author intend to read this?"*
Determining an Author's Point of View: *"What is the author's position on this issue?"*
Determining an Author's Tone: *"What do the author's choice of words and style of writing reveal about his or her attitude toward the topic?"*
Determining an Author's Intended Meaning: *"What is the author's real meaning?"*
Evaluating Whether Statements in Written Material Are Facts or Opinions: *"Can the information the author presents be proved, or does it represent a judgment?"*
Making Inferences: *"What logical inference (conclusion) can I make, based on what the author has stated?"*

Vocabulary   Chapter 2

Vocabulary in Context: *"Are there clues within the sentence or surrounding sentences that can help me deduce the meaning of an unfamiliar word?"*
Word-Structure Clues: *"Are there roots, prefixes, or suffixes that give me clues to the meaning of an unfamiliar word?"*
Connotative Meaning: *"Is there a positive or negative association in addition to the literal meaning of a word?"*
Figurative Language: *"Should these words or this expression be interpreted figuratively?"*

Evaluating an Author's Argument   Chapter 9

Identifying the Issue: *"What controversial topic is this passage about?"*
Determining the Author's Argument: *"What is the author's position on the issue?"*
Determining the Author's Bias: *"Which side of the issue does the author support?"*
Identifying the Author's Assumptions: *"What does the author take for granted?"*
Identifying Support: *"What types of support does the author present?"*
Deciding Whether an Author's Support Is Relevant: *"Does the support pertain directly to the argument?"*
Evaluating Whether an Author's Argument Is Objective and Complete: *"Is the argument based on facts and other appropriate evidence? Did the author leave out information that might weaken or disprove the argument?"*
Evaluating Whether an Author's Argument Is Valid and Credible: *"Is the author's argument logical and believable?"*
Identifying Propaganda Devices: *"Has the author tried to unfairly influence me to accept his or her point of view?"*